Y0-BZE-158

Joseph White

Statistics and Computing

Series Editors:
J. Chambers
W. Eddy
W. Härdle
S. Sheather
L. Tierney

Springer
New York
Berlin
Heidelberg
Hong Kong
London
Milan
Paris
Tokyo

Statistics and Computing

Dalgaard: Introductory Statistics with R.

Gentle: Elements of Computational Statistics.

Gentle: Numerical Linear Algebra for Applications in Statistics.

Gentle: Random Number Generation and Monte Carlo Methods.

Härdle/Klinke/Turlach: XploRe: An Interactive Statistical Computing Environment.

Krause/Olson: The Basics of S and S-PLUS, 3rd Edition.

Lange: Numerical Analysis for Statisticians.

Loader: Local Regression and Likelihood.

Ó Ruanaidh/Fitzgerald: Numerical Bayesian Methods Applied to Signal Processing.

Pannatier: VARIOWIN: Software for Spatial Data Analysis in 2D.

Pinheiro/Bates: Mixed-Effects Models in S and S-PLUS.

Venables/Ripley: Modern Applied Statistics with S, 4th Edition.

Venables/Ripley: S Programming.

Wilkinson: The Grammar of Graphics.

James E. Gentle

Elements of
Computational Statistics

With 86 Illustrations

 Springer

James E. Gentle
Department of Computational
    Sciences and Informatics
George Mason University
Fairfax, VA 22030-4444
USA
jgentle@gmu.edu

Series Editors:

J. Chambers
Bell Labs, Lucent Technologies
600 Mountain Avenue
Murray Hill, NJ 07974
USA

W. Eddy
Department of Statistics
Carnegie Mellon University
Pittsburgh, PA 15213
USA

W. Härdle
Institut für Statistik und Ökonometrie
Humboldt-Universität zu Berlin
Spandauer Str. 1
D-10178 Berlin
Germany

S. Sheather
Australian Graduate School
    of Management
University of New South Wales
Sydney, NSW 2052
Australia

L. Tierney
School of Statistics
University of Minnesota
Vincent Hall
Minneapolis, MN 55455
USA

Library of Congress Cataloging-in-Publication Data
Gentle, James E., 1943–
        Elements of computational statistics / James E. Gentle.
            p. cm. — (Statistics and computing)
        Includes bibliographical references and index.
        ISBN 0-387-95489-9 (alk. paper)
            1. Statistics—Data processing. I. Title. II. Series.
        QA276.4 .G455 2002
        519.5—dc21   2002067018

ISBN 0-387-95489-9   Printed on acid-free paper.

© 2002 Springer-Verlag New York, Inc.
All rights reserved. This work may not be translated or copied in whole or in part without the
written permission of the publisher (Springer-Verlag New York, Inc., 175 Fifth Avenue, New York,
NY 10010, USA), except for brief excerpts in connection with reviews or scholarly analysis. Use
in connection with any form of information storage and retrieval, electronic adaptation, computer
software, or by similar or dissimilar methodology now known or hereafter developed is forbidden.
The use in this publication of trade names, trademarks, service marks, and similar terms, even if
they are not identified as such, is not to be taken as an expression of opinion as to whether or not
they are subject to proprietary rights.

Printed in the United States of America.

9 8 7 6 5 4 3 2 1   SPIN 10876754

Typesetting pages created from the author's camera-ready copy.

www.springer-ny.com

Springer-Verlag   New York Berlin Heidelberg
A member of BertelsmannSpringer Science+Business Media GmbH

To María

Preface

In recent years, developments in statistics have to a great extent gone hand in hand with developments in computing. Indeed, many of the recent advances in statistics have been dependent on advances in computer science and technology. Many of the currently interesting statistical methods are computationally intensive, either because they require very large numbers of numerical computations or because they depend on visualization of many projections of the data. The class of statistical methods characterized by computational intensity and the supporting theory for such methods constitute a discipline called "computational statistics". (Here, I am following Wegman, 1988, and distinguishing "computational statistics" from "statistical computing", which we take to mean "computational methods, including numerical analysis, for statisticians".)

The computationally intensive methods of modern statistics rely heavily on the developments in statistical computing and numerical analysis generally. This book discusses methods of computational statistics; for statistical computing, the reader is referred to a book such as Lange (1999) or the older book by Kennedy and Gentle (1980).

Computational statistics shares two hallmarks with other "computational" sciences, such as computational physics, computational biology, and so on. One is a characteristic of the methodology: it is computationally intensive. The other is the nature of the tools of discovery. Tools of the scientific method have generally been logical deduction (theory) and observation (experimentation). The computer, used to explore large numbers of scenarios, constitutes a new type of tool. Use of the computer to simulate alternatives and present the research worker with information about these alternatives is a characteristic of the computational sciences. In some ways, this usage is akin to experimentation. The observations, however, are generated from an assumed model, and those simulated data are used to evaluate and study the model.

Advances in computing hardware and software have changed the nature of the daily work of statisticians. Data analysts and applied statisticians rely on computers for storage of data, analysis of the data, and production of reports describing the analysis. Mathematical statisticians (and even probabilists) use the computer for symbolic manipulations, evaluation of expressions, ad hoc simulations, and production of research reports and papers. Some of the effects on statisticians have been subtle, such as the change from the use of "critical values" of test statistics to the use of "p-values", whereas others have been more fundamental, such as the use of multivariate and/or nonlinear models instead of univariate linear models, which might formerly have been used as approximations because they were computationally tractable. More recently, computational inference using Monte Carlo methods has been replacing asymptotic approximations. Another major effect that developments in computing have had on the practice of statistics is that many Bayesian methods that were formerly impractical have entered the mainstream of statistical applications.

The ease of computations has given the statistician a new attitude about the nature of statistical research. Experimentation has been put in the toolbox of the mathematical statistician. Ideas can be explored via "quick and dirty" computations. Ideas that appear promising after an initial evaluation can be pursued more rigorously.

Larger scale computing systems have also given the statistician a new attitude about the nature of discovery. Science has always moved ahead by finding something that was not being sought. Exploratory methods can be applied to very large datasets. Data mining of massive datasets has enabled statisticians to increase the rate of finding things that are not being sought.

In computational statistics, computation is viewed as an instrument of discovery; the role of the computer is not just to store data, perform computations, and produce graphs and tables, but additionally to suggest to the scientist alternative models and theories. Many alternative graphical displays of a given dataset are usually integral features of computational statistics. Another characteristic of computational statistics is the computational intensity of the methods; even for datasets of medium size, high-performance computers may be required to perform the computations. Large-scale computations can replace asymptotic approximations in statistical inference.

This book describes techniques used in computational statistics, and considers some of the areas of application, such as density estimation and model building, in which computationally intensive methods are useful. The book grew out of a semester course in "Computational Statistics" and various courses called "Topics in Computational Statistics" that I have offered at George Mason University over the past several years. The book is part of a much larger tome that also covers many topics in numerical analysis; see http://www.science.gmu.edu/~jgentle/cmpstbk/.

Many of the topics addressed in this book could easily be (and are) subjects for full-length books. My intent in this book is to describe these methods in a general manner and to emphasize commonalities among them. An example of a basic tool used in a variety of settings in computational statistics is the decomposition of a function so that it has a probability density as a factor. We encounter this technique in Monte Carlo methods (page 52), in function estimation (Chapters 6 and 9), and in projection pursuit (Chapters 10).

Most of the statistical methods and applications discussed in this book are computationally intensive, and that is why we consider them to be in the field called computational statistics. As mentioned earlier, however, the attitude with which we embark on a statistical analyses is a hallmark of computational statistics. The computations are often viewed as experiments and the computer is used as a tool of discovery.

I assume that the reader has a background in mathematical statistics at roughly the level of an advanced undergraduate- or beginning graduate-level course in the subject, and, of course, the mathematical prerequisites for such a course, which include advanced calculus, some linear algebra, and the basic notions of optimization. Except for that prerequisite, the text is essentially self-contained.

Part **??** addresses in a general manner the methods and techniques of computational statistics. The first chapter reviews some basic notions of statistical inference and some of the computational methods. The subject of a statistical analysis is viewed as a *data-generating process*. The immediate object of the analysis is a set of data that arose from the process. A wealth of standard statistical tools are available for analyzing the dataset and for making inferences about the process. Important tools in computational statistics involve simulations of the data-generating process. These simulations are used for *computational inference*. The standard principles of statistical inference are employed in computational inference. The difference is in the source of the data and how the data are treated.

The second chapter is about Monte Carlo simulation and some of its uses in computational inference, including Monte Carlo tests, in which artificial data are generated according to a hypothesis. Some parts of Chapter 2 are revised versions of material that originally appeared in Gentle (1998a). Chapters 3 and 4 discuss computational inference using resampling and partitioning of a given dataset. In these methods, a given dataset is used, but the Monte Carlo sampling is employed repeatedly on the data. These methods include randomization tests, jackknife techniques, and bootstrap methods, in which data are generated from the empirical distribution of a given sample, that is, the sample is resampled.

Chapter 5 discusses methods of projecting higher-dimensional data into lower dimensions; Chapter 6 covers some of the general issues in function estimation; and Chapter 7 presents a brief overview of some graphical methods, especially those concerned with multidimensional data. The more complicated the structure of the data and the higher the dimension, the more ingenuity is required for visualization of the data; it is, however, in just those situations that graphics is most important. The orientation of the discussion on graphics is that of computational statistics; the emphasis is on discovery; and the important issues that should be considered in making presentation graphics are not addressed. The tools discussed in Chapter 5 will also be used for clustering and classification, and, in general, for exploring structure in data.

Identification of interesting features, or "structure", in data is an important activity in computational statistics. In Part I, I consider the problem of identification of structure and the general problem of estimation of probability densities. In simple cases, or as approximations in more realistic situations, structure may be described in terms of functional relationships among the variables in a dataset.

The most useful and complete description of a random data generating process is the associated probability density, if it exists. Estimation of this special type of function is the topic of Chapters 8 and 9, building on general methods discussed in earlier chapters, especially Chapter 6. If the data follow a parametric distribution, or rather, if we are willing to assume that the data follow a parametric distribution, identification of the probability density is accomplished by estimation of the parameters. Nonparametric density estimation is considered in Chapter 9.

Features of interest in data include clusters of observations and relationships among variables that allow a reduction in the dimension of the data. I discuss methods for identification of structure in Chapter 10, building on some of the basic measures introduced in Chapter 5.

Higher-dimensional data have some surprising and counterintuitive properties, and I discuss some of the interesting characteristics of higher dimensions.

In Chapter 11, I discuss asymmetric relationships among variables. For such problems, the objective often is to estimate or predict a response for a given set of explanatory or predictive variables, or to identify the class to which an observation belongs. The approach is to use a given dataset to develop a model or a set of rules that can be applied to new data. Statistical modeling may be computationally intensive because of the number of possible forms considered or because of the recursive partitioning of the data used in selecting a model. In computational statistics, the emphasis is on *building* a model rather than just estimating the parameters in the model. Parametric estimation of course plays an important role in building models.

People in various disciplines have contributed to the development of the clustering and classification methods discussed in Chapters 10 and 11. Different terminology is used in different disciplines. Some people, especially in the field that was once called artificial intelligence, attempt to identify some methods— usually only the simpler ones—as "statistical", and other methods as something else, including "machine learning". I do not understand these distinctions. I take the view that any method of analyzing data is a statistical method. The major objective of statistics is to development knowledge (and maybe wisdom) from data. Another problem in this area is the profusion of names that often denote the same method, or a trivial variation in a method. Many research workers in this field have a propensity to "nail the flag to the mast", and then to defend the "flag" as representing minute distinctions from other flags.

As in Chapters 8 and 9, a simple model may be a probability distribution for some variable of interest. If, in addition, the relationship among variables is of interest, a model may contain a systematic component that expresses that relationship approximately and a random component that attempts to account for deviations from the relationship expressed by the systematic component.

I often take the view that a model describes a generation mechanism for data. A better understanding of a model can be assessed by taking this view:

use the model to simulate artificial data, and examine the artificial data for conformity to our expectations or to some available real data. In the text and in the exercises of this chapter, I often use a model to generate data. The data are then analyzed using the model. This process, which is characteristic of computational statistics, helps to evaluate the *method* of the analysis. It helps us understand the role of the individual components of the model: its functional form, the parameters, and the nature of the stochastic component.

Monte Carlo methods are widely used in the research literature to evaluate properties of statistical methods. Appendix A addresses some of the considerations that apply to this kind of study. It is emphasized that the study uses an *experiment*, and the principles of scientific experimentation should be observed. Appendix B describes some of the software and programming issues that may be relevant for conducting a Monte Carlo study. Some parts of these appendices are revised and updated versions of material that originally appeared in Gentle (1998a).

After this summary of what is in the book, I feel compelled to mention some things that *are not* in the book—but which are relevant to computational statistics. I realize that in many places throughout the book, I have skimped on details. When I teach the material, I find myself providing details, or else, preferably, having students work out details. Some important topics such as FFTs and wavelets are only mentioned in this book. Several other topics, perhaps most notably the bootstrap, classification methods, and model-building, are discussed only in an introductory manner. A full treatment of any of these topics would require by itself a longer book than this one. My goal has been to introduce a number of topics and devote an appropriate proportion of pages to each. I have given a number of references for more in-depth study of most of the topics. For most of these topics, I have more extensive class notes, but I felt that their inclusion would result in an unwieldy book. Many of the class notes are available through the web pages for some of the classes I teach (CSI 771 and CSI 779).

The exercises contain an important part of the information that is to be conveyed. Many exercises require use of the computer, in some cases to perform routine calculations and in other cases to conduct experiments on simulated data. The exercises range from the trivial or merely mechanical to the very challenging. I have not attempted to indicate which is which. Some of the Monte Carlo studies suggested in the exercises could be the bases for research publications.

When I teach this material, I use more examples, and more extensive examples, than what I have included in the text. Some of my examples form the basis for some of the exercises; but it is important to include discussion of them in the class lectures. Additional examples, datasets, and programs are available through links from the web page for this book.

The text covers more material than can reasonably be included in a one-semester course. A reasonable approach, however, is just to begin at the beginning and proceed sequentially through the book. For students with more background in statistics, Chapter 1 can be skipped. The book can serve as text for two courses in computational statistics if more emphasis is placed on the student projects and/or on numerical computations.

In most classes I teach in computational statistics, I give Exercise A.3 in Appendix A (page 348) as a term project. It is to replicate and extend a Monte Carlo study reported in some recent journal article. Each student picks an article to use. The statistical methods studied in the article must be ones that the student understands, but that is the only requirement as to the area of statistics addressed in the article. I have varied the way in which the project is carried out, but it usually involves more than one student working together. A simple way is for each student to referee another student's first version (due midway through the term) and to provide a report for the student author to use in a revision. Each student is both an author and a referee. In another variation, I have students be coauthors. One student selects the article and designs and performs the Monte Carlo experiment, and another student writes the article, in which the main content is the description and analysis of the Monte Carlo experiment.

Software Systems

What software systems a person needs to use depends on the kinds of problems addressed and what systems are available. In this book, I do not intend to teach any software system; and although I do not presume competence with any particular system, I will use examples from various systems, primarily S-Plus. Most of the code fragments will also work in R.

Some exercises suggest or require a specific software system. In some cases, the required software can be obtained from either `statlib` or `netlib` (see the Bibliography). The online help system should provide sufficient information about the software system required. As with most aspects of computer usage, a spirit of experimentation and adventure makes the effort easier and more rewarding.

Software and "Reproducible Research"

Software has become an integral part of much of scientific research. It is not just the software system; it is the details of the program. A basic tenet of the scientific method is the requirement that research be reproducible by other scientists. The work of experimental scientists has long been characterized by meticulous notes describing all details that may possibly be relevant to the environment in which the results were obtained. That kind of care generally requires that computer programs with complete documentation be preserved. This requirement for reproducible research has been enunciated by Jon Claerbout (`http://sepwww.stanford.edu/`), and described and exemplified by Buckheit and Donoho (1995).

Taking care to preserve and document the devilish details of computer programs pays dividends not only in the communication with other scientists, but also for the person conducting the research. Most people begin writing programs before they become serious about their research; hence preservation and documentation are skills that must be acquired after bad habits have already developed.

A Word about Notation

I try to be very consistent in notation. Most of the notation is "standard". Appendix C contains a list of notation, but a general summary here may be useful. Terms that represent mathematical objects, such as variables, functions, and parameters, are generally printed in an italic font. The exceptions are the standard names of functions, operators, and mathematical constants, such as sin, log, E (the expectation operator), d (the differential operator), e (the base of the natural logarithm), and so on.

I tend to use Greek letters for parameters and English letters for almost everything else, but in a few cases, I am not consistent in this distinction.

I do not distinguish vectors and scalars in the notation; thus, "x" may represent either a scalar or a vector, and x_i may represent either the ith element of an array or the ith vector in a set of vectors. I use uppercase letters for matrices and the corresponding lowercase letters with subscripts for elements of the matrices.

I generally use uppercase letters for random variables and the corresponding lowercase letters for realizations of the random variables. Sometimes I am not completely consistent in this usage, especially in the case of random samples and statistics.

Acknowledgements

I thank the participants in our Friday afternoon seminars on computational statistics, in particular, Cliff Sutton, for enjoyable discussions on statistical methodology, both during the seminar and in post-seminar visits to local pubs. For the past few years, I have enjoyed pleasant Tuesday lunches with Ryszard Michalski, and I'm sure some of our discussions have affected parts of this book.

I thank John Kimmel of Springer for his encouragement and advice on this book and other books he has worked with me on. I also thank the reviewers for their comments and suggestions.

I thank my wife María, to whom this book is dedicated, for everything.

I used TEX via LATEX to write the book, and I used S-Plus and R to generate the graphics. I did all of the typing, programming, etc., myself, so all mistakes are mine. I would appreciate receiving notice of errors as well as suggestions for improvement.

Material relating to courses I teach in the computational sciences is available over the World Wide Web at the URL,
    `http://www.science.gmu.edu/`

Notes on this book, including errata, are available at
    `http://www.science.gmu.edu/~jgentle/cmstbk/`

Fairfax County, Virginia   James E. Gentle
                                                                        May 26, 2002

Contents

Preface   vii

I   Methods of Computational Statistics   1

Introduction to Part I   3

1   Preliminaries   5
   1.1   Discovering Structure: Data Structures and Structure in Data . .   6
   1.2   Modeling and Computational Inference   8
   1.3   The Role of the Empirical Cumulative Distribution Function . .   11
   1.4   The Role of Optimization in Inference   15
   1.5   Inference about Functions   30
   1.6   Probability Statements in Statistical Inference   32
   Exercises   35

2   Monte Carlo Methods for Statistical Inference   39
   2.1   Generation of Random Numbers   40
   2.2   Monte Carlo Estimation   53
   2.3   Simulation of Data from a Hypothesized Model:
        Monte Carlo Tests   58
   2.4   Simulation of Data from a Fitted Model:
        "Parametric Bootstraps"   60
   2.5   Random Sampling from Data   60
   2.6   Reducing Variance in Monte Carlo Methods   61
   2.7   Acceleration of Markov Chain Monte Carlo Methods   65
   Exercises   66

3   Randomization and Data Partitioning   69
   3.1   Randomization Methods   70
   3.2   Cross Validation for Smoothing and Fitting   74
   3.3   Jackknife Methods   76
   Further Reading   82
   Exercises   83

4 Bootstrap Methods   **85**
  4.1 Bootstrap Bias Corrections 86
  4.2 Bootstrap Estimation of Variance 88
  4.3 Bootstrap Confidence Intervals 89
  4.4 Bootstrapping Data with Dependencies 93
  4.5 Variance Reduction in Monte Carlo Bootstrap 94
  Further Reading 96
  Exercises 97

5 Tools for Identification of Structure in Data   **99**
  5.1 Linear Structure and Other Geometric Properties 100
  5.2 Linear Transformations 101
  5.3 General Transformations of the Coordinate System 108
  5.4 Measures of Similarity and Dissimilarity 109
  5.5 Data Mining 123
  5.6 Computational Feasibility 124
  Exercises 125

6 Estimation of Functions   **127**
  6.1 General Methods for Estimating Functions 128
  6.2 Pointwise Properties of Function Estimators 143
  6.3 Global Properties of Estimators of Functions 146
  Exercises 150

7 Graphical Methods in Computational Statistics   **153**
  7.1 Viewing One, Two, or Three Variables 155
  7.2 Viewing Multivariate Data 168
  7.3 Hardware and Low-Level Software for Graphics 184
  7.4 Software for Graphics Applications 186
  Further Reading 188
  Exercises 188

II Exploring Data Density and Structure   **191**

Introduction to Part II   **193**

**8 Estimation of Probability Density Functions Using Parametric
    Models**   **197**
  8.1 Fitting a Parametric Probability Distribution 198
  8.2 General Families of Probability Distributions 199
  8.3 Mixtures of Parametric Families 202
  Exercises 203

9 Nonparametric Estimation of Probability Density Functions 205
   9.1 The Likelihood Function 206
   9.2 Histogram Estimators 208
   9.3 Kernel Estimators 217
   9.4 Choice of Window Widths 222
   9.5 Orthogonal Series Estimators 222
   9.6 Other Methods of Density Estimation 224
   Exercises 226

10 Structure in Data   233
   10.1 Clustering and Classification 237
   10.2 Ordering and Ranking Multivariate Data 255
   10.3 Linear Principal Components 264
   10.4 Variants of Principal Components 276
   10.5 Projection Pursuit 281
   10.6 Other Methods for Identifying Structure 289
   10.7 Higher Dimensions 290
   Exercises 294

11 Statistical Models of Dependencies   299
   11.1 Regression and Classification Models 301
   11.2 Probability Distributions in Models 308
   11.3 Fitting Models to Data 311
   Exercises 333

Appendices   336

A Monte Carlo Studies in Statistics   337
   A.1 Simulation as an Experiment 338
   A.2 Reporting Simulation Experiments 339
   A.3 An Example 340
   A.4 Computer Experiments 347
   Exercises 349

B Software for Random Number Generation   351
   B.1 The User Interface for Random Number Generators 353
   B.2 Controlling the Seeds in Monte Carlo Studies 354
   B.3 Random Number Generation in IMSL Libraries 354
   B.4 Random Number Generation in S-Plus and R 357

C Notation and Definitions   363

D Solutions and Hints for Selected Exercises   377

Bibliography   **385**
  Literature in Computational Statistics 386
  Resources Available over the Internet   387
  References for Software Packages 389
  References to the Literature 389

Author Index   **409**

Subject Index   **415**

Part I

Methods of Computational Statistics

Introduction to Part I

The field of computational statistics includes a set of statistical methods that are computationally intensive. These methods may involve looking at data from many different perspectives and looking at various subsets of the data. Even for moderately sized datasets, the multiple analyses may result in a large number of computations. Statistical methods may be computationally intensive also because the dataset is extremely large. With the ability to collect data automatically, ever-larger datasets are available for analysis.

Viewing data from various perspectives often involves transformations such as projections onto multiple lower-dimensional spaces. Interesting datasets may consist of subsets that are different in some important way from other subsets of the given data. The identification of different subsets and the properties that distinguish them is computationally intensive because of the large number of possible combinations.

Another type of computationally intensive method useful in a wide range of applications involves simulation of the data-generating process. Study of many sets of artificially generated data helps to understand the process that generates real data. This is an exciting method of computational statistics because of the inherent possibilities of unexpected discoveries through experimentation.

Monte Carlo experimentation is the use of simulated random numbers to estimate some functional of a probability distribution. In simple applications of Monte Carlo, a problem that does not naturally have a stochastic component may be posed as a problem with a component that can be identified with an expectation of some function of a random variable. The problem is then solved by estimating the expected value by use of a simulated sample from the distribution of the random variable. In such applications, Monte Carlo methods are similar to other methods of numerical analysis.

Monte Carlo methods differ from other methods of numerical analysis in yielding an *estimate* rather than an *approximation*. The "numerical error" in a Monte Carlo estimate is due to a pseudovariance associated with a pseudorandom variable; but the numerical error in standard numerical analysis is associated with approximations, including discretization, truncation, and roundoff.

Monte Carlo methods can also be used to make inferences about parameters of models and to study random processes. In statistical inference, real data are used to estimate parameters of models and to study random processes assumed

3

to have generated the data. Some of the statistical methods discussed in Part I use simulated data in the analysis of real data. There are several ways this can be done.

If the simulated data are used just to estimate one or more parameters, rather than to study the probability model more generally, we generally use the term *Monte Carlo* to refer to the method. Whenever simulated data are used in the broader problem of studying the complete process and building models, the method is often called *simulation*. This distinction between a simulation method and a Monte Carlo method is by no means universally employed; and we will sometimes use the terms "simulation" and "Monte Carlo" synonymously.

In either simulation or Monte Carlo, an actual dataset may be available; but it may be supplemented with artificially generated data. The term *"resampling"* is related to both "simulation" and "Monte Carlo", and some authors use it synonymously with one or both of the other terms. In this text, we generally use the term "resampling" to refer to a method in which random subsamples of a given dataset are generated.

In the first chapter, we discuss the general objectives in statistical analyses and, in particular, those objectives for which computationally intensive methods are appropriate. We also describe briefly some of the methods of statistical inference that are applicable generally whether in computational statistics or not. Then, in the following chapters, we discuss the general methods of computational statistics. These include:

- Monte Carlo methods and simulation;

- randomization and use of subsets of the data;

- bootstrap methods;

- projection and other methods of transforming data and approximating functions;

- graphical methods.

Chapter 1

Preliminaries

The purpose of an exploration of data may be rather limited and ad hoc, or the purpose may be more general, perhaps to gain understanding of some natural phenomenon. The questions addressed may be somewhat open-ended. The process of understanding often begins with general questions about the structure of the data. At any stage of the analysis, our understanding is facilitated by means of a *model*.

A model is a description that embodies our current understanding of a phenomenon. In an operational sense, we can formulate a model either as a description of a *data-generating process*, or as a prescription for processing data. The model is often expressed as a set of equations that relate data elements to each other. It may include probability distributions for the data elements. If any of the data elements are considered to be realizations of random variables, the model is a *stochastic model*.

A model should not limit our analysis; rather, the model should be able to evolve. The process of understanding involves successive refinements of the model. The refinements proceed from vague models to more specific ones. An exploratory data analysis may begin by mining the data to identify interesting properties. These properties generally raise questions that are to be explored further.

A class of models may have a common form within which the members of the class are distinguished by values of *parameters*. For example, the class of normal probability distributions has a single form of a probability density function that has two parameters. If this form of model is chosen to represent the properties of a dataset, we may seek confidence intervals for values of the two parameters or perform statistical tests of hypothesized values of the parameters.

In models that are not as mathematically tractable as the normal probability model—and many realistic models are not—computationally intensive methods involving simulations, resamplings, and multiple views may be used to make inferences about the parameters of a model.

1.1 Discovering Structure: Data Structures and Structure in Data

The components of statistical datasets are "observations" and "variables". In general, "data structures" are ways of organizing data to take advantage of the relationships among the variables constituting the dataset. Data structures may express hierarchical relationships, crossed relationships (as in "relational" databases), or more complicated aspects of the data (as in "object-oriented" databases).

In data analysis, "structure in the data" is of interest. Structure in the data includes such nonparametric features as modes, gaps, or clusters in the data, the symmetry of the data, and other general aspects of the shape of the data. Because many classical techniques of statistical analysis rely on an assumption of normality of the data, the most interesting structure in the data may be those aspects of the data that deviate most from normality.

Sometimes, it is possible to express the structure in the data in terms of mathematical models. Prior to doing this, graphical displays may be used to discover qualitative structure in the data. Patterns observed in the data may suggest explicit statements of the structure or of relationships among the variables in the dataset. The process of building models of relationships is an iterative one, and graphical displays are useful throughout the process. Graphs comparing data and the fitted models are used to refine the models.

Multiple Analyses and Multiple Views

Effective use of graphics often requires multiple views. For multivariate data, plots of individual variables or combinations of variables can be produced quickly and used to get a general idea of the properties of the data. The data should be inspected from various perspectives. Instead of a single histogram to depict the general shape of univariate data, for example, multiple histograms with different bin widths and different bin locations may provide more insight.

Sometimes, a few data points in a display can completely obscure interesting structure in the other data points. A zooming window to restrict the scope of the display and simultaneously restore the scale to an appropriate viewing size can reveal structure. A zooming window can be used with any graphics software whether the software supports it or not; zooming can be accomplished by deletion of the points in the dataset outside of the window.

Scaling the axes can also be used effectively to reveal structure. The relative scale is called the "aspect ratio". In Figure 1.1, which is a plot of a bivariate dataset, we form a zooming window that deletes a single observation. The greater magnification and the changed aspect ratio clearly show a relationship between X and Y in a region close to the origin that may not hold for the full range of data. A simple statement of this relationship would not extrapolate outside the window to the outlying point.

The use of a zooming window is not "deletion of outliers"; it is focusing in on a subset of the data and is done independently of whatever is believed about the data outside of the window.

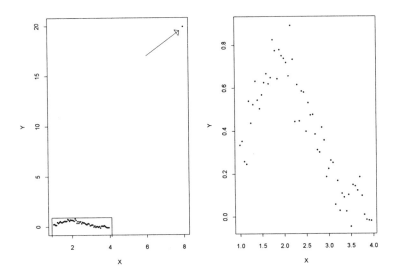

Figure 1.1: Scales Matter

One type of structure that may go undetected is that arising from the order in which the data were collected. For data that are recognized as a time series by the analyst, this is obviously not a problem, but often there is a time dependency in the data that is not recognized immediately. "Time" or "location" may not be an explicit variable on the dataset, even though it may be an important variable. The index of the observation within the dataset may be a surrogate variable for time, and characteristics of the data may vary as the index varies. Often it is useful to make plots in which one axis is the index number of the observations. More subtle time dependencies are those in which the values of the variables are not directly related to time, but relationships among variables are changing over time. The identification of such time dependencies is much more difficult, and often requires fitting a model and plotting residuals. Another strictly graphical way of observing changes in relationships over time is by using a sequence of graphical displays.

Simple Plots May Reveal the Unexpected

A simple plot of the data will often reveal structure or other characteristics of the data that numerical summaries do not.

An important property of data that is often easily seen in a graph is the unit of measurement. Data on continuous variables are often rounded or measured on a coarse grid. This may indicate other problems in the collection of the data. The horizontal lines in Figure 1.2 indicate that the data do not come from a continuous distribution. Whether we can use methods of data analysis that assume continuity depends on the coarseness of the grid or measurement; that is, on the extent to which the data are discrete or the extent to which they have been discretized.

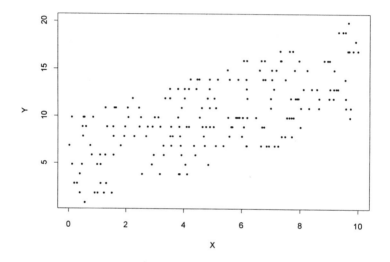

Figure 1.2: Discrete Data, Rounded Data, or Data Measured Imprecisely

We discuss graphics further in Chapter 7. The emphasis is on the use of graphics for discovery. The field of statistical graphics is much broader, of course, and includes many issues of design of graphical displays for conveying (rather than discovering) information.

1.2   Modeling and Computational Inference

The process of building models involves successive refinements. The evolution of the models proceeds from vague, tentative models to more complete ones, and our understanding of the process being modeled grows in this process.

The usual statements about statistical methods regarding bias, variance, and so on are made in the context of a model. It is not possible to measure bias or variance of a procedure to *select* a model, except in the relatively simple case of selection from some well-defined and simple set of possible models. Only within the context of rigid assumptions (a "metamodel") can we do a precise statistical analysis of model selection. Even the simple cases of selection of variables in linear regression analysis under the usual assumptions about the distribution of residuals (and this is a highly idealized situation) present more problems to the analyst than are generally recognized. See Kennedy and Bancroft (1971) and Speed and Yu (1993), for example, for some discussions of these kinds of problems in building regression models.

Descriptive Statistics, Inferential Statistics, and Model Building

We can distinguish statistical activities that involve:

- data collection;

- descriptions of a given dataset;

- inference within the context of a model or family of models; and

- model selection.

In any given application, it is likely that all of these activities will come into play. Sometimes (and often, ideally!), a statistician can specify how data are to be collected, either in surveys or in experiments. We will not be concerned with this aspect of the process in this text.

Once data are available, either from a survey or designed experiment, or just observational data, a statistical analysis begins by considering general descriptions of the dataset. These descriptions include ensemble characteristics, such as averages and spreads, and identification of extreme points. The descriptions are in the form of various summary statistics and graphical displays. The descriptive analyses may be computationally intensive for large datasets, especially if there are a large number of variables. The computationally intensive approach also involves multiple views of the data, including consideration of a large number of transformations of the data. We discuss these methods in Chapters 5 and 7 and in Part II.

A stochastic model is often expressed as a probability density function or as a cumulative distribution function of a random variable. In a simple linear regression model with normal errors,

$$Y = \beta_0 + \beta_1 x + E,$$

for example, the model may be expressed by use of the probability density function for the random variable E. (Notice that Y and E are written in uppercase because they represent random variables.) The probability density function for Y is

$$p(y) = \frac{1}{\sqrt{2\pi}\sigma} e^{-(y-\beta_0-\beta_1 x)^2/(2\sigma^2)}.$$

In this model, x is an observable covariate; σ, β_0, and β_1 are unobservable (and, generally, unknown) parameters; and 2 and π are constants. Statistical inference about parameters includes estimation or tests of their values or statements about their probability distributions based on observations of the elements of the model.

The elements of a stochastic model include observable random variables, observable covariates, unobservable parameters, and constants. Some random variables in the model may be considered to be "responses". The covariates may be considered to affect the response; they may or may not be random variables. The parameters are variable within a class of models, but for a specific data model the parameters are constants. The parameters may be considered to be unobservable random variables, and in that sense, a specific data model is defined by a realization of the parameter random variable. In the model, written as

$$Y = f(x; \beta) + E,$$

we identify a "systematic component", $f(x; \beta)$, and a "random component", E. The selection of an appropriate model may be very difficult, and almost always involves not only questions of how well the model corresponds to the observed data, but also the tractability of the model. The methods of computational statistics allow a much wider range of tractability than can be contemplated in mathematical statistics.

Statistical analyses generally are undertaken with the purpose of making a decision about a dataset, about a population from which a sample dataset is available, or in making a prediction about a future event. Much of the theory of statistics developed during the middle third of the twentieth century was concerned with formal inference; that is, use of a sample to make decisions about stochastic models based on probabilities that would result if a given model was indeed the data-generating process. The heuristic paradigm calls for rejection of a model if the probability is small that data arising from the model would be similar to the observed sample. This process can be quite tedious because of the wide range of models that should be explored and because some of the models may not yield mathematically tractable estimators or test statistics. Computationally intensive methods include exploration of a range of models, many of which may be mathematically intractable.

In a different approach employing the same paradigm, the statistical methods may involve direct simulation of the hypothesized data-generating process rather than formal computations of probabilities that would result under a given model of the data-generating process. We refer to this approach as *computational inference*. We discuss methods of computational inference in Chapters 2, 3, and 4. In a variation of computational inference, we may not even attempt to develop a model of the data-generating process; rather, we build decision rules directly from the data. This is often the approach in clustering and classification, which we discuss in Chapter 10. Computational inference is rooted in classical statistical inference. In subsequent sections of the current chapter, we discuss general techniques used in statistical inference.

1.3 The Role of the Empirical Cumulative Distribution Function

Methods of statistical inference are based on an assumption (often implicit) that a discrete uniform distribution with mass points at the observed values of a random sample is asymptotically the same as the distribution governing the data-generating process. Thus, the distribution function of this discrete uniform distribution is a model of the distribution function of the data-generating process.

For a given set of univariate data, $y_1, \ldots, y_n$, the *empirical cumulative distribution function*, or ECDF, is

$$P_n(y) = \frac{\#\{y_i, \text{ s.t. } y_i \leq y\}}{n}.$$

The ECDF is the basic function used in many methods of computational inference.

Although the ECDF has similar definitions for univariate and multivariate random variables, it is most useful in the univariate case. An equivalent expression for univariate random variables, in terms of intervals on the real line, is

$$P_n(y) = \frac{1}{n} \sum_{i=1}^{n} I_{(-\infty, y]}(y_i), \tag{1.1}$$

where I is the indicator function. (See page 368 for the definition and some of the properties of the indicator function. The measure $dI_{(-\infty, a]}(x)$, which we use in equation (1.6), for example, is particularly interesting.)

It is easy to see that the ECDF is pointwise unbiased for the CDF; that is, for a given y,

$$
\begin{aligned}
E\big(P_n(y)\big) &= E\left(\frac{1}{n} \sum_{i=1}^{n} I_{(-\infty, y]}(Y_i)\right) \\
&= \frac{1}{n} \sum_{i=1}^{n} E\left(I_{(-\infty, y]}(Y_i)\right) \\
&= \Pr(Y \leq y) \\
&= P(y). \tag{1.2}
\end{aligned}
$$

Similarly, we find

$$V\big(P_n(y)\big) = P(y)\big(1 - P(y)\big)/n; \tag{1.3}$$

indeed, at a fixed point y, $nP_n(y)$ is a binomial random variable with parameters n and $\pi = P(y)$. Because P_n is a function of the order statistics, which form a complete sufficient statistic for P, there is no unbiased estimator of $P(y)$ with smaller variance.

We also define the *empirical probability density function* (EPDF) as the derivative of the ECDF:

$$p_n(y) = \frac{1}{n} \sum_{i=1}^{n} \delta(y - y_i), \tag{1.4}$$

where δ is the Dirac delta function. The EPDF is just a series of spikes at points corresponding to the observed values. It is not as useful as the ECDF. It is, however, unbiased at any point for the probability density function at that point.

The ECDF and the EPDF can be used as estimators of the corresponding population functions, but there are better estimators (see Chapter 9).

Statistical Functions of the CDF and the ECDF

In many models of interest, a parameter can be expressed as a functional of the probability density function or of the cumulative distribution function of a random variable in the model. The mean of a distribution, for example, can be expressed as a functional Θ of the CDF P:

$$\Theta(P) = \int_{\mathbb{R}^d} y \, dP(y). \tag{1.5}$$

A functional that defines a parameter is called a *statistical function*.

Estimation of Statistical Functions

A common task in statistics is to use a random sample to estimate the parameters of a probability distribution. If the statistic T from a random sample is used to estimate the parameter θ, we measure the performance of T by the magnitude of the bias,

$$|E(T) - \theta|,$$

by the variance,

$$V(T) = E\left((T - E(T))^2\right),$$

by the mean squared error,

$$E\left((T - \theta)^2\right),$$

and by other expected values of measures of the distance from T to θ. (These expressions are for the scalar case, but similar expressions apply to vectors T and θ, in which case the bias is a vector, the variance is the variance-covariance matrix, and the mean squared error is a dot product and hence a scalar.)

If $E(T) = \theta$, T is unbiased for θ. For sample size n, if $E(T) = \theta + O(n^{-1/2})$, T is said to be *first-order accurate* for θ; if $E(T) = \theta + O(n^{-1})$, it is *second-order accurate*. (See page 369 for the definition of $O(\cdot)$. Convergence of $E(T)$ can also be expressed as a stochastic convergence of T, in which case we use the notation $O_P(\cdot)$.)

The order of the mean squared error is an important characteristic of an estimator. For good estimators of location, the order of the mean squared error is typically $O(n^{-1})$. Good estimators of probability densities, however, typically have mean squared errors of at least order $O(n^{-4/5})$ (see Chapter 9).

Estimation Using the ECDF

There are many ways to construct an estimator and to make inferences about the population. In the univariate case especially, we often use data to make inferences about a parameter by applying the statistical function to the ECDF. An estimator of a parameter that is defined in this way is called a *plug-in estimator*. A plug-in estimator for a given parameter is the same functional of the ECDF as the parameter is of the CDF.

For the mean of the model, for example, we use the estimate that is the same functional of the ECDF as the population mean in equation (1.5),

$$
\begin{aligned}
\Theta(P_n) &= \int_{-\infty}^{\infty} y \, \mathrm{d}P_n(y) \\
&= \int_{-\infty}^{\infty} y \, \mathrm{d}\frac{1}{n}\sum_{i=1}^{n} \mathrm{I}_{(-\infty,y]}(y_i) \\
&= \frac{1}{n}\sum_{i=1}^{n}\int_{-\infty}^{\infty} y \, \mathrm{d}\mathrm{I}_{(-\infty,y]}(y_i) \\
&= \frac{1}{n}\sum_{i=1}^{n} y_i \\
&= \bar{y}. \tag{1.6}
\end{aligned}
$$

The sample mean is thus a plug-in estimator of the population mean. Such an estimator is called a *method of moments estimator*. This is an important type of plug-in estimator. The method of moments results in estimates of the parameters $E(Y^r)$ that are the corresponding sample moments.

Statistical properties of plug-in estimators are generally relatively easy to determine. In some cases, the statistical properties, such as expectation and variance, are optimal in some sense.

In addition to estimation based on the ECDF, other methods of computational statistics make use of the ECDF. In some cases, such as in bootstrap methods, the ECDF is a surrogate for the CDF. In other cases, such as Monte Carlo methods, an ECDF for an estimator is constructed by repeated sampling, and that ECDF is used to make inferences using the observed value of the estimator from the given sample.

Viewed as a statistical function, Θ denotes a specific functional form. Any functional of the ECDF is a function of the data, so we may also use the notation $\Theta(Y_1, \ldots, Y_n)$. Often, however, the notation is cleaner if we use another letter to denote the function of the data; for example, $T(Y_1, \ldots, Y_n)$, even if it might

be the case that
$$T(Y_1, \ldots, Y_n) = \Theta(P_n).$$
We will also often use the same letter that denotes the functional of the sample to represent the random variable computed from a random sample; that is, we may write
$$T = T(Y_1, \ldots, Y_n).$$
As usual, we will use t to denote a realization of the random variable T.

Use of the ECDF in statistical inference does not require many assumptions about the distribution. Other methods discussed below are based on information or assumptions about the data-generating process.

Empirical Quantiles

For $\alpha \in (0, 1)$, the α *quantile* of the distribution with CDF P is the value $y_{(\alpha)}$ such that $P(y_{(\alpha)}) = \alpha$. (For a univariate random variable, this is a single point. For a d-variate random variable, it is a $(d-1)$-dimensional object that is generally nonunique.) For a discrete distribution the quantile may not exist for a given value of α.

We also use the term in a slightly different way: if $P(y) = \alpha$, we say the *quantile of y is α*.

This definition of a quantile applied to the ECDF leads to a quantile of 0 for the smallest sample value, $y_{(1)}$, and a quantile of 1 for the largest sample value, $y_{(n)}$. These values for quantiles are not so useful if the distribution is continuous, because it is likely that the range of the distribution extends beyond the smallest and largest observed values.

We define the *empirical quantile*, or *sample quantile*, corresponding to the ith order statistic, $y_{(i)}$, in a sample of size n as
$$\frac{i - \iota}{n + \nu} \tag{1.7}$$
for $\iota, \nu \in [0, \frac{1}{2}]$. Values of ι and ν that make the empirical quantiles of a random sample correspond closely to those of the population depend on the distribution of the population, which, of course, is generally unknown. A certain symmetry may be imposed by requiring $\nu = 1 - 2\iota$. Common choices are $\iota = \frac{1}{2}$ and $\nu = 0$.

We use empirical quantiles in Monte Carlo inference, in nonparametric inference, and in graphical displays for comparing a sample with a standard distribution or with another sample. Empirical quantiles can be used as estimators of the population quantiles, but there are other estimators. Some, such as the Kaigh-Lachenbruch estimator and the Harrell-Davis estimator (see Kaigh and Lachenbruch, 1982, and Harrell and Davis, 1982), use a weighted combination of multiple data points instead of just a single one, as in the simple estimators above. See Dielman, Lowry, and Pfaffenberger (1994) for comparisons of various quantile estimators. If a covariate is available, it may be possible to use it to improve the quantile estimate. This is often the case in simulation studies. See Hesterberg and Nelson (1998) for a discussion of this technique.

1.4 The Role of Optimization in Inference

Important classes of estimators are defined as the point at which some function that involves the parameter and the random variable achieves an optimum. There are, of course, many functions that involve the parameter and the random variable; an example is the probability density.

In the use of function optimization in inference, once the objective function is chosen, observations on the random variable are taken and are then considered to be fixed; the parameter in the function is considered to be a variable (the "decision variable", in the parlance often used in the literature on optimization). The function is then optimized with respect to the parameter variable. The nature of the function determines the meaning of "optimized"; if the function is the probability density, for example, "optimized" would logically mean "maximized". (This leads to maximum likelihood estimation, which we discuss below.)

In discussing the use of optimization in statistical estimation, we must be careful to distinguish between a symbol that represents a fixed parameter and a symbol that represents a "variable" parameter. When we denote a probability density function as $p(y \mid \theta)$, we generally expect "θ" to represent a fixed, but possibly unknown, parameter. In an estimation method that involves optimizing this function, however, "θ" is a variable placeholder. In the following discussion, we will generally consider θ to be a variable. We will use θ_* to represent the true value of the parameter on which the random variable observed is conditioned. We may also use θ_0, θ_1, and so on to represent specific fixed values of the variable. In an iterative algorithm, we use $\theta^{(k)}$ to represent a fixed value in the kth iteration.

Some Comments on Optimization

The solution to an optimization problem is in some sense "best" for that problem and its objective functions; this may mean it is considerably less good for some other optimization problem. It is often the case, therefore, that an optimal solution is not robust to assumptions about the phenomenon being studied. Use of optimization methods is likely to magnify the effects of the assumptions.

In the following pages we discuss two general ways in which optimization is used in statistical inference. One is to minimize deviations of observed values from what a model would predict. This is an intuitive procedure which may be chosen without regard to the nature of the data-generating process. The justification for a particular form of the objective function, however, may arise from assumptions about a probability distribution underlying the data-generating process. Another way in which optimization is used in statistical inference is in maximizing the "likelihood", which we will discuss more precisely beginning on page 22. The correct likelihood function depends on the probability distribution underlying the data-generating process, which, of course, is not known and can only be assumed. How poor the maximum likelihood estimator is depends on both the true distribution and the assumed distribution.

In the discussion below, we briefly describe particular optimization techniques that assume that the objective function is a continuous function of the decision variables, or the parameters. We also assume that there are no a priori constraints on the values of the parameters. Techniques appropriate for other situations, such as for discrete optimization and constrained optimization, are available in the general literature on optimization.

We must also realize that mathematical expressions below do not necessarily imply computational methods. There are many additional considerations for the numerical computations. A standard example of this point is in the solution of the linear full-rank system of n equations in n unknowns: $Ax = b$. While we may write the solution as $x = A^{-1}b$, we would almost never compute the solution by forming the inverse and then multiplying b by it (see Gentle, 1998b, page 87).

Estimation by Minimizing Residuals

In many applications, we can express the expected value of a random variable as a function of a parameter (which might be a vector, of course):

$$E(Y) = f(\theta_*). \tag{1.8}$$

The expectation may also involve covariates, so in general we may write $f(x, \theta_*)$. The standard linear regression model is an example: $E(Y) = x^T\beta$. If the covariates are observable, they can be subsumed into $f(\theta)$.

The more difficult and interesting problems, of course, involve the determination of the form of the function $f(\theta)$. In these sections, however, we concentrate on the simpler problem of determining an appropriate value of θ, assuming that the form of the function f is known.

If we can obtain observations $y_1, \ldots, y_n$ on Y (and observations on the covariates if there are any), a reasonable estimator of θ_* is a value $\widehat{\theta}$ that minimizes the residuals,

$$r_i(\theta) = y_i - f(\theta), \tag{1.9}$$

over all possible choices of θ. This is a logical approach because we expect the observed y's to be close to $f(\theta_*)$.

There are, of course, several ways we could reasonably "minimize the residuals". In general, we seek to minimize some norm of $r(\theta)$, the n-vector of residuals. The optimization problem is

$$\min_{\theta} \|r(\theta)\|. \tag{1.10}$$

We often choose the norm as the L_p norm, so we minimize a function of an L_p norm of the residuals,

$$s_p(\theta) = \sum_{i=1}^{n} |y_i - f(\theta)|^p, \tag{1.11}$$

for some $p > 1$, to obtain an L_p *estimator*. Simple choices are the sum of the absolute values and the sum of the squares. The latter choice yields the *least squares estimator*. More generally, we could minimize

$$s_p(\theta) = \sum_{i=1}^{n} \rho(y_i - f(\theta))$$

for some nonnegative function $\rho(\cdot)$ to obtain an *"M estimator"*. (The name comes from the similarity of this objective function to the objective function for some maximum likelihood estimators.)

Standard techniques for optimization can be used to determine estimates that minimize various functions of the residuals, that is, for some appropriate function of the residuals $s(\cdot)$, to solve

$$\min_{\theta} s(\theta). \tag{1.12}$$

Except for special forms of the objective function, the algorithms to solve expression (1.12) are iterative. If s is twice differentiable, one algorithm is Newton's method, in which the minimizing value of θ, $\hat{\theta}$, is obtained as a limit of the iterates

$$\theta^{(k)} = \theta^{(k-1)} - \left(H_s\left(\theta^{(k-1)}\right)\right)^{-1} \nabla s\left(\theta^{(k-1)}\right), \tag{1.13}$$

where $H_s(\theta)$ denotes the Hessian of s and $\nabla s(\theta)$ denotes the gradient of s, both evaluated at θ. (Newton's method is sometimes called the Newton-Raphson method, for no apparent reason.)

The function $s(\cdot)$ is usually chosen to be differentiable, at least piecewise.

For various computational considerations, instead of the exact Hessian, a matrix $\widetilde{H}_s$ approximating the Hessian is often used. In this case, the technique is called a quasi-Newton method.

Newton's method or a quasi-Newton method often overshoots the best step. The *direction*

$$\theta^{(k)} - \theta^{(k-1)}$$

may be the best direction, but the distance

$$\|\theta^{(k)} - \theta^{(k-1)}\|$$

may be too great. A variety of methods using Newton-like iterations involve a system of equations of the form

$$\widetilde{H}_s(\theta)\, d = \nabla s(\theta). \tag{1.14}$$

These equations are solved for the direction d, and the new point is taken as the old θ plus αd, for some damping factor α.

There are various ways of deciding when an iterative optimization algorithm has converged. In general, convergence criteria are based on the size of the change in $\theta^{(k)}$ from $\theta^{(k-1)}$, or the size of the change in $s(\theta^{(k)})$ from $s(\theta^{(k-1)})$. See Kennedy and Gentle (1980, page 435 and following) for a discussion of termination criteria in multivariate optimization.

Statistical Properties of Minimum-Residual Estimators

It is generally difficult to determine the variance or other high-order statistical properties of an estimator defined as above (that is, defined as the minimizer of some function of the residuals). In many cases, all that is possible is to approximate the variance of the estimator in terms of some relationship that holds for a normal distribution. (In robust statistical methods, for example, it is common to see a "scale estimate" expressed in terms of some mysterious constant times a function of some transformation of the residuals.)

There are two issues that affect both the computational method and the statistical properties of the estimator defined as the solution to the optimization problem. One consideration has to do with the acceptable values of the parameter θ. In order for the model to make sense, it may be necessary that the parameter be in some restricted range. In some models, a parameter must be positive, for example. In these cases, the optimization problem has constraints. Such a problem is more difficult to solve than an unconstrained problem. Statistical properties of the solution are also more difficult to determine. More extreme cases of restrictions on the parameter may require the parameter to take values in a countable set. Obviously, in such cases, Newton's method cannot be used because the derivatives cannot be defined. In those cases, a combinatorial optimization algorithm must be used instead. Other situations in which the function is not differentiable also present problems for the optimization algorithm. In such cases, if the domain is continuous, a descending sequence of simplexes can be used. See Rustagi (1994) for a discussion of these methods.

Secondly, it may turn out that the optimization problem (1.12) has local minima. This depends on the nature of the function $f(\cdot)$ in equation (1.8). Local minima present problems for the computation of the solution because the algorithm may get stuck in a local optimum. Local minima also present conceptual problems concerning the appropriateness of the estimation criterion itself. As long as there is a unique global optimum, it seems reasonable to seek it and to ignore local optima. It is not so clear what to do if there are multiple points at which the global optimum is attained.

Least Squares Estimation

Least squares estimators are generally more tractable than estimators based on other functions of the residuals. They are more tractable both in terms of solving the optimization problem to obtain the estimate and in approximating statistical properties of the estimators, such as their variances.

Assume that θ is an m-vector and that $f(\cdot)$ is a smooth function. Letting y be the n-vector of observations, we can write the least squares objective function corresponding to equation (1.11) as

$$s(\theta) = \big(r(\theta)\big)^{\mathrm{T}} r(\theta), \tag{1.15}$$

where the superscript T indicates the transpose of a vector or matrix.

The gradient and the Hessian for a least squares problem have special structures that involve the Jacobian of the residuals, $J_r(\theta)$. The gradient of s is

$$\nabla s(\theta) = \big(J_r(\theta)\big)^{\mathrm{T}} r(\theta). \tag{1.16}$$

Taking derivatives of $\nabla s(\theta)$, we see that the Hessian of s can be written in terms of the Jacobian of r and the individual residuals:

$$H_s(\theta) = \big(J_r(\theta)\big)^{\mathrm{T}} J_r(\theta) + \sum_{i=1}^{n} r_i(\theta) H_{r_i}(\theta). \tag{1.17}$$

In the vicinity of the solution $\widehat{\theta}$, the residuals $r_i(\theta)$ should be small, and $H_s(\theta)$ may be approximated by neglecting the second term:

$$H_s(\theta) \approx \big(J_r(\theta)\big)^{\mathrm{T}} J_r(\theta).$$

Using equation (1.16) and this approximation for equation (1.17) in the gradient descent equation (1.14), we have the system of equations

$$\big(J_r(\theta^{(k-1)})\big)^{\mathrm{T}} J_r(\theta^{(k-1)})\, d^{(k)} = -\big(J_r(\theta^{(k-1)})\big)^{\mathrm{T}} r(\theta^{(k-1)}) \tag{1.18}$$

to be solved for $d^{(k)}$, where

$$d^{(k)} \propto \theta^{(k)} - \theta^{(k-1)}.$$

It is clear that the solution $d^{(k)}$ is a descent direction; that is, if $\nabla s(\theta^{(k-1)}) \neq 0$,

$$\begin{aligned}
(d^{(k)})^{\mathrm{T}} \nabla s(\theta^{(k-1)}) &= -\Big(\big(J_r(\theta^{(k-1)})\big)^{\mathrm{T}} d^{(k)}\Big)^{\mathrm{T}} \big(J_r(\theta^{(k-1)})\big)^{\mathrm{T}} d^{(k)} \\
&< 0.
\end{aligned}$$

The update step is determined by a line search in the appropriate direction:

$$\theta^{(k)} - \theta^{(k-1)} = \alpha^{(k)} d^{(k)}.$$

This method is called the *Gauss-Newton algorithm*. (The method is also sometimes called the "modified Gauss-Newton algorithm" because many years ago no damping was used in the Gauss-Newton algorithm, and $\alpha^{(k)}$ was taken as the constant 1. Without an adjustment to the step, the Gauss-Newton method tends to overshoot the minimum in the direction $d^{(k)}$.) In practice, rather than a full search to determine the best value of $\alpha^{(k)}$, we just consider the sequence of values $1, \frac{1}{2}, \frac{1}{4}, \ldots$ and take the largest value so that $s(\theta^{(k)}) < s(\theta^{(k-1)})$. The algorithm terminates when the change is small.

If the residuals are not small or if $J_r(\theta^{(k)})$ is poorly conditioned, the Gauss-Newton method can perform very poorly. One possibility is to add a conditioning matrix to the coefficient matrix in equation (1.18). A simple choice is $\tau^{(k)} I_m$, and the equation for the update becomes

$$\Big(\big(J_r(\theta^{(k-1)})\big)^{\mathrm{T}} J_r(\theta^{(k-1)}) + \tau^{(k)} I_m\Big) d^{(k)} = -\big(J_r(\theta^{(k-1)})\big)^{\mathrm{T}} r(\theta^{(k-1)}),$$

where I_m is the $m \times m$ identity matrix. A better choice may be an $m \times m$ scaling matrix, $S^{(k)}$, that takes into account the variability in the columns of $J_r(\theta^{(k-1)})$; hence, we have for the update

$$\left(\left(J_r(\theta^{(k-1)}) \right)^T J_r(\theta^{(k-1)}) + \lambda^{(k)} \left(S^{(k)} \right)^T S^{(k)} \right) d^{(k)} = -\left(J_r(\theta^{(k-1)}) \right)^T r(\theta^{(k-1)}).$$

(1.19)

The basic requirement for the matrix $\left(S^{(k)} \right)^T S^{(k)}$ is that it improve the condition of the coefficient matrix. There are various ways of choosing this matrix. One is to transform the matrix $\left(J_r(\theta^{(k-1)}) \right)^T J_r(\theta^{(k-1)})$ so that it has 1's along the diagonal (this is equivalent to forming a correlation matrix from a variance-covariance matrix), and to use the scaling vector to form $S^{(k)}$. The nonnegative factor $\lambda^{(k)}$ can be chosen to control the extent of the adjustment. The sequence $\lambda^{(k)}$ must go to 0 for the algorithm to converge.

Equation (1.19) can be thought of as a Lagrange multiplier formulation of the constrained problem,

$$\min_x \quad \tfrac{1}{2} \left\| J_r(\theta^{(k-1)})x + r(\theta^{(k-1)}) \right\|$$

(1.20)

$$\text{s.t.} \quad \left\| S^{(k)}x \right\| \leq \delta_k.$$

The Lagrange multiplier $\lambda^{(k)}$ is zero if $d^{(k)}$ from equation (1.18) satisfies $\|d^{(k)}\| \leq \delta_k$; otherwise, it is chosen so that $\left\| S^{(k)} d^{(k)} \right\| = \delta_k$.

Use of an adjustment such as in equation (1.19) is called the *Levenberg-Marquardt algorithm*. This is probably the most widely used method for nonlinear least squares.

Variance of Least Squares Estimators

If the distribution of Y has finite moments, the sample mean $\overline{Y}$ is a consistent estimator of $f(\theta_*)$. Furthermore, the minimum residual norm $\left(r(\widehat{\theta}) \right)^T r(\widehat{\theta})$ divided by $(n - m)$ is a consistent estimator of the variance of Y, say σ^2, that is

$$\sigma^2 = \mathrm{E}(Y - f(\theta))^2.$$

We denote this estimator as $\widehat{\sigma^2}$:

$$\widehat{\sigma^2} = \left(r(\widehat{\theta}) \right)^T r(\widehat{\theta})/(n - m).$$

The variance of the least squares estimator $\widehat{\theta}$, however, is not easy to work out, except in special cases. In the simplest case, f is linear and Y has a normal distribution, and we have the familiar linear regression estimates of θ and of the variance of the estimator of θ. The estimator of the variance is $\widehat{\sigma^2}/(n - m)$, where $\widehat{\sigma^2}$ is an estimator of the variance of the residuals.

Without the linearity property, however, even with the assumption of normality, it may not be possible to write a simple expression for the variance-covariance matrix of an estimator that is defined as the solution to the least squares optimization problem. Using a linear approximation, however, we may estimate an approximate variance-covariance matrix for $\widehat{\theta}$ as

$$\left(\left(J_r(\widehat{\theta})\right)^{T} J_r(\widehat{\theta})\right)^{-1} \widehat{\sigma^2}. \tag{1.21}$$

Compare this linear approximation to the expression for the estimated variance-covariance matrix of the least squares estimator $\widehat{\beta}$ in the linear regression model $E(Y) = X\beta$, in which $J_r(\widehat{\beta})$ is just X. The estimate of σ^2 is taken as the sum of the squared residuals divided by $n - m$, where m is the number of estimated elements in θ.

If the residuals are small, the Hessian is approximately equal to the cross-product of the Jacobian, as we see from equation (1.17), so an alternate expression for the estimated variance-covariance matrix is

$$\left(H_r(\widehat{\theta})\right)^{-1} \widehat{\sigma^2}. \tag{1.22}$$

This latter expression is more useful if Newton's method or a quasi-Newton method is used instead of the Gauss-Newton method for the solution of the least squares problem because in these methods the Hessian or an approximate Hessian is used in the computations.

Iteratively Reweighted Least Squares

Often in applications, the residuals in equation (1.9) are not given equal weight for estimating θ. This may be because the reliability or precision of the observations may be different. For *weighted least squares*, instead of equation (1.15) we have the objective function

$$s_w(\theta) = \sum_{i=1}^{n} w_i \left(r_i(\theta)\right)^2. \tag{1.23}$$

The weights add no complexity to the problem, and the Gauss-Newton methods of the previous section apply immediately, with

$$\tilde{r}(\theta) = W r(\theta),$$

where W is a diagonal matrix containing the weights.

The simplicity of the computations for weighted least squares suggests a more general usage of the method. Suppose that we are to minimize some other L_p norm of the residuals r_i, as in equation (1.11). The objective function can be written as

$$s_p(\theta) = \sum_{i=1}^{n} \frac{1}{|y_i - f(\theta)|^{2-p}} |y_i - f(\theta)|^2. \tag{1.24}$$

This leads to an iteration on the least squares solutions. Beginning with $y_i - f(\theta^{(0)}) = 1$, we form the recursion that results from the approximation

$$s_p(\theta^{(k)}) \approx \sum_{i=1}^{n} \frac{1}{\left| y_i - f(\theta^{(k-1)}) \right|^{2-p}} \left| y_i - f(\theta^{(k)}) \right|^2.$$

Hence, we solve a weighted least squares problem, and then form a new weighted least squares problem using the residuals from the previous problem. This method is called *iteratively reweighted least squares*, or IRLS. The iterations over the residuals are outside the loops of iterations to solve the least squares problems, so in nonlinear least squares, IRLS results in nested iterations.

There are some problems with the use of reciprocals of powers of residuals as weights. The most obvious problem arises from very small residuals. This is usually handled by use of a fixed large number as the weight.

Iteratively reweighted least squares can also be applied to other norms,

$$s_\rho(\theta) = \sum_{i=1}^{n} \rho(y_i - f(\theta)),$$

but the approximations for the updates may not be as good.

Estimation by Maximum Likelihood

One of the most commonly used approaches to statistical estimation is *maximum likelihood*. The concept has an intuitive appeal, and the estimators based on this approach have a number of desirable mathematical properties, at least for broad classes of distributions.

Given a sample $y_1, \ldots, y_n$ from a distribution with probability density or probability mass function $p(y \mid \theta_*)$, a reasonable estimate of θ is the value that maximizes the joint density or joint probability with variable θ at the observed sample value: $\prod_i p(y_i \mid \theta)$. We define the *likelihood function* as a function of a variable in place of the parameter:

$$L_n(\theta \,; y) = \prod_{i=1}^{n} p(y_i \mid \theta). \qquad (1.25)$$

Note the reversal in roles of variables and parameters. The likelihood function appears to represent a "posterior probability", but, as emphasized by R. A. Fisher who made major contributions to the use of the likelihood function in inference, that is not an appropriate interpretation. See Albert (2002) and Edwards (1992) for discussions of the interpretation of likelihood.

Just as in the case of estimation by minimizing residuals, the more difficult and interesting problems involve the determination of the form of the function $p(y_i \mid \theta)$. In these sections, as above, however, we concentrate on the simpler problem of determining an appropriate value of θ, assuming that the form of p is known.

The value of θ for which L attains its maximum value is the *maximum likelihood estimate* (MLE) of θ_* for the given data, y. The data—that is, the realizations of the variables in the density function—are considered as fixed, and the parameters are considered as variables of the optimization problem,

$$\max_{\theta} L_n(\theta\,;y). \tag{1.26}$$

This optimization problem can be much more difficult than the optimization problem (1.10) that results from an estimation approach based on minimization of some norm of a residual vector. As we discussed in that case, there can be both computational and statistical problems associated either with restrictions on the set of possible parameter values or with the existence of local optima of the objective function. These problems also occur in maximum likelihood estimation.

Applying constraints in the optimization problem to force the solution to be within the set of possible parameter values is called *restricted maximum likelihood estimation*, or REML estimation. In addition to problems due to constraints or due to local optima, other problem may arise if the likelihood function is bounded. The conceptual difficulties resulting from an unbounded likelihood are much deeper. In practice, for computing estimates in the unbounded case, the general likelihood principle may be retained, and the optimization problem redefined to include a penalty that keeps the function bounded. Adding a penalty to form a bounded objective function in the optimization problem, or to dampen the solution is called *penalized maximum likelihood estimation*.

For a broad class of distributions, the maximum likelihood criterion yields estimators with good statistical properties. The conditions that guarantee certain optimality properties are called the "regular case". The general theory of the regular case is discussed in a number of texts, such as Lehmann and Casella (1998). Various nonregular cases are discussed by Cheng and Traylor (1995).

Although in practice, the functions of residuals that are minimized are almost always differentiable, and the optimum occurs at a stationary point, this is often not the case in maximum likelihood estimation. A standard example in which the MLE does not occur at a stationary point is a distribution in which the range depends on the parameter, and the simplest such distribution is the uniform $U(0,\theta)$. In this case, the MLE is the max order statistic.

An important family of probability distributions are those whose probability densities are members of the *exponential family*, that is, densities of the form

$$
\begin{aligned}
p(y\,|\,\theta) &= h(y)\exp\!\left(\theta^{\mathrm{T}}g(y)-a(\theta)\right), \quad \text{if} \quad y\in\mathcal{Y},\\
&= 0, \quad \text{otherwise}, \tag{1.27}
\end{aligned}
$$

where $\mathcal{Y}$ is some set, θ is an m-vector, and $g(\cdot)$ is an m-vector-valued function. Maximum likelihood estimation is particularly straightforward for distributions in the exponential family. Whenever $\mathcal{Y}$ does not depend on θ, and $g(\cdot)$ and $a(\cdot)$

are sufficiently smooth, the MLE has certain optimal statistical properties. This family of probability distributions includes many of the familiar distributions, such as the normal, the binomial, the Poisson, the gamma, the Pareto, and the negative binomial.

The *log-likelihood function*,

$$l_{L_n}(\theta\,;\,y) = \log L_n(\theta\,;\,y), \tag{1.28}$$

is a sum rather than a product. The form of the log-likelihood in the exponential family is particularly simple:

$$l_{L_n}(\theta\,;\,y) = \sum_{i=1}^{n} \theta^{\mathrm{T}} g(y_i) - n\,a(\theta) + c,$$

where c depends on the y_i but is constant with respect to the variable of interest.

The logarithm is monotone, so the optimization problem (1.26) can be solved by solving the maximization problem with the log-likelihood function:

$$\max_{\theta} l_{L_n}(\theta\,;\,y). \tag{1.29}$$

In the following discussion, we will find it convenient to drop the subscript n in the notation for the likelihood and the log-likelihood. We will also often work with the likelihood and log-likelihood as if there is only one observation. (A general definition of a likelihood function is any nonnegative function that is proportional to the density or the probability mass function; that is, it is the same as the density or the probability mass function except that the arguments are switched, and its integral or sum over the domain of the random variable need not be 1.)

If the likelihood is twice differentiable and if the range does not depend on the parameter, Newton's method (see equation (1.14)) could be used to solve the optimization problem (1.29). Newton's equation

$$H_{l_L}(\theta^{(k-1)}\,;\,y)\, d^{(k)} = \nabla l_L(\theta^{(k-1)}\,;\,y) \tag{1.30}$$

is used to determine the step direction in the kth iteration. A quasi-Newton method, as we mentioned on page 17, uses a matrix $\widetilde{H}_{l_L}(\theta^{(k-1)})$ in place of the Hessian $H_{l_L}(\theta^{(k-1)})$. At this point, we should remind the reader of the comments on page 16. Mathematical expressions do not necessarily imply computational methods. There are many additional considerations for the numerical computations, and the expression below rarely should be used directly in a computer program.

The log-likelihood function relates directly to useful concepts in statistical inference. If it exists, the derivative of the log-likelihood is the relative rate of change, with respect to the parameter placeholder θ, of the probability density function at a fixed observation. If θ is a scalar, some positive function of the derivative such as its square or its absolute value is obviously a measure of the effect of change in the parameter or in the estimate of the parameter. More generally, an outer product of the derivative with itself is a useful measure of the changes in the components of the parameter at any given point in the parameter space:

$$\nabla l_L(\theta \, ; \, y) \; (\nabla l_L(\theta \, ; \, y))^{\mathrm{T}}.$$

The average of this quantity with respect to the probability density of the random variable Y,

$$I(\theta \,|\, Y) = \mathrm{E}_\theta \left(\nabla l_L(\theta \,|\, Y) \; (\nabla l_L(\theta \,|\, Y))^{\mathrm{T}} \right), \tag{1.31}$$

is called the *information matrix*, or the Fisher information matrix, that an observation on Y contains about the parameter θ.

The optimization problem (1.26) or (1.29) can be solved by Newton's method, equation (1.13) on page 17, or by a quasi-Newton method. (We should first note that this is a maximization problem, so the signs are reversed from our previous discussion of a minimization problem.)

If θ is a scalar, the square of the first derivative is the negative of the second derivative,

$$\left(\frac{\partial}{\partial \theta} l_L(\theta \, ; \, y) \right)^2 = -\frac{\partial^2}{\partial \theta^2} l_L(\theta \, ; \, y),$$

or, in general,

$$\nabla l_L(\theta \, ; \, y) \; (\nabla l_L(\theta \, ; \, y))^{\mathrm{T}} = -\mathrm{H}_{l_L}(\theta \, ; \, y). \tag{1.32}$$

This is interesting because the second derivative, or an approximation of it, is used in a Newton-like method to solve the maximization problem.

A common quasi-Newton method for optimizing $l_L(\theta \, ; \, y)$ is *Fisher scoring*, in which the Hessian in Newton's method is replaced by its expected value. The expected value can be replaced by an estimate, such as the sample mean. The iterates then are

$$\theta^{(k)} = \theta^{(k-1)} - \left(\widetilde{E}\big(\theta^{(k-1)}\big) \right)^{-1} \nabla l_L\big(\theta^{(k-1)} \, ; \, y\big), \tag{1.33}$$

where $\widetilde{E}(\theta^{(k-1)})$ is an estimate or an approximation of

$$\mathrm{E}\left(\mathrm{H}_{l_L} \big(\theta^{(k-1)} \,|\, Y\big) \right), \tag{1.34}$$

which is itself an approximation of $\mathrm{E}_{\theta_*}(\mathrm{H}_{l_L}(\theta \,|\, Y))$. By equation (1.32), this is the negative of the Fisher information matrix *if* the differentiation and expectation operators can be interchanged. (This is one of the "regularity conditions" we alluded to earlier.) The most common practice is to take $\widetilde{E}(\theta^{(k-1)})$ as the Hessian evaluated at the current value of the iterations on θ; that is, as $\mathrm{H}_{l_L}(\theta^{(k-1)} \, ; \, y)$. This is called the *observed* information matrix.

In some cases a covariate x_i may be associated with the observed y_i, and the distribution of Y with given covariate x_i has a parameter μ that is a function of x_i and θ. (The linear regression model is an example, with $\mu_i = x_i^T \theta$.) We may in general write $\mu = x_i(\theta)$. In these cases, another quasi-Newton method may be useful. The Hessian in equation (1.30) is replaced by

$$\left(X(\theta^{(k-1)})\right)^{\mathrm{T}} K(\theta^{(k-1)}) \, X(\theta^{(k-1)}), \tag{1.35}$$

where $K(\theta^{(k-1)})$ is a positive definite matrix that may depend on the current value $\theta^{(k-1)}$. (Again, think of this in the context of a regression model, but not necessarily linear regression.) This method was suggested by Jörgensen (1984) and is called the *Delta algorithm* because of its similarity to the delta method for approximating a variance-covariance matrix (described on page 31).

In some cases, when θ is a vector, the optimization problem (1.26) or (1.29) can be solved by alternating iterations on the elements of θ. In this approach, iterations based on equations such as (1.30) are

$$\widetilde{H}_{l_L}\left(\theta_i^{(k-1)} \; ; \; \theta_j^{(k-1)}, y\right) d_i^{(k)} = \nabla l_{l_L}\left(\theta_i^{(k-1)} \; ; \; \theta_j^{(k-1)}, y\right), \tag{1.36}$$

where $\theta = (\theta_i, \theta_j)$ (or (θ_j, θ_i)), d_i is the update direction for θ_i, and θ_j is considered to be constant in this step. In the next step, the indices i and j are exchanged. This is called componentwise optimization. For some objective functions, the optimal value of θ_i for fixed θ_j can be determined in closed form. In such cases, componentwise optimization may be the best method.

Sometimes, we may be interested in the MLE of θ_i given a fixed value of θ_j, so the iterations do not involve an interchange of i and j as in component-wise optimization. Separating the arguments of the likelihood or log-likelihood function in this manner leads to what is called *profile likelihood*, or *concentrated likelihood*.

As a purely computational device, the separation of θ into smaller vectors makes for a smaller optimization problem for which the number of computations is reduced by more than a linear amount. The iterations tend to zigzag toward the solution, so convergence may be quite slow. If, however, the Hessian is block diagonal, or almost block diagonal (with sparse off-diagonal submatrices), two successive steps of the alternating method are essentially equivalent to one step with the full θ. The rate of convergence would be the same as that with the full θ. Because the total number of computations in the two steps is less than the number of computations in a single step with a full θ, the method may be more efficient in this case.

Statistical Properties of MLE

Under suitable regularity conditions we referred to earlier, maximum likelihood estimators have a number of desirable properties. For most distributions used as models in practical applications, the MLEs are consistent. Furthermore, in those cases, the MLE $\widehat{\theta}$ is asymptotically normal (with mean θ_*) with variance-covariance matrix

$$\left(E_{\theta_*} \left(-H_{l_L} \left(\theta_* \mid Y \right) \right) \right)^{-1}, \tag{1.37}$$

which is the inverse of the Fisher information matrix. A consistent estimator of the variance-covariance matrix is the Hessian at $\widehat{\theta}$. (Note that there are two kinds of asymptotic properties and convergence issues. Some involve the iterative algorithm, and the others are the usual statistical asymptotics in terms of the sample size.)

EM Methods

As we mentioned above, the computational burden in a single iteration for solving the MLE optimization problem can be reduced by more than a linear amount by separating θ into two subvectors. The MLE is then computed by alternating between computations involving the two subvectors, and the iterations proceed in a zigzag path to the solution. Each of the individual sequences of iterations is simpler than the sequence of iterations on the full θ.

Another alternating method that arises from an entirely different approach alternates between updating $\theta^{(k)}$ using maximum likelihood and conditional expected values. This method is called the *EM method* because the alternating steps involve an expectation and a maximization. The method was described and analyzed by Dempster, Laird, and Rubin (1977). Many additional details and alternatives are discussed by McLachlan and Krishnan (1997) who also work through about thirty examples of applications of the EM algorithm.

The EM methods can be explained most easily in terms of a random sample that consists of two components, one observed and one unobserved or missing. A simple example of missing data occurs in life-testing, when, for example, a number of electrical units are switched on and the time when each fails is recorded. In such an experiment, it is usually necessary to curtail the recordings prior to the failure of all units. The failure times of the units still working are unobserved. The data are said to be *left censored*. The number of censored observations and the time of the censoring obviously provide information about the distribution of the failure times.

The missing data can be missing observations on the same random variable that yields the observed sample, as in the case of the censoring example; or the missing data can be from a different random variable that is related somehow to the random variable observed.

Many common applications of EM methods do involve missing-data problems, but this is not necessary. Often, an EM method can be constructed based on an artificial "missing" random variable to supplement the observable data.

Let $Y = (U, V)$, and assume that we have observations on U but not on V. We wish to estimate the parameter θ, which figures in the distribution of both components of Y. An EM method uses the observations on U to obtain a value of $\theta^{(k)}$ that increases the likelihood and then uses an expectation based on V that increases the likelihood further.

Let $L_c(\theta ; u, v)$ and $l_{L_c}(\theta ; u, v)$ denote, respectively, the likelihood and the log-likelihood for the complete sample. The likelihood for the observed U is

$$L(\theta ; u) = \int L_c(\theta ; u, v) \, dv,$$

and $l_L(\theta ; u) = \log L(\theta ; u)$. The EM approach to maximizing $L(\theta ; u)$ has two alternating steps. The first one begins with a value $\theta^{(0)}$. The steps are iterated until convergence.

- E step : compute $q^{(k)}(\theta) = E_{V|u,\theta^{(k-1)}}\big(l_{L_c}(\theta \mid u, V)\big)$.

- M step : determine $\theta^{(k)}$ to maximize $q^{(k)}(\theta)$, subject to any constraints on acceptable values of θ.

The sequence $\theta^{(1)}, \theta^{(2)}, \ldots$ converges to a local maximum of the observed-data likelihood $L(\theta ; u)$ under fairly general conditions (including, of course, the nonexistence of a local maximum near enough to $\theta^{(0)}$). The EM method can be very slow to converge, however. See Wu (1983) for discussion of the convergence conditions.

For a simple example of the EM method, see Exercise 1.9, in which the problem in Dempster, Laird, and Rubin (1977) is described. As a further example of the EM method, consider an experiment described by Flury and Zoppè (2000). It is assumed that the lifetime of light bulbs follows an exponential distribution with mean θ. To estimate θ, n light bulbs were tested until they all failed. Their failure times were recorded as $u_1, \ldots, u_n$. In a separate experiment, m bulbs were tested, but the individual failure times were not recorded. Only the number of bulbs, r, that had failed at time t was recorded. The missing data are the failure times of the bulbs in the second experiment, $v_1, \ldots, v_m$. We have

$$l_{L_c}(\theta ; u, v) = -n(\log \theta + \bar{u}/\theta) - \sum_{i=1}^{m}(\log \theta + v_i/\theta).$$

The expected value, $E_{V|u,\theta^{(k-1)}}$, of this is

$$q^{(k)}(\theta) = -(n+m)\log \theta - \frac{1}{\theta}\left(n\bar{u} + (m-r)(t + \theta^{(k-1)}) + r(\theta^{(k-1)} - th^{(k-1)})\right),$$

where the hazard $h^{(k-1)}$ is given by

$$h^{(k-1)} = \frac{e^{t/\theta^{(k-1)}}}{1 - e^{t/\theta^{(k-1)}}}.$$

The kth M step determines the maximum, which, given $\theta^{(k-1)}$, occurs at

$$\theta^{(k)} = \frac{1}{n+m}n\bar{u} + (m-r)(t + \theta^{(k-1)}) + r(\theta^{(k-1)} - th^{(k-1)}).$$

Starting with a positive number $\theta^{(0)}$, this equation is iterated until convergence.

This example is interesting because if we assume that the distribution of the light bulbs is uniform, $U(0, \theta)$ (such bulbs are called "heavybulbs"!), the EM algorithm cannot be applied. As we have pointed out above, maximum likelihood methods must be used with some care whenever the range of the distribution depends on the parameter. In this case, however, there is another problem. It is in computing $q^{(k)}(\theta)$, which does not exist for $\theta < \theta^{(k-1)}$.

Although in the paper that first provided a solid description of the EM method (Dempster, Laird, and Rubin, 1977), specific techniques were used for the computations in the two steps, it is not necessary for the EM method to use those same inner-loop algorithms. There are various other ways to perform each of these computations. A number of papers since 1977 have suggested specific methods for the computations and have given new names to methods based on those inner-loop computations.

For the expectation step, there are not as many choices. In the happy case of an exponential family or some other nice distributions, the expectation can be computed in closed form. Otherwise, computing the expectation is a numerical quadrature problem. There are various procedures for quadrature, including Monte Carlo (see page 53). Wei and Tanner (1990) call an EM method that uses Monte Carlo to evaluate the expectation an MCEM method. (If a Newton-Cotes method is used, however, we do not call it an NCEM method.) The additional Monte Carlo computations add a lot to the overall time required for convergence of the EM method. Even the variance-reducing methods discussed in Section 2.6 can do little to speed up the method. In order to reduce the costs of Monte Carlo sampling in MCEM, Levine and Casella (2001) suggest reuse of Monte Carlo samples from previous expectation steps.

An additional problem in using Monte Carlo in the expectation step may be that the distribution of Y is difficult to simulate. The versatile Gibbs method (page 50) is often useful in this context (see Chan and Ledolter, 1995). The convergence criterion for optimization methods that involve Monte Carlo generally should be tighter than for deterministic methods.

For the maximization step, there are more choices, as we have seen in the discussion of maximum likelihood estimation above.

For the maximization step, Dempster, Laird, and Rubin (1977) suggested requiring only an increase in the expected value; that is, take $\theta^{(k)}$ so that $q_k(\theta^{(k)}) \geq q_{k-1}(\theta^{(k-1)})$. This is called a generalized EM algorithm, or GEM. Rai and Matthews (1993) suggest taking $\theta^{(k)}$ as the point resulting from a single Newton step and called this method EM1.

Meng and Rubin (1993) describe a GEM algorithm in which the M-step is a componentwise maximization, as in the update step of equation (1.36) on page 26; that is, if $\theta = (\theta_1, \theta_2)$, first $\theta_1^{(k)}$ is determined to maximize q subject to the constraint $\theta_2 = \theta_2^{(k-1)}$; then $\theta_2^{(k)}$ is determined to maximize q subject to the constraint $\theta_1 = \theta_1^{(k)}$. They call this an expectation conditional maximization, or ECM, algorithm. This sometimes simplifies the maximization problem so that it can be done in closed form. Jamshidian and Jennrich (1993) discuss acceleration of the EM algorithm using conjugate gradient methods and using quasi-Newton methods (Jamshidian and Jennrich, 1997).

Kim and Taylor (1995) describe an EM method when there are linear restrictions on the parameters.

As is usual for estimators defined as solutions to optimization problems, we may have some difficulty in determining the statistical properties of the estimators. Louis (1982) suggested a method of estimating the variance-covariance matrix of the estimator by use of the gradient and Hessian of the complete-data log-likelihood, $l_{L_c}(\theta\,;\,u,v)$. Meng and Rubin (1991) use a "supplemented" EM method, SEM, for estimation of the variance-covariance matrix. Kim and Taylor (1995) also described ways of estimating the variance-covariance matrix using computations that are part of the EM steps.

It is interesting to note that under certain assumptions on the distribution, the iteratively reweighted least squares method discussed on page 22 can be formulated as an EM method (see Dempster, Laird, and Rubin, 1980).

1.5   Inference about Functions

Functions of Parameters and Functions of Estimators

Suppose that instead of estimating the parameter θ, we wish to estimate $g(\theta)$, where $g(\cdot)$ is some function. If the function $g(\cdot)$ is monotonic or has certain other properties estimators, it may be the case that the estimator that results from the minimum residuals principle or from the maximum likelihood principle is invariant; that is, the estimator of $g(\theta)$ is merely the function $g(\cdot)$ evaluated at the solution to the optimization problem for estimating θ. The statistical properties of a T for estimating θ, however, do not necessarily carry over to $g(T)$ for estimating $g(\theta)$.

As an example of why a function of an unbiased estimator may not be unbiased, consider a simple case in which T and $g(T)$ are scalars. Let $R = g(T)$ and consider $\mathrm{E}(R)$ and $g(\mathrm{E}(T))$ in the case in which g is a convex function. (A function g is a *convex function* if for any two points x and y in the domain of g, $g(\frac{1}{2}(x+y)) \leq \frac{1}{2}(g(x)+g(y))$.) In this case, obviously

$$\mathrm{E}(R) \leq g(\mathrm{E}(T)), \qquad (1.38)$$

so R is biased for $g(\theta)$. (This relation is *Jensen's inequality.*) An opposite inequality obviously also applies to a concave function, in which case the bias is positive.

It is often possible to adjust R to be unbiased for $g(\theta)$; and properties of T, such as sufficiency for θ, may carry over to the adjusted R. Some of the applications of the jackknife and the bootstrap that we discuss later are in making adjustments to estimators of $g(\theta)$ that are based on estimators of θ.

The variance of $R = g(T)$ can often be approximated in terms of the variance of T. Let T and θ be m-vectors and R be a k-vector. In a simple but common case, we may know that T in a sample of size n has an approximate normal distribution with mean θ and some variance-covariance matrix, say $V(T)$, and g is a smooth function (that is, it can be approximated by a truncated Taylor series about θ):

$$\begin{aligned} R_i &= g_i(T) \\ &\approx g_i(\theta) + J_{g_i}(\theta)(T - \theta) + \frac{1}{2}(T - \theta)^{\mathrm{T}} H_{g_i}(\theta)(T - \theta). \end{aligned}$$

Because the variance of T is $O(n^{-1})$, the remaining terms in the expansion go to zero in probability at the rate of at least n^{-1}.

This yields the approximations

$$E(R) \approx g(\theta) \tag{1.39}$$

and

$$V(R) \approx J_g(\theta) \, V(T) \left(J_g(\theta) \right)^{\mathrm{T}}. \tag{1.40}$$

This method of approximation of the variance is called the *delta method*.

A common form of a simple estimator that may be difficult to analyze and may have unexpected properties is a ratio of two statistics,

$$R = \frac{T}{S},$$

where S is a scalar. An example is a studentized statistic, in which T is a sample mean and S is a function of squared deviations. If the underlying distribution is normal, a statistic of this form may have a well-known and tractable distribution. In particular, if T is a mean and S is a function of an independent chi-squared random variable, the distribution is that of a Student's t. If the underlying distribution has heavy tails, however, the distribution of R may have unexpectedly light tails. An asymmetric underlying distribution may also cause the distribution of R to be very different from a Student's t distribution. If the underlying distribution is positively skewed, the distribution of R may be negatively skewed (see Exercise 1.10).

Linear Estimators

A functional Θ is *linear* if, for any two functions f and g in the domain of Θ and any real number a,

$$\Theta(af + g) = a\Theta(f) + \Theta(g).$$

A statistic is linear if it is a linear functional of the ECDF. A linear statistic can be computed from a sample using an online algorithm, and linear statistics from two samples can be combined by addition. Strictly speaking, this definition excludes statistics such as means, but such statistics are *essentially linear* in the sense that they can be combined by a linear combination if the sample sizes are known.

1.6 Probability Statements in Statistical Inference

There are two important instances in statistical inference in which statements about probability are associated with the decisions of the inferential methods. In hypothesis testing, under assumptions about the distributions, we base our inferential methods on probabilities of two types of errors. In confidence intervals the decisions are associated with probability statements about coverage of the parameters. For both cases the probability statements are based on the distribution of a random sample, $Y_1, \ldots, Y_n$. In computational inference, probabilities associated with hypothesis tests or confidence intervals are estimated by simulation of a hypothesized data-generating process or by resampling of an observed sample.

Tests of Hypotheses

Often statistical inference involves testing a "null" hypothesis, H_0, about the parameter. In a simple case, for example, we may test the hypothesis

$$H_0 : \quad \theta = \theta_0$$

versus an alternative hypothesis that θ takes on some other value or is in some set that does not include θ_0. The straightforward way of performing the test involves use of a test statistic, T, computed from a random sample of data, $Y_1, \ldots, Y_n$. Associated with T is a rejection region C such that if the null hypothesis is true, $\Pr(T \in C)$ is some preassigned (small) value, α, and $\Pr(T \in C)$ is greater than α if the null hypothesis is not true. Thus, C is a region of more "extreme" values of the test statistic if the null hypothesis is true. If $T \in C$, the null hypothesis is rejected. It is desirable that the test have a high probability of rejecting the null hypothesis if indeed the null hypothesis is not true. The probability of rejection of the null hypothesis is called the power of the test.

A procedure for testing that is mechanically equivalent to this is to compute the test statistic t and then to determine the probability that T is more extreme than t. In this approach, the realized value of the test statistic determines a region C_t of more extreme values. The probability that the test statistic is in C_t if the null hypothesis is true, $\Pr(T \in C_t)$, is called the "p-value" or "significance level" of the realized test statistic.

If the distribution of T under the null hypothesis is known, the critical region or the p-value can be determined. If the distribution of T is not known, some other approach must be used. A common method is to use some approximation to the distribution. The objective is to approximate a quantile of T under the null hypothesis. The approximation is often based on an asymptotic distribution of the test statistic. In Monte Carlo tests, discussed in Section 2.3, the quantile of T is estimated by simulation of the distribution of the underlying data.

Confidence Intervals

Our usual notion of a confidence interval relies on a frequency approach to probability, and it leads to the definition of a $1 - \alpha$ confidence interval for the (scalar) parameter θ as the random interval (T_L, T_U) that has the property

$$\Pr(T_L \leq \theta \leq T_U) = 1 - \alpha. \tag{1.41}$$

This is also called a $(1 - \alpha)100\%$ confidence interval. The endpoints of the interval, T_L and T_U, are functions of a sample, $Y_1, \ldots, Y_n$. The interval (T_L, T_U) is not uniquely determined.

The concept extends easily to vector-valued parameters. Rather than taking vectors T_L and T_U, however, we generally define an ellipsoidal region, whose shape is determined by the covariances of the estimators.

A realization of the random interval, say (t_L, t_U), is also called a confidence interval. Although it may seem natural to state that the "probability that θ is in (t_L, t_U) is $1 - \alpha$", this statement can be misleading unless a certain underlying probability structure is assumed.

In practice, the interval is usually specified with respect to an estimator of θ, T. If we know the sampling distribution of $T - \theta$, we may determine c_1 and c_2 such that

$$\Pr(c_1 \leq T - \theta \leq c_2) = 1 - \alpha; \tag{1.42}$$

and hence

$$\Pr(T - c_2 \leq \theta \leq T - c_1) = 1 - \alpha.$$

If either T_L or T_U in equation (1.41) is infinite or corresponds to a bound on acceptable values of θ, the confidence interval is one-sided. For two-sided confidence intervals, we may seek to make the probability on either side of T to be equal, to make $c_1 = -c_2$, and/or to minimize $|c_1|$ or $|c_2|$. This is similar in spirit to seeking an estimator with small variance.

For forming confidence intervals, we generally use a function of the sample that also involves the parameter of interest, $f(T, \theta)$. The confidence interval is then formed by separating the parameter from the sample values.

Whenever the distribution depends on parameters other than the one of interest, we may be able to form only conditional confidence intervals that depend on the value of the other parameters. A class of functions that are particularly useful for forming confidence intervals in the presence of such nuisance parameters are called *pivotal* values, or pivotal functions. A function $f(T, \theta)$ is said to be a pivotal function if its distribution does not depend on any unknown parameters. This allows exact confidence intervals to be formed for the parameter θ. We first form

$$\Pr\left(f_{(\alpha/2)} \leq f(T, \theta) \leq f_{(1-\alpha/2)}\right) = 1 - \alpha, \tag{1.43}$$

where $f_{(\alpha/2)}$ and $f_{(1-\alpha/2)}$ are quantiles of the distribution of $f(T, \theta)$; that is,

$$\Pr(f(T, \theta) \leq f_{(\pi)}) = \pi.$$

If, as in the case considered above, $f(T, \theta) = T - \theta$, the resulting confidence interval has the form

$$\Pr\left(T - f_{(1-\alpha/2)} \leq \theta \leq T - f_{(\alpha/2)}\right) = 1 - \alpha.$$

For example, suppose that $Y_1, \ldots, Y_n$ is a random sample from a $N(\mu, \sigma^2)$ distribution, and $\overline{Y}$ is the sample mean. The quantity

$$f(\overline{Y}, \mu) = \frac{\sqrt{n(n-1)}\,(\overline{Y} - \mu)}{\sqrt{\sum (Y_i - \overline{Y})^2}} \tag{1.44}$$

has a Student's t distribution with $n - 1$ degrees of freedom, no matter what is the value of σ^2. This is one of the most commonly used pivotal values.

The pivotal value in equation (1.44) can be used to form a confidence value for θ by first writing

$$\Pr\left(t_{(\alpha/2)} \leq f(\overline{Y}, \mu) \leq t_{(1-\alpha/2)}\right) = 1 - \alpha,$$

where $t_{(\pi)}$ is a percentile from the Student's t distribution. Then, after making substitutions for $f(\overline{Y}, \mu)$, we form the familiar confidence interval for μ:

$$\left(\overline{Y} - t_{(1-\alpha/2)}\, s/\sqrt{n}, \quad \overline{Y} - t_{(\alpha/2)}\, s/\sqrt{n}\right), \tag{1.45}$$

where s^2 is the usual sample variance, $\sum (Y_i - \overline{Y})^2/(n - 1)$.

Other similar pivotal values have F distributions. For example, consider the usual linear regression model in which the n-vector random variable Y has a $N_n(X\beta, \sigma^2 I)$ distribution, where X is an $n \times m$ known matrix, and the m-vector β and the scalar σ^2 are unknown. A pivotal value useful in making inferences about β is

$$g(\widehat{\beta}, \beta) = \frac{\left(X(\widehat{\beta} - \beta)\right)^{\mathrm{T}} X(\widehat{\beta} - \beta)/m}{(Y - X\widehat{\beta})^{\mathrm{T}}(Y - X\widehat{\beta})/(n - m)}, \tag{1.46}$$

where

$$\widehat{\beta} = (X^{\mathrm{T}} X)^+ X^{\mathrm{T}} Y.$$

The random variable $g(\widehat{\beta}, \beta)$ for any finite value of σ^2 has an F distribution with m and $n - m$ degrees of freedom.

For a given parameter and family of distributions, there may be multiple pivotal values. For purposes of statistical inference, such considerations as unbiasedness and minimum variance may guide the choice of a pivotal value to use. Alternatively, it may not be possible to identify a pivotal quantity for a particular parameter. In that case, we may seek an approximate pivot. A function is asymptotically pivotal if a sequence of linear transformations of the function is pivotal in the limit as $n \to \infty$.

If the distribution of T is known, c_1 and c_2 in equation (1.42) can be determined. If the distribution of T is not known, some other approach must be used. A method for computational inference, discussed in Section 4.3, is to use "bootstrap" samples from the ECDF.

Exercises

1.1. (a) How would you describe, in nontechnical terms, the structure of the dataset displayed in Figure 1.1, page 7?

   (b) How would you describe the structure of the dataset in more precise mathematical terms? (Obviously, without having the actual data, your equations must contain unknown quantities. The question is meant to make you think about *how* you would do this—that is, what would be the components of your model.)

1.2. Show that the variance of the ECDF at a point y is the expression in equation (1.3) on page 11. *Hint:* Use the definition of the variance in terms of expected values, and represent $E\left((P_n(y))^2 \right)$ in a manner similar to how $E(P_n(y))$ was represented in equations (1.2).

1.3. The variance functional.

   (a) Express the variance of a random variable as a functional of its CDF as was done in equation (1.5) for the mean.

   (b) What is the same functional of the ECDF?

   (c) What is the plug-in estimate of the variance?

   (d) What are the statistical properties of the plug-in estimate of the variance? (Is it unbiased? Is it consistent? Is it an MLE?, etc.)

1.4. Assume a random sample of size 10 from a normal distribution. With $\nu = 1 - 2\iota$ in equation (1.7), determine the value of ι that makes the empirical quantile of the 9th order statistic unbiased for the normal quantile corresponding to 0.90.

1.5. Give examples of

   (a) a parameter that is defined by a linear functional of the distribution function, and

   (b) a parameter that is not a linear functional of the distribution function.

   (c) Is the variance a linear functional of the distribution function?

1.6. Consider the least squares estimator of β in the usual linear regression model, $E(Y) = X\beta$.

   (a) Use expression (1.21) on page 21 to derive the variance-covariance matrix for the estimator.

   (b) Use expression (1.22) to derive the variance-covariance matrix for the estimator.

1.7. Assume a random sample $y_1, \ldots, y_n$ from a gamma distribution with parameters α and β.

   (a) What are the least squares estimates of α and β? (Recall $E(Y) = \alpha\beta$ and $V(Y) = \alpha\beta^2$.)

   (b) Write a function in a language such as R, Matlab, or Fortran that accepts a sample of size n and computes the least squares estimator of α and β and an approximation of the variance-covariance matrix using both expression (1.21) and expression (1.22).

(c) Try out your program in Exercise 1.7b by generating a sample of size 500 from a gamma(2,3) distribution and then computing the estimates. (See Appendix B for information on software for generating random deviates.)

(d) Formulate the optimization problem for determining the MLE of α and β. Does this problem have a closed-form solution?

(e) Write a function in a language such as R, Matlab, or Fortran that accepts a sample of size n and computes the least squares estimator of α and β and computes an approximation of the variance-covariance matrix using expression (1.37), page 27.

(f) Try out your program in Exercise 1.7e by computing the estimates from an artificial sample of size 500 from a gamma(2,3) distribution.

1.8. For the random variable Y with a distribution in the exponential family and whose density is expressed in the form of equation (1.27) on page 23, and assuming that the first two moments of $g(Y)$ exist and $a(\cdot)$ is twice differentiable, show that

$$E(g(Y)) = \nabla a(\theta)$$

and

$$V(g(Y)) = H_a(\theta).$$

Hint: First show that

$$E(\nabla \log(p(Y \mid \theta))) = 0,$$

where the differentiation is with respect to θ.

1.9. Dempster, Laird, and Rubin (1977) consider the multinomial distribution with four outcomes, that is, the multinomial with probability function,

$$p(x_1, x_2, x_3, x_4) = \frac{n!}{x_1! x_2! x_3! x_4!} \pi_1^{x_1} \pi_2^{x_2} \pi_3^{x_3} \pi_4^{x_4},$$

with $n = x_1 + x_2 + x_3 + x_4$ and $1 = \pi_1 + \pi_2 + \pi_3 + \pi_4$. They assumed that the probabilities are related by a single parameter, θ:

$$\pi_1 = \frac{1}{2} + \frac{1}{4}\theta$$

$$\pi_2 = \frac{1}{4} - \frac{1}{4}\theta$$

$$\pi_3 = \frac{1}{4} - \frac{1}{4}\theta$$

$$\pi_4 = \frac{1}{4}\theta,$$

where $0 \le \theta \le 1$. (This model goes back to an example discussed by Fisher, 1925, in *Statistical Methods for Research Workers*.) Given an observation (x_1, x_2, x_3, x_4), the log-likelihood function is

$$l(\theta) = x_1 \log(2 + \theta) + (x_2 + x_3) \log(1 - \theta) + x_4 \log(\theta) + c$$

and

$$dl(\theta)/d\theta = \frac{x_1}{2 + \theta} - \frac{x_2 + x_3}{1 - \theta} + \frac{x_4}{\theta}.$$

The objective is to estimate θ.

(a) Determine the MLE of θ. (Just solve a simple polynonial equation.) Evaluate the estimate using the data that Dempster, Laird, and Rubin used: $n = 197$ and $x = (125, 18, 20, 34)$.

(b) Although the optimum is easily found as in the previous part of this exercise, it is instructive to use Newton's method (equation (1.13) on page 17). Write a program to determine the solution by Newton's method, starting with $\hat{\theta}^{(0)} = 0.5$.

(c) Write a program to determine the solution by scoring (which is the quasi-Newton method given in equation (1.33) on page 25), again starting with $\hat{\theta}^{(0)} = 0.5$.

(d) Write a program to determine the solution by the EM algorithm, again starting with $\hat{\theta}^{(0)} = 0.5$.

(e) How do these methods compare? (Remember, of course, that this is a particularly simple problem.)

1.10. Assume that $\{X_1, X_2\}$ is a random sample of size 2 from an exponential distribution with parameter θ. Consider the random variable formed as a Student's t,

$$T = \frac{\overline{X} - \theta}{\sqrt{S^2/2}},$$

where $\overline{X}$ is the sample mean and S^2 is the sample variance,

$$\frac{1}{n-1} \sum (X_i - \overline{X})^2.$$

(Note that $n = 2$.)

(a) Show that the distribution of T is negatively skewed (although the distribution of X is positively skewed).

(b) Give a heuristic explanation of the negative skewness of T.

The properties illustrated in the exercise relate to the robustness of statistical procedures that use Student's t. While those procedures may be robust to some departures from normality, they are often not robust to skewness. These properties also have relevance to the use of statistics like a Student's t in the bootstrap.

1.11. A function T of a random variable X with distribution parametrized by θ is said to be *sufficient* for θ if the conditional distribution of X given $T(X)$ does not depend on θ. Discuss (compare and contrast) pivotal and sufficient functions. (Start with the basics: Are they statistics? In what way do they both depend on some universe of discourse, that is, on some family of distributions?)

1.12. Use the pivotal value $g(\hat{\beta}, \beta)$ in equation (1.46) on page 34 to form a $(1-\alpha)100\%$ confidence region for β in the usual linear regression model.

1.13. Assume a random sample $y_1, \ldots, x_n$ from a normal distribution with mean μ and variance σ^2. Determine an unbiased estimator of σ based on the sample variance, s^2. (Note that s^2 is sufficient and unbiased for σ^2.)

Chapter 2

Monte Carlo Methods for Statistical Inference

Monte Carlo methods are experiments. Monte Carlo experimentation is the use of simulated random numbers to estimate some functional of a probability distribution. A problem that does not have a stochastic component sometimes may also be posed as a problem with a component that can be identified with an expectation of some function of a random variable. The problem is then solved by estimating the expected value by use of a simulated sample from the distribution of the random variable.

Monte Carlo methods use random numbers, so to implement a Monte Carlo method it is necessary to have a source of random numbers. On the computer, we generally settle for *pseudorandom* numbers, that is, numbers that *appear to be* random but are actually deterministic.

Often, our objective is not to simulate random sampling directly, but rather to estimate a specific quantity related to the distribution of a given sample. In this case, we may want to ensure that a chosen sample closely reflects the distribution of the population we are simulating. Because of random variation, a truly random sample or a pseudorandom sample that simulates a random sample would not necessarily have this property. Sometimes, therefore, we generate a *quasirandom* sample, which is a sample constrained to reflect closely the distribution of the population we are simulating, rather than to exhibit the variability that would result from random sampling. Because in either case we proceed to treat the samples as if they were random, we will refer to both pseudorandom numbers and quasirandom numbers as "random numbers", except when we wish to emphasize the "pseudo" or "quasi" nature.

In the first section of this chapter, we briefly discuss how random numbers are generated on the computer. In Chapters 1, 2, and 3 of Gentle (1998a), there are more extensive discussions of these methods. In subsequent sections of this chapter, we discuss various ways random numbers are used in statistical inference. Monte Carlo methods are also used in many of the techniques described in later chapters. More extensive uses of Monte Carlo methods are discussed in the book by Robert and Casella (1999).

2.1   Generation of Random Numbers

A sequence of pseudorandom numbers generated by a computer program is determined by a *seed*; that is, an initial state of the program. A given seed generates the same sequence of pseudorandom numbers every time the program is run. The ability to control the sequence is important because this allows the experimenter to reproduce results exactly and also to combine experiments that use pseudorandom numbers.

There are various algorithms for generating pseudorandom numbers, and various computer programs that implement these algorithms. Some algorithms and programs are better than others. Statistical tests for randomness applied to samples of pseudorandom numbers generated by good random number generators yield results consistent with hypotheses of randomness. The pseudorandom numbers simulate random samples. See Chapter 6 of Gentle (1998a) for discussions of quality of random number generators and for methods of testing their quality. Two sets of tests for random number generators are "DIEHARD", developed by Marsaglia (1985, 1995), and the NIST Test Suite, described in NIST (2000).

Although the algorithms for random number generation seem fairly simple, there are a number of issues that must be taken into account when implementing these algorithms in computer programs. See pages 19 through 22 of Gentle (1998a) for discussions of some of these considerations. Rather than writing code from scratch, it is generally better to use existing computer code. Appendix B describes available software in Fortran or C and in R or S-Plus.

The random numbers that can be generated directly and easily on the computer have a uniform distribution over the open interval $(0, 1)$. We denote this distribution by $U(0, 1)$. There are several methods for generating uniform numbers. Most of these methods are sequential congruential methods; that is methods in which if a subsequence of length j is given, the next value in the sequence is

$$u_k = f(u_{k-1}, \ldots u_{k-j}) \bmod m$$

for some function f and some number m. In this recursion, j is often chosen as 1. See Gentle (1998a, Chapter 1) for a further discussion of recursive methods for generating sequences of $U(0, 1)$ random numbers.

Samples from other distributions are generated by using transformations of sequences of a stream of $U(0, 1)$ random numbers, as described in Gentle (1998a, Chapters 2 and 3). We will briefly describe some of these methods below. These techniques are sometimes called "sampling methods".

To generate a realization of a random variable, X, with any given distribution, we seek a transformation of one or more independent $U(0, 1)$ random variables, $U_1, \ldots, U_k$,

$$X = f(U_1, \ldots, U_k),$$

such that X has the desired distribution. In some cases, the transformation f may be a simple transformation of a single uniform variable. For example, to obtain a standard exponential random variable, the transformation

$$X = -\log(U)$$

yields one exponential for each uniform variable. In other cases, the transformation may involve multiple stages in which we first transform a set of uniform variables to a set of variables with some other joint distribution and then identify a marginal or conditional distribution that corresponds to the desired distribution.

Inverse CDF Method

If X is a scalar random variable with a continuous cumulative distribution function (CDF) P_X, then the random variable

$$U = P_X(X)$$

has a U(0, 1) distribution.

This fact provides a very simple relationship with a uniform random variable U and a random variable X with distribution function P_X, namely,

$$X = P_X^{-1}(U), \tag{2.1}$$

where the inverse of the CDF exists. Use of this straightforward transformation is called the *inverse CDF* technique. The log transformation mentioned above that yields an exponential random variable uses the inverse CDF.

For a discrete random variable, although the inverse of the CDF does not exist, the inverse CDF method can still be used. The value of the discrete random variable is chosen as the smallest value within its countable range such that the CDF is no less than the value of the uniform variate.

For a multivariate random variable, the inverse CDF method yields a level curve in the range of the random variable; hence, the method is not directly useful for multivariate random variables. Multivariate random variates can be generated using the inverse CDF method first on a univariate marginal and then on a sequence of univariate conditionals.

Acceptance/Rejection Methods

Acceptance/rejection methods for generating realizations of a random variable X make use of realizations of another random variable Y whose probability density g_Y is similar to the probability density of X, p_X. The random variable Y is chosen so that we can easily generate realizations of it and so that its density

g_Y can be scaled to majorize p_X using some constant c; that is, $cg_Y(x) \geq p_X(x)$ for all x. The density g_Y is called the *majorizing* density, and cg_Y is called the majorizing function. The majorizing density is also called the "proposal density". The density of interest, p_X, is called the "target density". The support of the target density must be contained in the support of the majorizing density; for densities with infinite support, the majorizing density must likewise have infinite support. In the case of infinite support, it is critical that the majorizing density not approach zero faster than the target density.

Acceptance/rejection methods can also be used for discrete random variables. We use the term "probability density" to include a probability mass function, and all of the discussion in this section applies equally to probability functions and probability densities.

Unlike the inverse CDF method, acceptance/rejection methods apply immediately to multivariate random variables.

Algorithm 2.1 The Acceptance/Rejection Method to Convert Uniform Random Numbers

1. Generate y from the distribution with density function g_Y.

2. Generate u from a uniform $(0,1)$ distribution.

3. If $u \leq p_X(y)/cg_Y(y)$, then
    3.a. take y as the desired realization;
   otherwise,
    3.b. return to step 1.   ∎

It is easy to see that Algorithm 2.1 produces a random variable with the density p_X. Let Z be the random variable delivered. For any x, because Y (from the density g) and U are independent, we have

$$
\begin{aligned}
\Pr(Z \leq x) &= \Pr\left(Y \leq x \mid U \leq \frac{p_X(Y)}{cg_Y(Y)}\right) \\
&= \frac{\int_{-\infty}^{x} \int_{0}^{p_X(t)/cg_Y(t)} g_Y(t)\, ds\, dt}{\int_{-\infty}^{\infty} \int_{0}^{p_X(t)/cg_Y(t)} g_Y(t)\, ds\, dt} \\
&= \int_{-\infty}^{x} p_X(t)\, dt,
\end{aligned}
$$

which is the CDF corresponding to p_X. (Differentiating this quantity with respect to x yields $p_X(x)$.) Therefore, Z has the desired distribution.

It is easy to see that the random variable corresponding to the number of passes through the steps of Algorithm 2.1 until the desired variate is delivered has a geometric distribution.

A straightforward application of the acceptance/rejection method is very simple. For distributions with finite support, the density g can always be chosen as a uniform. For example, to generate deviates from a beta distribution with parameters α and β—that is, the distribution with density,

$$p(x) = \frac{1}{B(\alpha, \beta)} x^{\alpha-1}(1-x)^{\beta-1}, \quad \text{for } 0 \leq x \leq 1,$$

where $B(\alpha, \beta)$ is the complete beta function—we could use a uniform majorizing density, as shown in Figure 2.1.

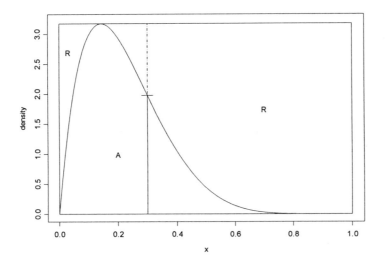

Figure 2.1: Beta (2, 7) Density with a Uniform Majorizing Density

The value of c by which we scale the uniform density should be as small as possible to minimize the frequency with which we reject the candidate points. This requires determination of the maximum value of the beta density, which we can compute very easily in S-Plus or R just by evaluating the density at the mode:

```
xmode <- (alpha-1.)/(alpha+beta-2.)
dmax  <- xmode^(alpha-1.)*(1-xmode)^(beta-1)*gamma(alpha+beta) /
         (gamma(alpha)*gamma(beta))
```

To generate deviates from the beta using the uniform majorizing density, we could write the following S-Plus statements:

```
y<-runif(1000)
x<-na.omit(ifelse(runif(1000)<=dbeta(y,alpha,beta)/dmax, y, NA))
```

Of course, in these statements, the number of beta variates delivered in x will not be known a priori; in fact, the number will vary with different executions of the statements. Instead of using a program that holds all the values in vectors, we generally form an explicit loop in the program to obtain a set number of deviates.

Just as an example, in one execution of these statements, with $\alpha = 2$ and $\beta = 7$, only 331 deviates were accepted. A histogram of the 331 deviates is shown in Figure 2.2 together with the beta density.

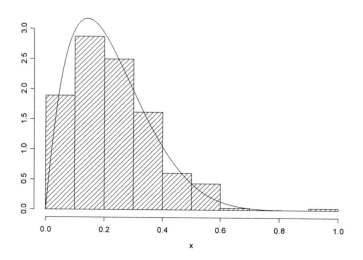

Figure 2.2: Histogram of an Acceptance/Rejection Sample from Beta $(2, 7)$

Considering the large area between a scaled uniform density and the beta density shown in Figure 2.1, it is clear that the uniform is not a very efficient density to use for the majorizing density, even though it is extremely easy to use. When a random uniform point falls in the areas marked "R", the point is rejected; when it falls in the area marked "A", the point is accepted. Only 1 out of dmax (≈ 3.18) will be accepted. As another example, consider the use of a normal with mean 0 and variance 2 as a majorizing density for a normal with mean 0 and variance 1, as shown in Figure 2.3. A majorizing density like this whose shape more closely approximates that of the target density is more efficient. The problem in this case, obviously, is that if we could generate deviates from the $N(0, 2)$ distribution, we could generate ones from the $N(0, 1)$ distribution.

The value of c required to make the density of $N(0, 2)$ majorize that of $N(0, 1)$ is $\sqrt{2}$. Hence, one out of ≈ 1.41 candidate points will be accepted.

Although the acceptance/rejection method can be used for multivariate random variables, in that case the majorizing distribution must also be multivariate. For higher dimensions, another problem is the relationship of the rejection

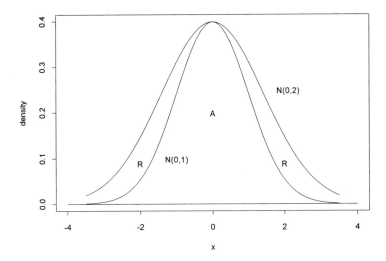

Figure 2.3: Normal $(0, 1)$ Density with a Normal $(0, 2)$ Majorizing Density

region to the acceptance region. In the one-dimensional case, as shown in Figure 2.3, the acceptance region is the area under the lower curve, and the rejection region is the thin shell between the two curves. In higher dimensions, even a thin shell contains most of the volume, so the rejection proportion would be high. See Section 10.7, page 290, and Exercise 10.10, page 297.

Use of Conditional Distributions

Sometimes, the density of interest, p_X, can be represented as a marginal density of some joint density, p_{XY}, that has tractable conditional densities, $p_{X|Y}$ and $p_{Y|X}$. If we can generate realizations from the conditional distributions, observations on X can often be generated as a discrete-time Markov process whose elements have densities

$$p_{Y_i|X_{i-1}}, \quad p_{X_i|Y_i}, \quad p_{Y_{i+1}|X_i}, \quad p_{X_{i+1}|Y_{i+1}}, \quad \cdots \cdot \qquad (2.2)$$

This is possible if the distribution of the X_i in the sequence converges to that of X. (A note on terminology: If the support of X or Y is continuous, the state space of the bivariate sequence $\{(X_i, Y_i)\}$ is uncountable, and the general term "Markov process" is traditionally applied. Current terminology in random number generation for such a process, however, is "Markov chain". Tierney, 1994, 1996, discusses some of the additional complexities arising from a continuous state space that are relevant to the use of such processes in random number generation.)

The transition kernel of X_i in the Markov chain is

$$p_{X_i|X_{i-1}}(x_i|x_{i-1}) = \int p_{X_i|Y_i}(x_i|y)\, p_{Y_i|X_{i-1}}(y|x_{i-1})\, dy.$$

Starting with X_0 and stepping through the transitions, we have

$$p_{X_i|X_0}(x|x_0) = \int p_{X_i|X_{i-1}}(x|t)\, p_{X_{i-1}|X_0}(t|x_0)\, dt. \qquad (2.3)$$

As $i \to \infty$, the density in equation (2.3) converges to p_X under very mild regularity conditions on the densities p_{X_i} and $p_{Y_i|X_i}$. (Existence and absolute continuity are sufficient; see, for example, Nummelin, 1984.) The problem is analogous to the more familiar one involving a discrete-state Markov chain, where convergence is assured if all of the entries in the transition matrix $T_{X|X} = T_{Y|X}T_{X|Y}$ are positive.

The usefulness of this method depends on identifying a joint density with conditionals that are easy to simulate.

For example, if the distribution of interest is a standard normal, the joint density

$$p_{XY}(x,y) = \frac{1}{\sqrt{2\pi}}\frac{1}{e^{-x^2/2}}, \quad \text{for } -\infty < x < \infty,\ 0 < y < e^{-x^2/2},$$

has a marginal density corresponding to the distribution of interest, and it has simple conditionals. The conditional distribution of $Y|X$ is $U(0, e^{-X^2/2})$, and the conditional of $X|Y$ is $U(-\sqrt{-2\log Y}, \sqrt{-2\log Y})$. Starting with x_0 in the range of X, we generate y_1 as a uniform conditional on x_0, then x_1 as a uniform conditional on y_1, and so on.

The auxiliary variable Y that we introduce just to simulate X is called a "latent variable". Use of conditional distributions to generate random variables is called *Gibbs sampling*.

A chain of conditional distributions can also be used for discrete random variables. In that case, the Markov process is a discrete-state Markov chain, and the analysis is even simpler.

Conditional distributions can also be used for a multivariate random variable, and in fact that is one of the most important applications of the method. We discuss the Gibbs algorithm further, for generation of multivariate random variables, on page 50.

Acceptance/Rejection Method Using a Markov Chain

A discrete-time Markov chain is the basis for several schemes for generating random numbers, either continuous or discrete, and multivariate as well as univariate. The differences in the various methods using Markov processes come from differences in the transition kernel. Sometimes, the transition kernel incorporates an acceptance/rejection decision. The elements of the chain can be accepted or rejected in such a way as to form a different chain whose stationary distribution is the distribution of interest. Simulation methods that make use of a Markov chain to generate samples are called Markov chain Monte Carlo, or MCMC, methods. The interest is not in the sequence of the Markov chain itself. Methods based on Markov chains are *iterative* because several steps must be taken before the stationary distribution is achieved. In practice, it is very difficult to determine the length of the "burn-in" period, that is, to determine when a stationary distribution has been achieved.

For a distribution with density p, the Metropolis algorithm, introduced by Metropolis et al. (1953), generates a random walk and performs an acceptance/rejection based on p evaluated at successive steps in the walk. In the simplest version, the walk moves from the point y_i to the point $y_{i+1} = y_i + s$, where s is a realization from $U(-a, a)$, and accepts y_{i+1} if

$$p(y_{i+1}) / p(y_i) \geq u, \qquad (2.4)$$

where u is an independent realization from $U(0, 1)$. If the range of the distribution is finite, the random walk is not allowed to go outside of the range.

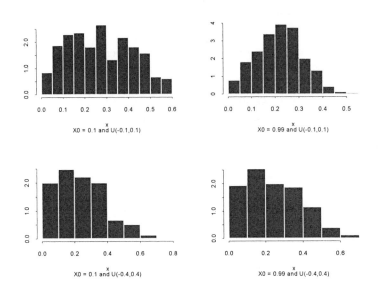

Figure 2.4: Histograms of Random Walk Samples from Beta (2, 7)

It is obvious that this kind of Markov process will favor points near the mode of the distribution.

Hastings (1970) developed an algorithm that is based on a transition kernel with a more general acceptance/rejection decision. The *Metropolis-Hastings sampler* to generate deviates from a distribution with density p_X uses deviates

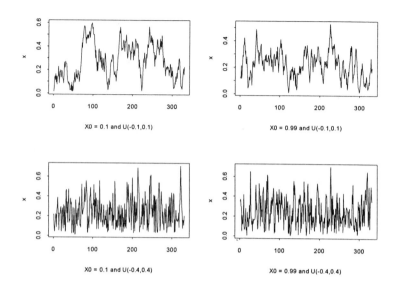

Figure 2.5: Random Walk Sampling from Beta (2, 7) that Yielded the Histograms Shown in Figure 2.4

from a Markov chain with a completely different density, $g_{Y_{t+1}|Y_t}$. The conditional density $g_{Y_{t+1}|Y_t}$ is chosen so that it is easy to generate deviates from it, and realizations from this distribution are selectively chosen as realizations from the distribution with density p_X.

Algorithm 2.2 Metropolis-Hastings Algorithm

0. Set $i = 0$ and choose x_i in the support of p.

1. Generate y from the density $g_{Y_{t+1}|Y_t}(y|x_i)$.

2. Set r:
$$r = p_X(y) \frac{g_{Y_{t+1}|Y_t}(x_i|y)}{p_X(x_i)g_{Y_{t+1}|Y_t}(y|x_i)}.$$

3. If $r \geq 1$, then
      3.a. set $x_{i+1} = y$;
   otherwise
      3.b. generate u from the uniform(0,1) distribution and
         if $u < r$, then
            3.b.i. set $x_{i+1} = y$,
         otherwise
            3.b.ii. set $x_{i+1} = x_i$.

4. Set $i = i + 1$ and go to step 1. ∎

The r in step 2 is called the "Hastings ratio", and step 3 is called the "Metropolis rejection". The conditional density, $g_{Y_{t+1}|Y_t}(\cdot|\cdot)$, is called the "proposal density" or the "candidate generating density". Notice that because the majorizing function contains p_X as a factor, we only need to know p_X to within a constant of proportionality. This is an important characteristic of the Metropolis algorithms.

We can illustrate the use of the Metropolis-Hastings algorithm in using a Markov chain in which the density of X_{t+1} is normal with a mean of X_t and a variance of σ^2. Let us use this density to generate a sample from a standard normal distribution (that is, a normal with a mean of 0 and a variance of 1). We start with x_0, chosen arbitrarily. We take logs and cancel terms in the expression for r. The output from an S-Plus implementation of the method is shown in Figure 2.6. Notice that the values descend very quickly from the

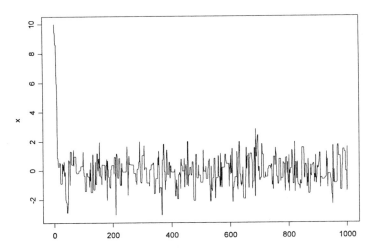

Figure 2.6: Sequential Output from a N(0,1) Distribution Using a Markov Chain, N(X_t, σ^2)

starting value, which would be a very unusual realization of a standard normal. In practice, we generally cannot expect such a short burn-in period. Notice also the horizontal line segments where the underlying Markov chain did not advance.

Generation of Multivariate Random Variates

For multivariate distributions with a very large number of variables, the standard acceptance/rejection method is difficult to apply because it is difficult to determine a usable majorizing density. In addition, the acceptance/rejection method is not very efficient because of the high rejection rate, as we mentioned when discussing Figure 2.3.

The most common ways of generating multivariate random variates are by use of either i.i.d. (independent, identically distributed) univariates followed by a transformation or else a sequence of conditional univariates.

If $Y_1, \ldots, Y_d$ is a sequence of i.i.d. univariate random variables with variance 1, the variance-covariance matrix of the random d-vector Y composed of those elements is I. Assume that the mean of Y is 0. This is without loss of generality because the mean can always be adjusted by an addition. Consider the random d-vector X, where $X = AY$ for the nonsingular matrix A. The variance-covariance matrix of this transformed random variable is AA^{T}. Suppose that we want to determine a transformation of i.i.d. random variables with unit variances that yields a random variable with variance-covariance matrix Σ. If Y is the vector of the i.i.d. random variables, and A is a matrix such that $AA^{\mathrm{T}} = \Sigma$, then $X = AY$ is the transformation. The matrix A could be the Cholesky factor (or square root) of Σ, for example (see Gentle, 1998b, Section 3.2.2).

This transformation is a very good way of generating multivariate normal random variables. For other multivariate distributions, however, its usefulness is much more limited.

The other common way of generating a multivariate random number is by use of a sequence of univariate random numbers from conditional univariate distributions that combine to yield the desired multivariate distribution.

Again, for the multivariate normal distribution, this is a simple method. For example, consider a multivariate normal with mean of 0 and variance-covariance matrix Σ, with elements σ_{ij}. If

X_1 is generated as N$(0, \sigma_{11})$,
X_2 is generated as N$(\sigma_{12}X_1/\sigma_{11}, \ \sigma_{22} - \sigma_{12}^2/\sigma_{11})$,
and so on,

then

$$X = (X_1, X_2, \ldots)$$

has a multivariate normal distribution with variance-covariance matrix Σ. Some other multivariate distributions can also be easily generated by a sequence of conditional distributions, but for many distributions, the method may be considerably more complicated.

Gibbs Sampling

In some cases, it is possible to reduce the problem to a sequence that begins with a univariate marginal distribution and then builds up the random vector by conditional distributions that include the generated elements one at a time. This is possible by decomposing the multivariate density into a marginal and then a sequence of conditionals:

$$p_{X_1 X_2 X_3 \cdots X_d} = p_{X_1 | X_2 X_3 \cdots X_d} \cdot p_{X_2 | X_3 \cdots X_d} \cdots p_{X_d}.$$

In other cases, we may have a full set of conditionals:

$$p_{X_i | \{X_j ; j \neq i\}}.$$

In this case, we can sample from a Markov process by updating individual random variables given the values of the other random variables at a previous time, in the same way as the process (2.2) on page 45. This iterative technique is called "Gibbs sampling". It was introduced by Geman and Geman (1984) and further developed by Gelfand and Smith (1990).

The Gibbs sampler begins with an arbitrary starting point, $x_1^{(0)}, x_2^{(0)}, \ldots, x_d^{(0)}$; generates $x_1^{(1)}$ from knowledge of $p_{X_1^{(1)} | x_2^{(0)}, \ldots, x_d^{(0)}}$; generates $x_2^{(1)}$ from knowledge of $p_{X_2^{(1)} | x_1^{(1)}, x_3^{(0)}, \ldots, x_d^{(0)}}$; and so on.

The process is then iterated in this systematic fashion to get $x_1^{(2)}, x_2^{(2)}, \ldots, x_d^{(2)}$, and so on. A full iteration requires generation of k random variables.

Geman and Geman showed that $(X_1^{(i)}, X_2^{(i)}, \ldots, X_d^{(i)})$ converges in distribution to $(X_1, X_2, \ldots, X_d)$ so that each component individually converges. This result does not depend on the conditional generations at each iteration being done in the same order.

Algorithm 2.3 Gibbs Method

0. Set $k = 0$ and choose $x^{(0)}$.

1. Generate $x_1^{(k+1)}$ conditionally on $x_2^{(k)}, x_3^{(k)}, \ldots, x_d^{(k)}$,
   Generate $x_2^{(k+1)}$ conditionally on $x_1^{(k+1)}, x_3^{(k)}, \ldots, x_d^{(k)}$,
   . . .
   Generate $x_{d-1}^{(k+1)}$ conditionally on $x_1^{(k+1)}, x_2^{(k+1)}, \ldots, x_d^{(k)}$,
   Generate $x_d^{(k+1)}$ conditionally on $x_1^{(k+1)}, x_2^{(k+1)}, \ldots, x_{d-1}^{(k+1)}$.

2. If convergence has occurred, then
      2.a. deliver $x = x^{(k+1)}$;
   otherwise,
      2.b. set $k = k + 1$, and go to step 1. ∎

Gibbs sampling must be used with caution because it can be extremely slow to converge. Furthermore, it is often difficult to determine when convergence has occurred (see the discussion beginning on page 56). The method is not practical when there are even relatively small correlations among the variables (see Exercise 2.5).

Probability Densities Known Only Proportionally

It is often easy to specify a model up to a constant of proportionality. An example is the family of Gibbs distributions that arises in spatial statistics. (This is the distribution that gave the Gibbs sampler its name.) Let t be a vector-valued statistic on the sample space and

$$h(x) = e^{\langle t(x), \theta \rangle},$$

where $\langle t(x), \theta \rangle$ denotes the dot product of $t(x)$ and θ. This specifies a family of densities

$$f_\theta(x) = \frac{1}{c(\theta)} e^{\langle t(x), \theta \rangle},$$

where

$$c(\theta) = \int e^{\langle t(x), \theta \rangle} \, d\mu(x).$$

In general, if h is a nonnegative integrable function that is not zero almost everywhere, a probability density p can be defined by normalizing h:

$$p(x) = \frac{1}{c} h(x),$$

where

$$c = \int h(x) \, d\mu(x).$$

We may know h but not c, and c may not be easy to evaluate, especially if h is multivariate. Markov chain Monte Carlo methods are particularly useful in dealing with such multivariate distributions that have densities known up to a constant of proportionality. In the Hastings ratio in Algorithm 2.2, the constant c would not be required; h alone could be used to simulate realizations from p.

There are many problems in Bayesian inference in which densities are known only up to a constant of proportionality. In such problems h is the likelihood times the prior. Normalizing h—that is, determining the integral c—may be difficult, but Markov chain Monte Carlo methods allow simulations of realizations from the posterior without knowing c.

Data-Based Random Number Generation

Often we have a set of data and wish to generate pseudorandom variates from the same data-generating process that yielded the given data. How we do this depends on how much we know or what assumptions we make about the data-generating process. At one extreme, we may assume full knowledge of the data-generating process; for example, we may assume that the given set of data came from a normal distribution with known mean and variance. In this case, we use the well-known techniques for generating pseudorandom variates from a $N(\mu, \sigma^2)$ distribution.

A slightly weaker assumption is that the data came from a normal distribution, but we do not know the mean or variance. In this case, a simple approach may be to use the given data to estimate the mean and standard deviation and then proceed as if the estimates were the true values. (Notice that if we want the process to be unbiased, we cannot use the square root of the sample variance as the estimate of the standard deviation.) Use of a parametric model, such as the normal distribution, with given or estimated values of the parameters, is a *parametric* approach. We discuss the use of estimated parameters in Section 2.5 on page 60. This method is sometimes called a "parametric bootstrap".

A strong assumption that does not involve parameters in the usual sense is that the given data resulted from a discrete data-generating process (that is, one that can yield only a countable set of distinct values). In this case, we would generate pseudorandom variates by sampling (or "resampling") the given set of data.

It may be appropriate to assume that the given data resulted from a continuous data-generating process, but we have only very limited knowledge about the process. In this case, we use a *nonparametric* approach.

For a given sample of univariate data, the ECDF could be used in place of the CDF in a standard inverse CDF method, as described on page 41. We discuss direct use of the ECDF in Section 2.5. As we mentioned on page 14, however, the ECDF defines a distribution with a finite range $[y_{(1)}, y_{(n)}]$ corresponding to the smallest and largest order statistics of the data. Instead of using the ECDF to generate random data, we may choose to use the empirical quantiles defined in equation (1.7) for some choice of ι and ν.

For a given sample of multivariate data, our pseudorandom samples must capture probabilities of general regions. The correlations in the given sample must be replicated. See Section 3.3 in Gentle (1998a) for methods for generating random variates to simulate a general multivariate distribution.

2.2 Monte Carlo Estimation

The general objective in Monte Carlo simulation is to estimate some characteristic of a random variable X. Often, the objective is to calculate the expectation of some function g of X.

Estimation of a Definite Integral

Monte Carlo inference, as for statistical inference generally, can be formulated as estimation of either a definite integral

$$\theta = \int_D f(x)\mathrm{d}x \qquad (2.5)$$

or, given the integral θ, of a domain D, or of a function f that satisfies certain optimality conditions. If the integral can be evaluated in closed form, there is no need for Monte Carlo methods. If D is of only one or two dimensions, there are several good, straightforward numerical quadrature methods available to solve the problem. For domains of higher dimension, Monte Carlo estimation is sometimes the best method for the quadrature. For more discussion of the quadrature problem, the reader is referred to texts on numerical analysis.

Function Decomposition

If the function f is decomposed to have a factor that is a probability density function, say

$$f(x) = g(x)p(x),   \tag{2.6}$$

where

$$\int_D p(x)\mathrm{d}x = 1$$

and $p(x) \geq 0$, then the integral θ is the expectation of the function g of the random variable with probability density p; that is,

$$\theta = \mathrm{E}(g(X)) = \int_D g(x)p(x)\mathrm{d}x.   \tag{2.7}$$

With a random sample $x_1, \ldots, x_m$ from the distribution with probability density p, an estimate of θ is

$$\widehat{\theta} = \frac{\sum g(x_i)}{m}.   \tag{2.8}$$

We use this technique in many settings in statistics. There are three steps:

1. decompose the function of interest to include a probability density function as a factor;

2. identify an expected value;

3. use a sample (simulated or otherwise) to estimate the expected value.

The decomposition is not unique, of course, and sometimes a particular decomposition is more useful than another. In the Monte Carlo application, it is necessary to be able to generate random numbers easily from the distribution with the given density. As we will see in the discussion of importance sampling on page 62, there are other considerations for efficient Monte Carlo estimation.

We should note here that the use of Monte Carlo procedures for numerical quadrature is rarely the best method for lower-dimensional integrals. Use of Newton-Cotes or Gaussian quadrature is usually better. For higher-dimensional integrals, however, Monte Carlo quadrature is often a viable alternative.

Estimation of the Variance

A Monte Carlo estimate usually has the form of the estimator of θ in equation (2.8). An estimate of the variance of this estimator is

$$\widehat{V}(\widehat{\theta}) = \frac{\sum \left(g(x_i) - \overline{g(x)}\right)^2}{m - 1}. \tag{2.9}$$

This is because the elements of the set of random variables $\{g(X_i)\}$, on which we have observations $\{g(x_i)\}$, are (assumed to be) independent and thus to have zero correlations.

Estimating the Variance Using Batch Means

If the $g(X_i)$ do not have zero correlations, the estimator (2.9) has an expected value that includes the correlations; that is, it is biased for estimating $V(\widehat{\theta})$. This situation arises often in simulation. In many processes of interest, however, observations are "more independent" of observations farther removed within the sequence than they are of observations closer to them in the sequence. A common method for estimating the variance in a sequence of nonindependent observations, therefore, is to use the means of successive subsequences that are long enough that the observations in one subsequence are almost independent of the observations in another subsequence. The means of the subsequences are called "batch means".

If $G_1, \ldots, G_b, G_{b+1}, \ldots, G_{2b}, G_{2b+1}, \ldots, G_{kb}$ is a sequence of random variables such that the correlation of G_i and G_{i+b} is approximately zero, an estimate of the variance of the mean, $\overline{G}$, of the $m = kb$ random variables can be developed by observing that

$$\begin{aligned}
V(\overline{G}) &= V\left(\frac{1}{m}\sum G_i\right) \\
&= V\left(\frac{1}{k}\sum_{j=1}^{k}\left(\frac{1}{b}\sum_{i=(j-1)b+1}^{jb}G_i\right)\right) \\
&\approx \frac{1}{k^2}\sum_{j=1}^{k}V\left(\frac{1}{b}\sum_{i=(j-1)b+1}^{jb}G_i\right) \\
&\approx \frac{1}{k}V(\overline{G}_b),
\end{aligned}$$

where $\overline{G}_b$ is the mean of a batch of length b. If the batches are long enough, it may be reasonable to assume that the means have a common variance. An estimator of the variance of $\bar{G}_b$ is the standard sample variance from k observations, $\bar{g}_1, \bar{g}_2, \ldots, \bar{g}_k$:

$$\frac{\sum(\bar{g}_j - \bar{g})^2}{k - 1}.$$

Hence, the batch-means estimator of the variance of $\bar{G}$ is

$$\hat{V}(\overline{G}) = \frac{\sum(\bar{g}_j - \bar{g})^2}{k(k-1)}. \tag{2.10}$$

This batch-means variance estimator should be used if the Monte Carlo study yields a stream of nonindependent observations, such as in a time series or when the simulation uses a Markov chain. The size of the subsamples should be as small as possible and still have means that are independent. A test of the independence of the $\bar{G}_b$ may be appropriate to help in choosing the size of the batches.

Batch means are useful in variance estimation whenever a Markov chain is used in the generation of the random deviates.

Convergence of Iterative Monte Carlo and Mixing of the Markov Chain

In ordinary Monte Carlo simulation, estimation relies on the fact that for independent, identically distributed variables $X_1, X_2, \ldots$ from the distribution P of X,

$$\frac{1}{n} \sum_{i=1}^{n} g(X_i) \to E(g(X))$$

almost surely as n goes to infinity. This convergence is a simple consequence of the law of large numbers in the case of i.i.d. random variables. In Monte Carlo simulation, a random number generator simulates an independent stream. When X is multivariate or a complicated stochastic process, however, it may be difficult to simulate independent realizations.

The mean of a sample from an irreducible Markov chain $X_1, X_2, \ldots$ that has P as its equilibrium distribution also converges to the desired expectation. For this fact to have relevance in applications, the finite sampling from a Markov chain in the application must be concentrated in the equilibrium distribution; that is, the burn-in sample must not dominate the results. We mention below some methods for assessing convergence of MCMC samples to the stationary distribution, but it is not easy to determine when the Markov chain has begun to resemble its stationary distribution.

Once convergence to the stationary distribution is achieved, however, subsequent iterations are from that distribution. In Gibbs sampling, if

$$X_1, \ldots, X_{i-1},\ X_{i+1}, \ldots, X_d$$

have the marginal stationary distribution and X_i is given a new realization from the correct conditional distribution given the rest, then all of them still have the correct joint distribution.

In MCMC we must be concerned with more than just the length of a burn-in period and convergence to the stationary distribution, however. We must also be concerned with the *mixing* of the Markov chain, that is, how independently states X_i and X_{i+k} behave. Rapid mixing of the chain (meaning X_i and X_{i+k} are "relatively independent" for small k) ensures that the regions in the state-space will be visited in relatively small sequences with a frequency similar to long-term frequencies in the stationary distribution.

Some of the most important issues in MCMC concern the rate of convergence, that is, the length of the burn-in, and how fast the sampler mixes. These issues are more difficult to assess for multivariate distributions, but it is for multivariate distributions that MCMC is most important. Gelman and Rubin (1992) give examples in which the burn-in is much longer than a quick analysis might lead us to expect.

Various diagnostics have been proposed to assess convergence. A general approach to assess convergence is to use multiple simultaneous simulations of the chain and compare the output of the simulations. Large differences in the output would indicate that one or more of the simulations is in the burn-in phase. A related approach using only a single simulation is to inspect and compare separate subsequences or blocks of the output. Large differences in relatively long blocks would indicate that convergence has not occurred.

The results of a method for assessing convergence may strongly indicate that convergence *has not* occurred, but they cannot strongly indicate that convergence *has* occurred. Different methods may be more or less reliable in different settings, but no single method is completely dependable. In practice, the analyst generally should use several different methods and conclude that convergence has occurred only if no method indicates a lack of convergence.

Cowles and Carlin (1996) provide a comparative review of several convergence diagnostics. Additional reviews are given in Brooks and Roberts (1999) and the collection of articles in Robert (1998b). Mengersen, Robert, and Guihenneuc-Jouyaux (1999) give a classification of methods and review their performance. They also propose a Web site on which links to reviews, software, and related topics will be provided. The site currently is

`http://www.ensae.fr/crest/statistique/robert/McDiag`

Robert (1998a) provides a benchmark case for evaluation of convergence assessment techniques. Rosenthal (1995) provides some general methods for placing bounds on the length of runs required to give satisfactory results.

Unfortunately, the current methodology for assessing convergence of MCMC methods is not sufficiently reliable to allow decisions to be made on the basis of any standard set of tests. The careful analyst chooses and performs various ad hoc assessments, often based on exploratory graphics.

Monte Carlo, Iterative Monte Carlo, and Simulation

Convergence of the Monte Carlo estimator $\frac{1}{n}\sum_{i=1}^{n} g(X_i)$ to its expectation $\mathrm{E}(g(X))$ is not the only issue. If the constant c is such that

$$g(c) = \mathrm{E}(g(X)),$$

a random number generator that yields $x_i = c$ in each iteration would yield a very good estimate of $E(g(X))$. Usually, however, our objectives in using Monte Carlo include obtaining other estimates or assessing the behavior of a random process that depends on the distribution P of X. The degenerate generator yielding $x_i = c$ would not provide these other results. Although it may not be efficient, sometimes it is very important to simulate the underlying random process.

Whenever a correlated sequence such as a Markov chain is used, variance estimation must be performed with some care. In the more common cases of positive autocorrelation, the ordinary variance estimators are negatively biased. The method of batch means or some other method that attempts to account for the autocorrelation should be used.

If the noniterative approach is possible, it is to be preferred. There are many situations in which an MCMC method is easy to devise but performs very poorly. See Robert (1998a) for an example of such a problem.

2.3   Simulation of Data from a Hypothesized Model: Monte Carlo Tests

One of the most straightforward methods of computational inference is the Monte Carlo test. Barnard (1963) suggested use of Monte Carlo methods to estimate quantiles of a test statistic, T, under the null hypothesis. In Barnard's Monte Carlo test, m random (or pseudorandom) samples of the same size as the given sample are generated under the null hypothesis, and the test statistic is computed from each sample. This yields a sample of test statistics, $t_1^*, \ldots, t_m^*$. The ECDF, P_m^*, of the sample of test statistics is used as an estimate of the CDF of the test statistic, P_T; and the critical region for the test or the p-value of the observed test statistic can be estimated from P_m^*.

An estimate of the p-value of the observed test statistic can be taken as the proportion of the number of simulated values that exceed the observed value. If the distribution of the test statistic is continuous, and r is the number that exceed the observed value,

$$r/m$$

is an unbiased estimate of the p-value. Because this quantity can be 0, we usually use

$$\frac{r+1}{m+1}$$

as an estimate of the p-value associated with the upper tail of the test statistic. This is also the simple empirical quantile if, as under the null hypothesis, the observed value is from the same distribution. For test statistics with discrete distributions, we must estimate the probability of the observed value, and allocate that proportionally to the rejection and acceptance regions.

Hope (1968) and Marriott (1979) studied the power of the test and found that the power of Monte Carlo tests can be quite good even for relatively small values of m. In simple situations (testing means, for example), $m = 99$ may be a good choice. This allows the p-value to be expressed simply in two decimal places. In more complicated situations (inference concerning higher moments or relationships between variables), a value of $m = 999$ may be more appropriate. The p-value resulting from a Monte Carlo test is an estimate based on a sample of size m, so in general the larger m is, the better the estimate. In practical applications, it is not likely that a decision, other than to gather additional data, would be made based on more than two significant digits in a p-value.

To use a Monte Carlo test, the distribution of the random component in the assumed model must be known, and it must be possible to generate pseudorandom samples from that distribution under the null hypothesis. Notice that a Monte Carlo test is based on an *estimate* of a critical value of the test statistic rather than on an *approximation* of it.

In many applications of statistics, there is no simple model of the phenomenon being studied. If a simple approximation is chosen as the model, subsequent decisions rely on the adequacy of the approximation. On the other hand, if a more realistic model is chosen, the distributions of the statistics used in making inferences are intractable. The common approach is to approximate the distributions using asymptotic approximations. Monte Carlo tests provide an alternative; the distributional properties can be estimated by simulation. Computational inference can replace asymptotic inference. (Of course, in many complicated models, both approaches may be used.) Hall and Titterington (1989) studied the power of Monte Carlo tests compared to that of tests that use asymptotic approximations. If the sample size is not compatible with the order of the asymptotic approximation, an inferential procedure using Monte Carlo methods is clearly better than one using the approximation.

Several applications of Monte Carlo tests are reported in the literature. Many involve spatial distributions of species of plants or animals. Manly (1997), for example, describes several uses of Monte Carlo tests in biology. Brown and Rothery (1978) and Dryden, Taylor, and Faghihi (1999) discuss methods of using interpoint distances to assess randomness in a spatial distribution. In Exercise 2.11, you are asked to devise a Monte Carlo test for spatial independence. Agresti (1992) and Senchaudhuri, Mehta, and Patel (1995) describe Monte Carlo tests in contingency tables. Forster, McDonald, and Smith (1996) describe conditional Monte Carlo tests based on Gibbs sampling in log-linear and logistic models. Besag and Clifford (1989, 1991) describe randomized significance tests with exact p-values using Markov chain Monte Carlo methods.

The ECDF of the simulated test statistic provides us with more information about the test statistic than just the critical values. It allows us to make other inferences about the distribution of the test statistic under the null hypothesis, such as an estimate of the variance of the test statistic, its symmetry, and so on.

Monte Carlo methods of inference are particularly useful in implicit statistical models. In this kind of model, it is often possible to generate random events that drive other, events that are observable, but no explicit relationship among the events is assumed.

An obvious problem with a Monte Carlo test is that the null hypothesis, together with underlying assumptions, must fully specify the distribution at least up to any pivotal quantity used in the test. In Chapter 4, we discuss Monte Carlo methods that involve *resampling* from the given sample; hence, a complete specification of an underlying distribution is not necessary.

2.4   Simulation of Data from a Fitted Model: "Parametric Bootstraps"

Instead of using the hypothesized value of the parameter, another approach in computational inference is to use an estimate of the parameter from the sample. In a similar manner as in the previous section, we can simulate samples from the fitted model to obtain a sample of test statistics $t_1^*, \ldots, t_m^*$. Again, the ECDF, P_m^*, of the sample of test statistics can be used as an estimate of the CDF of the test statistic, P_T; and critical regions for a test, p-values of the observed test statistic, or other properties of the distribution of the test statistic can be estimated from P_m^*. In this case, of course, the distributional properties are not those that hold under a particular hypothesis; rather they are the properties under a model whose parameters correspond to values fitted from the data. This kind of approach to statistical inference is sometimes called a *parametric bootstrap*.

In the parametric bootstrap, the CDF of the population of interest, P, is assumed known up to a finite set of parameters, θ. The estimate of the CDF, $\widehat{P}$, is P with θ replaced by an estimate $\widehat{\theta}$ obtained from the given sample. Hence, the first step is to obtain estimates of the parameters that characterize the distribution within the assumed family. After this, the procedure is to generate m random samples each of size n from the estimated distribution, and for each sample, compute an estimator T_j^* of the same functional form as the original estimator T. The distribution of the T_j^*'s is used to make inferences about the CDF of T. The estimate of the CDF of T can be used to test hypotheses about θ, using the observed value of T from the original sample. If $f(T, \theta)$ is a pivotal quantity when the distribution of T is known, the estimate of the CDF of T can be used to form confidence intervals for θ.

2.5   Random Sampling from Data

Some statistical methods involve formation of subsets of the data or randomization of the data. The number of subsets or permutations can be very large. For this reason, in the application of such methods, rather than using all possible subsets or all possible permutations, we generally resort to generating random samples of subsets or permutations. Some methods we discuss in Chapters 3 and 4 necessitate use of Monte Carlo sampling.

The discrete uniform population defined by the data is a useful surrogate for the population from which the data were drawn. Properties of the discrete population are used in making an inference about the "real" population. The analysis of the discrete population is often facilitated by drawing samples from it. This is, in effect, a *resampling* of the given data, which is a sample from the "real" population. Some of the bootstrap methods discussed in Chapter 4 use Monte Carlo procedures in this way.

Many other statistical methods involve sampling from the data. For example, in survey sampling, the dataset often includes incomplete records or missing data. In the missing-data problem, we think of the full dataset as being represented by an $n \times d$ matrix Y (that is, n observations, each of which contains d elements), of which a certain portion, Y^{mis}, is actually not observed. The missing portion together with the observed portion, Y^{obs}, constitute the full dataset. For analyzing the data and providing descriptive statistics of the population, it is often desirable to fill in the missing data using complete records as "donors" to impute the missing data. There are various approaches to this problem. In one approach, called *multiple imputation*, m simulated values, $Y_1^{mis*}, \ldots, Y_m^{mis*}$, of the missing data are generated from an appropriate population, and the complete datasets, $Y_1^*, \ldots, Y_m^*$, are analyzed. This procedure provides a measure of the uncertainty due to the missing data. (In order for this approach to be valid, the simulated missing data must come from a distribution with certain properties. See Rubin, 1987, or Schafer, 1997, for discussions of these properties.) Because multiple imputation only simulates from the missing data portion of the dataset and because the simulation variance is likely to be relatively small compared to the overall sampling variance, the value of m does not need to be large. A value of $m = 3$ is often adequate in multiple imputation.

2.6 Reducing Variance in Monte Carlo Methods

Monte Carlo methods involve an inference from random (or pseudorandom) samples. The usual principles of inference apply. We seek procedures with small (generally zero) bias and small variance. As with other methods for statistical inference, various procedures with differing bias and variance are available. In sampling from artificially generated random numbers on the computer, just as in taking observations of other events, an objective is to devise a sampling plan that will yield estimators with small variance. It is often possible to modify a procedure to reduce the bias or the variance. There are a number of ways of reducing the variance in Monte Carlo sampling.

As with any statistical estimation procedure, an objective is to choose an estimator and/or a sampling design that will have a small, possibly minimum, variance. The first principle in achieving this objective is to remove or reduce sampling variation wherever possible. This principle is *analytic reduction*. An example that has been considered in the literature (see Ripley, 1987) is the estimation of the probability that a Cauchy random variable is larger than 2;

that is, the evaluation of the integral

$$\int_2^\infty \frac{1}{\pi(1+x^2)}\mathrm{d}x.$$

This integral can be transformed analytically to

$$\int_0^{1/2} \frac{y^{-2}}{\pi(1+y^{-2})}\mathrm{d}y,$$

and the variance of a simple estimator of the latter integral using a sample from $U(0, \frac{1}{2})$ is only about one-thousandth the variance of a simple estimator of the former integral using a sample from a Cauchy distribution. Inspection of the original integral, however, reveals that the antiderivative of the integrand is the arctangent. If reasonable software for evaluating trigonometric functions is available, one should not estimate the integral in the original problem. The rule is *do not resort to Monte Carlo methods unnecessarily.*

Although generally we want to construct Monte Carlo estimators with small variance, we must be aware that sometimes it is very important to simulate the underlying random process in such a way that variances of the Monte Carlo stream are representative of variances within the process.

Importance Sampling

Given the integral $\int_D f(x)\mathrm{d}x$, there may be a number of ways that we can decompose f into g and a probability density function p. This decomposition determines the variance of our estimator $\hat{\theta}$. The intuitive rule is to sample more heavily where $|f|$ is large. This principle is called *importance sampling*. As we do following equation (2.5) on page 53, we write the integral as

$$\begin{aligned}
\theta &= \int_D f(x)\,\mathrm{d}x \\
&= \int_D \frac{f(x)}{p(x)}p(x)\,\mathrm{d}x.
\end{aligned}$$

where $p(x)$ is a probability density over D. The density $p(x)$ is called the *importance function.*

From a sample of size m from the distribution with density p, we have the estimator,

$$\hat{\theta} = \frac{1}{m}\sum \frac{f(x_i)}{p(x_i)}. \tag{2.11}$$

It is clear that $\hat{\theta}$ is unbiased for θ (assuming, of course, that the integral exists). The variance of this estimator is

$$\mathrm{V}(\hat{\theta}) = \frac{1}{m}\mathrm{V}\left(\frac{f(X)}{p(X)}\right),$$

where the variance is taken with respect to the distribution of the random variable X with density $p(x)$. The variance of the ratio can be expressed as

$$\mathrm{V}\left(\frac{f(X)}{p(X)}\right) = \mathrm{E}\left(\frac{f^2(X)}{p^2(X)}\right) - \left(\mathrm{E}\left(\frac{f(X)}{p(X)}\right)\right)^2.$$

The objective in importance sampling is to choose p so this variance is minimized. Because

$$\left(\mathrm{E}\left(\frac{f(X)}{p(X)}\right)\right)^2 = \left(\int_D f(x)\,\mathrm{d}x\right)^2,$$

the choice involves only the first term in the expression above for the variance. By Jensen's inequality, we have a lower bound on that term:

$$\mathrm{E}\left(\frac{f^2(X)}{p^2(X)}\right) \geq \left(\mathrm{E}\left(\frac{|f(X)|}{p(X)}\right)\right)^2$$
$$= \left(\int_D |f(x)|\,\mathrm{d}x\right)^2.$$

That bound is obviously achieved when

$$p(x) = \frac{|f(x)|}{\int_D |f(x)|\,\mathrm{d}x}.$$

Of course, if we knew $\int_D |f(x)|\,\mathrm{d}x$, we would probably know $\int_D f(x)\,\mathrm{d}x$ and would not even be considering the Monte Carlo procedure to estimate the integral. In practice, for importance sampling, we generally seek a probability density w that is nearly proportional to $|f|$ (that is, such that $|f(x)|/p(x)$ is nearly constant).

Control Variates

Another way of reducing the variance, just as in ordinary sampling, is to use covariates, or control variates, as they are often called in Monte Carlo sampling. Any variable that is correlated with the variable of interest has potential value as a control variate. The control variate is useful if it is easy to generate and if it has properties that are known or that can be computed easily.

As an example, consider a method of using control variates to reduce the variance in Monte Carlo tests in two-way contingency tables described by Senchaudhuri, Mehta, and Patel (1995). An $r \times c$ contingency table can be thought of as an $r \times c$ matrix, A, whose nonnegative integer elements a_{ij} represent the counts in the cells of the table. For such tables, we may be interested in patterns of values in the cells. Specifically, we ask whether, given the marginal totals

$$a_{\bullet j} = \sum_{i=1}^{r} a_{ij}$$

and

$$a_{i\bullet} = \sum_{j=1}^{c} a_{ij},$$

the cells are independent. (Here, we use the "dot notation" for summation: $a_{\bullet j}$ is the sum of the counts in the jth column, for example, and $a_{\bullet\bullet}$ is the grand total.) There are several statistical tests that address this question or aspects of it under various assumptions. The test statistic is some function of the observed table, $T(A)$. The objective is to compute the p-value of the observed value of the test statistic. The distributions of most test statistics for this problem are very complicated, so either an approximation is used or a Monte Carlo test is performed.

A Monte Carlo test involves generation of a large number of random tables that satisfy the null hypothesis and for each table computing the test statistic to determine if it is more extreme than that of the observed table. The problem with the Monte Carlo test, however, is the large amount of computation involved. Both generation of the tables and computation of the test statistic are tedious.

Senchaudhuri, Mehta, and Patel (1995) suggested use of an additional statistic related to the test statistic of interest to serve as a control variate. The auxiliary statistic, which is easy to compute, has a known mean.

The relationship between the auxiliary statistic and the test statistic relies on a "separability property" of the test statistic that allows the test statistic to be written as

$$T(A) = \sum_{j=1}^{c} T_j(a_j),$$

where a_j is the jth column of A. Given this representation, form $\widetilde{T}_j(a_j)$ as the contribution $T_j(a_j)$ rounded to p digits,

$$\widetilde{T}_j(a_j) = \lfloor T_j(a_j) \times 10^p + 0.5 \rfloor \times 10^{-p},$$

and form the new test statistic as

$$\widetilde{T}(A) = \sum_{j=1}^{c} \widetilde{T}_j(a_j). \tag{2.12}$$

As an example, consider Pearson's test, a common test for lack of dependence between the rows and columns that uses the test statistic

$$T(A) = \sum_{i=1}^{r} \sum_{j=1}^{c} \frac{(a_{ij} - a_{i\bullet}a_{\bullet j}/a_{\bullet\bullet})^2}{a_{i\bullet}a_{\bullet j}/a_{\bullet\bullet}}.$$

The distribution of this statistic is complicated, but under the null hypothesis, the statistic has an asymptotic chi-squared distribution with $(r-1)(c-1)$

degrees of freedom. The exact significance level of an observed value of this test statistic is often determined by Monte Carlo methods.

Pearson's test statistic has the separability property, so the procedure described above can be used.

Hesterberg and Nelson (1998) also discuss methods for using control variates in Monte Carlo applications involving the estimation of a significance level or a quantile.

Identification of appropriate control variates and other techniques of variance reduction often requires some ingenuity. The techniques are often ad hoc. See Huzurbazar and Butler (1998) for an example of variance reduction that involves importance sampling in Monte Carlo tests.

2.7 Acceleration of Markov Chain Monte Carlo Methods

In MCMC, not only are we concerned with the variance of estimators, but also with the convergence of the chain. Until the stationary distribution is reached, the Monte Carlo sample may not be representative of the target distribution. Even after the stationary distribution is reached, the Monte Carlo samples must be large enough that the Markov chain moves through the statespace sufficiently to ensure that the sample is representative. In many practical applications, MCMC is extremely slow.

The efficiency of MCMC may vary depending on the approach. In some cases, the Gibbs algorithm is more efficient because there is no rejection step as there is in the Metropolis-Hastings method. The setup step in the Gibbs method is more complicated, however, and unless the sampling from the one-dimensional conditionals is very fast, there may be simple Metropolis-Hastings methods that will run faster.

Geyer (1991) suggested running parallel sequences in which each sequence is updated, or at least tested for updating, in turn. Following each iteration through all sequences, the states of two sequences are considered for exchange. Geyer called this the Metropolis-coupled Markov chain Monte Carlo method, because of the way the decision was made whether to exchange the state of two chains. Geyer and Thompson (1995) described a modification of this method that they called simulated tempering because the distributions in the separate chains were associated with "temperatures" that are randomly chosen. (The terminology is motivated by that of simulated annealing in which the temperature decreases deterministically.) Liu and Sabatti (1999) observed a propensity of the simulated tempering method to spend time in low-density regions of multimodal distributions and suggested a method in which the separate distributions relate to grids of differing mesh size. They called this method simulated sintering. The reader is referred to the papers for the details of the methods.

Several other approaches have been suggested to speed up MCMC methods. These include the so-called Swendsen-Wang algorithm (see Swendsen and Wang,

1987; Gray, 1994; and Fishman, 1999), resampling adaptive methods of Gelfand and Sahu (1994), and hybrids of Gibbs and Metropolis-Hastings methods (see Sargent, Hodges, and Carlin, 2000). Frigessi, Martinelli, and Stander (1997) discuss some general principles for acceleration of convergence.

Exercises

2.1. Prove that if X is a random variable with an absolutely continuous distribution function P_X, the random variable $P_X(X)$ has a U$(0, 1)$ distribution.

2.2. Acceptance/rejection methods.

   (a) Give an algorithm to generate a normal random deviate using the acceptance/rejection method with the double exponential density as the majorizing density. After you have obtained the acceptance/rejection test, try to simplify it.

   (b) What would be the problem with using a normal density to make a majorizing function for the double exponential distribution (or using a half-normal for an exponential)?

   (c) Write a program to generate bivariate normal deviates with mean $(0, 0)$, variance $(1, 1)$, and correlation ρ. Use a bivariate product double exponential density as the majorizing density. Now, set $\rho = 0.5$ and generate a sample of 1,000 bivariate normals. Compare the sample statistics with the parameters of the simulated distribution.

2.3. Consider a modification of the acceptance/rejection method given in Algorithm 2.1, in which steps 1 and 2 are reversed and the branch in step 3 is back to the new step 2; that is:

   (a) Generate u from a uniform $(0,1)$ distribution.

   (b) Generate y from the distribution with density function g_Y.

   (c) If $u \le p_X(y)/cg_Y(y)$, then take y as the desired realization; otherwise, return to step 2.

   Is this a better method? Let Q be the number of passes through these three steps until the desired variate is delivered. Determine the mean and variance of Q. (This method was suggested by Sibuya, 1961.)

2.4. Use the Metropolis-Hastings algorithm (page 48) to generate a sample of standard normal random variables. Use as the candidate generating density, $g(x|y)$, a double exponential density in x with mean y; that is, $g(x|y) = \frac{1}{2}e^{-|x-y|}$. Experiment with different burn-in periods and different starting values. Plot the sequences generated. Test your samples for goodness-of-fit to a normal distribution. (Remember that they are correlated.) Experiment with different sample sizes.

2.5. Consider the use of Gibbs sampling to generate samples from a bivariate normal distribution. Let the means be 0, the variances be 1, and the correlation be ρ. Both conditional distributions have the same form, which is given in the discussion of the use of marginal/conditional distributions on page 50. Let

$\rho = 0, .1, .2, .3, .4, .5$. Generate samples with varying lengths of burn-in and assess the fidelity of the samples by computing summary statistics and by plots of your samples. Is Gibbs sampling a viable method for this problem?

2.6. Use Monte Carlo methods to study least squares/normal drift. Let $\mu = 0$ and $\sigma^2 = 1$, and generate a sample of size 100 from a $N(\mu, \sigma^2)$ distribution. From this sample, compute $\bar{y}^{(1)}$ and $\bar{s}^{2(1)}$. Now let $\mu = \bar{y}^{(1)}$ and $\sigma^2 = \bar{s}^{2(1)}$; generate a sample of size 100 and compute $\bar{y}^{(2)}$ and $\bar{s}^{2(2)}$. Continue in this way, generating the sequences $\{\bar{y}^{(k)}\}$ and $\{\bar{s}^{2(k)}\}$. Describe these stochastic processes.

2.7. Assume that we have a sample, $x_1, \ldots, x_n$ from a $N(\mu, \sigma^2)$ distribution, and we wish to test the hypothesis

$$H_0: \quad \mu = 0$$

versus

$$H_1: \quad \mu \neq 0.$$

(a) Describe a Monte Carlo test for this hypothesis. *Hint:* Use the standard test statistic for this situation.

(b) How would you study the power of this test?

2.8. Suppose a random sample of size n is taken from what is believed to be a double exponential distribution, that is, a distribution with density

$$f(y) = \frac{1}{2\theta} e^{-|y|/\theta}.$$

All you have available from the sample are the mean m and the second and fourth central moments:

$$m_2 = \sum (y_i - m)^2/n,$$

$$m_4 = \sum (y_i - m)^4/n.$$

Describe a test, at the 0.05 level of significance, of the hypothesis that the original sample came from a distribution with that density.

2.9. Consider a common application in statistics: three different treatments are to be compared by applying them to randomly selected experimental units. This, of course, usually leads us to "analysis of variance" using a model such as $y_{ij} = \mu + \alpha_i + e_{ij}$ with the standard meanings of these symbols and the usual assumptions about the random component e_{ij} in the model. Suppose that instead of the usual assumptions, we assume that the e_{ij} have independent and identical double exponential distributions centered on zero.

(a) Describe how you would perform a Monte Carlo test instead of the usual AOV test. Be clear in stating the alternative hypothesis.

(b) Is the Monte Carlo test that you described nonparametric? Describe some other computer-intensive test that you could use even if you make no assumptions about the distribution of the e_{ij}.

2.10. It is often said in statistical hypothesis testing that "if the sample size is large enough, any test will be significant". Is that true?

Study this by Monte Carlo methods. Use a two-sample t test for equality of means on some data you generate from $N(\mu, \sigma^2)$ and $N(\mu+\delta, \sigma^2)$. Set $\delta = 0$, and generate various sizes of samples n_1 and n_2. Does the size of your test increase as the sample sizes increase? (It should not, despite the quote from the folklore.) What about the power? (It should, of course; that is, the sensitivity of the test to δ should increase.) There are, of course, valid reasons to be aware of the increasing chance of rejecting the null hypothesis because of a large sample size. The analyst must balance statistical significance with practical significance.

2.11. A biologist studying the distribution of maple trees within New England forests is interested in how the trees tend to cover areas within the forests. The question is whether mature trees tend to be at maximal spatial separation or tend to cluster by some spatial measure (perhaps due to prevailing winds or other environmental factors). The biologist plotted a given area in a forest of mature maple trees and located each tree in a rectangular coordinate system. The area contained 47 trees.

   (a) Describe how the biologist might construct a Monte Carlo test of the null hypothesis that the trees are randomly distributed. There are several possibilities for constructing a Monte Carlo test. There are also many alternative procedures that do not involve Monte Carlo tests. See Cressie (1991, pages 579–618) for a discussion of possibilities. Monte Carlo tests for this kind of application were discussed by Besag and Diggle (1977) and Besag and Clifford (1989). The observations that constitute your sample might be various functions of the cartesian coordinates of the trees (such as distances between trees).

   (b) Now, to be specific and to change the problem to be much smaller, suppose that in a given area on which a coordinate system has been imposed in such a way that the area constitutes a unit square, trees were observed at the following 5 points:

   (.2, .3)
   (.8, .3)
   (.3, .7)
   (.4, .5)
   (.7, .9)

   Using this random sample, develop and perform a Monte Carlo test that the positions of the trees are independent of one another.

2.12. Suppose that we want to use Monte Carlo methods to compare the variances of two estimators, T_1 and T_2. In a simple approach to the problem, we wish to estimate the sign of $V(T_1) - V(T_2)$. Suppose that it is known that both of the estimators are unbiased. Why is it better to compute the Monte Carlo estimate as $V(T_1 - T_2)$ rather than as $V(T_1) - V(T_2)$?

Chapter 3

Randomization and Data Partitioning

Although subsampling, resampling, or otherwise rearranging a given dataset cannot increase its information content, these procedures can sometimes be useful in extracting information. Randomly rearranging the observed dataset, for example, can give an indication of how unusual the dataset is with respect to a null hypothesis. This idea leads to randomization tests.

There are many useful procedures for data analysis that involve partitioning the original sample. Using subsets of the full sample, we may be able to get an estimate of the bias or the variance of the standard estimator or test statistic without relying too heavily on the assumptions that led to that choice of estimator or test statistic. It is often useful to partition the dataset into two parts and use the data in the "training set" or "estimation set" to arrive at a preliminary estimate or fit and then use the data in the "validation set" or "test set" to evaluate the fit. This kind of approach is particularly appropriate when we are unsure of our model of the data-generating process. In actual applications, of course, we are always at least somewhat unsure of our model. If the full dataset is used to fit the model, we are very limited in the extent to which we can validate the model.

Subsets of the data can be formed systematically or they can be formed as random samples from the given dataset. Sometimes the given dataset is viewed as a set of mass points of a finite distribution whose distribution function is the same as the empirical distribution function of the given dataset. In this case, the data partitioning may be done in such a way that observations may occur multiple times in the various partitions. In most cases, when we speak of "sets" or "subsets", we mean "multisets" (that is, collections in which items may occur more than once and are distinguished in each occurrence).

3.1   Randomization Methods

The basic idea of randomization tests is to compare an observed configuration of outcomes with all possible configurations. The randomization procedure does not depend on assumptions about the underlying probability distribution, so it is usable in a wide range of applications. When a hypothesis of interest does not have an obvious simple test statistic, a randomization test may be useful. It is important to note, however, that the procedure does depend on the overall data-generating process. The data collection process and the sampling design must be respected in any randomization of the data. For clinical trials, for example, it is unlikely that randomization methods could be used in the analysis.

Randomization tests have been used on small datasets for a long time. R. A. Fisher's famous "lady tasting tea" experiment (Fisher, 1935) used a randomization test. Because such tests can require very extensive computations, however, their use has been limited until recently. Edgington (1995) gives an extensive description of randomization tests and their applications.

In straightforward applications of randomization tests, the null hypothesis for the test is that all outcomes are equally likely, and the null hypothesis is rejected if the observed outcome belongs to a subset that has a low probability under the null hypothesis but a relatively higher probability under the alternative hypothesis.

A simple example of a randomization test is a test of whether the means of two data-generating processes are equal. The decision would be based on observations of two samples of results using the two treatments. There are several statistical tests for this null hypothesis, both parametric and nonparametric, that might be used. Most tests would use either the differences in the means of the samples, the number of observations in each sample that are greater than the overall mean or median, or the overall ranks of the observations in one sample. Any of these test statistics could be used as a test statistic in a randomization test. Consider the difference in the two sample means, for example. Without making any assumptions about the distributions of the two populations, the significance of the test statistic (that is, a measure of the extremeness of the observed difference) can be estimated by considering all configurations of the observations among the two treatment groups. This is done by computing the same test statistic for each possible arrangement of the observations, and then ranking the observed value of the test statistic within the set of all computed values.

More precisely, consider two samples,

$$x_1, \ldots, x_{n_1},$$

$$y_1, \ldots, y_{n_2},$$

for which we want to test the equality of the respective population means. We choose the unscaled test statistic $t_0 = \bar{x} - \bar{y}$. Now consider a different configuration of the same set of observations,

$$y_1, \ldots, x_{n_1},$$

$$x_1, \ldots, y_{n_2},$$

in which an observation from each set has been interchanged with one from the other set. The same kind of test statistic, namely the difference in the sample means, is computed. Let t_1 be the value of the test statistic for this combination. Now, consider a different configuration in which other values of the original samples have been switched. Again, compute the test statistic. Continuing this way through the full set of x's, we would eventually obtain $\binom{n_1 + n_2}{n_2}$ different configurations and a value of the test statistic for each one of these artificial samples. Without making any assumptions about the distribution of the random variable corresponding to the test statistic, we can consider the set of computed values to be a realization of a random sample from that distribution under the null hypothesis. The empirical "significance" of the value corresponding to the observed configuration could then be computed simply as the rank of the observed value in the set of all values.

In Exercise 2.11 on page 68, we considered the problem of deciding whether the locations of trees within a field were randomly distributed. This question can be addressed by a Monte Carlo test, as suggested in the exercise, or by a randomization test (or by several other methods, as described by Cressie, 1991, pages 579–618). Mead (1974) described a randomization test based on counts within nested grids. If the field is divided into four quadrants as shown by the solid lines in Figure 3.1, and then each quadrant is divided as shown by the dashed lines, the uniformity of the distribution can be assessed by comparing the counts within the two levels of gridding.

Mead suggested a ratio of measures of variation of counts within the larger grids to variation of counts within the smaller grids. Let n_{ij} be the count of observations within the jth grid cell of the ith large cell, and let $\bar{n}_{i\bullet}$ be the mean within the ith large cell and $\bar{n}_{\bullet\bullet}$ be the overall mean, using the common AOV notation. There are various measures that could be used. One measure of overall variation among the small grids is the total sum of squares,

$$t = \sum_i \sum_j (n_{ij} - \bar{n}_{\bullet\bullet})^2,$$

and a measure of variation among the small grids within the larger grids is the sum of squares,

$$w = 4 \sum_i (\bar{n}_{i\bullet} - \bar{n}_{\bullet\bullet})^2.$$

A test statistic is

$$Q = w/t.$$

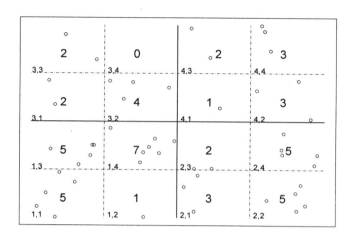

Figure 3.1: Quadrants and Subquadrants i, j with Cell Counts for a Randomization Test

Notice the similarity of Q to the F statistic in ANOVA. The numerator in both is the pooled among-sums-of-squares, but in Q the denominator is the total-sum-of-squares, rather than the error-sum-of-squares.

Clearly, values of Q that are either very small (close to 0) or very large (close to 1) indicate nonuniformity. In the example shown in Figure 3.1, $Q = 0.321$.

Although an approximation to the distribution of Q under the null hypothesis may be possible, a randomization approach can provide an accurate value for the significance level of the observed statistic. We consider values of Q computed by all possible arrangements of the small grid cells into the large grid. The total number of arrangements of the 16 counts and the ways of organizing them into 4 quadrants with 4 subquadrants is $16!/(4!)^4$, which is a very large number. (Of course, in our small example, because of the duplication of counts, the effective number of arrangements is much smaller.) Instead of computing Q for all possible arrangements, we may consider only a random sample of the arrangements. In this sampling for the randomization test, we generally do sampling with replacement because of the bookkeeping involved otherwise.

In this example, in a sample of 5,000 arrangements, the observed value of Q was near the second quartile, so this partitioning provided no evidence of nonrandomness. Mead's test, however, proceeds to further subdivisions. Each of the quadrants in Figure 3.1 could be divided into quadrants and subquadrants, and Q statistics could be computed for each as shown in Figure 3.2.

There are various ways to handle the statistics for the smaller quadrants.

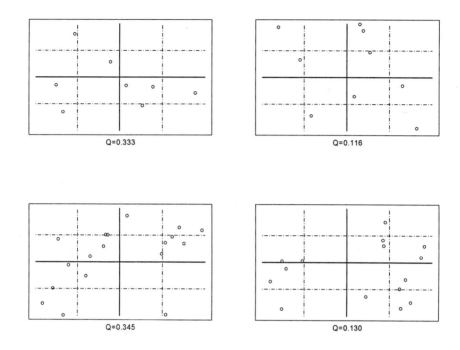

Figure 3.2: Further Subdivision into Quadrants and Subquadrants

One way is to take the average of the individual values as a single value for Q. There are many ways of doing the randomization that results in an unbiased test. It is difficult to make statements about the omnibus power of this test or any other test for randomness.

If tests from different levels of subdivision are combined, some kind of Bonferroni bound may be used on the significance level. Randomization, however, can allow us to avoid complications of multiple tests if the statistics computed in each randomization are the same as those computed on the observed sample.

Mead's test may have some difficulties caused by edge effects that occur because of the original square (or rectangular) outline we impose on the field. See Manly (1997) for a further discussion of this test.

In many applications of randomization methods, as in the one above, because there may be a very large number of all possible configurations, it may be necessary to sample randomly from the possible configurations rather than considering them all. When a sample of the configurations is used, the test is sometimes called an "approximate randomization test".

3.2   Cross Validation for Smoothing and Fitting

Cross validation methods are used with a variety of statistical procedures, such as regression, time series analysis, and density estimation, that yield a "fit" at each observation.

Consider the problem of fitting Y using X; that is, the problem of determining a function $g_{X,Y}(x)$ such that $Y \sim g_{X,Y}(X)$. For a given point, (x_0, y_0), how well does $g_{X,Y}(x_0)$ match y_0? The goodness of the match probably depends on whether the point (x_0, y_0) was used in determining the function g. If that point is used in fitting, then it is likely that $g_{X,Y}(x_0)$ is closer to y_0 than it would be if the point (x_0, y_0) is not used in the fitting. Our interest, of course, is in how well our fitted model $g_{X,Y}(x)$ would perform at new points; that is, how useful the model is in *prediction*.

Let $R(y, g)$ be a measure of the error between an observed value y and the predicted value g. (Often, R is the L_2 norm of the difference of the observed and the predicted. In the univariate case, this is the square, $(y - g)^2$.) We are interested in the expected value of this error. More precisely we are interested in the expected value with respect to the conditional distribution of Y given X; that is,

$$\mathrm{E}_{P_{Y|X}}\Big(R(Y_0,\ g_{X,Y}(x_0))\Big).$$

Of course, we do not know $P_{Y|X}$.

The fitted function $g_{X,Y}(x)$ provides an estimate of the conditional distribution of Y given X, $\widehat{P}_{Y|X}$, so we can evaluate the expectation with respect to this distribution. We could estimate it as the sample average:

$$\mathrm{E}_{\widehat{P}_{Y|X}}\Big(R(Y_0,\ g_{X,Y}(x_0))\Big) = \frac{1}{n}\sum_{i=1}^{n} R(y_i,\ g_{X,Y}(x_i)). \tag{3.1}$$

This quantity, which is easy to compute, is the "apparent error". It is typically smaller than the true error at any point x_0 whether or not a point corresponding to x_0 was in the dataset used in fitting $g_{X,Y}$. The fit is usually chosen to minimize a sum such as in equation (3.1).

We may arrive at a better estimate if we partition the dataset into two parts, say S_1 and S_2, and use the data in the training set or "estimation set" S_1 to get the fit $g_{1X,Y}$ and then use the data in the "validation set" or "test set" S_2 to estimate the error:

$$\mathrm{E}_{\widehat{P}_{1Y|X}}\Big(R(Y_0,\ g_{X,Y}(X_0))\Big) = \frac{1}{\#(S_1)}\sum_{i \in S_2} R(y_i,\ g_{1X,Y}(x_i)). \tag{3.2}$$

This quantity is likely to be larger than the quantity in equation (3.1).

We can also get an estimate after exchanging the roles of S_1 and S_2 and then combine the estimates:

$$E_{\widetilde{P}_{Y|X}}\left(R(Y_0, g_{X,Y}(X_0))\right) =$$

$$\frac{1}{n}\left(\sum_{i \in S_2} R(y_i, g_{1X,Y}(x_i)) + \sum_{i \in S_1} R(y_i, g_{2X,Y}(x_i))\right). \tag{3.3}$$

This is an old idea. An extension and related idea is balanced half-sampling, which is a technique that is often used in finite-population sampling.

This kind of data partitioning is the idea behind cross validation. Instead of dividing the sample in half, we could form multiple partial datasets with overlap. One way would be to leave out just one observation at a time. The idea is to hold out one (or more) observation(s) at a time, apply the basic procedure, and compare the fitted value with the observed value. In K-fold cross validation, the sample is divided into K approximately equal-sized subsets, and each subset is used to get a measure of the prediction error by using the fit from all of the rest of the data. The average from the K subsets is then taken as the estimate of the prediction error.

Cross validation can be useful in model building. In regression model building, the standard problem is, given a set of potential regressors, to choose a relatively small subset that provides a good fit to the data. Standard techniques include "stepwise" regression and all best subsets. One of the main problems in model building is overfitting. In regression models, the more independent variables are included in the model, the better the fit unless the observations on the added variables do not increase the rank of the coefficient matrix. This is a simple consequence of having more decision variables in the optimization problem that is used to fit the model. Various statistics, such as the adjusted R^2 or C_p, can be used to determine when the improvement of the fit due to an additional variable is "worthwhile". These statistics are based on penalties for the number of variables in the model.

Allen (1971, 1974) suggested a cross-validation "prediction sum of squares", PRESS, to aid in variable selection in full-rank linear models that are fit using a least squares criterion. PRESS is similar to the sums in equation (3.3) except that instead of just one partition into two sets, the dataset is partitioned n times into an estimation set with $n-1$ observation and a test set with only one observation. In the linear model $y = X\beta$, where y is an n-vector of observations, X is an $n \times m$ matrix of corresponding observations, and β is an m-vector of parameters, using the notation $\widehat{\beta}_{-j}$ to denote the least squares estimate of β based on all but the jth observation, PRESS is defined as

$$\sum_{j=1}^{n}(y_j - x_j^{\text{T}}\widehat{\beta}_{-j})^2, \tag{3.4}$$

where x_j^{T} is the jth row of X (that is, the one that was not used in computing $\widehat{\beta}_{-j}$).

As more variables are added to the model, PRESS may decrease initially and then begin to increase when overfitting occurs. It is important to understand that variable selection and model fitting are very different from inferential statistical procedures. Our usual concerns about bias, power, significance levels, and so on just do not apply. The problem is because to make statements about such things we must have a model, which we do not have if we are building a model.

Although computation of PRESS involves n regression fits, when efficient updating and downdating techniques are used, the additional amount of computation is only about twice the amount of computation to do a single regression fit (see, for example, Gentle, 1998b).

In fitting models to data, it is often appropriate to limit the range of influence of observations. For example, in estimation of a probability density function, observations at one extreme of the distribution may provide very little information about the shape of the density in a different range of the distribution. The range of influence of observations in a statistical procedure is often controlled by "smoothing" parameters. A smoothing parameter may be the width of an interval to use in constructing a frequency function, for example. Another example of a smoothing parameter is the number of knots in splines. Cross validation is a common method of selecting smoothing parameters. Further examples of smoothing parameters include such things as bin widths in histograms or window sizes for various kernel methods (see examples in Kohn, Ansley, and Tharm, 1991, and Thomas, 1991). Xiang and Wahba (1996) discuss a generalized approximate cross validation method for use in smoothing splines.

3.3   Jackknife Methods

Jackknife methods make use of systematic partitions of a dataset to estimate properties of an estimator computed from the full sample. Quenouille (1949, 1956) suggested the technique to estimate the bias of an estimator. John Tukey coined the term "jackknife" to refer to the method, and showed that the method is also useful in estimating the variance of an estimator.

Suppose that we have a random sample, $Y_1, \ldots, Y_n$, from which we compute a statistic T as an estimator of a parameter θ in the population from which the sample was drawn. In the jackknife method, we partition the given dataset into r groups, each of size k. (For simplicity, we will assume that the number of observations n is kr.)

Now, we remove the jth group from the sample and compute the estimator from the reduced sample. Let $T_{(-j)}$ denote the estimator computed from the sample with the jth group of observations removed. (This sample is of size $n - k$.) The estimator $T_{(-j)}$ has properties similar to those of T. For example, if T is unbiased, so is $T_{(-j)}$. If T is not unbiased, neither is $T_{(-j)}$; its bias, however, is likely to be different.

The mean of the $T_{(-j)}$,

$$\overline{T}_{(\bullet)} = \frac{1}{r} \sum_{j=1}^{r} T_{(-j)}, \tag{3.5}$$

can be used as an estimate of θ. The $T_{(-j)}$ can also be used in some cases to obtain more information about the estimator T from the full sample. (For the case in which T is a linear functional of the ECDF, then $\overline{T}_{(\bullet)} = T$, so the systematic partitioning of a random sample will not provide any additional information.)

Consider the weighted differences in the estimate for the full sample and the reduced samples:

$$T_j^* = rT - (r-1)T_{(-j)}. \tag{3.6}$$

The T_j^* are called "pseudovalues". (If T is a linear functional of the ECDF, then $T_j^* = T(x_j)$; that is, it is the estimator computed from the single observation, x_j.) We call the mean of the pseudovalues the "jackknifed" T and denote it as $J(T)$:

$$
\begin{aligned}
J(T) &= \frac{1}{r} \sum_{j=1}^{r} T_j^* \\
&= \overline{T}^*.
\end{aligned}
\tag{3.7}
$$

We can also write $J(T)$ as

$$J(T) = T + (n-1)\left(T - \overline{T}_{(\bullet)}\right)$$

or

$$J(T) = nT - (n-1)\overline{T}_{(\bullet)}. \tag{3.8}$$

In most applications of the jackknife, it is common to take $k = 1$, in which case $r = n$. It has been shown that this choice is optimal under certain assumptions about the population (see Rao and Webster, 1966).

Jackknife Variance Estimate

Although the pseudovalues are not independent (except when T is a linear functional), we treat them as if they were independent, and use $V(J(T))$ as an estimator of the variance of T, $V(T)$. The intuition behind this is simple: a small variation in the pseudovalues indicates a small variation in the estimator. The sample variance of the mean of the pseudovalues can be used as an estimator of $V(T)$:

$$\widehat{V(T)}_J = \frac{\sum_{j=1}^{r}\left(T_j^* - J(T)\right)^2}{r(r-1)}. \tag{3.9}$$

(Notice that when T is the mean and $k = 1$, this is the standard variance estimator.) From expression (3.9), it may seem more natural to take V_J as an estimator of the variance of $J(T)$, and indeed it often is.

A variant of this expression for the variance estimator uses the original estimator T:

$$\frac{\sum_{j=1}^{r}(T_j^* - T)^2}{r(r-1)}. \tag{3.10}$$

There are several methods of estimating or approximating the variances of estimators, including the delta method we discussed on page 31, which depends on knowing the variance of some simpler statistic; Monte Carlo methods, discussed in Chapter 2; and bootstrap methods, discussed in Chapter 4. How good any of these variance estimates are depends on the estimator T and on the underlying distribution. Monte Carlo studies indicate that $\widehat{V(T)}_J$ is often conservative; that is, it often overestimates the variance (see Efron, 1982). The alternate expression (3.10) is greater than or equal to $\widehat{V(T)}_J$, as is easily seen; hence, it is an even more conservative estimator (see Exercises 3.4 and 3.5).

Jackknife Bias Correction

In the following, for simplicity, we will consider the group sizes to be 1; that is, we assume that $r = n$. As we mentioned above, this is the most common case in practice, and it has certain optimality properties.

Suppose that we can represent the bias of T as a power series in n^{-1}; that is,

$$
\begin{aligned}
\text{Bias}(T) &= \text{E}(T) - \theta \\
&= \sum_{q=1}^{\infty} \frac{a_q}{n^q},
\end{aligned}
$$

where the a_q do not involve n. If all $a_q = 0$, the estimator is unbiased. If $a_1 \neq 0$, the order of the bias is n^{-1}. (Such an estimator is sometimes called "second-order accurate". "First-order" accuracy implies a bias of order $n^{-1/2}$.)

Using the power series representation for the bias of T, we see that the bias of the jackknife estimator is

$$
\begin{aligned}
\text{Bias}(\text{J}(T)) &= \text{E}(\text{J}(T)) - \theta \\
&= n(\text{E}(T) - \theta) - \frac{n-1}{n}\sum_{j=1}^{n}\text{E}(T_{(-j)}) - \theta) \\
&= n\sum_{q=1}^{\infty}\frac{a_q}{n^q} - (n-1)\left(\sum_{q=1}^{\infty}\frac{a_q}{(n-1)^q}\right) \\
&= a_2\left(\frac{1}{n} - \frac{1}{n-1}\right) + a_3\left(\frac{1}{n^2} - \frac{1}{(n-1)^2}\right) + \cdots \\
&= -a_2\left(\frac{1}{n(n-1)}\right) + a_3\left(\frac{1}{n^2} - \frac{1}{(n-1)^2}\right) + \cdots;
\end{aligned}
$$

that is, the bias of the jackknife estimator, Bias($J(T)$), is at most of order n^{-2}. If $a_q = 0$ for $q = 2, \ldots$, the jackknife estimator is unbiased.

This reduction in the bias is a major reason for using the jackknife. Any explicit analysis of the bias reduction, however, depends on a representation of the bias in a power series in n^{-1} with constant coefficients. This may not be possible, of course.

From

$$E(J(T)) - \theta = E(T) - \theta + (n-1)\left(E(T) - \frac{1}{n}\sum_{j=1}^{n} E(T_{(-j)})\right),$$

we have the jackknife estimator of the bias in T,

$$B_J = (n-1)\left(\overline{T}^* - T\right), \tag{3.11}$$

and the jackknife bias-corrected estimator of θ,

$$T_J = nT - (n-1)\overline{T}^*. \tag{3.12}$$

Higher-Order Bias Corrections

Suppose that we pursue the bias correction to higher orders by using a second application of the jackknife. The pseudovalues are

$$T_j^{**} = nJ(T) - (n-1)J(T_{(-j)}).$$

Assuming the same series representations for the bias as before, a second-order jackknife estimator,

$$J^2(T) = \frac{n^2 J(T) - (n-1)^2 \sum_{j=1}^{n} J(T)_{(-j)}/n}{n^2 - (n-1)^2}, \tag{3.13}$$

is unbiased to order $O(n^{-3})$.

There are two major differences between this estimator and the first-order jackknifed estimator. For the first-order jackknife, $J(T)$ differs from T by a quantity of order n^{-1}; hence, if T has variance of order n^{-1} (as we usually hope), the variance of $J(T)$ is asymptotically the same as that of T. In other words, the bias reduction carries no penalty in increased variance. This is not the case for higher-order bias correction of $J^2(T)$.

The other difference is that in the bias expansion,

$$E(T) - \theta = \sum_{q=1}^{\infty} a_q/n^q,$$

if $a_q = 0$ for $q \geq 2$, then the first-order jackknifed estimator is unbiased. For the second-order jackknifed estimator, even if $a_q = 0$ for $q \geq 3$, the estimator may not be unbiased. Its bias is

$$\text{Bias}(J^2(T)) = \frac{a_2}{(n-1)(n-2)(2n-1)};$$

that is, it is still of order n^{-3}.

The Generalized Jackknife

Schucany, Gray, and Owen (1971) suggested a method of systematically reducing the bias by combining higher-order jackknifes. First, consider two biased estimators of θ, T_1 and T_2. Let

$$w = \frac{\text{Bias}(T_1)}{\text{Bias}(T_2)}.$$

Now, consider the estimator

$$T_w = \frac{T_1 - wT_2}{1 - w}.$$

We have

$$
\begin{aligned}
\text{E}(T_w) &= \frac{1}{1 - w}\text{E}(T_1) - \frac{w}{1 - w}\text{E}(T_2) \\
&= \frac{1}{1 - w}(\theta + \text{Bias}(T_1)) - \frac{w}{1 - w}(\theta + \text{Bias}(T_2)) \\
&= \theta,
\end{aligned}
$$

so this weighted combination of the estimators is unbiased.

Now, consider the biases of the jackknifed estimators,

$$\text{Bias}(\text{J}(T)) - \theta = -\frac{a_2}{n(n - 1)} + \text{O}(n^{-3})$$

and

$$\text{Bias}(\text{J}^2(T)) - \theta = -\frac{a_2}{(n - 1)(n - 2)(2n - 1)} + \text{O}(n^{-3}),$$

and let

$$w = \frac{\text{Bias}(\text{J}(T))}{\text{Bias}(\text{J}^2(T))}.$$

Notice that if $w = (n - 1)/n$, then the jackknife estimator,

$$nT - (n - 1)\overline{T}_{(-j)},$$

is unbiased. This suggests a different second-order jackknife instead of the one in equation (3.13). Schucany, Gray, and Owen (1971) therefore set

$$
\begin{aligned}
w &= \frac{\frac{1}{n(n-1)}}{\frac{1}{(n-1)(n-2)}} \\
&= \frac{n - 2}{n}
\end{aligned}
$$

and take

$$\text{J}^2(T) = \frac{n}{2}\text{J}(T) - \frac{n - 2}{2}\sum_{j=1}^{n} T_{(-j)}^*/n.$$

as the second-order jackknifed estimator.

So, generalizing, and writing $T_1 = T$ and $T_2 = \overline{T}_{(-j)}$, we jackknife T_1 by the ratio of the determinants

$$J(T_1) = \frac{\begin{vmatrix} T_1 & T_2 \\ 1/n & 1/(n-1) \end{vmatrix}}{\begin{vmatrix} 1 & 1 \\ 1/n & 1/(n-1) \end{vmatrix}}.$$

Suppose that for two estimators, T_1 and T_2, we can express the biases as

$$E(T_1) - \theta = f_1(n)b$$

and

$$E(T_2) - \theta = f_2(n)b.$$

We define the generalized jackknife of T_1 as

$$\begin{aligned} J(T_1) &= \frac{\begin{vmatrix} T_1 & T_2 \\ f_1(n) & f_2(n) \end{vmatrix}}{\begin{vmatrix} 1 & 1 \\ f_1(n) & f_2(n) \end{vmatrix}} \\ &= \frac{1}{1-w}T_1 - \frac{w}{1-w}T_2, \end{aligned}$$

where

$$w = \frac{f_1(n)}{f_2(n)}.$$

The higher-order generalized jackknife estimators can be developed by writing the bias of the jth estimator as

$$E(T_j) - \theta = \sum_{i=1}^{\infty} f_{ij}(n)b_i$$

for $j = 1, \ldots, k+1$. Then

$$J(T_k) = \frac{\begin{vmatrix} T_1 & T_2 & \cdots & T_{k+1} \\ f_{11}(n) & f_{12}(n) & \cdots & T_{1,k+1}(n) \\ & & \vdots & \\ f_{k1}(n) & f_{k2}(n) & \cdots & T_{k,k+1}(n) \end{vmatrix}}{\begin{vmatrix} 1 & 1 & \cdots & 1 \\ f_{11}(n) & f_{12}(n) & \cdots & T_{1,k+1}(n) \\ & & \vdots & \\ f_{k1}(n) & f_{k2}(n) & \cdots & T_{k,k+1}(n) \end{vmatrix}},$$

where $T_2, \ldots, T_{k+1}$ are the means of the estimators of the successive jackknifed estimators from the reduced samples.

The generalized jackknife reduces the order of the bias by $1/n$ in each application and if all terms beyond the kth in the expansion of the bias are zero, then $J(T_k)$ is unbiased. The variance of the jackknifed estimator may increase, however. See Gray and Schucany (1972) and Sharot (1976) for further discussions of the generalized jackknife.

The Delete-k Jackknife

Although as we mentioned earlier it has been shown that deleting one observation at a time is optimal under certain assumptions about the population (see Rao and Webster, 1966), this does not lead to a consistent procedure for some estimators that are not differentiable functions of the sample. An example, considered by Efron and Tibshirani (1993), is the jackknife estimate of the variance of the sample median. Because in leaving out one observation at a time, the median of the reduced samples will only take on at most two different values, the jackknife procedure cannot lead to a good estimate of the variance. This is obviously the case, no matter how large is the sample size.

In a practical sense, the consistency is not the issue. The jackknife does not perform well in finite samples in this case. (Note that "performing well" in real applications may not be very closely related to consistency.)

Instead of deleting a single observation, we can form pseudo-observations by deleting k observations. This leads to the "delete-k jackknife". The delete-k jackknifed estimator may be consistent for a wider range of estimators than is the delete-one jackknife. The delete-k jackknifed estimator is consistent in the case of estimation of the variance of the median under certain conditions. The asymptotics require that k also gets large. For the median, the requirements are $n^{1/2}/k \to 0$ and $n - k \to \infty$; see Efron and Tibshirani (1993). (See also Shao and Tu, 1995, for further discussion of properties of the delete-k jackknife.)

In the delete-k jackknife, if each subset of size k is deleted, this could lead to a large number of pseudo-observations; we have the number of combinations of k items from a set of n items. The large number of pseudo-observations can be accommodated by random sampling, however; that is, we do not form the exact mean of all pseudo-observations.

Further Reading

The idea of partitioning data is an old one. It may be done prior to collecting data and, in this case, the statistician may use principles of experimental design to enhance the power of the procedure. "Half samples" have been used for many years in sampling finite populations. The immediate purpose is to get better estimates of variances, but a more general purpose is to assess the validity of assumptions and the quality of estimates.

In building a model of a data-generating process, generally the more complicated we allow the model to become, the better the model will appear to fit a given set of data. Rather than using some measure of the goodness-of-fit that depends on all of the data at once, such as an R-squared, it is much more sensible to use a criterion such as PRESS that depends on the ability of the model to fit data that were not included in the fitting process. The latter approach uses partitions of the data. Picard and Berk (1990) discuss and give examples of various uses of data partitioning in statistical inference.

The use of a training set and a test set has been standard procedure in classification and machine learning for years. More recently, various ways of selecting and using multiple training sets have been proposed; see Amit and Geman (1997) and Breiman (2001), for example.

Exercises

3.1. Consider again the problem of Exercise 2.11 on page 68, in which we must decide whether the locations of trees within a field were randomly distributed. In that exercise, you were to develop a Monte Carlo test, possibly based on distances between pairs of trees.

    (a) Write a program in Fortran, C, or a higher-level language to compute the randomization test statistic of Mead, allowing three levels of nested grids.

    (b) Design and conduct a small Monte Carlo study to compare the Monte Carlo test of Exercise 2.11 with the Mead randomization test. The important issue here is the omnibus alternative hypothesis (that the distribution is not randomly uniform). There are many ways that the distribution could be nonrandom, and it is possible that the relative performance of the tests is dependent on the nature of the nonrandomness. Define and study at least three different types of nonrandomness. One simple type you may include is due to a neighborhood exclusion, in which one tree exerts an inhibition on other trees within a neighborhood of radius r. Obviously, the larger r is, the less random is the distribution. A generalization of this is a Strauss process, in which there are nonuniform probabilities of multiple occurrences within a neighborhood. See Ripley (1979a, 1981) for general discussions of randomness in locations of points, and see Ripley (1979b) for a program to generate points according to a Strauss process.

3.2. PRESS.

    (a) Write a program in Fortran, C, or a higher-level language that computes PRESS efficiently.

    (b) Generate n observations according to the polynomial model

$$y_i = 1 + x_i + x_i^2 + e_i,$$

where e_i is from a normal distribution with a variance of 1. Let $n = 50$, and let x_i be from a standard normal distribution. Compute PRESS for each of the models:

$$
\begin{aligned}
y_i &= \beta_0 + \beta_1 x_i + e_i, \\
y_i &= \beta_0 + \beta_1 x_i + \beta_2 x_i^2 + e_i, \\
y_i &= \beta_0 + \beta_1 x_i + \beta_2 x_i^2 + \beta_3 x_i^3 + e_i.
\end{aligned}
$$

3.3. For $r = n$, show that the jackknife variance estimate, V_J (equation (3.9), page 77), can be expressed as

$$\frac{n-1}{n} \sum_{j=1}^{n} \left(T_{(-j)} - \widehat{T}_{(\bullet)}\right)^2.$$

3.4. Show that

$$V_J \leq \frac{\sum_{j=1}^{n}(T_j^* - T)^2}{n(n-1)}.$$

3.5. The statistic

$$b_2 = \frac{\sum(y_i - \bar{y})^4}{\left(\sum(y_i - \bar{y})^2\right)^2}$$

is sometimes used to decide whether a least squares estimator is appropriate (otherwise, a robust method may be used). What is the jackknife estimate of the standard deviation of b_2?

Design and conduct a Monte Carlo study of the performance of the jackknife estimator of the standard deviation of b_2 in two specific cases: a normal distribution and a double exponential distribution. In each case, use only one sample size, $n = 100$, but for each case, use both $k = 1$ and $k = 5$ (nonoverlapping partitions). Be specific about the basis on which you assess the performance of the jackknife estimator.

3.6. Jackknife bias reduction. Assume that $Y_1, \ldots, Y_n$ are i.i.d.

(a) Consider $M_2 = \sum Y_i^2/n$ as an estimator of the second raw population moment, $\mu_2 = \mathrm{E}(Y^2)$. What is the jackknife bias-reduced estimator of μ_2? Is it unbiased?

(b) Consider $M_3 = \sum Y_i^3/n$ as an estimator of the third raw population moment, $\mu_3 = \mathrm{E}(Y^3)$. What is the jackknife bias-reduced estimator of μ_3? Is it unbiased?

Chapter 4

Bootstrap Methods

Resampling methods involve the use of many samples, each taken from a single sample that was taken from the population of interest. Inference based on resampling makes use of the conditional sampling distribution of a new sample (the "resample") drawn from a given sample. Statistical functions on the given sample, a finite set, can easily be evaluated. Resampling methods therefore can be useful even when very little is known about the underlying distribution.

A basic idea in bootstrap resampling is that, because the observed sample contains all the available information about the underlying population, the observed sample can be considered *to be* the population; hence, the distribution of any relevant test statistic can be simulated by using random samples from the "population" consisting of the original sample.

Suppose that a sample $y_1, \ldots, y_n$ is to be used to estimate a population parameter, θ. For a statistic T that estimates θ, as usual, we wish to know the sampling distribution so as to correct for any bias in our estimator or to set confidence intervals for our estimate of θ. The sampling distribution of T is often intractable in applications of interest.

A basic bootstrapping method formulated by Efron (1979) uses the discrete distribution represented by the sample to study the unknown distribution from which the sample came. The basic tool is the empirical cumulative distribution function. The ECDF is the CDF of the finite population that is used as a model of the underlying population of interest.

The functional of the CDF that defines a parameter defines a plug-in estimator of that parameter when the functional is applied to the ECDF. A functional of a population distribution function, $\Theta(P)$, defining a parameter θ can usually be expressed as

$$\begin{aligned} \theta &= \Theta(P) \\ &= \int g(y)\, \mathrm{d}P(y). \end{aligned}$$

The plug-in estimator T is the same functional of the ECDF:

$$
\begin{aligned}
T &= T(P_n) \\
&= \Theta(P_n) \\
&= \int g(y)\, \mathrm{d}P_n(y).
\end{aligned}
$$

(In both of these expressions, we are using the integral in a general sense. In the second expression, the integral is a finite sum. It is also a countable sum in the first expression if the random variable is discrete. Note also that we use the same symbol to denote the functional and the random variable.) Various properties of the distribution of T can be estimated by use of "bootstrap samples", each of the form $\{y_1^*, \ldots, y_n^*\}$, where the y_i^*'s are chosen from the original y_i's with replacement.

We define a *resampling vector*, p^*, corresponding to each bootstrap sample as the vector of proportions of the elements of the original sample in the given bootstrap sample. The resampling vector is a realization of a random vector P^* for which nP^* has an n-variate multinomial distribution with parameters n and $(1/n, \ldots, 1/n)$. The resampling vector has random components that sum to 1. For example, if the bootstrap sample $(y_1^*, y_2^*, y_3^*, y_4^*)$ happens to be the sample (y_2, y_2, y_4, y_3), the resampling vector p^* is

$$(0,\ 1/2,\ 1/4,\ 1/4).$$

The bootstrap replication of the estimator T is a function of p^*, $T(p^*)$. The resampling vector can be used to estimate the variance of the bootstrap estimator. By imposing constraints on the resampling vector, the variance of the bootstrap estimator can be reduced.

The *bootstrap principle* involves repeating the process that leads from a population CDF to an ECDF. Taking the ECDF P_n to be the CDF of a population, and resampling, we have an ECDF for the new sample, $P_n^{(1)}$. (In this notation, we could write the ECDF of the original sample as $P_n^{(0)}$.) The difference is that we know more about $P_n^{(1)}$ than we know about P_n. Our knowledge about $P_n^{(1)}$ comes from the simple discrete uniform distribution, whereas our knowledge about P_n depends on knowledge (or assumptions) about the underlying population.

The bootstrap resampling approach can be used to derive properties of statistics, regardless of whether any resampling is done. Most common uses of the bootstrap involve computer simulation of the resampling; hence, bootstrap methods are usually instances of computational inference.

4.1   Bootstrap Bias Corrections

For an estimator T that is the same functional of the ECDF as the parameter is of the CDF, the problem of bias correction is to find a functional f_T that allows us to relate the distribution function of the sample P_n to the population distribution function P, that is, such that

$$E(f_T(P, P_n) \mid P) = 0. \tag{4.1}$$

Correcting for the bias is equivalent to finding b that solves the equation

$$
\begin{aligned}
f_T(P, P_n) &= \Theta(P_n) - \Theta(P) + b \\
&= T(P_n) - T(P) + b
\end{aligned}
$$

so that f_T has zero expectation with respect to P.

Using the bootstrap principle, we look for $f_T^{(1)}$ so that

$$E\left(f_T^{(1)}(P_n, P_n^{(1)}) \mid P_n\right) = 0, \tag{4.2}$$

where $P_n^{(1)}$ is the empirical cumulative distribution function for a sample from the discrete distribution formed from the original sample.

We know more about the items in equation (4.2) than those in equation (4.1), so we now consider the simpler problem of finding b_1 so that

$$E\left(T(P_n^{(1)}) - T(P_n) + b_1 \mid P_n\right) = 0.$$

We can write the solution as

$$b_1 = T(P_n) - E\left(T(P_n^{(1)}) \mid P_n\right). \tag{4.3}$$

An estimator with less bias is therefore

$$T_1 = 2T(P_n) - E\left(T(P_n^{(1)}) \mid P_n\right). \tag{4.4}$$

Suppose, for example, that

$$
\begin{aligned}
\theta &= \Theta(P) \\
&= \int y \, dP(y),
\end{aligned}
$$

and we wish to estimate θ^2. From a random sample of size n, the plug-in estimator of θ is

$$
\begin{aligned}
\Theta(P_n) &= \int y \, dP_n(y) \\
&= \bar{y}.
\end{aligned}
$$

A candidate estimator for θ^2 is the square of the sample mean, that is, $\bar{y}^2$. Because P_n completely defines the sample, we can represent the estimator as a functional $T(P_n)$, and we can study the bias of T by considering the problem of estimating the square of the mean of a discrete uniform distribution with mass points $y_1, \ldots, y_n$. We do this using a single sample of size n from this distribution, $y_1^*, \ldots, y_n^*$. For this sample, we merely work out the expectation of $(\sum y_i^*/n)^2$. You are asked to complete these computations in Exercise 4.1.

In general, to correct the bias, we must evaluate

$$\mathrm{E}\Big(T(P_n^{(1)}) \,\Big|\, P_n\Big) \tag{4.5}$$

in equation (4.4). We may be able to compute $\mathrm{E}\Big(T(P_n^{(1)}) \mid P_n\Big)$, as in the simple example above, or we may have to resort to Monte Carlo methods to estimate it.

The Monte Carlo estimate is based on m random samples each of size n, taken with replacement from the original sample. This is a nonparametric procedure. Specifically, the basic nonparametric Monte Carlo bootstrap procedure for bias correction is

- take m random samples each of size n, *with replacement* from the given set of data, the original sample $y_1, \ldots, y_n$;

- for each sample, compute an estimate T^{*j} of the same functional form as the original estimator T.

The mean of the T^{*j}, $\overline{T}^*$, is an unbiased estimator of $\mathrm{E}\Big(T(P_n^{(1)}) \mid P_n\Big)$.

The distribution of T^{*j} is related to the distribution of T. The variability of T about θ can be assessed by the variability of T^{*j} about T; the bias of T can be assessed by the mean of $T^{*j} - T$.

4.2   Bootstrap Estimation of Variance

From a given sample $y_1, \ldots, y_n$, suppose that we have an estimator $T(y)$. The estimator T^* computed as the same function T, using a bootstrap sample (that is, $T^* = T(y^*)$), is a *bootstrap observation* of T.

The bootstrap estimate of some function of the estimator T is a plug-in estimate that uses the empirical distribution P_n in place of P. This is the bootstrap principle, and this bootstrap estimate is called the *ideal bootstrap*.

For the variance of T, for example, the ideal bootstrap estimator is the variance $\mathrm{V}(T^*)$. This variance, in turn, can be estimated from bootstrap samples. The bootstrap estimate of the variance, then, is the sample variance of T^* based on the m samples of size n taken from P_n:

$$\widehat{\mathrm{V}}(T) \;=\; \widehat{\mathrm{V}}(T^*) \tag{4.6}$$

$$\qquad\quad =\; \frac{1}{m-1}\sum(T^{*j} - \overline{T}^*)^2, \tag{4.7}$$

where T^{*j} is the jth bootstrap observation of T. This, of course, can be computed by Monte Carlo methods by generating m bootstrap samples and computing T^{*j} for each.

If the estimator of interest is the sample mean, for example, the bootstrap estimate of the variance is $\widehat{V}(Y)/n$, where $\widehat{V}(Y)$ is an estimate of the variance of the underlying population. (This is true no matter what the underlying distribution is, as long as the variance exists.) The bootstrap procedure does not help in this situation.

4.3 Bootstrap Confidence Intervals

As in equation (1.43) on page 33, a method of forming a confidence interval for a parameter θ is to find a pivotal quantity that involves θ and a statistic T, $f(T, \theta)$, and then to rearrange the terms in a probability statement of the form

$$\Pr\left(f_{(\alpha/2)} \leq f(T, \theta) \leq f_{(1-\alpha/2)}\right) = 1 - \alpha. \tag{4.8}$$

When distributions are difficult to work out, we may use bootstrap methods for estimating and/or approximating the percentiles, $f_{(\alpha/2)}$ and $f_{(1-\alpha/2)}$.

Basic Intervals

For computing confidence intervals for a mean, the pivotal quantity is likely to be of the form $T - \theta$. The simplest application of the bootstrap to forming a confidence interval is to use the sampling distribution of $T^* - T_0$ as an approximation to the sampling distribution of $T - \theta$; that is, instead of using $f(T, \theta)$, we use $f(T^*, T_0)$, where T_0 is the value of T in the given sample. The percentiles of the sampling distribution determine $f_{(\alpha/2)}$ and $f_{(1-\alpha/2)}$ in the expressions above. If we cannot determine the sampling distribution of $T^* - t$, we can easily estimate it by Monte Carlo methods.

For the case $f(T, \theta) = T - \theta$, the probability statement above is equivalent to

$$\Pr\left(T - f_{(1-\alpha/2)} \leq \theta \leq T - f_{(\alpha/2)}\right) = 1 - \alpha. \tag{4.9}$$

The $f_{(\pi)}$ may be estimated from the percentiles of a Monte Carlo sample of $T^* - T_0$.

Bootstrap-t Intervals

Methods of inference based on a normal distribution often work well even when the underlying distribution is not normal. A useful approximate confidence interval for a location parameter can often be constructed using as a template the familiar confidence interval for the mean of a normal distribution,

$$\left(\overline{Y} - t_{(1-\alpha/2)} \, s/\sqrt{n}, \quad \overline{Y} - t_{(\alpha/2)} \, s/\sqrt{n}\right),$$

where $t_{(\pi)}$ is a percentile from the Student's t distribution, and s^2 is the usual sample variance.

A confidence interval for any parameter constructed in this pattern is called a *bootstrap-t interval*. A bootstrap-t interval has the form

$$\left(T - \widehat{t}_{(1-\alpha/2)} \sqrt{\widehat{V}(T)}, \quad T - \widehat{t}_{(\alpha/2)} \sqrt{\widehat{V}(T)} \right), \tag{4.10}$$

where $\widehat{t}_{(\pi)}$ is the estimated percentile from the studentized statistic,

$$\frac{T^* - T_0}{\sqrt{\widehat{V}(T^*)}}.$$

For many estimators T, no simple expression is available for $\widehat{V}(T)$. The variance could be estimated using a bootstrap and equation (4.6). This bootstrap nested in the bootstrap to determine $\widehat{t}_{(\pi)}$ increases the computational burden multiplicatively.

If the underlying distribution is normal and T is a sample mean, the interval in expression (4.10) is an exact $(1 - \alpha)100\%$ confidence interval of shortest length. If the underlying distribution is not normal, however, this confidence interval may not have good properties. In particular, it may not even be of size $(1 - \alpha)100\%$. An asymmetric underlying distribution can have particularly deleterious effects on one-sided confidence intervals (see Sutton, 1993). Exercise 1.10 on page 37, provides some insight as to why this is the case.

If the estimators T and $\widehat{V}(T)$ are based on sums of squares of deviations, the bootstrap-t interval performs very poorly when the underlying distribution has heavy tails. This is to be expected, of course. Bootstrap procedures can be no better than the statistics used.

Bootstrap Percentile Confidence Intervals

Given a random sample $(y_1, \ldots, y_n)$ from an unknown distribution with CDF P, we want an interval estimate of a parameter, $\theta = \Theta(P)$, for which we have a point estimator, T.

A bootstrap estimator for θ is T^*, based on the bootstrap sample $(y_1^*, \ldots, y_n^*)$. Now, if $G_{T^*}(t)$ is the distribution function for T^*, then the exact upper $1 - \alpha$ confidence limit for θ is the value $t_{(1-\alpha)}^*$, such that $G_{T^*}(t_{(1-\alpha)}^*) = 1 - \alpha$. This is called the *percentile upper confidence limit*. A lower limit is obtained similarly, and an interval is based on the lower and upper limits.

In practice, we generally use Monte Carlo and m bootstrap samples to estimate these quantities. The probability-symmetric bootstrap percentile confidence interval of size $(1 - \alpha)100\%$ is thus

$$\left(t_{(\alpha/2)}^*, \quad t_{(1-\alpha/2)}^* \right),$$

where $t_{(\pi)}^*$ is the $[\pi m]^{\text{th}}$ order statistic of a sample of size m of T^*. (Note that we are using T and t, and hence T^* and t^*, to represent estimators and estimates in general; that is, $t^*_{(\pi)}$ here does not refer to a percentile of the Student's t distribution.) This percentile interval is based on the ideal bootstrap and may be estimated by Monte Carlo simulation.

Confidence Intervals Based on Transformations

Suppose that there is a monotonically increasing transformation g and a constant c such that the random variable

$$W = c(g(T^*) - g(\theta)) \tag{4.11}$$

has a symmetric distribution about zero. Here $g(\theta)$ is in the role of a mean and c is a scale or standard deviation.

Let H be the distribution function of W, so

$$G_{T^*}(t) = H\big(c(g(t) - g(\theta))\big) \tag{4.12}$$

and

$$t^*_{(1-\alpha/2)} = g^{-1}\big(g(t^*) + w_{(1-\alpha/2)}/c\big), \tag{4.13}$$

where $w_{(1-\alpha/2)}$ is the $(1 - \alpha/2)$ quantile of W. The other quantile $t^*_{(\alpha/2)}$ would be determined analogously.

Instead of approximating the ideal interval with a Monte Carlo sample, we could use a transformation to a known W and compute the interval that way. Use of an exact transformation g to a known random variable W, of course, is just as difficult as evaluation of the ideal bootstrap interval. Nevertheless, we see that forming the ideal bootstrap confidence interval is equivalent to using the transformation g and the distribution function H.

Because transformations to approximate normality are well-understood and widely used, in practice, we generally choose g as a transformation to normality. The random variable W above is a standard normal random variable, Z. The relevant distribution function is Φ, the normal CDF. The normal approximations have a basis in the central limit property. Central limit approximations often have a bias of order $O(n^{-1})$, however, so in small samples, the percentile intervals may not be very good.

Correcting the Bias in Intervals Due to Bias in the Estimator or to Lack of Symmetry

It is likely that the transformed statistic $g(T^*)$ in equation (4.11) is biased for the transformed θ, even if the untransformed statistic is unbiased for θ. We can account for the possible bias by using the transformation

$$Z = c(g(T^*) - g(\theta)) + z_0,$$

and, analogous to equation (4.12), we have

$$G_{T^*}(t) = \Phi\big(c(g(t) - g(\theta)) + z_0\big).$$

The bias correction z_0 is $\Phi^{-1}(G_{T^*}(t))$.

Even when we are estimating θ directly with T^* (that is, g is the identity), another possible problem in determining percentiles for the confidence interval is the lack of symmetry of the distribution about z_0. We would therefore need to make some adjustments in the quantiles instead of using equation (4.13) without some correction.

Rather than correcting the quantiles directly, we may adjust their levels. For an interval of confidence $(1 - \alpha)$, instead of $(t^*_{(\alpha/2)},\ t^*_{(1-\alpha/2)})$, we take

$$\left(t^*_{(\alpha_1)},\ t^*_{(\alpha_2)}\right),$$

where the adjusted probabilities α_1 and α_2 are determined so as to reduce the bias and to allow for the lack of symmetry.

As we often do, even for a nonnormal underlying distribution, we relate α_1 and α_2 to percentiles of the normal distribution.

To allow for the lack of symmetry—that is, for a scale difference below and above z_0—we use quantiles about that point. Efron (1987), who developed this method, introduced an "acceleration", a, and used the distance $a(z_0 + z_{(\pi)})$. Using values for the bias correction and the acceleration determined from the data, Efron suggested the quantile adjustments

$$\alpha_1 = \Phi\left(\widehat{z}_0 + \frac{\widehat{z}_0 + z_{(\alpha/2)}}{1 - \widehat{a}(\widehat{z}_0 + z_{(\alpha/2)})}\right)$$

and

$$\alpha_2 = \Phi\left(\widehat{z}_0 + \frac{\widehat{z}_0 + z_{(1-\alpha/2)}}{1 - \widehat{a}(\widehat{z}_0 + z_{(1-\alpha/2)})}\right).$$

Use of these adjustments to the level of the quantiles for confidence intervals is called the bias-corrected and accelerated, or "BC_a", method. This method automatically takes care of the problems of bias or asymmetry resulting from transformations that we discussed above.

Note that if $\widehat{a} = \widehat{z}_0 = 0$, then $\alpha_1 = \Phi(z_{(\alpha)})$ and $\alpha_2 = \Phi(z_{(1-\alpha)})$. In this case, the BC_a is the same as the ordinary percentile method.

The problem now is to estimate the acceleration a and the bias correction z_0 from the data.

The bias-correction term z_0 is estimated by correcting the percentile near the median of the m bootstrap samples:

$$\widehat{z}_0 = \Phi^{-1}\left(\frac{1}{m}\sum_j I_{(-\infty,T]}\left(T^{*j}\right)\right).$$

The idea is that we approximate the bias of the median (that is, the bias of a central quantile) and then adjust the other quantiles accordingly.

Estimating a is a little more difficult. The way we proceed depends on the form the bias may take and how we choose to represent it. Because one cause of bias may be skewness, Efron (1987) adjusted for the skewness of the distribution of the estimator in the neighborhood of θ. The skewness is measured by a function of the second and third moments of T. We can use the jackknife to estimate those moments. The expression is

$$\widehat{a} = \frac{\sum\left(\mathrm{J}(T) - T_{(i)}\right)^3}{6\left(\sum\left(\mathrm{J}(T) - T_{(i)}\right)^2\right)^{3/2}}. \tag{4.14}$$

Bias resulting from other departures from normality, such as heavy tails, is not addressed by this adjustment.

The S-Plus program `boot.ci` developed by A. J. Canty (see Davison and Hinkley, 1997) computes BC_a confidence intervals. It is available from `statlib`.

Obuchowski and Lieber (1998) used Monte Carlo to compare bootstrap-t and BC_a confidence intervals of the difference in the means of two groups. The distributions that they studied included both discrete and continuous random variables with various properties. For moderate and approximately equal sample sizes, they found that the coverage of BC_a intervals was closest to the nominal confidence level but that, for samples with very different sizes, the bootstrap-t intervals were better in the sense of coverage frequency. Because of the variance of the components in the BC_a method, it generally requires relatively large numbers of bootstrap samples. For location parameters, for example, we may need $m = 1,000$.

Another method for bootstrap confidence intervals introduced by DiCiccio and Efron (1992) is based on a delta method approximation (equation (1.40)) for the standard deviation of the estimator. This method yields *approximate bootstrap confidence*, or ABC, intervals. Terms in the Taylor series expansions are used for computing $\widehat{a}$ and $\widehat{z}_0$ rather than using bootstrap estimates for these terms. As with the BC_a method, bias resulting from other departures from normality, such as heavy tails, is not addressed.

The S-Plus program `abc.ci` developed by A. J. Canty (see Davison and Hinkley, 1997) computes ABC confidence intervals. It is available from `statlib`.

4.4 Bootstrapping Data with Dependencies

When there are relationships among the variables originally sampled, resampling methods must preserve these relationships.

In analyzing data in a regression model,

$$y = X\beta + \epsilon,$$

we may resample the (y_i, x_i) observations (note x_i is a vector), or we may attempt to resample the ϵ_i. The former approach is generally less efficient. The latter approach uses the fitted $\widehat{\beta}$ to provide a set of residuals, which are then resampled and added to the $x_i^T \widehat{\beta}$ to obtain y_i^*. This approach is more efficient, but it relies more strongly on the assumption that the distribution of ϵ is the same in all regions of the model.

Another common case in which dependencies do not allow a straightforward application of the bootstrap is in time series data, or data with serial correlations. This problem can often be addressed by forming subsequences in batches whose summary statistics are (almost) independent. The method of batch means described on page 55 in Chapter 2 is one way of doing this.

Bootstrapping is critically dependent on reproducing the variance in the original population. A correlated sample will not reproduce this variance, so the first step in bootstrapping data with serial correlations is to model out the dependencies as well as any serial trend. This can be done with various time series models. The simplest model assumes that residuals from the means of disjoint blocks of data are essentially independent (batch means). A linear model or a higher-degree polynomial model may be useful for removal of trends. Politis and Romano (1992, 1994) describe the "stationary bootstrap" and other methods of blocking to overcome serial dependencies. Sherman and Carlstein (1996) describe the use of diagnostic plots based on histograms of block means to assess the success of blocking schemes.

Li and Maddala (1996) discuss the general problem of bootstrapping time series data and describe various approaches.

In more complicated problems with dependencies, such as the problem of selection of variables in a regression model, bootstrapping is rarely useful. Other methods, such as cross validation, that provide comparative measures must be used. Bootstrapping does not provide such measures.

4.5   Variance Reduction in Monte Carlo Bootstrap

Monte Carlo bootstrap estimators have two sources of variation: one is due to the initial sampling, and the other is due to the bootstrap sampling.

Jackknife After Bootstrap

The first problem, of course, is to estimate the variance of the bootstrap estimator. One way of estimating the variance is to use a jackknife. The brute force way would be to do n separate bootstraps on the original sample with a different observation removed each time.

A more computationally efficient way, called jackknife-after-bootstrap, was suggested by Efron (1992). The procedure is to store the indices of the sample included in each bootstrap sample (an $n \times m$ matrix) and then, for each bootstrap sample that does not contain a given element y_j of the original sample, treat that bootstrap sample as if it had been obtained from an original sample from which y_j had been omitted. The two bootstrap samples do indeed have the same distribution; that is, the distribution of a bootstrap sample conditioned on not containing y_j is the same as the unconditional distribution of a bootstrap sample from a given sample that does not contain y_j.

This procedure would have problems, of course, if it so happened that for a given y_j, every bootstrap sample contained y_j. Efron (1992) shows that the probability of this situation is extremely small, even for n as small as 10 and m as small as 20. For larger values of m relative to n, the probability is even lower.

Efron and Tibshirani (1993) report on a small Monte Carlo study that indicates that the jackknife-after-bootstrap tends to overestimate the variance of the bootstrap estimator, especially for small values of m. Efron and Tibshirani attribute this to the overestimation by the jackknife of the resampling variance caused by using the same set of m bootstrap samples to obtain the n jackknife estimates. The jackknife-after-bootstrap should only be used for large values of m, where "large" is subject to user discretion but generally is of the order of 1,000.

The Bootstrap Estimate of the Bias of a Plug-In Estimator

The Monte Carlo estimate of the bootstrap estimate of the bias can be improved if the estimator whose bias is being estimated is a plug-in estimator.

Consider the resampling vector, $p^{*0} = (1/n, \ldots, 1/n)$.

Such a resampling vector corresponds to a permutation of the original sample. If the estimator is a plug-in estimator, then its value is invariant to permutations of the sample; and, in fact,

$$T(p^{*0}) = T(P_n),$$

so the Monte Carlo estimate of the bootstrap estimate of the bias can be written as

$$\sum_{j=1}^{m} s(y_1^{*j}, \ldots, y_n^{*j})/m \; - \; T(p^{*0}).$$

Instead of using $T(p^{*0})$, however, we can increase the precision of the Monte Carlo estimate by using the mean of the individual p^*'s actually obtained:

$$\sum s(y_1^{*j}, \ldots, y_n^{*j})/m \; - \; T(\bar{p}^*),$$

where

$$\bar{p}^* = \sum p^{*j}/m.$$

Notice that for an unbiased plug-in estimator (e.g., the sample mean), this quantity is 0.

If the objective in Monte Carlo experimentation is to estimate some quantity, just as in any estimation procedure, we want to reduce the variance of our estimator (while preserving its other good qualities).

The basic idea is usually to reduce the problem analytically as far as possible and then to use Monte Carlo methods on what is left.

Beyond that general reduction principle, in Monte Carlo experimentation, there are several possibilities for reducing the variance, as discussed in Section 2.6 on page 61. The two main types of methods are judicious use of an auxiliary variable and use of probability sampling. Auxiliary variables may be:

- control variates (any correlated variable, either positively or negatively correlated);

- antithetic variates (in the basic uniform generator);

- regression covariates.

Probability sampling is:

- stratified sampling in the discrete case;

- importance sampling in the continuous case.

Balanced Resampling

Another way of reducing the variance in Monte Carlo experimentation is to constrain the sampling so that some aspects of the samples reflect precisely some aspects of the population.

We may choose to constrain $\bar{p}^*$ to equal p^{*0}. This makes $T(\bar{p}^*) = T(p^{*0})$ and hopefully makes $\sum s(y_1^{*j}, \ldots, y_n^{*j})/m$ closer to its expected value while preserving its correlation with $T(\bar{p}^*)$. This is called *balanced resampling*.

Hall (1990) has shown that the balanced-resampling Monte Carlo estimator of the bootstrap estimator has a bias $O(m^{-1})$ but that the reduced variance generally more than makes up for it.

Further Reading

Standard references on the bootstrap are Efron and Tibshirani (1993) and Davison and Hinkley (1997). With each of these texts is associated a library of S-Plus software for bootstrap computations. Both libraries are available from `statlib`. (See page 388 in the bibliography for more information.) Chernick (1999) provides a very extensive bibliography on the bootstrap. The volume edited by LePage and Billard (1992) contains a number of articles that describe situations requiring special care in the application of the bootstrap. Other texts addressing bootstrap methods are Barbe and Bertail (1995), Hall (1992), and Shao and Tu (1995). Li and Maddala (1996) discuss many problems and consideration for bootstrapping in time series models and other applications in economics.

Exercises

4.1. Use equation (4.3) to determine the bias of the square of the sample mean for estimating the square of the population mean.

4.2. Consider a bootstrap estimate of the variance of an estimator T. Show that the estimate from a bootstrap sample of size m has the same expected value as the ideal bootstrap estimator but that its variance is greater than or equal to that of the ideal bootstrap estimate. (This is the variance of the variance estimator. Also, note that the expectation and variance of these random variables should be taken with respect to the true distribution, not the empirical distribution.)

4.3. Show that the bootstrap estimate of the bias of the sample second central moment is $\sum (y_i - \bar{y})^2/n^2$. (Notice that here the y's are used to denote the realization of the random sample rather than the random sample.)

4.4. Show that, for the sample mean, both the bootstrap estimate of the bias and the Monte Carlo estimate of the bootstrap estimate of the bias using the mean resampling vector are 0. Is this also true for the ordinary Monte Carlo estimate?

4.5. Let $S = \{y_1, \ldots, y_n\}$ be a random sample from a population with mean μ, variance σ^2, and distribution function P. Let $\widehat{P}$ be the empirical distribution function. Let $\bar{y}$ be the sample mean for S. Let $S_j = \{y_1^*, \ldots, y_n^*\}$ be a random sample taken with replacement from S. Let $\bar{y}^{*j}$ be the sample mean for S_j.

(a) Show that
$$E_{\widehat{P}}(\bar{y}^{*j}) = \bar{y}.$$

(b) Show that
$$E_P(\bar{y}^{*j}) = \mu.$$

(c) Note that in the questions above there was no replication of the bootstrap sampling. Now, suppose that we take m samples S_j, compute $\bar{y}^{*j}$ for each, and compute
$$V = \frac{1}{m-1} \sum_j \left(\bar{y}^{*j} - \overline{\bar{y}^{*j}} \right)^2.$$
Derive $E_{\widehat{P}}(V)$.

(d) Derive $E_P(V)$.

4.6. Conduct a Monte Carlo study of confidence intervals for the variance in a normal distribution. (This is similar to a study reported by Schenker, 1985.) Use samples of size 20, 35, and 100 from a normal distribution with variance of 1. Use the nonparametric percentile, the BCa, and the ABC methods to set 90% confidence intervals, and estimate the coverage probabilities using Monte Carlo methods. You can use the S-Plus library boot developed by A. J. Canty (see Davison and Hinkley, 1997) to compute the confidence intervals. The library is available from statlib. Use bootstrap $m = 1,000$ and 1,000 Monte Carlo replications. Prepare a two-way table of the estimated coverage percentages:

n	Percentile	BCa	ABC
20	__%	__%	__%
35	__%	__%	__%
100	__%	__%	__%

Explain the difference in the confidence intervals for the mean and for the variance in terms of pivotal quantities.

4.7. Let $(y_1, y_2, ..., y_{20})$ be a random sample from an exponential distribution with mean $\theta = 1$. Based on a Monte Carlo sample size of 400 and bootstrap sizes of 200, construct a table of percentages of coverages of 95% confidence intervals based on:

  - a standard normal approximation;
  - a nonparametric percentile method;
  - the BCa method;
  - the nonparametric ABC method.

4.8. Show that, for the sample mean, both the bootstrap estimate of the bias and the Monte Carlo estimate of the bootstrap estimate of the bias using the mean resampling vector are 0. Is this also true for the ordinary Monte Carlo estimate?

4.9. Assume that we have a random sample, $Y_1, \ldots, Y_n$ from a gamma distribution with shape parameter α and scale parameter 1.

  (a) Describe how you would use a parametric bootstrap to set a 95% lower one-sided confidence interval for the standard deviation, $\sqrt{\alpha}$.

  (b) Carefully describe how you would perform a Monte Carlo test at the 0.05 significance level for
  $$H_0 : \sqrt{\alpha} \leq 10$$
  versus
  $$H_1 : \sqrt{\alpha} > 10.$$

  (c) What is the relationship (if any) between the answers to the previous two questions?

  (d) What estimator would you use for $\sqrt{\alpha}$? Your estimator is probably biased. Describe how you would use the jackknife to reduce the bias of the estimator.

  (e) Describe how you would use the jackknife to estimate the variance of your estimator.

  (f) Now, assume that you have the same sample as before, but you do not assume a particular form of the distribution. Describe how you would use a nonparametric bootstrap to set a 95% two-sided confidence interval for the standard deviation. (Use any type of nonparametric bootstrap confidence interval you wish.) Clearly specify the interval limits. Is your interval symmetric in any sense?

4.10. Assume a sample of size n. Write a program to generate m resampling vectors p^{*j} so that $\bar{p}^* = (1/n, \ldots, 1/n)$.

Chapter 5

Tools for Identification of Structure in Data

In recent years, with our increased ability to collect and store data have come enormous datasets. These datasets may consist of billions of observations and millions of variables. Some of the classical methods of statistical inference, in which a parametric model is studied, are neither feasible nor relevant for analysis of these datasets. The objective is to identify interesting structures in the data, such as clusters of observations, or relationships among the variables. Sometimes, the structures allow a reduction in the dimensionality of the data.

Many of the classical methods of multivariate analysis, such as principal components analysis, factor analysis, canonical correlations analysis, and multidimensional scaling, are useful in identifying interesting structure. These methods generally attempt to combine variables in such a way as to preserve information yet reduce the dimension of the dataset. Dimension reduction generally carries a loss of some information. Whether the lost information is important is the major concern in dimension reduction.

Another set of methods for reducing the complexity of a dataset attempts to group observations together, combining observations, as it were.

In the following we will assume that an observation consists of a vector $x = (x_1, \ldots, x_m)$. In most cases, we will assume that $x \in \mathbb{R}^m$. In statistical analysis, we generally assume that we have n observations, and we use X to denote an $n \times m$ matrix in which the rows correspond to observations.

In practice, it is common for one or more of the components of x to be measured on a nominal scale; that is, one or more of the variables represents membership in some particular class. We refer to such variables as "categorical variables". Although sometimes it is important to make finer distinctions among types of variables (see Stevens, 1946, who identified nominal, ordinal, interval, and ratio types), we often need to make a simple distinction between variables whose values can be modeled by $\mathbb{R}$ and those whose values essentially indicate membership in some class. We may represent the observation x as being composed of these two types, "real" or "numerical", and "categorical":

$$x = (x^{\mathrm{r}},\ x^{\mathrm{c}}).$$

In the following, we often use the phrase "numerical data" to indicate that each element of the vector variable takes on values in $\mathbb{R}$, that the operations of $\mathbb{R}$ are available, and that the properties of the reals apply.

Major concerns for methods of identifying structure are the number of computations and amount of storage required.

In this chapter, we introduce some of the tools that are used for identifying structure in data. We encounter examples of applications of these tools for producing graphical displays in Chapter 7. (particularly beginning on page 179) and for more general methods of exploring data in Chapter 10.

5.1   Linear Structure and Other Geometric Properties

Numerical data can conveniently be represented as geometric vectors. We can speak of the length of a vector, or of the angle between two vectors, and relate these geometric characteristics to properties of the data. We will begin with definitions of a few basic terms.

The *Euclidean length* or just the *length* of an n-vector x is the square root of the sum of the squares of the elements of the vector. We generally denote the Euclidean length of x as $\|x\|_2$ or just as $\|x\|$.

$$\|x\| = \left(\sum_{i=1}^{n} x_i^2 \right)^{1/2}.$$

The Euclidean length is a special case of a more general real-valued function of a vector called a "norm", which is defined on page 114.

The *dot product* or *inner product* of two vectors x and y that have the same number of elements n is denoted by $\langle x, y \rangle$ and is defined by

$$\langle x, y \rangle = \sum_{i=1}^{n} x_i y_i.$$

The *angle* θ between the vectors x and y is defined in terms of the cosine by

$$\cos(\theta) = \frac{\langle x, y \rangle}{\sqrt{\langle x, x \rangle \langle y, y \rangle}}.$$

Linear structures in data are the simplest and the most interesting. Linear relationships can also be used to approximate other more complicated structures.

Flats

The set of points x whose components satisfy a linear equation

$$b_1 x_1 + \cdots b_d x_d = c$$

is called a flat. Such linear structures often occur (approximately) in observational data, leading to a study of the linear regression model,

$$x_d = \beta_0 + \beta_1 x_1 + \cdots + \beta_m x_m + \epsilon.$$

A flat through the origin, that is, a set of points whose components satisfy

$$b_1 x_1 + \cdots b_d x_d = 0,$$

is a vector space. Such equations allow simpler transformations, so we often transform regression models into the form

$$x_d - \bar{x}_d = \beta_1(x_1 - \bar{x}_1) + \cdots + \beta_m(x_m - \bar{x}_m) + \epsilon.$$

The data are centered to correspond to this model.

5.2 Linear Transformations

Linear transformations play a major role in analyzing numerical data and identifying structure.

A linear transformation of the vector x is the vector Ax, where A is a matrix with as many columns as the elements of x. If the number of rows of A is different, the resulting vector has a dimension different from x.

Orthogonal Transformations

An important type of linear transformation is an orthogonal transformation, that is, a transformation in which the matrix of the transformation, Q, is square and has the property that

$$Q^{\mathrm{T}} Q = I,$$

where Q^{T} denotes the transpose of Q, and I denotes the identity matrix.

If Q is orthogonal, for the vector x, we have

$$\|Qx\| = \|x\|. \tag{5.1}$$

(This is easily seen by writing $\|Qx\|$ as $\sqrt{(Qx)^{\mathrm{T}} Qx}$, which is $\sqrt{x^{\mathrm{T}} Q^{\mathrm{T}} Qx}$.) Thus, we see that orthogonal transformations preserve Euclidean lengths.

If Q is orthogonal, for vectors x and y, we have

$$\langle Qx, Qy \rangle = (xQ)^{\mathrm{T}}(Qy) = x^{\mathrm{T}} Q^{\mathrm{T}} Qy = x^{\mathrm{T}} y = \langle x, y \rangle,$$

hence,

$$\arccos\left(\frac{\langle Qx, Qy \rangle}{\|Qx\|_2 \|Qy\|_2}\right) = \arccos\left(\frac{\langle x, y \rangle}{\|x\|_2 \|y\|_2}\right). \tag{5.2}$$

Thus, we see that orthogonal transformations preserve angles.

Gram-Schmidt Orthogonalization

Given two nonnull, linearly independent vectors, x_1 and x_2, it is easy to form two orthonormal vectors, $\tilde{x}_1$ and $\tilde{x}_2$, that span the same space:

$$\tilde{x}_1 = \frac{x_1}{\|x_1\|_2},$$

$$\tilde{x}_2 = \frac{(x_2 - \tilde{x}_1^T x_2 \tilde{x}_1)}{\|x_2 - \tilde{x}_1^T x_2 \tilde{x}_1\|_2}. \tag{5.3}$$

These are called *Gram-Schmidt transformations*. It is easy to confirm by multiplication that $\tilde{x}_1$ and $\tilde{x}_2$ are orthonormal. Further, because they are orthogonal and neither is 0, they must be independent. More generally, we can see that they are independent by observing

$$[\tilde{x}_1 \tilde{x}_2] = A\,[x_1 x_2],$$

where A is an upper triangular (that is, full rank) matrix.

The Gram-Schmidt transformations can easily be extended to more than two vectors. Given a third linearly independent vector, x_3, a third orthonormal vector, $\tilde{x}_3$, would be

$$\tilde{x}_3 = \frac{(x_3 - \tilde{x}_1^T x_3 \tilde{x}_1 - \tilde{x}_2^T x_3 \tilde{x}_2)}{\|x_3 - \tilde{x}_1^T x_3 \tilde{x}_1 - \tilde{x}_2^T x_3 \tilde{x}_2\|_2}.$$

Geometric Transformations

In many important applications of linear algebra, a vector represents a point in space, with each element of the vector corresponding to an element of a coordinate system, usually a cartesian system. A set of vectors describes a geometric object. Algebraic operations are geometric transformations that rotate, deform, or translate the object. Although these transformations are often used in the two or three dimensions that correspond to the easily perceived physical space, they have similar applications in higher dimensions.

Important characteristics of these transformations are what they leave *unchanged* (that is, their *invariance properties*). We have seen, for example, that an orthogonal transformation preserves lengths of vectors (equation (5.1)) and angles between vectors (equation (5.2)). A transformation that preserves lengths and angles is called an *isometric transformation*. Such a transformation also preserves areas and volumes.

Another isometric transformation is a *translation*, which for a vector x is just the addition of another vector:

$$\tilde{x} = x + t.$$

A transformation that preserves angles is called an *isotropic transformation*. An example of an isotropic transformation that is not isometric is a uniform scaling or dilation transformation, $\tilde{x} = ax$, where a is a scalar.

The transformation $\tilde{x} = Ax$, where A is a diagonal matrix with not all elements the same, does not preserve angles; it is an *anisotropic* scaling.

Another anisotropic transformation is a *shearing transformation*, $\tilde{x} = Ax$, where A is the same as an identity matrix except for a single row or column that has a one on the diagonal but possibly nonzero elements in the other positions; for example,

$$\begin{bmatrix} 1 & 0 & a_1 \\ 0 & 1 & a_2 \\ 0 & 0 & 1 \end{bmatrix}.$$

Although they do not preserve angles, both anisotropic scaling and shearing transformations preserve parallel lines. A transformation that preserves parallel lines is called an *affine transformation*. Preservation of parallel lines is equivalent to preservation of collinearity, so an alternative characterization of an affine transformation is one that preserves collinearity. More generally, we can combine nontrivial scaling and shearing transformations to see that the transformation Ax for any nonsingular matrix A is affine. It is easy to see that addition of a constant vector to all vectors in a set preserves collinearity within the set, so a more general affine transformation is $\tilde{x} = Ax + t$ for a nonsingular matrix A and a vector t.

All of these transformations are *linear transformations* because they preserve straight lines. A *projective transformation*, which uses the homogeneous coordinate system of the projective plane, preserves straight lines but does not preserve parallel lines. These transformations are very useful in computer graphics (see Riesenfeld, 1981). Mortenson (1995) describes all of these types of transformations and discusses their applications in geometric modeling.

Rotations

Two major tools in seeking linear structure are rotations and projections of the data matrix X. Rotations and projections of the observations are performed by postmultiplication of X by special matrices. In this section, we briefly review these types of matrices for use in multivariate data analysis.

The simplest rotation of a vector can be thought of as the rotation of a plane defined by two coordinates about the other principal axes. Such a rotation changes two elements of all vectors in that plane and leaves all of the other elements, representing the other coordinates, unchanged. This rotation can be described in a two-dimensional space defined by the coordinates being changed, without reference to the other coordinates.

Consider the rotation of the vector x through the angle θ into $\tilde{x}$. The length is preserved, so we have $\|\tilde{x}\| = \|x\|$. Referring to Figure 5.1, we can write

$$\begin{aligned} \tilde{x}_1 &= \|x\| \cos(\phi + \theta), \\ \tilde{x}_2 &= \|x\| \sin(\phi + \theta). \end{aligned}$$

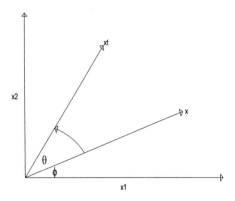

Figure 5.1: Rotation of x

Now, from elementary trigonometry, we know that

$$
\begin{aligned}
\cos(\phi + \theta) &= \cos\phi\cos\theta - \sin\phi\sin\theta, \\
\sin(\phi + \theta) &= \sin\phi\cos\theta + \cos\phi\sin\theta.
\end{aligned}
$$

Because $\cos\phi = x_1/\|x\|$ and $\sin\phi = x_2/\|x\|$, we can combine these equations to get

$$
\begin{aligned}
\tilde{x}_1 &= x_1\cos\theta - x_2\sin\theta, \\
\tilde{x}_2 &= x_1\sin\theta + x_2\cos\theta.
\end{aligned}
\tag{5.4}
$$

Hence, multiplying x by the orthogonal matrix

$$
\begin{bmatrix}
\cos\theta & -\sin\theta \\
\sin\theta & \cos\theta
\end{bmatrix}
$$

performs the rotation of x.

This idea easily extends to the rotation of a plane formed by two coordinates about all of the other (orthogonal) principal axes. The $m \times m$ orthogonal matrix

$$
Q_{pq}(\theta) =
\begin{bmatrix}
1 & 0 & \cdots & 0 & 0 & 0 & \cdots & 0 & 0 & 0 & \cdots & 0 \\
0 & 1 & \cdots & 0 & 0 & 0 & \cdots & 0 & 0 & 0 & \cdots & 0 \\
 & & \ddots & & & & & & & & & \\
0 & 0 & \cdots & 1 & 0 & 0 & \cdots & 0 & 0 & 0 & \cdots & 0 \\
0 & 0 & \cdots & 0 & \cos\theta & 0 & \cdots & 0 & \sin\theta & 0 & \cdots & 0 \\
0 & 0 & \cdots & 0 & 0 & 1 & \cdots & 0 & 0 & 0 & \cdots & 0 \\
 & & & & & & \ddots & & & & & \\
0 & 0 & \cdots & 0 & 0 & 0 & \cdots & 1 & 0 & 0 & \cdots & 0 \\
0 & 0 & \cdots & 0 & -\sin\theta & 0 & \cdots & 0 & \cos\theta & 0 & \cdots & 0 \\
0 & 0 & \cdots & 0 & 0 & 0 & \cdots & 0 & 0 & 1 & \cdots & 0 \\
 & & & & & & & & & & \ddots & \\
0 & 0 & \cdots & 0 & 0 & 0 & \cdots & 0 & 0 & 0 & \cdots & 1
\end{bmatrix},
\tag{5.5}
$$

in which p and q denote the rows and columns that differ from the identity, rotates the data vector x_i through an angle of θ in the plane formed by the pth and q^{th} principal axes of the m-dimensional cartesian coordinate system. This rotation can be viewed equivalently as a rotation of the coordinate system in the opposite direction. The coordinate system remains orthogonal after such a rotation. In the matrix XQ, all of the observations (rows) of X have been rotated through the angle θ.

How a rotation can reveal structure can be seen in Figures 5.2 and 5.3. In the original data, there do not appear to be any linear relationships among the variables. After applying a rotation about the third axis, however, we see in the scatter plot in Figure 5.3 a strong linear relationship between the first and third variables of the rotated data.

Rotations of the data matrix provide alternative views of the data. There is usually nothing obvious in the data to suggest a particular rotation; however, dynamic rotations coupled with projections that are plotted and viewed as they move are very useful in revealing structure.

A rotation of any plane can be formed by successive rotations of planes formed by two principal axes. Furthermore, any orthogonal matrix can be written as the product of a finite number of rotation matrices; that is, any orthogonal transformation can be viewed as a sequence of rotations.

Projections

Another way of getting useful alternative views of the data is to project the data onto subspaces. A symmetric idempotent matrix P *projects* vectors onto the subspace spanned by the rows (or columns) of P. Except for the identity matrix, a projection matrix is of less than full rank; hence, it projects a full-rank matrix into a space of lower dimension. Although we may only know that the rows of the data matrix X are in $\mathbb{R}^m$, the rows of XP are in the subspace spanned by

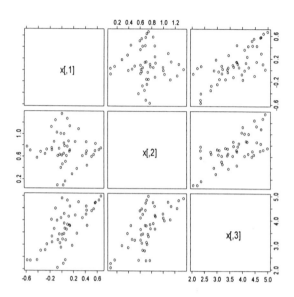

Figure 5.2: Scatter Plot Matrix of Original Data

the rows of P. It may be possible to identify relationships and structure in this space of lower dimension that are obscured in the higher-dimensional space.

Translations

Translations are relatively simple transformations involving the addition of vectors. Rotations, as we have seen, and other geometric transformations such as shearing, as we have indicated, involve multiplication by an appropriate matrix. In applications where several geometric transformations are to be made, it would be convenient if translations could also be performed by matrix multiplication. This can be done by using *homogeneous coordinates*.

Homogeneous coordinates, which form the natural coordinate system for projective geometry, have a very simple relationship to cartesian coordinates. The point with cartesian coordinates $(x_1, x_2, \ldots, x_d)$ is represented in homogeneous coordinates as $(x_0^h, x_1^h, x_2^h, \ldots, x_d^h)$, where, for arbitrary x_0^h not equal to zero, $x_1^h = x_0^h x_1$, $x_2^h = x_0^h x_2$, and so on.

Each value of x_0^h corresponds to a hyperplane in the ordinary cartesian coordinate system. The special plane $x_0^h = 0$ does not have a meaning in the cartesian system. It corresponds to a hyperplane at infinity in the projective geometry. (Alternatively, of course, the homogeneous coordinate defining the hyperplane could be written at the end of the set of coordinates; that is, it could be taken to be x_{d+1}^h.)

Because the point is the same, the two different symbols represent the same

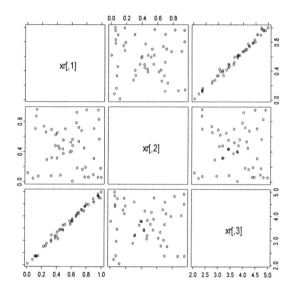

Figure 5.3: Scatter-Plot Matrix of Rotated Data

thing, and we have

$$(x_1, x_2, \ldots, x_d) = (x_0^h, x_1^h, x_2^h, \ldots, x_d^h). \tag{5.6}$$

An advantage of the homogeneous coordinate system is that we can easily perform translations. We can effect the translation $\tilde{x} = x + t$ by first representing the point x as $(1, x_1, x_2, \ldots, x_d)$ and then multiplying by the matrix

$$T = \begin{bmatrix} 1 & t_1 & \cdots & t_d \\ 0 & 1 & \cdots & 0 \\ & & \cdots & \\ 0 & 0 & \cdots & 1 \end{bmatrix}.$$

We will use the symbol x^h to represent the vector of corresponding homogeneous coordinates:

$$x^h = (1, x_1, x_2, \ldots, x_d).$$

The translated point can be represented as $\tilde{x} = T x^h$.

We must be careful to distinguish the point x from the vector of coordinates that represents the point. In cartesian coordinates, there is a natural correspondence, and the symbol x representing a point may also represent the vector $(x_1, x_2, \ldots, x_d)$. The vector of homogeneous coordinates of the result $T x^h$ corresponds to the vector of cartesian coordinates of $\tilde{x}$, $(x_1 + t_1, x_2 + t_2, \ldots, x_d + t_d)$.

Homogeneous coordinates are used extensively in computer graphics not only for the ordinary geometric transformations but also for projective transformations, which model visual properties. Riesenfeld (1981) and Morten-son (1997) describe many of these applications.

5.3   General Transformations of the Coordinate System

Although the transformations that we have discussed above can be thought of either as transforming the data within a fixed coordinate system or as trans-forming the coordinate system, the coordinate system itself remains essentially a cartesian coordinate system. Homogeneous coordinates correspond in a sim-ple way to cartesian coordinates, as we see in equation (5.6).

We can make more general transformations of the coordinate system that can be useful in identifying structure in the data. Two kinds of coordinate transformations especially useful in graphical displays are parallel coordinates, which we discuss on page 175, and Fourier curves, which we discuss on page 176.

Polar coordinates are useful in a variety of applications. They are par-ticularly simple for bivariate data, but they can be used in any number of dimensions. The point

$$x = (x_1, x_2, \ldots, x_d)$$

is represented in polar coordinates by a length,

$$r = \|x\|,$$

and $d - 1$ angles, $\theta_1, \ldots, \theta_{d-1}$. There are various ways that the relationships among the cartesian coordinates and the polar coordinates could be defined. One way is given by Kendall (1961). The relationships among the coordinates are given by

$$
\begin{aligned}
x_1 &= r \cos\theta_1 \quad\quad \cdots \quad\quad \cos\theta_{d-2} \cos\theta_{d-1} \\
x_2 &= r \cos\theta_1 \quad\quad \cdots \quad\quad \cos\theta_{d-2} \sin\theta_{d-1} \\
&\vdots \\
x_j &= r \cos\theta_1 \cdots \cos\theta_{d-j} \sin\theta_{d-j+1} \\
&\vdots \\
x_{d-1} &= r \cos\theta_1 \sin\theta_2 \\
x_d &= r \sin\theta_1,
\end{aligned}
\tag{5.7}
$$

where

$$-\pi/2 \le \theta_j \le \pi/2, \quad \text{for} \quad j = 1, 2, \ldots, d - 2,$$

and

$$0 \le \theta_{d-1} \le 2\pi.$$

In a variation of this definition, the sines and cosines are exchanged, with an appropriate change in the limits on the angles. In this variation, for $d = 2$, we have the usual polar coordinates representation; and for $d = 3$, we have what is sometimes called the spherical coordinates representation.

5.4 Measures of Similarity and Dissimilarity

There are many ways of measuring the similarity or dissimilarity between two observations or between two variables. For numerical data, the most familiar measures of similarity are covariances and correlations.

Dissimilarities in numerical data are generally distances of some type. The dissimilarity or distance function is often a *metric,* which is a function Δ from $\mathbb{R}^m \times \mathbb{R}^m$ into $\mathbb{R}$ satisfying the properties

- $\Delta(x_1, x_2) \geq 0$ for all $x_1, x_2 \in \mathbb{R}^m$,

- $\Delta(x_1, x_2) = 0$ if and only if $x_1 = x_2$,

- $\Delta(x_1, x_2) = \Delta(x_2, x_1)$ for all $x_1, x_2 \in \mathbb{R}^m$,

- $\Delta(x_1, x_3) \leq \Delta(x_1, x_2) + \Delta(x_2, x_3)$ for all $x_1, x_2, x_3 \in \mathbb{R}^m$.

The last property is called the "triangle inequality".

Other measures of dissimilarity can often be useful. Nonmetric functions, such as ones allowing ties and that do not obey the triangle inequality, can also be used for defining dissimilarity, especially in applications in which there is some noise or in which there is some subjectivity in the data. Distance measures defined on a finite set of points, $x_1, x_2, \ldots, x_n$, may use, instead of the triangle inequality, the "ultrametric" inequality:

$$\Delta(x_i, x_k) \leq \max_j \big(\Delta(x_i, x_j), \Delta(x_j, x_k)\big).$$

Ultrametric distances are sometimes used as dissimilarity measures in clustering applications.

Other measures of both similarity and dissimilarity must be used for categorical data or for mixed data (that is, for data consisting of some numerical variables and categorical variables),

$$x = (x^{\mathrm{r}}, \ x^{\mathrm{c}}).$$

The measures may involve ratings of judges, for example. The measures may not be metrics.

In some cases, it is useful to allow distance measures to be asymmetic. If $d(x_i, x_j)$ represents the cost of moving from point x_i to point x_j it may be the case that $d(x_i, x_j) \neq d(x_j, x_i)$. If the distance represents a perceptual difference, it may also be the case that $d(x_i, x_j) \neq d(x_j, x_i)$. Sullivan (2002) has developed a theory for asymmetric measures of dissimilarity, and explored their use in clustering and other applications.

Similarities: Covariances and Correlations

Measures of similarity include covariances, correlations, rank correlations, and cosines of the angles between two vectors. Any measure of dissimilarity, such as the distances discussed in the next section, can be transformed into a measure of similarity by use of a decreasing function, such as the reciprocal. For example, whereas the cosine of the angle formed by two vectors can be considered a measure of similarity, the sine can be considered a measure of dissimilarity.

Although we can consider similarities/dissimilarities between either columns (variables) or rows (observations), in our common data structures, we often evaluate covariances and correlations between columns and distances among rows. We speak of the covariance or the correlation between columns or between variables. The covariance between a column (variable) and itself is its variance.

For an $n \times m$ data matrix X, we have the $m \times m$ *variance-covariance matrix* (or just the *covariance matrix*):

$$
S = \begin{bmatrix}
s_{11} & s_{12} & \cdots & s_{1m} \\
s_{21} & s_{22} & \cdots & s_{2m} \\
\vdots & \vdots & \vdots & \vdots \\
s_{m1} & s_{m2} & \cdots & s_{mm}
\end{bmatrix},
\tag{5.8}
$$

where

$$
s_{jk} = s_{kj} = \frac{\sum_{i=1}^{n}(x_{ij} - \bar{x}_j)(x_{ik} - \bar{x}_k)}{n-1}.
\tag{5.9}
$$

If $\overline{X}$ is the matrix in which each column consists of the mean of the corresponding column of X, we see that

$$
S = \frac{1}{n-1}(X - \overline{X})^{\mathrm{T}}(X - \overline{X}).
$$

The matrix S is therefore nonnegative definite. The matrix $X - \overline{X}$ is called the "centered data matrix"; each column sums to 0.

Assuming none of the variables is constant, the correlation is often a more useful measure because it is scaled by the variances. For an $n \times m$ data matrix, the $m \times m$ *correlation matrix* is

$$
R = \begin{bmatrix}
1 & r_{12} & \cdots & r_{1m} \\
r_{12} & 1 & \cdots & r_{2m} \\
\vdots & \vdots & \vdots & \vdots \\
r_{1m} & r_{2m} & \cdots & 1
\end{bmatrix},
\tag{5.10}
$$

where

$$
r_{jk} = r_{kj} = \frac{s_{jk}}{\sqrt{s_{jj}s_{kk}}};
\tag{5.11}
$$

that is,

$$
R = \left(\mathrm{diag}(\sqrt{s_{11}}, \sqrt{s_{22}}, \ldots, \sqrt{s_{mm}})\right)^{-1} S \left(\mathrm{diag}(\sqrt{s_{11}}, \sqrt{s_{22}}, \ldots, \sqrt{s_{mm}})\right)^{-1}.
$$

The data matrix X together with either S or R is a complete graph in which the columns of X constitute the vertices.

Notice that covariances and correlations are based on the L_2 norm. They are sometimes called "product-moment" covariances and correlations.

Because the concepts of covariance and correlation are also used to refer to properties of random variables, we sometimes refer to the quantities that we have defined above as "sample covariance" or "sample correlation" to distinguish them from the "population" quantities of abstract variables.

There are variations of these such as rank correlations and robust covariances. Rank correlations are computed by first replacing the elements of each column of X by the ranks of the elements within the column and then computing the correlation as above. Robust covariances and correlations are computed either by using a different measure than the L_2 norm or by scaling of the covariance matrix based on an expectation taken with respect to a normal (or Gaussian) distribution. ("Robustness" usually assumes a normal or Gaussian distribution as the reference standard.) See page 121 for a specific robust alternative to S.

Similarities When Some Variables Are Categorical

If all of the variables are measured on a scale that can be modeled as a real number, covariances and/or correlations or similar measures are the obvious choice for measuring the similarity between two points, x_j and x_k. If, however, some of the variables are categorical variables, that is, if the generic x can be represented in the notation introduced earlier,

$$x = (x^\mathrm{r},\ x^\mathrm{c}),$$

a different measure of similarity must be chosen.

Sometimes, the values of the categorical variables represent such different situations that it does not make sense to consider similarities between observations from different groups. In such a case, the similarity between

$$x_j = (x_j^\mathrm{r},\ x_j^\mathrm{c})$$

and

$$x_k = (x_k^\mathrm{r},\ x_k^\mathrm{c})$$

may be measured by the function

$$s(x_j, x_k) \;=\; \frac{\sum_{i=1}^{n}(x_{ij}^\mathrm{r} - \bar{x}_j^\mathrm{r})(x_{ik}^\mathrm{r} - \bar{x}_k^\mathrm{r})}{n-1}, \quad \text{if } x_j^\mathrm{c} = x_k^\mathrm{c},$$

$$\;=\; 0, \quad \text{otherwise.} \tag{5.12}$$

Instead of requiring an exact match of the categorical variables, we can allow some degrees of similarity between observations with different values of their categorical variables. One way would be by using the count of how many variables within x_j^c and x_k^c agree. Such a simple count can be refined to take into account the number of possible values each of the categorical variables can assume. The measure can also be refined by incorporating some measure of the similarity of different classes.

Similarities among Functional Observations

Interest-bearing financial instruments such as bonds or U.S. Treasury bills have prices that depend on the spot or current interest rate and so-called forward rates at future points in time. (A forward rate at a future time t_1 can be thought of as the value of cash or a riskless security at time $t_2 > t_1$ discounted back to time t_1.) The forward rates depend on, among other things, the investors' perception of future spot or actual rates. At any point, a set of forward rates together with the spot rate determine the "yield curve" or the "term structure" for a given financial instrument:

$$r(t).$$

Observational data for measuring and comparing term structures consist of functions for a set of securities measured at different time points.

Another example of observations that are functions are the measurements on various units of individual features of developing organisms taken over time. For example, the observational unit may be a developing organism, the features may be gene expressions, and the data elements may be measures of these expressions taken at fixed times during the development of the organism. The observations on feature j may consist of measurements $(x_{j1}, x_{j2}, \ldots, x_{jm})$ taken at times $t_1, t_2, \ldots, t_m$. The overall patterns of the measurements may be of interest. The underlying model is a continuous function,

$$x(t).$$

The observation on each feature is a discrete function, evaluated at discrete points in its time domain.

Consider, for example, the three observations

$$x_1 = (1, \ 2, \ 1),$$

$$x_2 = (1, \ 2, \ 3),$$

and

$$x_3 = (4, \ 8, \ 4).$$

Because of the obvious patterns, we may wish to consider x_1 and x_3 more similar than are x_1 and x_2.

There are several ways to define a similarity measure to capture this kind of relationship. A very simple one in this case is the relative changes over time. We may first of all augment the existing data with measures of changes. In the example above, taking a simplistic approach of just measuring changes and scaling them, and then augmenting the original vectors, we have

$$\tilde{x}_1 = \left(1,\ 2,\ 1,\ \bigg|\ 1,\ -\frac{1}{2}\right),$$

$$\tilde{x}_2 = \left(1,\ 2,\ 3,\ \bigg|\ 1,\ \frac{1}{2}\right),$$

and

$$\tilde{x}_3 = \left(4,\ 8,\ 4,\ \bigg|\ 1,\ -\frac{1}{2}\right).$$

After transforming the data in this way, we may employ some standard similarity measure, possibly one that downweights the first three elements of each observation.

Another approach is to fit a smoothing curve to each observational vector and then form a new vector by evaluating the smoothing curve at fixed points. A standard similarity measure would then be applied to the transformed vectors.

There are many issues to consider when comparing curves. Whereas the data-generating process may follow a model $x(t)$, the data are of the form $x_i(t_{ij})$. In the model, the variable t (usually "time") may not be measured in an absolute sense, but rather may be measured relative to a different starting point for each observational unit. Even when this shift is taken into consideration two responses that are similar overall may not begin at the same relative time; that is, one observational unit may follow a model $x(t)$ and another $x(t + \delta)$. To proceed with the analysis of such data, it is necessary to *register* the data (that is, to shift the data to account for such differences in the time). More generally, two observational units may follow the same functional process under some unknown transformation of the independent variable:

$$x_1(t) = x_2(h(t)).$$

Unraveling this transformation is a more difficult process of registration. Ramsay and Silverman (1997) discuss methods of registration in the general context of functional data analysis.

We may want to base similarity among observations on some more general relationship satisfied by the observations. Suppose, for example, that a subset of some bivariate data lies in a circle. This pattern may be of interest, and we may want to consider all of the observations in the subset lying in the circle to be similar to one another and different from observations not lying in the circle.

Many such similarity measures depend on the context (that is, on a subset of variables or observations, not just on the relationship between two variables or two observations). Similarities defined by a context are of particular use in pattern recognition.

Similarities between Groups of Variables

We may want to combine variables that have similar values across all observations into a single variable, perhaps a linear combination of some of the original variables. This is an objective of the methods discussed in Sections 10.3 and 10.4.

The general problem of studying linear relationships between two sets of variables is addressed by the method of *canonical correlations*. We will not pursue that topic here. The interested reader is referred to Kennedy and Gentle (1980) for the relevant computations.

Dissimilarities: Distances

There are several ways of measuring dissimilarity. One measure of dissimilarity is distance, and there are several ways of measuring distance. Some measures of distance between two points are based only on the elements of the vectors defining those two points. These distances, which are usually defined by a commutative function, are useful in a homogeneous space. Other measures of distance may be based on a structure imposed by a set of observations.

In a homogeneous space, there are several commonly used measures of distance between two observations. Most of these are based on some *norm* of the difference between the two numeric vectors representing the observations. For a set of objects S that has an addition-type operator, $+_S$, a corresponding additive identity, 0_S, and a scalar multiplication (that is, a multiplication of the objects by a real (or complex) number), a *norm* is a function, $\| \cdot \|$, from S to $\mathbb{R}$ that satisfies the following three conditions:

- nonnegativity and mapping of the identity:
  if $x \neq 0_S$, then $\|x\| > 0$, and $\|0_S\| = 0$;

- relation of scalar multiplication to real multiplication:
  $\|ax\| = |a| \|x\|$ for real a;

- triangle inequality:
  $\|x +_S y\| \leq \|x\| + \|y\|$.

A norm of the difference between two vectors is a metric.

Some of the commonly used measures of distance between observations of numerical data represented in the vectors x_i and x_k are the following:

- Euclidean distance, the root sum of squares of differences:

$$\|x_i - x_k\|_2 \tag{5.13}$$

  or

$$\left(\sum_{j=1}^{m} (x_{ij} - x_{kj})^2 \right)^{1/2} .$$

The Euclidean distance is sometimes called the L_2 norm.

- maximum absolute difference:

$$\|x_i - x_k\|_\infty \tag{5.14}$$

or

$$\max_j |x_{ij} - x_{kj}|.$$

- Manhattan distance, the sum of absolute differences:

$$\|x_i - x_k\|_1 \tag{5.15}$$

or

$$\sum_{j=1}^m |x_{ij} - x_{kj}|.$$

- Minkowski or L_p distance:

$$\|x_i - x_k\|_p \tag{5.16}$$

or

$$\left(\sum_{j=1}^m |x_{ij} - x_{kj}|^p \right)^{1/p}.$$

The L_p distance is the L_p norm of the difference in the two vectors. Euclidean distance, maximum difference, and Manhattan distance are special cases, with $p = 2$, $p \to \infty$, and $p = 1$, respectively.

- Canberra distance (from Lance and Williams, 1966):

$$\sum_{j=1}^m \frac{|x_{ij} - x_{kj}|}{|x_{ij}| + |x_{kj}|}, \tag{5.17}$$

as long as $|x_{ij}| + |x_{kj}| \neq 0$; otherwise, 0 (sometimes normalized by m to be between 0 and 1).

- correlation-based distances:

$$f(r_{ik}).$$

The correlation between two vectors r_{ik} (equation (5.11)) can also be used as a measure of dissimilarity. Values close to 0 indicate small association. The absolute value of the correlation coefficient is a decreasing function in what is intuitively a dissimilarity, so a distance measure based on it, $f(r_{ik})$, should be a decreasing function of the absolute value. Two common choices are

$$1 - |r_{ik}|$$

and

$$1 - r_{ik}^2.$$

- distances based on angular separation:

$$\frac{x_i^T x_k}{\|x_i\|_2 \|x_k\|_2} \tag{5.18}$$

or

$$\frac{\sum_{j=1}^m x_{ij} x_{kj}}{\sqrt{\sum_{j=1}^m x_{ij}^2 \sum_{j=1}^m x_{kj}^2}}.$$

This measure of angular separation is the cosine of the angle; hence, it is a decreasing function in what is intuitively a dissimilarity. Other quantities, such as the sine of the angle, can be used instead. For centered data, the angular separation is the same as the correlation of equation (5.11).

For categorical data, other measures of distance must be used. For vectors composed of zeros and ones, for example, there are two useful distance measures:

- Hamming distance: the number of bits that are different in the two vectors;

- binary difference: the proportion of non-zeros that two vectors do not have in common (the number of occurrences of a zero and a one, or a one and a zero divided by the number of times at least one vector has a one).

Lance and Williams (1967a, 1967b, and 1968) provide a general framework for definitions of distances and discuss the differences in the measures in cluster analysis.

Notice that generally the *distances* are between the *observations*, whereas the *covariances* discussed above are between the *variables*.

The distances are elements of the $n \times n$ dissimilarity matrix,

$$D = \begin{bmatrix} 0 & d_{12} & d_{13} & \cdots & \cdots & d_{1n} \\ d_{21} & 0 & d_{23} & \cdots & \cdots & d_{2n} \\ \vdots & \vdots & \vdots & \vdots & \vdots & \vdots \\ \vdots & \vdots & \vdots & \vdots & \vdots & \vdots \\ \vdots & \vdots & \vdots & \vdots & \vdots & \vdots \\ d_{n1} & d_{n2} & d_{n3} & \cdots & \cdots & 0 \end{bmatrix}. \tag{5.19}$$

All of the distance measures discussed above are metrics (in particular, they satisfy $\Delta(x_1, x_2) = \Delta(x_2, x_1)$ for all $x_1, x_2 \in \mathbb{R}^m$), so any matrix D, in which the elements correspond to those measures, is symmetric.

The data matrix X together with D is a complete graph. In this graph, the rows of X constitute the vertices.

The measures of distance listed above are appropriate in a homogeneous space in which lengths have the same meaning in all directions. A scaling of the units in any of the cardinal directions (that is, a change of scale in the measurement of a single variable) may change the distances. In many applications, the variables have different meanings. Because many statistical techniques give preferential attention to variables with larger variance, it is often useful to scale all variables to have the same variance. Sometimes, it is more useful to scale the variables so that all have the same range.

Notice that the angular separation, as we have defined it, is based on the L_2 norm. A transformation that preserves L_2 distances and angles is called an "isometric transformation". If Q is an orthogonal matrix, the Euclidean distance between Qx_i and Qx_k and the angular separation between those two vectors are the same as the distance and angle between x_i and x_k. Hence, an orthogonal matrix is called an isometric matrix because it preserves Euclidean distances and angles.

Other Dissimilarities Based on Distances

The various distance measures that we have described can be used to define dissimilarities in other ways. For example, we may define the distance from x_j to x_k, $d^R(x_j, x_k)$, as the rank of an ordinary distance d_{jk} in the set of all distances d_{ji}. If x_k is the point closest to x_j, then $d^R(x_j, x_k) = 1$. This type of dissimilarity depends on the "direction"; that is, in general,

$$d^R(x_j, x_k) \neq d^R(x_k, x_j).$$

A distance measure such as $d^R(\cdot, \cdot)$ is dependent on the neighboring points, or the "context". Measures such as this were proposed and studied by Gowda and Krishna (1977).

If we think of the distance between two points as the cost or effort required to get from one point to another, the distance measure often may not be symmetric. (It is therefore not a metric.) Common examples in which distances measured this way are not symmetric arise in anisotropic media under the influence of a force field (say, electrical or gravitational) or in fluids with a flow (see Exercise 5.6).

Dissimilarities in Anisometric Coordinate Systems: Sphering Data

If the elements of the observation vectors represent measurements made on different scales, it is usually best to scale the variables so that all have the same variance or else have the same range. A scaling of the data matrix X so that all columns have a variance of 1 is achieved by postmultiplication by a diagonal matrix whose elements are the square roots of the diagonal elements of S in equations (5.8). If this is applied to the centered data, we have the "standardized" data matrix:

$$X_S = (X - \bar{X}) \operatorname{diag}(\sqrt{s_{ii}}). \tag{5.20}$$

This scaling is what is done in computing correlations. The correlation matrix in equation (5.10) can be computed as $X_S^T X_S / (n - 1)$.

If there are relationships among the variables whose observations comprise the columns of X, and if there are more rows than columns (that is, $n > m$), it may be appropriate to perform an oblique scaling,

$$X_W = (X - \bar{X})H, \tag{5.21}$$

where H is the Cholesky factor of S^{-1} (equation (5.8)); that is,

$$\begin{aligned} H^T H &= (n-1)((X - \bar{X})^T (X - \bar{X}))^{-1} \\ &= S^{-1}. \end{aligned}$$

(If the matrix S is not of full rank, the generalized inverse is used in place of the inverse. In any case, the matrix is nonnegative definite, so the decomposition exists.) The matrix X_W is a *centered and sphered* matrix. It is sometimes called a *white* matrix. The matrix is orthonormal; that is, $X_W^T X_W = I$.

In general, a structure may be imposed on the space by $(X - \bar{X})^T (X - \bar{X})$ or S. A very useful measure of the distance between two vectors is the *Mahalanobis distance*. The Mahalanobis distance between the ith and k^{th} observations, x_i and x_k (the ith and k^{th} rows of X) is

$$(x_i - x_k)^T S^{-1} (x_i - x_k). \tag{5.22}$$

Notice that the Mahalanobis distance is the squared Euclidean distance after using S to scale the data. It is the squared Euclidean distance between rows in the X_S matrix above.

There are other types of distance. Certain paths from one point to another can be specified. The distance can be thought of as the cost of getting from one node on a graph to another node. Although distances are usually considered to be symmetric (that is, the distance from point x_i to point x_k is the same as the distance from point x_k to point x_i), a more general measure may take into account fluid flow or elevation gradients, so the dissimilarity matrix would not be symmetric.

Another type of data that presents interesting variations for measuring dissimilarities or similarities is directional data, or circular data (that is, data that contain a directional component). The angular separation (5.18) measures this, of course, but often in directional data, one of the data elements is a plane angle. As the size of the angle increases, ultimately it comes close to a measure of 0. A simple example is data measured in polar coordinates. When one of the data elements is an angle, the component of the overall distance between two observations i and j attributable to their angles, θ_i and θ_j, could be taken as

$$d_{ij}^d = 1 - \cos(\theta_i - \theta_j).$$

The directional component must be combined additively with a component due to Euclidean-like distances, d_{ij}^r. In polar coordinates, the radial component is already a distance, so d_{ij}^r may just be taken as the absolute value of the difference in the radial components r_i and r_j. The overall distance d_{ij} may be formed from d_{ij}^d and d_{ij}^r in various ways that weight the radial distance and the angle differently.

There are many examples, such as wind direction in meteorology or climatology, in which directional data arise. See Lund (1999) for a further discussion of measures of similarity and dissimilarity and their use in clustering directional data.

Properties of Dissimilarities

A dissimilarity measure based on a metric conforms generally to our intuitive ideas of distance. The norm of the difference between two vectors is a metric, that is, if

$$\Delta(x_1, x_2) = \|x_1 - x_2\|,$$

then $\Delta(x_1, x_2)$ is a metric. Distance measures such as the L_p distance and the special cases of Euclidean distance, maximum difference, and Manhattan distance, which are based on norms of the difference between two vectors, have useful properties, such as satisfying the triangle inequality:

$$d_{ik} \leq d_{ij} + d_{jk}.$$

There are many different measures that may be useful in different applications. Gower and Legendre (1986) discuss several metric distances and other measures of dissimilarity and the properties of the measures.

Dissimilarities between Groups of Observations

In clustering applications, we need to measure distances between groups of observations. We are faced with two decisions. First, we must choose the distance metric to use, and then the points in the two groups between which we measure the distance. Any of the distance measures discussed above could be used.

Once a distance measure is chosen, the distance between two groups can be defined in several ways, such as the following;

- the distance between a central point, such as the mean or median, in one cluster and the corresponding central point in the other cluster;

- the minimum distance between a point in one cluster and a point in the other cluster;

- the largest distance between a point in one cluster and a point in the other cluster;

- the average of the distances between the points in one cluster and the points in the other cluster.

The average of all of the pairwise point distances is the most common type of measure used in some applications. This type of measure is widely used in genetics, where the distance between two populations is based on the differences in frequencies of chromosomal arrangements (for example, Prevosti's distance) or on DNA matches or agreement of other categorical variables (for example, Sanghvi's distance).

Effects of Transformations of the Data

In the course of an analysis of data, it is very common to apply various transformations to the data. These transformations may involve various operations on real numbers, such as scaling a variable (multiplication), summing all values of a variable (addition), and so on. Do these kinds of operations have an effect on the results of the data analysis? Do they change the relative values of such things as measures of similarity and dissimilarity?

Consider a very simple case in which a variable represents length, for example. The actual data are measurements such as 0.11 meters, 0.093 meters, and so on. These values are recorded simply as the real numbers 0.11, 0.093, and so on. In analyzing the data, we may perform certain operations (summing the data, squaring the data, and so on) in which we merely assume that the data behave as real numbers. (Notice that 0.11 is a real number but 0.11 meters is not a real number — 0.11 meters is a more complicated object.) After noting the range of values of the observations, we may decide that millimeters would be better units of measurement than meters. The values of the variable are then scaled by 1,000. Does this affect any data analysis we may do?

Although, as a result of scaling, the mean goes from approximately μ (for some value μ) to $1,000\mu$, and the variance goes from σ^2 (for some value σ) to $1,000,000\sigma^2$, the scaling certainly should not affect any analysis that involves that variable alone.

Suppose, however, that another variable in the dataset is also length and that typical values of that variable are 1,100 meters, 930 meters, and so on. For this variable, a more appropriate unit of measure may be kilometers. To change the unit of measurement results in dividing the data values by 1,000. The differential effects on the mean and variance are similar to the previous effects when the units were changed from meters to millimeters; the effects on the means and on the variances differ by a factor of 1,000. Again, the scaling certainly should not affect any analysis that involves that variable alone.

This scaling, however, does affect the relative values of measures of similarity and dissimilarity. Consider, for example, the Euclidean distance between two observations, $x_1 = (x_{11}, x_{12})$ and $x_2 = (x_{21}, x_{22})$. The squared distance prior to the scaling is

$$(x_{11} - x_{21})^2 + (x_{12} - x_{22})^2.$$

Following the scaling, it is

$$10^6(x_{11} - x_{21})^2 + 10^{-6}(x_{12} - x_{22})^2.$$

The net effect depends on the relative distances between x_1 and x_2 as measured by their separate components.

As we mention above, an orthogonal transformation preserves Euclidean distances and angular separations; that is, it is an isometric transformation. An orthogonal transformation also preserves measures of similarity based on the L_2 norm. An orthogonal transformation, however, does not preserve other measures of similarity or distance.

Outlying Observations and Collinear Variables

Many methods of data analysis may be overly affected by observations that lie at some distance from the other observations. Using a least squares criterion for locating the center of a set of observations, for example, can result in a "central point" that is outside of the convex hull of all of the data except for just one observation. As an extreme case, consider the mean of 100 univariate observations, all between 0 and 1 except for one outlying observation at 15. The mean of this set of data is larger than 99% of the data.

An outlier may result in one row and column in the dissimilarity matrix D having very large values compared to the other values in the dissimilarity matrix. This is especially true of dissimilarities based on the L_2 norm. Dissimilarities based on other norms, such as the L_1 norm, may not be as greatly affected by an outlier.

Methods of data analysis that are not as strongly affected by outlying observations are said to be "robust". (There are various technical definitions of robustness, which we will not consider here.) The variance-covariance matrix S in equation (5.8), because it is based on squares of distances from unweighted means, may be strongly affected by outliers. A robust alternative is

$$S_{\mathrm{R}} = (s_{\mathrm{R}jk}), \qquad (5.23)$$

where the $s_{\mathrm{R}jk}$ are robust alternatives to the s_{jk} in equation (5.9). There are various ways of defining the $s_{\mathrm{R}jk}$. In general, they are formed by choosing weights for the individual observations to decrease the effect of outlying points; for example,

$$s_{\mathrm{R}jk} = \frac{\sum_{i=1}^{n} w_i^2 (x_{ij} - \bar{x}_{\mathrm{R}j})(x_{ik} - \bar{x}_{\mathrm{R}k})}{\sum_{i=1}^{n} w_i^2 - 1},$$

where

$$\bar{x}_{\mathrm{R}j} = \sum_{i=1}^{n} w_i x_{ij} \Big/ \sum_{i=1}^{n} w_i,$$

for a given function ω,

$$w_i = \omega(d_i)/d_i,$$

and

$$d_i = (x_i - \bar{x}_{\mathrm{R}})^{\mathrm{T}} S_{\mathrm{R}}^{-1}(x_i - \bar{x}_{\mathrm{R}}).$$

(In this last expression, x_i represents the m-vector of the ith observation, and $\bar{x}_R$ represents the m-vector of the weighted means. These expressions are circular and require iterations to evaluate them.)

The function ω is designed to downweight outlying observations. One possibility, for given constants b_1 and b_2, is

$$\begin{aligned} \omega(d) &= d & \text{if} \quad d \le d_0 \\ &= d_0 e^{-\frac{1}{2}(d-d_0)^2/b_2^2} & \text{if} \quad d > d_0, \end{aligned}$$

where $d_0 = \sqrt{m} + b_1/\sqrt{2}$. See Campbell (1980) and Marazzi (1993) for further discussions on robust covariances and correlations. Ammann (1989, 1993) discusses the effects of outlying observations on multivariate analysis procedures such as principal components and projection pursuit. He recommends using robust measures of association and then modifying the procedures by adaptive weighting to make them resistant to outliers.

A problem of a different type arises when the variables are highly correlated. In this case, the covariance matrix S and the correlation matrix R, which are based on the L_2 norm, are both ill-conditioned. The ranking transformation mentioned on page 111 results in a correlation matrix that is better conditioned.

Multidimensional Scaling: Determining Observations that Yield a Given Distance Matrix

Given an $n \times n$ distance matrix such as D in equation (5.19), could we reconstruct an $n \times m$ data matrix X that yields D for some metric $\Delta(\cdot, \cdot)$? The question, of course, is constrained by m (that is, by the number of variables). The problem is to determine the elements of rows of X such that

$$\begin{aligned} \tilde{d}_{ij} &= \Delta(x_i, x_j) \\ &\approx d_{ij}. \end{aligned}$$

This is called *multidimensional scaling*.

The approximation problem can be stated precisely as an optimization problem to minimize

$$\frac{\sum_i \sum_j f(\tilde{d}_{ij} - d_{ij})}{\sum_i \sum_j f(d_{ij})},$$

where $f(\cdot)$ is some function that is positive for nonzero arguments and is monotone increasing in the absolute value of the argument, and $f(0) = 0$. An obvious choice is $f(t) = t^2$. Clarkson and Gentle (1986) describe an alternating iteratively reweighted least squares algorithm to compute the minimum when f is of the form $f(t) = |t|^p$. If the distances in D do not arise from a metric, they discussed ways of transforming the dissimilarities so that the least squares approach would still work.

The larger the value of m, of course, the closer the $\tilde{d}_{ij}$ will be to the d_{ij}. If $m \ll n$ and the approximations are good, significant data reduction is achieved.

There are various modifications of the basic multidimensional scaling problem, and software programs are available for different ones. The S-Plus and R function `cmdscale` performs computations for multidimensional scaling when the dissimilarities are Euclidean distances. (In R, `cmdscale` is in the `mva` package.)

5.5   Data Mining

It is now common to search through datasets and compute summary statistics from various items that may indicate relationships that were not previously recognized. The individual items or the relationships among them may not have been of primary interest when the data were originally collected. This process of prowling through the data is sometimes called *data mining* or *knowledge discovery in databases* (KDD). (The names come and go with current fads; there is very little of substance indicated by use of different names.) The objective is to discover characteristics of the data that may not be expected based on the existing theory. In the language of the database literature, the specific goals of data mining are:

- classification of observations;

- linkage analysis;

- deviation detection;

and finally

- predictive modeling.

Of course, the first three of these are the objectives of any exploratory statistical data analysis. Data mining is exploratory data analysis (EDA) applied to large datasets. An objective of an exploratory analysis is often to generate hypotheses, and exploratory analyses are generally followed by more formal confirmatory procedures. The explorations in massive datasets must be performed without much human intervention. Searching algorithms need to have some means of learning and adaptively improving. This will be a major area of research for some time.

Predictive modeling uses inductive reasoning rather than the more common deductive reasoning, which is much easier to automate.

In the statistical classification of observations, the dataset is partitioned recursively. The partitioning results in a classification tree, which is a decision tree, each node of which represents a partition of the dataset. The decision at each node is generally based on the values of a single variable at a time, as in the two most commonly used procedures, CART (see Breiman et al., 1984) and C4.5, or its successors, See5 and C5.0 (see Quinlan, 1993).

CART can also build nodes based on linear combinations of the variables. This is sometimes called "oblique partitioning" because the partitions are not parallel to the axes representing the individual variables. Seeking good linear combinations of variables on which to build oblique partitions is a much more computationally intensive procedure than just using single variables. Heath, Kasif, and Salzberg (1993) and Murthy, Kasif, and Salzberg (1994) describe methods that use randomization in selecting oblique partitions.

Linkage analysis is often the most important activity of data mining. In linkage analysis, relationships among different variables are discovered and analyzed. This step follows partitioning and is the interpretation of the partitions that were formed.

It is also important to identify data that do not fit the patterns that are discovered. The deviation of some subsets of the data often makes it difficult to develop models for the remainder of the data.

An overview of some of the issues in mining large datasets is given in Fayyad, Piatetsky-Shapiro, and Smyth (1996) in the book edited by Fayyad et al. (1996), which contains several articles addressing specific aspects and approaches to the problem. Glymour et al. (1996) discuss some possible roles for statistical inference in data mining. There are several commercially available software packages that implement data mining, usually of datasets in some standard format.

5.6   Computational Feasibility

Data must be stored, transported, sorted, searched, and otherwise rearranged, and computations must be performed on it. The size of the dataset largely determines whether these actions are feasible. Huber (1994, 1996) proposed a classification of datasets by the number of bytes required to store them (see also Wegman, 1995). Huber described as "tiny" those requiring on the order of 10^2 bytes; as "small" those requiring on the order of 10^4 bytes; as "medium" those requiring on the order of 10^6 bytes (one megabyte); as "large", 10^8 bytes; "huge", 10^{10} bytes (10 gigabytes); and as "massive", 10^{12} bytes (one terabyte). ("Tera" in Greek means "monster".) This log scale of two orders of magnitude is useful to give a perspective on what can be done with data. Online or out-of-core algorithms are generally necessary for processing massive datasets.

For processing massive datasets, the order of computations is a key measure of feasibility. We can quickly determine that a process whose computations are $O(n^2)$ cannot be reasonably contemplated for massive (10^{12} bytes) datasets. If computations can be performed at a rate of 10^{12} per second (teraflop), it would take over three years to complete the computations. (A rough order of magnitude for quick "year" computations is $\pi \times 10^7$ seconds equals approximately one year.) A process whose computations are $O(n \log n)$ could be completed in 230 milliseconds for a massive dataset. This remarkable difference in time required for $O(n^2)$ and $O(n \log n)$ processes is the reason that the fast Fourier transform (FFT) algorithm was such an important advance.

Exponential orders can make operations even on tiny (10^2 bytes) datasets infeasible. A process whose computations require time of $O(2^n)$ may not be completed in four centuries.

Sometimes, it is appropriate to reduce the size of the dataset by forming groups of data. "Bins" can be defined, usually as nonoverlapping intervals covering $\mathbb{R}^d$, and the number of observations falling into each bin can be determined. This process is linear in the number of observations. The amount of information loss, of course, depends on the sizes of the bins. Binning of data has long been used for reducing the size of a dataset, and earlier books on statistical analysis usually had major sections dealing with "grouped data".

Another way of reducing the size of a dataset is by sampling. This must be done with some care, and often, in fact, sampling is not a good idea. Sampling is likely to miss the unusual observations, and it is precisely these outlying observations that are most likely to yield new information.

Advances in computer hardware continue to expand what is computationally feasible. It is interesting to note, however, that the order of computations is determined by the problem to be solved and the algorithm to be used, not by the hardware. Advances in algorithm design have reduced the order of computations for many standard problems, while advances in hardware have not changed the order of the computations. Hardware advances change the constant in the order of time.

We discuss methods of identifying structure in multivariate data in Chapter 10. Anderson (1984) and Gnanadesikan (1997) are two good general references on multivariate methods.

Exercises

5.1. Determine the rotation matrix that transforms the vector $x = (5, 12)$ into the vector $\tilde{x} = (0, 13)$.

5.2. Consider the relative interpoint distances between the three 3-vectors

$$x_1 = (x_{11}, x_{12}, x_{13}),$$

$$x_2 = (x_{21}, x_{22}, x_{23}),$$

and

$$x_3 = (x_{31}, x_{32}, x_{33}).$$

Give specific values (small integers) for the x_{ij} such that, for the Euclidean distance, the distance between the first and second, d_{12}, is less than the distance between the second and third, d_{23}, but for all of the other distance measures listed on pages 115 and 116, $d_{12} > d_{23}$. For the Hamming and binary distances, use the binary representations of the elements.

5.3. Show that the Mahalanobis distance (5.22), on page 118, between any two observations is nonnegative.

5.4. Show that the norm of the difference between two vectors is a metric; that is, if

$$\Delta(x_1, x_2) = \|x_1 - x_2\|,$$

$\Delta(x_1, x_2)$ is a metric.

5.5.   (a) Show that all of the distance measures in equations (5.13) through (5.18), as well as the Hamming distance and the binary difference, are metrics.

(b) Which of those distance measures are norms?

5.6.   Consider a two-dimensional surface with an orthogonal coordinate system over which there is a fluid flow with constant velocity $f = (f_1, f_2)$. Suppose that an object can move through the fluid with constant velocity v with respect to the fluid and measured in the same units as f. (The magnitude of the velocity is $\|v\| = \sqrt{v_1^2 + v_2^2}$.) Assume that $\|v\| > \|f\|$.

(a) Define a distance measure, d, over the surface such that for two points x_i and x_j, the distance from x_i to x_j is proportional to the time required for the object to move from x_i to x_j.

(b) Compare your distance measure with those listed on page 114.

(c) What properties of a norm does your distance measure possess?

5.7.   Consider the problem of a dissimilarity measure for two-dimensional data represented in polar coordinates, as discussed on page 118. One possibility, of course, is to transform the data to cartesian coordinates and then use any of the distance measures for that coordinate system. Define a dissimilarity measure based on d_{ij}^d and d_{ij}^r. Is your measure a metric?

5.8.   Given two n-vectors, x_1 and x_2, form a third vector, x_3, as $x_3 = a_1 x_1 + a_2 x_2 + \epsilon$, where ϵ is a vector of independent $N(0, 1)$ realizations. Although the matrix $X = [x_1 \ x_2 \ x_3]$ is in $\mathbb{R}^{n \times 3}$, the linear structure, even obscured by the noise, implies a two-dimensional space for the data matrix (that is, the space $\mathbb{R}^{n \times 2}$).

(a) Determine a rotation matrix that reveals the linear structure. In other words, determine matrices Q and P such that the rotation XQ followed by the projection $(XQ)P$ is a noisy line in two dimensions.

(b) Generate x_1 and x_2 as realizations of a $U(0, 1)$ process and x_3 as $5x_1 + x_2 + \epsilon$, where ϵ is a realization of a $N(0, 1)$ process. What are Q and P from the previous question?

5.9.   Given the distance matrix

$$
D = \begin{bmatrix}
0 & 4.34 & 4.58 & 7.68 & 4.47 \\
4.34 & 0 & 1.41 & 4.00 & 4.36 \\
4.58 & 1.41 & 0 & 5.10 & 5.00 \\
7.68 & 4.00 & 5.10 & 0 & 6.56 \\
4.47 & 4.36 & 5.00 & 6.56 & 0
\end{bmatrix},
$$

where the elements are Euclidean distances, determine a $5 \times m$ matrix with a small value of m that has a distance matrix very close to D.

Chapter 6

Estimation of Functions

An interesting problem in statistics, and one that is generally difficult, is the estimation of a continuous function such as a probability density function. The statistical properties of an estimator of a function are more complicated than statistical properties of an estimator of a single parameter or even of a countable set of parameters. In this chapter we will discuss the properties of an estimator in the general case of a real scalar-valued function over real vector-valued arguments (that is, a mapping from $\mathbb{R}^d$ into $\mathbb{R}$). One of the most common situations in which these properties are relevant is in nonparametric probability density estimation, which we discuss in Chapter 9. The global statistical properties discussed in Section 6.3 are the measures by which we evaluate probability density estimators.

First, we say a few words about notation. We may denote a function by a single letter, f, for example, or by the function notation, $f(\cdot)$ or $f(x)$. When $f(x)$ denotes a function, x is merely a placeholder. The notation $f(x)$, however, may also refer to the value of the function at the point x. The meaning is usually clear from the context.

Using the common "hat" notation for an estimator, we use $\widehat{f}$ or $\widehat{f}(x)$ to denote the estimator of f or of $f(x)$. Following the usual terminology, we use the term "estimator" to denote a random variable, and "estimate" to denote a realization of the random variable. The hat notation is also used to denote an estimate, so we must determine from the context whether $\widehat{f}$ or $\widehat{f}(x)$ denotes a random variable or a realization of a random variable. The estimate or the estimator of the value of the function at the point x may also be denoted by $\widehat{f}(x)$. Sometimes, to emphasize that we are estimating the ordinate of the function rather than evaluating an estimate of the function, we use the notation $\widehat{f(x)}$. In this case also, we often make no distinction in the notation between the realization (the estimate) and the random variable (the estimator). We must determine from the context whether $\widehat{f}(x)$ or $\widehat{f(x)}$ denotes a random variable or a realization of a random variable. In most of the following discussion, the hat notation denotes a random variable that depends on the underlying random variable that yields the sample from which the estimator is computed.

The usual optimality properties that we use in developing a theory of estimation of a finite-dimensional parameter must be extended for estimation of a general function. As we will see, two of the usual desirable properties of point estimators, namely unbiasedness and maximum likelihood, cannot be attained in general by estimators of functions.

There are many similarities in *estimation* of functions and *approximation* of functions, but we must be aware of the fundamental differences in the two problems. Estimation of functions is similar to other estimation problems: we are given a sample of observations; we make certain assumptions about the probability distribution of the sample; and then we develop estimators. The estimators are random variables, and how useful they are depends on properties of their distribution, such as their expected values and their variances. Approximation of functions is an important aspect of numerical analysis. Functions are often approximated to interpolate functional values between directly computed or known values. Functions are also approximated as a prelude to quadrature. Methods for estimating functions often use methods for approximating functions.

Discussions of methods for function approximation are available in texts on numerical methods, such as Rice (1993). Extensive discussions of methods of function estimation are available in Ramsay and Silverman (1997) and Efromovich (1999). Small (1996) describes statistical methods for the related problem of data defining shapes.

6.1   General Methods for Estimating Functions

In the problem of function estimation, we may have observations on the function at specific points in the domain, or we may have indirect measurements of the function, such as observations that relate to a derivative or an integral of the function. In either case, the problem of function estimation has the competing goals of providing a good fit to the observed data and predicting values at other points. In many cases, a smooth estimate satisfies this latter objective. In other cases, however, the unknown function itself is not smooth. Functions with different forms may govern the phenomena in different regimes. This presents a very difficult problem in function estimation, and it is one that we will not consider in any detail here.

There are various approaches to estimating functions. Maximum likelihood (see page 22) has limited usefulness for estimating functions because in general the likelihood is unbounded. A practical approach is to assume that the function is of a particular form and estimate the parameters that characterize the form. For example, we may assume that the function is exponential, possibly because of physical properties such as exponential decay. We may then use various estimation criteria, such as least squares, to estimate the parameter. An extension of this approach is to assume that the function is a mixture of other functions. The mixture can be formed by different functions over different domains or by weighted averages of the functions over the whole domain. Estimation of the function of interest involves estimation of various parameters as well as the weights.

Another approach to function estimation is to represent the function of interest as a linear combination of basis functions, that is, to represent the function in a series expansion. The basis functions are generally chosen to be orthogonal over the domain of interest, and the observed data are used to estimate the coefficients in the series. We discuss the use of basis functions beginning on page 133.

It is often more practical to estimate the function value at a given point. (Of course, if we can estimate the function at any given point, we can effectively have an estimate at all points.) One way of forming an estimate of a function at a given point is to take the average at that point of a filtering function that is evaluated in the vicinity of each data point. The filtering function is called a kernel, and the result of this approach is called a kernel estimator. We discuss the use of kernel filters on page 142.

In the estimation of functions, we must be concerned about the properties of the estimators at specific points and also about properties over the full domain. Global properties over the full domain are often defined in terms of integrals or in terms of suprema or infima.

Before proceeding to discuss methods of approximation and estimation, we need to develop some methods for comparing functions. Much of this material can be considered as an extension of the material in Chapter 5 to uncountable spaces.

Inner Products and Norms

The dot product of functions is naturally defined in terms of integrals of the products of the functions, analogously to the definition of the dot product of vectors. Just as the dot product of vectors is limited to vectors with the same length, the dot product of functions is defined over some fixed range of integration (possibly infinite). The dot product of either functions or vectors is a type of a more general mapping from a linear space into the nonnegative reals called an inner product.

The *inner product* or *dot product* of the real functions f and g over the domain D, denoted by $\langle f, g \rangle_D$ or usually just by $\langle f, g \rangle$, is defined as

$$\langle f, g \rangle_D = \int_D f(x)g(x)\,\mathrm{d}x \tag{6.1}$$

if the (Lebesque) integral exists.

Dot products of functions (as well as of vectors and matrices) over the complex number field are defined in terms of integrals (or sums) of complex conjugates,

$$\langle f, g \rangle_D = \int_D f(x)\bar{g}(x)\,\mathrm{d}x,$$

if the integral exists. The notation $\bar{g}(\cdot)$ denotes the complex conjugate of the function $g(\cdot)$. Often, even if the vectors and matrices in data analysis have real elements, many functions of interest are complex.

To avoid questions about integrability, we generally restrict attention to functions whose dot products with themselves exist; that is, to functions that are square Lebesque integrable over the region of interest. The set of such square integrable functions is denoted $L^2(D)$. In many cases, the range of integration is the real line, and we may use the notation $L^2(\mathbb{R})$, or often just L^2, to denote that set of functions and the associated inner product.

The Cauchy-Schwarz inequality holds for the inner products of functions, just as for vectors, that is,

$$\langle f, g \rangle \leq \langle f, f \rangle^{1/2} \langle g, g \rangle^{1/2}.$$

This is easy to see by first observing that for every real number t,

$$
\begin{aligned}
0 \quad &\leq \quad (\langle (tf + g), (tf + g) \rangle)^2 \\
&= \quad \langle f, f \rangle t^2 + 2\langle f, g \rangle t + \langle g, g \rangle \\
&= \quad at^2 + bt + c,
\end{aligned}
$$

where the constants a, b, and c correspond to the inner products in the preceding equation. This nonnegative quadratic in t cannot have two distinct real roots, hence the discriminant, $b^2 - 4ac$, must be less than or equal to zero; that is,

$$\left(\frac{1}{2} b \right)^2 \leq ac.$$

By substituting and taking square roots, we get the Cauchy-Schwarz inequality. It is also clear from this proof that equality holds only if $f = 0$ or if $g = rf$ for some scalar r.

Just as we sometimes define vector inner products and vector norms in terms of a weight vector or matrix, we likewise define function inner products with respect to a weight function, $w(x)$, or with respect to the measure μ, where $d\mu = w(x)dx$,

$$\langle f, g \rangle_{(\mu;D)} = \int_D f(x)\bar{g}(x)w(x)\, dx,$$

if the integral exists. Often, both the weight and the range are assumed to be fixed, and the simpler notation $\langle f, g \rangle$ is used.

Scalar multiplication and function addition distribute over an inner product; if a is a scalar and f, g, and h are functions,

$$\langle af + g, h \rangle = a\langle f, h \rangle + \langle g, h \rangle. \tag{6.2}$$

This *linearity* is an important property of an inner product.

The *norm of a function* f, denoted generically as $\| f \|$, is a mapping into the nonnegative reals such that

- if $f \neq 0$ over an interval in which $w > 0$, then $\|f\| > 0$ and $\|0\| = 0$;

- $\|af\| = |a|\|f\|$ for a real scalar a; and

- $\|f + g\| \leq \|f\| + \|g\|$.

(This is just a special case of the norm defined on page 114.) Because of the linearity of a norm, a space together with a norm is called a *normed linear space*.

A norm of a function $\|f\|$ is often defined as some nonnegative, strictly increasing function of the inner product of f with itself, $\langle f, f \rangle$. Not all norms are defined in terms of inner products, however. The most common type of norm for a real-valued function is the L_p norm, denoted as $\|f\|_p$, which is defined similarly to the L_p vector norm as

$$\|f\|_p = \left(\int_D |f(x)|^p w(x) \, dx \right)^{1/p}, \tag{6.3}$$

if the integral exists. The set of functions for which these integrals exist is often denoted by $L^p_{(\mu;D)}$. It is clear that $\|f\|_p$ satisfies the properties that define a norm.

Often μ is taken as Lebesgue measure, and $w(x)dx$ becomes dx. This is a uniform weighting.

A common L_p function norm is the L_2 norm, which is often denoted simply by $\|f\|$. This norm is related to the inner product:

$$\|f\|_2 = \langle f, f \rangle^{1/2}. \tag{6.4}$$

The space consisting of the set of functions whose L_2 norms over $\mathbb{R}$ exist together with this norm is denoted L^2.

Another common L_p function norm is the L_∞ norm, especially as a measure of the difference between two functions. This norm, which is called the *Chebyshev norm* or the *uniform norm*, is the limit of equation (6.3) as $p \to \infty$. This norm has the simpler relationship

$$\|f\|_\infty = \sup |f(x)w(x)|.$$

How well one function approximates another function is usually measured by a norm of the difference in the functions over the relevant range. If g approximates f, $\|g - f\|_\infty$ is likely to be the norm of interest. This is the norm most often used in numerical analysis when the objective is interpolation or quadrature. In problems with noisy data, or when g may be very different from f, $\|g - f\|_2$ may be the more appropriate norm. This is the norm most often used in estimating probability density functions (see Chapter 9) or in projection pursuit (see Section 10.5), for example.

To emphasize the measure of the weighting function, the notation $\|f\|_\mu$ is sometimes used. (The ambiguity of the possible subscripts on $\| \cdot \|$ is usually resolved by the context.) For functions over finite domains, the weighting function is most often the identity.

A *normal function* is one whose norm is 1. Although this term can be used with respect to any norm, it is generally reserved for the L_2 norm (that is, the norm arising from the inner product). A function whose integral (over a relevant range, usually $\mathbb{R}$) is 1 is also called a normal function. (Although this latter definition is similar to the standard one, the latter is broader because it may include functions that are not square-integrable.) Density and weight functions are often normalized (that is, scaled to be normal).

Complete Spaces

For approximation methods, it may be important to know that a sequence of functions (or vectors) within a given space converges to a function (or vector) in that space.

A sequence $\{f^{(i)}\}$ in an inner product space is said to converge to f^* if, given $\epsilon > 0$, there exists an integer M such that $\|f^{(i)} - f^*\| \le \epsilon$ for all $i \ge M$. (This convergence of the norm is uniform convergence. There is also a condition of pointwise convergence of a sequence of functions, which depends on the argument of each function in the sequence.)

A sequence is said to be a Cauchy sequence if, given $\epsilon > 0$, there exists an integer M such that $\|f^{(i)} - f^{(j)}\| \le \epsilon$ for all $i, j \ge M$.

A space in which every Cauchy sequence converges to a member of the space is said to be *complete*.

A complete space together with a norm defined on the space is called a *Banach space*. A closed Banach space in which the norm arises from an inner product is called a *Hilbert space*.

The finite-dimensional vector space $\mathbb{R}^d$ and the space of square-integrable functions L^2 are both Hilbert spaces. They are, by far, the two most important Hilbert spaces for our purposes. The convergence properties of the iterative methods we often employ in smoothing and in optimization methods generally derive from the fact that we are working in Hilbert spaces.

Measures for Comparing Two Functions

Statistical properties such as bias and consistency are defined in terms of the difference of the estimator and what is being estimated. For an estimator of a function, first we must consider some ways of measuring this difference. These are general measures for functions and are not dependent on the distribution of a random variable.

The most common measure of the difference between two functions, $g(x)$ and $f(x)$, is a norm of the function

$$e(x) = g(x) - f(x).$$

When one function is an estimate or approximation of the other function, we may call this difference the "error". We will discuss some norms of errors in Section 6.3.

Basis Sets in Function Spaces

If each function in a linear space can be expressed as a linear combination of the functions in a set G, then G is said to be a *generating set*, a *spanning set*, or a *basis set* for the linear space. (These three terms are synonymous.) The basis sets for finite-dimensional vector spaces are finite; for most function spaces of interest, the basis sets are infinite.

A set of functions $\{q_k\}$ is *orthogonal over the domain D with respect to the nonnegative weight function $w(x)$* if the inner product with respect to $w(x)$ of q_k and q_l, $\langle q_k, q_l \rangle$, is 0 if $k \neq l$; that is,

$$\int_D q_k(x)\bar{q}_l(x)w(x)\mathrm{d}x = 0 \quad k \neq l. \tag{6.5}$$

If, in addition,

$$\int_D q_k(x)\bar{q}_k(x)w(x)\mathrm{d}x = 1,$$

the functions are called *orthonormal.*

In the following, we will be concerned with real functions of real arguments, so we can take $\bar{q}_k(x) = q_k(x)$.

The weight function can also be incorporated into the individual functions to form a different set,

$$\tilde{q}_k(x) = q_k(x)w^{1/2}(x).$$

This set of functions also spans the same function space and is orthogonal over D with respect to a constant weight function.

Basis sets consisting of orthonormal functions are generally easier to work with and can be formed from any basis set. Given two nonnull, linearly independent functions, q_1 and q_2, two orthonormal vectors, $\tilde{q}_1$ and $\tilde{q}_2$, that span the same space can be formed as

$$\tilde{q}_1(\cdot) = \frac{1}{\|q_1\|} q_1(\cdot),$$

$$\tilde{q}_2(\cdot) = \frac{1}{\|q_2 - \langle \tilde{q}_1, q_2 \rangle \tilde{q}_1\|} \left(q_2(\cdot) - \langle \tilde{q}_1, q_2 \rangle \tilde{q}_1(\cdot) \right). \tag{6.6}$$

These are the Gram-Schmidt function transformations, which are essentially the same as the vector transformations we discuss on page 102. They can easily be extended to more than two functions to form a set of orthonormal functions from any set of linearly independent functions.

Series Expansions in Basis Functions

Our objective is to represent a function of interest, $f(x)$, over some domain D, as a linear combination of "simpler" functions, $q_0(x), q_1(x), \ldots$:

$$f(x) = \sum_{k=0}^{\infty} c_k q_k(x). \tag{6.7}$$

There are various ways of constructing the q_k functions. If they are developed through a linear operator on a function space, they are called *eigenfunctions*, and the corresponding c_k are called eigenvalues.

We choose a set $\{q_k\}$ that spans some class of functions over the given domain D. A set of orthogonal basis functions is often the best choice because they have nice properties that facilitate computations and a large body of theory about their properties is available.

If the function to be estimated, $f(x)$, is continuous and integrable over a domain D, the orthonormality property allows us to determine the coefficients c_k in the expansion (6.7):

$$c_k = \langle f, q_k \rangle. \tag{6.8}$$

The coefficients $\{c_k\}$ are called the *Fourier coefficients* of f with respect to the orthonormal functions $\{q_k\}$.

In applications, we *approximate* the function using a truncated orthogonal series. The error due to finite truncation at j terms of the infinite series is the residual function $f - \sum_{k=1}^{j} c_k f_k$. The *mean squared error* over the domain D is the scaled, squared L_2 norm of the residual,

$$\frac{1}{d} \left\| f - \sum_{k=0}^{j} c_k q_k \right\|^2, \tag{6.9}$$

where d is some measure of the domain D. (If the domain is the interval $[a, b]$, for example, one choice is $d = b - a$.)

A very important property of Fourier coefficients is that they yield the minimum mean squared error for a given set of basis functions $\{q_i\}$; that is, for any other constants, $\{a_i\}$, and any k,

$$\left\| f - \sum_{k=0}^{j} c_k q_k \right\|^2 \leq \left\| f - \sum_{k=0}^{j} a_k q_k \right\|^2 \tag{6.10}$$

(see Exercise 6.4).

In applications of statistical data analysis, after forming the approximation, we then *estimate* the coefficients from equation (6.8) by identifying an appropriate probability density that is a factor of the function of interest, f. (Note again the difference in "approximation" and "estimation".) Expected values can be estimated using observed or simulated values of the random variable and the approximation of the probability density function.

The basis functions are generally chosen to be easy to use in computations. Common examples include the Fourier trigonometric functions $\sin(kt)$ and $\cos(kt)$ for $k = 1, 2, \ldots$, orthogonal polynomials such as Legendre, Hermite, and so on, splines, and wavelets. We discuss orthogonal polynomials below, and discuss splines beginning on page 139. For use of wavelets in estimating functions we refer the reader to Antoniadis, Gregoire, and McKeague (1994). More general applications of wavelets are considered in the articles in Antoniadis and Oppenheim (1995).

Orthogonal Polynomials

The most useful type of basis function depends on the nature of the function being estimated. The orthogonal polynomials are useful for a very wide range of functions. Orthogonal polynomials of real variables are their own complex conjugates. It is clear that for the kth polynomial in the orthogonal sequence, we can choose an a_k that does not involve x, such that

$$q_k(x) - a_k x q_{k-1}(x)$$

is a polynomial of degree $k - 1$.

Because any polynomial of degree $k - 1$ can be represented by a linear combination of the first k members of any sequence of orthogonal polynomials, we can write

$$q_k(x) - a_k x q_{k-1}(x) = \sum_{i=0}^{k-1} c_i q_i(x).$$

Because of orthogonality, all c_i for $i < k - 2$ must be 0. Therefore, collecting terms, we have, for some constants a_k, b_k, and c_k, the three-term recursion that applies to any sequence of orthogonal polynomials:

$$q_k(x) = (a_k x + b_k)q_{k-1}(x) - c_k q_{k-2}(x) = 0, \quad \text{for } k = 2, 3, \ldots. \tag{6.11}$$

This recursion formula is often used in computing orthogonal polynomials. The coefficients in this recursion formula depend on the specific sequence of orthogonal polynomials, of course.

This three-term recursion formula can also be used to develop a formula for the sum of products of orthogonal polynomials $q_i(x)$ and $q_i(y)$:

$$\sum_{i=0}^{k} q_i(x)q_i(y) = \frac{1}{a_{k+1}} \frac{q_{k+1}(x)q_k(y) - q_k(x)q_{k+1}(y)}{x - y}. \tag{6.12}$$

This expression, which is called the Christoffel-Darboux formula, is useful in evaluating the product of arbitrary functions that have been approximated by finite series of orthogonal polynomials.

There are several widely used complete systems of univariate orthogonal polynomials. The different systems are characterized by the one-dimensional intervals over which they are defined and by their weight functions. The Legendre, Chebyshev, and Jacobi polynomials are defined over $[-1, 1]$ and hence can be scaled into any finite interval. The weight function of the Jacobi polynomials is more general, so a finite sequence of them may fit a given function better, but the Legendre and Chebyshev polynomials are simpler and so are often used. The Laguerre polynomials are defined over the half line $[0, \infty)$, and the Hermite polynomials are defined over the reals, $(-\infty, \infty)$.

Any of these systems of polynomials can be developed easily by beginning with the basis set $1, x, x^2, \ldots$ and orthogonalizing them by use of equations (6.6) and their extensions.

Table 6.1 summarizes the ranges and weight functions for these standard orthogonal polynomials.

Table 6.1: Orthogonal Polynomials

Polynomial Series	Range	Weight Function
Legendre	$[-1, 1]$	1 (uniform)
Chebyshev	$[-1, 1]$	$(1 - x^2)^{1/2}$ (symmetric beta)
Jacobi	$[-1, 1]$	$(1 - x)^\alpha (1 + x)^\beta$ (beta)
Laguerre	$[0, \infty)$	$x^{\alpha-1} e^{-x}$ (gamma)
Hermite	$(-\infty, \infty)$	$e^{-x^2/2}$ (normal)

The *Legendre polynomials* have a constant weight function and are defined over the interval $[-1, 1]$. The first few (unnormalized) Legendre polynomials are

$$
\begin{aligned}
&P_0(t) = 1 &&P_1(t) = t \\
&P_2(t) = (3t^2 - 1)/2 &&P_3(t) = (5t^3 - 3t)/2 \\
&P_4(t) = (35t^4 - 30t^2 + 3)/8 \quad&&P_5(t) = (63t^5 - 70t^3 + 15t)/8
\end{aligned}
\tag{6.13}
$$

Graphs of these polynomials are shown in Figure 6.1.

The normalizing constant for the kth Legendre polynomial is determined by noting

$$
\int_{-1}^{1} (P_k(t))^2 \mathrm{d}x = \frac{2}{2k + 1}.
$$

The recurrence formula for the Legendre polynomials is

$$
P_k(t) = \frac{2k - 1}{k} t P_{k-1}(t) - \frac{k - 1}{k} P_{k-2}(t).
\tag{6.14}
$$

The *Hermite polynomials* are orthogonal with respect to a Gaussian, or standard normal, weight function. A series using these Hermite polynomials is often called a Gram-Charlier series. (These are not the standard Hermite polynomials, but they are the ones most commonly used by statisticians because the weight function is proportional to the normal density.)

The first few Hermite polynomials are

$$
\begin{aligned}
&H_0^e(t) = 1 &&H_1^e(t) = t \\
&H_2^e(t) = t^2 - 1 &&H_3^e(t) = t^3 - 3t \\
&H_4^e(t) = t^4 - 6t^2 + 3 \quad&&H_5^e(t) = t^5 - 10t^3 + 15t
\end{aligned}
\tag{6.15}
$$

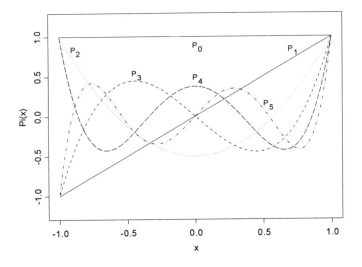

Figure 6.1: Legendre Polynomials

The recurrence formula for the Hermite polynomials is

$$H_k^e(t) = tH_{k-1}^e(t) - kH_{k-2}^e(t). \tag{6.16}$$

As an example of the use of orthogonal polynomials to approximate a given function, consider the expansion of $f(x) = e^{-x}$ over the interval $[-1, 1]$. The coefficients are determined by equation (6.8). Graphs of the function and the truncated series approximations using up to six terms $(j = 0, 1, \ldots, 5)$ are shown in Figure 6.2. Each truncated series is the best linear combination of the Legendre polynomials (in terms of the L_2 norm) of the function using no more than $j + 1$ terms.

Multivariate Orthogonal Polynomials

Multivariate orthogonal polynomials can be formed easily as tensor products of univariate orthogonal polynomials. The tensor product of the functions $f(x)$ over D_x and $g(y)$ over D_y is a function of the arguments x and y over $D_x \times D_y$:

$$h(x, y) = f(x)g(y).$$

If $\{q_{1,k}(x_1)\}$ and $\{q_{2,l}(x_2)\}$ are sequences of univariate orthogonal polynomials, a sequence of bivariate orthogonal polynomials can be formed as

$$q_{kl}(x_1, x_2) = q_{1,k}(x_1)q_{2,l}(x_2). \tag{6.17}$$

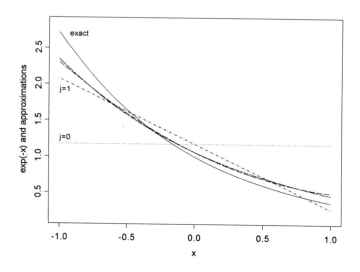

Figure 6.2: Approximations with Legendre Polynomials

These polynomials are orthogonal in the same sense as in equation (6.5), where the integration is over the two-dimensional domain. Similarly as in equation (6.7), a bivariate function can be expressed as

$$f(x_1, x_2) = \sum_{k=0}^{\infty} \sum_{l=0}^{\infty} c_{kl} q_{kl}(x_1, x_2),\qquad(6.18)$$

with the coefficients being determined by integrating over both dimensions.

Although obviously such product polynomials, or radial polynomials, would emphasize features along coordinate axes, they can nevertheless be useful for representing general multivariate functions. Often, it is useful to apply a rotation of the coordinate axes, as we discussed in Section 5.2. A general reference on multivariate orthogonal polynomials is Dunkl and Yu (2001).

The weight functions, such as those for the Jacobi polynomials, that have various shapes controlled by parameters can also often be used in a mixture model of the function of interest. This is the way the Bernstein polynomials (7.3) are used in Bézier curves, as discussed on page 163, except in that case the coefficients are determined to interpolate a fixed set of points. The weight function for the Hermite polynomials can be generalized by a linear transformation (resulting in a normal weight with mean μ and variance σ^2), and the function of interest may be represented as a mixture of general normals.

Function Decomposition and Estimation of the Coefficients in an Orthogonal Expansion

We use the techniques discussed in relation to equation (2.5) on page 53; that is, we decompose the function of interest to have a factor that is a probability density function, p, as in equation (2.6),

$$f(x) = g(x)p(x). \tag{6.19}$$

From equation (6.8), we have

$$
\begin{aligned}
c_k &= \langle f, q_k \rangle \\
&= \int_D q_k(x)g(x)p(x)\mathrm{d}x \\
&= E(q_k(X)g(X)), \tag{6.20}
\end{aligned}
$$

where X is a random variable whose probability density function is p.

If we can obtain a random sample, $x_1, \ldots, x_n$, from the distribution with density p, the c_k can be unbiasedly estimated by

$$\widehat{c}_k = \frac{1}{n} \sum_{i=1}^n q_k(x_i)g(x_i).$$

The series estimator of the function for all x therefore is

$$\widehat{f}(x) = \frac{1}{n} \sum_{k=0}^j \sum_{i=1}^n q_k(x_i)g(x_i)q_k(x) \tag{6.21}$$

for some truncation point j.

The random sample, $x_1, \ldots, x_n$, may be an observed dataset, or it may be the output of a random number generator.

Splines

The approach to function approximation that we pursued in the previous section makes use of a finite subset of an infinite basis set consisting of polynomials of degrees $p = 0, 1, \ldots$. This approach yields a smooth approximation $\widehat{f}(x)$. ("Smooth" means an approximation that is continuous and has continuous derivatives. These are useful properties of the approximation.) The polynomials in $\widehat{f}(x)$, however, cause oscillations that may be undesirable. The approximation oscillates a number of times one less than the highest degree of the polynomial used. Also, if the function being approximated has quite different shapes in different regions of its domain, the global approach of using the same polynomials over the full domain may not be very effective.

Another approach is to subdivide the interval over which the function is to be approximated and then on each subinterval use polynomials with low degree.

The approximation at any point is a sum of one or more piecewise polynomials. Even with polynomials of very low degree, if we use a large number of subintervals, we can obtain a good approximation to the function. Zero-degree polynomials, for example, would yield a piecewise constant function that could be very close to a given function if enough subintervals are used. Using more and more subintervals, of course, is not a very practical approach. Not only is the approximation a rather complicated function, but it may be discontinuous at the interval boundaries. We can achieve smoothness of the approximation by imposing continuity restrictions on the piecewise polynomials and their derivatives. This is the approach in *spline* approximation and smoothing.

The polynomials are of degree no greater than some specified number, often just 3. This means, of course, that the class of functions for which these piecewise polynomials form a basis is the set of polynomials of degree no greater than the degree of polynomial in the basis; hence, we do not begin with an exact representation as in equation (6.7).

In spline approximation, the basis functions are polynomials over given intervals and zero outside of those intervals. The polynomials have specified contact at the endpoints of the intervals; that is, their derivatives of a specified order are continuous at the endpoints. The endpoints are called "knots". The finite approximation therefore can be smooth and, with the proper choice of knots, is close to the function being approximated at any point. The approximation, $\widehat{f}(x)$, formed as a sum of such piecewise polynomials is called a "spline". The "order" of a spline is the number of free parameters in each interval. (For polynomial splines, the order is the degree plus 1.)

There are three types of spline basis functions commonly used:

- *truncated power functions* (or just power functions). For k knots and degree p, there are $k + p + 1$ of these:

$$1, x, ..., x^p, ((x - z_1)_+)^p, ..., ((x - z_k)_+)^p.$$

   Sometimes, the constant is not used, so there are only $k + p$ functions. These are nice when we are adding or deleting knots. Deletion of the ith knot, z_i, is equivalent to removal of the basis function $((x - z_i)_+)^p$.

- *B-splines.* B-splines are probably the most widely used set of splines, and they are available in many software packages. The IMSL Library, for example, contains three routines for univariate approximations using B-splines, with options for variable knots or constraints, and routines for two- and three-dimensional approximations using tensor product B-splines. The influence of any particular B-spline coefficient extends over only a few intervals, so B-splines can provide good fits to functions that are not smooth. The B-spline functions also tend to be better conditioned than the power functions. The mathematical development of B-splines is more complicated than the power functions. De Boor (2002) provides a comprehensive development, an extensive discussion of their properties, and several Fortran routines for using B-splines and other splines.

- *"natural" polynomial splines.* These basis functions are such that the second derivative of the spline expansion is 0 for all x beyond the boundary knots. This condition can be imposed in various ways. An easy way is just to start with any set of basis functions and replace the degrees of freedom from two of them with the condition that every basis function have zero second derivative for all x beyond the boundary knots. For natural cubic splines with k knots, there are k basis functions. There is nothing "natural" about the natural polynomial splines. A way of handling the end conditions that is usually better is to remove the second and the penultimate knots and to replace them with the requirement that the basis functions have contact one order higher. (For cubics, this means that the third derivatives match.)

Some basis functions for various types of splines over the interval $[-1, 1]$ are shown in Figure 6.3.

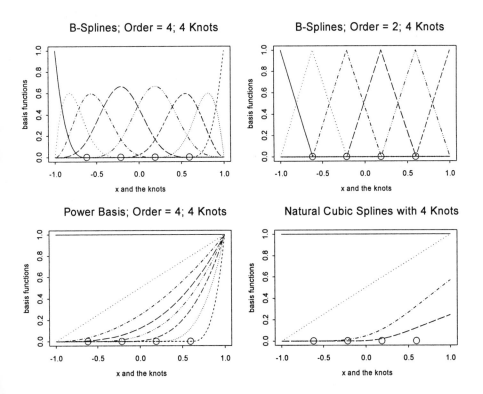

Figure 6.3: Spline Basis Functions

Interpolating Splines

Splines can be used for interpolation, approximation, and estimation. An interpolating spline fit matches each of a given set of points. Each point is usually taken as a knot, and the continuity conditions are imposed at each point. It makes sense to interpolate points that are known to be exact.

The reason to use an interpolating spline is usually to approximate a function at points other than those given (maybe for quadrature), so applied mathematicians may refer to the results of the interpolating spline as an "approximation". An interpolating spline is used when a set of points are assumed to be known exactly (more or less).

Smoothing Splines

The other way of using splines is for approximation or smoothing. The individual points may be subject to error, so the spline may not go through any of the given points. In this usage, the splines are evaluated at each abscissa point, and the ordinates are fitted by some criterion (such as least squares) to the spline.

Choice of Knots in Smoothing Splines

The choice of knots is a difficult problem when the points are measured subject to error. One approach is to include the knots as decision variables in the fitting optimization problem. This approach may be ill-posed. A common approach is to add (pre-chosen) knots in a stepwise manner. Another approach is to use a regularization method (addition of a component to the fitting optimization objective function that increases for roughness or for some other undesirable characteristic of the fit).

Multivariate Splines

Multivariate splines are easily formed as tensor products of univariate splines in the same way as the bivariate orthogonal polynomials were formed from univariate polynomials in equation (6.17). A good introduction to multivariate splines is given by Chui (1988).

Kernel Methods

Another approach to function estimation and approximation is to use a *filter* or *kernel* function to provide local weighting of the observed data. This approach ensures that at a given point the observations close to that point influence the estimate at the point more strongly than more distant observations. A standard method in this approach is to convolve the observations with a unimodal function that decreases rapidly away from a central point. This function is the filter or the kernel. A kernel has two arguments representing the two points in the convolution, but we typically use a single argument that represents the distance between the two points.

Some examples of univariate kernel functions are shown below.

uniform: $K_u(t) = 0.5$,   for $|t| \leq 1$,
quadratic: $K_q(t) = 0.75(1 - t^2)$,   for $|t| \leq 1$,
normal: $K_n(t) = \frac{1}{\sqrt{2\pi}} e^{-t^2/2}$,   for all t.

The kernels with finite support are defined to be 0 outside that range. Often, multivariate kernels are formed as products of these or other univariate kernels.

In kernel methods, the locality of influence is controlled by a *window* around the point of interest. The choice of the size of the window is the most important issue in the use of kernel methods. In practice, for a given choice of the size of the window, the argument of the kernel function is transformed to reflect the size. The transformation is accomplished using a positive definite matrix, V, whose determinant measures the volume (size) of the window.

To estimate the function f at the point x, we first decompose f to have a factor that is a probability density function, p, as in equation (6.19),

$$f(x) = g(x)p(x).$$

For a given set of data, $x_1, \ldots, x_n$, and a given scaling transformation matrix V, the kernel estimator of the function at the point x is

$$\widehat{f(x)} = (n|V|)^{-1} \sum_{i=1}^{n} g(x)K\left(V^{-1}(x - x_i)\right). \tag{6.22}$$

In the univariate case, the size of the window is just the width h. The argument of the kernel is transformed to s/h, so the function that is convolved with the function of interest is $K(s/h)/h$. The univariate kernel estimator is

$$\widehat{f(x)} = \frac{1}{nh} \sum_{i=1}^{n} g(x)K\left(\frac{x - x_i}{h}\right).$$

We discuss kernel methods in more detail in Section 9.3 in the context of estimating a probability density function.

6.2   Pointwise Properties of Function Estimators

The statistical properties of an estimator of a function at a given point are analogous to the usual statistical properties of an estimator of a scalar parameter. The statistical properties involve expectations or other properties of random variables. In the following, when we write an expectation, $E(\cdot)$, or a variance, $V(\cdot)$, the expectations are usually taken with respect to the (unknown) distribution of the underlying random variable. Occasionally, we may explicitly indicate the distribution by writing, for example, $E_p(\cdot)$, where p is the density of the random variable with respect to which the expectation is taken.

Bias

The bias of the estimator of a function value at the point x is

$$E\big(\widehat{f}(x)\big) - f(x).$$

If this bias is zero, we would say that the estimator is unbiased at the point x. If the estimator is unbiased at every point x in the domain of f, we say that the estimator is pointwise unbiased. Obviously, in order for $\widehat{f}(\cdot)$ to be pointwise unbiased, it must be defined over the full domain of f.

Variance

The variance of the estimator at the point x is

$$V\big(\widehat{f}(x)\big) = E\left(\big(\widehat{f}(x) - E(\widehat{f}(x))\big)^2 \right).$$

Estimators with small variance are generally more desirable, and an optimal estimator is often taken as the one with smallest variance among a class of unbiased estimators.

Mean Squared Error

The mean squared error, MSE, at the point x is

$$\text{MSE}\big(\widehat{f}(x)\big) = E\left(\big(\widehat{f}(x) - f(x)\big)^2 \right). \tag{6.23}$$

The mean squared error is the sum of the variance and the square of the bias:

$$
\begin{aligned}
\text{MSE}\big(\widehat{f}(x)\big) &= E\left(\big(\widehat{f}(x)\big)^2 - 2\widehat{f}(x)f(x) + \big(f(x)\big)^2 \right) \\
&= V\big(\widehat{f}(x)\big) + \left(E(\widehat{f}(x)) - f(x) \right)^2. \tag{6.24}
\end{aligned}
$$

Sometimes, the variance of an unbiased estimator is much greater than that of an estimator that is only slightly biased, so it is often appropriate to compare the mean squared error of the two estimators. In some cases, as we will see, unbiased estimators do not exist, so rather than seek an unbiased estimator with a small variance, we seek an estimator with a small MSE.

Mean Absolute Error

The mean absolute error, MAE, at the point x is similar to the MSE:

$$\text{MAE}\big(\widehat{f}(x)\big) = E\left(\big|\widehat{f}(x) - f(x)\big| \right). \tag{6.25}$$

It is more difficult to do mathematical analysis of the MAE than it is for the MSE. Furthermore, the MAE does not have a simple decomposition into other meaningful quantities similar to the MSE.

Consistency

Consistency of an estimator refers to the convergence of the expected value of the estimator to what is being estimated as the sample size increases without bound. A point estimator T_n, based on a sample of size n, is consistent for θ if

$$E(T_n) \to \theta \quad \text{as } n \to \infty.$$

The convergence is stochastic, of course, so there are various types of convergence that can be required for consistency. The most common kind of convergence considered is weak convergence, or convergence in probability.

In addition to the type of stochastic convergence, we may consider the convergence of various measures of the estimator. In general, if m is a function (usually a vector-valued function that is an elementwise norm), we may define consistency of an estimator T_n in terms of m if

$$E(m(T_n - \theta)) \to 0. \tag{6.26}$$

For an estimator, we are often interested in *weak convergence in mean square* or *weak convergence in quadratic mean*, so the common definition of consistency of T_n is

$$E((T_n - \theta)^{\mathrm{T}}(T_n - \theta)) \to 0,$$

where the type of convergence is convergence in probability. Consistency defined by convergence in mean square is also called L_2 consistency.

If convergence does occur, we are interested in the rate of convergence. We define rate of convergence in terms of a function of n, say $r(n)$, such that

$$E(m(T_n - \theta)) = O(r(n)).$$

A common form of $r(n)$ is n^α, where $\alpha < 0$. For example, in the simple case of a univariate population with a finite mean μ and finite second moment, use of the sample mean $\bar{x}$ as the estimator T_n, and use of $m(z) = z^2$, we have

$$\begin{aligned} E(m(\bar{x} - \mu)) &= E((\bar{x} - \mu)^2) \\ &= \mathrm{MSE}(\bar{x}) \\ &= O(n^{-1}). \end{aligned}$$

See Exercise 6.7, page 151.

In the estimation of a function, we say that the estimator $\widehat{f}$ of the function f is *pointwise consistent* if

$$E(\widehat{f}(x)) \to f(x) \tag{6.27}$$

for every x the domain of f. Just as in the estimation of a parameter, there are various kinds of pointwise consistency in the estimation of a function. If the convergence in expression (6.27) is in probability, for example, we say that the estimator is weakly pointwise consistent. We could also define other kinds of pointwise consistency in function estimation along the lines of other types of consistency.

6.3 Global Properties of Estimators of Functions

Often, we are interested in some measure of the statistical properties of an estimator of a function over the full domain of the function. The obvious way of defining statistical properties of an estimator of a function is to integrate the pointwise properties discussed in the previous section.

Statistical properties of a function, such as the bias of the function, are often defined in terms of a norm of the function.

For comparing $\widehat{f}(x)$ and $f(x)$, the L_p norm of the error is

$$\left(\int_D |\widehat{f}(x) - f(x)|^p \, dx \right)^{1/p}, \tag{6.28}$$

where D is the domain of f. The integral may not exist, of course. Clearly, the estimator $\widehat{f}$ must also be defined over the same domain.

Three useful measures are the L_1 norm, also called the *integrated absolute error*, or IAE,

$$\text{IAE}(\widehat{f}) = \int_D \left| \widehat{f}(x) - f(x) \right| \, dx, \tag{6.29}$$

the square of the L_2 norm, also called the *integrated squared error*, or ISE,

$$\text{ISE}(\widehat{f}) = \int_D \left(\widehat{f}(x) - f(x) \right)^2 \, dx, \tag{6.30}$$

and the L_∞ norm, the *sup absolute error*, or SAE,

$$\text{SAE}(\widehat{f}) = \sup \left| \widehat{f}(x) - f(x) \right|. \tag{6.31}$$

The L_1 measure is invariant under monotone transformations of the coordinate axes, but the measure based on the L_2 norm is not. See Exercise 6.2 on page 150.

The L_∞ norm, or SAE, is the most often used measure in general function approximation. In statistical applications, this measure applied to two cumulative distribution functions is the *Kolmogorov distance*. The measure is not so useful in comparing densities and is not often used in density estimation.

Other measures of the difference in $\widehat{f}$ and f over the full range of x are the Kullback-Leibler measure,

$$\int_D \widehat{f}(x) \log \left(\frac{\widehat{f}(x)}{f(x)} \right) \, dx,$$

and the Hellinger distance,

$$\left(\int_D \left(\widehat{f}^{1/p}(x) - f^{1/p}(x) \right)^p \, dx \right)^{1/p}.$$

For $p = 2$, the Hellinger distance is also called the Matusita distance.

Integrated Bias and Variance

We now want to develop global concepts of bias and variance for estimators of functions. Bias and variance are statistical properties that involve expectations of random variables. The obvious global measures of bias and variance are just the pointwise measures integrated over the domain. In the case of the bias, of course, we must integrate the absolute value, otherwise points of negative bias could cancel out points of positive bias.

The estimator $\widehat{f}$ is pointwise unbiased if

$$E\big(\widehat{f}(x)\big) = f(x) \quad \text{for all } x \in \mathbb{R}^d.$$

Because we are interested in the bias over the domain of the function, we define the *integrated absolute bias* as

$$\text{IAB}\big(\widehat{f}\big) = \int_D \left| E\big(\widehat{f}(x)\big) - f(x) \right| dx \tag{6.32}$$

and the *integrated squared bias* as

$$\text{ISB}\big(\widehat{f}\big) = \int_D \left(E\big(\widehat{f}(x)\big) - f(x) \right)^2 dx. \tag{6.33}$$

If the estimator is unbiased, both the integrated absolute bias and integrated squared bias are 0. This, of course, would mean that the estimator is pointwise unbiased almost everywhere. Although it is not uncommon to have unbiased estimators of scalar parameters or even of vector parameters with a countable number of elements, it is not likely that an estimator of a function could be unbiased at almost all points in a dense domain. ("Almost" means all except possibly a set with a probability measure of 0.)

The *integrated variance* is defined in a similar manner:

$$
\begin{aligned}
\text{IV}\big(\widehat{f}\big) &= \int_D V\big(\widehat{f}(x)\big)\, dx \\
&= \int_D E\Big(\big(\widehat{f}(x) - E(\widehat{f}(x))\big)^2 \Big)\, dx. \tag{6.34}
\end{aligned}
$$

Integrated Mean Squared Error and Mean Absolute Error

As we suggested above, global unbiasedness is generally not to be expected. An important measure for comparing estimators of funtions is, therefore, based on the mean squared error.

The *integrated mean squared error* is

$$
\begin{aligned}
\text{IMSE}\big(\widehat{f}\big) &= \int_D E\Big(\big(\widehat{f}(x) - f(x)\big)^2 \Big)\, dx \\
&= \text{IV}\big(\widehat{f}\big) + \text{ISB}\big(\widehat{f}\big) \tag{6.35}
\end{aligned}
$$

(compare equations (6.23) and (6.24)).

If the expectation integration can be interchanged with the outer integration in the expression above, we have

$$
\begin{aligned}
\text{IMSE}(\widehat{f}) &= \text{E}\left(\int_D \left(\widehat{f}(x) - f(x)\right)^2 dx\right) \\
&= \text{MISE}(\widehat{f}),
\end{aligned}
$$

the *mean integrated squared error*. We will assume that this interchange leaves the integrals unchanged, so we will use MISE and IMSE interchangeably.

Similarly, for the *integrated mean absolute error*, we have

$$
\begin{aligned}
\text{IMAE}(\widehat{f}) &= \int_D \text{E}\left(\left|\widehat{f}(x) - f(x)\right|\right) dx \\
&= \text{E}\left(\int_D \left|\widehat{f}(x) - f(x)\right| dx\right) \\
&= \text{MIAE}(\widehat{f}),
\end{aligned}
$$

the *mean integrated absolute error*.

Mean SAE

The *mean sup absolute error*, or MSAE, is

$$
\text{MSAE}(\widehat{f}) = \int_D \text{E}\left(\sup|\widehat{f}(x) - f(x)|\right) dx. \tag{6.36}
$$

This measure is not very useful unless the variation in the function f is relatively small. For example, if f is a density function, $\widehat{f}$ can be a "good" estimator, yet the MSAE may be quite large. On the other hand, if f is a cumulative distribution function (monotonically ranging from 0 to 1), the MSAE may be a good measure of how well the estimator performs. As mentioned earlier, the SAE is the *Kolmogorov distance*. The Kolmogorov distance (and, hence, the SAE and the MSAE) does poorly in measuring differences in the tails of the distribution.

Large-Sample Statistical Properties

The pointwise consistency properties are extended to the full function in the obvious way. In the notation of expression (6.26), consistency of the function estimator is defined in terms of

$$
\int_D \text{E}\left(m(\widehat{f}(x) - f(x))\right) dx \to 0.
$$

The estimator of the function is said to be *mean square consistent* or L_2 *consistent* if the MISE converges to 0; that is,

$$
\int_D \text{E}\left((\widehat{f}(x) - f(x))^2\right) dx \to 0.
$$

If the convergence is weak, that is, if it is convergence in probability, we say that the function estimator is weakly consistent; if the convergence is strong, that is, if it is convergence almost surely or with probability 1, we say the function estimator is strongly consistent.

The estimator of the function is said to be L_1 *consistent* if the mean integrated absolute error (MIAE) converges to 0; that is,

$$\int_D \mathrm{E}\Big(\big|\widehat{f}(x) - f(x)\big|\Big)\, \mathrm{d}x \;\to\; 0.$$

As with the other kinds of consistency, the nature of the convergence in the definition may be expressed in the qualifiers "weak" or "strong".

As we have mentioned above, the integrated absolute error is invariant under monotone transformations of the coordinate axes, but the L_2 measures are not. As with most work in L_1, however, derivation of various properties of IAE or MIAE is more difficult than for analogous properties with respect to L_2 criteria.

If the MISE converges to 0, we are interested in the rate of convergence. To determine this, we seek an expression of MISE as a function of n. We do this by a Taylor series expansion.

In general, if $\widehat{\theta}$ is an estimator of θ, the Taylor series for $\mathrm{ISE}(\widehat{\theta})$, equation (6.30), about the true value is

$$\mathrm{ISE}(\widehat{\theta}) = \sum_{k=0}^{\infty} \frac{1}{k!} \left(\widehat{\theta} - \theta\right)^k \mathrm{ISE}^{k'}(\theta), \tag{6.37}$$

where $\mathrm{ISE}^{k'}(\theta)$ represents the kth derivative of ISE evaluated at θ.

Taking the expectation in equation (6.37) yields the MISE. The limit of the MISE as $n \to \infty$ is the *asymptotic mean integrated squared error*, AMISE. One of the most important properties of an estimator is the order of the AMISE.

In the case of an unbiased estimator, the first two terms in the Taylor series expansion are zero, and the AMISE is

$$\mathrm{V}(\widehat{\theta})\,\mathrm{ISE}''(\theta)$$

to terms of second order.

Other Global Properties of Estimators of Functions

There are often other properties that we would like an estimator of a function to possess. We may want the estimator to weight given functions in some particular way. For example, if we know how the function to be estimated, f, weights a given function r, we may require that the estimate $\widehat{f}$ weight the function r in the same way; that is,

$$\int_D r(x)\widehat{f}(x)\mathrm{d}x = \int_D r(x)f(x)\mathrm{d}x.$$

We may want to restrict the minimum and maximum values of the estimator. For example, because many functions of interest are nonnegative, we may want to require that the estimator be nonnegative.

We may want to restrict the variation in the function. This can be thought of as the "roughness" of the function. A reasonable measure of the variation is

$$\int_D \left(f(x) - \int_D f(x)dx \right)^2 dx.$$

If the integral $\int_D f(x)dx$ is constrained to be some constant (such as 1 in the case that $f(x)$ is a probability density), then the variation can be measured by the square of the L_2 norm,

$$S(f) = \int_D \left(f(x) \right)^2 dx. \tag{6.38}$$

We may want to restrict the derivatives of the estimator or the smoothness of the estimator. Another intuitive measure of the roughness of a twice-differentiable and integrable univariate function f is the integral of the square of the second derivative:

$$\mathcal{R}(f) = \int_D \left(f''(x) \right)^2 dx. \tag{6.39}$$

Often, in function estimation, we may seek an estimator $\hat{f}$ such that its roughness (by some definition) is small.

Exercises

6.1. Derive equation (6.8) from equation (6.7).

6.2. Show that the L_1 norm of $f_a(ax)$, for any given $a \neq 0$, is the same as the L_1 norm of $f(x)$, and show that the L_2 norm of $f_a(ax)$ is not the same as the L_2 norm of $f(x)$.

6.3. Let $\{q_k : k = 1, \dots, m\}$ be a set of orthogonal functions. Show that

$$\left\| \sum_{k=1}^m q_k \right\|^2 = \sum_{k=1}^m \|q_k\|^2.$$

What is the common value of the expressions above if the q_k are orthonormal? In these expressions, $\|\cdot\|$ represents an L_2 norm. Would a similar equation hold for a general L_p norm?

6.4. Prove that the Fourier coefficients form the finite expansion in basis functions with the minimum mean squared error (that is, prove inequality (6.10) on page 134). *Hint:* Write $\|f - a_0 q_0\|^2$ as a function of a_0, $\langle f, f \rangle - 2a_0 \langle f, q_0 \rangle + a_0^2 \langle q_0, q_0 \rangle$, differentiate, set to zero for the minimum, and determine $a_0 = c_0$ (equation (6.8)). This same approach can be done in multidimensions for $a_0, a_1, \dots, a_k$, or else induction can be used from a_1 on.

6.5. Using equations (6.6) and their extensions and beginning with $T_0(t) = 1$ and $T_1(t) = t$, derive the first four Chebyshev polynomials, $T_0(t)$, $T_1(t)$, $T_2(t)$, and $T_3(t)$.

6.6. Approximate $f(t) = e^t$ over $[-1, 1]$ as

$$\sum_{k=0}^{3} c_k P_k(t),$$

where the $P_k(t)$ are the Legendre polynomials.

(a) Graph the function and your approximation.

(b) Determine the error at $t = 0$.

(c) Determine the integrated squared error.

(d) Would some more general sequence of Jacobi polynomials form a better approximation? Why do you think so? What values of α and β might be more approriate?

(e) For reasonable values of α and β from the previous question, derive $J_0^{(\alpha,\beta)}(t)$, $J_1^{(\alpha,\beta)}(t)$, $J_2^{(\alpha,\beta)}(t)$, and $J_3^{(\alpha,\beta)}(t)$. Now, approximate $f(t) = e^t$ over $[-1, 1]$ with your polynomials and determine the error at $t = 0$ and the integrated squared error.

6.7. Consider the problem of estimating μ and σ (the mean and standard deviation) in a normal distribution. For estimators in a sample of size n, we will use the sample mean, $\bar{y}_n$, and the sample standard deviation, s_n. Assume that

$$\text{MSE}(\bar{y}_n) = \text{O}(n^\alpha)$$

and

$$\text{MSE}(s_n) = \text{O}(n^\beta).$$

Perform a Monte Carlo experiment to estimate α and β. Plot your data on log-log axes, and use least squares to estimate α and β. Now, derive the exact values for α and β and compare them with your estimates.

6.8. Using equations (6.35), (6.34), and (6.33) to show that $\text{MISE}(\hat{f}) = \text{IV}(\hat{f}) + \text{ISB}(\hat{f})$.

6.9. Some problems in function estimation are relatively easy. Conside the problem of estimation of

$$f(t) = \alpha + \beta t,$$

for $t \in [0, 1]$. Suppose, for $t_1, \ldots, t_n$ we observe $f(t_1) + \epsilon_1, \ldots, f(t_n) + \epsilon_n$, where the ϵ_i are independent realizations from a $\text{N}(0, \sigma^2)$ distribution. As we know, a good estimator of $f(t)$ is $\hat{f}(t) = \hat{\alpha} + \hat{\beta} t$, where $\hat{\alpha}$ and $\hat{\beta}$ are the least squares estimators from the data. Determine $\text{MISE}(\hat{f})$.

6.10. Compute roughness measures of your Legendre-polynomial approximation in Exercise 6.6. Compute both $\mathcal{S}(\hat{f})$ in equation (6.38) and $\mathcal{R}(\hat{f})$ in equation (6.39).

6.11. Let

$$p(x) = \frac{1}{\sqrt{2\pi}\sigma} e^{-x^2/(2\sigma^2)}$$

(the normal density with mean equal to 0).

(a) Compute $\mathcal{S}(p)$.

(b) Compute $\mathcal{S}(p')$.

(c) Compute $\mathcal{S}(p'') = \mathcal{R}(p)$.

6.12. Develop an extension of the roughness definition given in equation (6.39) for functions of more than one variable. (You obviously use the Hessian. How do you map it to $\mathbb{R}$?)

Chapter 7

Graphical Methods in Computational Statistics

One of the first steps in attempting to understand data is to visualize it. Visualization of data and information provides a wealth of psychological tools that can be used in detecting features, in discovering relationships, and finally in retaining the knowledge gained.

Graphical displays have always been an important part of statistical data analysis, but with the continuing developments in high-speed computers and high-resolution devices, the usefulness of graphics has greatly increased. Higher resolution makes for a more visually pleasing display, and occasionally it allows features to be seen that could not be distinguished otherwise. The most important effects of the computer on graphical methods in statistics, however, arise from the ease and speed with which graphical displays can be produced. Rapid production of graphical displays has introduced motion and articulated projections and sections into statistical graphics. Such graphical methods are important tools of computational statistics. The multiple views are tools of discovery, not just ways of displaying a set of data that has already been analyzed.

Proper design of a graphical display depends on the context of the application and the purpose of the graphics, whether it is for the analyst to get a better understanding of the data or to present a picture that conveys a message. Our emphasis in the following discussion is on methods useful in exploratory graphics.

One thing that seems to be lagging in the statistical literature is the use of color in graphical displays. The first mainstream statistical article to include color graphics was in 1979 (Fienberg, 1979), but we have yet to see the widespread use of color graphics in statistical articles. The simple mechanics used in producing popular magazines are yet to be incorporated in the production of learned journals. Journals available in electronic form do not have these production problems.

Data of three or fewer dimensions can be portrayed on a two-dimensional surface fairly easily, but for data of higher dimensions, various transformations must be employed. The simplest transformations are just projections, but transformations of points into other geometric objects may often reveal salient features. It is useful to have multiple views of the data in which graphical objects are linked by color or some other visual indicator.

The number of variables and the number of observations may determine the way that graphical displays are constructed. If the number of observations is large we may first make a few plots of samples of the full dataset. Even for multivariate data, some initial plots of single variables may be useful. For univariate data $x_1, x_2, \ldots$, quick insights can be obtained by a "4-plot" (Filliben, 1982) that consists of the following four plots:

- plot of x_i versus i to see if there is any trend in the way the data are ordered, which is likely to be the order in which the data were collected;

- plot of x_{i+1} versus x_i to see if there are systematic lags (again, this is done because of possible effects of the order in which the data were collected);

- histogram;

- normal probability plot of the data.

A preliminary 4-plot for each variable on a dataset can be a useful, automatic part of almost any analysis of data.

In this chapter, we begin with basic elements of a graphical display and then discuss methods of plotting a small number of variables. Graphical displays of one, two, or three variables are relatively straightforward. Displays of multivariate data are much more complicated. It is, however, in higher dimensions that visualization offers the greatest benefits in understanding data. We will briefly discuss the visualization of multivariate data. Young, Faldowski, and McFarlane (1993) provide more extensive discussions of issues in multivariate visualization. Banchoff (1996) discusses the geometry of higher dimensions and its applications to computer graphics.

Most often we are interested in graphical representations of a dataset, but we can distinguish three basic types of objects that a graphical display may represent:

- discrete data;

- mathematical functions;

- geometrical objects.

The graphical elements that represent discrete data are simple plotting symbols: dots, circles, and so on. The graphical elements that represent functions or geometrical objects may be curves or surfaces. Because of the discrete nature of the picture elements (pixels) of a graphical display, both continuous functions and geometrical objects must be converted to discrete data to produce a graph.

Hence, beginning with either functions or geometrical objects, we arrive at the task of graphing discrete data. The data, at the lowest level, correspond to adjacent pixels.

The basic activity in producing a graphical display is to translate data represented in a "world coordinate system" into a representation in a graphics "device coordinate system". Positions in the world coordinate system are represented in the computer in its floating-point scheme. Positions in the device coordinate system correspond to picture elements, or "pixels", which can appear as black or white dots or dots of various colors. The graphical display is the pointillistic image produced by the pixels. The type of the coordinate system used, cartesian or homogeneous, may depend on the types of transformations on the data to be performed in the graphical analysis (see Riesenfeld, 1981).

The images themselves are usually constructed in one of two ways: as a raster or as a vector. A raster image is a fixed set of pixels. It is resolution-dependent, so if it is displayed at a higher resolution or its size is increased, jagged edges may appear. A vector image is made up of mathematically defined lines and curves. The definitions do not depend on the resolution. Modifications to the image, such as moving it or changing its size, are relatively simple and scalable because they are made to the mathematical definition.

7.1 Viewing One, Two, or Three Variables

Plots of one or two variables are easy to construct and often easy to interpret. Plots of three variables can use some of the same techniques as for one or two variables. For datasets with more variables, it is often useful to look at the variables one, two, or three at a time, or to look at projections of all variables into a two- or three-dimensional subspace.

One of the most important properties of data is the shape of its distribution, that is, a general characterization of the density of the data. The density of the data is measured by a nonnegative real number. The density is thus an additional variable on the dataset. The basic tool for looking at the shape of the distribution of univariate data is the *histogram*. A histogram is a graph of the counts or the relative frequency of the data within contiguous regions called bins. Graphs such as histograms that represent the density have one more dimension than the dimension of the original dataset.

A *scatter plot*, which is just a plot of the points on cartesian axes representing the variables, is useful for showing the distribution of two-dimensional data. The dimension of the scatter plot is the same as the dimension of the data. In a scatter plot, data density is portrayed by the density of the points in the plot.

We use the phrases "two-dimensional" and "three-dimensional" in reference to graphical displays to refer to the dimension of the space that the display depicts in a cartesian system. Thus, the dimension of a scatter plot of either two or three variables is the same as the dimension of the data, although in either case the actual display either on a monitor or on paper is two-dimensional.

In statistical displays, we often are interested in an additional dimension that represents the distribution or density of the data. As noted above, plots representing densities have one more dimension than the data.

A three-dimensional plot on a two-dimensional surface is sometimes called a "perspective plot". Important characteristics of a perspective plot are the viewing angle and the assumed position of the eye that is viewing the plot. In a perspective plot, the simulated location of the eye determines the viewing angle or line of sight and also affects the perspective.

An effective simple way of reducing a three-dimensional display to a two-dimensional one is by use of contour lines, or contour bands (usually of different colors). A contour line represents a path over which the values in the dimension not represented are constant.

Histograms and Variations

A histogram is a presentation, either graphical or tabular, of the counts of binned or discrete data. The vertical axis in a histogram may be the counts in the bins or may be proportions such that the total area adds up to 1.

The formation of bins for grouping data is one of the most fundamental aspects of visualizing and understanding data. The bins in a histogram generally all have the same width, but this is not necessary; sometimes, if there are only a small number of observations over a wide range, the bins over that range can be made wider to smooth out the roughness of the variation in the small counts.

The number of bins in a histogram can markedly affect its appearance, especially if the number of observations is small. In Figure 7.1, four histograms are shown, each of the same dataset. The data are a pseudorandom sample of size 30 from a gamma distribution with shape parameter 3 and scale parameter 10. In this simple example, we get different pictures of the overall shape of the data depending on the number of bins. It is worthwhile to consider this example of a small dataset because the same issues may arise even in very large datasets in high dimensions. In such cases, we also have "small sample" problems.

More bins give a rougher appearance of the histogram. Either too few or too many bins can obscure structure in the data. In Figure 7.1, when only three or four bins are used, the curvature of the density is not apparent; conversely, when twelve bins are used, it is difficult to ascertain any simple pattern in the data. In general, the number of bins should be greater for a larger number of observations. A simple rule for the approximate number of bins to use is

$$1 + \log_2 n,$$

where n is the number of observations.

Figure 7.2 shows the same data as used in Figure 7.1 and with the same cutpoints for the bins as the histogram with seven bins, except that the last two bins have been combined. The appearance of the histogram is smoother

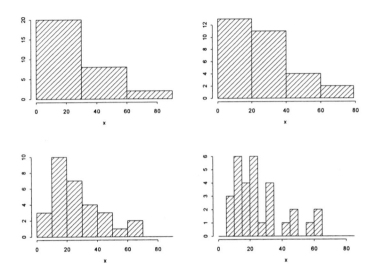

Figure 7.1: Histograms of the Same Data with Different Fixed Bin Sizes (Data from a Gamma Distribution)

and, in fact, is closer to the appearance expected of a histogram of a sample from a gamma distribution with a shape parameter of 3.

Exploring the data by using histograms with different bin widths is useful in understanding univariate data. The objective, of course, is not to match some known or desired distribution but rather to get a better view of the structure of the data. Obviously, the histogram of a random sample from a particular distribution may never look like the density of that distribution. Exploration of the data for gaining a better understanding of it is not to be confused with manipulation of the data for presentation purposes.

The appearance of a histogram can also be affected by the location of the cutpoints of the bins. The cutpoints of the histogram in the lower left of Figure 7.1, which has seven bins, are

$$0, 10, 20, 30, 40, 60, 70.$$

Shifting the cutpoints by 2, so that the cutpoints are

$$2, 12, 22, 32, 42, 62, 72,$$

results in the histogram in the upper right-hand corner of Figure 7.3, and further shifts in the cutpoints result in the other histograms in that figure. Notice the changes in the apparent structure in the data. See Simonoff (1995) for further discussion and examples of the effects of shifting the bin cutpoints. Simonoff

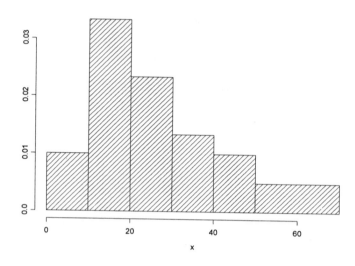

Figure 7.2: Density Histogram of the Gamma Data with Bins of Variable Widths

and Udina (1997) define an index of the stability of a histogram of a given dataset with a given number of bins.

The use of histograms with different widths and locations of bins is an example of a method of computational statistics. In the analysis of a dataset, we should consider a number of different views of the same data. The emphasis is on exploration of the data rather than on confirmation of hypotheses or graphical presentation.

In the toy example that we considered, we could attribute the problems to the relatively small sample size and so perhaps decide that the problems are not very relevant. These same kinds of problems, however, can occur in very large datasets if the number of variables is large.

The Empirical Cumulative Distribution Function and q-q Plots

The empirical cumulative distribution function, or ECDF, is one of the most useful summaries of a univariate sample. The ECDF is a step function, with a saltus of $\frac{1}{n}$ at each point in a sample of size n. A variation of the ECDF, the broken-line ECDF, with lines connecting the points, is often more useful. A plot of the broken-line ECDF is shown in the graph on the left-hand side in Figure 7.4.

Another variation of an ECDF plot is one that is folded at the median. Such a plot is called a *mountain plot*. It is often easier to see certain properties, such as symmetry, in a mountain plot (see Monti, 1995). A folded ECDF plot, or

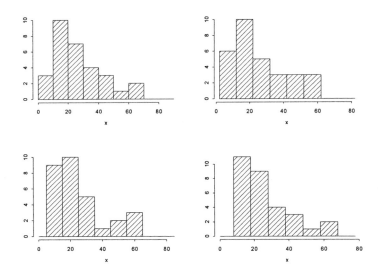

Figure 7.3: Histograms of the Same Set of Gamma Data with Different Locations of Bins

mountain plot, is shown on the right in Figure 7.4.

The plot of the ECDF provides a simple comparison of the sample with the uniform distribution. If the sample were from a uniform distribution, the broken-line ECDF would be close to a straight line, and the folded ECDF would be close to an isosceles triangle. The ECDF of a unimodal sample is concave. The ECDF of a multimodal sample is convex over some intervals. The plots of the sample of gamma variates in Figure 7.4 show a skewed, unimodal pattern.

A sample can be compared to some other distribution very easily by a transformation of the vertical axis so that it corresponds to the cumulative distribution function of the given distribution. If the vertical axis is transformed in this way, a broken-line ECDF plot of a sample from that distribution would be close to a straight line. A plot with a transformed vertical axis is called a probability plot. Many years ago, it was common to have graph paper in which the scale of the vertical axis corresponded to the quantiles of a standard distribution such as the normal or the Weibull distribution.

A related plot is the quantile-quantile plot or q-q plot. In this kind of plot, the quantiles or "scores" of the reference distribution are plotted against the sorted data. The $1/n^{\mathrm{th}}$ quantile is plotted against the first order statistic in the sample of size n, and so on. As we mentioned on page 14, there are different ways of defining the empirical quantiles. The kth smallest value should correspond to a value of p approximately equal to k/n or to $(k-1)/n$. A common way is

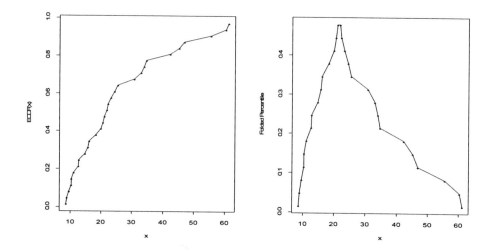

Figure 7.4: Plots of a Broken-Line ECDF and a Folded ECDF or Mountain Plot of Data from a Gamma Distribution

just to split the difference and use

$$p_k = (k - 1/2)/n.$$

The kth smallest value in the sample is called the p_k^{th} *sample quantile*.

Another way of defining the kth quantile is as

$$p_k = (k - 3/8)/(n + 1/4).$$

This corresponds to values that match quantiles of a normal distribution. (Compare equation (1.7) on page 14.)

However the probability is chosen, the p_k^{th} *quantile* (or "population quantile") is the value, x_{p_k}, of the random variable, X, such that

$$\Pr(X \le x_{p_k}) = p_k.$$

In the case of the normal distribution, this value is also called the p_k^{th} *normal score*.

A q-q plot with a vertical axis corresponding to the quantiles of a gamma distribution with a shape parameter of 4 is shown on the left-hand side in Figure 7.5. This plot was produced by the S-Plus statement

```
plot(qgamma(ppoints(length(x)),4),sort(x))
```

If the relative values of the sample quantiles correspond closely to the distribution quantiles, the points fall along a straight line, as in the plot on the

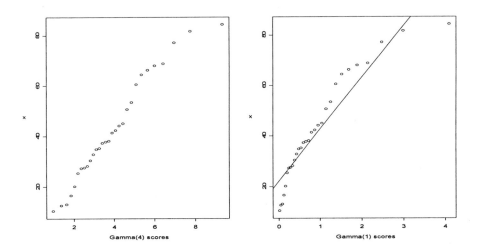

Figure 7.5: Quantile-Quantile Plot for Comparing the Sample to Gamma Distributions

left-hand side in Figure 7.5. The data shown were generated from a gamma distribution with a shape parameter of 4. When the sample quantiles are compared with the quantiles of a gamma distribution with a shape parameter of 1, as in the plot on the right-hand side in Figure 7.5, the extremes of the sample do not match the quantiles well. The pattern that we observe for the smaller observations (that is, that they are below a straight line that fits most of the data) is characteristic of data with a heavier left tail than the reference distribution to which it is being compared. Conversely, the larger observations, being below the straight line, indicate that the data have a lighter right tail than the reference distribution.

The sup absolute difference between the ECDF and the reference CDF is the *Kolmogorov distance*, which is the basis for the Kolmogorov test (and the Kolmogorov-Smirnov test) for distributions. The Kolmogorov distance, however, does poorly in measuring differences in the tails of the distribution. A q-q plot, on the other hand, generally is very good in revealing differences in the tails.

An important property of the q-q plot is that its shape is independent of the location and the scale of the data. In Figure 7.5, the sample is from a gamma distribution with a scale parameter of 10, but the distribution quantiles are from a population with a scale parameter of 1.

For a random sample from the distribution against whose quantiles it is plotted, the points generally deviate most from a straight line in the tails. This is because of the larger variability of the extreme order statistics. Also, because the distributions of the extreme statistics are skewed, the deviation from a straight line is in a specific direction (toward lighter tails) more than half of the time (see Exercise 7.2, page 188).

Plots based on the ECDF for of a multivariate dataset are generally difficult to interpret.

Smoothing

In typical applications, the observed data represent points along some continuous range of possibilities. Hence, although we begin with discrete data, we wish to graph a continuous function. We assume a continuous function as an underlying model of the process that generated the data. The process of determining a continuous function from the data is called *smoothing*.

Smoothing is often an integral process of graphing discrete data. A smooth curve helps us to visualize relationships and trends.

Graphing Continuous Functions

There are two common situations in statistics that lead to analysis of functions. Sometimes, one of the variables in a dataset is modeled as a stochastic function of the other variables, and a model of the form

$$y \approx f(x) \tag{7.1}$$

is used. The "dependent" or "response" variable y is related to the variable x by an unknown function f.

In another type of situation, the variable x is assumed to be a realization of a random variable X, and we are interested in the probability density function

$$p_X(x). \tag{7.2}$$

In both of these cases, x may be a vector.

In the former case, in which relationships of variables are being modeled as in model (7.1), the dataset consists of pairs (y_i, x_i). A smooth curve or surface that represents an estimate or an approximation of f helps us to understand the relationship between y and x. Fitting this curve smooths the scatter plot of y_i versus x_i. There are, of course, several ways of smoothing the data, as discussed in a number of texts, such as Bowman and Azzalini (1997), Eubank (1999), and Simonoff (1996).

Bézier Curves

In graphical applications and in geometric modeling, Bézier curves are used extensively because they are quickly computed. Bézier curves are smooth curves in two dimensions that connect two given points with a shape that depends on points in between (see Bézier, 1986, and Mortenson, 1997). For a given set of points in two dimensions, $p_0, p_1, \ldots, p_n$, called control points, Bézier curves are required to satisfy two conditions:

1. The two endpoints p_0 and p_n must be interpolated.

2. The rth derivatives at p_0 and p_n are determined by r adjacent points to produce a smooth curve. The first derivative at p_0, for example, is the line determined by p_0 and p_1.

These conditions obviously do not uniquely determine the curves.

The Bézier curve is defined as the set of points p (that is, in two dimensions, $p = (x, y)$), defined by

$$p(u) = \sum_{i=0}^{n} p_i B_{i,n}(u),$$

where, for integers i and n with $0 \le i \le n$, p_i is one of the points to be interpolated, and $B_{i,n}(u)$ is the Bernstein polynomial,

$$B_{i,n}(u) = \frac{n!}{i!(n-i)!} u^i (1-u)^{n-i} \quad \text{for} \quad u \in [0,1]. \tag{7.3}$$

For example,

$$
\begin{aligned}
B_{0,3}(u) &= (1-u)^3, \\
B_{1,3}(u) &= 3u(1-u)^2, \\
B_{2,3}(u) &= 3u^2(1-u), \\
B_{3,3}(u) &= u^3.
\end{aligned}
$$

The Bernstein polynomials are essentially the same as the beta weight function used in defining the Jacobi polynomials (see page 136). (The difference in the finite ranges can easily be accommodated by a linear transformation.)

For $n + 1$ data points, $(x_0, y_0), (x_1, y_1), \ldots, (x_n, y_n)$, we use the series of Bernstein polynomials $B_{i,n}(u)$ for $i = 0 \ldots n$.

Note that because of the form of the Bernstein polynomials, the sequence of points could be reversed without changing the curve.

Two quadratic Bézier curves, each determined by three control points, are shown in Figure 7.6.

Continuous Densities

If no particular variable is considered a dependent variable, we may be interested in the probability density function p that describes the distribution of a random variable. A histogram is one representation of the probability density. The histogram is one of the oldest methods of smoothing data, but the histogram itself can be smoothed in various ways, or, alternatively, other smooth estimates of the density can be computed.

Fitting models using observed data is an important aspect of statistical data analysis. Distributional assumptions may be used to arrive at precise

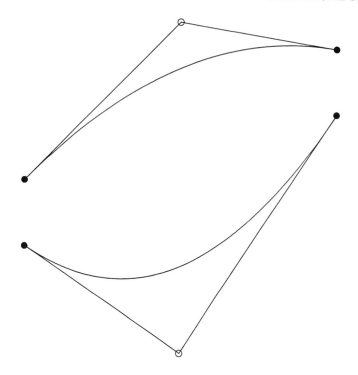

Figure 7.6: Quadratic Bézier Curves and Control Points

statements about parameters in the model. Smoothing for graphical displays is generally less formal. The purpose is to help us to visualize relationships and distributions without making formal inferences about models.

Representation of the Third Dimension

Contours represent one extra dimension, so three-dimensional data are often represented on a two-dimensional surface in a *contour plot*. A contour plot is especially useful if one variable is a "dependent" variable (that is, one for which we are interested in its relationship or dependence on the two other variables). In a contour plot, lines or color bands are used to represent regions over which the values of the dependent variable are constant.

For representing three-dimensional data in which one variable is a dependent variable, an *image plot* is particularly useful. An image plot is a plot of three-dimensional data in which one dimension is represented by color or by a gray scale.

Image plots are especially useful in identifying structural dependencies. They are often used when the two "independent" variables are categorical. In such cases, the ordering of the categories along the two axes has a major effect on the appearance of the plot. Figure 7.7 shows four image plots of the same

set of data representing gene expression activity for 500 genes from cells from
60 different locations in a human patient. In the plot in the upper left, the
cells and genes are arbitrarily positioned along the axes, whereas in the other
plots there has been an attempt to arrange the cells and/or genes along their
respective axes to discover whether patterns may be present.

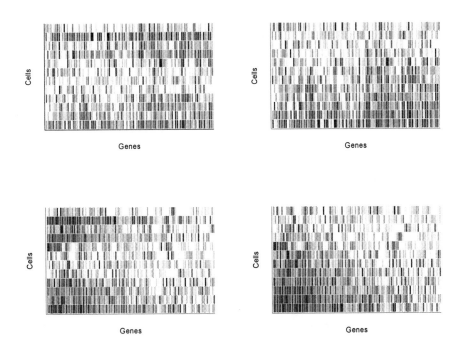

Figure 7.7: Image Plots with Different Orderings of the Categorical Variables

Exploration with image plots is a powerful tool for discovering structure
and relationships. Clustering methods discussed in Chapter 10 can be used to
suggest orderings of the categorical variables. A "clustered image map" can
be particularly useful in detecting structural differences. See the programs and
data at

http://discover.nci.nih.gov

Both contour plots and image plots can be effective for large datasets in
which overplotting would be a serious problem in other types of plots.

Contour plots are produced by the **contour** function in both S-Plus and R,
and image plots are produced by the **image** function in both packages.

Other methods of representing the third dimension use color or some other
noncartesian property, such as discussed for general multivariate data beginning

on page 172. Another approach for three-dimensional data is to simulate a visual perception of depth.

Some methods of representing three-dimensional data attempt to simulate a geometric object. These methods include *direct volume rendering* and *surface rendering*. In either case, an important consideration is the point, called the viewpoint, from which the space is viewed. In some cases, the viewpoint may be a pair of points corresponding to the viewer's two eyes.

In direct volume rendering, we attempt to display the density of material or data along imaginary rays from the viewer's eyes through the dataset. This procedure is called ray tracing. The volume is rendered by assigning values to voxels (three-dimensional equivalents of pixels). In one form, called binary voxel volume rendering, the first object along the ray from the viewer's eye results in an opaque voxel that hides objects farther along the ray. Binary rendering is often done by "z-buffering". In this technique, a value representing the depth of each point (discretized as a pixel) is stored, and the minimum such depth (discretized) from the viewpoint is stored in a "z-buffer". (It is called this because in graphics for three dimensions, a cartesian coordinate system (x, y, z) is commonly used, and by custom the plane of the display is the x-y plane, or that plane moved slightly.) A point is hidden if its depth is greater than the value in the z-buffer for that direction. In another form, called semitransparent volume rendering, a transparency is assigned to a voxel based on the value of the parameter that is being rendered. This allows visualization of the interior of an object. This technique is widely used in medical imaging.

The simplest method of representing a surface is by use of a "wire frame", which is a grid deformed to lie on the surface. Generally, in a wire frame, the grid lines on regions of surfaces that would be obscured by other surfaces are not shown. This is usually done by z-buffering. Sometimes, however, it is useful to show the hidden lines in a wire frame. Sewell (1988a, 1988b) describes a wire frame composed of thin bands instead of wires or single lines. Using bands, it is possible to show lines that would be hidden but make clear that those lines are in the background. It is often useful to combine a wire frame with a contour plot on the flat surface representing the plane of two variables.

Other ways of depicting the surface, which use a continuous representation, require consideration of the surface texture and the source of light that the surface reflects. We refer the reader to the texts by Foley et al. (1990) or by Wolff and Yaeger (1993) for discussions of the lighting models that lead to various ways of depicting a surface.

A perception of depth or a third dimension in a two-dimensional display can be induced by use of two horizontally juxtaposed displays of the same set of points and a mechanism to cause one of the viewer's eyes to concentrate on one display and the other eye to concentrate on the other display. The stereo pair may be in different colors, and the viewer uses glasses with one lens of one color and the other lens of the other color (the colors are chosen so that a lens of one color cancels the other color). Such a pair is called an *anaglyph*. Another type of stereo pair, called a *stereogram*, requires the viewer to defocus each separate view and fuse the two views into a single view. This fusion can be aided by special glasses that present one view to one eye and the other view to the other eye. Many people can perform the fusion without the aid of glasses by focusing their eyes on a point either beyond the actual plane of the display or in front of the plane. Either way works. The perspective in one way is the reverse of the perspective in the other way. For some displays and for some people, one way is easier than the other. In either type of stereo pair, the features on the two displays are offset in such a way as to appear in perspective.

Figure 7.8 shows a stereogram of data with three variables, x, y, and z. The stereoscopic display is formed by two side-by-side plots of x and y in which x is on the horizontal axes and z determines the depth. The perception of depth occurs because the values of x are offset by an amount proportional to the depth. The depth at the ith point is

$$d_i = c \cdot \left(z_{\max} - z_i\right) \frac{x_{\max} - x_{\min}}{z_{\max} - z_{\min}}. \tag{7.4}$$

The choice of c in equation (7.4) depends on the separation of the displays and on the units of measurement of the variables. The left-hand plot is of the vectors $x - d$ and y, and the right-hand plot is of $x + d$ and y. If the eyes are focused behind the plane of the paper, the vertex that is lowest on the graphs in Figure 7.8 is at the front of the image; if the eyes are focused in front of the plane of the paper (that is, if the eyes are crossed) the vertex that is highest on the graphs in Figure 7.8 is at the front of the image. See Carr and Littlefield (1983) for additional details on the construction of stereo plots.

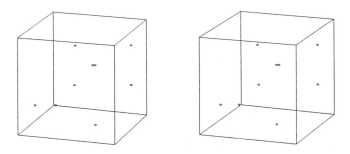

Figure 7.8: Trivariate Data in a Stereogram

Tsianco et al. (1981) describe a computer program that provides both anaglyphs and stereograms for statistical graphics. Although statisticians have experimented with anaglyphs and stereograms for many years, these visual devices have generally had more value as entertainment than as effective as tools of discovery. They may be useful, however, for displaying features of the data that are already known.

The perception of depth can also be induced by rotating a single three-dimensional scatter plot on a monitor. The perception of a third dimension ceases when the movement stops, however. One way of preserving the motion and hence the depth perception while still maintaining the viewing angle is to rock the scatter plot (that is, to rotate the scatter plot back and forth through a small angle).

Use of rotations to visualize a third dimension often prompts discoveries of structure in the data. For example, observations that are outliers in a direction that does not correspond to the axis of any single variable may become apparent when a three-dimensional scatter plot is rotated.

Different people have differing abilities to interpret graphical displays. The stereoscopic devices discussed above are not very useful for people with vision in only one eye and for the growing number of people who use artificial lenses to provide near vision in one eye and distance vision in the other.

Contours in Three Dimensions

Contour plots in three dimensions are surfaces that represent constant values of a fourth variable. Methods for drawing contours for three-dimensional data are similar to those for two-dimensional data; a three-dimensional mesh is formed, and the values of the function or of a fourth variable at the lattice points of the mesh are used to decide whether and how a contour surface may cut through the mesh volume element. The most widely used method for drawing contours in three dimensions is "the marching cubes" method, described by Lorensen and Cline (1988). (See also Schroeder, Martin, and Lorensen, 1996, for a good description of the method.)

Contours of three-dimensional data can also be represented in stereograms using the same offsets as in equation (7.4). See Scott (1992, pages 22 and 26) for examples.

7.2   Viewing Multivariate Data

Graphical displays are essentially limited to the two dimensions of a computer monitor or a piece of paper. Various devices that simulate depth allow visualization of a third dimension using just the two-dimensional surface. The simplest such devices are reference objects, such as color saturation or perspective lines, that provide a sense of depth. Because of our everyday experience in a three-dimensional world with an atmosphere, visual clues such as diminished color or converging lines readily suggest distance from the eye. Other, more complicated mechanisms making use of the stereo perspective of the two human eyes may suggest depth more effectively, as we discuss on page 166. There are not many situations in which these more complicated devices have provided more understanding of data than would be available by looking at various two-dimensional views.

There are basically two ways of displaying higher-dimensional data on a two-dimensional surface. One is to use multiple two-dimensional views, each of which relates a point in a cartesian plane with a projection of a point in higher dimensions. The number of separate two-dimensional views of d-dimensional data is $O(d^2)$.

The other way is to use graphical objects that have characteristics other than just cartesian coordinates that are associated with values of variables in the data. These graphical objects may be other geometric mappings, or they may be icons or glyphs whose shapes are related to specific values of variables. The number of graphical objects is n, the number of observations, so some of these methods of displaying high-dimensional data are useful only if the number of observations is relatively small.

Projections

Numeric data can easily be viewed two variables at a time using scatter plots in two-dimensional cartesian coordinates. An effective way of arranging these two-dimensional scatter plots of multidimensional data is to lay them out in a square (or triangular) pattern. All scatter plots in one row of the pattern have the same variable on the vertical axis, and all scatter plots in one column of the pattern have the same variable on the horizontal axis, as shown in Figure 7.9. Tukey and Tukey (1981a) demonstrated the utility of multiple views organized in this way, and named it a "draftsman's display". Each view is a two-dimensional projection of a multidimensional scatter plot, so all observations are represented in each view. This arrangement is sometimes called a scatter plot matrix, or "SPLOM". One is shown in Figure 7.9. The plot shows pairwise relationships among the variables and also that the observations fall into distinct groups. (The plot in Figure 7.9 was produced by the S-Plus function **splom**. The **pairs** function in both S-Plus and R produces a similar plot. The plot uses the "Fisher iris data". This is a relatively small dataset that has been widely studied. The data are four measurements on each of 50 iris plants from each of three species. The data are given as dataset number 33 of Hand et al., 1994.)

The two-dimensional scatter plots represent the data in the $n \times 2$ matrix, $X_{jk} = X[e_j | e_k]$, where $[e_j | e_k]$ is a $d \times 2$ matrix and e_i is the ith unit column vector of length d. More general two-dimensional projections of the d-dimensional data may also be useful. The $n \times d$ matrix X that contains the data is post-multiplied by a $d \times d$ projection matrix of rank 2, and then the data are plotted on cartesian axes that form an orthogonal basis of the two-dimensional space. (As discussed in Chapter 5, a projection matrix is any real symmetric idempotent matrix. The projection matrix used in the formation of X_{jk} above, if $j < k$, is the $d \times d$ matrix consisting of all zeros except for ones in the (j, j) and (k, k) positions.)

The scatter plots in a SPLOM as described above are plots of unadjusted marginal values of the individual variables. Davison and Sardy (2000) suggest use of a partial scatter plot matrix (that is, scatter plots of residuals from

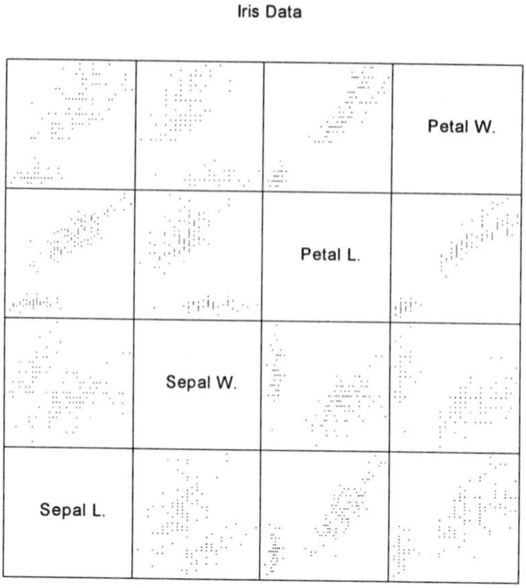

Iris Data

Figure 7.9: Scatter Plot Matrix of Fisher Iris Data

linearly adjusting each variable for all others except the other one in the current scatter plot). This has the advantage of showing more precisely the relationship between the two variables, because they are conditioned on the other variables that may be related. Davison and Sardy also suggest forming a scatter plot matrix using the marginal values in one half (say, the plots above the diagonal) and using the adjusted values or residuals in the other half of the matrix.

A sequence of projections is useful in identifying interesting properties of data. In a "grand tour", a plane is moved through a d-dimensional scatter plot (see Asimov, 1985). As the plane moves through the space, all points are projected onto the plane in directions normal to the plane. We discuss the grand tour on page 180. Projection pursuit, as discussed in Section 10.5, is another technique for successively considering lower-dimensional projections of a dataset in order to identify interesting features of the data.

Projections cannot reveal structure of a higher dimension than the dimension of the projection. Consider, for example, a sphere, which is a three-dimensional structure. A two-dimensional projection of the sphere is the same as that of a ball; that is, the projection does not reveal the hollow interior.

Another type of lower-dimension view of a dataset is provided by a *section*. A section of a space of d dimensions is the intersection of the space with a lower-dimensional object. The lower-dimensional object is often chosen as a hyperplane.

A two-dimensional section of a three-dimensional sphere can reveal the hollow interior if the section passes through the sphere. The ability of a section to determine a feature depends on where the section is relative to the feature. Furnas and Buja (1994) discuss the usefulness of projections and sections together in identifying structure in data, and they suggest that their complementary abilities be utilized in compositions of projections and sections, which they call "prosections".

A matrix of image plots can be useful in simultaneously exploring the relationship of a response variable to pairs of other variables. The plot in Figure 7.10 is an image plot matrix, or IMPLOM, showing values of a response variable in gray scale at various combinations of levels of three independent variables. In Figure 7.10, the ordering of each of the independent variables is the same above the diagonal as below it, but this is not necessary. Orderings can be compared by using different ones in the two images that correspond to the same two independent variables.

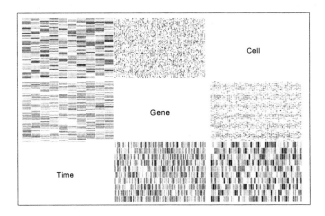

Figure 7.10: Matrix of Image Plots

Conditioning Plots

When a multivariate dataset has different subsets of interest, perhaps determined by the values of a nominal variable, it is convenient to view the data in separate panels corresponding to the different subsets. Such a multipaneled graphic is called a "casement display".

Graphics composed of panels corresponding to values of a variable that is not directly displayed in the plots are called conditioning plots, or coplots. They are "conditioned" on the values of a variable. The conditioning values can also be ranges of continuous variables. In this case, we display "slices" of the data (see Jacoby, 1998).

In a conditioning plot, the overall graphical display is divided into two parts, a panel for the conditioning slices and a set of *dependence panels* showing the bivariate relationship between the dependent variable and the panel variable, at each level of the conditioning slices.

Conditioning is performed by the "splitting" operation in the graph algebra of Wilkinson (1997, 1999). The "trellis" displays of S-Plus are designed to do this. See Becker, Cleveland, and Shyu (1996) and Theus (1995) for descriptions of trellis displays.

The `coplot` function in both S-Plus and R produces conditioning plots.

Noncartesian Displays

One way of dealing with multivariate data is to represent each observation as a more complicated object than just a point. The values of the individual variables comprising the observation are represented by some aspect of the object. For some kinds of displays, each observation takes up a lot of space, so the use of those techniques is generally limited to datasets with a small number of observations. Other displays use curves to represent observations, and those kinds of displays can be used with larger datasets.

A limitation to the usefulness of noncartesian displays is that the graphical elements may not have any natural correspondence to the variables. This sometimes makes the plot difficult to interpret until the viewer has established the proper association between the graphical features and the variables. Even so, it often is not easy to visualize the data using the icons or curves.

We will use the small dataset in Table 7.1 to illustrate some of the types of displays.

Table 7.1: Data for Examples of Noncartesian Displays

Observation	x_1	x_2	x_3	x_4	x_5	x_6	x_7
1	6	5	4	3	2	1	2
2	1	2	3	4	5	6	5
3	4	4	6	4	3	3	3
4	2	2	2	3	6	6	6
Minimum	1	2	2	3	2	1	2
Maximum	6	5	6	4	6	6	6

Glyphs and Icons

Various kinds of glyphs and icons can be used to represent multivariate data. In many cases, a separate glyph or icon is used for each observation. One of the most typical is a star diagram, of which there are several variations. In a star diagram, for each observation of d-dimensional data, rays pointing from a central point in d equally spaced directions represent the values of the variables.

An issue in noncartesian displays is how to represent magnitudes. In one variation of the star diagram, the lengths of the rays correspond to the magnitude of the value of the variable. In another variation, sometimes called "snowflakes", the lengths of the rays are linearly scaled individually so that the minimum of any variable in the dataset becomes 0 and the maximum becomes 1. Thus, for x_1 in Table 7.1, the values become

$$1.0, \ 1.0, \ 0.5, \ 0.0, \ 0.0, \ 0.0, \ 0.0.$$

Once the rays are drawn, their endpoints are connected. This is the default method in the S-Plus **stars** function. The star diagrams for the four observations of Table 7.1 are shown in Figure 7.11. Observation number one has only three rays because four of its elements correspond to zero. Once a mental association is made between a direction and the variable that corresponds to it, one can get a quick idea of the relative values of the variables in a given observation. Star diagrams are widely used to make comparisons between objects.

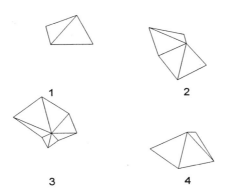

Figure 7.11: Star Diagrams of Data in Table 7.1

Chernoff (1973) suggested the use of stylized human faces for representing multivariate data. Each variable is associated with some particular feature of the face, such as height, width, shape of the mouth, and so on. Because of our visual and mental ability to process facial images rapidly, it is likely that by viewing observations represented as faces, we can identify similarities among observations very quickly. A set of Chernoff faces for the data in Table 7.1 are shown in Figure 7.12.

As with star diagrams, the features of Chernoff faces can be associated with the variables and their values in different ways. The faces shown in Figure 7.12 are just as they are produced by the S-Plus function **faces** using the default settings, in which the area of face corresponds to the first variable, the shape

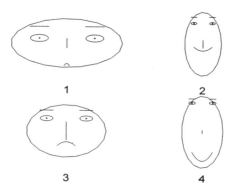

Figure 7.12: Chernoff Faces of Data in Table 7.1

of face to the second, the length of nose to the third, the location of mouth to the fourth, the curve of smile to the fifth, the width of mouth to the sixth, and the location of eyes to the seventh.

In star diagrams, each variable is represented in the same way: as a ray. The stars have different appearances based only on the order in which the variables are assigned to rays. In faces, however, the variables correspond to very different features of the diagram, so there are many more differences in appearance that can result from the same dataset. Perhaps for this reason, faces are not used nearly as often as stars.

Anderson (1957) proposed use of a glyph consisting of a circle and from one to seven rays emanating from its top. Kleiner and Hartigan (1981) discuss various other icons, including "trees" and "castles", which they felt are less sensitive to the ordering of the variables on the dataset. Matlab provides several types of glyph plots, including "feather plots", "compass plots", and "rose plots". Sparr et al. (1993) describe several other types of icons and glyphs that can be used for representing multivariate data.

Stars, faces, and other kinds of icons that individually represent a single observation are not very useful if the number of observations is more than 20 or 30. The usefulness of such graphics results from their ability to represent 20 or 30 variables.

Carr and Nicholson (1987) describe a method of visualizing four-dimensional data using stereo-ray glyphs, which are pairs of dots with rays emanating from them. The centers of the dots represent the first two variables, the stereo depth represents the third variable, as illustrated in Figure 7.8 on page 167, and the angle of the ray represents the fourth variable. The program EXPLOR4, described by Carr and Nicholson, produces stereo-ray glyphs as well as other graphics for exploring four-dimensional data.

Further discussion of glyphs and icons, together with many examples of their use, is provided by Chambers et al. (1983).

Parallel Coordinates: Points Become Broken Line Segments

Another type of curve for representing a multivariate observation is a piecewise linear curve joining the values of the variables on a set of parallel axes, each of which represents values of a given variable. This type of plot, called "parallel coordinates", for viewing multivariate data was introduced by Inselberg (1985) (see also Inselberg and Dimsdale, 1988, Wegman, 1990, and Inselberg, 1998). A parallel coordinates plot is similar to a nomogram. A parallel coordinates plot of the four observations in Table 7.1 is shown in Figure 7.13.

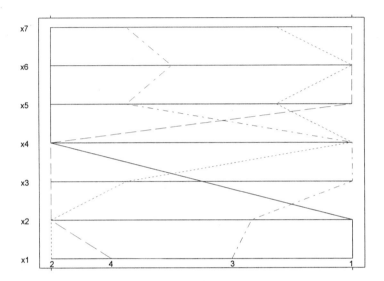

Figure 7.13: Parallel Coordinates Plot of Data in Table 7.1

With parallel coordinates, a point in the multidimensional space becomes a curve (a broken line) in a two-dimensional space. The scales on the horizontal lines in a parallel coordinates plot are generally scaled linearly to cover the range of the value in the sample. Thus, in Figure 7.13, the scale on the lowest of the parallel coordinate lines, which represents the first variable, is a linear scale from 1 to 6. The scale on the second line from the bottom, which represents the second variable, corresponds to values from 2 to 5. The first observation in the example dataset has a value of 6 for the first variable and a value of 5 for the second variable. The line in the plot representing the first observation is vertical between the bottom coordinate line and the second coordinate line. The fourth coordinate line represents values only from 3 to 4 because those are the minimum and maximum values, respectively, of the fourth variable in the dataset.

Parallel coordinates help to identify relationships between variables. Pairwise positive correlations between variables represented by adjacent coordinate lines result in the line segments of the observations having similar slopes, whereas negative correlations yield line segments with different slopes. Correlations between variables on adjacent coordinate lines are most easily recognized. If the columns in the dataset are reordered, the adjacency pattern in the parallel coordinates plot changes, so other relationships may be observed.

Observations that are similar tend to have lines that have similar tracks. Parallel coordinates plots are therefore useful in identifying groups in data. If a variable on the dataset indicates group membership, all of the lines will go through the points on that coordinate that represent the (presumably small number of) groups. The visual impact is enhanced by placing this special coordinate either at the top or the bottom of the parallel coordinates plot (although if this special coordinate is placed in the middle, sometimes the groups are more obvious, because there may be fewer line crossings).

Trigonometric Series: Points Become Curves

Another way of depicting a multivariate observation is with a curve in two dimensions. One type of curve is built by a sum of trigonometric functions. Plots of this type are called "Fourier series curves", or "Andrews curves" after Andrews (1972). An Andrews curve representing the point

$$x = (x_1, x_2, \ldots, x_d)$$

is

$$s(t) = x_1/\sqrt{2} + x_2 \sin t + x_3 \cos t + x_4 \sin(2t) + x_5 \cos(2t) + \ldots. \qquad (7.5)$$

A set of Andrews curves for the data in Table 7.1 are shown in Figure 7.14. As t goes from 0 to 2π, the curve traces out a full period, so the plot is shown just over that range. It is often useful, however, to make plots of two full periods of these periodic curves.

In Andrews curves, the value of the first variable determines the overall height of the curve. Thus, in the example in Figure 7.14, the curve representing observation number 1 is the highest overall, and the curve representing observation number 3 is next highest. The values of the next two variables determine the amplitude of a periodic component of period 2π, the values of the fourth and fifth variables determine the amplitude of a periodic component of period π, and so on. Andrews curves are also sometimes plotted in polar coordinates, resulting in a star-shaped figure with four arms.

Cone Plots

Representations in polar coordinates can often be useful in graphics.

Dawkins (1995) introduced "cone plots", based on polar coordinates, for displaying multivariate data. The polar coordinates could be defined in different ways, but however they are defined, their use allows for easy computation of angles, which are a basic component of cone plots. The cone plot is based on two

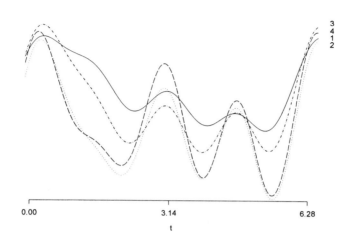

Figure 7.14: Fourier Curves Plot of Data in Table 7.1

fixed points in the space of the data, v, the "vertex", and a, the "apocenter". A multivariate point x is plotted as the two-dimensional cartesian point

$$(r_v \cos \phi, \; r_v \sin \phi),$$

where r_v is the distance from v to x, and ϕ is the angle that the line segment from v to x makes with the line segment from v to a, as shown in Figure 7.15. The line segment from the vertex v to the apocenter a is called the baseline.

Various points may be chosen as the vertex and apocenter. Each different pair of points gives a different picture of the data. Dawkins (1995) recommends taking the apocenter as the centroid of the data and producing cone plots with different observations as the vertices. A full complement of cone plots formed in that way would be as many as the number of observations on the dataset. Different views may make different features visible. Interesting features of the dataset can often be observed from just a few cone plots. Knowing which view will highlight a specific feature requires considerable experience with cone plots. It is generally better to look at all cone plots formed with observations at the vertex or at least at a large subset of them. For skewed data, use of some other measure of the center of the data rather than the centroid may yield different views.

Cone plots of the data in Table 7.1 are shown in Figure 7.16. The data were first of all standardized to have column means of 0 and variances of 1. The apocenter in each plot was taken as the centroid, 0. Then, in turn, each observation was taken as the vertex, and cone plots of all observations were

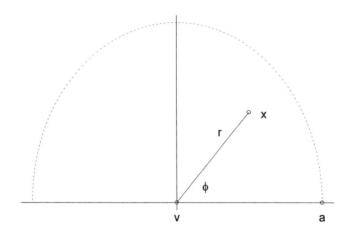

Figure 7.15: A Point in a Cone Plot

produced.

Geometrical shapes in d dimensions have some interesting representations in cone plots, as Dawkins (1995) points out. A d-dimensional cylinder, for example, is a horizontal line in the cone plot. A hypersphere is a semicircle. The fact that some higher-dimensional structures can be seen in the two-dimensional cone plot makes this kind of plot a useful supplement to both projections and sections (see Exercise 7.7).

Exploring Data with Noncartesian Displays

Noncartesian displays are often developed to aid in identification of specific features. The box plot is very useful in seeing the overall shape of the data density and in highlighting univariate outliers (see Cleveland, 1995). The stalactite plot described by Atkinson and Mulira (1993) can be useful in the detection of multivariate outliers. (See Atkinson and Mulira, 1993, for a description of this type of plot.)

Roping, Brushing, and Linking

If all points in a graphical display are identified by observation number or some other label, it is likely that the display will become so cluttered that the information content is obscured. It is easy to allow labeling of selected points, and when the graphical display is viewed on a computer monitor, interesting points can be selected after the entire dataset is viewed. It is often desired to

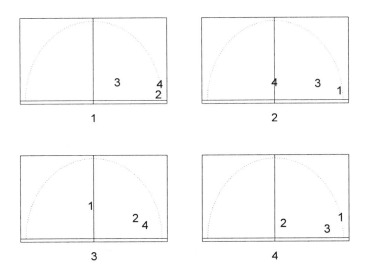

Figure 7.16: Cone Plots of Data in Table 7.1, with Each Observation in Turn Taken as the Apocenter

focus in on a set of points that are interesting, perhaps because they form an outlying cluster. An interactive graphics program may allow these points to be "roped" by the data analyst. This may be done by use of a pointing device to draw a curve around the representations of the observations. The analyst may then wish to magnify the region of the graph containing these special observations or perform other transformations selectively.

Whenever a single dataset is displayed in multiple views, it is useful to have some way of linking selected observations in the different views, as suggested by Newton (1978). Becker and Cleveland (1987) described "brushing" methods for the scatter plot matrix (Figure 7.9, page 170) to allow identification of single observations or subsets of observations simultaneously in all views. When the analyst associates a particular color or other identifying attribute with given observations in one view, those same observations are given the same attribute in the other views. (See papers in Buja and Tukey, 1991, for examples.)

Rotations and Dynamical Graphics

When a cluster of points or a surface in three dimensions is rotated (or alternatively, when the viewing direction, or position of the "eye", is changed), patterns and structures in the data may be more easily recognized. The program PRIM-9, developed by Friedman, Fisherkeller, and Tukey in the early 1970s (see Fisherkeller, Friedman, and Tukey, 1988), is an interactive program

that allows the user to view multivariate data from various perspectives. The
system provides Picturing, Rotation, Isolation, and Masking. The purpose is
to allow discovery of interesting features in the data.

Rotations are orthogonal transformations that preserve norms of the data
vectors and angles between the vectors. The simplest rotation to describe is that
of a plane defined by two coordinates about the other principal axes. Such a
rotation changes two elements of a vector that represents cartesian coordinates
in the plane that is rotated and leaves all the other elements, representing the
other coordinates, unchanged. A rotation matrix, as shown in equation (5.5)
on page 105, is the same as an identity matrix with four elements changed.

A generalized rotation matrix, Q, can be built as a product of $(d^2 - d)/2$
such Q_{ij} simple rotation matrices,

$$Q = Q_{12}Q_{13}\cdots Q_{1d}Q_{23}Q_{24}\cdots Q_{2d}\cdots Q_{d-1,d}.$$

Rotating a plot in all directions, along with various projections, is called
a "grand tour". Asimov (1985) described three different ways of performing a
grand tour. In one method, the angles for the rotations are taken as

$$t\phi_{ij} \bmod 2\pi,$$

where the ϕ_{ij} are fixed constants that are linearly independent over the integers;
that is, if for any set of integers $k_{12}, k_{13}, \ldots, k_{d-1,d}$,

$$\left(\sum_{i=1}^{d-1}\sum_{j=i+1}^{d} k_{ij}\phi_{ij}\right) \bmod 2\pi = 0,$$

then all $k_{ij} = 0$. As t is stepped over time, the angle in the rotation matrix Q_{ij}
is taken as $t\phi_{ij}$ and the generalized rotation matrix is computed and applied to
the dataset.

The rotated datasets can be viewed in various ways. In the most common grand tour, the point cloud is projected onto a representation of a three-
dimensional cartesian system. In the grand tour, the data points appear to
be in continuous motion on the computer monitor. The motion of the system,
or equivalently, the apparent continuous rotations of the data, provide a perception of the third dimension. Buja and Asimov (1986) discuss some of the
desirable properties of the motion in a grand tour.

Rotated datasets can also be viewed using parallel coordinates, cone plots,
or Andrews curves. Structure appears in various ways in these plots. A hyperplane, for example, appears as a point on a parallel coordinate axis that corresponds to the coefficients of the hyperplane. Figure 7.17 shows 1,000 points in
three-space that were generated by a random number generator called RANDU.
The data have been rotated by postmultiplication by a 3×3 orthogonal matrix
whose second column is proportional to $(9, -6, 1)$. We see from the figure that
there are exactly 15 planes in that rotation. (See Gentle, 1998a, page 13, for

further discussion of data generated by RANDU. Because of the sharp indentations between the axes in the plot in Figure 7.17, we may conclude that there are strong negative correlations between these orthogonal linear combinations of the original data. This is a further indication that the random number generator is not a good one. In Exercise 7.4 on page 189, you are asked to consider similar problems.) You are asked to develop systematic rotation and plotting methods for producing Andrews curves and cone plots in Exercises 7.9 and 7.10.

Figure 7.17: 1,000 Triples from RANDU Rotated onto Interesting Coordinates

There is another way of "touring the data" by using the Andrews curves, $s(t)$, of equation (7.5) on page 176. These representations have a natural dynamic quality. The variable t in $s(t)$ of equation (7.5) on page 176 can be interpreted as "time" and varied continuously.

Wegman and Shen (1993) modify and generalize the Andrews curves as

$$r(t) = x_1 \sin(\omega_1 t) + x_2 \cos(\omega_1 t) + x_3 \sin(\omega_2 t) + x_4 \cos(\omega_2 t) + \ldots$$
$$= a^{\mathrm{T}}(t)x,$$

where
$$a^{\mathrm{T}}(t) = \big(\sin(\omega_1 t),\ \cos(\omega_1 t),\ \sin(\omega_2 t),\ \cos(\omega_2 t),\ \ldots\big).$$

If the ω's are chosen so that ω_i/ω_j is irrational for all i and j not equal (i and j range from 1 to $\lceil d/2 \rceil$), a richer set of orientations of the data are encountered when t is varied. The generalized curves are not periodic in this case. Wegman and Shen (1993) then consider an orthogonal linear combination, $q(t) = b^{\mathrm{T}}(t)x$, where
$$b^{\mathrm{T}}(t) = \big(\cos(\omega_1 t),\ -\sin(\omega_1 t),\ \cos(\omega_2 t),\ -\sin(\omega_2 t),\ \ldots\big).$$

They define a two-dimensional "pseudo grand tour" as the plots of $r(t)$ and $q(t)$ as t varies continuously. For the pseudo grand tour, they suggest defining $a(t)$ and $b(t)$ so that each has an even number of elements (if d is odd, the data vector x can be augmented with a 0 as its last element) and then normalizing both $a(t)$ and $b(t)$. They also recommend centering the data vectors about 0.

The S-Plus function spin can be used for controlled rotations of a three-dimensional point cloud in cartesian coordinates. Other specialized graphics software provides even better interaction and allows "guided tours" using controlled rotations as described by Young, Kent, and Kuhfeld (1988), Hurley and Buja (1990), and Young and Rheingans (1991). In a guided tour, the data analyst, using knowledge of the dataset or information provided by previous views of the data, actively decides which portions of the data space are explored.

Projection pursuit, as discussed in Section 10.5 on page 281, can be used to determine the rotations in any grand tour using either the standard cartesian coordinates or the other types of displays. Cook et al. (1995) described such a scheme and called it a projection pursuit guided tour.

Displays of Large Data Sets

As the number of observations increases, information should increase. A problem with many graphical displays, however, is that large amounts of data result in too dense a graph, and there may actually be a loss of information. Data points are overplotted. There is too much "ink" and too little information. If there were no low-dimensional structure in the data shown in Figure 7.17, for example, the plot, which represents only 1,000 points, would just be an almost solid blob.

When overplotting occurs for only a relatively small number of points, and especially if the data are not continuous (that is, data points occur only on a relatively coarse lattice), the overplotting problem can be solved by jittering, which is the process of plotting the data at nearby points rather than at the exact point ("exact" subject to the resolution of the plot).

The number of observations in a dataset may be even larger than the number of pixels. Keim (1996) describes various approaches for large datasets by associating each observation with a single pixel.

For very large datasets where the number of observations is greater than the number of pixels, it is clear that some other approach must be used to represent the data. It is necessary either to sample the data, to smooth the data and plot the smoothed function, and/or to plot a representation of the density of the data. Carr et al. (1987) used gray scale or relative sizes of the plotting symbols to represent the data density. This is effective for univariate or bivariate data. It can also be used in two-dimensional projections of multivariate data.

Image plots are useful for large trivariate datasets and for multivariate data in three-dimensional projections displayed in an IMPLOM.

Smoothing and graphing of data are activities that go well together. Smoothing provides a better visual display, and conversely, the display of the smoothed data provides a visual assessment of smoothing. See Marron and Tsybakov (1995) for a discussion of the use of the display in determining an appropriate amount of smoothing.

Datasets that are large because of the number of variables present a more difficult problem, as we have already discussed. The nature of the variables may allow special representations that are useful for that type of data. Hartigan and Kleiner (1981) and Friendly (1994) have developed methods for graphically representing data from multiway contingency tables.

Data Analysis and Human Perception

Visual perception by humans is a complex process. Wandell (1995) considers the activity to be composed of three fairly distinct aspects. The first is the physical and physiological, the optics, the retinal photoreceptors and their responses, and the matching of colors. The second phase is the representation, that is, the analysis of images in the neural retina and the visual cortex. This involves sensitivity to and recognition of patterns, requiring multiresolution of images. The third aspect is the interpretation of information in the visual representation. Perception of color, motion, and depth plays an important role in all of these phases. Julesz (1986, 1994) gives detailed descriptions of factors that affect perception and how these factors are interpreted by the human nervous system.

Cleveland (1993) discusses the impact of various details of a graphical display on the overall perception and, consequently, on the understanding of the data.

Although color can be very useful in the visual representation of data, poorly chosen colors are a major distraction in statistical graphics. Many statisticians and other data analysts are aware of the importance of carefully chosen colors for enhancing visual displays. There are two issues that need emphasis, however. One is the differences in the effects of color in different media. A color scheme that appears very useful on one computer monitor may not be appropriate on other monitors or on printed media. Another problem arises from the not insignificant proportion of persons who are color-blind but in all other ways are normally-sighted. Color-blindness usually involves only two colors, often complementary ones. The most common type of color-blindness in America is red-green; that is, the inability to distinguish red and green. For normally-sighted persons, however, these two colors show up well and are easily distinguished; hence, they are obvious choices for use in color graphics.

Other senses, such as hearing and touch may, be usefully employed in coming to a better understanding of a set of data.

Immersive techniques in which data are used to simulate a "virtual reality" may help in understanding complicated data. A system called CAVE provides an immersive experience for exploring data or geometric objects. The system consists of various projectors, mirrors, and speakers; eyeglasses with alternating shutters; and user controls for feedback. Symanzik et al. (1997) provide a description of various immersive techniques in the CAVE system.

7.3   Hardware and Low-Level Software for Graphics

Computer graphics has been an active area of research and development in computer science for years. Foley et al. (1990) provide a thorough discussion of the hardware aspects of computer graphics.

Hardware for graphics includes the computational engine, input devices, and various display devices. Rapid advances are being made for almost all types of graphics hardware, and the advances in the quality and capabilities of the hardware are being accompanied by decreases in the costs of the equipment.

The two most common display devices are monitors, either using a cathode ray tube or a liquid crystal display (LCD) screen, and printers, usually based on a laser technology. In either case, the image is the result of the collage of pixels.

Software for graphics often interacts very closely with the hardware, taking advantage of specific design features of the hardware.

Speed and Resolution

Because a graph may require many computations to produce lines and surfaces that appear smooth, the speed of the computational engine is very important. The appropriate pixels must be identified and set to the proper value to make the entire graph appear correctly to the human eye. The need for computer speed is even greater if the object being displayed is to appear to move smoothly.

A typical computer monitor has a rectangular array of approximately one to two million pixels. (Common monitors currently are 1,280 by 1,024 or 1,600 by 1,200.) This is approximately 100 pixels per inch. This resolution allows arbitrary curves to appear fairly smooth. Whether graphical displays can respond to real-time motion depends on how fast the computer can perform the calculations necessary to update 10^6 pixels fast enough for the latency period of the human eye.

Representation of Color

Color is determined by the wavelength of light. Violet is the shortest and red the longest. (Here, "color" is assumed to refer to something visible.) White color is a mixture of waves of various lengths.

Most light sources generate light of various wavelengths. Our perception of color depends on the mix of wavelengths. A single wavelength in light is a highly saturated single color. Multiple wavelengths reduce the saturation and affect the overall hue and lightness. Multiple wavelengths are perceived as a different single color that is a combination of the individual colors.

A given color can be formed by combining up to three basic colors. Red, green, and blue are often used as the basic colors. Colors can be combined additively using different light sources or in a subtractive way by filters or absorptive surfaces.

To specify a given color or mix of colors and other characteristics of the light, we use a *color system*. Color values are defined in the given color system and then used by the software and hardware to control the colors on the output device. Different systems use different combinations of values to describe the same color and the same overall effect. The common color systems are RGB (red, green, blue), CMY (cyan, magenta, yellow), HLS (hue, lightness, saturation), and HSV (hue, saturation, value).

The RGB color system uses a vector of three elements ranging in value from 0 to 255. The system can be illustrated as in Figure 7.18 by a cube whose sides are 255 units long. Three corners correspond to the primary colors of red, green, and blue; three corners correspond to the secondary colors of cyan, magenta, and yellow; and two corners correspond to black and white. Each color is represented by a point within or on the cube. The point $(255, 255, 255)$ represents an additive mixture of the full intensity of each of the three primary colors. Points along the main diagonal are shades of gray because the intensity of each of the three primaries is equal.

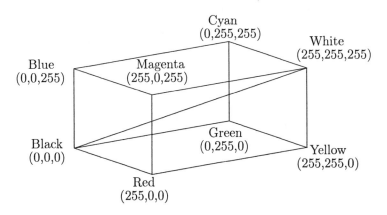

Figure 7.18: RGB Color Cube

Digital display devices represent each component of an RGB color coordinate in binary as an integer in the range of 0 to $2^n - 1$, for some n. Each displayable color is an RGB coordinate triple of n-bit numbers, so the total number of representable colors is 2^{3n}, including black and white. An m-bit pixel can represent 2^m different colors. If m is less than $3n$, a *color translation table* (or just *color table*) with 2^m entries is used to map color triples to values of the pixels.

Low-Level Software

Software for producing graphics must interact very closely with the display devices. Because the devices vary in their capabilities, the approach generally taken is to design and produce the software at various levels so that graphics software at one level will interface with different software at another level in different environments.

The lowest-level software includes the *device drivers*, which are programs in the machine language of the particular display device. The next level of software provides the primitive graphics operations, such as illuminating a pixel or drawing a line. There have been a number of efforts to standardize the interface for this set of graphics primitives. Lower-level standards include GKS and PHIGS. Standards for GKS and PHIGS have been adopted by both the American National Standards Institute (ANSI) and the International Standards Organization (ISO). The Open Graphics Library, or OpenGL, is a library of primitive graphics functions developed by Silicon Graphics, Inc. It is now a standard controlled by the OpenGL Architecture Review Board (1992). For each of these sets of standard graphics functions there are bindings for Fortran, C, and C++. Glaeser and Stachel (1999) describe the use of OpenGL in a C++ graphics system called Open Geometry.

The most common software to control the appearance of graphics on a computer monitor running under Unix is X Windows. An important platform at a slightly higher level is Motif, which interacts with X Windows. The Microsoft Windows platform, or MS Windows, which is a complete operating system rather than just a windowing system, provides windows management similar to Motif.

An important system that provides capabilities for arranging multiple displays on a page is PostScript. Another system that is used for graphical displays over the internet is the Virtual Reality Modeling Language, or VRML. VRML is based on OpenGL.

Although the word "standard" is sometimes used in reference to these software systems, they exhibit aggravating variability from one environment to another.

7.4   Software for Graphics Applications

There are a number of higher-level graphics systems ranging from Fortran, C, or Java libraries to interactive packages that allow modification of the display as it is being produced. Many graphics packages have a number of preconstructed color tables from which the user can select to match the colors a given device produces to the desired colors.

The IMSL Exponent Graphics allows programming in Fortran, C, or X, but also has an interactive interface to customize the graphical displays. Java 3D is a Java-based library for three-dimensional graphics developed by Sun Microsystems.

Gnuplot is an interactive plotting package that provides a command-driven interface for making a variety of data- and function-based graphs. The system is primarily for two-dimensional graphics, but there are some three-dimensional plotting capabilities. The graphs produced can be exported into a number of formats. The package is freeware and is commonly available on both Unix systems and MS Windows.

Xfig is a graphics package for Unix windowing systems (X11) that provides capabilities for the basic objects of vector graphics, including lines and various curves such as Bézier curves.

GIMP (the GNU Image Manipulation Program) is a freely distributed software package for image manipulation. It can be used for simple "painting" (drawing and coloring), photo retouching, image rendering, and image format conversion. GIMP is available on Unix platforms. Various similar tools such as Photoshop are available on MS Windows systems.

Advanced Visual Systems, Inc., develops and distributes a widely used set of graphics and visualization systems, AVS5 and AVS/Express together with various associated products. These systems run on most of the common platforms.

XGobi is an interactive graphics system that emphasizes dynamic graphics. See Swayne, Cook, and Buja (1991) for a description of the XGobi system.

The Visualization Toolkit, or vtk, developed by Schroeder, Martin, and Lorensen (1996), is an object-oriented system that emphasizes three-dimensional graphics. The software manual also has good descriptions of the algorithms implemented.

Because making graphical displays is generally not an end in itself, graphics software is usually incorporated into the main application software. Software systems for statistical data analysis, such as S-Plus, R, and SAS, have extensive graphics capabilities. The graphical capabilities in S-Plus and R are similar. Most features in one package are available in the other package, but there are differences in how the two packages interact with the operating system, and this means that there are some differences in the way that graphics files are produced. The function `expression` in R is a useful feature for producing text containing mathematical notation or Greek letters The function can be used in most places that expect text, such as `xlab`. For example,

```
main = expression(paste("Plot of ",
                Gamma(x)," versus",hat(beta) x^hat(gamma)))
```

produces the main title

$$\text{Plot of } \Gamma(x) \text{ versus } \widehat{\beta} \, x^{\widehat{\gamma}}$$

The actual appearance is device dependent and in any event is unlikely to have the beauty of a display produced by T$_{\text{E}}$X.

Other software systems for more general scientific applications, such as Matlab and PV-Wave, have abilities for the usual plots and images and are also very useful for creating graphics.

Jacoby (1998, page 92) provides a table of the graphical procedures available in a variety of statistical analysis packages, including Data Desk, JMP, SAS,

S-Plus, SPSS, Stata, Statistica, and SYSTAT. Of course, any such software summary becomes out of date very quickly.

Further Reading

There is a wealth of statistical literature on graphics, and visualization is being used ever more widely in data analysis. Accounts of the history of development and use of graphical methods in statistics are given in Funkhauser (1938), Beniger and Robyn (1978), and Fienberg (1979). Developments in statistical graphics are reported in several journals, most notably, perhaps, *Journal of Computational and Graphical Statistics*, as well as in unrefereed conference proceedings and newsletters, such as *Statistical Computing & Graphics Newsletter*, published quarterly by the Statistical Computing and the Statistical Graphics sections of the American Statistical Association. Many of the advances in computer graphics are reported at the annual ACM SIGGRAPH Conference. The proceedings of these conferences, with nominal refereeing, are published as *Computer Graphics, ACM SIGGRAPH xx Conference Proceedings* (where "xx" is a two-digit representation of the year). The texts by Foley et al. (1990) and by Wolff and Yaeger (1993) describe the principles of computer graphics and applications in imaging. Taylor (1992) provides a good background to the geometries useful in computer graphics. Ware (2000) discusses principles of human perception that determine the effectiveness of a graphical display.

Exercises

7.1. Generate a sample of size 200 of pseudorandom numbers from a mixture of two univariate normal distributions. Let the population consist of 80% from a N(0, 1) distribution and 20% from a N(3, 1) distribution. Plot the density of this mixture. Notice that it is bimodal. Now plot a histogram of the data using nine bins. Is it bimodal? Choose a few different numbers of bins and plot histograms. (Compare this with Exercise 9.9 of Chapter 9 on page 228.)

7.2. Generate a sample of pseudorandom numbers from a normal (0,1) distribution and produce a quantile plot of the sample against a normal (0,1) distribution, similar to Figure 7.5 on page 161. Do the tails of the sample seem light? (How can you tell?) If they do not, generate another sample and plot it. Does the erratic tail behavior indicate problems with the random number generator? Why might you expect often (more than 50% of the time) to see samples with light tails?

7.3. Stereoscopic displays.

   (a) Show that equation (7.4) on page 167, is the offset, in the plane of the display, for each eye in viewing points at a depth z. *Hint:* Draw rays representing the lines of sight through the plane of the graph.

   (b) Using any graphics software, reproduce the stereogram in Figure 7.19 that represents a cone resting on its base being viewed from above. (If the eyes focus in front of the plane of the paper, the view of the cone is from below.)

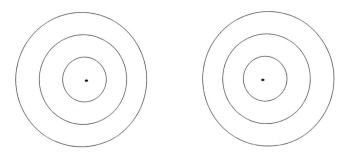

Figure 7.19: A Cone Resting on Its Base

7.4. Write a program for the simple linear congruential random number generator

$$x_i \equiv 35x_{i-1} \bmod 2^{15}.$$

Generate a sequence of length 1008. Look for structure in d-tuples of sequential values, $(x_i, x_{i+1}, \ldots, x_{i+d-1})$, for $3 \le d \le 1005$.

(a) Use a program that plots points in three dimensions and rotates the axes. Now, look for structure in higher dimensions. *Hint:* All of the points lie on the hyperplanes

$$x_{i+3} - 9x_{i+2} + 27x_{i+1} - 27x_i = j,$$

where j is an integer.

(b) Examine this structure using parallel coordinates.

7.5. Write a program for the simple linear congruential random number generator

$$x_i \equiv 259x_{i-1} \bmod 2^{15}.$$

Generate a sequence of length 1,008. Look for structure in triples of sequential values, (x_i, x_{i+1}, x_{i+2}), by plotting two-dimensional sections of a three-dimensional scatter plot.

7.6. Plot the ellipse $x^2 + 4y^2 = 5$ in cartesian coordinates. Now, plot it in parallel coordinates. What is the shape of the parallel coordinates plot of an ellipse?

7.7. Generate 1,000 pseudorandom 4-variate normal deviates with mean 0 and the identity as the variance-covariance matrix. Now, delete from the dataset all deviates whose length is less than 2. This creates a dataset with a "hole" in it. Try to find the hole using various graphic displays. Do you see it with cone plots? How can you tell?

7.8. Generate 100 pseudorandom trivariate normal variates with mean 0 and variance-covariance matrix

$$\begin{bmatrix} 1.00 & -.90 & .90 \\ -.90 & 1.81 & -1.71 \\ .90 & -1.71 & 2.62 \end{bmatrix}.$$

The Cholesky factor of the variance-covariance matrix is

$$\begin{bmatrix} 1.00 & & \\ -.90 & 1.00 & \\ .90 & -.90 & 1.00 \end{bmatrix}.$$

(a) Plot the data using parallel coordinates. What shapes result from the correlations?

(b) Plot the data using Andrews curves. What shapes result from the correlations?

7.9. Develop a grand tour in Andrews curves. Apply it to data generated by the random number generator in Exercise 7.4. What is the difference in the grand tour and the pseudo grand tour in Andrews curves discussed on page 182?

7.10. Develop a grand tour in cone plots. Apply it to data generated by the random number generator in Exercise 7.4.

7.11. Program a modification of parallel coordinates in which there is a common scale for all coordinates (that is, one in which a vertical line would pass through the same value on all parallel coordinate lines). Plot the data in Table 7.1 (page 172) and compare them with Figure 7.13. Now, try some other datasets. How would you recommend that the scales on the parallel coordinate lines be constructed? What are the advantages and disadvantages of a fixed scale for all lines?

7.12. Data exploration.

(a) Generate 25 numbers independently from $U(0, 1)$, and form five five-dimensional vectors, x_i, from them by taking the first five, the second five, and so on. Now, using Gram-Schmidt orthogonalization, form a set of orthogonal vectors y_i from the x's. You now have two multivariate datasets with very different characteristics. See if you can discover the difference graphically using either cartesian or noncartesian displays.

(b) Now, generate five n-dimensional vectors, for n relatively large. Do the same thing as in the previous part. (Now, you can decide what is meant by "n relatively large".) In this exercise, you have two datasets, each with five variables and n observations. Your graphical displays have been of the *variables* instead of the *observations*.

(c) Now, use the two datasets of the previous part and graph them in the traditional way using displays in which the upper-level graphical objects are the n observations.

Part II

Exploring Data Density and Structure

Introduction to Part II

A canonical problem in statistics is to gain understanding of a given random sample,

$$y_1, \ldots, y_n,$$

to understand the process that yielded the data. The specific objective is to make inferences about the population from which the random sample arose. In many cases, we wish to make inferences only about some finite set of parameters, such as the mean and variance, that describe the population. In other cases, we want to predict a future value of an observation. Sometimes, the objective is more difficult: we want to estimate a *function* that characterizes the distribution of the population. The cumulative distribution function (CDF) or the probability density function (PDF) provides a complete description of the population, so we may wish to estimate these functions.

In the simpler cases of statistical inference, we assume that the form of the CDF P is known and that there is a parameter, $\theta = \Theta(P)$, of finite dimension that characterizes the distribution within that assumed family of forms. An objective in such cases may be to determine an estimate $\widehat{\theta}$ of the parameter θ. The parameter may completely characterize the probability distribution of the population, or it may just determine an important property of the distribution, such as its mean or median. If the distribution or density function is assumed known up to a vector of parameters, the complete description is provided by the parameter estimate. For example, if the distribution is assumed to be normal, then the form of P is known. It involves two parameters, the mean μ and the variance σ^2. The problem of completely describing the distribution is merely the problem of estimating $\theta = (\mu, \sigma^2)$. In this case, the estimates of the CDF, $\widehat{P}$, and the density, $\widehat{p}$, are the normal CDF and density with the estimate of the parameter, $\widehat{\theta}$, plugged in.

If no assumptions, or only weak assumptions, are made about the form of the distribution or density function, the estimation problem is much more difficult. Because the distribution function or density function is a characterization from which all other properties of the distribution could be determined, we expect the estimation of the function to be the most difficult type of statistical inference. "Most difficult" is clearly a heuristic concept and here may mean that the estimator is most biased, most variable, most difficult to compute, most mathematically intractable, and so on.

Estimators such as $\widehat{\theta}$ for the parameter θ or $\widehat{p}$ for the density p are usually random variables; hence, we are interested in the statistical properties of these estimators. If our approach to the problem treats θ and p as fixed (but unknown), then the distribution of $\widehat{\theta}$ and $\widehat{p}$ can be used to make informative statements about θ and p. Alternatively, if θ and p are viewed as realizations of random variables, then the distribution of $\widehat{\theta}$ and $\widehat{p}$ can be used to make informative statements about conditional distributions of the parameter and the function, given the observed data.

Although the CDF in some ways is more fundamental in characterizing a probability distribution (it always exists and is defined the same for both continuous and discrete distributions), the probability density function is more familiar to most data analysts. Important properties such as skewness, modes, and so on can be seen more readily from a plot of the probability density function than from a plot of the CDF. We are therefore usually more interested in estimating the density, p, than the CDF, P. Some methods of estimating the density, however, are based on estimates of the CDF. The simplest estimate of the CDF is the empirical cumulative distribution function, the ECDF, which is defined as

$$P_n(y) = \frac{1}{n} \sum_{i=1}^{n} I_{(-\infty, y]}(y_i).$$

(See page 368 for the definition and properties of the indicator function $I_S(\cdot)$ in the ECDF.) As we have seen on page 11, the ECDF is pointwise unbiased for the CDF.

The derivative of the ECDF, the empirical probability density function (EPDF),

$$p_n(y) = \frac{1}{n} \sum_{i=1}^{n} \delta(y - y_i),$$

where δ is the Dirac delta function, is just a series of spikes at points corresponding to the observed values. It is not very useful as an estimator of the probability density. It is, however, unbiased for the probability density function at any point.

In the absence of assumptions about the form of the density p, the estimation problem may be computationally intensive. A very large sample is usually required in order to get a reliable estimate of the density. The goodness of the estimate depends on the dimension of the random variable. Heuristically, the higher the dimension, the larger the sample required to provide adequate representation of the sample space.

Density estimation generally has more modest goals than the development of a mathematical expression that yields the probability density function p everywhere. Although we may develop such an expression, the purpose of the estimate is usually a more general understanding of the population:

- to identify structure in the population, its modality, tail behavior, skewness, and so on;

- to classify the data and to identify different subpopulations giving rise to it; or

- to make a visual presentation that represents the population density.

There are several ways to approach the probability density estimation problem. In a parametric approach mentioned above, the parametric family of distributions, such as a normal distribution or a beta distribution, is assumed. The density is estimated by estimating the parameters of the distribution and substituting the estimates into the expression for the density. In a nonparametric approach, only very general assumptions about the distribution are made. These assumptions may only address the shape of the distribution, such as an assumption of unimodality or an assumption of continuity or other degrees of smoothness of the density function. There are various semiparametric approaches in which, for example, parametric assumptions may be made only over a subset of the range of the distribution, or, in a multivariate case, a parametric approach may be taken for some elements of the random vector and a nonparametric approach for others. Another approach is to assume a more general family of distributions, perhaps characterized by a differential equation, for example, and to fit the equation by equating properties of the sample, such as sample moments, with the corresponding properties of the equation.

In the case of parametric estimation, we have a complete estimate of the density (that is, an estimate at all points). In nonparametric estimation, we generally develop estimates of the ordinate of the density function at specific points. After the estimates are available at given points, a smooth function can be fitted. In the next few chapters we will be concerned primarily with nonparametric estimation of probability densities and identification of structure in the data. In Chapter 11 we will consider building models that express asymmetric relationships between variables and making inferences about those models.

Chapter 8

Estimation of Probability Density Functions Using Parametric Models

There are some relatively simple standard distributions that have proven useful for their ability to model the distribution of observed data from many different areas of application. The normal distribution is a good model for symmetric, continuous data from various sources. For skewed data, the lognormal and gamma distributions often work very well. Discrete data are often modeled by the Poisson or binomial distributions. Distributions such as these are *families of distributions* that have various numbers of parameters to specify the distribution completely. To emphasize that the density is dependent on parameters, we may write the density as $p(y \mid \theta)$, where θ may be a vector.

A standard way of estimating a density is to identify appropriate characteristics, such as symmetry, modes, range, and so on, choose some well-known parametric distribution that has those characteristics, and then estimate the parameters of that distribution. For example, if the density is known or assumed to be zero below some point, to be unimodal, and to extend without limit along the positive axis, a three-parameter gamma distribution with density

$$p(y \mid \alpha, \beta, \gamma) = \frac{1}{\Gamma(\alpha)\beta^\alpha}(y - \gamma)^{\alpha-1}e^{-(y-\gamma)/\beta}, \quad \text{for } \gamma \le y,$$

may be used to model the data. The three parameters α, β, and γ are then estimated from the data.

If the probability density of interest has a finite range, a beta distribution may be used to model it, and if it has an infinite range at both ends, a normal distribution, a Student's t distribution, or a stable distribution may be a useful approximation.

8.1   Fitting a Parametric Probability Distribution

Fitting a parametric density to a set of data is done by estimating the parameters. The estimate of the density, $\widehat{p}(y)$, is formed by substitution of the estimate of the parameters:

$$\widehat{p}_P(y) = p(y \,|\, \widehat{\theta}). \tag{8.1}$$

There are several ways of estimating the parameters, and for more complicated models there are many issues that go beyond just estimating the parameters. Many of the methods of fitting the model involve minimization of residuals. To fit a parametric probability density, the most common ways of estimating the parameters are maximum likelihood, matching moments, and matching quantiles.

Maximum Likelihood Methods

The method of maximum likelihood involves the use of a *likelihood function* that comes from the joint density for a random sample. If $p(y \,|\, \theta)$ is the underlying density, the joint density is just $\prod_i p(y_i \,|\, \theta)$. The likelihood is a function of the parameter θ:

$$L(\theta; \, y_1, \ldots, y_n) = \prod_i p(y_i \,|\, \theta).$$

Note the reversal in roles of variables and parameters.

The mode of the likelihood (that is, the value of θ for which L attains its maximum value) is the *maximum likelihood estimate* of θ for the given data, y. The data, which are realizations of the variables in the density function, are considered as fixed and the parameters are considered as variables of the optimization problem in maximum likelihood methods.

Fitting by Matching Moments

Because many of the interesting distributions are uniquely determined by a few of their moments, another method of estimating the density is just parameters of a given family so that the population moments (or model moments) match the sample moments. In some distributions, the parameter estimates derived from matching moments are the same as the maximum likelihood estimates. In general, we would expect the number of moments that can be matched exactly to be the same as the number of parameters in the family of distributions being used.

Fitting by Matching Quantiles

The moments of distributions with infinite range may exhibit extreme variability. This is particularly true of higher-order moments. For that reason it is sometimes better to fit distributions by matching population quantiles with sample quantiles. In general, we would expect the number of quantiles that can be matched exactly to be the same as the number of parameters in the family of distributions being used. A quantile plot may be useful in assessing the goodness of the fit.

Statistical Properties of Parametric Family Estimators

The statistical properties of parametric density estimators depend on the properties of the estimators of the parameters. The true density is a function of the parameter, and the estimator of the density is a function of an estimator of the parameter, so, as we discussed on page 30, properties of the estimator such as unbiasedness do not carry over to the density estimator. This applies to the pointwise properties of the density estimator and so obviously applies to global properties.

The use of a parametric family of densities for estimating an unknown density results in good estimators if the unknown density is a member of that parametric family. If this is not the case, the density estimator is not robust to many types of departures from the assumed distribution. Use of a symmetric family, for example, would not yield a good estimator for a skewed distribution.

8.2 General Families of Probability Distributions

Instead of using some parametric family with relatively limited flexibility of shape, a more general parametric family may be defined. This approach is often used in simulation. The general families of distributions, such as the generalized lambda distributions, are useful in modeling an observed set of data in order to simulate observations from a similar population.

Because a probability density is a derivative of a function, a family of differential equations may be used to model the density. The Pearson family of distributions is based on a differential equation whose parameters allow a wide range of characteristics.

Pearson Curves

The univariate *Pearson family* of probability density functions is developed from the probability function of a hypergeometric random variable, Y,

$$p(y) = \Pr(Y = y)$$

$$= \frac{\binom{N\pi}{y}\binom{N(1-\pi)}{n-y}}{\binom{N}{n}}.$$

The difference equation at y is

$$\frac{\Delta p}{p} = \frac{\Pr(Y = y) - \Pr(Y = y - 1)}{\Pr(Y = y)}$$

$$= 1 - \frac{y(N(1 - \pi) - n + y)}{(N\pi - y + 1)(n - y + 1)}$$

$$= \frac{y - \frac{(n+1)(N\pi+1)}{N+2}}{-\frac{(n+1)(N\pi+1)}{N+2} + \frac{N\pi+n+2}{N+2}y - \frac{1}{N+2}y^2}$$

$$= \frac{(y - a)}{b + cy + dy^2},$$

and the associated differential equation is

$$\frac{d(\log p(y))}{dy} = \frac{(y - a)}{b + cy + dy^2}$$

or

$$(b + cy + dy^2)\,dp = (y - a)p\,dy. \tag{8.2}$$

The solution of the differential equation $(b + cy + dy^2)\,dp = (y - a)p\,dy$ depends on the roots of $(b + cy + dy^2) = 0$. Certain common parametric families correspond to particular situations. For example, if the roots are real and of opposite sign (that is, if $c^2 - 4bd > 0$ and $|c^2 - 4bd| > |b|$), then the corresponding density function is that of a beta distribution. This is called a Pearson Type I distribution.

If the roots are real, but of the same sign, the distribution is called a Pearson Type VI distribution. A familiar member of this family is the beta distribution of the second kind, which can be obtained from a common beta distribution by means of the transformation of a common beta random variable Y as $X = Y/(1 - Y)$.

Although Karl Pearson distinguished eleven types and subtypes based on the differential equation, the only other one that corresponds to a common distribution is the Pearson Type III, in which $d = 0$. After a translation of the origin, this is the gamma distribution.

The usefulness of the Pearson family of distributions arises from its ability to model many types of empirical data. By multiplying both sides of equation (8.2) by y^k, for $k = 1, 2, 3, 4$, and integrating (by parts), we can express the parameters a, b, c, d in terms of the first four moments. For modeling the distribution of observed data, the first four sample moments are used to determine the parameters of the Pearson system.

Other General Parametric Univariate Families of Distribution Functions

The *Johnson family* of distributions is based on transformations to an approximate normal distribution. There are three distributional classes, called S_B,

S_L, and S_U, based on the form of the transformation required to cause a given random variable Y to have an approximate normal distribution. Each type of transformation has four parameters. If Z is the random variable that has an approximate normal distribution, the transformations that define the distributional classes are

$$S_B: \quad Z = \gamma + \eta \log\left(\frac{Y-\epsilon}{\lambda+\epsilon-Y}\right), \quad \text{for } \epsilon \le Y \le \epsilon + \lambda, \tag{8.3}$$

$$S_L: \quad Z = \gamma + \eta \log\left(\frac{Y-\epsilon}{\lambda}\right), \quad \text{for } \epsilon \le Y, \tag{8.4}$$

$$S_U: \quad Z = \gamma + \eta \sinh^{-1}\left(\frac{Y-\epsilon}{\lambda}\right), \quad \text{for } -\infty \le Y \le \infty, \tag{8.5}$$

where $\eta, \lambda > 0$, and γ and ϵ are unrestricted.

Chou et al. (1994) identify the distributional classes and the appropriate transformations for a number of well-known distributions. Slifker and Shapiro (1980) describe a method for selection of the particular Johnson family based on ratios of quantiles of the density to be fitted.

An attractive property of the Johnson family is the ability to match it to empirical quantiles. Chou et al. (1994) give a method for fitting Johnson curves using quantiles. Devroye (1986) describes a method for simulating variates from a Johnson family.

The *Burr family* of distributions (Burr, 1942, and Burr and Cislak, 1968) is defined by the distribution function

$$P(y) = \frac{1}{1 + \exp(-G(y))},$$

where

$$G(y) = \int_{-\infty}^{y} g(t)\, dt,$$

and $g(y)$ is a nonnegative integrable function (a scaled density function). There are many forms that the Burr distribution function can take; for example,

$$P(y) = 1 - \frac{1}{(1+y^\alpha)^\beta} \quad \text{for } 0 \le y; 0 < \alpha, \beta.$$

John Tukey introduced a general distribution with a single parameter, called λ, for fitting a given set of data. Ramberg and Schmeiser (1974) extended this distribution to accommodate various amounts of skewness and kurtosis. The *generalized lambda family* of distributions is described by its inverse distribution function,

$$P^{-1}(u) = \lambda_1 + \frac{u^{\lambda_3} - (1-u)^{\lambda_4}}{\lambda_2}.$$

Karian, Dudewicz, and McDonald (1996) describe methods based on fitting moments to determine values of the λ parameters that fit a given set of data well. Karian and Dudewicz (1999, 2000) describe methods based on matching quantiles. The generalized lambda distribution is particularly useful in simulation because the percentiles can be taken as uniform random variables.

Albert, Delampady, and Polasek (1991) defined another family of distributions that is very similar to the lambda distributions with proper choice of the parameters. The family of distributions of Albert, Delampady, and Polasek is particularly useful in Bayesian analysis with location-scale models.

8.3   Mixtures of Parametric Families

Rather than trying to fit an unknown density $p(y)$ to a single parametric family of distributions, it may be better to fit it to a finite mixture of densities and to represent it as

$$p(y) \approx \sum_{j=1}^{m} w_j p_j(y \mid \theta_j),$$

where $\sum_{j=1}^{m} w_j = 1$. Such a linear combination provides great flexibility for approximating many distributions, even if the individual densities $p_j(y \mid \theta_j)$ are from a restricted class. For example, even if the individual densities are all normals, a skewed distribution can be approximated by a proper choice of the w_j.

The use of mixtures for density estimation involves *choice* of the number of terms m and the component families of densities $p_j(y \mid \theta_j)$ and *estimation* of the weights w_j and the parameters θ_j. The mixture density estimator is

$$\widehat{p}_M(y) = \sum_{j=1}^{\widehat{m}} \widehat{w}_j p_j(y \mid \widehat{\theta}_j). \tag{8.6}$$

Here, we have written the number of terms as $\widehat{m}$ because we can think of it as an estimated value under the assumption that the true density is a finite mixture of the p_j.

The choice of the number of terms is usually made adaptively; that is, after an initial arbitrary choice, terms are added or taken away based on the apparent fit of the data. Priebe (1994) describes an adaptive method of using mixtures to estimate a probability density. Solka, Poston, and Wegman (1995) describe visualization methods for selection of the mixture estimator.

The process of fitting a mixture of probability densities to a given dataset involves what is called "model-based clustering". Each observation is assigned to a particular distribution, and each set of observations from a given distribution is a cluster.

Everitt and Hand (1981) provide a good general discussion of the use of finite mixtures for representing distributions. Solka et al. (1998) describe how fitting mixtures to observed data can provide insight about the underlying structure of the data. Roeder and Wasserman (1997) describe the use of mixtures in Bayesian density estimation.

Exercises

8.1. Consider the $U(0, \theta)$ distribution. The maximum likelihood estimator of θ is the maximum order statistic, $x_{(n)}$, in a sample of size n. This estimator, which is biased, provides a parametric estimator of the function $p(x) = 1/\theta$, which is the probability density function corresponding to $U(0, \theta)$:

$$\widehat{p}_P(x) = 1/x_{(n)}, \quad \text{for } 0 < x < x_{(n)}.$$

(a) Determine the ISE of $\widehat{p}_P(x) = 1/x_{(n)}$. Remember that the domain is $(0, \theta)$.

(b) Determine the MISE of $\widehat{p}_P(x) = 1/x_{(n)}$ (with respect to $U(0, \theta)$).

(c) The bias in $x_{(n)}$ can be reduced by taking $\widehat{\theta} = cx_{(n)}$ for some $c > 1$. Determine the value of c that minimizes the MISE.

8.2. Repeat Exercises 8.1a, 8.1b, and 8.1c for the IAE and the MIAE instead of the ISE and the MISE.

8.3. Repeat Exercises 8.1a, 8.1b, and 8.1c for the SAE and the MSAE.

8.4. For the $U(0,1)$ distribution, compute the SAE and the MSAE of the ECDF as an estimtor of the CDF.

8.5. Given a random sample $x_1, x_2, \ldots, x_n$, where n is greater than 9, assume that the density of the population from which the sample was taken can be written as a mixture of three normal densities:

$$p(x) = \frac{w_1}{\sqrt{2\pi}\sigma_1} e^{(x-\mu_1)^2/2\sigma_1^2} + \frac{w_2}{\sqrt{2\pi}\sigma_2} e^{(x-\mu_2)^2/2\sigma_2^2} + \frac{w_3}{\sqrt{2\pi}\sigma_3} e^{(x-\mu_3)^2/2\sigma_3^2}.$$

(a) What is the likelihood function of w_i, μ_i, σ_i?

(b) Generate a random sample of size 100 from a gamma(2,3) distribution and compute the MLE.

(c) Using $\widehat{p}$ as the mixture above with the MLE substituted for the parameters, plot your estimated density and superimpose on it a histogram of the random sample you generated.

(d) Using a histogram with 10 bins, compute an estimate of the integrated error of your estimate.

Chapter 9

Nonparametric Estimation of Probability Density Functions

Estimation of a probability density function is similar to the estimation of any function, and the properties of the function estimators that we have discussed are relevant for density function estimators. A density function $p(y)$ is characterized by two properties:

- it is nonnegative everywhere;

- it integrates to 1 (with the appropriate definition of "integrate").

In this chapter, we consider several nonparametric estimators of a density; that is, estimators of a general nonnegative function that integrates to 1 and for which we make no assumptions about a functional form other than, perhaps, smoothness.

It seems reasonable that we require the density estimate to have the characteristic properties of a density:

- $\widehat{p}(y) \geq 0$ for all y;

- $\int_{\mathbb{R}^d} \widehat{p}(y) \, dy = 1$.

A probability density estimator that is nonnegative and integrates to 1 is called a *bona fide* estimator.

Rosenblatt (1956) showed that no unbiased bona fide estimator can exist for all continuous p. Rather than requiring an unbiased estimator that cannot be a bona fide estimator, we generally seek a bona fide estimator with small mean squared error or a sequence of bona fide estimators $\widehat{p}_n$ that are asymptotically unbiased; that is,

$$E_p(\widehat{p}_n(y)) \to p(y) \quad \text{for all } y \in \mathbb{R}^d \text{ as } n \to \infty.$$

9.1   The Likelihood Function

Suppose that we have a random sample, $y_1, \ldots, y_n$, from a population with density p. Treating the density p as a variable, we write the likelihood functional as

$$L(p; y_1, \ldots, y_n) = \prod_{i=1}^{n} p(y_i).$$

The *maximum likelihood method* of estimation obviously cannot be used directly because this functional is unbounded in p. We may, however, seek an estimator that maximizes some modification of the likelihood. There are two reasonable ways to approach this problem. One is to restrict the domain of the optimization problem. This is called *restricted maximum likelihood*. The other is to *regularize* the estimator by adding a penalty term to the functional to be optimized. This is called *penalized maximum likelihood*.

We may seek to maximize the likelihood functional subject to the constraint that p be a bona fide density. If we put no further restrictions on the function p, however, infinite Dirac spikes at each observation give an unbounded likelihood, so a maximum likelihood estimator cannot exist, subject only to the restriction to the bona fide class. An additional restriction that p be Lebesgue-integrable over some domain D (that is, $p \in L^1(D)$) does not resolve the problem because we can construct sequences of finite spikes at each observation that grow without bound.

We therefore must restrict the class further. Consider a finite dimensional class, such as the class of step functions that are bona fide density estimators. We assume that the sizes of the regions over which the step function is constant are greater than 0.

For a step function with m regions having constant values, $c_1, \ldots, c_m$, the likelihood is

$$
\begin{aligned}
L(c_1, \ldots, c_m; y_1, \ldots, y_n) &= \prod_{i=1}^{n} p(y_i) \\
&= \prod_{k=1}^{m} c_k^{n_k},
\end{aligned}
\tag{9.1}
$$

where n_k is the number of data points in the kth region. For the step function to be a bona fide estimator, all c_k must be nonnegative and finite. A maximum therefore exists in the class of step functions that are bona fide estimators.

If v_k is the measure of the volume of the kth region (that is, v_k is the length of an interval in the univariate case, the area in the bivariate case, and so on), we have

$$\sum_{k=1}^{m} c_k v_k = 1.$$

We incorporate this constraint together with equation (9.1) to form the Lagrangian,

$$L(c_1, \ldots, c_m) + \lambda \left(1 - \sum_{k=1}^{m} c_k v_k \right).$$

Differentiating the Lagrangian function and setting the derivative to zero, we have at the maximum point $c_k = c_k^*$, for any λ,

$$\frac{\partial L}{\partial c_k} = \lambda v_k.$$

Using the derivative of L from equation (9.1), we get

$$n_k L = \lambda c_k^* v_k.$$

Summing both sides of this equation over k, we have

$$nL = \lambda,$$

and then substituting, we have

$$n_k L = nL c_k^* v_k.$$

Therefore, the maximum of the likelihood occurs at

$$c_k^* = \frac{n_k}{n v_k}.$$

The restricted maximum likelihood estimator is therefore

$$
\begin{aligned}
\widehat{p}(y) &= \frac{n_k}{n v_k}, \quad \text{for } y \in \text{region } k, \\
&= 0, \qquad \text{otherwise.}
\end{aligned}
\tag{9.2}
$$

Instead of restricting the density estimate to step functions, we could consider other classes of functions, such as piecewise linear functions. For given subsets S_i of densities for which a maximum likelihood estimator exists, Grenander (1981) developed estimators based on sequences of such subsets, each containing its predecessor. The sequence is called a sieve, so the approach is called the method of sieves. Such sequences have been constructed that yield standard estimators of the density, such as histogram estimators and orthogonal series estimators (see Banks, 1989, for example).

We may also seek other properties, such as smoothness, for the estimated density. One way of achieving other desirable properties for the estimator is to use a penalizing function to modify the function to be optimized. Instead of the likelihood function, we may use a penalized likelihood function of the form

$$L_{\mathrm{p}}(p; y_1, \ldots, y_n) = \prod_{i=1}^{n} p(y_i) e^{-\mathcal{T}(p)},$$

where $\mathcal{T}(p)$ is a transform that measures some property that we would like to minimize. For example, to achieve smoothness, we may use the transform $\mathcal{R}(p)$ of equation (6.39) in the penalizing factor. To choose a function $\hat{p}$ to maximize $L_p(p)$ we would have to use some finite series approximation to $\mathcal{T}(\hat{p})$. (See Scott, Tapia, and Thompson, 1980, for an example of how this might be done. Their estimator is implemented in the IMSL routine despl.)

For densities with special properties there may be likelihood approaches that take advantage of those properties. For example, for nonincreasing densities, Grenander (1981) suggested use of the slope of the least concave majorant of the ECDF.

9.2   Histogram Estimators

Let us assume finite support D, and construct a fixed partition of D into a grid of m nonoverlapping bins T_k. (We can arbitrarily assign bin boundaries to one or the other bin.) Let v_k be the volume of the kth bin (in one dimension, v_k is a length and in this simple case is often denoted h_k; in two dimensions, v_k is an area, and so on). The number of such bins we choose, and consequently their volumes, depends on n, so we sometimes indicate that dependence in the notation: $v_{n,k}$. For the sample $y_1, \ldots, y_n$, the histogram estimator of the probability density function is defined as

$$
\begin{aligned}
\widehat{p}_H(y) &= \sum_{k=1}^{m} \frac{1}{v_k} \frac{\sum_{i=1}^{n} \mathrm{I}_{T_k}(y_i)}{n} \mathrm{I}_{T_k}(y), \quad \text{for } y \in D, \\
&= 0, \quad \text{otherwise.}
\end{aligned}
$$

The histogram is the restricted maximum likelihood estimator (9.2).

Letting n_k be the number of sample values falling into T_k,

$$
n_k = \sum_{i=1}^{n} \mathrm{I}_{T_k}(y_i),
$$

we have the simpler expression for the histogram over D,

$$
\widehat{p}_H(y) = \sum_{k=1}^{m} \frac{n_k}{n v_k} \mathrm{I}_{T_k}(y). \tag{9.3}
$$

As we have noted already, this is a bona fide estimator:

$$
\widehat{p}_H(y) \geq 0
$$

and

$$
\begin{aligned}
\int_{\mathbb{R}^d} \widehat{p}_H(y) \mathrm{d}y &= \sum_{k=1}^{m} \frac{n_k}{n v_k} v_k \\
&= 1.
\end{aligned}
$$

Although our discussion generally concerns observations on multivariate random variables, we should occasionally consider simple univariate observations. One reason why the univariate case is simpler is that the derivative is a scalar function. Another reason why we use the univariate case as a model is because it is easier to visualize. The density of a univariate random variable is two-dimensional, and densities of other types of random variables are of higher dimension, so only in the univariate case can the density estimates be graphed directly.

In the univariate case, we assume that the support is the finite interval $[a, b]$. We partition $[a, b]$ into a grid of m nonoverlapping bins $T_k = [t_{n,k}, t_{n,k+1})$ where

$$a = t_{n,1} < t_{n,2} < \ldots < t_{n,m+1} = b.$$

The univariate histogram is

$$\widehat{p}_H(y) = \sum_{k=1}^{m} \frac{n_k}{n(t_{n,k+1} - t_{n,k})} I_{T_k}(y). \tag{9.4}$$

If the bins are of equal width, say h (that is, $t_k = t_{k-1} + h$), the histogram is

$$\widehat{p}_H(y) = \frac{n_k}{nh}, \quad \text{for } y \in T_k.$$

This class of functions consists of polynomial splines of degree 0 with fixed knots, and the histogram is the maximum likelihood estimator over the class of step functions. Generalized versions of the histogram can be defined with respect to splines of higher degree. Splines with degree higher than 1 may yield negative estimators, but such histograms are also maximum likelihood estimators over those classes of functions.

The histogram as we have defined it is sometimes called a "density histogram", whereas a "frequency histogram" is not normalized by the n.

Some Properties of the Histogram Estimator

The histogram estimator, being a step function, is discontinuous at cell boundaries, and it is zero outside of a finite range. As we have seen (page 156 and Figure 7.3 on page 159), it is sensitive both to the bin size and to the choice of the origin.

An important advantage of the histogram estimator is its simplicity, both for computations and for analysis. In addition to its simplicity, as we have seen, it has two other desirable global properties:

- It is a bona fide density estimator.

- It is the unique maximum likelihood estimator confined to the subspace of functions of the form

$$
\begin{aligned}
g(t) &= c_k, \text{ for } t \in T_k, \\
&= 0, \text{ otherwise,}
\end{aligned}
$$

and where $g(t) \geq 0$ and $\int_{\cup_k T_k} g(t)\,dt = 1$.

Pointwise and Binwise Properties

Properties of the histogram vary from bin to bin. The expectation of at the point y in bin T_k is

$$E(\widehat{p}_H(y)) = \frac{p_k}{v_k}, \tag{9.5}$$

where

$$p_k = \int_{T_k} p(t)\,dt \tag{9.6}$$

is the probability content of the kth bin.

Some pointwise properties of the histogram estimator are the following:

- The **bias** of the histogram at the point y within the kth bin is

$$\frac{p_k}{v_k} - p(y). \tag{9.7}$$

Note that the bias is different from bin to bin, even if the bins are of constant size. The bias tends to decrease as the bin size decreases. We can bound the bias if we assume a regularity condition on p. If there exists γ such that for any $y_1 \neq y_2$ in an interval

$$|p(y_1) - p(y_2)| < \gamma \|y_1 - y_2\|,$$

we say that p is Lipschitz-continuous on the interval, and for such a density, for any ξ_k in the kth bin, we have

$$
\begin{aligned}
|\text{Bias}(\widehat{p}_H(y))| &= |p(\xi_k) - p(y)| \\
&\leq \gamma_k \|\xi_k - y\| \\
&\leq \gamma_k v_k.
\end{aligned} \tag{9.8}
$$

- The **variance** of the histogram at the point y within the kth bin is

$$
\begin{aligned}
V(\widehat{p}_H(y)) &= V(n_k)/(nv_k)^2 \\
&= \frac{p_k(1 - p_k)}{nv_k^2}.
\end{aligned} \tag{9.9}
$$

This is easily seen by recognizing that n_k is a binomial random variable with parameters n and p_k. Notice that the variance decreases as the bin size increases. Note also that the variance is different from bin to bin. We can bound the variance:

$$V(\widehat{p}_H(y)) \leq \frac{p_k}{nv_k^2}.$$

By the mean-value theorem, we have $p_k = v_k p(\xi_k)$ for some $\xi_k \in T_k$, so we can write

$$V(\widehat{p}_H(y)) \leq \frac{p(\xi_k)}{nv_k}.$$

Notice the tradeoff between bias and variance: *as h increases the variance, equation (9.9), decreases, but the bound on the bias, equation (9.8), increases.*

- The **mean squared error** of the histogram at the point y within the kth bin is

$$\text{MSE}(\widehat{p}_H(y)) = \frac{p_k(1 - p_k)}{nv_k^2} + \left(\frac{p_k}{v_k} - p(y)\right)^2. \qquad (9.10)$$

For a Lipschitz-continuous density, within the kth bin we have

$$\text{MSE}(\widehat{p}_H(y)) \leq \frac{p(\xi_k)}{nv_k} + \gamma_k^2 v_k^2. \qquad (9.11)$$

We easily see that the histogram estimator is L_2 pointwise consistent for a Lipschitz-continuous density if, as $n \to \infty$, for each k, $v_k \to 0$ and $nv_k \to \infty$. By differentiating, we see that the minimum of the bound on the MSE in the kth bin occurs for

$$h^*(k) = \left(\frac{p(\xi_k)}{2\gamma_k^2 n}\right)^{1/3}. \qquad (9.12)$$

Substituting this value back into MSE, we obtain the order of the optimal MSE at the point x,

$$\text{MSE}^*(\widehat{p}_H(y)) = O(n^{-2/3}).$$

Asymptotic MISE (or AMISE) of Histogram Estimators

Global properties of the histogram are obtained by summing the binwise properties over all of the bins.

The expressions for the integrated variance and the integrated squared bias are quite complicated because they depend on the bin sizes and the probability content of the bins. We will first write the general expressions, and then we will assume some degree of smoothness of the true density and write approximate expressions that result from mean values or Taylor approximations. We will assume rectangular bins for additional simplification. Finally, we will then consider bins of equal size to simplify the expressions further.

First, consider the integrated variance,

$$\begin{aligned} \text{IV}(\widehat{p}_H) &= \int_{\mathbb{R}^d} V(\widehat{p}_H(t)) \, dt \\ &= \sum_{k=1}^{m} \int_{T_k} V(\widehat{p}_H(t)) \, dt \end{aligned}$$

$$= \sum_{k=1}^{m} \frac{p_k - p_k^2}{nv_k}$$

$$= \sum_{k=1}^{m} \left(\frac{1}{nv_k} - \frac{\sum p(\xi_k)^2 v_k}{n} \right) + o(n^{-1})$$

for some $\xi_k \in T_k$, as before. Now, taking $\sum p(\xi_k)^2 v_k$ as an approximation to the integral $\int (p(t))^2 \, dt$, and letting $\mathcal{S}$ be the functional that measures the variation in a square-integrable function of d variables,

$$\mathcal{S}(g) = \int_{\mathbb{R}^d} (g(t))^2 \, dt, \tag{9.13}$$

we have the integrated variance,

$$\mathrm{IV}(\widehat{p}_H) \approx \sum_{k=1}^{m} \frac{1}{nv_k} - \frac{\mathcal{S}(p)}{n}, \tag{9.14}$$

and the asymptotic integrated variance,

$$\mathrm{AIV}(\widehat{p}_H) = \sum_{k=1}^{m} \frac{1}{nv_k}. \tag{9.15}$$

The measure of the variation, $\mathcal{S}(p)$, is a measure of the roughness of the density because the density integrates to 1.

Now, consider the other term in the integrated MSE, the integrated squared bias. We will consider the case of rectangular bins, in which $h_k = (h_{k_1}, \ldots, h_{k_d})$ is the vector of lengths of sides in the kth bin. In the case of rectangular bins, $v_k = \Pi_{j=1}^{d} h_{k_j}$.

We assume that the density can be expanded in a Taylor series, and we expand the density in the kth bin about $\bar{t}_k$, the midpoint of the rectangular bin. For $\bar{t}_k + t \in T_k$, we have

$$p(\bar{t}_k + t) = p(\bar{t}_k) + t^{\mathrm{T}} \nabla p(\bar{t}_k) + \frac{1}{2} t^{\mathrm{T}} \mathrm{H}_p(\bar{t}_k)t + \cdots, \tag{9.16}$$

where $\mathrm{H}_p(\bar{t}_k)$ is the Hessian of p evaluated at $\bar{t}_k$.

The probability content of the kth bin, p_k, from equation (9.6), can be expressed as an integral of the Taylor series expansion:

$$
\begin{aligned}
p_k &= \int_{\bar{t}_k + t \in T_k} p(\bar{t}_k + t) \, dt \\
&= \int_{-h_{kd}/2}^{h_{kd}/2} \cdots \int_{-h_{k1}/2}^{h_{k1}/2} \left(p(\bar{t}_k) + t^{\mathrm{T}} \nabla p(\bar{t}_k) + \ldots \right) dt_1 \cdots dt_d \\
&= v_k p(\bar{t}_k) + \mathrm{O}\left(h_{k*}^{d+2} \right),
\end{aligned} \tag{9.17}
$$

where $h_{k*} = \min_j h_{kj}$. The bias at a point $\bar{t}_k + t$ in the kth bin, after substituting equations (9.16) and (9.17) into equation (9.7), is

$$\frac{p_k}{v_k} - p(\bar{t}_k + t) = -t^{\text{T}} \nabla p(\bar{t}_k) + \text{O}(h_{k*}^2).$$

For the kth bin the integrated squared bias is

$\text{ISB}_k(\widehat{p}_H)$

$$= \int_{T_k} \left(\left(t^{\text{T}} \nabla p(\bar{t}_k) \right)^2 - 2\text{O}(h_{k*}^2) t^{\text{T}} \nabla p(\bar{t}_k) + \text{O}(h_{k*}^4) \right) \, dt$$

$$= \int_{-h_{kd}/2}^{h_{kd}/2} \cdots \int_{-h_{k1}/2}^{h_{k1}/2} \sum_i \sum_j t_{ki} t_{kj} \nabla_i p(\bar{t}_k) \nabla_j p(\bar{t}_k) \, dt_1 \cdots dt_d + \text{O}\left(h_{k*}^{4+d} \right).$$

$$(9.18)$$

Many of the expressions above are simpler if we use a constant bin size, v, or $h_1, \ldots, h_d$. In the case of constant bin size, the asymptotic integrated variance in equation (9.15) becomes

$$\text{AIV}(\widehat{p}_H) = \frac{1}{nv}. \tag{9.19}$$

In this case, the integral in equation (9.18) simplifies as the integration is performed term by term because the cross-product terms cancel, and the integral is

$$\frac{1}{12} (h_1 \cdots h_d) \sum_{j=1}^d h_j^2 \left(\nabla_j p(\bar{t}_k) \right)^2. \tag{9.20}$$

This is the asymptotic squared bias integrated over the kth bin.

When we sum the expression (9.20) over all bins, the $\left(\nabla_j p(\bar{t}_k) \right)^2$ become $\mathcal{S}(\nabla_j p)$, and we have the asymptotic integrated squared bias,

$$\text{AISB}(\widehat{p}_H) = \frac{1}{12} \sum_{j=1}^d h_j^2 \mathcal{S}(\nabla_j p). \tag{9.21}$$

Combining the asymptotic integrated variance, equation (9.19), and squared bias, equation (9.21), for the histogram with rectangular bins of constant size, we have

$$\text{AMISE}(\widehat{p}_H) = \frac{1}{n(h_1 \cdots h_d)} + \frac{1}{12} \sum_{j=1}^d h_j^2 \mathcal{S}(\nabla_j p). \tag{9.22}$$

As we have seen before, smaller bin sizes increase the variance but decrease the squared bias.

Bin Sizes

As we have mentioned and have seen by example, the histogram is very sensitive to the bin sizes, both in appearance and in other properties. Equation (9.22) for the AMISE assuming constant rectangular bin size is often used as a guide for determining the bin size to use when constructing a histogram. This expression involves $\mathcal{S}(\nabla_j p)$ and so, of course, cannot be used directly. Nevertheless, differentiating the expression with respect to h_j and setting the result equal to zero, we have the bin width that is optimal with respect to the AMISE,

$$
h_{j*} = \mathcal{S}(\nabla_j p)^{-1/2} \left(6 \prod_{i=1}^{d} \mathcal{S}(\nabla_i p)^{1/2} \right)^{\frac{1}{2+d}} n^{-\frac{1}{2+d}}. \tag{9.23}
$$

Substituting this into equation (9.22), we have the as optimal value of the AMISE

$$
\frac{1}{4} \left(36 \prod_{i=1}^{d} \mathcal{S}(\nabla_i p)^{1/2} \right)^{\frac{1}{2+d}} n^{-\frac{2}{2+d}}. \tag{9.24}
$$

Notice that the optimal rate of decrease of AMISE for histogram estimators is $O(n^{-\frac{2}{2+d}})$. Although histograms have several desirable properties, this order of convergence is not good compared to that of some other bona fide density estimators, as we will see in later sections.

The expression for the optimal bin width involves $\mathcal{S}(\nabla_j p)$, where p is the unknown density. An approach is to choose a value for $\mathcal{S}(\nabla_j p)$ that corresponds to some good general distribution. A "good general distribution", of course, is the normal with a diagonal variance-covariance matrix. For the d-variate normal with variance-covariance matrix $\Sigma = \mathrm{diag}(\sigma_1^2, \ldots, \sigma_d^2)$,

$$
\mathcal{S}(\nabla_j p) = \frac{1}{2^{d+1} \pi^{d/2} \sigma_j^2 |\Sigma|^{1/2}}.
$$

For a univariate normal density with variance σ^2,

$$
\mathcal{S}(p') = 1/(4\sqrt{\pi}\sigma^3)
$$

(Exercise 6.11b on page 152), so the optimal constant one-dimensional bin width under the AMISE criterion is

$$
3.49\sigma n^{-1/3}.
$$

In practice, of course, an estimate of σ must be used. The sample standard deviation s is one obvious choice. Freedman and Diaconis (1981a) proposed using a more robust estimate of the scale based on the sample interquartile range, r. The sample interquartile range leads to a bin width of $2rn^{-1/3}$. See Lax (1985) for several other scale estimators.

The AMISE is essentially an L_2 measure. The L_∞ criterion—that is, the sup absolute error (SAE) of equation (6.31)—also leads to an asymptotically optimal bin width that is proportional to $n^{-1/3}$. Based on that criterion, Freedman and Diaconis (1981b) derived the rule

$$1.66s \left(\frac{\log n}{n} \right)^{1/3},$$

where s is an estimate of the scale.

One of the most commonly used rules is for the number of bins rather than the width. Assume a symmetric binomial model for the bin counts, that is, the bin count is just the binomial coefficient. The total sample size n is

$$\sum_{k=0}^{m-1} \binom{m-1}{k} = 2^{k-1},$$

and so the number of bins is

$$m = 1 + \log_2 n.$$

Bin Shapes

In the univariate case, histogram bins may vary in size, but each bin is an interval. For the multivariate case, there are various possibilities for the shapes of the bins. The simplest shape is the direct extension of an interval, that is a hyperrectangle. The volume of a hyperrectangle is just $v_k = \prod h_{kj}$. There are, of course, other possibilities; any tessellation of the space would work. The objects may or may not be regular, and they may or may not be of equal size. Regular, equal-sized geometric figures such as hypercubes have the advantages of simplicity, both computationally and analytically. In two dimensions, there are three possible regular tessellations: triangles, squares, and hexagons.

For two dimensions, Scott (1988) showed that hexagons are slightly better than squares and triangles with respect to the AMISE (see Exercise 9.6 on page 228). Binning in hexagons can be accomplished using two staggered tessellations by rectangles, as indicated in Figure 9.1 (see also Exercise 9.7). The lattice determining one tessellation is formed by the points at the centers of the rectangles of the other tessellation. Newman and Barkema (1999) discuss data structures for working with hexagonal grids and a related type of grid formed by a Kagomé lattice. See Klinke (1997) for general discussions of data structures for computational statistics.

Various other tessellations may also work well, especially adaptive tessellations (see Hearne and Wegman, 1991). We discuss tessellations for use in clustering data beginning on page 246. General discussions of tessellations are given by Conway and Sloane (1999) (particularly Chapter 2 of that book) and by Okabe et al. (2000). Conway and Sloane (1982) give algorithms for binning data into lattices of various types for dimensions from 2 to 8.

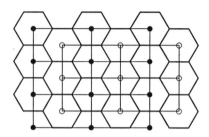

Figure 9.1: Regular Hexagonal Tiling of 2-Space with Two Rectangular Lattices Superimposed

For hyperrectangles of constant size, the univariate theory generally extends fairly easily to the multivariate case. The histogram density estimator is

$$\widehat{p}_H(y) = \frac{n_k}{nh_1 h_2 \cdots h_d}, \quad \text{for } y \in T_k,$$

where the h's are the lengths of the sides of the rectangles. The variance within the kth bin is

$$V(\widehat{p}_H(y)) = \frac{np_k(1 - p_k)}{(nh_1 h_2 \cdots h_d)^2}, \quad \text{for } y \in T_k,$$

and the integrated variance is

$$\text{IV}(\widehat{p}_H) \approx \frac{1}{nh_1 h_2 \cdots h_d} - \frac{\mathcal{S}(f)}{n}.$$

Other Density Estimators Related to the Histogram

There are several variations of the histogram that are useful as probability density estimators. The most common modification is to connect points on the histogram by a continuous curve. A simple way of doing this in the univariate case leads to the *frequency polygon*. This is the piecewise linear curve that connects the midpoints of the bins of the histogram. The endpoints are usually the zero values of two appended bins, one on either side.

The *histospline* is constructed by interpolating knots of the empirical CDF with a cubic spline and then differentiating it. More general methods use splines or orthogonal series, such as we discuss in Section 9.5, to fit the histogram.

As we have mentioned and have seen by example, the histogram is somewhat sensitive in appearance to the location of the bins, even for a fixed width of the bins (see also Simonoff, 1995). To overcome the problem of location of the bins, Scott and Thompson (1983) suggested a density estimator that is the average of several histograms with equal bin widths but different bin locations. This is called the *average shifted histogram*, or ASH. It also has desirable statistical properties, and it is computationally efficient in the multivariate case. See Scott (1992) for further discussions of ASH.

9.3 Kernel Estimators

Kernel methods are probably the most widely used technique for building non-parametric probability density estimators. They are best understood by developing them as a special type of histogram. The difference is that the bins in kernel estimators are centered at the points at which the estimator is to be computed. The problem of the choice of location of the bins in histogram estimators does not arise.

Rosenblatt's Histogram Estimator; Kernels

For the one-dimensional case, Rosenblatt (1956) defined a histogram that is shifted to be centered on the point at which the density is to be estimated. At the point y, Rosenblatt's histogram estimator is

$$\widehat{p}_R(y) = \frac{\#\{y_i \ : \ y_i \in (y - h/2, \quad y + h/2]\ \}}{nh}. \tag{9.25}$$

This histogram estimator avoids the ordinary histogram's constant-slope contribution to the bias. This estimator is a step function with variable lengths of the intervals that have constant value.

Rosenblatt's centered histogram can also be written in terms of the ECDF:

$$\widehat{p}_R(y) = \frac{P_n(y + h/2) - P_n(y - h/2)}{h},$$

where, as usual, P_n denotes the ECDF. As seen in this expression, Rosenblatt's estimator is a centered finite-difference approximation to the derivative of the empirical cumulative distribution function (which, of course, is not differentiable at the data points). We could, of course, use the same idea and form other density estimators using other finite-difference approximations to the derivative of P_n.

Another way to write Rosenblatt's shifted histogram estimator over bins of length h is

$$\widehat{p}_R(y) = \frac{1}{nh} \sum_{i=1}^{n} K\left(\frac{y - y_i}{h}\right), \tag{9.26}$$

where $K(t) = 1$ if $|t| < 1/2$ and $= 0$ otherwise. The function K is a kernel or filter. In Rosenblatt's estimator, it is a "boxcar" function, but other kernel functions could be used.

The estimator extends easily to the multivariate case. In the general kernel estimator, we usually use a more general scaling of $y - y_i$,

$$V^{-1}(y - y_i),$$

for some positive-definite matrix V. The determinant of V^{-1} scales the estimator to account for the scaling within the kernel function. The general kernel estimator is given by

$$\widehat{p}_K(y) = \frac{1}{n|V|} \sum_{i=1}^{n} K\left(V^{-1}(y - y_i)\right), \tag{9.27}$$

where the function K is called the *kernel*, and V is the *smoothing matrix*. The determinant of the smoothing matrix is exactly analogous to the bin volume in a histogram estimator. The univariate version of the kernel estimator is the same as Rosenblatt's estimator (9.26), in which a more general function K is allowed.

In practice, V is usually taken to be constant for a given sample size, but, of course, there is no reason for this to be the case, and indeed it may be better to vary V depending on the number of observations near the point y. The dependency of the smoothing matrix on the sample size n and on y is often indicated by the notation $V_n(y)$.

Properties of Kernel Estimators

The appearance of the kernel density estimator depends to some extent on the support and shape of the kernel. Unlike the histogram estimator, the kernel density estimator may be continuous and even smooth.

It is easy to see that if the kernel satisfies

$$K(t) \geq 0, \tag{9.28}$$

and

$$\int_{\mathbb{R}^d} K(t)\, \mathrm{d}t = 1 \tag{9.29}$$

(that is, if K is a density), then $\widehat{p}_K(y)$ is a bona fide density estimator.

There are other requirements that we may impose on the kernel either for the theoretical properties that result or just for their intuitive appeal. It also seems reasonable that in estimating the density at the point y, we would want to emphasize the sample points near y. This could be done in various ways, but one simple way is to require

$$\int_{\mathbb{R}^d} tK(t)\, \mathrm{d}t = 0. \tag{9.30}$$

In addition, we may require the kernel to be symmetric about 0.

For multivariate density estimation, the kernels are usually chosen as a radially symmetric generalization of a univariate kernel. Such a kernel can be formed as a product of the univariate kernels. For a product kernel, we have for some constant σ_K^2,

$$\int_{\mathbb{R}^d} tt^{\mathrm{T}} K(t)\, \mathrm{d}t = \sigma_K^2 I_d, \tag{9.31}$$

where I_d is the identity matrix of order d. We could also impose this as a requirement on any kernel, whether it is a product kernel or not. This makes the expressions for bias and variance of the estimators simpler. The spread of the kernel can always be controlled by the smoothing matrix V, so sometimes, for convenience, we sometimes require $\sigma_K^2 = 1$.

In the following, we will assume the kernel satisfies the properties in equations (9.28) through (9.31).

The pointwise properties of the kernel estimator are relatively simple to determine because the estimator at a point is merely the sample mean of n independent and identically distributed random variables. The expectation of the kernel estimator (9.27) at the point y is the convolution of the kernel function and the probability density function,

$$
\begin{aligned}
\mathrm{E}\left(\widehat{p}_K(y)\right) &= \frac{1}{|V|} \int_{\mathbb{R}^d} K\left(V^{-1}(y-t)\right) p(t)\, dt \\
&= \int_{\mathbb{R}^d} K(u) p(y - Vt)\, du,
\end{aligned}
\tag{9.32}
$$

where $u = V^{-1}(y-t)$ (and, hence, $du = |V|^{-1}dt$).

If we approximate $p(y - Vt)$ about y with a three-term Taylor series, using the properties of the kernel in equations (9.28) through (9.31) and using properties of the trace, we have

$$
\begin{aligned}
\mathrm{E}\left(\widehat{p}_K(y)\right) &\approx \int_{\mathbb{R}^d} K(u)\left(p(y) - (Vu)^{\mathrm{T}}\nabla p(y) + \frac{1}{2}(Vu)^{\mathrm{T}}\mathrm{H}_p(y)Vu\right) du \\
&= p(y) - 0 + \frac{1}{2}\mathrm{trace}\left(V^{\mathrm{T}}\mathrm{H}_p(y)V\right).
\end{aligned}
\tag{9.33}
$$

To second order in the elements of V (that is, $\mathrm{O}(|V|^2)$), the bias at the point y is therefore

$$
\frac{1}{2}\mathrm{trace}\left(VV^{\mathrm{T}}\mathrm{H}_p(y)\right).
\tag{9.34}
$$

Using the same kinds of expansions and approximations as in equations (9.32) and (9.33) to evaluate $\mathrm{E}\left((\widehat{p}_K(y))^2\right)$ to get an expression of order $\mathrm{O}(|V|/n)$, and subtracting the square of the expectation in equation (9.33), we get the approximate variance at y as

$$
\frac{p(y)}{n|V|} \int_{\mathbb{R}^d} (K(u))^2\, du,
$$

or

$$
\frac{p(y)}{n|V|} S(K).
\tag{9.35}
$$

Integrating this, we have

$$
\mathrm{AIV}(\widehat{p}_K) = \frac{S(K)}{n|V|},
\tag{9.36}
$$

and integrating the square of the asymptotic bias in expression (9.34), we have

$$
\mathrm{AISB}(\widehat{p}_K) = \frac{1}{4}\int_{\mathbb{R}^d}\left(\mathrm{trace}\left(V^{\mathrm{T}}\mathrm{H}_p(y)V\right)\right)^2 dy.
\tag{9.37}
$$

These expressions are much simpler in the univariate case, where the smoothing matrix V is the smoothing parameter or window width h. We have a simpler approximation for $E(\widehat{p}_K(y))$ than that given in equation (9.33),

$$E(\widehat{p}_K(y)) \approx p(y) + \frac{1}{2}h^2 p''(y) \int_{\mathbb{R}^d} u^2 K(u)\, du,$$

and from this we get a simpler expression for the AISB. After likewise simplifying the AIV, we have

$$\text{AMISE}(\widehat{p}_K) = \frac{S(K)}{nh} + \frac{1}{4}\sigma_K^4 h^4 \mathcal{R}(p), \tag{9.38}$$

where we have left the kernel unscaled (that is, $\int u^2 K(u)\, du = \sigma_K^4$).

Minimizing this with respect to h, we have the optimal value of the smoothing parameter

$$\left(\frac{S(K)}{n\sigma_K^4 \mathcal{R}(p)}\right)^{1/5}. \tag{9.39}$$

Substituting this back into the expression for the AMISE, we find that its optimal value in this univariate case is

$$\frac{5}{4}\mathcal{R}(p)(\sigma_K S(K))^{4/5}\, n^{-4/5}. \tag{9.40}$$

The AMISE for the univariate kernel density estimator is thus $O(n^{-4/5})$. Recall that the AMISE for the univariate histogram density estimator is $O(n^{-2/3})$ (expression (9.24) on page 214).

We see that the bias and variance of kernel density estimators have similar relationships to the smoothing matrix that the bias and variance of histogram estimators have. As the determinant of the smoothing matrix gets smaller (that is, as the window of influence around the point at which the estimator is to be evaluated gets smaller), the bias becomes smaller and the variance becomes larger. This agrees with what we would expect intuitively.

Choice of Kernels

Standard normal densities have these properties described above, so the kernel is often chosen to be the standard normal density. As it turns out, the kernel density estimator is not very sensitive to the form of the kernel.

Although the kernel may be from a parametric family of distributions, in kernel density estimation, we do not estimate those parameters; hence, the kernel method is a nonparametric method.

Sometimes, a kernel with finite support is easier to work with. In the univariate case, a useful general form of a compact kernel is

$$K(t) = \kappa_{rs}(1 - |t|^r)^s I_{[-1,1]}(t),$$

where

$$\kappa_{rs}(u) = \frac{rB(s+1, 1/r)}{2u^s(1-u)^{1/r}}, \quad \text{for } r > 0, \ s \geq 0,$$

and $B(a, b)$ is the complete beta function.

This general form leads to several simple specific cases:

- for $r = 1$ and $s = 0$, it is the rectangular kernel;

- for $r = 1$ and $s = 1$, it is the triangular kernel;

- for $r = 2$ and $s = 1$ ($\kappa_{rs} = 3/4$), it is the "Epanechnikov" kernel, which yields the optimal rate of convergence of the MISE (see Epanechnikov, 1969);

- for $r = 2$ and $s = 2$ ($\kappa_{rs} = 15/16$), it is the "biweight" kernel.

If $r = 2$ and $s \to \infty$, we have the Gaussian kernel (with some rescaling).

As mentioned above, for multivariate density estimation, the kernels are often chosen as a product of the univariate kernels. The product Epanechnikov kernel, for example, is

$$K(t) = \frac{d+2}{2c_d}(1 - t^T t)I_{(t^T t \leq 1)},$$

where

$$c_d = \frac{\pi^{d/2}}{\Gamma(d/2 + 1)}.$$

We have seen that the AMISE of a kernel estimator (that is, the sum of equations (9.36) and (9.37)) depends on $S(K)$ and the smoothing matrix V. As we mentioned above, the amount of smoothing (that is, the window of influence) can be made to depend on σ_K. We can establish an approximate equivalence between two kernels, K_1 and K_2, by choosing the smoothing matrix to offset the differences in $S(K_1)$ and $S(K_2)$ and in σ_{K_1} and σ_{K_2} (see Marron and Nolan, 1988 for a discussion of the univariate case).

Computation of Kernel Density Estimators

If the estimate is required at one point only, it is simplest just to compute it directly. If the estimate is required at several points, it is often more efficient to compute the estimates in some regular fashion.

If the estimate is required over a grid of points, a fast Fourier transform (FFT) can be used to speed up the computations. Silverman (1982) describes an FFT method using a Gaussian kernel. He first takes the discrete Fourier transform of the data (using a histogram on 2^k cells) and then inverts the product of that and the Fourier transform of the Gaussian kernel, $\exp(-h^2s^2/2)$.

9.4   Choice of Window Widths

An important problem in nonparametric density estimation is to determine the smoothing parameter, such as the bin volume, the smoothing matrix, the number of nearest neighbors, or other measures of locality. In kernel density estimation, the window width has a much greater effect on the estimator than the kernel itself does.

An objective is to choose the smoothing parameter that minimizes the MISE. We often can do this for the AMISE, as in equation (9.23) on page 214. It is not as easy for the MISE. The first problem, of course, is just to estimate the MISE.

In practice, we use cross validation with varying smoothing parameters and alternate computations between the MISE and AMISE.

In univariate density estimation, the MISE has terms such as $h^\alpha \mathcal{S}(p')$ (for histograms) or $h^\alpha \mathcal{S}(p'')$ (for kernels). We need to estimate the roughness of a derivative of the density.

Using a histogram, a reasonable estimate of the integral $\mathcal{S}(p')$ is a Riemann approximation,

$$
\begin{aligned}
\widehat{\mathcal{S}}(p') &= h \sum \left(\widehat{p}'(t_k) \right)^2 \\
&= \frac{1}{n^2 h^3} \sum (n_{k+1} - n_k)^2,
\end{aligned}
$$

where $\widehat{p}'(t_k)$ is the finite difference at the midpoints of the kth and $(k+1)^{\text{th}}$ bins; that is,

$$
\widehat{p}'(t_k) = \frac{n_{k+1}/(nh) - n_k/(nh)}{h}.
$$

This estimator is biased. For the histogram, for example,

$$
\mathrm{E}(\widehat{\mathcal{S}}(p')) = \mathcal{S}(p') + 2/(nh^3) + \ldots
$$

A standard estimation scheme is to correct for the $2/(nh^3)$ term in the bias and plug this back into the formula for the AMISE (which is $1/(nh) + h^2 \mathcal{S}(r')/12$ for the histogram).

We compute the estimated values of the AMISE for various values of h and choose the one that minimizes the AMISE. This is called *biased cross validation* because of the use of the AMISE rather than the MISE.

These same techniques can be used for other density estimators and for multivariate estimators, although at the expense of considerably more complexity.

Terrell (1990) found cross validation to be of limited value in selecting the window width because the sampling variability is too great.

9.5   Orthogonal Series Estimators

A continuous function $p(x)$, integrable over a domain D, can be represented over that domain as an infinite series in terms of a complete spanning set of orthogonal functions $\{f_k\}$ over D:

$$p(x) = \sum_k c_k f_k(x). \tag{9.41}$$

The orthogonality property allows us to determine the coefficients c_k in the expansion (9.41):

$$c_k = \langle p, \bar{f}_k \rangle. \tag{9.42}$$

Approximation using a truncated orthogonal series can be particularly useful in estimation of a probability density function because the orthogonality relationship provides an equivalence between the coefficient and an expected value. Expected values can be estimated using observed values of the random variable and the approximation of the probability density function. Assume that the probability density function p is approximated by an orthogonal series $\{q_k\}$ that has a constant weight function:

$$p(y) = \sum_k c_k q_k(y).$$

From equation (9.42), we have

$$
\begin{aligned}
c_k &= \langle p, \bar{q}_k \rangle \\
&= \int_D \bar{q}_k(y) p(y) \, dy \\
&= \mathrm{E}(\bar{q}_k(Y)),
\end{aligned} \tag{9.43}
$$

where Y is a random variable whose probability density function is p.

The c_k can therefore be unbiasedly estimated by

$$\hat{c}_k = \frac{1}{n} \sum_{i=1}^{n} \bar{q}_k(y_i).$$

The orthogonal series estimator is therefore

$$\hat{p}_S(y) = \frac{1}{n} \sum_{k=0}^{j} \sum_{i=1}^{n} \bar{q}_k(y_i) q_k(y) \tag{9.44}$$

for some truncation point j.

Without some modifications, this generally is not a good estimator of the probability density function. It may not be smooth, and it may have infinite variance. The estimator may be improved by shrinking the $\hat{c}_k$ toward the origin. The number of terms in the finite series approximation also has a major effect on the statistical properties of the estimator. Having more terms is not necessarily better. One useful property of orthogonal series estimators is that the convergence rate is independent of the dimension. This may make orthogonal series methods more desirable for higher-dimensional problems. See Tarter and

Kronmal (1970) for a discussion of the use of orthogonal series in multivariate problems.

There are several standard orthogonal series that could be used. These two most commonly used series are the Fourier and the Hermite. There is no consensus on which is preferable.

The Fourier series is commonly used for distributions with bounded support. It yields estimators with better properties in the L_1 sense.

Tarter, Freeman, and Hopkins (1986) gave a Fortran program for computing probability density estimates based on the Fourier series.

For distributions with unbounded support, the Hermite polynomials are most commonly used. Some of the Hermite polynomials are shown in equation (6.15) on page 136.

Other orthogonal systems can be used in density estimation. Walter and Ghorai (1992) describe the use of wavelets in density estimation, and discuss some of the problems in their use. Vidakovic (1999) also discusses density estimation and other applications of wavelets.

9.6   Other Methods of Density Estimation

There are several other methods of probability density estimation. Most of them are modifications of the ones we have discussed. In some cases, combinations of methods can be used effectively. Some methods work only in the univariate case, whereas others can be applied in multivariate density estimation.

All of the nonparametric methods of density estimation involve decisions such as window width, number of mixtures, number of terms in an expansion, and so on. All of these quantities can be thought of as smoothing parameters. There are, of course, various rules for making these decisions in an asymptotically optimal fashion for some known distributions, such as the window selection rule for kernel density estimates of Stone (1984). Absent assumptions about the nature of the true distribution, it is difficult to decide on the extent of smoothing. Much of the current work is on developing adaptive methods in which these choices are made based on the data.

Filtered Kernel Methods

As we mentioned earlier, it may be reasonable to vary the smoothing parameter in the kernel density estimator in such a way that the locality of influence is smaller in areas of high density and larger in sparser regions. Terrell and Scott (1992) discuss some of the issues and describe an adaptive approach to selection of variable windows in the univariate case.

Also for the univariate case, Marchette et al. (1996) describe an approach using an additional set of filter functions. In the filtered kernel density estimator a set of functions $f_1, f_2, \ldots, f_m$, such that $\sum f_j(x) = 1$, and associated window widths h_j, are used to weight the standard univariate kernel estimator. Analogous to the kernel estimator, which is of the same form as in equation (9.26), the univariate filtered kernel density estimator is

$$\widehat{p}_F(y) = \frac{1}{n} \sum_{i=1}^{n} \sum_{j=1}^{m} \frac{f_j(y_i)}{h_j} K\left(\frac{y - y_i}{h_j}\right). \tag{9.45}$$

If the kernel function is the standard normal density $\phi(t)$ and the filtering functions are weighted normal densities $\pi_j \phi(t \,|\, \mu_j, \sigma_j^2)$, we can express the filtered kernel density estimator as

$$\widehat{p}_F(y) = \frac{1}{n} \sum_{i=1}^{n} \sum_{j=1}^{m} \frac{\pi_j \phi(t \,|\, \mu_j, \sigma_j^2)}{h \sigma_k f_\bullet(y_i)} \phi\left(\frac{y - y_i}{h \sigma_j}\right),$$

where $f_\bullet(t) = \sum_{j=1}^{m} \pi_j \phi(t \,|\, \mu_j, \sigma_j^2)$. We now have the choices in the estimator as m, π_j, μ_j, and σ_j^2.

This approach is similar to a mixture approach in that the number of different filter functions must be chosen. Marchette et al. (1996) describe various adaptive methods for choosing the number of filter functions and their associated window widths.

Alternating Kernel and Mixture Methods

Priebe and Marchette (2000) suggested a density estimator formed by alternating between nonparametric filtered kernel estimators and parametric mixture estimators composed of the same number of terms (filter functions or component densities). The estimator is computed iteratively by beginning with a mixture estimator $\widehat{p}_M^{(1)}(y)$ of the form in equation (8.6) on page 202 and a filtered kernel estimator $\widehat{p}_F^{(1)}(y)$ of the form in equation (9.45) above. A new mixture estimator $\widehat{p}_M^{(2)}(y)$ is chosen as the mixture estimator closest to $\widehat{p}_F^{(1)}(y)$ (in some norm). The new mixture estimator is used to determine the choices for a new filtered kernel estimator. (In general, these are the f_j and the h_j in equation (9.45). For normal filters and kernels, they are the variances.) The process is continued until

$$\|\widehat{p}_M^{(k+1)}(y) - \widehat{p}_M^{(k)}(y)\|$$

is small.

The method of alternating kernel and mixture estimators can easily be used for multivariate density estimation.

Methods of Comparisons of Methods

Nonparametric probability density estimation involves the fundamental trade-off between a spike at each observation (that is, no smoothing) and a constant function over the range of the observations (that is, complete smoothing) ignoring differences in relative frequencies of observations in various intervals. It is therefore not surprising that the comparison of methods is not a trivial exercise.

One approach for comparing methods of estimation is to define broad classes of densities and to evaluate the performance of various estimators within those classes. Marron and Wand (1992) studied a number of general shapes of densities, such as unimodal symmetric, skewed, multimodal, and so on. These classes and other standard ones are regularly used for comparing density estimators. Farmen and Marron (1999) and Butucea (2001) are examples of such studies. In the study by Butucea (2001), ten densities were used:

- standard normal, $\phi(y \mid 0, 1)$;

- mixed normals, $p(y) = 0.7\phi(y \mid -2, 1.5) + 0.3\phi(y \mid 2, 0.5)$;

- standard Cauchy, $p(y) = 1/(\pi(1 + y^2))$;

- standard extreme value distribution, $p(y) = \exp(-e^{-y} - y)$;

- standard logistic, $p(y) = e^{-y}/(1 + e^{-y})^2$;

- standard Laplace, $p(y) = e^{-|y|/2}$;

- claw density

$$p(y) = \frac{1}{10}\Big(5\phi(y \mid 0, 1) + \phi(y \mid -1, 0.1) + \phi(y \mid -0.5, 0.1) +$$
$$\phi(y \mid 0, 0.1) + \phi(y \mid 0.5, 0.1) + \phi(y \mid 1, 0.1)\Big);$$

- smooth comb density

$$p(y) = \frac{32}{63}\phi\left(y \mid -\frac{31}{21}, \frac{32}{63}\right) + \frac{16}{63}\phi\left(y \mid \frac{17}{21}, \frac{16}{63}\right) + \frac{8}{63}\phi\left(y \mid \frac{41}{21}, \frac{8}{63}\right) +$$
$$\frac{4}{63}\phi\left(y \mid \frac{53}{21}, \frac{4}{63}\right) + \frac{2}{63}\phi\left(y \mid \frac{59}{21}, \frac{2}{63}\right) + \frac{1}{63}\phi\left(y \mid \frac{62}{21}, \frac{1}{63}\right);$$

- triangular density, $p(y) = (1 - |x|)_+$;

- saw-tooth density

$$g(y) = p(y + 9) + p(y + 7) + \cdots p(y - 7) + p(y - 9),$$

where p is the triangular density.

These densities cover a wide range of shapes.

Exercises

9.1. Use Monte Carlo methods to study the performance of the histogram density estimator $\widehat{p}_H(x)$ using univariate normal data. Generate samples of size 500 from a $N(0, 1)$ distribution. Use a Monte Carlo sample size of 100.

(a) Choose three different bin sizes. Tell how you chose them.

(b) For each bin size, estimate the variance of $\widehat{p}(0)$.

(c) For each bin size, compute the average MISE.

9.2. Use Monte Carlo methods to study the performance of the histogram density estimator $\widehat{p}_H(x)$ using a simple but nonstandard univariate distribution that has density

$$
\begin{aligned}
p(x) \quad &= \quad 3x \quad \text{for} \quad 0.0 \leq x < 0.5 \\
&= \quad 3 - 3x \quad \text{for} \quad 0.5 \leq x < 1.0 \\
&= \quad x - 1 \quad \text{for} \quad 1.0 \leq x < 1.5 \\
&= \quad 2 - x \quad \text{for} \quad 1.5 \leq x < 2.0 \\
&= \quad 0 \quad \text{otherwise.}
\end{aligned}
$$

The programs you will need to write are incremental; that is, the program written in one question may be used in another question.

(a) Generation of random variates.

    i. Describe a method for generating random variables from this distribution.

    ii. Write a program to generate random variables from this distribution.

(b) Use Monte Carlo methods to estimate the variance of $\widehat{p}_H(1)$ for a fixed sample size of 500, using three different bin widths: 0.2, 0.3, and 0.4. Use a Monte Carlo sample size of 100. If a cutpoint corresponds to $x = 1$, use the average of the two bins. (Notice that this is the variance of the density estimator at one point.)
Now, work out the true variance of $\widehat{p}_H(1)$ for this distribution when a bin width of 0.4 is used. (Tell what bin this point is in. It depends on how you set the cutpoints.)

(c) For each bin size in the previous question, compute an estimate of the MISE.

(d) Now, investigate the order of the MISE in the sample size for a given bin width that is dependent on the sample size. Choose the bin width as $0.84n^{-1/3}$.

    i. First, show that this bin width is optimal for the AMISE. (The coefficient is given to two decimal places.)

    ii. Use Monte Carlo methods to study the order of the MISE; that is, estimate α in AMISE $= O(n^{\alpha})$, for the given bin width sequence. Use sample sizes of 128, 256, 512, and 1,024. Compute the MISE at each sample size, and plot the MISE versus n on log-log axes. Estimate α using least squares.

9.3. Derive the variance of the histogram (equation (9.9) on page 210).

9.4. Derive the bin size that achieves the lower bound of the MSE for the histogram (equation (9.12), page 211).

9.5. Let

$$p(y) = \frac{1}{\Gamma(\alpha)\beta^\alpha} y^{\alpha-1} e^{-y/\beta} \quad \text{for } 0 \geq y,$$
$$= 0 \quad \text{elsewhere.}$$

(This is the probability density function for a gamma distribution.) Determine $\mathcal{S}(p')$, as in equation (9.13) on page 212.

9.6. Bivariate histograms over any of the three regular tessellations are relatively easy to construct. (The triangular and square tessellations are straightforward. See Exercise 9.7 for the hexagonal tessellation.) For a random sample from a density $p(y_1, y_2)$, show that a bivariate histogram has AMISE of the form

$$\frac{1}{nh^2} + ch^2 \big(\mathcal{S}(p_{y_1}) + \mathcal{S}(p_{y_2}) \big),$$

where h^2 is the area of the bin, $p_{y_1} = \partial p(y_1, y_2)/\partial y_1$ and $p_{y_2} = \partial p(y_1, y_2)/\partial y_2$. Notice that the number of bins is different for the three bin shapes. Determine the value of c for each of the regular tessellations. Which tesselation has the best AMISE, given equal bin sizes (but unequal numbers of bins)? See Scott (1988).

9.7. Write a program to count the bivariate observations for regular hexagonal bins. The input to your program is a set of observations, the bin definitions, and the bin counts from prior sets of observations. The output is the updated array of bin counts. Use the fact that the centers of the hexagons are the lattice points of two rectangular tilings of the plane. See Figure 9.1 on page 216. See Carr et al. (1987) for a Fortran program.

9.8. Frequency polygons.

(a) Show that the univariate frequency polygon is a bona fide estimator.

(b) Suppose that it is known that the true density is zero below a certain bound (for example, suppose that the nature of the phenomenon being modeled requires the data to be nonnegative, so the support is the positive half line). Derive an expression for the integrated squared bias of the frequency polygon density estimator. (The main thing to determine is the order of the bias in the bin width h.)

(c) For the density estimation problem when a fixed bound is known, suggest a modification to the frequency polygon that might reduce the bias. (Reflection is one possibility, but you may want to suggest a different approach.) Derive an expression for the integrated squared bias of your modified frequency polygon density estimator. Show whether your modified estimator is a bona fide estimator.

9.9. Use a random number generator to generate a sample of size 1,000 from a mixture of two univariate normal distributions to study the performance of a histogram density estimator and a kernel estimator. Among other things, the object of the study will be to assess the ability of the two types of estimators to identify mixtures. In each case, the width of the bins must be decided on empirically in such a way that the resulting density estimator is visually smooth (that is, so that it is not very jagged), yet may have more than one "hump".

(Of course, since you know the density, you can "cheat" a little on this.) Let the population consist of a fraction π from a $N(0, 1)$ distribution and a fraction $1 - \pi$ from a $N(\delta, 1)$ distribution. Let π take the values 0.5, 0.7, and 0.9. Let δ take two positive values, δ_1 and δ_2.

(a) For each value of π, choose δ_1 and δ_2 so that for δ_1 the distribution is unimodal and for δ_2 the distribution is bimodal. (δ is nested in π.) Choose δ_2 so that the minimum of the density between the two modes is at least 0.05. (Marron and Wand, 1992, describe general types of bimodal and multimodal families of distributions useful in assessing the performance of density estimators.)

(b) For each of the six combinations of π and δ, choose a sequence of bin widths, compute the estimates, and by visual inspection of plots of the estimates, choose an "optimal" bin size.

The functions `tabulate` and `density` in S-Plus can be used to compute the density estimates.

9.10. Using the univariate analogue of equation (9.33) on page 219, derive the AMISE for the kernel density estimator given in expression (9.38).

9.11. Suppose that we have a random sample as follows:

$$-1.8, \; -1.2, \; -.9, \; -.3, \; -.1, \; .1, \; .2, \; .4, \; .7, \; 1.0, \; 1.3, \; 1.9.$$

(Be aware that this sample is too small for any serious density estimation!)

(a) Compute the kernel density estimate at the point 0 using a normal kernel.

(b) Compute the kernel density estimate at the point 0 using the Epanechnikov kernel.

(c) Compute a smoothed kernel density estimate over the range $(-2, 2)$ using the Epanechnikov kernel.

(d) Compute the orthogonal series estimator of the probability density using Hermite polynomials in equation (9.44) and truncating at $j = 4$.

9.12. Given a random sample $y_1, \ldots, y_n$ from an unknown population, the basic problems in density estimation are to estimate $\Pr(Y \in S)$ for a random variable Y from that population, to estimate the density at a specific point, $p(y_0)$, or to estimate the density function p or the distribution function P at all points.

Suppose instead that the problem is to generate random numbers from the unknown population.

(a) Describe how you might do this. There are several possibilities that you might want to explore. Also, you should say something about higher dimensions.

(b) Suppose that we have a random sample as follows:

$$-1.8, \; -1.2, \; -.9, \; -.3, \; -.1, \; .1, \; .2, \; .4, \; .7, \; 1.0, \; 1.3, \; 1.9.$$

Generate a random sample of size 5 from the population that yielded this sample. There are obviously some choices to be made.
Describe your procedure in detail, and write a computer program to generate the random sample.

9.13. Consider another problem related to density estimation:

Given a random sample $y_1, \ldots, y_n$ from an unknown population, estimate the mode of that population.

(a) Describe how you might do this. Again, there are several possibilities that you might want to explore, and your solution will be evaluated on the basis of how you address the alternative possibilities and how you select a specific procedure to use. (You might also want to say something about higher dimensions.)

(b) Suppose that we have a random sample as follows:

$$-1.8, \ -1.2, \ -.9, \ -.3, \ -.1, \ .1, \ .2, \ .4, \ .7, \ 1.0, \ 1.3, \ 1.9.$$

Estimate the mode of the population that yielded this sample. Describe your procedure in detail, and write a computer program to estimate the mode.

9.14. Consider the three density estimators

$$\widehat{p}_1(y) = \frac{P_n(y) - P_n(y - h)}{h},$$

$$\widehat{p}_2(y) = \frac{P_n(y + h) - P_n(y)}{h},$$

$$\widehat{p}_3(y) = \frac{P_n(y + \frac{h}{2}) - P_n(y - \frac{h}{2})}{h},$$

where P_n is the empirical distribution function based on a random sample of size n. For each,

(a) putting the estimator in the form of a kernel density estimator, write out the kernel;

(b) compute the integrated variance; and

(c) compute the integrated squared bias.

9.15. The L_p error of bona fide density estimators.

(a) Show that the L_1 error is less than or equal to 2.

(b) Let g be a monotone, continuous function, and consider the random variable, $Z = g(Y)$. Show that the L_1 error is invariant to this change of variable. (Apply the same function g to the elements of the sample of y's.)

(c) By an example, show that the L_2 error has no bound.

9.16. A common way of fitting a parametric probability density function to data is to use estimates of the parameters that yield moments of the fitted density that match the sample moments. The second and higher moments used in this method of estimation are usually taken as the central moments. This means that if $\widehat{p}$ is the density estimated from the sample $y_1, \ldots, y_n$, then

$$E_{\widehat{p}}(Y) = \bar{y}$$

and, in the univariate case,

$$E_{\widehat{p}}(Y^r) = \frac{1}{n} \sum (y_i - \bar{y})^r$$

for $r = 2, \ldots$.

(a) For the univariate histogram estimator, $\widehat{p}_H$, and a sample $y_1, \ldots, y_n$, how does $E_{\widehat{p}_H}(Y^r)$ compare to the rth sample moment?

(b) For the univariate kernel estimator, $\widehat{p}_K$, with a rectangular kernel, how does $E_{\widehat{p}_K}(Y^r)$ compare to the rth sample moment?

9.17. Make a plot of each of the test densities shown on page 226.

Chapter 10

Structure in Data

A major objective in data analysis is to identify interesting features or structure in the data. In this chapter, we consider the use of some of the tools and measures discussed in Chapters 5 and 6 to identify interesting structure. The graphical methods discussed in Chapter 7 are also very useful in discovering structure, but we do not consider those methods further in the present chapter.

There are basically two ways of thinking about "structure". One has to do with *counts* of observations. In this approach, patterns in the *density* are the features of interest. We may be interested in whether the density is multimodal, whether it is skewed, whether there are holes in the density, and so on. The other approach seeks to identify relationships among the variables. The two approaches are related in the sense that if there are relationships among the variables, the density of the observations is higher in regions in which the relationships hold. Relationships among variables are generally not exact, and the relationships are identified by the higher density of observations that exhibit the approximate relationships.

An important kind of pattern in data is a relationship to time. Often, even though data are collected at different times, the time itself is not represented by a variable on the dataset. A simple example is one in which the data are collected sequentially at roughly equal intervals. In this case, the index of the observations may serve as a surrogate variable. Consider the small univariate dataset in Table 10.1, for example.

A static view of a histogram of these univariate data, as in Figure 10.1, shows a univariate bimodal dataset. Figure 10.2, however, in which the data are plotted against the index (by rows in Table 10.1), shows a completely different structure. The data appear to be sinusoidal with an increasing frequency. The sinusoidal responses at roughly equal sampling intervals result in a bimodal static distribution, which is the structure seen in the histogram.

Interesting structure may also be groups or clusters of data based on some measure of similarity, as discussed in Section 5.4. When there are separate groups in the data, but the observations do not contain an element or an in-

Table 10.1: Dataset with Two Interesting Structures

0.85	0.89	0.94	0.95	0.99	1.00	0.96	0.94	0.97	0.90
0.84	0.71	0.57	0.43	0.29	0.08	-0.09	-0.30	-0.49	-0.72
-0.83	-0.88	-1.02	-0.94	-0.95	-0.78	-0.60	-0.38	-0.04	0.26
0.55	0.77	0.97	1.04	0.91	0.69	0.41	0.02	-0.37	-0.70
-0.96	-1.01	-0.87	-0.50	-0.06	0.44	0.79	0.99	0.95	0.59
0.10	-0.46	-0.87	-0.95	-0.77	-0.22	0.36	0.89	1.03	0.66

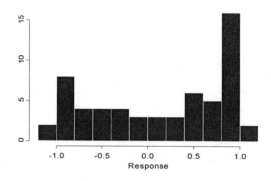

Figure 10.1: Histogram of the Data in Table 10.1

dex variable representing group membership, identifying nearby elements or
clusters in the data requires some measure of similarity (or, equivalently, of
dissimilarity).

Figure 10.3 shows four different bivariate datasets, each of which consists
of two clusters. The criteria that distinguish the clusters are different in the
datasets. In Figure 10.3(a), the clusters are defined by proximity; the points in
each cluster are closer to the respective cluster centroid than they are to the
centroid of the other cluster.

In Figures 10.3(b), 10.3(c), and 10.3(d), the definitions of the clusters are
somewhat more difficult. The clusters are defined by characteristics of the clusters themselves (that is, by structures that the clusters individually exhibit).
These clusters are sometimes called "conceptual clusters"; the points are members of a cluster because of some concept or holistic characteristic of the set of
points, such as lying close to a straight line.

The plots in Figure 10.3 also illustrate one of the problems in the identification of clusters: in some cases, although the clusters are obvious, there are a
few individual observations that could apparently belong to either cluster.

Figure 10.4 shows two different datasets whose members fall almost within
one-dimensional manifolds.

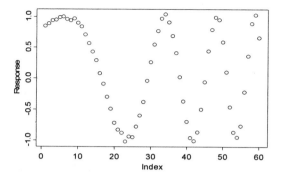

Figure 10.2: Data in Table 10.1 Plotted against Its Index

We may occasionally wish to identify any of the types of groups or structures shown in Figures 10.2, 10.3, and 10.4, but we will concentrate in this chapter on identifying the types of clusters shown in the first graph in Figure 10.3 (that is, clusters whose centroids are different).

Although we often assume that the data space is a subspace of $\mathbb{R}^m$, a data space may be more general. Data, for example, may be character strings such as names. The more general types of data may be mapped from the original data space to a "feature space", which is a subspace of $\mathbb{R}^m$. The variables may be measured on different scales; they may, of course, represent completely different phenomena, so measurement scales cannot be made the same. One way of reconciling the measurements, however, is to standardize the data using the transformation (5.20)

$$X_S = (X - \overline{X})\operatorname{diag}(1/\sqrt{s_{ii}}),$$

where $\overline{X}$ is the matrix whose constant columns contain the means of the corresponding columns of X, and $\sqrt{s_{ii}}$ is the sample standard deviation of the ith column of X.

We may be interested in finding the *nearest neighbors* of a given observation based on their similarity; or, alternatively, we may be interested in identifying all observations within a given degree of closeness to a given observation. This problem is called a "proximity search".

In the following sections, we consider general problems in multivariate data analysis. Our emphasis will be on exploratory analysis, and the main goals will be to identify clusters in data and to determine lower-dimensional structures in multidimensional data. We will use the methods and measurements that we discussed in Section 5.4.

Interesting structure may involve clusters of data, or it may be the result of the data lying on or near a space of reduced dimension. Interesting structure may also be defined generically as properties of the data that differ from

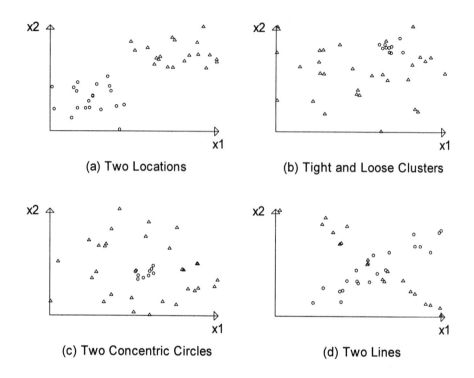

Figure 10.3: Clusters in Bivariate Datasets

expected properties if the data were a random sample from a multivariate normal distribution or from some other standard distribution. The normal (or Gaussian) distribution lies at the heart of many methods of data analysis. The heuristic definition of structure as a departure from normality can be motivated by the fact that most randomly selected low-dimensional projections of any high-dimensional dataset will appear similar to a random sample from a multivariate normal distribution (see Diaconis and Freedman, 1984).

The usual objective in cluster analysis is to divide the observations into groups that are close to each other or are more homogeneous than the full set of observations. An observation may consist of categorical variables that may (or may not) specify the class to which the observation belongs. In general, as we discuss on page 111, if the ith observation can be represented as

$$x_i = (x_i^{\text{r}},\ x_i^{\text{c}}), \qquad (10.1)$$

where the subvector x_i^{c} represents values of the categorical variables, we may wish to handle the x_i^{c} component separately. In Figure 10.3, for example, suppose that each observation consists of values for three variables, x_1 and x_2 as

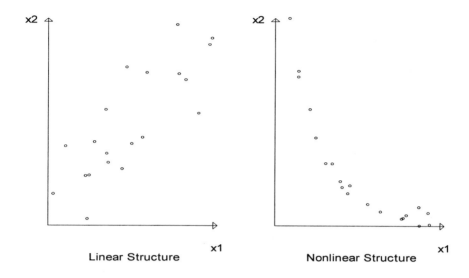

Figure 10.4: Relational Structures in Bivariate Datasets

shown and a third variable that represents group membership that corresponds to the symbol in the graphical depiction. In that case, the classes may already be defined, or we may want to allow the possibility that observations with different values of the categorical variable nevertheless belong to the same class. In most of the following, we will assume that none of the variables are categorical.

10.1 Clustering and Classification

Identifying groups of similar observations in a dataset is an important step in making sense of the data and in understanding the phenomena represented by the data. Clustering, classification, and discrimination are terms that describe this activity, which lies at the crossroads of a number of traditional disciplines, including statistics, computer science, artificial intelligence, and electrical engineering. Classification is sometimes called *machine learning*, especially in the more engineering-oriented disciplines. As is often the case when scientific methods are developed within diverse areas, there are several slight variations of theory and methodology, which are sometimes described as "statistical", "inductive", and so on. The slight variations lead to a variety of terms to describe the methods, and there is generally scant theory to support optimality of one method over another. The various approaches to clustering and classification also lead to the use of terms such as "hypothesis", "bias", and "variance" that have different meanings from their technical statistical definitions.

Clustering and classification make use of a wide range of statistical techniques, both descriptive methods utilizing simple summary statistics and graphics and methods of fitting equations to data. Statistical techniques in clustering and classification often emphasize uncertainty and the importance of dealing with noise in the data. A good general reference on clustering and classification, generally from a statistical perspective, is Gordon (1999). Hastie, Tibshirani, and Friedman (2001) discuss classification using terminology from both the statistics and machine learning disciplines.

The first step in forming groups is to develop a definition of the groups. This may be based on similarities of the observations or on closeness of the observations to one another.

Clustering

Cluster analysis is generally exploratory. It seeks to determine what groups are present in the data. If the groups are known from some training set, "discriminant analysis" seeks to understand what makes the groups different and then to provide a method of classifying observations into the appropriate groups. When discriminant analysis is used to "train" a clustering method, we refer to the procedure as "supervised" classification. Discriminant analysis is mechanically simpler than cluster analysis. Clustering is "unsupervised" classification. We will discuss classification in Chapter 11.

Because of the large number of possibilities for grouping a set of data into clusters, we generally must make some decisions to simplify the problem. One way is to decide a priori on the number of clusters; this is done in K-means clustering, discussed below. Another way is to do recursive clustering; that is, once trial clusters are formed, observations are not exchanged from one cluster to another. Two pairs of observations that are in different clusters at one stage of the clustering process would never be split so that at a later stage one member of each pair is in one cluster and the other member of each pair is in a different cluster.

There are two fundamentally different approaches to recursive clustering. One way is to start with the full dataset as a single group and, based on some reasonable criterion, partition the dataset into two groups. This is called divisive clustering. The criterion may be the value of some single variable; for example, any observation with a value of the third variable larger than 5 may be placed into one group and the other observations placed in the other group. Each group is then partitioned based on some other criterion, and the partitioning is continued recursively. This type of divisive clustering or partitioning results in a classification tree, which is a decision tree each node of which represents a partition of the dataset.

Another way of doing recursive clustering is to begin with a complete clustering of the observations into singletons. Initially, each cluster is a single observation, and the first multiple-unit cluster is formed from the two closest observations. This agglomerative, bottom-up approach is continued so that at each stage the two nearest clusters are combined to form one bigger cluster.

K-Means Clustering

The objective in K-means clustering is to find a partition of the observations into a preset number of groups, k, that minimizes the variation within each group. Each variable may have a different variation, of course. The variation of the jth variable in the gth group is measured by the within sum-of-squares,

$$s_{j(g)}^2 = \frac{\sum_{i=1}^{n_g} \left(x_{ij(g)} - \bar{x}_{j(g)} \right)^2}{n_g - 1}, \tag{10.2}$$

where n_g is the number of observations in the gth group, and $\bar{x}_{j(g)}$ is the mean of the jth variable in the gth group. There are m such quantities. The variation of the observations within the gth group is chosen as a linear combination of the sums-of-squares for all of the m variables. The coefficients in the linear combination determine the relative effects that the individual variables have on the clustering. The coefficients are usually chosen to be equal. The relative effects that the individual variables have on the clustering also depend on their scales.

Now, to state more precisely the objective in K-means clustering, it is to find a partition of the observations into a preset number of groups k that minimizes, over all groups, the total of the linear combinations of the within sum-of-squares for all variables. For linear combinations with unit coefficients, this quantity is

$$w = \sum_{g=1}^{k} \sum_{j=1}^{m} \sum_{i=1}^{n_g} \left(x_{ij(g)} - \bar{x}_{j(g)} \right)^2. \tag{10.3}$$

Determining the partitioning to minimize this quantity is a computationally intensive task.

In practice, we seek a local minimum (that is, a solution such that there is no single switch of an observation from one group to another group that will decrease the objective). Even the procedure used to achieve the local minimum is rather complicated. Hartigan and Wong (1979) give an algorithm (and Fortran code) for performing the clustering. Their algorithm forms a set of initial trial clusters and then transfers observations from one cluster to another while seeking to decrease the quantity in equation (10.3). Simulated annealing can also be used to do K-means clustering (see Zeger, Vaisey, and Gersho, 1992).

Most of the algorithms for K-means clustering will yield different results if the data are presented in a different order. Those using techniques, such as simulated annealing, that depend on random numbers may yield different results on different runs with the same data in the same order.

In either method for performing K-means clustering, it is necessary to choose initial points and then trial points to move around. Although in most algorithms these points are chosen arbitrarily, Faber (1994) has suggested that the points be chosen uniformly randomly. This choice gives preference to points in dense regions, which is consistent with an underlying concept of K-means clustering in which the inner two sums in expression (10.3) are similar to an expected value with respect to a distribution from which the observed data constitute a random sample.

The clustering depends on the variability of the variables. It may be necessary to scale the variables in order for the clustering to be sensible because the larger a variable's variance, the more impact it will have on the clustering. See page 251 for further discussion of the issue of scaling variables prior to clustering.

Choosing the Number of Clusters

A major issue is how many clusters should be formed. Hartigan (1975) discusses some ways of deciding this and some heuristic underlying theory and supporting empirical evidence. The question of the number of groups must generally be addressed in an ad hoc manner, however. The algorithms in current use form nonempty clusters. The objective function leads to exactly k clusters except in an extreme case of multiple observations with the same values, which yields multiple solutions. A modification to the objective function that penalizes the objective function for the number of groups and a modification to the algorithms that allows empty clusters would put less importance on the specification of k.

A number of statistics have been proposed for use in deciding how many clusters to use. These statistics can be used as stopping rules in the clustering methods such as hierarchical ones discussed below that present the user with a range of clusters of the given data. Milligan and Cooper (1985) performed a Monte Carlo study comparing 30 different procedures. The one they found that worked the best is the Calinski-Harabasz index,

$$\frac{b/(k-1)}{w/(n-k)},\tag{10.4}$$

where b is the between-groups sum-of-squares,

$$b = \sum_{g=1}^{k}\sum_{j=1}^{m}\left(\bar{x}_{j(g)} - \bar{x}_j\right)^2,$$

and w is the pooled within-groups sum-of-squares of equation (10.3).

Hierarchical Clustering

It is useful to consider a hierarchy of clusterings from a single large cluster to a large number of very small clusters. Hierarchical clustering yields these alternative clusterings.

The results of a hierarchical clustering can be depicted as a tree, as shown in Figure 10.5. Each point along the bottom of the tree may correspond to a single observation. Nodes higher up in the diagram represent successively larger groups. The number of clusters depends on the level in the tree, as indicated in the plot.

The vertical axis, which is not shown in Figure 10.5, corresponds to a distance metric, which could be based on any of the measures of distance described beginning on page 114. The actual units of the vertical axis must be interpreted in that context.

A hierarchical clustering can be depicted in a level tree such as in Figure 10.5 in which the lengths of the vertical lines indicate the weakness of the cluster, or the clustering can be shown with the leaves at different heights to indicate the strength or weakness of the cluster, as in the trees in Figure 10.7.

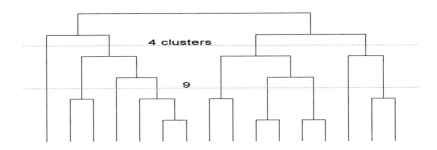

Figure 10.5: A Cluster Tree. Each Leaf Represents an Observation or a Group of Observations

Many of the algorithms for hierarchical clustering will yield different results if the data are presented in a different order.

Agglomerative Hierarchical Clustering

In agglomerative hierarchical clustering, we first begin with a large number of clusters, generally as many as the number of observations, so that each cluster consists of a single observation, and then we combine clusters that are nearest to each other.

To define distances between groups, we must first consider from what points within the groups to measure distance. As we mentioned on page 119, there are several ways of doing this. One way is to measure the distance between a central point in one group, such as the mean or median of the group, and the corresponding central point in the other group. These methods often do not work very well in hierarchical clustering. In agglomerative hierarchical clustering, the distance between two clusters is usually chosen in one of the following three ways.

- The minimum distance between a point in the first cluster and a point

in the second cluster. Using this criterion results in what is sometimes
called "single linkage" clustering.

- The distance between clusters is the average of the distances between the
  points in one cluster and the points in the other cluster.

- The largest distance between a point in one cluster and a point in the
  other cluster. Using this criterion results in what is sometimes called
  "complete linkage" clustering.

In addition to the choice of the two points to define the distance, different
distance metrics can be chosen. Any of the distances described beginning on
page 114 could be used, and in a given situation, one may be more appropriate
than another. Most clustering methods use an L_2 metric. Coleman et al. (1999)
considered an exploratory clustering problem in which a metric such as one
based on the linear discriminant is not chosen in advance but rather is selected
adaptively.

By changing the distance metric and the clustering method, several different
cluster trees can be created from a single dataset. No one method seems to be
useful in all situations.

We can see the differences in hierarchical clustering with different distance
measures between clusters using a simple example that consists of five observations with the distance matrix

$$D = \begin{bmatrix} & 2 & 3 & 4 & 5 \\ \hline 1 & 4.34 & 4.58 & 7.68 & 4.47 \\ 2 & & 1.41 & 4.00 & 4.36 \\ 3 & & & 5.10 & 5.00 \\ 4 & & & & 6.56 \end{bmatrix} . \tag{10.5}$$

Using either type of distance measure, the first cluster is formed from observations 2 and 3 because 1.41 is the minimum in any case. The subsequent clusters
are different in the three methods, as shown in Figure 10.6 by the matrices that
contain distances between clusters.

In this example, we have carried the clustering to a single final cluster. The
clusters at any intermediate stage except the first are different. Thus, in complete linkage, for example, after the cluster with observations 2 and 3 is formed,
a separate cluster with observations 1 and 5 is formed; then, these two clusters
are grouped into a cluster with four observations, and finally observation 4 is
added to form a single cluster.

Figure 10.7 shows the cluster trees that result from each method of clustering. The lengths of the vertical lines indicate the closeness of the clusters that
are combined. In each tree, for example, the first level of combination (between
observations 2 and 3) occurred at a measure of 1.41, as shown on the vertical
scale. In the connected linkage, as shown in the tree on the left-hand side, the
second step was to add observation 4 to the cluster containing observations 2
and 3. This combination occurred at a measure of 4.00. On the other hand,

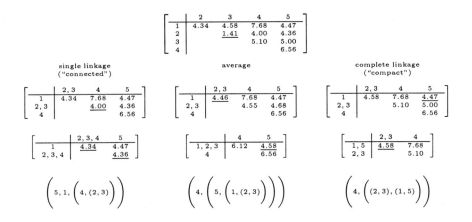

Figure 10.6: Hierarchical Clustering Using Three Different Methods

in the compact linkage, as shown in the tree on the right-hand side, the cluster containing observations 2 and 3 was unchanged and a second cluster was formed between observations 1 and 5 at a measure of 4.47.

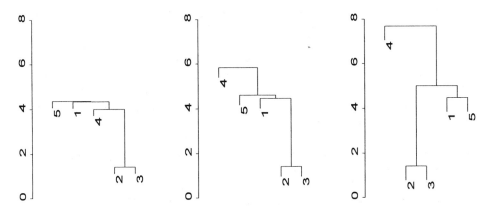

Figure 10.7: Cluster Trees Corresponding to the Methods in Figure 10.6

The cluster trees in Figure 10.7 differ in appearance from the one shown in Figure 10.5 in which the terminal nodes or leaves are all shown at the same level. This appearance is controlled by the **hang** keyword in the S-Plus plotting function **plclust**. The cluster trees in Figure 10.7 were produced with the following S-Plus commands:

```
plclust(hclust(D,method="connected"))
plclust(hclust(D,method="average"))
plclust(hclust(D,method="compact"))
```

Another agglomerative hierarchical clustering method proceeds by forming the clusters in such a way that each new cluster leads to a minimum increase in the total within-cluster sums of squares, equation (10.2). Beginning with all clusters consisting of single observations, this total is 0. The closest two points are combined to form the first cluster with two elements. In the example in Figure 10.6, this would be observations 2 and 3, the same as in all of the other methods. Assuming that the distances are Euclidean distances in D in equation (10.5), the increase in the sum of squares is $1.41^2/2$. (It is not possible to know what cluster is formed next without knowing the data that yielded the distance matrix D. Of course, as we have seen in Exercise 5.9, a data matrix could be determined using multidimensional scaling.) This is sometimes called Ward's method from Ward (1963).

The height h_{ik} at which the two observations i and k enter the same cluster is a measure of the closeness of the two observations. For any reasonable dissimilarity matrix and any reasonable method of linkage, the heights will satisfy the ultrametric inequality

$$h_{ik} \leq \max_j (h_{ij}, h_{kj}).$$

This property is trivially satisfied by the linkages illustrated in Figures 10.6 and 10.7, as may be easily checked.

Consideration of the heights in a hierarchical clustering may suggest the appropriate number of clusters. For example, the relative heights separating clusters in the first tree (on the left-hand side) in Figure 10.7 indicates that there may be four clusters: (5), (1), (4), and (2,3), three of which are singletons. (Remember that this is a toy dataset!) The tree on the right-hand side indicates that there may be three clusters: (4), (2,3), and (1,5).

The S-Plus function **agnes** also does agglomerative hierarchical clustering and provides more information about the levels at which clusters are combined.

It is important to note the computational and storage burdens in agglomerative hierarchical clustering that begins with individual observations. The size of the distance matrix (D in the example above) is of order $O(n^2)$.

Model-Based Hierarchical Clustering

In the general clustering problem, we may assume that the data come from several distributions, and our problem is to identify the distribution from which each observation arose. Without further restrictions, this problem is ill-posed; no solution is any better than any other. We may, however, impose the constraint that the distributions be of a particular type. We may then formulate the problem as one of fitting the observed data to a mixture of distributions of the given type. The problem posed thusly is similar to the problem of density estimation using parametric mixtures, as we discuss in Section 8.3 beginning on page 202.

Banfield and Raftery (1993) discussed the clustering problem in this context. They concentrated on the case in which the family of distributions is the normal (Gaussian) family with variable means and variances.

The S-Plus function `mclust` performs model-based clustering.

Divisive Hierarchical Clustering

Most hierarchical clustering schemes are agglomerative; that is, they begin with no clusters and proceed by forming ever-larger clusters. In divisive hierarchical clustering, we begin with a single large cluster and successively divide the clusters into smaller ones.

Kaufman and Rousseeuw (1990) have described a divisive hierarchy in which clusters are divided until each cluster contains only a single observation. At each stage, the cluster with the largest dissimilarity between any two of its observations is selected to be divided. To divide the selected cluster, the observation with the largest average dissimilarity to the other observations of the selected cluster is used to define a "splinter group". Next, observations that are closer to the splinter group than to their previous groups are assigned to the splinter group. This is continued until all observations have been assigned to a single cluster. The result is a hierarchical clustering. The S-Plus function `diana` determines clusters by this method.

Other Divisive Clustering Schemes

Because of the computational time required in agglomerative clustering or global partitioning such as by K-means, for large datasets, simpler methods are sometimes more useful. A recursive partitioning scheme can be efficient. One simple recursive method groups the observations into hyperrectangular regions based on the medians of the individual variables. In the first step of the median-split divisive scheme, the n observations are divided into two sets of $n/2$ based on the median of the variable with the largest range. The subsequent steps iterate that procedure. At any stage, the number of observations in all clusters is nearly equal. This procedure and the motivation for it are closely related to the k-d-tree (see below). A related scheme uses the mean rather than the median. This scheme is less intensive computationally. It does not have the property of almost equal-size clusters, however.

Wan, Wong, and Prusinkiewicz (1988) suggest an alternative divisive scheme that attempts to minimize the sum-of-squares, similar to K-means clustering. They provide empirical evidence that their method, although much faster than the K-means procedure, yields sums-of-squares very comparable to the local minima obtained by K-means. We refer the reader to their paper for details of their method.

Clustering and Classification by Space Tessellations

Groups in data can naturally be formed by partitioning a space in which the data are represented. If the data are represented in a cartesian coordinate system, for example, the groupings can be identified by polytopes that fill the space. Groups are separated by simple planar structures.

Groups may be formed by the values of only a subset of the variables. A simple example is data in which one or more variables represent geographic location. Clusters may be defined based on location, either by methods such as we have discussed above or by regions that tessellate the space. The tessellations may be preassigned regions, perhaps corresponding to administrative or geographical boundaries.

More interesting tessellations can be constructed from data. Let T be a set of points, possibly all of the observations in a dataset, a random sample of the data, or some statistics formed from subsets of the data. The set T may be used to form a tessellation that defines groups, and the tessellation may be used to classify additional data. The use of a subset of the data is related to the multipolar mapping defined by Kao, Bergeron, and Sparr (1998) for use in proximity searches. Formation of a subset of observations for classification is a form of dimension reduction, which, as we have noted with caveats, is one of the general approaches for understanding multivariate data.

A simple and useful tessellation constructed from a dataset is the *Dirichlet tessellation*, or the *Voronoi tessellation*. (The names are synonymous.) This tiling forms regions containing single points of T in such a way that all points within a region are closer to the given point than they are to any other point in T. The points in T that form the tessellation are called *generators*. The points on a boundary in a Dirichlet tessellation are equidistant to two points in T. This type of tessellation generalizes to higher dimensions.

The set of edges of the polygons (or faces of polyhedra or hyperpolyhedra) on which points are equidistant to two points in T is called the *Voronoi diagram*. The Dirichlet tessellation determined by a set of six points is shown in Figure 10.8.

The other points shown in Figure 10.8 are clustered with respect to the tessellation formed by the given six points.

A unique set of simplices is obtained by joining all nodes that share an edge in the Voronoi diagram. The set of triangles (which are simplices in two dimensions) formed by the Dirichlet tessellation in Figure 10.8 is shown in Figure 10.9. This construction is called a Delaunay triangulation. The triangulation is also a tessellation and is sometimes called a Delaunay tessellation. The Voronoi diagram and the Delaunay triangulation are duals of each other; one determines the other.

Ash et al. (1988), Aurenhammer (1991), and Okabe et al. (2000) discuss many interesting properties of the Dirichlet tessellation or Voronoi diagram and the Delaunay triangulation that hold in d dimensions. One important property of the Delaunay triangulation is that it is the unique triangulation

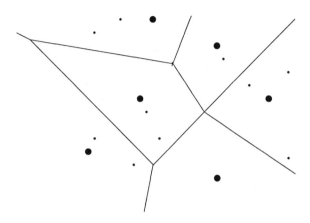

Figure 10.8: A Dirichlet Tessellation in a Plane Formed by Six Generator Points

that maximizes the minimum angle in a grid formed from a fixed set of vertices. This property is easy to see in two dimensions. (See Figure 10.10 for an example of another triangulation that obviously lacks this property when compared to Figure 10.9.) This property makes the Delaunay triangulation very useful in various fields of scientific computation. For example, it is a good way to form a set of solution points for the numerical solution of partial differential equations. (This is an "unstructured grid".)

Another property of the Voronoi diagram and the associated Delaunay triangulation in two dimensions is that a circle centered at a point where three Voronoi tiles meet and that passes through the vertices of the Delaunay triangle enclosing that point will not contain a vertex of any other triangle. (There are possible degeneracies when multiple points are collinear, but the property still holds when more than three tiles meet.) This property also holds in higher dimensions for spheres and hyperspheres.

The Bowyer-Watson algorithm exploits this property for computing a Delaunay triangulation (Bowyer, 1981, Watson, 1981). Starting with $d + 1$ points and a simplex, the algorithm proceeds by recursive insertion of nodes. For each new node:

1. Find any simplices whose circumscribed hyperspheres include the new node.

2. Create a cavity by eliminating these simplices (if there are any).

3. Create the new set of simplices by connecting the new point to the nodes that define this cavity.

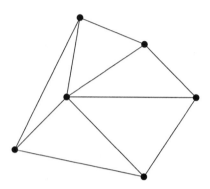

Figure 10.9: A Delaunay Triangulation

This triangulation is relatively simple to implement in two dimensions, as in the simple application of unstructured grids for the numerical solution of partial differential equations. O'Rourke (1998) and Lee (1999a, 1999b) provide general descriptions of computational methods for Delaunay triangulations as well as other problems in computational geometry. Various programs for performing the tessellations and other computations in d dimensions are available at

www.geom.umn.edu/software/download/

Renka (1997) gives an algorithm for computing the Delaunay tessellation on the surface of a sphere.

A special type of Voronoi tessellation is one in which the generators are the centroids of the regions of the tessellation. This is called a *centroidal Voronoi tessellation*. A centroidal Voronoi tessellation with k regions can be formed by an iterative routine in which a random set of k generators is chosen, the Voronoi tessellation is determined, and the centroids of the regions are taken as generators for a new tessellation. The generators, which were the centroids of the previous tessellation, will not in general be the centroids of the new tessellation, so the iterations are continued until a stopping criterion is achieved. See Lloyd (1982) for descriptions and properties of the process. Kieffer (1983) proved convergence of the process for a fairly restricted class of problems. General convergence properties are open questions.

A tessellation of a finite point set, T, can be defined in terms of a tiling over a continuous region. The points within a given tile form the finite set of points within a given tessellation of the set T. A K-means clustering is a centroidal Voronoi tessellation of a finite point set in which the means of the clusters are

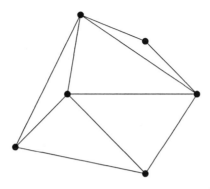

Figure 10.10: Another Triangulation

the generators. See Du, Faber, and Gunzburger (1999) for further discussion and applications.

A minimal spanning tree (see page 255) can also be used to cluster by tessellations, as shown in Figure 10.17 on page 263.

Meanings of Clusters; Conceptual Clustering

Identification of clusters in a dataset is usually only a small part of a larger scientific investigation. Another small step toward the larger objective of understanding the phenomenon represented by the data is to characterize the groups in the data by simple descriptions in terms of ranges of individual variables. Duran and Odell (1974) emphasized the importance of a summary of a cluster analysis in such terms, and, for the case of hierarchical clustering, suggested decision trees similar to Figure 11.3 on page 321 together with a set of rules as in Table 11.1 as a way of describing the clustering. The set of conjunctive rules that results can aid in understanding the phenomenon being studied. The rules that define classes can be formulated in terms of either numerical or categorical variables.

If the intent of an analysis is interpretation or understanding of the phenomenon that gave rise to the data, simplicity of the description of clusters has great value, even if it is achieved at some cost in accuracy. If, on the other hand, the objective is an ad hoc classification of the observations in a given dataset, simplicity is not important, and often an algorithmic "black box" is a more effective classifier (see Breiman, 2001).

We could formulate the clustering problem so that there are unobserved categorical variables whose values range over a predetermined set. In this situation, the observation x may be represented as

$$x = (x^{\mathrm{r}}, \, x^{\mathrm{c}}), \tag{10.6}$$

as we have discussed on page 236, but we may not observe x^{c} directly. We may know, however, that $x^{\mathrm{c}} \in \mathcal{C}$, where $\mathcal{C}$ is some given set of characteristics.

In another variation, we may have a set of characteristics of interest, $\mathcal{C}$, and wish to assign to each observation a variable x^{c} that takes a value in our previously identified set $\mathcal{C}$. The set $\mathcal{C}$ may consist of rules or general characteristics. The characteristics may be dependent on the context, as we discussed on page 113. The set of characteristics of interest may include such things as "lies on a straight line with negative slope", for example. The data represented by triangles in the graph in the lower left of Figure 10.3 on page 236 would have this characteristic, so all of those points are similar in that respect.

This kind of similarity cannot be identified by considering only pairwise similarity measurements. Michalski (1980) and Michalski and Stepp (1983) described methods for clustering using sets of characteristics, or "concepts". They called this approach conceptual clustering. Dale (1985) provides a comparison of conceptual clustering with other clustering methods.

Fuzzy Clustering

Fuzzy set theory has been applied to clustering, as it has to most problems that have a component of uncertainty. Instead of observations being grouped into definite or "crisp" clusters, they are given membership probabilities. The membership of the ith observation in the gth group is u_{ig}. The memberships satisfy

$$0 \le u_{ig} \le 1$$

and

$$\sum_{g=1}^{k} u_{ig} = 1 \quad \text{for all } i = 1, \ldots, n.$$

The quantity analogous to equation (10.3) in standard K-means clustering is

$$\sum_{g=1}^{k} \sum_{j=1}^{m} \sum_{i=1}^{n} u_{ig}^{2} \left(x_{ij} - \bar{x}_{j(g)} \right)^{2}, \tag{10.7}$$

where, as before, $\bar{x}_{j(g)}$ is the mean of the jth element of the vectors x_i that are in the gth group. Because group membership is a weight, however,

$$\bar{x}_{j(g)} = \frac{\sum_{i=1}^{n} u_{ig}^{2} x_{ij}}{\sum_{i=1}^{n} u_{ig}^{2}}.$$

Hathaway and Bezdek (1988) discuss the performance of algorithms that identify fuzzy clusters by minimizing the quantity (10.7) above. Seaver, Triantis, and Reeves (1999) describe an algorithm for fuzzy clustering that begins with a stage of hard clustering and in the second step treats cluster membership as fuzzy. Rousseeuw (1995) discusses concepts of fuzzy clustering, and Laviolette et al. (1995) discuss some general issues in fuzzy methods.

Clustering and Transformations of the Data

As we discuss on page 120, transformations on the data may change the relative values of measures of similarity. This, of course, affects any method of analysis that depends on measures of similarity. A severe limitation of clustering results from the dependence of the clusters on the scaling of the data. In many data-analytic procedures, we perform various linear transformations on the data, with predictable results on the analysis. For example, we often perform a simple univariate standardization of the data by subtracting the sample mean and dividing by the sample standard deviation. For the typical data matrix X whose columns represent variables and whose rows represent multivariate observations, we may standardize each variable by subtracting the column mean from each value in the column and dividing by the standardization of the column. Doing this, however, affects the clustering, as seen in Figure 10.11.

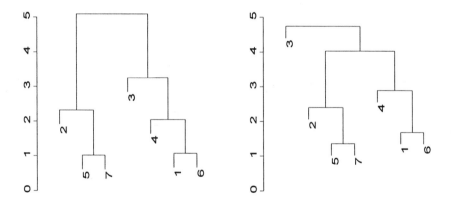

Figure 10.11: Cluster Trees; Raw Data and Standardized Data

The cluster trees in Figure 10.11 were produced with the following S-Plus commands that first create a matrix of seven observations with five variables and perform hierarchical clustering (using largest distances) and then standardize the data univariately and perform the same hierarchical clustering. (As mentioned in Appendix B, the same seed and **rnorm** function in R do not produce the same data as in S-Plus. Also, there is no guarantee that the S-Plus code executed on a different computer system will produce the same data.)

```
set.seed(2)
x <- matrix(rnorm(35),ncol=5)
plclust(hclust(dist(x)))
standard <- function(vec) (vec-mean(vec))/sqrt(var(vec))
y <- apply(x,2,standard)
plclust(hclust(dist(y)))
```

The dependence of the clustering on transformations of the data results from the effect on the distance measures discussed on page 109 and following. Whether one variable is measured in grams or kilograms affects the relative distance of any one observation to the other observations. If all variables in the dataset are of the same type (mass, say), it is easy to measure them all in the same units; if some are of one type and some are of another type, decisions on units are not as easy. These decisions, however, affect the results of clustering. We also observe effects of transformations of the data on other structures in the data, such as those we discuss in later sections.

Transformations are useful in finding other types of structure in data, as we will see in later sections. Even in the identification of clusters, transformations can help. The two clusters called "concentric circles" in Figure 10.3 on page 236 could be identified easily using any of the clustering methods discussed in the section if the data were centered and then transformed to polar coordinates. (Other methods for this kind of structure may involve "slicing" the data.)

Clustering of Variables

There is a basic duality between the m "variables" and the n "observations" of the dataset X. We have been discussing clustering of observational units. Clustering observations is done by measures of distance, possibly scaled by S. Consider reversing the roles of variables and observations. Suppose that we wish to cluster the variables (that is, we wish to know which variables have values that are strongly related to each other).

The relative values of the variables provide information on how similar or dissimilar the observations are; conversely, the relative values of the multivariate observations provide information on the similarity of the variables. Clustering of variables is conceptually and mechanically the same as clustering of observations. Instead of an $n \times n$ matrix of dissimilarities between observations, such as D in equation (5.19), we would use an $m \times m$ matrix of association between variables, such as S in equation (5.8) or R in equation (5.10).

There is one obvious difference in the variance-covariance matrix or the correlation matrix and the dissimilarity matrix: covariances and correlations can be positive or negative. Positive and negative covariances or correlations of the same magnitude, however, represent the same degree of association between the variables, so instead of S or R, similar matrices with all elements replaced by their absolute values are more useful for clustering variables. See Soffritti (1999) for some comparisons of various ways of using these and other measures of association for clustering variables.

Comparing Clusterings

As we have seen, various methods of clustering yield different results, and, furthermore, the same method yields different results if the data have been transformed. Which clustering is best cannot in general be determined by analysis of data with no context. The purpose of the clustering, after all, is to develop a better understanding of a phenomenon of which the data measure various aspects. Nevertheless, it is instructive to develop numerical measures of the agreement (or, equivalently, disagreement) of different clusterings of the same dataset.

A two-way contingency table can be used to represent agreement of two clusterings. (A p-way contingency table could be used to represent agreement of p clusterings.) If the classes of one clustering are denoted as $C_{11}, \ldots, C_{1k_1}$ and those of a second clustering as $C_{21}, \ldots, C_{2k_2}$, a two-way table of the numbers of units falling in the cells is constructed, as shown.

	C_{11}	$\cdots$	C_{1k_1}	
C_{21}	n_{11}	$\cdots$	n_{1k_1}	$n_{1\bullet}$
$\vdots$		$\ddots$		$\vdots$
C_{2k_2}	$n_{k_2 1}$	$\cdots$	$n_{k_2 k_1}$	$n_{k_2 \bullet}$
	$n_{\bullet 1}$	$\cdots$	$n_{\bullet k_2}$	n

The labeling of the clusters is arbitrary. (In a classification problem, the clusters correspond to classes, which are usually known and fixed, given the data.)

From the cluster trees shown in Figure 10.11, there appear to be two obvious clusters in the first clustering and three clusters in the second clustering. If we identify the clusters from left to right in each tree (so that, for example, the first cluster in the first tree contains the points 2, 5, and 7, and the first cluster in the second tree contains the single point 3), we would have the table below.

	C_{11}	C_{12}	
C_{21}	0	1	1
C_{22}	3	0	3
C_{23}	0	3	3
	3	4	7

The marginal totals are the counts for the corresponding clusters. The numbers in the cells indicate the extent of agreement of the two clusterings. Perfect agreement would yield, first of all, $k_1 = k_2$, and, secondly, a table in which each column and each row contains only one nonzero value.

Rand (1971) suggested a measure of the agreement of two clusterings by considering the number of pairs of points that are in common clusters. Of the total of $\binom{n}{2}$ pairs of points, each pair may be:

1. in the same cluster in both clusterings;

2. in different clusters in both clusterings;

3. in the same cluster in one clustering but in different clusters in the other clustering.

Both the first and second events indicate agreement of the clusterings, and the third indicates disagreement. Rand's statistic is a count of the number of pairs of the first and second types divided by the total number of pairs. This statistic is obviously in the interval $[0, 1]$, and a value of 0 indicates total disagreement and a value of 1 complete agreement. Rand gave a method of computing the total number of pairs of the first and second types by subtracting the count of the number of the third type from the total:

$$\binom{n}{2} - \frac{1}{2}\left(\sum_i n_{i\bullet}^2 - 2\sum_i\sum_j n_{ij}^2 + \sum_j n_{\bullet j}^2\right).$$

This can be seen by expanding $(\sum_i \sum_j n_{ij})^2$. Rand's statistic therefore is

$$R = 1 - \frac{\sum_i n_{i\bullet}^2 - 2\sum_i\sum_j n_{ij}^2 + \sum_j n_{\bullet j}^2}{n(n-1)}. \tag{10.8}$$

For the two clusterings shown in Figure 10.11, with two clusters in the first clustering and three clusters in the second, we see that the count of agreements is 18; hence, Rand's statistic is 6/7.

Statistical significance may be determined in terms of the distribution of such a statistic given random clusterings. Hubert and Arabie (1985) studied and modified Rand's measure to account for the expected values of random clusterings. Their statistic is

$$R_{HA} = \frac{\sum_i\sum_j \binom{n_{ij}}{2} - \sum_i \binom{n_{i\bullet}}{2}\sum_j \binom{n_{\bullet j}}{2}/\binom{n}{2}}{\left(\sum_i \binom{n_{i\bullet}}{2} + \sum_j \binom{n_{\bullet j}}{2}\right)/2 - \sum_i \binom{n_{i\bullet}}{2}\sum_j \binom{n_{\bullet j}}{2}/\binom{n}{2}}, \tag{10.9}$$

where the sums over i go to k_1 and the sums over j go to k_2. In practice, the statistical significance of such a comparison of two observed clusterings would be approximated by use of a few randomly formed clusterings.

An interesting problem that has received very little attention is to develop methods for drawing cluster trees to facilitate comparisons of clusterings.

There have been and will continue to be a multitude of Monte Carlo studies assessing the performance of various clustering procedures in various settings. The difficulty in making a simple statement about the performance of clustering methods arises from the multitude of possible clustering patterns. Milligan (1985) discussed the types of patterns of data and clusters that provide interesting test cases, and he gave an algorithm for randomly generating test clusters under a variety of design parameters.

Computational Complexity of Clustering

The task of identifying an unknown number of clusters that are distinguished by unknown features is an exceedingly complex problem. In practical clustering methods, there are generally trade-offs between how clusters are defined and the algorithm used to find the clusters. In the hierarchical clustering algorithms, the algorithm dominates the approach to the problem. In those hierarchical clustering methods, the definition of clusters at any level is merely what results from a specified algorithm. After the $O(mn^2)$ computations to compute the distance matrix, the algorithm requires only $O(n)$ computations. As we have discussed, identification of clusters may involve concepts and iterations requiring human interactions. Even with a fixed algorithm-based approach, however, the method is computationally intensive.

K-means clustering begins with a reasonable definition of clusters, assuming a known number of clusters. Even with the simplifying assumption that the number of clusters is known, the definition of clusters requires a very computationally intensive algorithm. Just to compute the objective function (10.3) on page 239 for a given trial clustering requires kmn computations. A trial clustering is defined by a permutation of the n data elements together with a choice of k nonnegative integers n_g such that $\sum n_g = n$. Clearly, the number of computations required to satisfy the definition of clusters, even under the assumption of a known number of clusters, is often not acceptable.

Development of clustering algorithms that are feasible for large datasets is an important current activity.

10.2 Ordering and Ranking Multivariate Data

The concept of order or rank within a multivariate dataset can be quite complicated. (See Barnett, 1976, and Eddy, 1985, for general discussions of the problem.) The simple approach of defining a "sort key" that consists of a priority ordering of the variables to use in ranking the data is not very useful except in simple, well-structured datasets.

Minimal Spanning Trees

A *spanning tree* for a graph is a tree subgraph that contains all nodes of the given graph. A spanning tree is not necessarily rooted. A useful graph of observations is the spanning tree whose edges have the least total distance. This is called a *minimal spanning tree*, or MST. It is obvious that the number of edges in a minimal spanning tree would be one less than the number of nodes. A minimal spanning tree may not be unique.

Kruskal (1956) gave the method shown in Algorithm 10.1 for forming a minimal spanning tree. The set of all edge distances should first be put into a minimum heap so that the updating can proceed more rapidly.

Algorithm 10.1 Formation of a Minimal Spanning Tree T from a Connected Graph with n Nodes and with Edge Distances in H

   0. Set $T = \emptyset$ (the empty set), and set $k = 0$.

1. Choose the edge e from H with shortest distance.

2. Remove e from H.

3. If e does not create a cycle in T, then add e to H and set $k = k + 1$.

4. If $k < n - 1$, go to step 1.   ∎

It is easy to see that the problem of determining an MST is $O(n^2)$ and Algorithm 10.1 is of that order. This is prohibitive for large datasets. Bentley and Friedman (1978) described an algorithm to approximate an MST that is $O(n \log n)$.

A tree that connects observations with nearby ones helps us to understand the distribution of the observations and to identify clusters of observations and outlying observations. The number of edges in the longest path starting at any node is called the *eccentricity* of that node or observation. The node most distant from a given node is called an *antipode* of the node, and the path between a node with greatest eccentricity and its antipode is called a *diameter* of the tree. The length of such a path is also called the diameter. (This word also carries both meanings in the familiar context of a circle.) A node with minimum eccentricity is called a *center* node or a *median*.

Minimal spanning trees have a variety of uses in multivariate analysis. Zahn (1971) and Bhavsar and Ling (1988) give examples of their use for discovering multivariate structure.

A related problem is to determine the shortest path between two given nodes. An algorithm to determine the shortest path, called Dijkstra's algorithm, is described in Horowitz, Sahni, and Rajasekaran (1998), for example.

In the following few pages, we will use a simple bivariate dataset for illustrations. The dataset is shown in Table 10.2. A plot of the data and a minimal spanning tree for this simple bivariate dataset is shown in Figure 10.12. In most cases, when we display this dataset we will suppress the scales on the axes.

The median of the tree shown in the right-hand plot in Figure 10.12 is observation number 6 (as labeled in the left-hand plot in Figure 10.12).

Although we cannot produce a useful visual graph of an MST in higher dimensions, the concept carries through, and the same algorithm applies.

Ranking Data Using Minimal Spanning Trees

Friedman and Rafsky (1979a) defined a method for sorting multivariate observations based on a minimal spanning tree. The procedure is to define a starting node at an endpoint of a tree diameter and then to proceed through the tree in such a way as to visit any shallow subtrees at a given node before proceeding to the deeper subtrees. For the tree shown in the right-hand plot in Figure 10.12, for example, if we choose to begin on the right of the tree, the next seven nodes are in the single path from the first one. Finally, at the eighth node, we choose the shallow subtree for the ninth and tenth nodes. The eleventh node is then the other node connected to the eighth one. This ordering is shown

Table 10.2: Dataset for Illustrations

Obs. Number	x_1	x_2
1	10	66
2	19	52
3	8	88
4	37	25
5	66	75
6	53	55
7	89	76
8	73	91
9	21	32
10	12	23
11	29	41
12	86	65
13	91	81
14	42	23
15	36	38
16	90	85

in the left-hand plot in Figure 10.13. Friedman and Rafsky (1979b) described an algorithm for this ranking, which they called a "linear" ranking. They also described another one-dimensional ranking that begins near the center of the minimal spanning tree and moves outward. This ranking, which they called a "radial" ranking, is shown in the right-hand plot in Figure 10.13. They called these one-dimensional rankings "linings".

Friedman and Rafsky (1979b) also defined a mapping of multivariate data to a plane in which the interpoint distances in the plane maintain the ordering of the interpoint distances of the multivariate data. They called this mapping a "planing". They give an algorithm for planing (Friedman and Rafsky, 1979b) and describe applications of planing for producing multivariate p-p plots (Friedman and Rafsky, 1981). After planing multivariate data, the data can be ranked using a two-dimensional scheme.

The S-Plus function `mstree` computes a minimal spanning tree, the x-y coordinates of a planing of multivariate data, and both the linear and radial orderings of the data.

Using orderings by minimal spanning trees, Friedman and Rafsky (1979b) developed tests for equality of distributions of two samples, and Friedman and Rafsky (1981) used them to define multivariate p-p plots for comparing two multivariate samples. Banks and Lavine (1992) defined nonparametric regression methods based on minimal spanning trees. Kwon and Cook (1998) used minimal spanning trees in grand tour visualization.

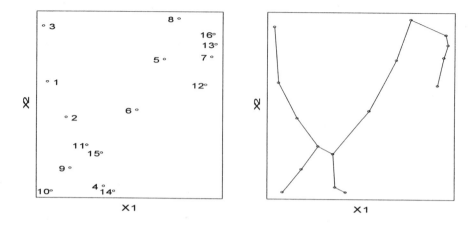

Figure 10.12: A Scatter Plot of the Bivariate Dataset (Table 10.2) and a Minimal Spanning Tree for It

There are, of course, several other ways of using a graph to define a sequence or ranking of multivariate data. (See Barnett, 1976, and Eddy, 1985, for general discussions of the problem.) A connected acyclic graph that contains only one path would be a reasonable possibility. (A cyclic path that includes every node exactly once is called a "Hamiltonian circuit".) Such a graph with minimal diameter is the solution to the traveling salesperson problem. The traveling salesperson problem is computationally more complex than determining the minimal spanning tree.

Ranking Data Using Convex Container Hulls

Another way to order data is by convex hull peeling (see Eddy, 1981, 1982). The idea behind convex hull peeling, which is due to John Tukey, is that the convex hull of a dataset identifies the extreme points, and the most extreme of these is the one whose removal from the dataset would yield a much "smaller" convex hull of the remaining data. In two dimensions, convex hull peeling takes as the most extreme observation the one on the convex hull with the smallest angle. Next, the convex hull of all remaining points is determined, and the second most extreme observation is the one on this convex hull with the smallest angle. This process continues until a total ordering of all observations is achieved. The first few steps are shown in Figure 10.14. The ordering by convex hull peeling tends to move around the edges of the set of points, often similar to the radial ordering in a minimal spanning tree.

An algorithm for computing the convex hull of a multivariate dataset is given by Barber, Dobkin, and Huhdanpaa (1996). Various programs for computing

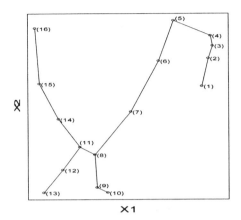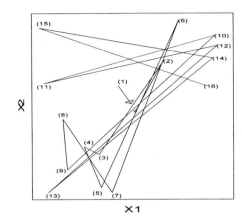

Figure 10.13: Two Orderings of the Dataset Using the MST

convex hulls and other problems in computational geometry are available at the site,

www.geom.umn.edu/software/download/

The convex hull of a two-dimensional dataset is particularly easy to compute (see Eddy, 1977, for example).

Instead of a convex hull, formed by planes, we may consider a smoothed figure such as an ellipsoid with minimum volume. Hawkins (1993a), Cook, Hawkins, and Weisberg (1993), and Woodruff and Rocke (1993) give algorithms for computing the minimum-volume ellipsoid. The algorithms in the last reference include various heuristic combinatorial algorithms, such as simulated annealing, genetic algorithms, and tabu searches. The minimum-volume ellipsoid that contains a given percentage of the data provides another way of ordering the points in a multivariate dataset.

Ranking Data Using Location Depth

A peeled convex hull or an ellipsoid containing a given percentage of data provides an ordering of the data from the outside in. Another approach to ordering data is to begin in the inside—that is, at the densest part of the data—and proceed outward. For bivariate data, John Tukey introduced the concept of *halfspace location depth* for a given point x_c relative to the dataset X whose rows are in $\mathbb{R}^2$. The halfspace location depth, $d_{\mathrm{hsl}}(x_c, X)$, is the smallest number of x_i contained in any closed halfplane whose boundary passes through x_c. The halfspace location depth is defined for datasets X whose rows are in $\mathbb{R}^m$ by immediate extension of the definition for the bivariate case. Figure 10.15

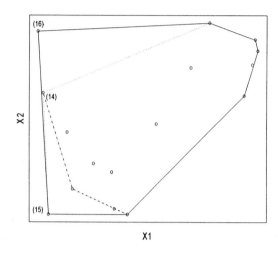

Figure 10.14: Ordering of the Dataset (Table 10.2) by Peeling the Convex Hull

shows some halfspaces defined by lines, together with the counts of points on either of the lines.

There are 15 possible pairs of counts for each point in Figure 10.15 (no three points in this dataset are collinear). Some halfplanes for which point A lies on the boundary contain as few as six points (one such halfplane is shown in the figure), but all contain at least six points. Thus,

$$d_{\mathrm{hsl}}(a, X) = 6.$$

Of all the points in this dataset, a has the greatest halfspace location depth. The halfspace location depth of point b, $d_{\mathrm{hsl}}(b, X)$, for example, is 4. The halfplane shown in Figure 10.15 with point b on the boundary contains five points. A clockwise rotation of that boundary line yields a halfplane containing four points.

The halfspace location depth provides another way of ordering the data. There are generally many ties in this ordering.

Rousseeuw and Ruts (1996) provide an algorithm for computing the halfspace location depth for bivariate data. (See also Ruts and Rousseeuw, 1996, who discuss contours of regions with equal location depth.)

Ordering by location depth emphasizes the interior points, whereas convex hull peeling emphasizes the outer points. The outer points have a halfspace location depth of 0, and generally the first few points removed in convex hull peeling, such as points 15 and 16 in Figure 10.14, have a location depth of 0. The point that is removed next, however, has a location depth of 1, whereas

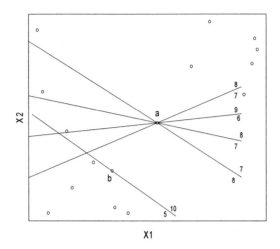

Figure 10.15: Halfplanes that Define Location Depths in the Dataset (Table 10.2)

there are other points in the dataset with location depths of 0.

If a single point has a greater location depth than any other point in the dataset, the point is called the *depth median*. If multiple points have the largest location depth of any in the dataset, the depth median is the centroid of all such points.

The depth median of the dataset shown in Figure 10.15 is the point labeled "a". That is the same as observation number 6 as labeled in the left-hand plot in Figure 10.12 (page 258), which was the median of the minimal spanning tree shown in the right plot in Figure 10.12.

Determination of the depth median is computationally intensive. Rousseeuw and Ruts (1998) give an algorithm for computing the depth median in a bivariate dataset, and Struyf and Rousseeuw (2000) give an approximate algorithm for higher-dimensional data.

There are other ways of defining data depth. One approach is to define a measure of distance of depth based on maximal one-dimensional projections. This measure can be used to order the data, and it is also useful as an inverse weight for robust estimators of location and scale. It is computationally intensive, and most methods in use depend on sampling of the data. Maronna and Yohai (1995) and Zuo and Serfling (2000a, 2000b) describe properties of this measure of depth. Liu (1990) defined the *simplicial location depth* as the proportion of data simplices (triangles formed by three observations in the bivariate case) that contain the given point. Rousseeuw and Hubert (1999) define and study a depth measure based on regression fits. Liu, Parelius, and Singh (1999) describe and compare measures of data depth and discuss various applications of data depth in multivariate analysis.

Ordering by Clustering

Clustering also provides a way of ordering or, especially, of partially ordering data. The ordering that arises from clustering, whether divisive or agglomerative, however, depends on local properties, and a global ordering is difficult to identify. A hierarchical clustering of the data in Table 10.2 is shown in Figure 10.16. The ordering, or partial ordering, would be from left to right (or from right to left) along the leaves of the tree. Comparison of the cluster tree with the scatter plot in Figure 10.12 (page 258) shows how nearby points are grouped first. In this dataset, the points closest together are on the periphery of the data cloud. For a cloud of points that is concentrated around the median, as is perhaps more common, the central points would be grouped first.

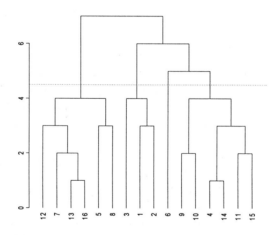

Figure 10.16: Hierarchical Clustering of the Dataset (Table 10.2)

Clustering by Ordering

The ordering of the data by the minimal spanning tree can be used to cluster the data. The minimal spanning tree shown in Figure 10.12 can be used to form the clusters indicated in Figure 10.17. The clusters are formed by a tessellation formed by boundaries perpendicular to the longer edges in the MST.

As it turns out, the four clusters shown in the MST correspond to the four clusters formed by the hierarchical clustering shown in Figure 10.16. It is not always the case that a clustering can be formed by simple cuts of the branches of a minimal spanning tree to correspond to the clustering formed by a particular hierarchical algorithm.

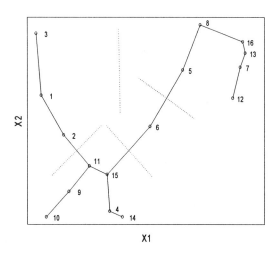

Figure 10.17: Clustering Using the MST of the Dataset (Table 10.2)

Nearest Neighbors and k-d-Trees

For a given observation, x_i, we may want to find its "nearest neighbor", x_k, where we define a nearest neighbor as one for which some function, $f(x_i, x_k)$, is minimized. For example, f may be the square of the Euclidean distance,

$$\sum_{j=1}^{m}(x_{ij} - x_{kj})^2.$$

To search bivariate data for a point that is close in Euclidean distance to a given point, a *quad tree* is useful (see Knuth, 1973).

For the more general problem of finding nearest neighbors in multivariate data, a k-d-tree developed by Friedman, Bentley, and Finkel (1977) may be more useful. A k-d-tree is a multivariate form of a B-tree; see Bentley and Friedman (1979).

Consider an $n \times m$ data matrix X in which columns represent variables and rows represent observations. A k-d-tree for X is defined by two arrays, v, which contains indicators of the variables to be used as discriminators, and p, which contains values of the corresponding variables to be used in forming partitions. Let b be the maximum bucket size (that is, the largest number of elements to be left at a terminal node).

Algorithm 10.2 Formation of a k-d-Tree

0. Set $l = 1$ and $h = n$.

1. Let $k = \lfloor (l+h)/2 \rfloor$.

2. Let v_k be the column number with maximum spread.

3. Let p_k be the median in the range $[l, h]$ of the v_k^{th} column.

4. Interchange the rows of X so that all rows of X with values in the v_k^{th} column less than or equal to p_k occur before (or at) the kth element.

5. If $k - l > b$, then form a submatrix with $h = k$.
   If $h - k - l > b$, then form a submatrix with $l = k + 1$ (with h as in step 4). Process steps 1 through 4 for each submatrix formed and then return to step 5. ■

Although trees are used often at a lower level, there is not much software available at the user level to form trees. The IMSL Fortran routine QUADT builds a k-d-tree and the routine NGHBR uses a k-d-tree to find nearest neighbors.

Murtagh (1984) provides a comparative review of algorithms for computing nearest neighbors.

Ordering and Ranking of Transformed Data

Minimal spanning trees depend on relative distances between points, so, as we would expect, the minimal spanning tree and any ordering based on it may be different if the data are transformed. Likewise, of course, orderings based on clustering may be changed by transformations of the data.

An important property of convex hulls and the depth of data is that they are not affected by affine transformations.

10.3   Linear Principal Components

In addition to clusters and orderings in data, other types of interesting structure are lower-dimensional relationships in the data. The information in observations that consists of m components may be adequately represented by transformed observations consisting of a smaller set of k components. This reduction in the dimension of the data may allow a reduction in the storage requirements, but, more importantly, it may help in understanding the data. Dimension reduction is useful in identifying structure in the data and also in discovering properties that the data do not measure directly. We may wish to extract features in the data that have been obscured by measurement error or other sources of noise.

A basic tenet of data analysis is that variation provides information, and an important approach in statistics is the analysis of variation. When many variables are present, however, it is often difficult to identify individual effects, so it may be useful to reduce the number of variables.

Another basic tenet is that covariance among a set of variables reduces the amount of information that the variables contain. We therefore seek to combine variables in such a way that their covariance is reduced or, more generally, that they are independent. For normal variables, of course, zero covariance is equivalent to independence.

The basic problem therefore is to transform the observed m-vectors x into k-vectors $\tilde{x}$ that, as a set, exhibit almost as much variation as the original set and are mutually independent or "almost" so.

Because of differences in the meanings of the variables, it is best first to standardize the data using the transformation (5.20)

$$X_S = (X - \overline{X}) \operatorname{diag}(\sqrt{s_{ii}}),$$

where $\overline{X}$ is the matrix whose constant columns contain the means of the corresponding columns of X, and $\sqrt{s_{ii}}$ is the sample standard deviation of the ith column of X.

There are various ways of combining a set of variables into a smaller set (that is, of transforming m-vectors into k-vectors). One of the simplest methods is to use linear transformations. If the linear transformations result in new variables that are orthogonal (that is, if they have zero sample correlation), and if the data are multivariate normal, then the new variables are independent. The linear combinations are called "principal components", "empirical orthogonal functions" or "EOF" (especially in meteorology and atmospheric research), "latent semantic indices" (especially in information retrieval), "factors" (especially in the social sciences), Karhunen-Loève transforms (especially in signal analysis), or "independent components" (also in signal analysis).

There are some differences among and within these methods. The differences have to do with assumptions about probability distributions and with the nature of the transformations. In factor analysis, which we discuss in Section 10.4, a rather strong stochastic model guides the analysis. In independent components analysis, rather than seeking only orthogonality, which yields zero correlations, and hence independence for normal data, transformations may be performed to yield zero cross moments of higher order. (Correlations are cross moments of second order.) Independent component analysis, therefore, may involve nonlinear transformations. Any of the methods mentioned above may also utilize nonlinear combinations of the observed variables.

Linear *principal components analysis* (PCA) is a technique for data reduction by constructing linear combinations of the original variables that account for as much of the total variation in those variables as possible. We discuss this method first.

The Probability Model Underlying Principal Components Analysis

Linear principal components is a method of "decorrelating" the elements of a vector random variable. The method depends on the variances of the individual elements, so it is generally best to perform transformations as necessary so that all elements have the same variance. In addition and without loss of generality, it is convenient to subtract the mean of each element of the random variable. The transformed vector is thus standardized so that the mean of each element is 0 and the variance of each element is 1.

Consider an m-vector random variable Y with variance-covariance matrix Σ, which has 1's along the diagonal. We will refer to the elements of the random variable as "variables". We seek a transformation of Y that produces a random vector whose elements are uncorrelated; that is, we seek a matrix W with m columns such that $V(WY)$ is diagonal. (Here, $V(\cdot)$ is the variance.) Now,

$$V(WY) = W\Sigma W^{\mathrm{T}},$$

so the matrix W must be chosen so that $W\Sigma W^{\mathrm{T}}$ is diagonal.

The obvious solution is to decompose Σ:

$$\Sigma = W^{\mathrm{T}}\Lambda W. \tag{10.10}$$

The spectral decomposition of the variance-covariance matrix is

$$\Sigma = \sum_{k}^{m} \lambda_k w_k w_k^{\mathrm{T}}, \tag{10.11}$$

with the eigenvalues λ_k indexed so that $0 \leq \lambda_m \leq \cdots \leq \lambda_1$ and with the w_k orthonormal; that is,

$$I = \sum_{k} w_k w_k^{\mathrm{T}}.$$

Now, consider the random variables

$$\widetilde{Y}_{(k)} = w_k^{\mathrm{T}} Y,$$

which we define as the *principal components* of Y.

The first principal component, $\widetilde{Y}_{(1)}$, is the projection of Y in the direction in which the variance is maximized, the second principal component, $\widetilde{Y}_{(2)}$, is the projection of Y in an orthogonal direction with the largest variance, and so on.

It is clear that the variance of $\widetilde{Y}_{(k)}$ is λ_k and that the $\widetilde{Y}_{(k)}$ are uncorrelated; that is, the variance-covariance matrix of the random vector $(\widetilde{Y}_{(1)}, \ldots, \widetilde{Y}_{(m)})$ is $\mathrm{diag}(\lambda_1, \ldots, \lambda_m)$. Heuristically, the kth principal component accounts for the proportion

$$\frac{\lambda_k}{\sum \lambda_j}$$

of the "total variation" in the original random vector Y.

The linear combinations $\widetilde{Y}_{(k)}$ that correspond to the largest eigenvalues are most interesting. If we consider only the ones that account for a major portion of the total variation, we have reduced the dimension of the original random variable without sacrificing very much of the potential explanatory value of the probability model. Thus, using only the p largest eigenvalues, instead of the m-vector Y, we form the transformation matrix W as

$$
W = \begin{bmatrix} w_1^\mathrm{T} \\ w_2^\mathrm{T} \\ \vdots \\ w_p^\mathrm{T} \end{bmatrix}.
$$

This produces the p-vector $\widetilde{Y} = (\widetilde{Y}_{(1)}, \ldots, \widetilde{Y}_{(p)})$.

The matrix

$$
\Sigma_p = \sum_k^p \lambda_k w_k w_k^\mathrm{T}
$$

is the variance-covariance matrix of $\widetilde{Y}$.

Eckart and Young (1936) proved an interesting fact about Σ_p as an approximation to Σ. It is the matrix of rank p closest to Σ as measured by the Frobenius norm,

$$
\|\Sigma - \Sigma_p\|_\mathrm{F}.
$$

Although all of the statements above are true for any distribution for which the first two moments exist, the properties of the principal components are even more useful if the underlying random variable Y has a multivariate normal distribution. In this case, the principal components vector $\widetilde{Y}$ also has a multivariate normal distribution, and the elements of $\widetilde{Y}$ are independent.

Principal Components Analysis of Data

In the basic multivariate data structure of X, we often consider the rows to be realizations of some multivariate random variable, such as Y in the discussion above. Because of differences in the meanings of the variables in the data matrix X, it is best first to standardize the data using the transformation (5.20) on page 117:

$$
X_\mathrm{S} = (X - \overline{X}) \operatorname{diag}(\sqrt{s_{ii}}).
$$

In the following, we will assume that this has been done. We will assume that X has been standardized and not continue to use the notation X_S.

Using S as an estimate of Σ, we can perform a principal components analysis of the data that follows the same techniques as above for a random variable.

We determine the spectral decomposition of S just as we did for Σ in equation (10.11):

$$S = \sum_j \hat{\lambda}_j \hat{w}_j \hat{w}_j^T.$$ (10.12)

The principal components of the vector of observed variables x are

$$\tilde{x}_{(j)} = \hat{w}_j^T x.$$ (10.13)

Corresponding to the generic data vector x is the generic vector of principal components,

$$\tilde{x} = (\tilde{x}_{(1)}, \ldots, \tilde{x}_{(m)}).$$

For each observation x_i, we can compute a value of the principal components vector, $\tilde{x}_i$. From the spectral decomposition that yields the principal components, it is easy to see that the sample variance-covariance matrix of the principal components is diagonal.

Figure 10.19 shows the marginal distributions of the elliptical data cloud shown in Figure 10.18 in the original coordinates x_1 and x_2 and in the coordinates of the principal components z_1 and z_2.

The first principal component is the hyperplane that minimizes the orthogonal distances to the hyperplane as discussed on page 318, and illustrated in Figure 11.2.

The principal components are transformations of the original system of coordinate axes. It is difficult to relate any of the new axes to the old axes, however. To aid in their interpretability, Hausman (1982) suggests a constrained PCA in which each principal component is approximated by a linear combination of the original axes with coefficients of the combination being $+1$, -1, or 0. Presumably, a combination in which the original variables are just added or subtracted is easier to interpret in terms of the quantities measured by the original variables.

In the same spirit, Vines (2000) and Jolliffe and Uddin (2000) describe methods to determine "simple components". In Vines's approach, "simplicity preserving" transformations—that is, linear combinations with integer coefficients (but not just $+1$, -1, or 0)—are applied sequentially in such a way that the combination with the largest variance has a larger variance than that of the original variable with the largest variance. The allowable combinations result from a fixed set of coefficients or from a rule that defines allowable coefficients. After fixing that combination as the first simple component, another simple component is chosen similarly. There are several different criteria that could be applied to determine the order of all of the transformations, and more studies are needed to evaluate various ways of proceeding. Of course, underlying any decision on the exact algorithm is the question of what is a "simple" component.

In the method of Jolliffe and Uddin (2000), instead of choosing a priori a set of allowable combinations, a penalty function is used to push the combinations, which are determined sequentially, toward simplicity. The reader is referred to

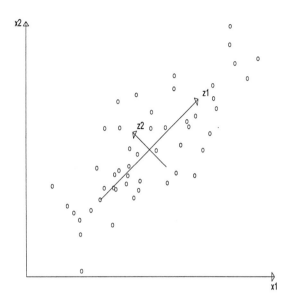

Figure 10.18: Principal Components of Some Bivariate Data

the papers of Vines (2000) and Jolliffe and Uddin (2000) for further discussions of the methods.

Dimension Reduction by Principal Components Analysis

We can reduce the dimension of the data by considering the transformed variables $\tilde{x}_{(i)}$, each of which is a vector formed using the eigenvectors corresponding only to the p largest eigenvalues. As before, we form the $p \times m$ transformation matrix $\widehat{W}$,

$$
\widehat{W} = \begin{bmatrix} \hat{w}_1^{\mathrm{T}} \\ \hat{w}_2^{\mathrm{T}} \\ \vdots \\ \hat{w}_p^{\mathrm{T}} \end{bmatrix}.
$$

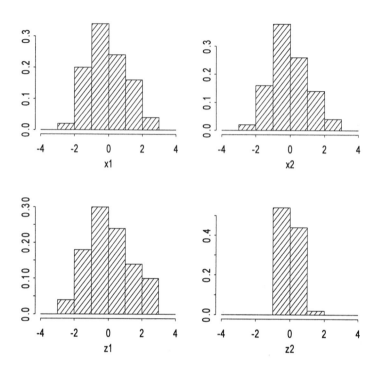

Figure 10.19: Univariate Histograms of the Original Coordinates and the Principal Components

For the ith observation x_i, this produces the p-vector $\tilde{x}_i = (\tilde{x}_{i(1)}, \ldots, \tilde{x}_{i(p)})$. The application of this transformation matrix is often called the (discrete) Karhunen-Loève transform in signal analysis after independent work by K. Karhunen and M. Loève in the late 1940s or the Hotelling transform after the work of H. Hotelling in the 1930s.

The question arises, naturally, of how to choose p. This is the question of how much we can reduce the dimensionality of the original dataset. A simple approach that is often employed is to choose p as the number of the ranked eigenvalues just prior to a large gap in the list. For example, if $m = 6$ and the eigenvalues are 10.0, 9.0, 3.0, 2.5, 2.1, and 2.0, a logical choice of p may be 2, because of the large decrease after the second eigenvalue. A plot of these ordered values or of the values scaled by their total may be useful in identifying the point at which there is a large dropoff in effect. Such a plot, called a scree plot, is shown as the left-hand plot in Figure 10.20. The scree plot can be either a line plot as in the figure or a bar chart in which the heights of the bars represent the relative values of the eigenvalues. The key feature in a scree plot is an "elbow", if one exists. A plot of the accumulated "total variation" accounted for by the principal components, as shown in the right-hand plot in Figure 10.20, may also be useful.

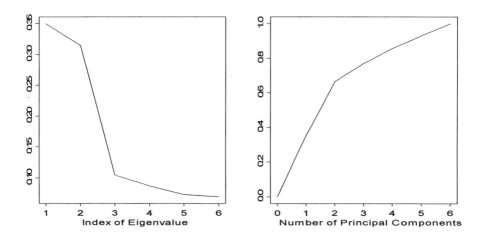

Figure 10.20: Scree Plot of Scaled Eigenvalues and Plot of Proportion of "Total Variance"

The effect of each of the original variables (the elements of x) on each principal component is measured by the correlation between the variable and the principal component. This is called the "component loading" of the variable on the principal component. The component loading of the jth variable on the kth principal component is the correlation

$$\frac{w_{kj}\sqrt{\hat{\lambda}_k}}{\sqrt{s_{jj}}}.$$

(Note that w_{kj} is the jth element of the kth eigenvector.)

Principal Components and Transformations of the Data

As we mentioned at the outset, variation provides information. Variables with large sample variances will tend to predominate in the first principal component. Consider the extreme case in which the variables are uncorrelated (that is, in which S is diagonal). The principal components are determined exactly by the variances, from largest to smallest. This is a natural and desirable consequence of the fact that variation provides information. In principal components analysis, the relative variation from one variable to another is the important factor in determining the rankings of the components. It is difficult, however, to measure the relative variation from one variable to another. The variance of a variable depends on the units of measurement. Suppose that one variable represents linear measurements in meters. If, for some reason, the unit of measurement is changed to centimeters, the effect of that variable in determining the principal components will increase one hundredfold.

The component loadings can help in understanding the effects of data reduction through principal components analysis. Notice that the component loadings are scaled by the square root of the variance. Another approach to scaling problems resulting from the choice of unit of measurement is to use the correlation matrix, R (see equation (5.10)), rather than the variance-covariance matrix. The correlations result from scaling the covariances by the square roots of the variances. The obvious should be noted, however: *the principal components resulting from the use of R are not the same as those resulting from the use of S.*

Change of units of measurement is just one kind of simple scaling transformation. Transformations of any kind are likely to change the results of a multivariate analysis, as we see, for example, in the case of clustering on page 251.

Principal Components of Observations

Just as in Section 10.1, on page 252, we observed the basic symmetry between the "variables" and the "observations" of the dataset X, we can likewise reverse their roles in principal components analysis. Suppose, for example, that the observational units are individual persons and the variables are responses to psychological tests. Principal components analysis as we have described it would identify linear combinations of the scores on the tests. These principal components determine relationships among the test scores. If we replace the data matrix X by its transpose and proceed with a principal components analysis as described above, we identify important linear combinations of the observations that, in turn, identify relationships among the observational units. In the social sciences, a principal components analysis of variables is called an "R-Type" analysis and the analysis identifying relationships among the observational units is called "Q-Type".

In the usual situation, as we have described, the number of observations, n, is greater than the number of variables, m. If X has rank m, then the variance-covariance matrix and the correlation matrix are of full rank. In a reversal of the roles of observations and variables, the corresponding matrix would not be of full rank. Of course, the analysis could proceed mechanically as we have described, but the available information for identifying meaningful linear combinations of the observations would be rather limited. This problem could perhaps be remedied by collecting more data on each observational unit (that is, by defining and observing more variables).

Principal Components Directly from the Data Matrix

Formation of the S or R matrix emphasizes the role that the sample covariances or correlations play in principal component analysis. However, there is no reason to form a matrix such as $(X - \overline{X})^{\mathrm{T}}(X - \overline{X})$, and indeed we may introduce significant rounding errors by doing so.

The singular value decomposition (SVD) of the $n \times m$ matrix $X - \overline{X}$ yields the square roots of the eigenvalues of $(X - \overline{X})^{\mathrm{T}}(X - \overline{X})$ and the same eigenvectors. (The eigenvalues of $(X - \overline{X})^{\mathrm{T}}(X - \overline{X})$ are $(n-1)$ times the eigenvalues of S.) We will assume that there are more observations than variables (that is, that $n > m$). In the SVD of the centered data matrix, we write

$$(X - \overline{X})^{\mathrm{T}}(X - \overline{X}) = UAV^{\mathrm{T}},$$

where U is an $n \times m$ matrix with orthogonal columns, V is an $m \times m$ orthogonal matrix, and A is an $m \times m$ diagonal matrix with nonnegative entries, called the singular values of $X - \overline{X}$.

The spectral decomposition in terms of the singular values and outer products of the columns of the factor matrices is

$$X - \overline{X} = \sum_{i}^{m} \sigma_i u_i v_i^{\mathrm{T}}. \tag{10.14}$$

The vectors u_i, called the "left eigenvectors" or "left singular vectors" of $X - \overline{X}$, are the same as the eigenvectors of S in equation (10.12). The vectors v_i, the "right eigenvectors", are the eigenvectors that would be used in a Q-type principal components analysis. The reduced-rank matrix that approximates $X - \overline{X}$ is

$$\tilde{X}_p = \sum_{i}^{p} \sigma_i u_i v_i^{\mathrm{T}} \tag{10.15}$$

for some $p < \min(n, m)$.

Computational Issues

For the eigenanalysis computations in PCA, if the sample variance-covariance matrix S is available, it is probably best to proceed with the decomposition of it as in equations (10.12). Because the interest is generally only in the largest eigenvalues, the power method (see Gentle, 1998b, page 124) may be the best method to use. If S is not available, there is generally no reason to compute it just to perform PCA. The computations to form S are $O(m^3)$. Not only do these computations add significantly to the overall computational burden, but S is more poorly conditioned than X (or $X - \overline{X}$). The SVD decomposition (10.14) is therefore the better procedure.

Artificial neural nets have been proposed as a method for computing the singular values in equation (10.14). A study by Nicole (2000), however, indicates that neural nets may not perform very well for identifying any but the first principal component.

PCA for Clustering

An objective of principal components analysis is to identify linear combinations of the original variables that are useful in accounting for the variation in those original variables. This is effectively a clustering of the variables. For many purposes, these derived features carry a large amount of the information that is available in the original larger set of variables. For other purposes, however, the principal component may completely lose the relevant information. For example, the information carried by the smaller set of features identified in PCA may be useless in clustering the observations. Consider the bivariate dataset in Figure 10.21. There are two clusters in this dataset, each of which appears to be a sample from an elliptical bivariate normal distribution with a small positive correlation. The two clusters are separated by a displacement of the mean of the second component. The two principal components are shown in Figure 10.21. As would be expected, the first principal component is in the direction of greater spread of the data, and the second principal component is orthogonal to the first.

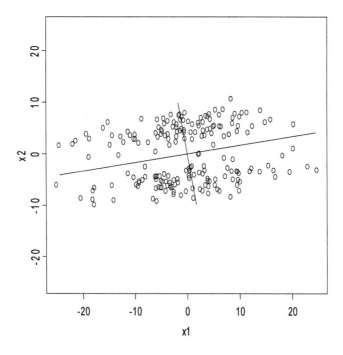

Figure 10.21: Principal Components of a Bivariate Dataset with Two Clusters

The first principal component contains no information about the clusters in the data. Figure 10.22 shows histograms of the data projected onto the two principal components. The second principal component carries information about the two clusters, but the first principal component appears to be a single normal sample.

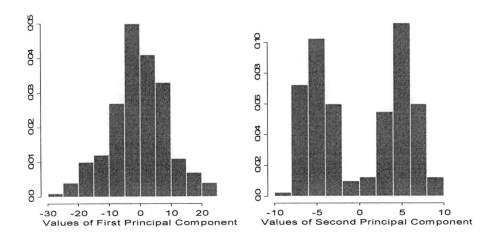

Figure 10.22: Histograms of Projections of Bivariate Dataset onto the Two Principal Components

Principal components analysis emphasizes the direction of maximum variation. If the main source of variation in the dataset is the variation between clusters, then PCA will identify the clusters. This is not always the case, and the principal component may not lie in the most informative direction. Other techniques, such as projection pursuit (see Section 10.5), seek projections of the data in directions that exhibit other interesting structure, such as the bimodality in the direction of the second principal component in this example.

Robustness of Principal Components

As we have mentioned above, outlying observations or (nearly) collinear variables can present problems in data analysis. Principal components is one way of dealing with collinear variables. These variables have large correlations among themselves. The dimension of the space of principal components will likely be reduced so that all variables that are collinear with each other are replaced by a single variable.

Outlying observations, however, may have a major effect on the principal components analysis. The first few principal components are very sensitive to these outlying observations. If the outliers were not present, or if they were perturbed slightly, a different set of the first few principal components would likely result.

There are generally two ways of dealing with outlying observations. One way is to identify the outliers and remove them temporarily. Another way is to use methods that are not much affected by outliers. Campbell (1980) suggests using the robust sample variance-covariance, S_R, in equation 5.23 on page 121. The principal components resulting from S_R are less affected by outliers than those resulting from the usual sample variance-covariance, S.

If outliers can be identified and removed temporarily, a standard analysis can be performed. This identification, removal, and analysis procedure can be applied in stages. The major problem, of course, is that as extreme observations are removed, the variability in the dataset is reduced, so other, valid observations are more likely to appear as outliers. In general, a data analyst must assume that every observation carries useful information, and no observation must be discarded until its information is incorporated into the analysis. (See Barnett and Lewis, 1994, for methods of dealing with outliers.)

For purposes of PCA, outliers can be identified in a preliminary step using a clustering procedure or even by using Q-type principal components analysis. Caroni (2000) describes a way of using the robust PCA based on S_R to identify outliers.

10.4   Variants of Principal Components

Factor Analysis

Factor analysis is mechanically similar to principal components analysis. The main differences involve the probability model. In the following sections we will briefly discuss factor analysis. For more discussion on the subject, the reader is referred to Reyment and Jöreskog (1996).

The Probability Model Underlying Factor Analysis

In factor analysis, we begin with a model that relates a centered m-vector random variable Y (observable) to an underlying, unobservable k-vector random variable, whose elements are called "factors". The factors have a mean of 0. In this model, the observable vector Y consists of linear combinations of the factors plus an independent random vector of "unique errors", which is modeled by a random variable with a mean of 0. The unique errors are independent of the factors. Now, letting F represent the vector of factors and E represent the errors, we have

$$Y - \mu = \Gamma F + E, \tag{10.16}$$

where μ is the mean of Y and Γ is an $m \times k$ fixed (but unknown) matrix, called the "factor loadings" matrix. Generally, the number of factors is less than the number of the observable variables. In some applications, such as in psychology, the factors may be related to some innate characteristics that are manifested in observable behavior.

We denote the variance-covariance matrix of Y by Σ, that of F by Σ_F, and that of E by Ψ, which is diagonal by the assumptions in the model. We therefore have the relationship

$$\Sigma = \Gamma \Sigma_F \Gamma^{\mathrm{T}} + \Psi.$$

Now, if we let $\widetilde{\Gamma} = \Gamma \Sigma_F^{\frac{1}{2}}$ and $\widetilde{F} = (\Sigma_F^{\frac{1}{2}})^{-1} F$, we have

$$\Sigma = \widetilde{\Gamma} \widetilde{\Gamma}^{\mathrm{T}} + \Psi.$$

Hence, a model equivalent to equation (10.16) is one in which we assume that the underlying factors have the identity as their variance-covariance matrix, and so we have

$$\Sigma = \Gamma \Gamma^{\mathrm{T}} + \Psi. \tag{10.17}$$

The diagonal elements of Ψ are called the *specific variances* of the factors and the diagonal elements of $\Gamma \Gamma^{\mathrm{T}}$ are called the *commonalities* of the factors.

The transformations above that indicate that $\Gamma \Gamma^{\mathrm{T}}$ can be used instead of $\Gamma \Sigma_F \Gamma^{\mathrm{T}}$ raise the issue of more general transformations of the factors, leading to an indeterminacy in the analysis.

If we decompose $\Sigma - \Psi$ as we did in PCA in equation (10.10) on page 266, (with Δ replacing Λ) we have

$$\Sigma - \Psi = W^{\mathrm{T}} \Lambda W. \tag{10.18}$$

The factor-loading matrix therefore is

$$\Gamma = W^{\mathrm{T}} \Lambda^{\frac{1}{2}}. \tag{10.19}$$

Factor Analysis of Data

In practical applications of factor analysis, we must begin with a chosen value of k, the number of factors. This is similar to choosing the number of principal components in PCA, and there are some ways of adaptively choosing k, but the computational approaches that we discuss below assume a fixed value for k. As usual, we consider the rows of the data matrix X to be realizations of a multivariate random variable. In factor analysis, the random variable has the same relationships to other random variables as Y above; hence, the observation x (a row of X) is related to the realization of two other random variables, f and e, by

$$x - \bar{x} = \Gamma f + e.$$

The objective in factor analysis is to estimate the parameters in the model (10.16)—that is, the factor loadings, Γ, and the variances, Σ and Ψ, in equation (10.17). There are several methods for estimating these parameters. In one method, the estimation criterion is *least squares* of the sum of the differences in the diagonal elements of Σ and S, that is, minimize the function g:

$$g(\Gamma, \Psi) = \mathrm{trace}((S - \Sigma)^2). \tag{10.20}$$

This criterion leads to the *principal factors method*. The minimization proceeds by first choosing a value $\widehat{\Psi}^{(0)}$ and then performing a decomposition similar to that in principal components, except that instead of decomposing the sample variance-covariance matrix S, an eigenanalysis of $S - \widehat{\Psi}^{(0)}$ as suggested by equation (10.18) is performed:

$$S - \widehat{\Psi}^{(0)} = \left(\widehat{W}^{(0)}\right)^{\mathrm{T}} \widehat{\Lambda}^{(0)} \, \widehat{W}^{(0)}. \qquad (10.21)$$

This yields the value for Γ, analogous to equation (10.19):

$$\widehat{\Gamma}^{(0)} = \left(\widehat{W}^{(0)}\right)^{\mathrm{T}} \left(\widehat{\Lambda}^{(0)}\right)^{\frac{1}{2}}.$$

Next, the minimization problem (10.20) is solved for Ψ with the fixed value of $\widehat{\Gamma}^{(0)}$, that is,

$$\min g\!\left(\widehat{\Gamma}^{(0)}, \Psi\right). \qquad (10.22)$$

Newton's method is usually used to solve this problem, leading to $\widehat{\Psi}^{(1)}$. The steps are then repeated; that is, $S - \widehat{\Psi}^{(1)}$ is decomposed, leading to

$$\widehat{\Gamma}^{(1)} = \left(\widehat{W}^{(1)}\right)^{\mathrm{T}} \left(\widehat{\Lambda}^{(1)}\right)^{\frac{1}{2}},$$

which is used in the next application of Newton's method to solve $\min g\!\left(\widehat{\Gamma}^{(1)}, \Psi\right)$. Convergence criteria are usually chosen based on norms of the change in the estimates from one iteration to the next.

A simple method that is often used to get started is to take $\widehat{\psi}_{jj}^{(0)}$ as

$$\left(1 - \frac{k}{2m}\right)\left(S_{jj}^{-1}\right)^{-1},$$

where S_{jj}^{-1} is the jth diagonal element of S^{-1} if S is full rank; otherwise, take $\widehat{\psi}_{jj}^{(0)}$ as $s_{jj}/2$.

The factors derived using the principal factors method (that is, the linear combinations of the original variables) are the same as would be obtained in ordinary PCA if the variance of the noise (the unique errors) were removed from the variance-covariance of the observations prior to performing the PCA.

Another common method for estimating Γ, Σ, and Ψ uses the *likelihood criterion* that results from the asymptotic distributions. Using the negative of the log of the likelihood, we have the minimization problem,

$$\min l(\Gamma, \Psi) = \min\!\left(\log\left|\Sigma^{-1} S\right| - \mathrm{trace}\!\left(\Sigma^{-1} S\right)\right). \qquad (10.23)$$

This criterion results in the method of maximum likelihood. In this method, we require that S be positive definite.

Solution of the minimization problem (10.23) is also done in iterations over two stages, as we did in the least squares method above. First, we choose a starting value $\widehat{\Psi}^{(0)}$. Its Cholesky factor, $\left(\widehat{\Psi}^{(0)}\right)^{\frac{1}{2}}$, is symmetric. We then decompose $\left(\widehat{\Psi}^{(0)}\right)^{\frac{1}{2}} S^{-1}\left(\widehat{\Psi}^{(0)}\right)^{\frac{1}{2}}$ as in equation (10.21):

$$\left(\widehat{\Psi}^{(0)}\right)^{\frac{1}{2}} S^{-1}\left(\widehat{\Psi}^{(0)}\right)^{\frac{1}{2}} = \left(\widehat{W}^{(0)}\right)^{\mathrm{T}} \widehat{\Lambda}^{(0)}\, \widehat{W}^{(0)}. \tag{10.24}$$

Using the relationship (10.17) and equation (10.19), we get a value for Γ:

$$\widehat{\Gamma}^{(0)} = \left(\widehat{\Psi}^{(0)}\widehat{W}^{(0)}\right)^{\mathrm{T}}\left(\widehat{\Lambda}^{(0)} - I\right)^{\frac{1}{2}}.$$

Next, the minimization problem (10.23) is solved for Ψ with the fixed value of $\widehat{\Gamma}^{(0)}$. This problem may be rather ill-conditioned, and the convergence can be rather poor. The transformations

$$\theta_j = \psi_{jj}$$

can help. (The ψ_{jj} are the only variable elements of the diagonal matrix Ψ.) Hence, the minimization problem is

$$\min l\left(\widehat{\Gamma}^{(0)}, \theta\right). \tag{10.25}$$

An advantage of the maximum likelihood method is that it is independent of the scales of measurement. This results from the decomposition of $\widehat{\Psi}^{\frac{1}{2}} S^{-1} \widehat{\Psi}^{\frac{1}{2}}$ in equation (10.24). Suppose that we make a scale transformation on the random variable, Y, in equation (10.16); that is, we form $T = YD$, where D is a fixed diagonal matrix with positive entries. The resulting variance-covariance matrix for the unique errors, Ψ_T, is $D\Psi D^{\mathrm{T}}$. Likewise, the corresponding sample variance-covariance matrix, S_T, is DSD^{T}. The matrix to be decomposed as in equation (10.24) is

$$
\begin{aligned}
\left(\widehat{\Psi}_T^{(0)}\right)^{\frac{1}{2}} S_T^{-1}\left(\widehat{\Psi}_T^{(0)}\right)^{\frac{1}{2}} &= \left(D\widehat{\Psi}^{(0)}D^{\mathrm{T}}\right)^{\frac{1}{2}}\left(DSD^{\mathrm{T}}\right)^{-1}\left(D\widehat{\Psi}^{(0)}D^{\mathrm{T}}\right)^{\frac{1}{2}} \\
&= \left(\widehat{\Psi}^{(0)}\right)^{\frac{1}{2}} D^{\mathrm{T}}\left(D^{\mathrm{T}}\right)^{-1} S^{-1} D^{-1} D\left(\widehat{\Psi}^{(0)}\right)^{\frac{1}{2}} \\
&= \left(\widehat{\Psi}^{(0)}\right)^{\frac{1}{2}} S^{-1}\left(\widehat{\Psi}^{(0)}\right)^{\frac{1}{2}},
\end{aligned}
$$

which is the same as the one for the untransformed data.

Other common methods for factor analysis include generalized least squares, image analysis (of two different types), and alpha factor analysis.

The methods for factor analysis begin with the computation of the sample variance-covariance matrix S or the sample correlation matrix R. As we noted in the case of PCA, the results are different, just as the results are generally different following any transformation of the data.

Note that the model (10.16) does not define the factors uniquely; any rotation of the factors would yield the same model. In principal components analysis, a similar indeterminacy could also occur if we allow an arbitrary basis for the PCA subspace defined by the chosen k principal components.

The factors are often rotated to get a basis with some interesting properties. A common criterion is parsimony of representation, which roughly means that the matrix has few significantly nonzero entries. This principle has given rise to various rotations, such as the varimax, quartimax, and oblimin rotations.

Factor analysis is often applied to grouped data under a model with the same factors in each group, called a common factor model.

In general, because of the stronger model, factor analysis should be used with more caution than principal components analysis.

An appendix in the book by Reyment and Jöreskog (1996) contains Matlab scripts to perform many of the computations for factor analysis.

Latent Semantic Indexing

An interesting application of the methods of principal components, called *latent semantic indexing*, is used in matching keyword searches with documents. The method begins with the construction of a term-document matrix, X, whose rows correspond to keywords, whose columns correspond to documents (web pages, for example), and whose entries are the frequencies of occurrences of the keywords in the documents. A singular value decomposition is performed on X (or on $X - \overline{X}$) as in equation (10.14), and then a reduced-rank matrix $\widetilde{X}_p$ is defined, as in equation (10.15). A list of keywords is matched to documents by representing the keyword list as a vector, q, of 0's and 1's corresponding to the rows of X. The vector $\widetilde{X}_p^{\mathrm{T}} q$ is a list of scores for the documents. Documents with larger scores are those deemed relevant for the search.

A semantic structure for the set of documents can also be identified by $\widetilde{X}_p$. Semantically nearby documents are mapped onto the same singular vectors. See Berry and Browne (1999) for further discussion of latent semantic indexing and its use in document retrieval.

A variation of latent semantic indexing is called probabilistic latent semantic indexing, or nonnegative-part factorization. This approach assumes a set of hidden variables whose values in the matrix H correspond to the columns of X by a *nonnegative matrix factorization*,

$$X = WH,$$

where W is a matrix with nonnegative elements. See Lee and Seung (1999) for a description of this factorization and its use.

Hofmann (1999) describes a similar approach from a different perspective. The relationship of the model in probabilistic latent semantic indexing to the standard latent semantic indexing model is similar to the differences in factor analysis and principal components analysis.

Linear Independent Components Analysis

Independent components analysis (ICA) is similar to principal components analysis and factor analysis. Both PCA and ICA have nonlinear extensions. In linear PCA and ICA, the objective is to find a linear transformation W of a random vector Y so that the elements of WY have small correlations. In linear PCA, the objective then is to find W so that $V(WY)$ is diagonal, and, as we have seen, this is simple to do. If the random vector Y is normal, then 0 correlations imply independence. The objective in linear ICA is slightly different; instead of just the elements of WY, attention may be focused on chosen transformations of this vector, and instead of small correlations, independence is the goal. Of course, because most multivariate distributions other than the normal are rather intractable, in practice small correlations are usually the objective in ICA. The transformations of WY are often higher-order sample moments. The projections that yield diagonal variance-covariance matrices are not necessarily orthogonal.

In the literature on ICA, which is generally in the field of signal processing, either a "noise-free ICA model", similar to the simple PCA model, or a "noisy ICA model", similar to the factor analysis model, is used. Most of the research has been on the noise-free ICA model. The reader is referred to Comon (1994) for further descriptions of ICA and an iterative algorithm. We discuss independent components analysis further in Section 10.6.

10.5   Projection Pursuit

The objective in projection pursuit is to find "interesting" projections of multivariate data. Interesting structure in multivariate data may be identified by analyzing projections of the data onto lower-dimensional subspaces. The projections can be used for optimal visualization of the clustering structure of the data or for density estimation or even regression analysis. The approach is related to the visual approach of the grand tour (page 180). Reduction of dimension is also an important objective, especially if the use of the projections is in visualization of the data. Projection pursuit requires a measure of the "interestingness" of a projection.

Diaconis and Freedman (1984) showed that a randomly selected projection of a high-dimensional dataset onto a low-dimensional space will tend to appear similar to a sample from a multivariate normal distribution with that lower dimension. This result, which may be thought of as a central limit theorem for projections, implies that a multivariate normal dataset is the least "interesting". A specific projection of the given dataset, however, may reveal interesting features of the dataset. In projection pursuit, therefore, the objective is to find departures from normality in linear projections of the data.

Departures from normality may include such things as skewness and "holes" in the data, or multimodality. The projection whose histogram is shown on the right-hand side of Figure 10.22 on page 275 exhibits a departure from normality, whereas the histogram on the left-hand side appears to be of normal univariate data. The projections are of the same dataset.

The Probability Model Underlying Projection Pursuit

Consider an m-vector random variable Y. In general, we are interested in a k-dimensional projection of Y, say A^TY, such that the random variable A^TY is very different from a k-variate normal distribution.

Because all one-dimensional marginals of a multivariate normal are normal, and cross products of normals are multivariate normal, we will concentrate on one-dimensional projections of Z. Our problem is to find $Z = a^TY$ such that the random variable Y is "most different" from a normal random variable. Two-dimensional projections are also of particular interest, especially in graphics. We will discuss just the one-dimensional projections, and refer the interested reader to Cook, Buja, and Cabrera (1993) for more discussion of two-dimensional projections and their applications.

The structure of interest (that is, a departure from normality) can be considered separately from the location, variances, and covariances of the vector Y; therefore, we will assume that $E(Y) = 0$ and $V(Y) = I$. Prior to applying projection pursuit to data, we center and sphere the data so that the sample characteristics are consistent with these assumptions.

To quantify the objectives in projection pursuit, we need a measure, or index, of the departure from normality.

Projection Indexes for the Probability Model

One way to quantify departure from normality is to consider the probability density function of the projected variable and compare it to the probability density function ϕ of a standard normal random variable. If p is the density of Z, we want it to be very different from ϕ. This is an opposite problem from the function approximation problem, but the approaches are related. Whereas in function approximation, the Chebyshev norm is generally of most interest in seeking a function that is "different", an L_2 norm,

$$\int_{-\infty}^{\infty} (p(z) - \phi(z))^2 \mathrm{d}z, \tag{10.26}$$

makes more sense as a measure of the difference.

The objective in projection pursuit is to find an a that maximizes this norm. It has become common practice in the literature on projection pursuit to name indexes of departure from normality by the type of orthogonal polynomials used in approximating the index. The index in expression (10.26) is called the *Hermite index* because Hermite polynomials are appropriate for approximation over the unbounded domain (see Table 6.1 on page 136). It is also called *Hall's index* because it was studied by Hall (1989).

For a given a, Friedman (1987) proposed first mapping $Z = a^T Y$ into $[-1, 1]$ by the transformation

$$R = 2\Phi(Z) - 1,$$

where Φ is the CDF of a standard normal distribution. If p_Z is the probability density of Z, then the probability density of R is

$$p_R(r) = \frac{\frac{1}{2} p_Z \left(\Phi^{-1} \left(\frac{r+1}{2} \right) \right)}{\phi \left(\Phi^{-1} \left(\frac{r+1}{2} \right) \right)}.$$

If Z has a normal distribution with a mean of 0 and variance of 1, R has a uniform distribution over $(-1, 1)$ and so has a constant density of $\frac{1}{2}$. (This is the idea behind the inverse CDF method of random number generation.) Hence, the problem is to find a such that the density, p_R, of R is very different from $\frac{1}{2}$. The relevant L_2 norm is

$$L(a) = \int_{-1}^{1} \left(p_R(r) - \frac{1}{2} \right)^2 dr,$$

which simplifies to

$$L(a) = \int_{-1}^{1} p_R^2(r) dr - \frac{1}{2}. \tag{10.27}$$

This norm, which is a scalar function of a and a functional of p_R, is sometimes called the *Legendre index* because Legendre polynomials are natural approximating series of orthogonal polynomials for functions over finite domains (see Table 6.1, on page 136). It is also called Friedman's Legendre index.

Cook, Buja, and Cabrera (1993) suggested another index based on the L_2 norm in equation (10.26) being weighted with the normal density:

$$H(a) = \int_{-\infty}^{\infty} (p(z) - \phi(z))^2 \phi(z) dz. \tag{10.28}$$

Cook, Buja, and Cabrera call this the *natural Hermite index*. The index is evaluated by expanding both $p(z)$ and $\phi(z)$ in the Hermite polynomials that are orthogonal with respect to $e^{-x^2/2}$ over $(-\infty, \infty)$. (These are not the standard Hermite polynomials, but they are the ones most commonly used by statisticians because the weight function is proportional to the normal density.) These Hermite polynomials are the H_k^e in equations (6.15) on page 136. The index is called "natural" because the difference in p and ϕ is weighted by the normal density. The natural Hermite index has some desirable invariance properties for two-dimensional projections. See Cook, Buja, and Cabrera (1993) for a discussion of these properties.

Various other measures of departure from normality are possible; Jones (see Jones and Sibson, 1987) suggested an index based on ratios of moments of a standard normal distribution, and Huber (1985) suggested indexes based on entropy (called Shannon entropy or differential entropy):

$$- \int_{\mathbb{R}^m} p(z) \log p(z) dz.$$

The entropy is maximized among the class of all random variables when the density p is the standard multivariate normal density (mean of zero and variance-covariance matrix equal to the identity). For any other distribution, the entropy is strictly smaller.

Other kinds of measures of departure from normality can be contemplated. Almost any goodness-of-fit criterion could serve as the basis for a projection index. Posse (1990, 1995a, 1995b) suggests a projection index based on a chi-squared measure of departure from normality. It has an advantage of computational simplicity.

Naito (1997) considers other elliptically symmetric distributions as the basis for comparisons. An elliptically symmetric distribution does not have an "interesting" structure. Nason (2001) suggested use of a circular multivariate t distribution following sphering of the data. Nason defined three indices similar to those in equations (10.26) and (10.28), but based on departures from an m-variate t distribution,

$$\int_{\mathbb{R}^m} (p(z) - t_{\nu,m}(z))^2 (t_{\nu,m}(z))^\alpha dz,$$

where $t_{\nu,m}(z)$ is the density function of a spherical m-variate t distribution with ν degrees of freedom, and α is 0, as in equation (10.26), $\frac{1}{2}$, or 1, as in equation (10.28). As Nason points out and confirms empirically, a procedure based on an index of departure from a multivariate t distribution is likely to be more robust to a small number of outlying observations than would a procedure based on a normal distribution.

Morton (1992) suggests an "interpretability index" that gives preference to simple projections (that is, to linear combinations in which a has more zeros), and when comparing two combinations a_1 and a_2, the vectors are (nearly) orthogonal. This work anticipated similar attempts in PCA to determine approximate principal components that are "simple" (see Vines, 2000, and Jolliffe and Uddin, 2000).

Sun (1992, 1993) reports comparisons of the use of Friedman's Legendre index, $L(a)$, and Hall's Hermite index (10.26). Cook, Buja, and Cabrera (1993) give comparisons of these two indexes and the natural Hermite index, $H(a)$. Posse (1990, 1995a, 1995b) and Nason (2001) also report comparisons of the various indices. The results of these comparisons were inconclusive; which index is better in identifying departures from normality (or from uninteresting structure) seems to depend on the nature of the nonnormality.

Projection Pursuit in Data

We now consider one-dimensional projection pursuit in a given set of data X (the familiar $n \times m$ matrix in our data analysis paradigm). For each projection a, we *estimate* the projection index associated with a under the assumption that the rows in X are independent realizations of a random variable Y. The vector Xa contains independent realizations of the scalar random variable $Z = a^T Y = Y^T a$.

The question is how similar the distribution of Z is to a normal distribution. The problem with measures of departure from normality is the difficulty in estimating the terms.

To estimate the projection index, we must *approximate* an integral. As we suggested above, the indexes lend themselves to approximation by standard series of orthogonal polynomials.

For $L(a)$, expanding one factor of p_R^2 in equation (10.27) in Legendre polynomials and leaving the other unexpanded, we have

$$L(a) = \int_{-1}^{1} \left(\sum_{k=0}^{\infty} c_k P_k(r) \right) p_R(r) \, dr - \frac{1}{2},$$

where P_k is the kth Legendre polynomial.

We have the Legendre coefficients for the expansion

$$c_k = \frac{2k + 1}{2} \int_{-1}^{1} P_k(r) p_R(r) \, dr.$$

Substituting this into the expression above, because of the orthogonality of the P_k, we have

$$L(a) = \sum_{k=0}^{\infty} \frac{2k + 1}{2} \left(E(P_k(R)) \right)^2 - \frac{1}{2}, \qquad (10.29)$$

where the expectation E is taken with respect to the distribution of the random variable R. Each term in equation (10.29) is an expectation and therefore can be estimated easily from a random sample. The sample mean is generally a good estimate of an expectation; hence, for the kth term, from the original observations x_i, the projection a, and the normal CDF transformation, we have

$$
\begin{aligned}
\widehat{E}\left(P_k(R)\right) &= \frac{1}{n} \sum_{i=1}^{n} P_k(r_i) \\
&= \frac{1}{n} \sum_{i=1}^{n} P_k(2\Phi(a^T x_i) - 1).
\end{aligned}
$$

A simple estimate of the squared expectation is just the square of this quantity.

Obviously, in practice, we must use a finite approximation to the infinite expansion of p_R. After terminating the expansion at j, we have the truncated Legendre projection index, $L_j(a)$,

$$L_j(a) = \sum_{k=0}^{j} \frac{2k + 1}{2} \left(E\left(P_k(R)\right) \right)^2 - \frac{1}{2}. \qquad (10.30)$$

The approximation in equation (10.30) can be estimated easily from the sample:

$$\widehat{L}_j(a) = \sum_{k=0}^{j}(2k+1)\left(\frac{1}{n}\sum_{i=1}^{n}P_k(2\Phi(a^{\mathrm{T}}x_i)-1)\right)^2 - \frac{1}{2}. \tag{10.31}$$

This expression is easily evaluated. The first six Legendre polynomials are shown in equation (6.13) on page 136. We usually use the recurrence relationship, equation (6.14), in computing the truncated Legendre index, especially if we are using more than three or four terms.

The problem now is to determine

$$\max_{a} \widehat{L}_j(a).$$

Scaling of a is not relevant, so we may restrict a so that the sum of its elements is some given value, such as 1. In general, this is not an easy optimization problem. There are local minima. Use of an optimization method such as Newton's method may require multiple starting points. An optimization method such as simulated annealing may work better.

After both $p(z)$ and $\phi(z)$ are expanded in the Hermite polynomials, the natural Hermite index of Cook, Buja, and Cabrera, equation (10.28), reduces to

$$\sum_{k=0}^{\infty}(d_k - b_k)^2,$$

where the d_k are the coefficients of the expansion of $p(z)$ and the b_k are the coefficients of the expansion of $\phi(z)$. The b_k can be evaluated analytically. From Cook, Buja, and Cabrera, they are, for $k = 0, 1, \ldots,$

$$b_{2k} = \frac{(-1)^k((2k)!)^{1/2}}{2^{2k+1}k!\sqrt{\pi}}$$
$$b_{2k+1} = 0.$$

The d_k can be represented as expected values, and are estimated from the data in a similar manner as done for the Legendre index above. The estimates are given by

$$\hat{d}_k = \sum_{i=1}^{n}H_k^e(x_i)\phi(x_i). \tag{10.32}$$

The index is the truncated series

$$\sum_{k=0}^{j}(\hat{d}_k - b_k)^2.$$

The first six Hermite polynomials are shown in equation (6.15) on page 136. We usually use the recurrence relationship, equation (6.16), in computing the truncated Hermite index, especially if we are using more than three or four terms.

Although the more terms retained in the orthogonal series expansions, the better is the approximation, it is not necessarily the case that the better-approximated index is more useful. Friedman (1987), Hall (1989), Sun (1992), and Cook, Buja, and Cabrera (1993) have addressed this anomaly. Hall develops an asymptotic theory that suggests that the optimal choice of j depends on the sample size and type of index. (He considers both the norm in expression (10.26) and that in equation (10.27).) Sun suggests the choice of j between 3 and 6 inclusive, with smaller values being chosen for smaller numbers of observations and smaller values being chosen for larger values of the dimension m. Cook, Buja, and Cabrera found that the discrimination ability of the index for different values of j depends on the nature of the nonnormality in the data.

Friedman (1987) addresses the statistical significance of $L(a)$ (that is, the question of whether the projection using random data is significantly different from a projection of normal data). He gives a method for computing a p-value for the projection. Sun (1991) further discusses the evaluation of p-values.

Exploratory Projection Pursuit

The most important use of projection pursuit is for initial exploratory analysis of multivariate datasets.

Cook et al. (1995) describe the use of projection pursuit in a grand tour. Cabrera and Cook (1992) discuss the relationship of projection pursuit to the fractal dimension of a dataset.

Different indexes may be useful in identifying different kinds of structure. The Legendre index is very sensitive to outliers in the data. If identification of the outliers is of specific interest, this may make the index useful. On the other hand, if the analysis should be robust to outliers, the Legendre index would not be a good one. The Laguerre-Fourier index, which is based on an expansion in Laguerre polynomials, is particularly useful in identifying clusters in the data.

Example

As an example of projection pursuit, consider the simple dataset shown in Figure 10.21. The obvious nonnormal structure in that dataset is the existence of two groups. Performing principal components analysis on the data resulted in a first principal component that completely obscured this structure (see Figure 10.22). As it turned out, the second principal component identified the structure very well.

In projection pursuit, the first step is generally to sphere the data. The result of the sphering is to make the variances in all directions almost equal. A "principal" component is no longer very relevant. As we have emphasized, sphering or any other transformation of the data is likely to have an effect on the results. Whether to sphere the data in projection pursuit is subject to some question; see the discussion following Jones and Sibson (1987).

The sphered data corresponding to those in Figure 10.21 are shown in Figure 10.23. (See Exercise 10.7 for the data.)

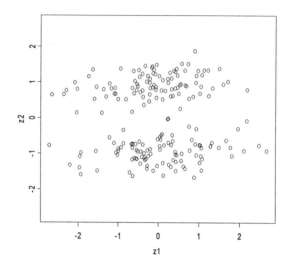

Figure 10.23: The Sphered Bivariate Dataset with Two Clusters

After sphering the data, the plot does not show the correlations or the elliptical scatter of Figure 10.21. The principal components would be along the axes. The sphered data do, however, continue to exhibit a bimodality, which is a departure from normality.

Now, consider the Legendre index for the principal components—that is, for the projections $a_1 = (1, 0)$ and $a_2 = (0, 1)$. Using equation (10.31) with $j = 5$, we obtain $\widehat{L}_5(a_1) = 1.03$ and $\widehat{L}_5(a_2) = 1.66$. Clearly, the projection onto z_2 exhibits the greater nonnormality.

In most applications of projection pursuit, of course, we have datasets of higher dimension.

Computational Issues

Posse (1990) and Sun (1992) discuss some of the computational issues in evaluating projection indexes, especially Friedman's Legendre index. Projection pursuit involves not only the computation of an index but the optimization of the index as a function of the linear combination vector. This approach is therefore computationally intensive.

The optimization problem is characterized by many local maxima. Rather than being interested in a global maximum, in data analysis with projection pursuit, we are generally interested in inspecting several projections, each of which exhibits an interesting structure—that is, some locally maximal departure from normality as measured by a projection index. This also adds to the computational intensity. Sun (1992) recommends use of NPSOL for solution of the problem to find the optimal projection.

10.6 Other Methods for Identifying Structure

Structure in data is defined in terms of transformations of the data. In PCA, for example, the linear structure that is identified consists of a set of one-dimensional linear projections that is ordered by the norm of the projection of the centered dataset. In projection pursuit, the linear structure is also a set of projections, but they are ordered by their deviation from normality.

Nonlinear structure is generally much more difficult to detect. One approach is to generalize the methods of PCA. Girard (2000) describes a nonlinear PCA based on manifolds instead of linear projections. Hastie and Stuetzle (1989) discuss the generalization of principal (linear) components to principal curves.

Independent Components Analysis

In PCA, the objective is to determine components (that is, combinations of the original variables) that have zero correlations. If the data are normally distributed, zero correlations imply independence. If the data are not normally distributed, independence does not follow. Independent components analysis (ICA) is similar to PCA except that the objective is to determine combinations of the original variables that are independent. In ICA, moments of higher order than two are used to determine base vectors that are statistically as independent as possible. PCA is often used as a preprocessing step in ICA.

The probability model underlying independent components analysis assumes the existence of k *independent* data-generating processes that yield an observable n-vector through an unknown mixing process. Because many applications of ICA involve a time series in the observed x, we often express the model as

$$x(t) = As(t),$$

where A is a mixing matrix. The problem of uncovering $s(t)$ is sometimes called *blind source separation*. Let x_i for $i = 1, \ldots, m$ be measured signals and s_j for $j = 1, \ldots, k$ be independent components (ICs) with the zero mean. The basic problem in ICA is to estimate the mixing matrix A and determine the components s in

$$x = As.$$

Independent components analysis is similar to principal components analysis and factor analysis, but much of the research on ICA has been conducted without reference to PCA and factor analysis. Both PCA and ICA have nonlinear extensions. In linear PCA and ICA, the objective is to find a linear transformation W of a random vector Y so that the elements of WY have small correlations. In linear PCA, the objective then is to find W so that $V(WY)$ is diagonal, and, as we have seen, this is simple to do. If the random vector Y is normal, then 0 correlations imply independence. The objective in linear ICA is slightly different; instead of just the elements of WY, attention may be focused on chosen transformations of this vector, and instead of small correlations, independence is the goal. Of course, because most multivariate distributions other than the normal are rather intractable, in practice, small correlations are usually the objective in ICA. The transformations of WY are often higher-order sample moments. The projections that yield diagonal variance-covariance matrices are not necessarily orthogonal.

In the literature on ICA, which is generally in the field of signal processing, either a "noise-free ICA model", similar to the simple PCA model, or a "noisy ICA model", similar to the factor analysis model, is used. Most of the research has been on the noise-free ICA model. Comon (1994) describes some of the similarities and differences between ICA and PCA. Hyvärinen, Karhunen, and Oja (2001) provide a comprehensive discussion of ICA.

10.7 Higher Dimensions

The most common statistical datasets can be thought of as rows, representing observations, and columns, representing variables. In traditional multiple regression and correlation and other methods of multivariate analysis, there are generally few conceptual hurdles in thinking of the observations as ranging over a multidimensional space. In multiple regression with m regressors, for example, it is easy to visualize the hyperplane in $m + 1$ dimensions that represents the fit $\widehat{y} = X\widehat{\beta}$. It is even easy to visualize the projection of the n-dimensional vector that represents a least-squares fit.

Many properties of one- and two-dimensional objects (lines and planes) carry over into higher-dimensional space just as we would expect.

Although most of our intuition is derived from our existence in a three-dimensional world, we generally have no problem dealing with one- or two-dimensional objects. On the other hand, it can be difficult to view a 3-D world from a two-dimensional perspective. The delightful fantasy, *Flatland*, written by Edwin Abbott in 1884, describes the travails of a two-dimensional person (one "A. Square") thrown into a three-dimensional world. (See also Stewart, 2001, *Flatterland, Like Flatland Only More So.*) The small book by Kendall (1961), *A Course in the Geometry of n Dimensions*, gives numerous examples in which common statistical concepts are elucidated by geometrical constructs.

There are many situations, however, in which our intuition derived from the familiar representations in one-, two-, and three-dimensional space leads us completely astray. This is particularly true of objects whose dimensionality is greater than three, such as volumes in higher-dimensional space. The problem is not just with our intuition, however; it is indeed the case that some properties do not generalize to higher dimensions. Exercise 10.11 in this chapter illustrates such a situation.

The *shape* of a dataset is the total information content that is invariant under translations, rotations, and scale transformations. Quantifying the shape of data is an interesting problem.

Data Sparsity in Higher Dimensions

We measure space both linearly and volumetrically. The basic cause of the breakdown of intuition in higher dimensions is that the relationship of linear measures to volumetric measures is exponential in dimensionality. The cubing we are familiar with in three-dimensional space cannot be used to describe the relative sizes of volumes (that is, the distribution of space). Volumes relative to the linear dimensions grow very rapidly. There are two consequences of this. One is that the volumes of objects with interior holes, such as thin boxes or thin shells, are much larger than our intuition predicts. Another is that the density of a fixed number of points becomes extremely small.

The density of a probability distribution decreases as the distribution is extended to higher dimensions by an outer product of the range. This happens fastest going from one dimension to two dimensions but continues at a decreasing rate for higher dimensions. The effect of this is that the probability content of regions at a fixed distance to the center of the distribution increases; that is, outliers or isolated data points become more common. This is easy to see in comparing a univariate normal distribution with a bivariate normal distribution. If $X = (X_1, X_2)$ has a bivariate normal distribution with mean 0 and variance-covariance matrix $\text{diag}(1, 1)$,

$$\Pr(|X_1| > 2) = 0.0455,$$

whereas

$$\Pr(\|X\| > 2) = 0.135.$$

The probability that the bivariate random variable is greater than two standard deviations from the center is much greater than the probability that the univariate random variable is greater than two standard deviations from the center. We can see the relative probabilities in Figure 10.24. The area under the univariate density that is outside the central interval shown is relatively small. It is about 5% of the total area. The volume under the bivariate density on the right-hand side in Figure 10.24 beyond the circle is relatively greater than the volume within the circle. It is about 13% of the total volume. The percentage increases with the dimensionality (see Exercises 10.9 and 10.10).

The consequence of these density patterns is that an observation in higher dimensions is more likely to appear to be an outlier than one in lower dimensions.

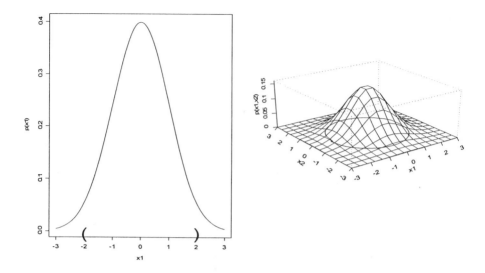

Figure 10.24: Univariate and Bivariate Extreme Regions

Volumes of Hyperspheres and Hypercubes

It is interesting to compare the volumes of regular geometrical objects and observe how the relationships of volumes to linear measures change as the number of dimensions changes. Consider, for example, that the volume of a sphere of radius a in d dimensions is

$$\frac{a^d \pi^{d/2}}{\Gamma(1+d/2)}.$$

The volume of a superscribed cube is $(2a)^d$. Now, compare the volumes. Consider the ratio

$$\frac{\pi^{d/2}}{d2^{d-1}\Gamma(d/2)}.$$

For $d = 3$ (Figure 10.25), this is 0.524; for $d = 7$, however, it is 0.037. As the number of dimensions increases, more and more of the volume of the cube is in the corners.

For two objects of different sizes but the same shape, with the smaller one centered inside the larger one, we have a similar phenomenon of the content of the interior object relative to the larger object. The volume of a thin shell as the ratio of the volume of the outer figure (sphere, cube, whatever) is

$$\frac{V_d(r) - V_d(r-\epsilon)}{V_d(r)} = 1 - \left(1 - \frac{\epsilon}{r}\right)^d.$$

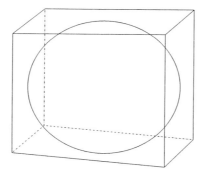

Figure 10.25: A Superscribed Cube

As the number of dimensions increases, more and more of the volume of the larger object is in the outer thin shell. This is the same phenomenon that we observed above for probability distributions. In a multivariate distribution whose density is the product of identical univariate densities (which is the density of a simple random sample), the relative probability content within extreme regions becomes greater as the dimension increases.

The Curse of Dimensionality

The computational and conceptual problems associated with higher dimensions have often been referred to as "the curse of dimensionality". How many dimensions cause problems depends on the nature of the application. Golub and Ortega (1993) use the phrase in describing the solution to the diffusion equation in three dimensions, plus time as the fourth dimensions, of course.

In higher dimensions, not only do data appear as outliers, but they also tend to lie on lower dimensional manifolds. This is the problem sometimes called "multicollinearity". The reason that data in higher dimensions are multicollinear, or more generally, concurve, is that the number of lower dimensional manifolds increases very rapidly in the dimensionality: the rate is 2^d.

Whenever it is possible to collect data in a well-designed experiment or observational study, some of the problems of high dimensions can be ameliorated. In computer experiments, for example, Latin hypercube designs can be useful for exploring very high dimensional spaces.

Data in higher dimensions carry more information in the same number of observations than data in lower dimensions. Some people have referred to the increase in information as the "blessing of dimensionality". The support vector machine approach in fact attempts to detect structure in data by mapping the data to higher dimensions.

Tiling Space

As we have mentioned in previous chapters, tessellations of the data space are useful in density estimation and in clustering and classification. Generally, regular tessellations, or tilings (objects with the same shapes), are used. Regular tessellations are easier both to form and to analyze.

Regular tessellations in higher dimensional space have counterintuitive properties. As an example, consider tiling by hypercubes, as illustrated in Figure 10.26 for squares in two dimensions.

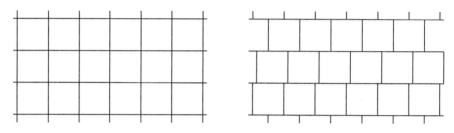

Figure 10.26: Hypercube (Square) Tilings of 2-Space

The tiling on the left-hand side in Figure 10.26 is a lattice tiling. In both tilings, we see that each tile has an entire side in common with at least one adjacent tile. This is a useful fact when we use the tiles as bins in data analysis, and it is always the case for a lattice tiling. It is also always the case in two dimensions. (To see this, make drawings similar to those in Figure 10.26.) In fact, in lower dimensions (up to six dimensions for sure), tilings by hypercubes of equal size always have the property that some adjacent tiles have an entire face (side) in common. It is an open question as to what number of dimensions ensures this property, but the property definitely does not hold in ten dimensions, as shown by Peter Shor and Jeff Lagarias. (See *What's Happening in the Mathematical Sciences, Volume 1*, American Mathematical Society, 1993, pages 21–25.)

Exercises

10.1. Consider the clusterings of the toy dataset depicted in Figure 10.7 on page 243.

    (a) How many clusters seem to be suggested by each?

    (b) Compute Rand's statistic (10.8) on page 254 and the modified Rand statistic (10.9) to compare the clustering on the left-hand side with that in the middle. Assume four clusters in each.

(c) Compute Rand's statistic and the modified Rand statistic to compare the clustering in the middle with that on the right-hand side. Assume four clusters in the middle, and three clusters on the right-hand side.

(d) Compute Rand's statistic and the modified Rand statistic to compare the clustering in the middle with that on the right-hand side. Assume two clusters in the middle, and three clusters on the right-hand side.

10.2. (a) Develop a combinatorial optimization algorithm, perhaps using simulated annealing or a genetic algorithm, to perform K-means clustering in such a way that less than k groups may be formed. The objective function would need to be penalized for the number of groups. Try a modification of expression (10.3),

$$\sum_{g=1}^{k} \sum_{j=1}^{m} \sum_{i=1}^{n_g} \left(x_{ij(g)} - \bar{x}_{j(g)} \right)^2 + \alpha k,$$

where α is a tuning parameter. Its magnitude depends on the sizes of the sums of squares, which of course are unknown a priori. Write a program to implement your algorithm. In the program, α is an input parameter. Use your program to form five or fewer clusters of the data:

$$\begin{bmatrix} x_1 \\ x_2 \\ x_3 \\ x_4 \\ x_5 \\ x_6 \\ x_7 \\ x_8 \\ x_9 \\ x_{10} \\ x_{11} \\ x_{12} \\ x_{13} \\ x_{14} \\ x_{15} \\ x_{16} \end{bmatrix} = \begin{bmatrix} 1 & 1 \\ 1 & 2 \\ 1 & 3 \\ 1 & 4 \\ 2 & 1 \\ 2 & 2 \\ 2 & 3 \\ 2 & 4 \\ 3 & 1 \\ 3 & 2 \\ 3 & 3 \\ 3 & 4 \\ 4 & 1 \\ 4 & 2 \\ 4 & 3 \\ 4 & 4 \end{bmatrix}$$

How many clusters do you get?

(b) Using the given data, do K-means clustering for $k = 1, 2, 3, 4, 5$. For each number of clusters, compute the Calinski-Harabasz index (10.4) on page 240. How many clusters are suggested?

10.3. What happens in cluster analysis if the data are sphered prior to the analysis? Sphere the data used in Figure 10.11 (page 251), and then do the hierarchical clustering. To do this, replace the statement

```
y <- apply(x,2,standard)
```

with

```
y <- x %*% solve(chol(var(x)))
```

The strange result in this case of clustering sphered data does not always occur, but the point is that sphering can have unexpected effects.

10.4. Consider the problem of identification of the "concentric circles" structure in Figure 10.3 on page 236. As we mentioned, representation of the data in polar coordinates provides one way of finding this structure. A dissimilarity measure consisting of an angular component d_{ij}^d and a radial component d_{ij}^r may be defined, as discussed on page 118 and in Exercise 5.7. Develop a procedure for clustering the concentric circles. Test your procedure using data similar to that in Figure 10.3, which can be generated in S-Plus by

```
x1<-rnorm(10)
x2<-rnorm(10)
x<-cbind(x1,x2)
y1<-rnorm(40,0,5)
y2<-rnorm(40,0,5)
sel<-y1^2+y2^2>25
y<-cbind(y1[sel],y2[sel])
```

10.5. Consider the problem of Exercise 5.8 on page 126; that is, given two n-vectors, x_1 and x_2, form a third vector x_3 as $x_3 = a_1 x_1 + a_2 x_2 + \epsilon$, where ϵ is a vector of independent $N(0, 1)$ realizations. Although the matrix $X = [x_1 \ x_2 \ x_3]$ is in $\mathbb{R}^{n \times 3}$, the linear structure, even obscured by the noise, implies a two-dimensional space for the data matrix (that is, the space $\mathbb{R}^{n \times 2}$). Generate x_1 and x_2 as realizations of a $U(0, 1)$ process, and x_3 as $5x_1 + x_2 + \epsilon$, where ϵ is a realization of a $N(0, 1)$ process. Do a principal components analysis (perhaps using prcomp or princomp in S-Plus) of the data. Make a scree plot of the eigenvalues (perhaps using screeplot in S-Plus, which produces a bar plot, rather than a line plot as shown in Figure 10.20). How many principal components would you choose?

10.6. (a) Write out the gradient and Hessian for the optimization problem (10.22) on page 278. Remember Ψ is a diagonal matrix.

(b) Write out the gradient and Hessian for the optimization problem (10.25) on page 279.

10.7. The data shown in Figure 10.21 and used in the PCA and the projection pursuit examples were generated by the S-Plus commands

```
n <- 200
x <- rnorm(n)
y <- rnorm(n)
xx <- 10*x + y
yy <- 2*y +x
n2 <- n/2
yy[1:n2] <- yy[1:n2] + 5
yy[(n2+1):n] <- yy[(n2+1):n] - 5
```

(a) Sphere this dataset and plot it. Your plot should look like that in Figure 10.23.

(b) Determine the optimal projection a using the estimated truncated Legendre index with $j = 4$.

10.8. Indexes for projection pursuit.

    (a) Derive equation (10.32) on page 286 for use in the natural Hermite index, equation (10.28). (Compare equation (10.31).)

    (b) Determine the optimal projection of the data in Exercise 10.7 using the estimated truncated natural Hermite index with $j = 4$.

10.9. Let X be a standard 10-variate normal random variable (the mean is 0 and the variance-covariance is diag$(1, 1, 1, 1, 1, 1, 1, 1, 1, 1)$. What is the probability that $\|X\| > 6$? In other words, what is the probability of exceeding six sigma? *Hint:* Use polar coordinates. (Even then, the algebra is messy.)

10.10. Consider the use of a d-variate multivariate normal density as a majorizing density for another d-variate multivariate normal in an acceptance/rejection application. (See Figure 2.3 on page 45 and the discussion concerning it.) To be specific, let $d = 1,000$, let the majorizing density have a diagonal variance-covariance matrix with constant diagonal terms of 1.1, and let the target density also have a diagonal variance-covariance matrix but with constant diagonal terms of 1. (As mentioned in the discussion concerning Figure 2.3, this is just an illustrative example. This kind of majorizing density would not make sense for the given target because if we could generate from the majorizing density we could generate directly from the target.)

    (a) Determine the value of c in Algorithm 2.1 on page 42.

    (b) Determine the probability of acceptance.

10.11. In d dimensions, construct 2^d hyperspheres centered at the points $(\pm 1, \ldots, \pm 1)$, and construct the hypercube with edges of length 2 that contains the unit hyperspheres. At the point $(0, \ldots, 0)$, construct the hypersphere that is tangent to the other 2^d spheres. In two dimensions, the spheres appear as

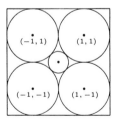

Is the interior hypersphere always inside the hypercube? (The answer is "No!") At what number of dimensions does the interior hypersphere poke outside the hypercube? (See *What's Happening in the Mathematical Sciences, Volume 1*, American Mathematical Society, 1993.)

10.12. Consider a cartesian coordinate system for $\mathbb{R}^d$, with $d \geq 2$. Let x be a point in $\mathbb{R}^d_+$ such that $\|x\|_2 = 1$ and x is equidistant from all axes of the coordinate system.

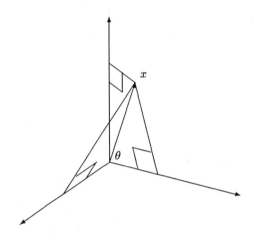

What is the angle between the line through x and any of the positive axes?
Hint: for $d = 2$, the angles are $\pm\pi/4$.
What are the angles as $d \to \infty$?

Chapter 11

Statistical Models of Dependencies

In previous chapters, we considered models for probability densities and the problem of fitting those models with observed data. We discussed various exploratory multivariate techniques and models associated with the methods. In this chapter, we consider other types of models, generally ones expressing dependence relationships among variables. These models relate the behavior of one variable, Y, possibly a vector, as a function of other variables. Models of this type that express dependencies are called regression models if Y is a numeric variable or classification models if Y is a categorical variable. If Y is a numeric variable that takes on only a countable number of values, the model can be considered either a regression model (sometimes a "generalized model") or a classification model.

Another important type of dependency arises in sequentially sampled variables. The distribution of a random variable at time t_k depends on the realization of that random variable at time t_{k-1}. There may also be covariates whose realizations affect the distribution of the variable of interest. A random process that possibly changes in time is called a *stochastic process*. Because change is of interest in such processes, the model is often expressed as a differential equation.

The development and use of a model is an iterative process that includes data collection and analysis. It requires looking at the data from various perspectives. The model embodies both knowledge and assumptions. The knowledge may result from first principles or from previous observations. A model can be strong (very specific) or weak (leaving open many possibilities).

If the range of possibilities in a model can be limited to a set of real numbers, the possibilities are represented by a *parameter*. Parametric statistical procedures involve inference about the parameters of a model. *Nonparametric methods* in statistics also rely on models that usually contain parameters; the phrase "nonparametric" often refers to a method that does not specify a family of probability distributions except in a very general way.

While some methods are referred to as "model-free", and the phrase "model-based approach" is sometimes used, implying that other, "non-model-based" approaches exist, in reality some model underlies all statistical analyses. The model is not immutable, however, and much of the effort of an analysis may go into developing and refining a model. In *exploratory data analysis*, or *EDA*, the model is quite weak. The patterns and other characteristics identified in an exploratory data analysis help to form a stronger model. In general, whenever the model is weak, a primary objective is usually to build a stronger model.

In data analysis (as in most human activities), the most fundamental question to be asked is "why is this being done?" Putting the activity in the context of its purpose often determines the approaches to be employed in the activity. In data analysis, the nature of the model relates directly to the purpose of the analysis. Often, the objective is prediction, and there is a large premium on making accurate predictions or classifications in a very short time. In such cases, modeling the data-generating process may not be relevant. An "algorithmic model" that prioritizes prediction accuracy given the data at hand may be more appropriate. See Breiman (2001) for further discussion of these two different approaches to modeling.

Model Inference Using Data

Data analysis usually proceeds through some fairly standard steps. Before much is known about the process being investigated, the statistician may just explore the data to arrive at a general understanding of its structure. This may involve many graphical displays in various coordinate systems and under various projections. When more than one variable is present, relationships among the variables may be explored and models describing these relationships developed.

One aspect of the modeling process is to fit a tentative model to observed data. In a parametric model, this means determination of values of parameters in the model so that the model corresponds in some way to the observations. The criteria for the model to correspond to the observations may be based on some distributional motivation or merely on some heuristic measure of the correspondence of pairs of points to an equation. These criteria include the following.

- Some model moments match the corresponding sample moments (method of moments).

- Some norm of the vector of deviations of observed values from mean model values is minimized (least squares, for example).

- The joint probability density function evaluated at the observed values is maximized (maximum likelihood).

- Observations that are similar have similar responses in the model (homogeneity of classes).

- If the data are partitioned into two sets and a model is fit based on one set, the model fits the data in the other set well (training set and test set, or cross validation). In this case, the emphasis is on classification or prediction accuracy (based on an appropriate definition and a suitable quantification).

These criteria are not mutually exclusive, and some combination of them may be used. The criteria can be viewed purely as intuitive guidelines, or the stochastic components of the model may be modeled by some family of statistical probability distributions, and the distributional properties of the estimators under various assumptions can determine the approach.

An important part of the modeling process is to perform statistical tests of the correspondence of the available data to the model that has been fit. Depending on the type of model, the goodness-of-fit testing may or may not be a relatively straightforward process. We should also understand that goodness-of-fit tests generally are rather ineffective for addressing the basic question of what is the correct model.

The distributions of estimators under various assumptions may be quite difficult to work out. Rather than basing inference on asymptotic approximations, we can use computational inference for confidence levels or statements of probability about model parameters. Computational inference using simulated datasets can also be useful in assessing the fidelity of the evolving models to the observed data.

11.1 Regression and Classification Models

In many applications, some subset of variables may be characterized as "dependent" on some other subset of variables; in fact, often there is just a single "dependent" variable, and our objective is to characterize its value in terms of the values of the other variables. (The word "dependent" is in quotes here because we do not wish necessarily to allow any connotation of causation or other stronger meanings of the word "dependence". In the following, we use "dependent" in this casual way but do not continue to emphasize that fact with quotation marks.) The dependent variable is often called the "response", and the other variables are often called "factors", "regressors", "independent variables", "carriers", "stimuli", or "covariates". (The word "independent" has some connotative difficulties because of its use in referring to a stochastic property, and some authors object to the use of "independent" here. Most choices of words have one kind of problem or another. A problem with "stimulus", for example, is the implication of causation. I am likely to use any one of these terms at various times. Fortunately, it does not matter; the meaning is always clear from the context.)

The asymmetric relationship between a random variable Y and a variable

x may be represented as a black box that accepts x as input and outputs Y:

$$Y \leftarrow \boxed{\text{unknown process}} \leftarrow x. \tag{11.1}$$

The relationship might also be described by a statement of the form

$$Y \leftarrow f(x)$$

or

$$Y \approx f(x). \tag{11.2}$$

If f has an inverse, the model (11.2) appears symmetric. Even in that case, however, there is an asymmetry that results from the role of random variables in the model; we model the response as a random variable. We may think of $f(x)$ as a *systematic* effect and write the model with an additive adjustment, or error, as

$$Y = f(x) + E \tag{11.3}$$

or with a multiplicative error as

$$Y = f(x)\Delta, \tag{11.4}$$

where E and Δ are assumed to be random variables. (The "E" is the Greek uppercase epsilon.) We refer to these as "errors", although this word does not indicate a mistake. Thus, the model is composed of a *systematic component* related to the values of x and a *random component* that accounts for the indeterminacy between Y and $f(x)$. In the case of the black-box model (11.1), both the systematic and random components are embedded in the box.

Models with multiplicative random effects are not as widely used. In the following, we will concentrate on models with additive random effects. In such models, E is also called the "residual".

Because the functional form f of the relationship between Y and x may contain a *parameter*, we may write the equation in the model as

$$Y = f(x; \theta) + E, \tag{11.5}$$

where θ is a parameter whose value determines a specific relationship within the family specified by f. In most cases, θ is a vector. In the usual linear regression model, for example, the parameter is a vector with two more elements than the number of elements in x,

$$Y = \beta_0 + x^{\mathrm{T}}\beta + E, \tag{11.6}$$

where $\theta = (\beta_0, \beta, \sigma^2)$.

A generalization of the linear model (11.6) is the *additive model*,

$$Y = \beta_0 + f_1(x_1, \beta_1) + \cdots + f_m(x_m, \beta_m) + E. \tag{11.7}$$

The specification of the distribution of the random component is a part of the model, and that part of the model can range from very general assumptions about the existence of certain moments or about the general shape of the density to very specific assumptions about the distribution. If the random component is additive, the mean, or more generally (because the moments may not exist) the appropriate location parameter, is assumed without loss of generality to be 0.

The model for the relationship between Y and x includes the equation (11.5) together with various other statements about Y and x such as the nature of the values that they may assume, statements about θ, and statements about the distribution of E. Thus, the *model* is

$$\begin{cases} Y = f(x; \theta) + E \\ \\ \text{additional statements about } Y, x, \theta, E. \end{cases} \qquad (11.8)$$

In the following, for convenience, we will often refer to just the equation as the "model".

Another way of viewing the systematic component of equation (11.5) is as a conditional expectation of a random variable,

$$E(Y|x; \theta) = f(x; \theta). \qquad (11.9)$$

This formulation is very similar to that of equations (11.3) and (11.4). The main differences are that in the formulation of equation (11.9) we do not distinguish between an additive error and a multiplicative one, and we consider the error to be a random variable with finite first moment. In equations (11.3) and (11.4), or equation (11.5), we do not necessarily make these assumptions about E or Δ.

If we assume a probability distribution for the random component, we may write the model in terms of a probability density for the response in terms of the systematic component of the model,

$$p(y|x, \theta). \qquad (11.10)$$

Cast in this way, the problem of statistical modeling is the same as fitting a probability distribution whose density depends on the values of a covariate.

Generalized Models

If the response can take on only a countable set of distinct values, a model of the form

$$Y = f(x; \theta) + E$$

may not be appropriate, especially if the covariate x is continuous.

Suppose, for example, that the response is binary (0 or 1) representing whether or not a person has had a heart attack, and x contains various biometric measures such as blood pressure, cholesterol level, and so on. The expected value $E(Y|x; \theta)$ is the probability that a person with x has had a heart attack. Even if a model such as

$$E(Y|x; \theta) = f(x; \theta),$$

with continuous regressor x, made sense, it would not be clear how to fit the model to data or to make inferences about the model. A simple transformation of the response variable, $\tau(Y)$, does not improve the data-analysis problem; if Y is binary, so is $\tau(Y)$.

A problem with the model in this form is that the value of $f(x; \theta)$ must range between 0 and 1 for all (reasonable) values of x and θ. A function f could of course be constructed to have this range, but another way is to model a transformation of $E(Y|x; \theta)$. This can often be done in a way that has a meaningful interpretation. For example, letting $\pi = E(Y|x; \theta)$, we introduce the transformation

$$
\begin{aligned}
g(\pi) &= \log\left(\frac{\pi}{1 - \pi}\right) \\
&= \text{logit}(\pi).
\end{aligned}
$$

The logit function is the odds ratio. We now can form a "generalized model" that is more similar to the forms of the models for continuous responses than a form that models Y directly. The function g is called the *link function*. The appropriate form of the link function depends on the nature of the probability distribution. The logit function is useful for a Bernoulli distribution. The generalized model formed using it is called a logistic regression model.

For certain classes of random variables that model the residual, Nelder and Wedderburn (1972) develop a relationship between the models used in these applications and a linear model (that is, a model in which $f(x; \theta)$ is linear in θ). The resulting model is called a *generalized linear model*.

Classification Models

In the generic model for the classification problem, the variables are the pairs (Y, x), where Y is a categorical variable representing the subclass of the population to which the observation belongs. The generalized models discussed above can be viewed as classification models. A generalized model yields the probability that an observation has a particular response, or that the observation is in a given category. The result can be viewed as a fuzzy classification. White and Reed (1989) explore other relationships between classification and logit models.

In the classification problem, we often consider x to be a realization of a random variable, and we represent the random variable pair as (G, X). (We often use G instead of Y to emphasize its meaning.) A classification rule, ϕ, is a mapping from $\mathcal{X}$, the space of X, to $\mathcal{G}$, the space of G. If we were to assume a particular distribution of the data, it may be possible to develop an optimal approach to the classification problem based on the distribution. Given a set of distributional assumptions, a *Bayes rule* is a classification rule that has a minimal expected misclassification rate. The key function is the conditional probability $p(g|x)$ that $G = g$, given $X = x$.

In applications of classification models, we generally have a dataset with known values of x and G and are interested in predicting the values of G in another dataset with known values of x only.

Classification is similar to the clustering problem for the x's that we have discussed in Section 10.1 beginning on page 237, except that in classification models, the value of one of the variables indicates the cluster or group to which the observation belongs.

Generally, we do not assume a specific distribution but rather that the training sets represent randomly chosen examples of the qualities for which we are trying to build a classification rule. This is sometimes called the *probably approximately correct*, or *PAC*, model of learning.

The starting point for studying the classification problem is classification into one of two groups. Bayes rules for the binary case are relatively simple to develop in a variety of scenarios. The multigroup problem is not as simple. One approach is a sequential one of classifying all unclassified observations into the ith group or the group consisting of all other groups and then continuing this process considering the observations in the group consisting of all other groups to be unclassified. This approach, however, does not necessarily yield an optimal classification, even if it is optimal at each stage.

As more data are collected, the properties of the groups may become known from the past training datasets, and future data can be classified in a supervised fashion. How well a classification scheme works can be assessed by observing the similarity of the new observations in each cluster. This process can also be applied to a single dataset by defining a subset of the data to be a training dataset. This type of cross validation is often useful in developing rules for classification.

Classification rules are often based on measures of distance to the means of the groups scaled by S, the sample variance-covariance matrix. The Mahalanobis distance of an observation x to the mean of the ith group, $\bar{x}_{(i)}$, is

$$(x - \bar{x}_{(i)})^{\text{T}} S^{-1} (x - \bar{x}_{(i)}).$$

This is the basis for a linear discriminant function for classification.

An observation can be classified by computing its Euclidean distance from the group means projected onto a subspace defined by a subset of the canonical variates. The observation is assigned to the closest group. For two groups, this is easy; the discriminant for the observation x is just

$$\phi(x) = \text{sign}\big(x^{\text{T}} S^{-1} (\bar{x}_{(1)} - \bar{x}_{(2)})\big).$$

A positive value of $\phi(x)$ assigns x to the first group, and a negative value assigns it to the second group. Under certain assumptions (for example, normality), this is a Bayes rule. For more than two groups, it is a little more complicated. In general, a classification rule based on the Mahalanobis distance is

$$\phi(x) = \text{argmin}_i\left((x - \bar{x}_{(i)})^\mathrm{T} S^{-1}(x - \bar{x}_{(i)})\right).$$

We could represent the data in the classification problem as $x = (x^\mathrm{r},\ x^\mathrm{c})$ as in equation (10.6) on page 250. The x^c are categorical variables. If x^c is a vector, some elements may be unobserved. We may know that $x^\mathrm{c} \in \mathcal{C}$, where $\mathcal{C}$ is some given set of general characteristics or rules. The characteristics may be dependent on the context, as we discussed on page 113. The set of characteristics of interest may include "concepts" (that is, something more general than just a class index). Hunt, Marin, and Stone (1966) called this kind of classification problem "concept learning", and developed concept-learning systems. (Their purpose was to study ways that humans learn more so than to address a given classification problem.) Michalski (1980) and Michalski and Stepp (1983) described conceptual clustering, which is a set of methods of classification that identifies sets of characteristics, or "concepts".

Models of Sequential Dependencies

A stochastic process is indexed by a time parameter, which may be a continuous variable over an interval or may be assumed to take on fixed values $\ldots, t_{k-1}, t_k, t_{k+1}, \ldots$. A model for a stochastic process may be written as

$$Y_{t_k} = f_{t_k}(x_{t_k}, y_{t_{k-1}}; \theta_{t_k}) + E_{t_k}. \tag{11.11}$$

The response variable in a stochastic process is often referred to as the *state* of the process.

In many applications of interest we can assume that f_{t_k}, θ_{t_k}, and the distribution of E_{t_k} do not change in time; that is, the model is *stationary*.

Another way of formulating a model of a stochastic process is to focus on the change in the dependent variable and to write a differential equation that represents the rate of change:

$$\frac{\mathrm{d}Y}{\mathrm{d}t} = g(x(t), Y(t); \theta(t)) + E(t). \tag{11.12}$$

In many cases, this is a natural way of developing a stochastic model from first principles of the theory underlying the phenomenon being studied. In other cases, such as financial applications, for the variable of interest there may be no obvious dependency on other variables. In financial analysis, the change in prices from day to day or from trade to trade is of interest, so the appropriate model is a differential equation.

Data and Models

The model (11.8) is expressed in terms of the general variables Y and x. The relationship for a particular pair of observed values of these variables may be written as

$$y_i = f(x_i; \theta) + \epsilon_i.$$

For a sample of n y_i's and x_i's, we may write the model as

$$y = f(X; \theta) + \epsilon, \tag{11.13}$$

where y is an n-vector, X is an $n \times m$ matrix of n observations on the m-vectors x_i, and ϵ is an n-vector. The usual linear regression model would be written as

$$y = X\beta + \epsilon, \tag{11.14}$$

where X is understood to contain a column of 1's in addition to the columns of values of the covariates.

The problem in data analysis is to select the relevant factors x, the functional form f, the value of θ, and properties of the random component that best fit the data. Depending on the assumptions of the distribution of E, its variance may be of interest.

If the form of the density is known, the theory of statistical inference can be used to assess properties of estimators or test procedures. Although the theory that allows identification of optimal procedures is interesting, the problem of model building is much more complicated than this. For each of the various models considered, however, it is useful to have simple theoretical guidelines for fitting a model, even if the model is tentative.

Transformations

Sometimes, the response of interest may not have a distribution that is amenable to analysis, but some transformation of the response variable may have a more tractable distribution. In such cases, rather than modeling the response Y, it may be preferable to model a transformation of the response, $\tau(Y)$. One reason for doing this is to remove dependence of various properties of the distribution of Y on x and θ. For example, if the variance of Y depends on $E(Y)$, it may be desirable to consider a transformation $\tau(Y)$ whose variance does not change as the mean changes as a function of x and θ.

If statistics of the forms

$$\bar{y}|x; \theta$$

and

$$\sum (y_i - \bar{y}|x; \theta)^2$$

are to be used in data analysis, our objective might be to determine the transformation so that $\tau(Y)$ has a normal distribution because that is the only way that the statistics

$$\overline{\tau(y)}|x; \theta$$

and

$$\sum (\tau(y_i) - \overline{\tau(y)}|x; \theta)^2$$

would be independent. We describe such transformations beginning on page 326.

As we discuss on page 327, we may also consider transformations of the independent variable x. Transformations of the variable x in the clustering problem often result in quite different clusters, as we discuss on page 251. This effect of transformations can be exploited in the classification problem.

Exploration of various transformations and functional forms, using both numerical computations and graphical displays, is computationally intensive. Choice of a functional form involves selection of variables for inclusion in the model. Evaluation of subsets of potential variables is computationally intensive. We discuss some of the issues of variable selection and transformations of variables later.

Piecewise Models

As we have seen in Chapter 6, sometimes it is best to approximate a function differently over different domains. This can be done by use of splines, for example. Likewise, different statistical models of dependencies over different domains of the independent variables may be appropriate. Although a systematic component in a model that has a single global function is useful because of its simplicity, the data may not follow a single form of the systematic component very well.

One approach to developing a model that is piecewise smooth is to use polynomials over subintervals. We can impose smoothness constraints at the knots separating the subintervals. The difficult modeling problem is the choice of where to locate the knots. Obviously, the more knots, the better the model can fit any given set of data. On the other hand, the more knots, the more variation the model will exhibit. One approach is to add knots in a stepwise manner while monitoring the improvement in the fit of the model to the data (measured by some function of the residuals, as discussed in Section 11.3, for example).

11.2   Probability Distributions in Models

Statistical inference (that is, estimation, testing, or prediction) is predicated on probability distributions. This means that the model (11.8) or (11.13) must include some specification of the distribution of the random component or the residual term, E. In statistical modeling, we often assume that the independent variables are fixed—not necessarily that there is no probability distribution associated with them, but that the set of observations we have are considered as given—and the random mechanism generating them is not of particular interest. This is another aspect of the asymmetry of the model. This distinction between what is random and what is not is a basic distinction between regression analysis and correlation analysis, although we do not wish to imply that this is a hard and fast distinction.

The probability distribution for the residual term determines a family of probability distributions for the response variable. This specification may be very complete, such as that $E \sim \mathrm{N}(0, \sigma^2 I)$, or it may be much less specific. If there is no a priori specification of the distribution of the residual term, the main point of the statistical inference may be to provide that specification. If the distribution of the residual has a first moment, it is taken to be 0; hence, the model (for an individual Y) can be written as

$$E(Y) = f(x;\ \theta);$$

that is, the expected value of Y is the systematic effect in the model. If the first moment does not exist, the median is usually taken to be 0 so that the median of y is $f(x;\ \theta)$. More generally, we can think of the model as expressing a conditional probability density for Y:

$$p_Y(y) = p(y \mid f(x; \theta)). \tag{11.15}$$

Hierarchical Models

The model (11.8) can be a component of a *hierarchical model*:

$$\begin{aligned} y &= f(x; \theta) + \epsilon, \\ x &= g(w; \tau) + \delta, \end{aligned} \tag{11.16}$$

or

$$\begin{aligned} y &= f(x; \theta) + \epsilon, \\ \theta &\sim D(\tau), \end{aligned} \tag{11.17}$$

where $D(\tau)$ is some distribution that may depend on a parameter, τ. Either of these models could be part of a larger hierarchy, of course.

Hierarchical models of the form (11.16) arise in various applications, such as population dynamics, where the components are often called "compartments", or in situations where the independent variables are assumed not to be observable or not to be measured without error.

Hierarchical models of the form (11.17) are useful in Bayesian statistics. In that case, we may identify the components of the model as various joint, marginal, and conditional distributions. For example, we may consider the joint distribution of the random variables Y and Θ (using an uppercase letter to emphasize that it is a random variable),

$$(Y, \Theta) \sim D_{Y,\Theta}(x, \tau),$$

the conditional distribution of Y given Θ,

$$Y \sim D_{Y|\theta}(f(x; \theta)),$$

or the conditional distribution of Θ given Y,

$$\Theta \sim D_{\Theta|y}(x, y, \tau). \tag{11.18}$$

In the analysis of data, the second component of model (11.17), which is a marginal distribution, which we rewrite as

$$\Theta \sim D_{\Theta}(\tau),$$

is called the *prior distribution*, and the conditional distribution of Θ given Y (11.18) is called the *posterior distribution*. The idea is that the conditional distribution represents knowledge of the "unknown parameter" that includes information from the observations y and the prior distribution of the parameter.

Probability Distributions in Models of Sequential Dependencies

There are two different ways to develop probability models for the dependent variable in a stochastic process, equation (11.11). In one approach, we consider a set of probability spaces indexed by t; that is, for each t, there is a different probability space that depends not only on t but also on the value of $Y(t - \epsilon)$.

In another approach, we define the outcome space to correspond to the sequence or path of values that can be assumed by Y_t. In a continuous stochastic process, the outcome space in the underlying probability space may be chosen to be the set of continuous mappings ("trajectories") of $[0, t]$ into $\mathbb{R}$. This approach is sometimes called the "canonical" setup.

The parameter space for these models includes time. The parameter that indexes time may be continuous, but it is often considered to be discrete.

We can develop a differential equation model of a stochastic process, as in equation (11.12), by starting with models of small changes. One of the simplest and most commonly used models developed in this way is called *Brownian motion*. In this model, the random variable, B_t, with a continuous index, t, has the following properties:

- the change ΔB_t during the small time interval Δt is

$$\Delta B_t = Z\sqrt{\Delta t},$$

  where Z is a random variable with distribution $N(0, 1)$;

- ΔB_{t_1} and ΔB_{t_2} are independent for $t_1 \neq t_2$.

From the definition, we see that $E(\Delta B_t) = 0$ and $V(\Delta B_t) = \Delta t$. Now, if $B_0 = 0$, and for the positive integer n we let $t = n\Delta t$, we have

$$B_t = \sum_{i=1}^{n} Z_i \sqrt{\Delta t}, \tag{11.19}$$

where the Z_i are i.i.d. $N(0, 1)$, so B_t has a $N(0, t)$ distribution.

In the limit as $\Delta t \to 0$, $\sqrt{\Delta t}$ becomes much larger than Δt, and the change in B_t (that is, ΔB_t) becomes relatively large compared to the change in t (that is, Δt). Therefore, as t moves through any finite interval:

- the expected length of the path followed by B_t is infinite; and

- the expected number of times B_t takes on any given value is infinite.

The limiting process is called a *Wiener process* and is denoted as dB_t.

There are some useful generalizations of this process. One, called a *generalized Wiener process*, is a linear combination of a Wiener process and a constant rate in t. This can be represented by

$$dY_t = u \, dt + v \, dB_t, \tag{11.20}$$

where u and v are constants and dB_t is a Wiener process. (An equation in differentials of the form (11.20) is called a *Langevin equation*.) Another generalization is an *Ornstein-Uhlenbeck process*, which is similar to a generalized Wiener process except that the change in time depends on the state. The Langevin equation is

$$dY_t = uY_t \, dt + v \, dB_t. \tag{11.21}$$

A further generalization is an *Itô process*, which is similar to a generalized Wiener process except that both coefficients are functions of Y_t (and, hence, at least implicitly, of t). The Langevin-type equation for an Itô process is

$$dY_t(\omega) = u(Y_t(\omega), t) \, dt + v(Y_t(\omega), t) \, dB_t(\omega), \tag{11.22}$$

where B_t is a Brownian motion. This model is widely used for the price of a financial asset, such as a stock. The simple form is just

$$dY = \mu Y \, dt + \sigma Y \, dB_t, \tag{11.23}$$

where the drift parameter μ is the rate of return of the stock per unit of time, and σ is the "volatility" of the stock price. (In general terms, ignoring the ambiguities of continuous time, volatility is the standard deviation of the relative change in the price.) This version of an Itô process is called *geometric Brownian motion*. Variations on geometric Brownian motion that attempt to capture additional aspects of stock price behavior include discrete changes in μ or σ, resulting in a "jump process", and imposition of stochastic constraints on the magnitude of Y, yielding a "mean-reverting process".

The extensive theory for stochastic differential equations is covered in a number of texts, such as Øksendal (1998).

11.3 Fitting Models to Data

Observational data help us to build a model. The model helps us to understand nature. Standard ways of developing our knowledge of nature involve estimation and tests of hypotheses—that is, statistical inference.

Inference about the model $y = f(X; \theta) + \epsilon$ involves estimation of the parameters θ, tests of hypotheses about θ, and inference about the probability distribution of ϵ. It may also involve further consideration of the model, the form of f, or other issues relating to the population, such as whether the population or the sample is homogeneous, whether certain observations are outliers, and so on.

The statistical characteristics of the estimator, such as its bias and variance, depend on how the model is fit (that is, on how the estimates are computed) and on the distribution of the random component. For a specific family of distributions of the random component and a specific form of f, it may be possible to determine estimators that are optimal with respect to some statistical characteristic such as mean squared error.

A unified approach to model inference involves a method of estimation that allows for statements of confidence and that provides the basis for the subsequent inference regarding the distribution of ϵ and the suitability of the model. In this section, we will be concerned primarily with methods of fitting the model rather than on the problem of statistical inference.

The Mechanics of Fitting

Fitting a model using data can be viewed simply as a mechanical problem of determining values of the parameters so that functional relationships expressed by the model are satisfied approximately by the given set of data. Fitting a model to data is often a step in statistical estimation, but estimation generally involves a deeper belief about the nature of the data. The data are realizations of a random variable whose distribution is related to or specified by the model. Statistical estimation also includes some assessment of the distribution of the estimator.

One of the first considerations is what approach to take in modeling. Is the objective to develop a model in the form of equations and statements about distributions of elements of the model, as in equation (11.8), or is it acceptable to have a black box of the form (11.1) together with an algorithm that accepts x and produces a good prediction of Y? Often, a set of rules is sufficient. Because there is no particular restriction on the complexity of the rules as there would be if we attempt to express the rules in a single equation, the black box together with a prediction algorithm performs best. A neural net, which can be quite complicated yet provides no insight into identifiable functions and parameters, often yields excellent predictions of the response for a given input x. See Ripley (1993, 1994, 1996) for discussion of neural nets in modeling applications.

An additional consideration is whether the fit is to be global or local (that is, whether a single model describes the data over the full domain and all observations are used at once to fit the model, or whether different models apply in different domains and only "local" observations are used to fit the model within each domain).

On page 300, we listed five basic approaches for fitting models using data: method of moments, minimizing residuals, maximizing the likelihood, homogeneity of modeled classes, and predictive accuracy in partitioned data. Any of these approaches can be applied in fitting models that have a continuous-valued response. (We can assess class homogeneity if one or more of the covariates is a classification variable, or we may be able to discretize the response into meaningful groups.) If the model has a discrete-valued response, or if the purpose is classification, there are two possibilities. One is the use of a generalized model, which effectively makes the response continuous-valued and can yield a probability-based or fuzzy classification. Otherwise, the fitting problem can be addressed directly, and the class purity is the primary criterion. In the classification problem, the predictive accuracy in partitioned data is almost alway considered in the model fitting. The dataset can be partitioned either randomly or systematically, as we discuss in Chapter 3. Whatever method is used to fit a model, it may be followed by some further steps to bring the model and the data into closer agreement. Individual observations that do not agree well with the fitted model may be treated specially in some way. Some outlying observations may be modified or even removed from the dataset, and then the model is refit using the cleaned data.

Estimation by Minimizing Residuals

Of the basic approaches for fitting models using data, listed on page 300, perhaps the most intuitive is fitting based on minimizing the residuals. This is the method most often used by data analysts and scientists to fit a curve to data without any assumptions about probability distributions.

For a given function f, the fit is accomplished by solving an optimization problem involving some function of the vector of residuals,

$$r = y - f(X; \theta),$$

where y is the vector of observed responses and X is the matrix of corresponding observations of the covariates. The decision variable in the optimization problem is θ.

Notice that the r_i are vertical distances as shown in Figure 11.1 for a simple linear model. Another way of measuring residuals in a model is indicated by the orthogonal residuals shown in Figure 11.2.

For a given set of data $\{(y_i, x_i)\}$, the residuals r_i are functions of f and θ. Clearly, the space of functions from which to select f must be restricted in some way; otherwise, the problem is not well-defined. We generally restrict the function space to contain only relatively tractable functions, such as low-degree polynomials, often just linear functions, exponential functions, or functions that can be formed from common basis functions, as we discuss in Chapter 6. Once a general form of f is chosen, the residuals are functions of θ, $r_i(\theta)$.

As we discussed on pages 16 to 22, there are many reasonable choices as to

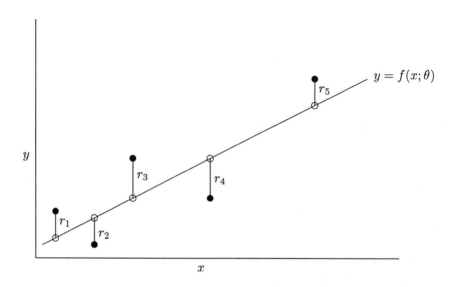

Figure 11.1: Residuals

how to minimize the $r_i(\theta)$. In general, we can minimize the sum

$$\sum \rho(r_i(\theta)),$$ (11.24)

where $\rho(t)$ is some nonnegative, nondecreasing function in $|t|$, at least near $t = 0$. A value of θ that minimizes the sum (11.24) is called an *M-estimator* because log-likelihood equations for common distributions often have a form similar to the negative of this sum. Most common choices of $\rho(\cdot)$ are such that the sum is a norm of the residual vector r:

$$\sum \rho(r_i(\theta)) = \|r\|.$$ (11.25)

(A vector norm is defined on page 114.) The L_p norm (see page 115) is commonly used. For $p = 2$ this is least squares, for $p = 1$ this is least absolute values, and for $p \to \infty$ this is least maximum value (minimax). For data from a normal distribution, least squares is the optimal minimal-residual criterion by various other criteria, such as maximum likelihood. It is, however, subject to strong effects of outliers or observations that have large (positive or negative) residuals. The least absolute values criterion, on the other hand, is not strongly affected by outlying observations.

The computations for determining the minimizer of (11.24) are discussed on pages 17 to 22. The most common method is some type of quasi-Newton algorithm. Another iterative method that is very simple to implement is one in which the individual elements of the m-vector θ are updated one at a time.

Beginning with some starting value for $\theta^{(0)}$, we have a one-dimensional minimization problem, and letting j range over the indices of θ, we take

$$\theta_j^{(k)} = \text{argmin}_{\theta_j} \sum \rho(r_i(\theta_1^{(k-1)}, \ldots, \theta_j, \ldots, \theta_m^{(k-1)})). \tag{11.26}$$

We then iterate on k until convergence. These kinds of iterations are especially useful in fitting an additive model such as equation (11.7) on page 302, in which

$$r_i = y_i - \beta_0 - \sum_{l \neq j} f_l(x_{li}, \beta_l) - f_j(x_{ji}, \beta_j).$$

Various iterative methods for such problems are described in Gentle (1998b, beginning on page 103).

In Chapter 1, in addition to outlining the basic quasi-Newton computations, we also discuss how those computations may yield estimates of the variance of the estimator of θ. Other methods of estimating the variance of estimators of θ are based on computational inference utilizing data partitioning (Chapter 3) or bootstrapping (Chapter 4).

Minimizing the sum (11.24) in the case of a generalized model may be quite difficult. If, however, we restrict attention to certain classes of link functions and to a simple form of ρ, such as a square, the computations are relatively stable, and a quasi-Newton method, a Gauss-Newton method, or iteratively reweighted least squares can be used. The optimization problem for estimation of the parameters in a generalized model is usually formulated as a likelihood to be maximized rather than a sum of functions of the residuals to be minimized. For the link function and ρ of simple forms, the MLE and the minimum-residual estimates are the same.

Variations on Minimizing Residuals

When data are contaminated with some (unidentified) observations from a different data-generating process, it is desirable to reduce or eliminate the effect of these contaminants. Even if all of the observations arise from the same data-generating process, if that process is subject to extreme variance, it may be desirable to reduce the effect of observations that lie far from the mean of the model. It is not possible, of course, to know which observations are which in either of these cases. Both situations can be addressed, however, by assuming that the bulk of the observations are close to the mean values of the model and fit the model allowing such observations to have larger relative effect on the fit. The objective is to obtain an estimator that is "robust" or resistant to contamination.

A useful variation on the sum (11.24) is

$$\sum w_i \rho(r_i(\theta)). \tag{11.27}$$

If the w_i are just given constants that do not depend on $\rho(r_i(\theta))$, the expression (11.27) is a simple weighted sum and presents no difficulties, either computational or inferential, beyond those of the unweighted sum (11.24). If, on the other hand, we want to choose smaller weights for the y's and x's that do not fit the model, w_i may be some function $w(x_i, \theta, \rho(r_i(\theta)))$. The problems, both computational and inferential, are more difficult in this case.

Another way of approaching this problem is to define a function ρ in the sum (11.24) that depends on y, x, and a given model determined by θ:

$$\rho(t; y, x, \theta) = \begin{cases} \rho_1(t) & \text{if } \theta \text{ provides a "good" fit for } x \text{ and } y, \\ \rho_2(t) & \text{otherwise.} \end{cases} \tag{11.28}$$

This heuristic approach is appealing, but to carry it out would require some preliminary fits and some definition of what it means for "θ to provide a good fit for x and y". Once that meaning is quantified, this approach may be computationally intensive, but it is easily done. In one simple approach, for example, we could define a function ρ in the sum (11.24) that is a square near zero (small model residuals) and smoothly becomes an absolute value at some data-dependent distance from zero:

$$\rho(t; y, x, \theta) = \begin{cases} \frac{1}{2}t^2 & \text{if } |t| \leq c, \\ |t|c - \frac{1}{2}c^2 & \text{if } |t| > c, \end{cases} \tag{11.29}$$

where $c = c(y, x, \theta)$ is some function of the data. The $\frac{1}{2}$ factor is included to make the derivative continuous. (This form of ρ was suggested by Huber, and the resulting estimator of θ is called a *Huber estimator*. Various forms of $c(y, x, \theta)$ have been proposed and studied.)

We can easily modify this basic idea to define other estimators. Suppose that $\rho(t)$ is defined to be 0 for $|t| > c$. If for $|t| \leq c$, $\rho(t) = t^2$, minimizing the sum (11.24) yields the least trimmed squares estimate; if for $|t| \leq c$, $\rho(t) = t^2$, minimizing (11.24) yields the least trimmed absolute values estimate. Because of the dependence of c, computation of such estimators is more difficult. The basic approach consists of two-step iterations; at the jth iteration, set $c^{(j)} = c(y, x, \theta^{(j)})$, which determines $\rho^{(j)}$, and then determine $\theta^{(j+1)}$ as the solution to

$$\min_{\theta} \sum \rho^{(j)}(r_i(\theta)). \tag{11.30}$$

The iterations can be started with some value of $\theta^{(0)}$ that is computed without any trimming. If the functional form of $\rho(t)$ for $|t| \leq c$ is t^2 or some other simple form with second derivatives, quasi-Netwon methods (see pages 17 and following) can be used to solve for $\theta^{(j+1)}$. Hawkins and Olive (1999) give an algorithm for the least trimmed absolute values case.

Instead of defining ρ_1 and ρ_2 in equation (11.28) based on the size of the residuals, we could define ρ based on order statistics of the residuals; that is, decrease the effects of the smallest and largest order statistics. This is the idea behind the commonly used univariate trimmed mean and winsorized mean statistics, in which the contributions to the estimator of a certain percentage of the smallest and largest order statistics are attenuated. If the percentage approaches 50%, the estimators become the median.

Following this same idea, we could either define weights in expression (11.27) or a ρ_1 in equation (11.28) to reduce the effects on the estimator of the observations whose residuals are the smallest and largest order statistics of all residuals. In the extreme case of eliminating the effect of all but one observation, we can write the optimization problem as

$$\min_{\theta} \operatorname{median}(\rho(r_i(\theta))). \tag{11.31}$$

If $\rho(t) = t^2$, this yields the least median of squares estimator proposed by Rousseeuw (1984).

See Rousseeuw and Leroy (1987), Rousseeuw and van Zomeren (1990), and Bassett (1991) for discussions of statistical properties and uses of this estimator. Hettmansperger and Sheather (1992) and Davies (1993) point out some potential problems and situations in which the estimator performs very poorly. The estimator is obviously computationally intensive. Hawkins (1993b) gives a feasible set algorithm, and Xu and Shiue (1993) give a parallel algorithm.

Other variations on the basic approach of minimizing residuals involve some kind of regularization, which may take the form of an additive penalty on the objective function (11.24). Regularization often results in a shrinkage of the estimator toward 0. One of the most common types of shrinkage estimator is the ridge regression estimator in linear regression, which for the model $y = X\beta + \epsilon$ is the solution of the normal equations $(X^{\mathsf{T}}X + \lambda I)\beta = X^{\mathsf{T}}y$ (see Frank and Friedman, 1993, for example). These normal equations correspond to the least squares approximation

$$\begin{pmatrix} y \\ 0 \end{pmatrix} \approx \begin{bmatrix} X \\ \sqrt{\lambda}I \end{bmatrix} \beta.$$

As a side comment, and as an indication of the form of ridge regression in a more general setting, we note that the Levenberg-Marquardt scaling matrix $S^{(k)}$ in the Gauss-Newton update (1.19) on page 20 can be thought of as a regularization of a standard Gauss-Newton step. The formulation as a constrained optimization problem in equation (1.20) emphasizes this view. The general ridge regression objective function can be formulated in a similar manner. In both the Gauss-Newton method with a scaling matrix and ridge regression, the computations can be performed efficiently by recognizing that the system is the normal equations for the least squares fit of

$$\begin{pmatrix} r(\theta^{(k)}) \\ 0 \end{pmatrix} \approx \begin{bmatrix} J_r(\theta^{(k)}) \\ \sqrt{\lambda^{(k)}}(S^{(k)}) \end{bmatrix} p,$$

where p is the update step.

Comparisons of Estimators Defined by Minimum Residuals

It is easy to describe estimators determined by minimizing various functions of the residuals. What is difficult is understanding when to use which one. Because of the range of possibilities of forms of models and of distributions, it is also difficult to summarize what is known about the relative performance of various estimators.

Because of the difficulty of working out exact distributions, Monte Carlo methods are often used in comparing the performance of various estimators. An example is described in Appendix A that compares the power of a statistical hypothesis test for which the test statistic is computed by minimizing an L_2 norm with a test for which the test statistic is computed by minimizing an L_1 norm. Dielman and Rose (1997) and Meintanis and Donatos (1997) present useful results from more extensive simulation studies of the performance of various criteria for fitting regression models. Dodge and Jureckova (2000) provide a review of various methods of fitting regression models using adaptive methods of minimizing residuals.

Orthogonal Residuals

The d_i are orthogonal distances as shown in Figure 11.2. The model is fit to minimize the sum of some function of the d_i. The function is usually the square, so the fit is "orthogonal least squares".

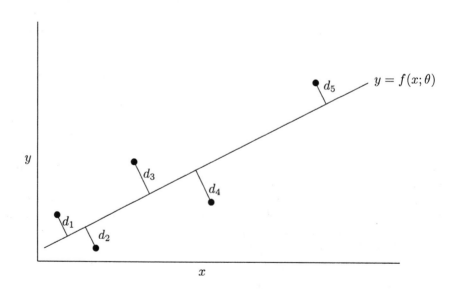

Figure 11.2: Orthogonal Distances

Fitting a model by minimizing the sum of the squared distances is called *orthogonal distance regression*, and the criterion is sometimes called *total least squares*.

Orthogonal distances have been studied most extensively in the case of the linear model,

$$y \approx X\beta.$$

This criterion is sometimes suggested for the errors-in-variables model. This model has the form

$$y = (X + \Delta)\beta + E,$$

where both Δ and E are random variables. See Fuller (1987) for a discussion of the errors-in-variables model.

Golub and Van Loan (1980) and Van Huffel and Vandewalle (1991) discuss some of the computational details of total least squares. Boggs et al. (1989) provided software for weighted orthogonal distance regression.

Ammann and Van Ness (1988, 1989) describe an iterative method that is applicable to any norm, as long as a method is available to compute a value of β that minimizes the norm of the vertical distances in the model. The method is

1. determine $b^{(k)}$ that minimizes the norm of $(y^{(k-1)} - X^{(k-1)}\beta)$;

2. transform the matrix $\left[y^{(k-1)}|X^{(k-1)}\right]$ to $\left[y^{(k)}|X^{(k)}\right]$ by a rotation matrix that makes the kth fit horizontal;

3. set $k = k + 1$ and go to 1.

This is repeated until there is only a small change. An appropriate rotation matrix is Q in the QR decomposition of

$$\begin{bmatrix} I_m & 0 \\ (b^{(k)})^{\text{T}}X & 1 \end{bmatrix}.$$

Projection Pursuit Regression

In Chapter 10, we discussed several methods for analyzing multivariate data with the objective of identifying structure in the data or perhaps reducing the dimension of the data. Two projection methods discussed were principal components and projection pursuit. In models for dependencies, we often apply these multivariate methods just to the independent variables. In linear regression, principal components can be used to reduce the effects of multicollinearity among the independent variables. The dependent variable is regressed on a smaller number of linear combinations of the original set of independent variables.

Projection pursuit is a method of finding interesting projections of data. In the discussion of projection pursuit beginning on page 281, it was applied to a multivariate dataset with the objective of identifying structure in the data.

Friedman and Stuetzle (1981) applied projection pursuit to the independent variables in a regression model.

In regression modeling, projection pursuit is often applied to an additive model of the form

$$Y = \beta_0 + \sum_j^m f_j(x_j, \beta) + E.$$

The idea is to seek lower-dimensional projections of the independent variables, that is, to fit the model

$$Y = \beta_0 + \sum_j^m f_j(\alpha_j^T x) + E.$$

Projection pursuit regression involves the same kind of iterations described beginning on page 284 except that they are applied to the model residuals. Even for the linear model, these computations can be extensive. The R or S-Plus function `ppreg` performs the computations for linear projection pursuit regression.

Classification and Regression Trees

A rooted tree that is used to define a process based on a sequence of choices is called a *decision tree*. Decision trees that are used for classifying observations are called *classification trees*. They are similar to the cluster tree shown in Figure 10.5 on page 241 except that the nodes in the classification trees represent decisions based on values of the independent variables. Decision trees that are used for predicting values of a continuous response variable are called *regression trees*. The terminal nodes correspond to predicted values or intervals of predicted values of the response variable.

The objective in building a classification tree is to determine a sequence of simple decisions that would ultimately divide the set of observations into the given groups. Each decision is generally in the form of a test based on the values of the variables that constitute an observation. Often, the test involves only a single variable. If the variable takes on only a countable number of values, the test based on the variable may be chosen to have as many possible outcomes as the values associated with the variable. If the variable has a continuous range of values, the test is generally chosen to have a binary outcome corresponding to observations above or below some cutpoint. Trees with exactly two branches emanating from each nonterminal node are called *binary trees*. The terminal nodes of a classification tree represent groups or classes that are not to be subdivided further.

How well a test divides the observations is determined by the "impurity" of the resulting groups. There are several ways of measuring the impurity or how well a test divides the observations. Breiman et al. (1984) describe some methods, including a "twoing rule" for a binary test. For classifying the observations into k groups, at a node with n observations to classify, this rule assigns a value to a test based on the formula

$$n_L n_R \left(\sum_{i=1}^{k} |L_i n_L - R_i n_R|/n \right)^2,$$

where n_L and n_R are the number of observations that the test assigns to the left and right child nodes, respectively, and L_i and R_i are the number of group i assigned to the left and right, respectively. Murthy, Kasif, and Salzberg (1994) discuss this and compare it with several other measures.

The classification tree can be built by a greedy divide-and-conquer recursive partitioning scheme, as shown in Algorithm 11.1. See Quinlan (1986) for further discussion of such schemes and their implementation on parallel processors.

Algorithm 11.1 Recursive Partitioning for Classification Using a Training Set

1. Evaluate all tests that divide the given set into mutually exclusive sets.

2. Choose the test that scores highest, and divide the set based on this test.

3. For any subset that contains observations from more than one group, repeat beginning at step 1. ∎

The results of a binary partitioning may be presented as a tree, as shown in Figure 11.3, in which the rule for splitting at each node is shown. In this example, there are three groups and two numerical variables.

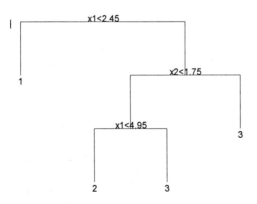

Figure 11.3: A Classification Tree

The process of building a tree by recursive binary partitioning continues until either the data at the terminal nodes are sufficiently homogeneous or consist of a small number of observations. Homogeneity is measured (negatively) by *deviance*. For continuous response variables, deviance is the sum of squares; for factor variables, it is two times the log-likelihood of the full model (that is, all categories) minus the log-likelihood of the current model.

The S-Plus function `tree` uses binary recursive partitioning to build a classification tree. Two widely used stand-alone programs that use recursive partitioning are CART (see Breiman et al., 1984) and C4.5 or its successors C5.0 and See5 (see Quinlan, 1993).

The rules in a decision tree can be used to define each of the classes by conjunctive combinations of the rules at each node. In the example of Figure 11.3, we can define the classes as in the following table, where "∧" represents "and" and "∨" represents "or". Rules expressed in these forms are called conjunctive normal forms, or CNFs (if the major conjunctions are all ∧) or disjunctive normal forms, or DNFs. (A formula in DNF is one written as a disjunction of terms, each of which may be a conjunction.)

Table 11.1: Rules Defining the Clusters Shown in Figure 11.3

cluster	rule(s)
1	$x_1 < 2.45$
2	$(2.45 \leq x_1) \wedge (x_1 < 4.95) \wedge (x_2 < 1.75)$
3	$((2.45 \leq x_1) \wedge (1.75 \leq x_2)) \vee ((4.95 \leq x_1) \wedge (x2 < 1.75))$

Rules such as these are useful in describing the result of the classification, and they also aid in our understanding of the basis for the classification.

A variety of other classification tree programs have been developed. Some classification tree programs perform multilevel splits rather than binary splits. One type of classification tree with multilevel splits was proposed by Morgan and Sonquist (1963). Their method has come to be called "automatic interaction detection", or AID, and a number of modifications have been developed, including CHAID, for "chi-square automatic interaction detection", by Kass (1980) (see Hawkins and Kass, 1982). Other classification procedures that perform multilevel splits include FACT ("Fast Algorithm for Classification Trees"), described by Loh and Vanichestakul (1988). (See also Kademan, Loh, and Vanichsetakul, 1989, for an interface to S.)

A multilevel split can be represented as a series of binary splits, and because with multilevel splits predictor variables are used for splitting only once, the resulting classification trees may be unrealistically short. Another problem with multilevel splitting is the effect of the order in which the variables are used in splitting. The number of levels for splits of variables affects the interpretation of the classification tree. These effects are sometimes referred to in a nontechnical sense as "bias".

Instead of splitting on a single variable at each node, we can form splits based on combinations of values of several variables. The most obvious way of doing this is to use some linear combination of the variables, such as the principal components (see Section 10.3, page 264). Splits based on linear combinations of the variables are called *oblique linear splits*. Seeking good linear combinations of variables on which to build oblique partitions is a much more computationally intensive procedure than just using single variables. Siu (1988) describes a recursive partitioning to produce a piecewise linear model. Heath, Kasif, and Salzberg (1993) and Murthy, Kasif, and Salzberg (1994) describe methods that use randomization in selecting oblique partitions.

Combining Classifications

Classification methods tend to be unstable; that is, small perturbations in the training datasets may yield large differences in the classification rules (see Breiman, 1996a). To overcome the instability, which manifests itself in large variability of the classes (called "variance"), perturbations or resampling and averaging methods may help. The averaging is essentially a "voting" by the various classifications formed following resampling. The idea of averaging is an old one; in this context it is sometimes called "stacked generalization" (Wolpert, 1992). A similar idea in linear regression in which subsamples of minimal size are used is called "elemental regression". (The minimal size in linear regression is a dataset that has the same number of observations as variables. See Hawkins, 1993c, for examples and discussion.) The coefficient estimates are averaged over the subsamples. Henery (1997) gives a review of methods of combining classification procedures. Some examples of applications in classification in which combined classifiers had superior performance are described by Richeldi and Rossotto (1997) and by Westphal and Nakhaeizadeh (1997).

Breiman (1996b) describes a method of forming random training sets by bootstrapping the given dataset. He calls this process "bagging". For a given "bag", the classification tree is constructed by randomly choosing subsets of the features to use in forming the branches from nodes. The process is continued until the full tree is formed (that is, the tree is not "pruned").

Schapire (1990) suggested an iterative method of "boosting" the classification ability by reweighting the variables. Freund and Schapire (1997) further developed this method in an algorithm called AdaBoost. Breiman (1998) described and compared similar methods. He referred to his type of method as an "arc", for "adaptively resample and combine". Breiman (1998) and Ho (1998) gave comparisons of these methods on several different datasets. There does not appear to be a method that is consistently best. Some methods are better on some datasets than others, and there is no simple way of describing the optimality properties.

Amit and Geman (1997) and Ho (1998) suggested forming classification trees from random subsamples of the given data and then combining the individual trees by some averaging process. The collection of random trees is called a random forest.

Breiman (2000) suggested another approach based on randomly perturbing only the output (that is, the classes) and then averaging. This method, surprisingly, also seems to improve the classification.

Kernel Methods and Support Vector Machines

Identification of nonlinear structure in data is often preceded by a nonlinear mapping from the m-dimensional data space to a p-dimensional "feature space". The feature space may have more, even many more, dimensions than the data space. The mapping carries the basic data m-vector x to a p-vector $f(x)$. The feature space is a subspace of $\mathbb{R}^p$ and thus is an inner-product space. (The original data space may be more general.) This is essentially the approach of *support vector machines* (see Cristianini and Shawe-Taylor, 2000, and Vapnik, 1999b).

A simple type of mapping that may be used in support vector machines is one defined by an inner product, called a kernel function. A *kernel function* is an inner product of the feature mappings of two data vectors; that is, for data vectors x and y and a mapping to the feature space f, a kernel K is the function

$$K(x, y) = \langle f(x), f(y) \rangle.$$

See Cristianini and Shawe-Taylor (2000) and Vapnik (1999a) for more discussions of kernel methods in this context. Schölkopf, Smola, and Müller (1999) describe a nonlinear PCA based on kernel methods. Wahba (1999) discusses the connections of cross validation and support vector machines.

Although support vector machines can be used for exploratory clustering, most of the applications are for classification with a given training set.

Fitting Models of Sequential Dependencies

Models for dependencies within a sequence such as a time series often are regression models in which an independent variable is the same as the dependent variable at a previous point in time. Data for fitting such models can be put in the same form as data for other regression models by simply adding variables that represent lagged values.

The model for sequential dependency often expresses a rate in a differential equation, such as equation (11.23) (in a slightly different form),

$$\frac{\mathrm{d}Y}{Y} = \mu \, \mathrm{d}t + \sigma \, \mathrm{d}B_t. \tag{11.32}$$

A rate cannot be directly observed; the data for fitting such a model are observations at discrete points in time, and derivatives are approximated by ratios of finite differences. In applications to financial data, for example, this model is fit by selecting a fixed time interval Δt, such as a day, and observing ΔY_t and Y_t at a set of points in time. (In this application, there are obvious problems because of time restrictions on the underlying process; stocks are not traded on weekends and market holidays.) The parameters in the model, μ and σ, are generally estimated by the method of moments. If B_t is a Brownian motion—that is, if the random variable has a normal distribution—the method of moments estimator is also the maximum likelihood estimator.

The geometric Brownian motion model leads to a lognormal distribution of prices with an expected value that decreases proportionally to the variance of the rate of return (see Exercise 11.5). The importance of this model is not because of the stock prices themselves but for applications in pricing derivatives.

A derivative is a financial instrument whose value depends on values of other financial instruments or on some measure of the state of the economy or of nature. The most common types of derivatives available to individuals are call options on stocks, which are rights to purchase the stock at a fixed price, and put options on stocks, which are rights to sell the stock at a fixed price. Both of these types of derivatives have expiration dates at which the rights terminate. There are many variations on calls and puts that are useful in academic analyses, but in application a call option conveys to the owner the right to buy a stated number of shares of the underlying stock at a fixed price anytime before the expiration date, and a put option conveys to the owner the right to sell a stated number of shares of the underlying stock at a fixed price anytime before the expiration date. (For no particular reason, such options are called "American options". Options that cannot be exercised prior to the expiration time are called "European options". Although European options are rare, their values are easier to analyze.) Stock options are *rights*, not obligations, so the value, and consequently the price, cannot be negative. Much study has been devoted to determining the appropriate price of a call or a put.

Based on use of equation (11.32) and the associated assumptions of normality with constant μ and σ as a pricing model, with certain assumptions about financial markets (no arbitrage and the existence of a riskless investment, for example) and additional assumptions about the underlying stock (no dividends, for example), a differential equation for the price of European options can be developed. This is called the Black-Scholes differential equation; it has a fairly simple solution (see Hull, 2000, for example).

The failure of any one of the assumptions can invalidate the Black-Scholes differential equation. In some cases, there is no simple differential equation that can take its place. In other cases, the resulting differential equation cannot be solved easily.

More realistic versions of equation (11.32), such as ones with jumps, or ones that are mean-reverting, can easily be simulated. Likewise, more realistic assumptions about exercise times, dividend payouts, and so on can easily be accommodated in a simulation. Our ability to simulate the process allows us to use Monte Carlo methods to study whether the assumptions about the process correspond to observable behavior.

If our assumptions about the process do indeed correspond to reality, we can use Monte Carlo simulation to determine various features of the process, including the appropriate prices of derivative assets. The way this is done is one of the standard techniques of the Monte Carlo method; that is, we express the quantity of interest as an expected value, simulate the process many times, each time computing the outcome, and then estimate the expected value as the mean of the outcomes.

Transformations to Make Data Fit Models

Often, a model is so tractable, both statistically and computationally, that even if it is not a good representation of observed reality, it may be worth using it as an approximation. Sometimes, the approximation can be made even better by transforming the data.

The most common types of transformations are those that attempt to make the low-order moments of the transformed variable correspond to the assumptions in the model. In real data, often the second moment (the variance) increases as the first moment increases, but a common assumption is that the moments are constant; hence, we may seek a transformation that stabilizes the variance. Another common assumption in the model is that the distribution is symmetric. A transformation based on the third moment may make the data more symmetric.

The use of transformations to make the data fit simple models is an old idea. See Bartlett (1947) for a discussion. Tukey (1957) gives a systematic description of transformations and associated distributional characteristics.

Variance Stabilization

A transformation may be suggested by some pattern in the observations. For example, certain types of measurements are often observed to exhibit greater variability as the magnitude of the observations becomes larger. For a probability distribution such as the normal distribution, there are two distinct parameters for the mean and the variance, and we may wish to model populations with different means using normal distributions with the same variance. To use data pooled from the different populations, a *variance stabilizing* transformation may be useful. It may turn out, for example, that if the variance of y tends to be proportional to its magnitude, the variance of $y^{1/2}$ is relatively constant. In this case, the square root transformation is a variance-stabilizing transformation.

In general, if the variance of Y is some function V of the mean of Y, a transformation $h(Y)$ to stabilize the variance would have the property

$$\frac{\partial h(y)}{\partial y} \propto \frac{1}{\sqrt{V(y)}};$$

therefore, the appropriate transformation $h(y)$ is the integral of $1/\sqrt{V(y)}$.

In addition to assumptions in the model about the variance, there are generally assumptions about covariances, either among the variables or among the same variables in different observations. Young (1992) discusses methods for finding transformations to reduce correlations.

Transformations of the Independent Variables

In addition to problems with the random component of the model not corresponding well with the data, the systematic component also may not fit the data. This may suggest transformations of either the independent or the dependent variables. Box and Tidwell (1962) discuss various transformations of the independent variables. For a linear model such as equation (11.6), with the independent variables taking only positive values, they suggest use of a power transformation,

$$w_j = \left\{ \begin{array}{ll} x_j^{\alpha_j} & \alpha_j \neq 0 \\ \log x_j & \alpha_j = 0 \end{array} \right. , \tag{11.33}$$

and give an iterative procedure for determining the α_j's, that minimizes the residual sum of squares.

Transformations of the Box-Cox Type

Box and Cox (1964) study power transformations of the dependent variable (assumed to be positive) and suggest use of a maximum likelihood method to determine the power. The power transformation of equation (11.33) can be made continuous in the power by making a slight modification. This results in the *Box-Cox transformation*,

$$\tau(y; \lambda) = \left\{ \begin{array}{ll} (y^\lambda - 1)/\lambda & \lambda \neq 0 \\ \log y & \lambda = 0 \end{array} \right. . \tag{11.34}$$

If τ is the dependent variable in a linear model such as equation (11.14) and the elements of ϵ are from independent normals with mean 0 and variance σ^2, the log-likelihood function is

$$l(\lambda, \beta, \sigma; y) = -n \log \sigma - \frac{(\tau(y; \lambda) - X\beta)^{\mathrm{T}}(\tau(y; \lambda) - X\beta)}{2\sigma^2} - (\lambda - 1) \sum_i^n \log y_i.$$

$$\tag{11.35}$$

(Recall that the y_i's are assumed to be positive.) For a fixed value of λ, the maximum of equation (11.35) with respect to β and σ yields the usual least squares estimates, with $\tau(y; \lambda)$ as the dependent variable. The function $\widehat{l}(\lambda; \widehat{\beta}, \widehat{\sigma}, y)$ is called the *profile likelihood*. In practice, the profile likelihood is often computed for a fixed set of values of λ, and the maximum with respect to λ may be chosen based on an inspection of the plot of the function. The choice of λ is often restricted to $\ldots, -2, -1\frac{1}{2}, -1, -\frac{1}{2}, 0, \frac{1}{2}, 1, 1\frac{1}{2}, 2, \ldots$. The maximum of $\widehat{l}$ with respect to λ is the same as the maximum of l with respect to λ, β, and σ. If one really believes the likelihood from which equation (11.35) is derived, confidence intervals on λ could be computed based on the asymptotic chi-squared distribution of the log-likelihood.

There are several obvious extensions to the transformations discussed above. The transformations can be applied whether the systematic component of the model is linear or of the more general form in equation (11.8). Instead of the power transformations in equations (11.33) and (11.34), more general transformations could be used, and the λ in $\tau(y; \lambda)$ could represent a much more general parameter. Both the Box-Tidwell transformations of the independent variables and the Box-Cox transformations of the dependent variables could be applied simultaneously. Carroll and Ruppert (1984) proposed such simultaneous general transformations. They called such a method "transform both sides" and used the same transformation for both the dependent variable and the systematic component, although obviously different transformations could be used.

Weisberg (1985), Draper and Smith (1998), and Carroll and Ruppert (1988) all have extensive discussions of various transformations for linear models.

Velilla (1995) discusses multivariate Box-Cox transformations, as well as the robustness of the transformations to outliers and diagnostics for detecting the effect of outliers.

Alternating Conditional Expectation

In any model, we want to include independent variables that have strong relationships to the dependent variable. We may seek transformations of all of the variables to achieve stronger relationships.

Breiman and Friedman (1985a, 1985b) describe and study a method of fitting an additive model (11.7) that relates the independent variables to a transformation of the dependent variable:

$$\tau(Y) \approx \beta_0 + f_1(x_1) + \cdots f_m(x_m).$$

The f's are just transformations of the x's. The basic approach is to transform the variables iteratively using τ and the f's to maximize the sample correlation of the transformed variables.

The procedure is called *alternating conditional expectations*, or ACE. It attempts to maximize the sample correlation between $\tau(y)$ and $\sum_{j=1}^{m} f_j(x_j)$ or to minimize

$$e^2(\tau, f_1, \ldots, f_m) = \frac{M\left(\left(\tau(y) - \alpha - \sum_{j=1}^{m} f_j(x_j)\right)^2\right)}{S(\tau(y))},$$

where $M(\cdot)$ is the sample mean and $V(\cdot)$ is the sample variance. The method is shown in Algorithm 11.2, in which we write $e^2(\tau, f_1, \ldots, f_m)$ as $e^2(\tau, f)$.

Algorithm 11.2 Alternating Conditional Expectation (ACE)

0. Set $k = 0$. Set $\tau^{(k)}(y) = (y - M(y))/(S(y))^{1/2}$.

1. Set $k = k + 1$.

2. Fit the additive model with $\tau^{(k-1)}(y)$ (see page 315) to obtain $f_j^{(k)}$.

3. Set

$$\tau^{(k)}(y) = \frac{M\left(f^{(k)}(x) \mid y\right)}{\left(S\left(f^{(k)}(x) \mid y\right)\right)^{1/2}}.$$

4. If $e^2\left(\tau^{(k)}, f^{(k)}\right) < e^2\left(\tau^{(k-1)}, f^{(k-1)}\right)$, then go to step 1; otherwise terminate. ∎

If there is only one explanatory variable x, step 2 is just to compute

$$f^{(k)}(x) = M\left(\tau^{(k-1)}(y) \mid x\right).$$

When the algorithm terminates, the sample of y's and of the x vectors have been transformed so that the simple additive model provides a good fit.

Additivity and Variance Stabilization

Transformations to stabilize the variance of the residuals can be performed simultaneously with the transformations that achieve the strong additive relationship. Tibshirani (1988) introduced a technique called additivity and variance stabilization (AVAS) that attempts to do this.

Algorithm 11.3 Additivity and Variance Stabilization (AVAS)

0. Set $k = 0$. Set

$$\tau^{(k)}(y) = \frac{y - M(y)}{(S(y))^{1/2}}.$$

1. Set $k = k + 1$.

2. Fit the additive model with $\tau^{(k-1)}(y)$ (see page 315) to obtain $f_j^{(k)}$.

3. Determine the variance function

$$v(u) = S\left(\tau^{(k-1)}(y) \mid \sum f_j^{(k-1)}(x_j) = u\right);$$

compute the variance-stabilizing function (see page 326)

$$h(t) = \int_0^t v(u)^{-1/2}\, du;$$

set

$$\tilde{\tau}^{(k-1)}(t) = h(\tau^{(k-1)}(t));$$

set

$$\tau^{(k)}(t) = \frac{\tilde{\tau}^{(k-1)}(t) - M(\tilde{\tau}^{(k-1)}(y))}{S(\tilde{\tau}^{(k-1)}(y))}.$$

4. If

$$e^2\left(\tau^{(k)}, f^{(k)}\right) < e^2\left(\tau^{(k-1)}, f^{(k-1)}\right),$$

then go to step 1;
otherwise terminate.   ■

Wang and Ruppert (1995) introduce a semiparametric version of AVAS (SPAVAS) in which the structural form of the systematic component, $f(x; \theta)$, is assumed known.

Algorithm 11.4 Semiparametric AVAS

0. Set $k = 0$, set $\tau^{(k)}(\cdot)$ to the identity function, and set $y^{(0)} = y$.

1. Set $k = k + 1$.

2. Determine $\widehat{y}^{(k)}$ as the least squares fit of $\tau^{(k-1)}(y^{(k-1)})$ to $\tau^{(k-1)}(f(x; \theta))$.

3. Let $r^{(k)} = \tau^{(k-1)}(y^{(k-1)}) - \widehat{y}^{(k)}$ and smooth $(r^{(k)})^2$ against $\widehat{y}^{(k)}$ to estimate the conditional variance V of $\tau^{(k)}(y^{(k)})$ given $\tau^{(k)}(f(x; \widehat{\theta}))$, where $\widehat{\theta}$ is the ordinary least squares estimate.

4. Compute the variance stabilizing function

$$h(t) = \int_0^t v(u)^{-1/2}\, du;$$

set

$$\tilde{\tau}^{(k-1)}(t) = h\left(\tau^{(k-1)}(t)\right);$$

set

$$\tau^{(k)}(t) = \frac{\tilde{\tau}^{(k-1)}(t) - M(\tilde{\tau}^{(k-1)}(y))}{S(\tilde{\tau}^{(k-1)}(y))}.$$

5. If

$$e^2\left(\tau^{(k)}(y^{(k)}) - \tau^{(k)}(f(x; \theta))\right) < e^2\left(\tau^{(k-1)}(y^{(k-1)}) - \tau^{(k-1)}(f(x; \theta))\right)$$

then go to step 1;
otherwise terminate.   ■

Local Fitting

Often, a single model of the form $Y \approx f(x; \theta)$ over the full range of interest either does not provide a very good fit or the form of f is overly complicated. If the functional form is complicated, it is unlikely that it provides insights into the relationship of Y and x. We may achieve a better fit and more accuracy in predictions if we abandon the global model. We could, of course, seek a piecewise model of the

$$Y \approx f_j(x; \theta_j) \quad \text{for } x \in R_j.$$

This may be a useful approach, but, of course, we are faced with the problem of determining the ranges R_j. In some applications, there may be first principles that suggest particular functional forms over certain ranges.

Two other ways of doing local fitting that we discuss in Chapter 6 (page 139) are by using splines or kernels. Rather than developing single functional forms, we can think of the problem as simply one of providing a rule that for a given x_0 provides a predicted $\widehat{Y}_0$. The rule may be expressed in the form of a regression tree (page 320) in which each terminal node is the predicted value of Y within the region defined by the path to the terminal node.

An even simpler approach is just to divide the range of x into convenient sets R_j and take $\widehat{Y}$ in that region to be the mean of the observed values of Y in that region. This is called a *bin smoother*. A variation on a bin smoother is a *running smoother*, which, at any given point x_0, uses weighted averages of observed values of Y corresponding to observed values of x near x_0. This is the idea behind *kernel smoothers*. A smoothing procedure based on local averaging directly uses the fact that the systematic component of the model is a conditional expectation of y, given x. The fitted systematic component then takes the form

$$\widehat{f}(x) = \sum K(x, x_i) y_i,$$

where $K(x, x_i)$ is a kernel. The kernel is often taken as a radially symmetric function of a scalar, and we can express the kernel smooth at x as

$$\widehat{f}_V(x) = \frac{\sum K_V(\|V^{-1}(x - x_i)\| y_i)}{\sum K_V(\|V^{-1}(x - x_i)\|)},$$

where V is a scaling matrix, perhaps one that also spheres the data (see page 117). The scaling matrix V controls the locality of influence of observations around x. As in the case of density estimation (see page 222), the scaling matrix, or the window width, has a major effect on the performance of the estimates. A wide window makes for a very smooth regression surface, whereas a very small window results in a highly variable surface.

Use of kernels is a common method in nonparametric regression. See Green and Silverman (1994), Härdle (1990, 1991), Simonoff (1996), and Wand and Jones (1995) for further discussions of kernel methods in nonparametric regression.

Another approach to local fitting is to use splines. A way to do this is to evaluate each of the spline basis functions b_j at each x_i, yielding $\tilde{x}_{ij}$, where

$$\tilde{x}_{ij} = b_j(x_i).$$

The observations on the dependent variable y_i are then fit to the spline function values. The fit can be based on any of the criteria that we have discussed. A least squares fit is most commonly used. See Eubank (1999) for an extensive discussion of the use of splines in regression modeling.

Assessing the Fit of a Model

We have described various approaches to fitting a model using data, such as maximum likelihood, based on an assumed probability distribution, fitting by minimizing the residuals, and fitting by matching moments. Each of these methods has its place. In some cases, a particular type of one of these general schemes is identical to a particular type of another; for example, maximum likelihood under a normal distribution is equivalent to minimizing the sum of the squares of the residuals. Whatever method is used in fitting the model, we are interested in the *goodness* of the fit. If the method of fit is to mimimize some norm of the residuals, intuitively it would seem that the proportional reduction in the norm of the residuals by fitting a model gives some indication of the goodness of that model. In other words, we compare the norm of the "residuals" with no model (that is, just the responses themselves) with the norm of the residuals after fitting the model,

$$\frac{\|r\|}{\|y\|},$$

which should be small if the fit is good or, looking at it another way,

$$\frac{\|y\| - \|r\|}{\|y\|}, \tag{11.36}$$

which should be close to 1 if the fit is good. Expression (11.36) is the familiar R^2 statistic from least squares linear regression.

Although a particular method of fitting a model may yield a relatively small norm of the residual vector, certain observations may have very large residuals. In some cases of model fitting, deleting one or more observations may have a very large effect on the model fit. If one or more observations have very large residuals (the meaning of "very large" is not specified here), we may question whether the model is appropriate for these anomalous observations, even if the model is useful for the rest of the dataset. We may also question whether the method of fit is appropriate. The method of fit should come under special scrutiny if deleting one or more observations has a very large effect on the model fit.

Quantile plots are especially useful in assessing the validity of assumptions in a model. If the residuals are ranked from smallest to largest, the pattern should be similar to a pattern of ranked normal random variables. Given a sample of n residuals,

$$r_{(1)} \leq \cdots \leq r_{(n)},$$

we compare the observed values with the theoretical values corresponding to probabilities

$$p_{(1)} \leq \cdots \leq p_{(n)}.$$

Although the sample distribution of the residuals may give some indication of how well the data fit the model, because of the interactions of the residuals with the fitting process, the problem of assessing whether the model is appropriate is ill-posed. The most we can generally hope for is to assess the predictive ability of the model by use of partitioned data and cross validation, as discussed in Section 3.2.

Exercises

11.1. Consider the use of a simple model of the probability density for univariate data:

$$f(y; \theta_1, \theta_2) = \frac{\theta_1}{2} e^{-\theta_1 |y - \theta_2|} \quad \text{for} \ -\infty \le y \le \infty.$$

(This is the double exponential.) Choose

$$\theta_1 = 10,$$
$$\theta_2 = 100,$$

and generate a random sample of size 100.

(a) Write out the likelihood function of θ_1 and θ_2, and use an optimization program to maximize it. Make appropriate transformations prior to optimizing a function.

(b) For the moment, ignore θ_1, and estimate θ_2 by minimizing various functions of the residuals $y - \theta_2$. Use iteratively reweighted least squares to obtain the L_1, $L_{1.5}$, and L_2 estimates of θ_2. Now, in each case, obtain an estimate of θ_1. Using your estimate of θ_1 and rescaling, which of the L_p estimates is closest to the MLE above? Which one would you expect to be closest?

(c) Obtain 95% confidence intervals for both θ_1 and θ_2 using your L_p estimates. (Assume asymptotic normality of your location estimator.)

11.2. Consider the simple linear model

$$y_i = \beta_0 + \beta_1 x_i + \epsilon_i.$$

(a) Assume that the ϵ_i are independent realizations of a random variable that has a $N(0, \sigma^2)$ distribution. Taking

$$\beta_0 = 10,$$
$$\beta_1 = 10,$$

and x to be

$$0.0, 1.0, 2.0, \ldots, 100$$

(i.e., 101 observations equally spaced from 0 to 100):

i. Let $\sigma = 1$, generate the corresponding y's, estimate β_0 and β_1 by ordinary least squares, and plot the data and the fitted line.

     ii. Repeat with $\sigma = 100$.

  (b) Assume that the ϵ_i are independent realizations of a random variable with a Cauchy distribution with scale parameter a. Now, for $a = 1$ and $a = 100$, repeat the previous part of this exercise.

  (c) Repeat the previous part of this exercise, except use the L_1 criterion for estimating β_0 and β_1.

11.3. Conduct a Monte Carlo study to determine the size of the test for

$$\beta_{q+1} = \beta_{q+2} = \cdots = \beta_p = 0$$

in the linear model

$$y_i = \beta_0 + \beta_1 x_1 + \cdots + \beta_{q+1} x_{q+1} + \cdots + \beta_p x_{ip} + e_i$$

when the parameters are fitted using Huber M estimation. Conduct the test at the nominal significance level of 0.05. (The "size of the test" is the actual significance level.) Use a normal distribution, a double exponential distribution, and a Cauchy distribution for the error term.

11.4. Suppose that you have data on x and y that follow a model of the form

$$y^{p_y} = \beta_0 + \beta_1 x^{p_x} + \epsilon.$$

(Of course you would not know that the data follow this model.) Choose some representative values of the parameters in the model and, for each combination, generate artificial data to study some of the data transformations we have discussed. (This is not a Monte Carlo study; it is just an exercise to yield a better understanding of the methods.) The following R or S-Plus code would generate a useful example:

```
nmod   <- 50
beta0 <- 3
beta1 <- 2
esd    <- 2
xdat   <- runif(nmod,0,2)
px     <- 2
py     <- 2
xmod  <- xtmp^px
ymod  <- beta0 + beta1*xmod + esd*rnorm(nmod)
ydat   <- ymod^py
```

The data that would be observed are in xdat and ydat.

  (a) Plot the data.

  (b) Fit the linear model

$$y = \beta_0 + \beta_1 x + \epsilon.$$

    Plot the residuals, and notice that a quadratic model seems to be in order.

  (c) Fit the model

$$y = \beta_0 + \beta_1 x + \beta_2 x^2 + \epsilon.$$

    Plot the residuals, and notice that their variance seems to increase with the mean.

(d) Fit the model
$$w = \beta_0 + \beta_1 x + \beta_2 x^2 + \epsilon,$$
where $w = y^{1/2}$. Comment on what you have observed.

(e) Now, for a grid of values of λ, the model
$$w = \beta_0 + \beta_1 x + \beta_2 x^2 + \epsilon,$$
where $w = (y^\lambda - 1)/\lambda$. Compute a profile likelihood as a function of λ, and select a Box-Cox power transformation that seems appropriate.

(f) Apply ACE to x and y (ac <- ace(xdat,ydat)). Use the fit to determine a predicted value of y for $x = 1$. (You may have to go through series of smoothing transformations to do this.)

(g) Apply AVAS to x and y (av <- avas(xdat,ydat)). Use the fit to determine a predicted value of y for $x = 1$. (You may have to go through series of smoothing transformations to do this.) Compare the AVAS results with the ACE results.

(h) Using the original data, apply directly one step of the AVAS algorithm. (The interest here is in computing the variance-stabilizing transformation from the data.)

11.5. The geometric Brownian motion model for changes in stock prices (11.32) on page 324 leads to a lognormal distribution for the prices themselves with an expected value that decreases proportionally to the variance of the rate of return. Study this decrease by Monte Carlo methods beginning with the model for changes in price. Give an intuitive explanation why it should decrease.

11.6. Choose any ten stocks traded on the New York Stock Exchange. Do the price histories of these stocks over the past 5 years support the validity of the geometric Brownian motion model?

Appendix A

Monte Carlo Studies in Statistics

In previous chapters, we have seen how Monte Carlo methods can be used in statistical inference, including Monte Carlo tests and bootstrap methods. Simulation has also become one of the most important tools in the development of statistical theory and methods. If the properties of an estimator are very difficult to work out analytically, a Monte Carlo study may be conducted to estimate those properties.

Although high-speed computers have recently helped to expand the usage of Monte Carlo methods, there is a long history of such usage. Stigler (1991) describes Monte Carlo simulations by nineteenth-century scientists and suggests that "simulation, in the modern sense of that term, may be the oldest of the stochastic arts." One of the earliest documented Monte Carlo studies of a statistical procedure was by Erastus Lyman de Forest in the 1870s. Stigler (1978) describes how De Forest studied ways of smoothing a time series by simulating the data using cards drawn from a box.

Another early use of Monte Carlo was the sampling experiment (using biometric data recorded on pieces of cardboard) that led W. S. Gosset to the discovery of the distribution of the t-statistic and the correlation coefficient. (See Student, 1908a, 1908b. Of course, it was R. A. Fisher who later worked out the distributions.)

Often a Monte Carlo study is an informal investigation whose main purpose is to indicate promising research directions. If a "quick and dirty" Monte Carlo study indicates that some method of inference has good properties, it may be worth the time of the research worker in developing the method and perhaps doing the difficult analysis to confirm the results of the Monte Carlo study.

In addition to quick Monte Carlo studies that are mere precursors to analytic work, Monte Carlo studies often provide a significant amount of the available knowledge of the properties of statistical techniques, especially under various alternative models. A large proportion of the articles in the statistical literature

337

include Monte Carlo studies. In recent issues of the *Journal of the American Statistical Association*, for example, almost half of the articles report on Monte Carlo studies that supported the research.

A.1   Simulation as an Experiment

A simulation study that incorporates a random component is an experiment. The principles of statistical design and analysis apply just as much to a Monte Carlo study as they do to any other scientific experiment. The Monte Carlo study should adhere to the same high standards as any scientific experimentation:

- control;

- reproducibility;

- efficiency;

- careful and complete documentation.

In simulation, *control*, among other things, relates to the fidelity of a *nonrandom* process to a *random* process. The experimental units are only simulated. Questions about the computer model must be addressed (tests of the random number generators, and so on).

Likewise, *reproducibility* is predicated on good random number generators (or else on equally bad ones!). Portability of the random number generators enhances reproducibility and in fact can allow *strict* reproducibility. Reproducible research also requires preservation and documentation of the computer programs that produced the results (see Buckheit and Donoho, 1995).

The principles of good statistical design can improve the efficiency. Use of good designs (e.g., fractional factorials) can allow efficient simultaneous exploration of several factors. Also, there are often many opportunities to reduce the variance (improve the efficiency). Hammersley and Hanscomb (1964, page 8) note,

> ... statisticians were insistent that other experimentalists should design experiments to be as little subject to unwanted error as possible, and had indeed given important and useful help to the experimentalist in this way; but in their own experiments they were singularly inefficient, nay negligent in this respect.

Many properties of statistical methods of inference are analytically intractable. Asymptotic results, which are often easy to work out, may imply excellent performance, such as consistency with a good rate of convergence, but the finite sample properties are ultimately what must be considered. Monte Carlo studies are a common tool for investigating the properties of a statistical method, as noted above. In the literature, the Monte Carlo studies are sometimes called "numerical results". Some numerical results are illustrated by just one randomly generated dataset; others are studied by averaging over thousands of randomly generated sets.

In a Monte Carlo study, there are usually several different things ("treatments" or "factors") that we want to investigate. As in other kinds of experiments, a factorial design is usually more efficient. Each factor occurs at different "levels", and the set of all levels of all factors that are used in the study constitute the "design space". The measured responses are properties of the statistical methods, such as their sample means and variances.

The factors commonly studied in Monte Carlo experiments in statistics include the following.

- statistical method (estimator, test procedure, etc.);

- sample size;

- the problem for which the statistical method is being applied (that is, the "true" model, which may be different from the one for which the method was developed). Factors relating to the type of problem may be:

  - distribution of the random component in the model (normality?);

  - correlation among observations (independence?);

  - homogeneity of the observations (outliers?, mixtures?);

  - structure of associated variables (leverage?).

The factor whose effect is of primary interest is the statistical method. The other factors are generally just blocking factors. There is, however, usually an interaction between the statistical method and these other factors.

As in physical experimentation, observational units are selected for each point in the design space and measured. The measurements, or "responses" made at the same design point, are used to assess the amount of random variation, or variation that is not accounted for by the factors being studied. A comparison of the variation among observational units at the same levels of all factors with the variation among observational units at different levels is the basis for a decision as to whether there are real (or "significant") differences at the different levels of the factors. This comparison is called analysis of variance. The same basic rationale for identifying differences is used in simulation experiments.

A fundamental (and difficult) question in experimental design is how many experimental units to observe at the various design points. Because the experimental units in Monte Carlo studies are generated on the computer, they are usually rather inexpensive. The subsequent processing (the application of the factors, in the terminology of an experiment) may be very extensive, however, so there is a need to design an efficient experiment.

A.2 Reporting Simulation Experiments

The reporting of a simulation experiment should receive the same care and consideration that would be accorded the reporting of other scientific experiments.

Hoaglin and Andrews (1975) outline the items that should be included in a report of a simulation study. In addition to a careful general description of the experiment, the report should include mention of the random number generator used, any variance-reducing methods employed, and a justification of the simulation sample size. The *Journal of the American Statistical Association* includes these reporting standards in its style guide for authors.

Closely related to the choice of the sample size is the standard deviation of the estimates that result from the study. The sample standard deviations actually achieved should be included as part of the report. Standard deviations are often reported in parentheses beside the estimates with which they are associated. A formal analysis, of course, would use the sample variance of each estimate to assess the significance of the differences observed between points in the design space; that is, a formal analysis of the simulation experiment would be a standard analysis of variance.

The most common method of reporting the results is by means of tables, but a better understanding of the results can often be conveyed by graphs.

A.3 An Example

One area of statistics in which Monte Carlo studies have been used extensively is robust statistics. This is because the finite sampling distributions of many robust statistics are very difficult to work out, especially for the kinds of underlying distributions for which the statistics are to be studied. A well-known use of Monte Carlo mehtod is in the important study of robust statistics described by Andrews et al. (1972), who introduced and examined many alternative estimators of location for samples from univariate distributions. This study, which involved many Monte Carlo experiments, employed innovative methods of variance reduction and was very influential in subsequent Monte Carlo studies reported in the statistical literature.

As an example of a Monte Carlo study, we will now describe a simple experiment to assess the robustness of a statistical test in linear regression analysis. The purpose of this example is to illustrate some of the issues in designing a Monte Carlo experiment. The results of this small study are not of interest here. There are many important issues about the robustness of the procedures that we do not address in this example.

The Problem

Consider the simple linear regression model

$$Y = \beta_0 + \beta_1 x + E$$

where a response or "dependent variable", Y, is modeled as a linear function of a single regressor or "independent variable", x, plus a random variable, E, called the "error". Because E is a random variable, Y is also a random variable.

The statistical problem is to make inferences about the unknown, constant parameters, β_0 and β_1, and about distributional parameters of the random variable, E. The inferences are made based on a sample of n pairs, (y_i, x_i), associated with unobservable realizations of the random error, ϵ_i, and assumed to have the relationship

$$y_i = \beta_0 + \beta_1 x_i + \epsilon_i. \tag{A.1}$$

We also generally assume that the realizations of the random error are independent and are unrelated to the value of x.

For this example, let us consider just the specific problem of testing the hypothesis

$$H_0: \beta_1 = 0 \tag{A.2}$$

versus the universal alternative. If the distribution of E is normal and we make the additional assumptions above about the sample, the optimal test for the hypothesis is based on a least squares procedure that yields the statistic

$$t = \frac{\widehat{\beta}_1 \sqrt{(n-2) \sum (x_i - \bar{x})^2}}{\sqrt{\sum r_i^2}}, \tag{A.3}$$

where $\bar{x}$ is the mean of the x's, $\widehat{\beta}_1$ together with $\widehat{\beta}_0$ minimizes the function

$$\begin{aligned} L_2(b_0, b_1) &= \sum_{i=1}^{n}(y_i - b_0 - b_1 x_i)^2 \\ &= \|r(b_0, b_1)\|_2^2, \end{aligned}$$

and

$$\begin{aligned} r_i &= r_i(\widehat{\beta}_0, \widehat{\beta}_1) \\ &= y_i - (\widehat{\beta}_0 + \widehat{\beta}_1 x_i) \end{aligned}$$

(in the notation of equation (11.26)).

If the null hypothesis is true, t is a realization of a Student's t distribution with $n - 2$ degrees of freedom. The test is performed by comparing the p-value from the Student's t distribution with a preassigned significance level, α, or by comparing the observed value of t with a critical value. The test of the hypothesis depends on the estimates of β_0 and β_1 used in the test statistic t.

Another method of fitting the linear regression line that is robust to outliers in E is to minimize the absolute values of the deviations. The least absolute values procedure chooses estimates of β_0 and β_1 to minimize the function

$$\begin{aligned} L_1(b_0, b_1) &= \sum_{i=1}^{n}|y_i - b_0 - b_1 x_i| \\ &= \|r(b_0, b_1)\|_1. \end{aligned}$$

A test statistic analogous to the one in equation (A.3), but based on the least absolute values fit, is

$$t_1 = \frac{2\tilde{\beta}_1 \sqrt{\sum (x_i - \bar{x})^2}}{(e_{(k_2)} - e_{(k_1)})\sqrt{n-2}}, \tag{A.4}$$

where $\tilde{\beta}_1$ together with $\tilde{\beta}_0$ minimizes the function

$$L_1(b_0, b_1) = \sum_{i=1}^{n} |y_i - b_0 - b_1 x_i|,$$

$e_{(k)}$ is the kth order statistic from

$$e_i = y_i - (\tilde{\beta}_0 + \tilde{\beta}_1 x_i),$$

k_1 is the integer closest to $(n-1)/2 - \sqrt{n-2}$, and k_2 is the integer closest to $(n-1)/2 + \sqrt{n-2}$. This statistic has an approximate Student's t distribution with $n-2$ degrees of freedom (see Birkes and Dodge, 1993, for example).

If the distribution of the random error is normal, inference based on minimizing the sum of the absolute values is not nearly as efficient as inference based on least squares. This alternative to least squares should therefore be used with some discretion. Furthermore, there are other procedures that may warrant consideration. It is not our purpose here to explore these important issues in robust statistics, however.

The Design of the Experiment

At this point, we should have a clear picture of the problem: we wish to compare two ways of testing the hypothesis (A.2) under various scenarios. The data may have outliers, and there may be observations with large leverage. We expect that the optimal test procedure will depend on the presence of outliers, or more generally, on the distribution of the random error, and on the pattern of the values of the independent variable. The possibilities of interest for the distribution of the random error include:

- the family of the distribution (that is, normal, double exponential, Cauchy, and so on);

- whether the distribution is a mixture of more than one basic distribution and, if so, the proportions in the mixture;

- the values of the parameters of the distribution; that is, the variance, the skewness, or any other parameters that may affect the power of the test.

In textbooks on the design of experiments, a simple objective of an experiment is to perform a t test or an F test of whether different levels of response are associated with different treatments. Our objective in the Monte Carlo experiment that we are designing is to investigate and characterize the dependence of the performance of the hypothesis test on these factors. The principles of design are similar to those of other experiments, however.

It is possible that the optimal test of the hypothesis will depend on the sample size or on the true values of the coefficients in the regression model, so some additional issues that are relevant to the performance of a statistical test of this hypothesis are the sample size and the true values of β_0 and β_1.

In the terminology of statistical models, the factors in our Monte Carlo experiment are the estimation method and the associated test, the distribution of the random error, the pattern of the independent variable, the sample size, and the true value of β_0 and β_1. The estimation method together with the associated test is the "treatment" of interest. The "effect" of interest (that is, the measured response) is the proportion of times that the null hypothesis is rejected using the two treatments.

We now can see our objective more clearly: for each setting of the distribution, pattern, and size factors, we wish to measure the power of the two tests. These factors are similar to blocking factors, except that there is likely to be an interaction between the treatment and these factors. Of course, the power depends on the nominal level of the test, α. It may be the case that the nominal level of the test affects the relative powers of the two tests.

We can think of the problem in the context of a binary response model,

$$\mathrm{E}(P_{ijklqsr}) = f(\tau_i, \delta_j, \phi_k, \nu_l, \alpha_q, \beta_{1s}), \tag{A.5}$$

where the parameters represent levels of the factors listed above (β_{1s} is the sth level of β_1), and $P_{ijklqsr}$ is a binary variable representing whether the test rejects the null hypothesis on the rth trial at the $(ijklqs)^{\mathrm{th}}$ setting of the design factors. It is useful to write down a model like this to remind ourselves of the issues in designing an experiment.

At this point, it is necessary to pay careful attention to our terminology. We are planning to use a statistical procedure (a Monte Carlo experiment) to evaluate a statistical procedure (a statistical test in a linear model). For the statistical procedure that we will use, we have written a model (A.5) for the observations that we will make. Those observations are indexed by r in that model. Let m be the sample size for each combination of factor settings. This is the Monte Carlo sample size. It is not to be confused with the data sample size, n, that is one of the factors in our study.

We now choose the levels of the factors in the Monte Carlo experiment.

- For the estimation method, we have decided on two methods: least squares and least absolute values. Its differential effect in the binary response model (A.5) is denoted by τ_i, for $i = 1, 2$.

- For the distribution of the random error, we choose three general ones:

  1. Normal $(0, 1)$;
  2. Normal $(0, 1)$ with $c\%$ outliers from normal $(0, d^2)$;

3. Standard Cauchy.

We choose different values of c and d as appropriate. For this example, let us choose $c = 5$ and 20 and $d = 2$ and 5. Thus, in the binary response model (A.5), $j = 1, 2, 3, 4, 5, 6$.

- For the pattern of the independent variable, we choose three different arrangements:

    1. Uniform over the range;

    2. A group of extreme outliers;

    3. Two groups of outliers.

    In the binary response model (A.5), $k = 1, 2, 3$. We use fixed values of the independent variable.

- For the sample size, we choose three values: 20, 200, and 2,000. In the binary response model (A.5), $l = 1, 2, 3$.

- For the nominal level of the test, we choose two values: 0.01 and 0.05. In the binary response model (A.5), $q = 1, 2$.

- The true value of β_0 probably is not relevant, so we just choose $\beta_0 = 1$. We are interested in the power of the tests at different values of β_1. We expect the power function to be symmetric about $\beta_1 = 0$ and to approach 1 as $|\beta_1|$ increases.

The estimation method is the "treatment" of interest.

Restating our objective in terms of the notation introduced above, for each of two tests, we wish to estimate the power curve,

$$\Pr(\text{reject } H_0) = g(\beta_1 \mid \tau_i, \delta_j, \phi_k, \nu_l, \alpha_q),$$

for any combination $(\tau_i, \delta_j, \phi_k, \nu_l, \alpha_q)$. The minimum of the power curve should occur at $\beta_1 = 0$, and should be α. The curve should approach 1 symmetrically as $|\beta_1|$.

To estimate the curve, we use a discrete set of points, and because of symmetry, all values chosen for β_1 can be nonnegative. The first question is at what point the curve flattens out just below 1. We might arbitrarily define the region of interest to be that in which the power is less than 0.99 approximately. The abscissa of this point is the maximum β_1 of interest. This point, say β_1^*, varies, depending on all of the factors in the study. We could work this out in the least squares case for uncontaminated normal errors using the noncentral Student's t distribution, but for all other cases, it is analytically intractable. Hence, we compute some preliminary Monte Carlo estimates to determine the maximum β_1 for each factor combination in the study.

To do a careful job of fitting a curve using a relatively small number of points, we would choose points where the second derivative is changing rapidly and especially near points of inflection where the second derivative changes sign. Because the problem of determining these points for each combination of (i, j, k, l, q) is not analytically tractable (otherwise we would not be doing the study!), we may conveniently choose a set of points equally spaced between 0 and β_1^*. Let us decide on five such points, for this example. It is not important that the β_1^*'s be chosen with a great deal of care. The objective is that we be able to calculate two power curves between 0 and β_1^* that are meaningful for comparisons.

The Experiment

The observational units in the experiment are the values of the test statistics (A.3) and (A.4). The measurements are the binary variables corresponding to rejection of the hypothesis (A.2). At each point in the factor space, there will be m such observations. If z is the number of rejections observed, the estimate of the power is z/m, and the variance of the estimator is $\pi(1 - \pi)/m$, where π is the true power at that point. (z is a realization of a binomial random variable with parameters m and π.) This leads us to a choice of the value of m. The coefficient of variation at any point is $\sqrt{(1 - \pi)/(m\pi)}$, which increases as π decreases. At $\pi = 0.50$, a 5% coefficient of variation can be achieved with a sample of size 400. This yields a standard deviation of 0.025. There may be some motivation to choose a slightly larger value for m because we can assume that the minimum of π will be approximately the minimum of α. To achieve a 5% coefficient of variation at that point (i.e., at $\beta_1 = 0$) would require a sample of size approximately 160,000. That would correspond to a standard deviation of 0.0005, which is probably much smaller than we need. A sample size of 400 would yield a standard deviation of 0.005. Although that is large in a relative sense, it may be adequate for our purposes. Because this particular point (where $\beta_1 = 0$) corresponds to the null hypothesis, however, we may choose a larger sample size, say 4,000, at that special point. A reasonable choice therefore is a Monte Carlo sample size of 4,000 at the null hypothesis and 400 at all other points. We will, however, conduct the experiment in such a way that we can combine the results of this experiment with independent results from a subsequent experiment.

The experiment is conducted by running a computer program. The main computation in the program is to determine the values of the test statistics and to compare them with their critical values to decide on the hypothesis. These computations need to be performed at each setting of the factors and for any given realization of the random sample.

We design a program that allows us to loop through the settings of the factors and, at each factor setting, to use a random sample. The result is a nest of loops. The program may be stopped and restarted, so we need to be able to control the seeds (see Section B.2, page 354).

Recalling that the purpose of our experiment is to obtain estimates, we may now consider any appropriate methods of reducing the variance of those estimates. There is not much opportunity to apply methods of variance reduction, but at least we might consider at what points to use common realizations of the pseudorandom variables. Because the things that we want to compare most directly are the powers of the tests, we perform the tests on the same pseudorandom datasets. Also, because we are interested in the shape of the power curves we may want to use the same pseudorandom datasets at each value of β_1—that is, to use the same set of errors in the model (A.1). Finally, following similar reasoning, we may use the same pseudorandom datasets at each value of the pattern of the independent variable. This implies that our program of nested loops has the structure shown in Figure A.1.

Initialize a table of counts.
   Fix the data sample size. (Loop over the sample sizes $n = 20$, $n = 200$, and $n = 2,000$.)

      Generate a set of residuals for the linear regression model (A.1). (This is the loop of m Monte Carlo replications.)

         Fix the pattern of the independent variable. (Loop over patterns P_1, P_2, and P_3.)

            Choose the distribution of the error term. (Loop over the distributions D_1, D_2, D_3, D_4, D_5, and D_6.)

               For each value of β_1, generate a set of observations (the y values) for the linear regression model (A.1), and perform the tests using both procedures and at both levels of significance. Record results.
            End distributions loop.
         End patterns loop.
      End Monte Carlo loop.
   End sample size loop.
Perform computations of summary statistics.

Figure A.1: Program Structure for the Monte Carlo Experiment

After writing a computer program with this structure, the first thing is to test the program on a small set of problems and to determine appropriate values of β_1^*. We should compare the results with known values at a few points. (As mentioned earlier, the only points that we can work out correspond to the normal case with the ordinary t statistic. One of these points, at $\beta_1 = 0$, is easily checked.) We can also check the internal consistency of the results. For example, does the power curve increase? We must be careful, of course, in applying such consistency checks because we do not know the behavior of the tests in most cases.

Reporting the Results

The report of this Monte Carlo study should address as completely as possible the results of interest. The relative values of the power are the main points of interest. The estimated power at $\beta_1 = 0$ is of interest. This is the actual significance level of the test, and how it compares to the nominal level α is of particular interest.

The presentation should be in a form easily assimilated by the reader. This may mean several graphs. Two graphs, for the two test procedures, should be shown on the same set of axes. It is probably counterproductive to show a graph for each factor setting. (There are 108 combinations of factor settings.)

In addition to the graphs, tables may allow presentation of a large amount of information in a compact format.

The Monte Carlo study should be described so carefully that the study could be replicated exactly. This means specifying the factor settings, the loop nesting, the software and computer used, the seed used, and the Monte Carlo sample size. There should also be at least a simple statement explaining the choice of the Monte Carlo sample size.

As mentioned earlier, the statistical literature is replete with reports of Monte Carlo studies. Some of these reports (and likely the studies themselves) are woefully deficient. An example of a careful Monte Carlo study and a good report of the study are given by Kleijnen (1977). He designed, performed, and reported a Monte Carlo study to investigate the robustness of a multiple-ranking procedure. In addition to reporting on the study of the question at hand, another purpose of the paper was to illustrate the methods of a Monte Carlo study.

A.4 Computer Experiments

In many scientific investigations, we envision a relationship expressed by a model

$$y \approx f(x).$$

The quantity of interest y, usually called a "response" (although it may not be a response to any of the other entities), may be the growth of a crystal, the growth of a tumor, the growth of corn, the price of a stock one month hence, or some other quantity. The other variables, x, called "factors", "regressors", or just "input variables", may be temperature, pressure, amount of a drug, amount of a type of fertilizer, interest rates, or some other quantity. Both y and x may be vectors. An objective is to determine a suitable form of f and the nature of the approximation. The simplest type of approximation is one in which an additive deviation can be identified with a random variable:

$$Y = f(x) + E.$$

The most important objective, whatever the nature of the approximation, usually is to determine values of x that are associated with optimal realizations of Y. The association may or may not be one of causation.

One of the major contributions of the science of statistics to the scientific method is the experimental methods that efficiently help to determine f, the nature of an unexplainable deviation E, and the values of x that yield optimal values of y. Design and analysis of experiments is a fairly mature subdiscipline of statistics.

In computer experiments, the function f is a computer program, x is the input, and y is the output. The program implements known or supposed relationships among the phenomena of interest. In cases of practical interest, the function is very complicated, the number of input variables may be in the hundreds, and the output may consist of many elements. The objective is to find a tractable function, $\widehat{f}$, that approximates the true behavior, at least over ranges of interest, and to find the values of the input, say $\widehat{x}_0$, such that $\widehat{f}(\widehat{x}_0)$ is optimal. How useful $\widehat{x}_0$ is depends on how close $\widehat{f}(\widehat{x}_0)$ is to $f(x_0)$, where x_0 yields the optimal value of f.

What makes this an unusual statistical problem is that the relationships are deterministic. The statistical approach to computer experiments introduces randomness into the problem. The estimate $\widehat{f}(\widehat{x}_0)$ can then be described in terms of probabilities or variances.

In a Bayesian approach, randomness is introduced by considering the function f to be a realization of a random function, F. The prior on F may be specified only at certain points, say $F(x_0)$. A set of input vectors $x_1, \ldots, x_n$ is chosen, and the output $y_i = f(x_i)$ is used to estimate a posterior distribution for $F(x)$, or at least for $F(x_0)$. The Bayesian approach generally involves extensive computations for the posterior densities. In a frequentist approach, randomness is introduced by taking random values of the input, $x_1, \ldots, x_n$. This randomness in the input yields randomness in the output $y_i = f(x_i)$, which is used to obtain the estimates $\widehat{x}_0$ and $\widehat{f}(\widehat{x}_0)$ and estimates of the variances of the estimators. See Koehler and Owen (1996) for further discussion.

Latin Hypercube Sampling

Principles for the design of experiments provide a powerful set of tools for reducing the variance in cases where several factors are to be investigated simultaneously. Such techniques as balanced or partially balanced fractional factorial designs allow the study of a large number of factors while keeping the total experiment size manageably small. Some processes are so complex that even with efficient statistical designs, experiments to study the process would involve a prohibitively large number of factors and levels. For some processes, it may not be possible to apply the treatments whose effects are to be studied, and data are available only from observational studies. The various processes determining weather are examples of phenomena that are not amenable to traditional experimental study. Such processes can often be modeled and studied by computer experiments.

There are some special concerns in experimentation using the computer (see Sacks et al., 1989), but the issues of statistical efficiency remain. Rather than a model involving ordinary experimental units, a computer experimental model receives a fixed input and produces a deterministic output. An objective in computer experimentation (just as in any experimentation) is to provide a set of inputs that effectively (or randomly) span a space of interest. McKay, Conover, and Beckman (1979) introduce a technique called Latin hypercube sampling (as a generalization of the ideas of a Latin square design) for providing input to a computer experiment.

If each of k factors in an experiment is associated with a random input that is initially a $U(0,1)$ variate, a sample of size n that efficiently covers the factor space can be formed by selecting the ith realization of the jth factor as

$$v_j = \frac{\pi_j(i) - 1 + u_j}{n},$$

where

- $\pi_1(\cdot), \pi_2(\cdot), \ldots, \pi_k(\cdot)$ are permutations of the integers $1, \ldots, n$, sampled randomly, independently, and with replacement from the set of $n!$ possible permutations; and $\pi_j(i)$ is the ith element of the jth permutation.

- The u_j are sampled independently from $U(0,1)$.

It is easy to see that v_j are independent $U(0,1)$. We can see heuristically that such numbers tend to be "spread out" over the space. Use of Latin hypercube sampling is particularly useful in higher dimensions. See Owen (1998) for examples and further discussion.

Exercises

A.1. Write a computer program to implement the Monte Carlo experiment described in Section A.3. The S-Plus functions `lsfit` and `l1fit` or the IMSL Fortran subroutines `rline` and `rlav` can be used to calculate the fits. See Appendix B for discussions of other software you may use in the program.

A.2. Choose a recent issue of the *Journal of the American Statistical Association* and identify five articles that report on Monte Carlo studies of statistical methods. In each case, describe the Monte Carlo experiment.

   (a) What are the factors in the experiment?

   (b) What is the measured response?

   (c) What is the design space—that is, the set of factor settings?

   (d) What random number generators were used?

   (e) Critique the report in each article. Did the author(s) justify the sample size? Did the author(s) report variances or confidence intervals? Did the author(s) attempt to reduce the experimental variance?

A.3. Select an article you identified in Exercise A.2 that concerns a statistical method that you understand and that interests you. Choose a design space that is not a subspace of that used in the article but that has a nonnull intersection with it, and perform a similar experiment. Compare your results with those reported in the article.

Appendix B

Software for Random Number Generation

Random number generators are widely available in a variety of software packages. As Park and Miller (1988) state, however, "good ones are hard to find".

Basic Uniform Generators

Some programming languages, such as C, Fortran 90, and Ada 95, provide built-in random number generators. In C, the generator is the function `rand()` in `stdlib.h`. This function returns an integer in the range 0 through `RAND_MAX`, so the result must be normalized to the range $(0, 1)$. (The scaling should be done with care. It is desirable to have uniform numbers in $(0, 1)$ rather than $[0, 1]$.) The seed for the C random number generator is set in `srand()`.

In Fortran 90, the generator is the subroutine `random_number`, which returns $U(0, 1)$ numbers. (The user must be careful, however; the generator may yield either a 0 or a 1.) The seed can be set in the subroutine `random_seed`. The design of the Fortran 90 module as a subroutine yields a major advantage over the C function in terms of efficiency. (Of course, because Fortran 90 has the basic advantage of arrays, the module could have been designed as an array function and would still have had an advantage over the C function.)

A basic problem with the built-in generator of C, Fortran 90, and Ada 95 is lack of portability. The standards do not specify the algorithm. The bindings are portable, but none of these generators will necessarily generate the same sequence on different platforms.

Other Distributions

Given a uniform random number generator, it is usually not too difficult to generate variates from other distributions. For example, in Fortran 90, the inverse

CDF technique for generating a random deviate from a Bernoulli distribution with parameter π can be implemented by the code in Figure B.1.

```fortran
integer, parameter      :: n  = 100  ! INITIALIZE THIS
real, parameter (pi)    :: pi = .5   ! INITIALIZE THIS
real, dimension (n)     :: uniform
real, dimension (n)     :: bernoulli
call random_number (uniform)
where (uniform .le. pi)
      bernoulli = 1.0
elsewhere
      bernoulli = 0.0
endwhere
```

Figure B.1: A Fortran 90 Code Fragment to Generate n Bernoulli Random Deviates with Parameter π

Implementing one of the simple methods to convert a uniform deviate to that of another distribution may not be as efficient as a special method for the target distribution, and those special methods may be somewhat complicated. The IMSL Libraries and S-Plus and R have a number of modules that use efficient methods to generate variates from several of the more common distributions. Matlab has a basic uniform generator, **rand**, and a standard normal generator, **randn**. The Matlab Statistics Toolbox also contains generators for several other distributions.

A number of Fortran or C programs are available in collections published by *Applied Statistics* and by *ACM Transactions on Mathematical Software*. These collections are available online at **statlib** and **netlib**, respectively. See page 388 in the bibliography for more information.

The freely distributed GNU Scientific Library (GSL) contains several C functions for random number generation. There are several different basic uniform generators in the library. Utility functions in the library allow selection of a uniform generator for use by the functions that generate nonuniform numbers. In addition to a number of newer uniform generators, there are basic uniform generators that yield output sequences that correspond (or almost correspond) to legacy generators provided by various systems developers, such as the IBM **RANDU** and generators associated with various Unix distributions. Information about the GNU Scientific Library, including links to sites from which source code can be obtained, is available at

http://sources.redhat.com/gsl/

The Guide to Available Mathematical Software, or GAMS (see the Bibliography) can be used to locate special software for various distributions.

Choice of Software for Monte Carlo Studies

Monte Carlo studies typically require many repetitive computations, which are usually implemented through looping program-control structures. Some higher-level languages do not provide efficient looping structures. For this reason, it is usually desirable to conduct moderate- to large-scale Monte Carlo studies using a lower-level language such as C or Fortran. Some higher-level languages provide the capability to produce compiled code, which will execute faster. If Monte Carlo studies are to be conducted using an interpretive language, and if the production of compiled code is an option, that option should be chosen for the Monte Carlo work.

B.1 The User Interface for Random Number Generators

Software for random number generation must provide a certain amount of control by the user, including the ability to:

- set or retrieve the seed;
- select seeds that yield separate streams;
- possibly select the method from a limited number of choices.

Whenever the user invokes a random number generator for the first time in a program or session, the software should not require the specification of a seed but should allow the user to set it if desired. If the user does not specify the seed, the software should use some mechanism, such as accessing the system clock, to form a "random" seed. On a subsequent invocation of the random number generator, unless the user specifies a seed, the software should use the last value of the seed from the previous invocation. This means that the routine for generating random numbers must produce a "side effect"; that is, it changes something other than the main result. It is a basic tenet of software engineering that side effects must be carefully noted. At one time, side effects were generally to be avoided. In object-oriented programming, however, objects may encapsulate many entities, and as the object is acted upon, any of the components may change. Therefore, in object-oriented software, side effects are to be expected. In object-oriented software for random number generation, the state of the generator is an object.

Another issue to consider in the design of a user interface for a random number generator is whether the output is a single value (and an updated seed) or an array of values. Although a function that produces a single value as the C function **rand()** is convenient to use, it can carry quite a penalty in execution time because of the multiple invocations required to generate an array of random numbers. It is generally better to provide both single- and multivalued procedures for random number generation, especially for the basic uniform generator.

B.2   Controlling the Seeds in Monte Carlo Studies

There are three reasons why the user must be able to control the seeds in Monte Carlo studies: for testing of the program, for use of blocks in Monte Carlo experiments, and for combining results of Monte Carlo studies.

In the early phases of programming for a Monte Carlo study, it is very important to be able to test the output of the program. To do this, it is necessary to use the same seed from one run of the program to another.

Controlling seeds in a parallel random number generator is much more complicated than in a serial generator. Performing Monte Carlo computations in parallel requires some way of ensuring the independence of the parallel streams.

B.3   Random Number Generation in IMSL Libraries

For doing Monte Carlo studies, it is usually better to use a software system with a compilable programming language, such as Fortran or C. Not only do such systems provide more flexibility and control, but the programs built in the compiler languages execute faster. To do much work in such a system, however, a library or routines both to perform the numerical computations in the inner loop of the Monte Carlo study and to generate the random numbers driving the study are needed.

The IMSL Libraries contain a large number of routines for random number generation. The libraries are available in both Fortran and C, each providing the same capabilities and with essentially the same interface within the two languages. In Fortran the basic uniform generator is provided in both function and subroutine forms.

The uniform generator allows the user to choose among seven different algorithms: a linear congruential generator with modulus of $2^{31} - 1$ and with three choices of multiplier, each with or without shuffling, and the generalized feedback shift generator described by Fushimi (1990), which has a period of $2^{521} - 1$. The multipliers that the user can choose are the "minimal standard" one of Park and Miller (1988), which goes back to Lewis, Goodman, and Miller (1969) and two of the "best" multipliers found by Fishman and Moore (1982, 1986).

The user chooses which of the basic uniform generators to use by means of the Fortran routine **rnopt** or the C function **imsls_random_option**. For whatever choice is in effect, that form of the uniform generator will be used for whatever type of pseudorandom events are to be generated. The states of the generators are maintained in a **common** block (for the simple congruential generators, the state is a single seed; for the shuffled generators and the GFSR generator, the state is maintained in a table). There are utility routines for setting and saving states of the generators and a utility routine for obtaining a seed to skip ahead a fixed amount.

There are routines to generate deviates from most of the common distributions. Most of the routines are subroutines but some are functions. The algorithms used often depend on the values of the parameters to achieve greater efficiency. The routines are available in both single and double precision. (Double precision is more for the purpose of convenience for the user than it is for increasing accuracy of the algorithm.)

A single-precision IMSL Fortran subroutine for generating from a specific distribution has the form

rnname (number, parameter_1, parameter_2, ..., output_array)

where "*name*" is an identifier for the distribution, "*number*" is the number of random deviates to be generated, "*parameter_i*" are parameters of the distribution, and "*output_array*" is the output argument with the generated deviates. The Fortran subroutines generate variates from standard distributions, so location and scale parameters are not included in the argument list. The subroutine and formal arguments to generate gamma random deviates, for example, are

rngam (nr, a, r)

where a is the shape parameter (α) of the gamma distribution. The other parameter in the common two-parameter gamma distribution (usually called β) is a scale parameter. The deviates produced by the routine rngam have a scale parameter of 1; hence, for a scale parameter of b, the user would follow the call above with a call to a BLAS routine:

sscal (nr, b, r, 1)

Identifiers of distributions include those shown in Table B.1.

For general distributions, the IMSL Libraries provide routines for an alias method and for table lookup, for either discrete or continuous distributions. The user specifies a discrete distribution by providing a vector of the probabilities at the mass points and specifies a continuous distribution by giving the values of the cumulative distribution function at a chosen set of points. In the case of a discrete distribution, the generation can be done either by an alias method or by an efficient table lookup method. For a continuous distribution, a cubic spline is first fit to the given values of the cumulative distribution function, and then an inverse CDF method is used to generate the random numbers from the target distribution. Another routine uses the Thompson-Taylor data-based scheme (Taylor and Thompson, 1986) to generate deviates from an unknown population from which only a sample is available.

Other routines in the IMSL Libraries generate various kinds of time series, random permutations, and random samples. The routine rnuno, which generates order statistics from a uniform distribution, can be used to generate order statistics from other distributions.

All of the IMSL routines for random number generation are available in both Fortran and C. The C functions have more descriptive names, such as

Table B.1: Root Names for IMSL Random Number Generators

Continuous Distributions		Discrete Distributions	
un or unf	uniform	bin	binomial
nor, noa, or nof	normal	nbn	negative binomial
mvn	multivariate normal	poi	Poisson
chi	chi-squared	geo	geometric
stt	Student's t	hyp	hypergeometric
tri	triangular	lgr	logarithmic
lnl	lognormal	und	discrete uniform
exp	exponential	mtn	multinomial
gam	gamma	tab	two-way tables
wib	Weibull		
chy	Cauchy		
beta	beta		
vms	von Mises		
stab	stable		
ext	exponential mixture		
cor	correlation matrices		
sph	points on a circle or sphere		
nos	order statistics from a normal		
uno	order statistics from a uniform		
arm	ARMA process		
npp	nonhomogeneous Poisson process		

random_normal. Also, the C functions may allow specification of additional arguments, such as location and scale parameters. For example, random_normal has optional arguments IMSLS_MEAN and IMSLS_VARIANCE.

Controlling the State of the Generators

Figure B.2 illustrates the way to save the state of an IMSL generator and then restart it. The functions to save and to set the seed are rnget and rnset.

```
  call rnget (iseed)      ! save it
  call rnun (nr, y)       ! get sample, analyze, etc.
...
  call rnset (iseed)      ! restore seed
  call rnun (nr, yagain)  ! will be the same as y
```

Figure B.2: Fortran Code Fragment to Save and Restart a Random Sequence Using the IMSL Library

In a library of numerical routines such as the IMSL Libraries, it is likely that some of the routines will use random numbers in regular deterministic computations, such as an optimization routine generating random starting points. In a well-designed system, before a routine in the system uses a random number generator in the system, it will retrieve the current value of the seed if one has been set, use the generator, and then reset the seed to the former value. IMSL subprograms are designed this way. This allows the user to control the seeds in the routines called directly.

B.4 Random Number Generation in S-Plus and R

The software system called S was developed at Bell Laboratories in the mid-1970s. Work on S has continued at Bell Labs, and the system has evolved considerably since the early versions (see Becker, Chambers, and Wilks, 1988, and Chambers, 1997). S is both a data-analysis system and an object-oriented programming language.

S-Plus is an enhancement of S, developed by StatSci, Inc. (now a part of Insightful Corporation). The enhancements include graphical interfaces, more statistical analysis functionality, and support.

There is a freely available package, called R, that provides generally the same functionality in the same language as S (see Gentleman and Ihaka, 1997).

S-Plus and R do not use the same random number generators. *Monte Carlo studies conducted using one system cannot reliably be reproduced exactly in the other system.*

Random number generators in S-Plus are all based upon a single uniform random number generator that is a combination of a linear congruential generator and a Tausworthe generator. The original generator, called "Super-Duper", was developed by George Marsaglia in the 1970s. It is described in Learmonth and Lewis (1973). McCullough (1999) reports results of the DIEHARD tests on the S-Plus generator. The tests raise some questions about the quality of the generator.

Several choices for the basic uniform generator are available in R. The function RNGkind can be used to choose the generator. One of the choices is Super-Duper, but the implementation is slightly different from the implementation in S-Plus. The user can also specify a user-defined and programmed generator. The chosen (or default) basic uniform generator is used in the generation of nonuniform variates.

In S-Plus and R, there are some basic functions with the form

r*name* (*number* [, *parameters*])

where "*name*" is an identifier for the distribution, "*number*" is the number of random deviates to be generated, which can be specified by an array argument, in which case the number is the number of elements in the array, and "*parameters*" are parameters of the distribution, which may or may not be required.

For distributions with standard forms, such as the normal, the parameters may be optional, in which case they take on default values if they are not specified. For other distributions, such as the gamma or the t, there are required parameters. Optional parameters are both positional and keyword.

For example, the normal variate generation function is

```
rnorm (n, mean=0, sd=1)
```

so

rnorm (n)	yields n normal (0,1) variates
rnorm (n, 100, 10)	yields n normal (100,100) variates
rnorm (n, 100)	yields n normal (100,1) variates
rnorm (n, sd=10)	yields n normal (0,100) variates

(Note that S-Plus and R consider one of the natural parameters of the normal distribution to be the standard deviation or the scale rather than the variance, as is more common.)

For the gamma distribution, at least one parameter (the shape parameter) is required. The function reference

```
rgamma (100,5)
```

generates 100 random numbers from a gamma distribution with a shape parameter of 5 and a scale parameter of 1 (a standard gamma distribution).

Identifiers of distributions include those shown in Table B.2.

Table B.2: Root Names for S-Plus and R Functions for Distributions

Continuous Distributions		Discrete Distributions	
unif	uniform	binom	binomial
norm	normal	nbinom	negative binomial
mvnorm	multivariate normal	pois	Poisson
chisq	chi-squared	geom	geometric
t	t	hyper	hypergeometric
f	F	wilcox	Wilcoxon rank sum statistic
lnorm	lognormal		
exp	exponential		
gamma	gamma		
weibull	Weibull		
cauchy	Cauchy		
beta	beta		
logis	logistic		
stab	stable		

The function **sample** generates a random sample with or without replacement. Sampling with replacement is equivalent to generating random numbers from a (finite) discrete distribution. The mass points and probabilities can be specified in optional arguments:

```
xx <- sample(massp, n, replace=T, probs)
```

Order statistics in S-Plus and R can be generated using the beta distribution and the inverse distribution function. For example, 10 maximum order statistics from normal samples of size 30 can be generated by

```
x <- qnorm(rbeta(10,30,1))
```

Controlling the State of the Generators

Both S-Plus and R use an object called .Random.seed to maintain the state of the random number generators. In R, .Random.seed also maintains an indicator of which of the basic uniform random number generators is the current choice. Anytime random number generation is performed, if .Random.seed does not exist in the user's working directory, it is created. If it exists, it is used to initiate the pseudorandom sequence and then is updated after the sequence is generated. Setting a different working directory will change the state of the random number generator.

The function set.seed(i) provides a convenient way of setting the value of the .Random.seed object in the working directory to one of a fixed number of values. The argument i is an integer between 0 and 1023, and each value represents a state of the generator, which is "far away" from the other states that can be set in set.seed.

To save the state of the generator, just copy .Random.seed into a named object, and to restore, just copy the named object back into .Random.seed, as in Figure B.3.

```
oldseed <- .Random.seed   # save it
y <- rnunif(1000)         # get sample, analyze, etc.
...
.Random.seed <- oldseed   # restore seed
yagain <- rnorm(1000)     # will be the same as y
```

Figure B.3: Code Fragment to Save and Restart a Random Sequence Using S-Plus or R

A common situation is one in which computations for a Monte Carlo study are performed intermittently and are interspersed with other computations, perhaps broken over multiple sessions. In such a case, we may begin by setting the seed using the function set.seed(i), save the state after each set of computations in the study, and then restore it prior to resuming the computations, similar to the code shown in Figure B.4.

The built-in functions in S-Plus that use the random number generators have the side effect of changing the state of the generators, so the user must be

```
set.seed(10)              # set seed at beginning of study
... # perform some computations for the Monte Carlo study
MC1seed <- .Random.seed  # save the generator state
... # do other computations
.Random.seed <- MC1seed  # restore seed
... # perform some computations for the Monte Carlo study
MC1seed <- .Random.seed  # save the generator state
```

Figure B.4: Starting and Restarting Monte Carlo Studies in S-Plus or R

careful in Monte Carlo studies where the computational nuclei, such as `ltsreg` for robust regression, for example, invoke an S-Plus random number generator. In this case, the user must retrieve the state of the generator prior to calling the function and then reset the state prior to the next invocation of a random number generator.

To avoid the side effect of changing the state of the generator, when writing a function in S-Plus or R, the user can preserve the state upon entry to the function and restore it prior to exit. The assignment

```
.Random.seed <- oldseed
```

in Figure B.3, however, does not work if it occurs within a user-written function in S-Plus or R. Within a function, the assignment must be performed by the `<<-` operator. A well-designed S-Plus or R function that invokes a random number generator would have code similar to that in Figure B.5.

```
oldseed <- .Random.seed   # save seed on entry
...
.Random.seed <<- oldseed  # restore seed on exit
return(...)
```

Figure B.5: Saving and Restoring the State of the Generator within an S-Plus or R Function

Monte Carlo in S-Plus and R

Explicit loops in S-Plus or R execute slowly. (Loops in R generally seem to execute much faster than those in S-Plus.) In either package, it is best to use array arguments for functions rather than to loop over scalar values of the arguments. Consider, for example, the problem of evaluating the integral

$$\int_0^2 \log(x+1)x^2(2-x)^3 \, dx.$$

This could be estimated in a loop as follows:

```
# First, initialize n.
uu <- runif(n, 0, 2)
eu <- 0
for (i in 1:n) eu <- eu + log(uu[i]+1)*uu[i]^2*(2-uu[i])^3
eu <- 2*eu/n
```

A much more efficient way, without the `for` loop, but still using the uniform, is

```
uu <- runif(n, 0, 2)
eu <- 2*sum(log(uu+1)*uu^2*(2-uu)^3)/n
```

Alternatively, using the beta density as a weight function, we have

```
eb <- (16/15)*sum(log(2*rbeta(n,3,4)+1))/n
```

(Of course, if we recognize the relationship of the integral to the beta distribution, we would not use the Monte Carlo method for integration.)

For large-scale Monte Carlo studies, an interpretive language such as S-Plus or R may require an inordinate amount of running time. These systems are very useful for prototyping Monte Carlo studies, but it is often better to do the actual computations in a compiled language such as Fortran or C.

Appendix C

Notation and Definitions

All notation used in this work is "standard". I have opted for simple notation, which, of course, results in a one-to-many map of notation to object classes. Within a given context, however, the overloaded notation is generally unambiguous. I have endeavored to use notation consistently.

This appendix is not intended to be a comprehensive listing of definitions. The Subject Index, beginning on page 415, is a more reliable set of pointers to definitions, except for symbols that are not words.

General Notation

Uppercase italic Latin and Greek letters, A, B, E, Λ, and so on are generally used to represent either matrices or random variables. Random variables are usually denoted by letters nearer the end of the Latin alphabet, X, Y, Z, and by the Greek letter E. Parameters in models (that is, unobservables in the models), whether or not they are considered to be random variables, are generally represented by lowercase Greek letters. Uppercase Latin and Greek letters, especially P, in general, and Φ, for the normal distribution, are also used to represent cumulative distribution functions. Also, uppercase Latin letters are used to denote sets.

Lowercase Latin and Greek letters are used to represent ordinary scalar or vector variables and functions. **No distinction in the notation is made between scalars and vectors**; thus, β may represent a vector and β_i may represent the ith element of the vector β. In another context, however, β may represent a scalar. All vectors are considered to be column vectors, although we may write a vector as $x = (x_1, x_2, \ldots, x_n)$. Transposition of a vector or a matrix is denoted by a superscript ^{T}.

Uppercase calligraphic Latin letters, $\mathcal{F}$, $\mathcal{V}$, $\mathcal{W}$, and so on, are generally used to represent either vector spaces or transforms.

Subscripts generally represent indexes to a larger structure, for example, x_{ij} may represent the $(i, j)^{\text{th}}$ element of a matrix, X. A subscript in parentheses represents an order statistic. A superscript in parentheses represents an iteration, for example, $x_i^{(k)}$ may represent the value of x_i at the kth step of an iterative process.

x_i The ith element of a structure (including a sample, which is a multiset).

$x_{(i)}$ The ith order statistic.

$x^{(i)}$ The value of x at the ith iteration.

Realizations of random variables and placeholders in functions associated with random variables are usually represented by lowercase letters corresponding to the uppercase letters; thus, ϵ may represent a realization of the random variable E.

A single symbol in an italic font is used to represent a single variable. A Roman font or a special font is often used to represent a standard operator or a standard mathematical structure. Sometimes, a string of symbols in a Roman font is used to represent an operator (or a standard function); for example, exp represents the exponential function, but a string of symbols in an italic font on the same baseline should be interpreted as representing a composition (probably by multiplication) of separate objects; for example, exp represents the product of e, x, and p.

A fixed-width font is used to represent computer input or output; for example,

```
a = bx + sin(c).
```

In computer text, a string of letters or numerals with no intervening spaces or other characters, such as `bx` above, represents a single object, and there is no distinction in the font to indicate the type of object.

Some important mathematical structures and other objects are:

$\mathbb{R}$ The field of reals, or the set over which that field is defined.

$\mathbb{R}^d$ The usual d-dimensional vector space over the reals, or the set of all d-tuples with elements in $\mathbb{R}$.

$\mathbb{R}_+^d$ The usual d-dimensional vector space over the reals, or the set of all d-tuples with positive real elements.

$\mathbb{C}$ The field of complex numbers, or the set over which that field is defined.

Z   The ring of integers, or the set over which that ring is defined.

$\mathbb{G}(n)$ A Galois field defined on a set with n elements.

$C^0, C^1, C^2, \ldots$ The set of continuous functions, the set of functions with continuous first derivatives, and so forth.

i   The imaginary unit, $\sqrt{-1}$.

Notation Relating to Random Variables

A common function used with continuous random variables is a *density function*, and a common function used with discrete random variables is a *probability function*. The more fundamental function for either type of random variable is the *cumulative distribution function*, or CDF. The CDF of a random variable X, denoted by $P_X(x)$ or just by $P(x)$, is defined by

$$P(x) = \Pr(X \le x),$$

where "Pr", or "probability", can be taken here as a primitive (it is defined in terms of a measure). For vectors (of the same length), "$X \le x$" means that each element of X is less than or equal to the corresponding element of x. Both the CDF and the density or probability function for a d-dimensional random variable are defined over $\mathbb{R}^d$. (It is unfortunately necessary to state that "$P(x)$" means the "function P evaluated at x", and likewise "$P(y)$" means the *same* "function P evaluated at y", unless P has been redefined. Using a different expression as the argument *does not redefine* the function, despite the sloppy convention adopted by some statisticians.)

The density for a continuous random variable is just the derivative of the CDF (if it exists). The CDF is therefore the integral. To keep the notation simple, we likewise consider the probability function for a discrete random variable to be a type of derivative (a Radon-Nikodym derivative) of the CDF. Instead of expressing the CDF of a discrete random variable as a sum over a countable set, we often also express it as an integral. (In this case, however, the integral is over a set whose ordinary Lebesgue measure is 0.)

A useful analog of the CDF for a random sample is the *empirical cumulative distribution function*, or ECDF. For a sample of size n, the ECDF is

$$P_n(x) = \frac{1}{n} \sum_{i=1}^{n} I_{(-\infty, x]}(x_i)$$

for the indicator function $I_{(-\infty, x]}(\cdot)$.

Functions and operators such as Cov and E that are commonly associated with Latin letters or groups of Latin letters are generally represented by that letter in a Roman font.

$\Pr(A)$ The probability of the event A.

$p_X(\cdot)$
or $P_X(\cdot)$ The probability density function (or probability function), or the cumulative probability function, of the random variable X.

$p_{XY}(\cdot)$
or $P_{XY}(\cdot)$ The joint probability density function (or probability function), or the joint cumulative probability function, of the random variables X and Y.

$p_{X|Y}(\cdot)$
or $P_{X|Y}(\cdot)$ The conditional probability density function (or probability function), or the conditional cumulative probability function, of the random variable X given the random variable Y (these functions are random variables).

$p_{X|y}(\cdot)$
or $P_{X|y}(\cdot)$ The conditional probability density function (or probability function), or the conditional cumulative probability function, of the random variable X given the realization y.

  Sometimes, the notation above is replaced by a similar notation in which the arguments indicate the nature of the distribution; for example, $p(x, y)$ or $p(x|y)$.

$p_\theta(\cdot)$
or $P_\theta(\cdot)$ The probability density function (or probability function), or the cumulative probability function, of the distribution characterized by the parameter θ.

$Y \sim D_X(\theta)$ The random variable Y is distributed as $D_X(\theta)$, where X is the name of a random variable associated with the distribution, and θ is a parameter of the distribution. The subscript may take forms similar to those used in the density and distribution functions, such as $X|y$, or it may be omitted. Alternatively, in place of D_X, a symbol denoting a specific distribution may be used. An example is $Z \sim N(0, 1)$, which means that Z has a normal distribution with mean 0 and variance 1.

CDF   A cumulative distribution function.

ECDF   An empirical cumulative distribution function.

i.i.d.   Independent and identically distributed.

$X^{(i)} \xrightarrow{d} X$ or $X_i \xrightarrow{d} X$	The sequence of random variables $X^{(i)}$ or X_i converges in distribution to the random variable X. (The difference in the notation $X^{(i)}$ and X_i is generally unimportant. The former notation is often used to emphasize the iterative nature of a process.)
$\mathrm{E}(g(X))$	The expected value of the function g of the random variable X. The notation $\mathrm{E}_P(\cdot)$, where P is a cumulative distribution function or some other identifier of a probability distribution, is sometimes used to indicate explicitly the distribution with respect to which the expectation is evaluated.
$\mathrm{V}(g(X))$	The variance of the function g of the random variable X. The notation $\mathrm{V}_P(\cdot)$ is also often used.
$\mathrm{Cov}(X, Y)$	The covariance of the random variables X and Y. The notation $\mathrm{Cov}_P(\cdot, \cdot)$ is also often used.
$\mathrm{Cov}(X)$	The variance-covariance matrix of the vector random variable X.
$\mathrm{Corr}(X, Y)$	The correlation of the random variables X and Y. The notation $\mathrm{Corr}_P(\cdot, \cdot)$ is also often used.
$\mathrm{Corr}(X)$	The correlation matrix of the vector random variable X.
$\mathrm{Bias}(T, \theta)$ or $\mathrm{Bias}(T)$	The bias of the estimator T (as an estimator of θ); that is, $$\mathrm{Bias}(T, \theta) = \mathrm{E}(T) - \theta.$$
$\mathrm{MSE}(T, \theta)$ or $\mathrm{MSE}(T)$	The mean squared error of the estimator T (as an estimator of θ); that is, $$\mathrm{MSE}(T, \theta) = \big(\mathrm{Bias}(T, \theta)\big)^2 + \mathrm{V}(T).$$
$\mathrm{J}(T)$	The Jackknife estimator corresponding to the statistic T.

General Mathematical Functions and Operators

Functions such as sin, max, span, and so on that are commonly associated with groups of Latin letters are generally represented by those letters in a Roman font.

Generally, the argument of a function is enclosed in parentheses (for example, $\sin(x)$), but often, for the very common functions, the parentheses are omitted: $\sin x$. In expressions involving functions, parentheses are generally used for clarity, for example, $(E(X))^2$ instead of $E^2(X)$.

Operators such as d (the differential operator) that are commonly associated with a Latin letter are generally represented by that letter in a Roman font.

$|x|$ The modulus of the real or complex number x; if x is real, $|x|$ is the absolute value of x.

$\lceil x \rceil$ The ceiling function evaluated at the real number x: $\lceil x \rceil$ is the smallest integer greater than or equal to x.

$\lfloor x \rfloor$ The floor function evaluated at the real number x: $\lfloor x \rfloor$ is the largest integer less than or equal to x.

$\#S$ The cardinality of the set S.

$I_S(\cdot)$ The indicator function:

$$
\begin{aligned}
I_S(x) &= 1, \text{ if } x \in S, \\
&= 0, \text{ otherwise.}
\end{aligned}
$$

If x is a scalar, the set S is often taken as the interval $(-\infty, y]$, and in this case, the indicator function is the Heaviside function, H, evaluated at the difference of the argument and the upper bound on the interval:

$$I_{(-\infty,y]}(x) = H(y - x).$$

(An alternative definition of the Heaviside function is the same as this except that $H(0) = \frac{1}{2}$.) In higher dimensions, the set S is often taken as the product set,

$$
\begin{aligned}
A^d &= (-\infty, y_1] \times (-\infty, y_2] \times \cdots \times (-\infty, y_d] \\
&= A_1 \times A_2 \times \cdots \times A_d,
\end{aligned}
$$

and in this case,

$$I_{A^d}(x) = I_{A_1}(x_1) I_{A_2}(x_2) \cdots I_{A_d}(x_d),$$

where $x = (x_1, x_2, \ldots, x_d)$. The derivative of the indicator function is the Dirac delta function, $\delta(\cdot)$.

$\delta(\cdot)$

The Dirac delta "function", defined by

$$\delta(x) = 0, \quad \text{for } x \neq 0,$$
$$\int_{-\infty}^{\infty} \delta(t)\, dt = 1.$$

The Dirac delta function is not a function in the usual sense. We do, however, refer to it as a function. For any continuous function f, we have the useful fact

$$\int_{-\infty}^{\infty} f(y)\, dI_{(-\infty, y]}(x) = \int_{-\infty}^{\infty} f(y)\, \delta(y - x)\, dy$$
$$= f(x).$$

$\min f(\cdot)$ or $\min(S)$

The minimum value of the real scalar-valued function f, or the smallest element in the countable set of real numbers S.

$\operatorname{argmin} f(\cdot)$

The value of the argument of the real scalar-valued function f that yields its minimum value.

$O(f(n))$

Big O; $g(n) = O(f(n))$ means that there exists a positive constant M such that $|g(n)| \leq M|f(n)|$ as $n \to \infty$. $g(n) = O(1)$ means that $g(n)$ is bounded from above.

$o(f(n))$

Little o; $g(n) = o(f(n))$ means that $g(n)/f(n) \to 0$ as $n \to \infty$. $g(n) = o(1)$ means that $g(n) \to 0$ as $n \to \infty$.

$o_P(f(n))$

Convergent in probability; $X(n) = o_P(f(n))$ means that, for any positive ϵ, $\Pr(|X(n) - f(n)| > \epsilon) \to 0$ as $n \to \infty$.

d

The differential operator. The derivative with respect to the variable x is denoted by $\frac{d}{dx}$.

$f', f'', \ldots, f^{k'}$

For the scalar-valued function f of a scalar variable, differentiation (with respect to an implied variable) taken on the function once, twice, $\ldots$, k times.

f^T

For the vector-valued function f, the transpose of f (a row vector).

∇f

For the scalar-valued function f of a vector variable, the gradient (that is, the vector of partial derivatives), also often denoted as g_f or D_f.

∇f

For the vector-valued function f of a vector variable, the transpose of the Jacobian, which is often denoted as J_f, so $\nabla f = J_f^T$ (see below).

J_f For the vector-valued function f of a vector variable, the transpose of the Jacobian. The element in position (i, j) is

$$\frac{\partial f_i(x)}{\partial x_j}.$$

H_f For the scalar-valued function f of a vector variable, the Hessian.
or $\nabla\nabla f$ The Hessian is the transpose of the Jacobian of the gradient.
or $\nabla^2 f$ Except in pathological cases, it is symmetric. The element in position (i, j) is

$$\frac{\partial^2 f(x)}{\partial x_i \partial x_j}.$$

The symbol $\nabla^2 f$ is sometimes also used to denote the diagonal of the Hessian, in which case it is called the Laplacian.

$f \star g$ The convolution of the functions f and g,

$$(f \star g)(t) = \int f(x)g(t - x)\, dx.$$

The convolution is a function.

$\text{Cov}(f, g)$ For the functions f and g whose integrals are zero, the covariance of f and g at lag t;

$$\text{Cov}(f, g)(t) = \int f(x)g(t + x)\, dx.$$

The covariance is a function; its argument is called the lag. $\text{Cov}(f, f)(t)$ is called the autocovariance of f at lag t, and $\text{Cov}(f, f)(0)$ is called the variance of f.

$\text{Corr}(f, g)$ For the functions f and g whose integrals are zero, the correlation of f and g at lag t;

$$\text{Corr}(f, g)(t) = \frac{\int f(x)g(t + x)\, dx}{\sqrt{\text{Cov}(f, f)(0)\text{Cov}(g, g)(0)}}.$$

The correlation is a function; its argument is called the lag. $\text{Cov}(f, f)(t)$ is called the autocorrelation of f at lag t.

$f \otimes g$ The tensor product of the functions f and g,

$$(f \otimes g)(w) = f(x)g(y) \quad \text{for} \quad w = (x, y).$$

The operator is also used for the tensor product of two function spaces and for the Kronecker product of two matrices.

$f^{\mathcal{T}}$
or $\mathcal{T}f$ The transform of the function f by the functional $\mathcal{T}$.
$f^{\mathcal{F}}$ usually denotes the Fourier transform of f.
$f^{\mathcal{L}}$ usually denotes the Laplace transform of f.
$f^{\mathcal{W}}$ usually denotes a wavelet transform of f.

δ A perturbation operator. δx represents a perturbation of x and not a multiplication of x by δ, even if x is a type of object for which a multiplication is defined.

$\Delta(\cdot, \cdot)$ A real-valued difference function. $\Delta(x, y)$ is a measure of the difference of x and y. For simple objects, $\Delta(x, y) = |x - y|$; for more complicated objects, a subtraction operator may not be defined, and Δ is a generalized difference.

$\tilde{x}$ A perturbation of the object x; $\Delta(x, \tilde{x}) = \delta x$.

$\text{Ave}(S)$ An average (of some kind) of the elements in the set S.

$\langle f^r \rangle_p$ The rth moment of the function f with respect to the density p.

$\bar{x}$ The mean of a sample of objects generically denoted by x.

$\bar{x}$ The complex conjugate of the object x; that is, if $x = r + ic$, then $\bar{x} = r - ic$.

$\log x$ The natural logarithm evaluated at x.

$\sin x$ The sine evaluated at x (in radians) and similarly for other trigonometric functions.

$x!$ The factorial of x. If x is a positive integer, $x! = x(x-1) \cdots 2 \cdot 1$. For other values of x, except negative integers, $x!$ is often defined as

$$x! = \Gamma(x + 1).$$

$\Gamma(\alpha)$ The complete gamma function. For α not equal to a nonpositive integer,

$$\Gamma(\alpha) = \int_0^\infty t^{\alpha-1} e^{-t} \, dt.$$

We have the useful relationship, $\Gamma(\alpha) = (\alpha - 1)!$. An important argument is $\frac{1}{2}$, and $\Gamma(\frac{1}{2}) = \sqrt{\pi}$.

$\Gamma_x(\alpha)$ The incomplete gamma function:

$$\Gamma_x(\alpha) = \int_0^x t^{\alpha-1} e^{-t} \, dt.$$

$B(\alpha, \beta)$ The complete beta function:

$$B(\alpha, \beta) = \int_0^1 t^{\alpha-1}(1 - t)^{\beta-1} \, dt,$$

where $\alpha > 0$ and $\beta > 0$. A useful relationship is

$$B(\alpha, \beta) = \frac{\Gamma(\alpha)\Gamma(\beta)}{\Gamma(\alpha + \beta)}.$$

$B_x(\alpha, \beta)$ The incomplete beta function:

$$B_x(\alpha, \beta) = \int_0^x t^{\alpha-1}(1 - t)^{\beta-1} \, dt.$$

A^{T} For the matrix A, its transpose (also used for a vector to represent the corresponding row vector).

A^{H} The conjugate transpose of the matrix A; $A^{\mathrm{H}} = \bar{A}^{\mathrm{T}}$.

A^{-1} The inverse of the square, nonsingular matrix A.

A^{+} The g_4 inverse, or the Moore-Penrose inverse, or the pseudoinverse, of the matrix A.

$A^{\frac{1}{2}}$ For the nonnegative definite matrix A, the Cholesky factor; that is,

$$(A^{\frac{1}{2}})^{\mathrm{T}} A^{\frac{1}{2}} = A.$$

$\text{sign}(x)$ For the vector x, a vector of units corresponding to the signs

$$
\begin{aligned}
\text{sign}(x)_i &= 1 && \text{if } x_i > 0, \\
&= 0 && \text{if } x_i = 0, \\
&= -1 && \text{if } x_i < 0,
\end{aligned}
$$

with a similar meaning for a scalar. The sign function is also sometimes called the signum function and denoted $\text{sgn}(\cdot)$.

L_p For real $p \geq 1$, a norm formed by accumulating the pth powers of the moduli of individual elements in an object and then taking the $(1/p)^{\text{th}}$ power of the result.

$\| \cdot \|$ In general, the norm of the object $\cdot$. Often, however, specifically either the L_2 norm, or the norm defined by an inner product.

$\| \cdot \|_p$ In general, the L_p norm of the object $\cdot$.

$\|x\|_p$ For the vector x, the L_p norm:

$$
\|x\|_p = \left(\sum |x_i|^p \right)^{\frac{1}{p}}.
$$

$\|X\|_p$ For the matrix X, the L_p norm:

$$
\|X\|_p = \max_{\|v\|_p = 1} \|Xv\|_p.
$$

$\|f\|_p$ For the function f, the L_p norm:

$$
\|f\|_p = \left(\int |f(x)|^p \mathrm{d}x \right)^{\frac{1}{p}}.
$$

$\|X\|_{\mathrm{F}}$ For the matrix X, the Frobenius norm:

$$
\|X\|_{\mathrm{F}} = \sqrt{\sum_{i,j} x_{ij}^2}.
$$

$\langle x, y \rangle$ The inner product of x and y.

$\kappa_p(A)$ The L_p condition number of the nonsingular square matrix A with respect to inversion.

$\text{diag}(v)$ For the vector v, the diagonal matrix whose nonzero elements are those of v; that is, the square matrix, A, such that $A_{ii} = v_i$ and for $i \neq j$, $A_{ij} = 0$.

$\text{diag}(A_1, \ldots, A_k)$
: The block diagonal matrix whose submatrices along the diagonal are $A_1, \ldots, A_k$.

$\text{trace}(A)$
: The trace of the square matrix A; that is, the sum of the diagonal elements.

$\text{rank}(A)$
: The rank of the matrix A, that is, the maximum number of independent rows (or columns) of A.

$\det(A)$
: The determinant of the square matrix A, $\det(A) = |A|$.

$|A|$
: The determinant of the square matrix A, $|A| = \det(A)$.

Models and Data

A form of model used often in statistics and applied mathematics has three parts: a left-hand side representing an object of primary interest; a function of another variable and a parameter, each of which is likely to be a vector; and an adjustment term to make the right-hand side equal the left-hand side. The notation varies depending on the meaning of the terms. One of the most common models used in statistics, the linear regression model with normal errors, is written as

$$Y = \beta^{\text{T}} x + E. \tag{C.1}$$

The adjustment term is a random variable, denoted by an uppercase epsilon. The term on the left-hand side is also a random variable. This model does not represent observations or data. A slightly more general form is

$$Y = f(x; \theta) + E. \tag{C.2}$$

A single observation or a single data item that corresponds to model (C.1) may be written as

$$y = \beta^{\text{T}} x + \epsilon$$

or, if it is one of several,

$$y_i = \beta^{\text{T}} x_i + \epsilon_i.$$

Similar expressions are used for a single data item that corresponds to model (C.2). In these cases, rather than being a random variable, ϵ or ϵ_i may be a realization of a random variable, or it may just be an adjustment factor with no assumptions about its origin.

A set of n such observations is usually represented in an n-vector y, a matrix X with n rows, and an n-vector ϵ:

$$y = X\beta + \epsilon$$

or

$$y = f(X; \theta) + \epsilon.$$

The model is not symmetric in y and x. The error term is added to the systematic component that involes x. The has implications in estimation and model fitting (see Chapter 11).

Appendix D

Solutions and Hints for Selected Exercises

1.3b.

$$
\Psi(P_n) = \int_{-\infty}^{\infty} \left(y - \int_{-\infty}^{\infty} u \, dP_n(u) \right)^2 dP_n(y)
$$

$$
= \frac{1}{n} \sum_{i=1}^{n} (y_i - \bar{y})^2.
$$

1.5a. $E(X)$, $E(X^2)$.

1.5b. The median.

1.5c. No; it is a nonlinear combination of two linear functionals, $E(X)$ and $E(X^2)$.

1.7a. $\widehat{\alpha} = (n-2)\bar{y}^2 / \sum (y_i - \bar{y})^2$;
$\widehat{\beta} = \sum (y_i - \bar{y})^2 / ((n-2)\bar{y})$.

1.7d. It does not have a closed-form solution.

1.9b. The Hessian is

$$
\frac{x_1}{(2+\theta)^2} + \frac{x_2 + x_3}{(1-\theta)^2} + \frac{x_4}{\theta^2}.
$$

Coding this in Matlab and beginning at 0.5, we get the first few iterates
0.6364
0.6270
0.6268
0.6268

1.9c. The expected value of the information is

$$
\frac{n}{4} \left(\frac{1}{2+\theta} + \frac{2}{1-\theta} + \frac{1}{\theta} \right),
$$

which we obtain by taking $E(X_i)$ for each element of the multinomial random variable. Coding the method in Matlab and beginning at 0.5, we get the first few iterates
0.6332
0.6265
0.6268
0.6268

1.9d. To use the EM algorithm on this problem, we can think of a multinomial with five classes, which is formed from the original multinomial by splitting the first class into two with associated probabilities $1/2$ and $\theta/4$. The original variable x_1 is now the sum of x_{11} and x_{12}. Under this reformulation, we now have a maximum likelihood estimate of θ by considering $x_{12} + x_4$ (or $x_2 + x_3$) to be a realization of a binomial with $n = x_{12} + x_4 + x_2 + x_3$ and $\pi = \theta$ (or $1 - \theta$). However, we do not know x_{12} (or x_{11}). Proceeding as if we had a five-outcome multinomial observation with two missing elements, we have the log-likelihood for the complete data,

$$l_c(\theta) = (x_{12} + x_4)\log(\theta) + (x_2 + x_3)\log(1 - \theta),$$

and the maximum likelihood estimate for θ is

$$\frac{x_{12} + x_4}{x_{12} + x_2 + x_3 + x_4}.$$

The E-step of the iterative EM algorithm fills in the missing or unobservable value with its expected value given a current value of the parameter, $\theta^{(k)}$, and the observed data. Because $l_c(\theta)$ is linear in the data, we have

$$\mathrm{E}\left(l_c(\theta)\right) = \mathrm{E}(x_{12} + x_4)\log(\theta) + \mathrm{E}(x_2 + x_3)\log(1 - \theta).$$

Under this setup, with $\theta = \theta^{(k)}$,

$$
\begin{aligned}
\mathrm{E}_{\theta^{(k)}}(x_{12}) &= \frac{1}{4}x_1\theta^{(k)}/(\frac{1}{2} + \frac{1}{4}x_1\theta^{(k)}) \\
&= x_{12}^{(k)}.
\end{aligned}
$$

We now maximize $\mathrm{E}_{\theta^{(k)}}\left(l_c(\theta)\right)$. This maximum occurs at

$$\theta^{(k+1)} = (x_{12}^{(k)} + x_4)/(x_{12}^{(k)} + x_2 + x_3 + x_4).$$

The following Matlab statements execute a single iteration.

```
function [x12kp1,tkp1] = em(tk,x)
x12kp1 = x(1)*tk/(2+tk);
tkp1 = (x12kp1 + x(4))/(sum(x)-x(1)+x12kp1);
```

1.13. The distribution of $X = s^2/\sigma^2$ is a gamma with parameters $(n-1)/2$ and 2 (that is, chi-squared with $n - 1$ degrees of freedom). Using this fact, evaluate $\mathrm{E}(X^{1/2})$ and determine the scaling needed to form an unbiased estimator for σ.

2.3. Conditional on u, the distribution of T is geometric:

$$p_{T|u}(t) = \pi_u(1 - \pi_u)^{t-1}, \quad \text{for } t = 1, 2, \ldots,$$

where

$$\pi_u = \int \mathrm{H}\big(g_Y(y) - u\big)\,\frac{p_X(y)}{cg_Y(y)}\,dy,$$

and $\mathrm{H}(\cdot)$ is the Heaviside function. The marginal probability function for T is

$$p_T(t) = \int_0^1 \pi_u(1 - \pi_u)^{t-1}\,du, \quad \text{for } t = 1, 2, \ldots.$$

Therefore, we have

$$\mathrm{E}(T) = \int_0^1 \frac{1}{\pi_u}\,du$$

and

$$\mathrm{V}(T) = \int_0^1 \frac{1}{\pi_u}\left(\frac{2}{\pi_u} - 1\right)\,du - (\mathrm{E}(T))^2.$$

For certain densities these moments may be infinite. Assume, for example, that for some y_0, $g_Y(y_0) = 1$, and that we can expand g_Y about y_0:

$$g_Y(y_0 + \delta) = 1 - a\delta^2 + \mathrm{O}(\delta^3).$$

For u close to 1, π_u is approximately proportional to $2a^{-1/2}(1 - u)^{1/2}$, so $\mathrm{V}(T)$ is arbitrarily large (see Greenwood, 1976).

2.8. What we are to do is a goodness-of-fit test. These are hard (in the sense that there are too many alternatives). Just three $O(n)$ statistics cannot result in a very powerful omnibus test. Most reasonable tests, such as a Kolmogorov-Smirnov test, use at least $O(n \log n)$ test statistics. What we can do in this case are just some simple tests for specific aspects of the hypothesized distribution.

The unknown parameter θ complicates anything we might try; we cannot generate Monte Carlo samples without knowing this value. Therefore, we must consider two general approaches: one kind in which we use an estimate of θ, and another kind in which we address characteristics of the distribution that are independent of θ.

First of all, note that the distribution is symmetric; therefore, the mean is 0. Unfortunately, we cannot construct a test based on m unless we know θ or have an estimate of it.

Because $V(X) = 2\theta^2$, where X is a random variable with the hypothesized distribution, we can estimate θ with $m_2/(2(n-1))$. Using this estimate of θ, we can now construct various tests. We can, for example, do Monte Carlo tests on m, m_2, or m_4. These tests would in reality be on the population parameters corresponding to the expectations of the corresponding random variables (that is, the sample mean, the sample second central moment, and the sample fourth central moment). Each Monte Carlo test would be performed in the usual way by generating samples from a double exponential with the estimated value of θ, computing the appropriate statistic from each sample, and then comparing the single observed value of that statistic with the Monte Carlo set. To do a test at the α level, we have several possibilities. An easy way out is just to do one of the Monte Carlo tests described; the observed value of just one of the quantities m, m_2, and m_4 would be compared with the $\lfloor n\alpha/2 \rfloor^{\text{th}}$ and the $\lfloor n(1 - \alpha/2) \rfloor^{\text{th}}$ order statistics from the Monte Carlo sample of corresponding statistics. Another possibility would be to do three tests with appropriately adjusted significance levels. There are no (obvious) Bonferroni bounds, so the adjusted level would just be $\alpha/3$, and the rejection criterion would be rejection of any separate test.

Another approach would be to determine salient features of the hypothesized distribution that are independent of the unknown parameter. An example is the ratio of the fourth moment to the square of the second moment, which is 12. The expected value of m_4/m_2^2 is independent of θ. Therefore, we can choose an arbitrary value of θ and generate Monte Carlo samples. We would then do a Monte Carlo test using m_4/m_2^2. This test would compare the observed value of this ratio with the Monte Carlo sample of this ratio. (The test would not directly compare the observed value with the hypothesized population value of 12.)

3.4. Consider the numerator,

$$
\begin{aligned}
\sum_{j=1}^{n} \left(T_j^* - T \right)^2 &= \sum_{j=1}^{n} \left((T_j^* - \overline{T}^*) - (T - \overline{T}^*) \right)^2 \\
&= \sum_{j=1}^{n} \left(T_j^* - \overline{T}^* \right)^2 - 2\sum_{j=1}^{n} (T_j^* - \overline{T}^*)(T - \overline{T}^*) + \sum_{j=1}^{n} \left(T - \overline{T}^* \right)^2 \\
&= \sum_{j=1}^{n} \left(T_j^* - \overline{T}^* \right)^2 + \sum_{j=1}^{n} \left(T - \overline{T}^* \right)^2 \\
&\leq \sum_{j=1}^{n} \left(T_j^* - \overline{T}^* \right)^2,
\end{aligned}
$$

which is the numerator of V_J with $r = n$. The same arithmetic also holds for other values of r.

4.5a.

$$
\begin{aligned}
\mathrm{E}_{\widehat{P}}(\bar{x}_b^*) &= \mathrm{E}_{\widehat{P}}\left(\frac{1}{n}\sum_i x_i^*\right) \\
&= \frac{1}{n}\sum_i \mathrm{E}_{\widehat{P}}(x_i^*) \\
&= \frac{1}{n}\sum_i \bar{x} \\
&= \bar{x}.
\end{aligned}
$$

Note that the empirical distribution is a conditional distribution, given the sample. With the sample fixed, $\bar{x}$ is a "parameter", rather than a "statistic".

4.5d.

$$
\begin{aligned}
\mathrm{E}_P(V) &= \mathrm{E}_P(\mathrm{E}_{\widehat{P}}(V)) \\
&= \mathrm{E}_P\left(\frac{1}{n}\sum(x_i - \bar{x})^2 n\right) \\
&= \frac{1}{n}\frac{n-1}{n}\sigma_P^2.
\end{aligned}
$$

5.8a. The rotation matrix Q rotates (x_{1i}, x_{2i}, x_3) into $(a_1 x_{1i} + a_2 x_{2i}, 0, x_3)$. If

$$
Q = \begin{bmatrix} c & -s & 0 \\ s & c & 0 \\ 0 & 0 & 1 \end{bmatrix},
$$

then $a_2 c = a_1 s$ and $s = \sqrt{1 - c^2}$. Thus, we have two equations in two unknowns for which we can solve in terms of a_1 and a_2. The projection matrix is just

$$
P = \begin{bmatrix} 1 & 0 & 0 \\ 0 & 0 & 1 \end{bmatrix}.
$$

5.8b. The first thing to consider here is whether to use the known model (that is, in the notation of the previous question, $a_1 = 5$ and $a_2 = 1$), or to use the data to determine coefficients that better fit the data. (In the latter case, we would first regress x_3 on x_1 and x_2, and then use the estimates $\hat{a}_1$ and $\hat{a}_2$.) At this point, the problem is almost like Exercise 5.8a. This depends on the signal-to-noise (that is, on whether the variation in ϵ dominates the variation in $5x_1 + x_2$). If the noise dominates, it is not likely that a good projection exists.

5.9. $m = 3$, and

$$
X = \begin{bmatrix}
3.31 & 0.95 & -1.38 \\
-0.68 & 0.79 & 0.31 \\
-0.31 & 1.73 & 1.31 \\
-4.17 & -0.72 & -0.94 \\
1.85 & -2.74 & 0.69
\end{bmatrix}.
$$

6.2. For $x \in D$, consider the change of variable $y = ax$ for $a \neq 0$. The Jacobian of the inverse transformation, J, is $1/a$. Let D_a represent the domain of y. For the L_1 norm,

$$
\begin{aligned}
\int_{D_a} |f_a(y)|\,dy &= \int_{D_a} |f(y/a)||J|\,dy \\
&= \int_D |f(x)|\,dx.
\end{aligned}
$$

For the L_2 norm (squared),

$$\int_{D_a} (f_a(y))^2 dy = \int_{D_a} (f(y/a))^2 |J| dy$$

$$\neq \int_D (f(x))^2 dx.$$

As a specific example, let $f(x)$ be the density $2x$ over the interval $(0, 1)$, and let $a = 2$.

6.11a. $3/(8\sqrt{\pi}\sigma^5)$.

7.2. It is likely that the tails will be light because the median is smaller in absolute value than the mean.

Exercise 7.2': Generate a sample of size 50 of maximum order statistics from samples of size 100 from a normal $(0,1)$ distribution, and plot a histogram of it. Notice the skewed shape. Because much of our experience is with symmetric data, our expectations of the behavior of random samples often are not met when the data are skewed.

7.4. There are 63 planes in 4-D. They may be somewhat difficult to see because of the slicing and because of the relatively large number of planes.

8.1a.

$$\int_0^{x_{(n)}} \left(\frac{1}{x_{(n)}} - \frac{1}{\theta} \right)^2 dx + \int_{x_{(n)}}^{\theta} \left(0 - \frac{1}{\theta} \right)^2 dx = \frac{1}{x_{(n)}} - \frac{1}{\theta}.$$

8.1b. $\frac{1}{n-1}$ (remember that the ith order statistic from a uniform distribution has a beta distribution with i and $n - i + 1$).

8.1c. The minimum occurs at $c = 2^{1/(n-1)}$ (see Scott, 1992).

9.6. For regular triangles, $c = \frac{1}{6\sqrt{3}}$; for squares, $c = \frac{1}{12}$; and for regular triangles, $c = \frac{5}{36\sqrt{3}}$.

9.8a.

$$\int_{\mathbb{R}} \widehat{p}_F(y) dy = \frac{1}{2} \frac{n_1}{nv_1} v_1 + \sum_{k=1}^{m-1} \frac{1}{2} \left(\frac{n_{k+1}}{nv_{k+1}} v_{k+1} + \frac{n_k}{nv_k} v_k \right) + \frac{1}{2} \frac{n_m}{nv_m} v_m$$

$$= 1.$$

9.15c. Take the density $f(x) = 1$ on $[0, 1]$ and the estimator $\widehat{f}(x) = n$ on $\left[0, \frac{1}{n}\right]$.

9.16a. For the first moment,

$$\mathrm{E}_{\widehat{p}_H}(Y) = \int_D y\widehat{p}_H(y) dy$$

$$= \int_D y \sum_{k=1}^m \frac{n_k}{nv_k} I_{T_k}(y) dy$$

$$= \sum_{k=1}^m \int_{T_k} y \frac{n_k}{nv_k} dy$$

$$= \sum_{k=1}^m \frac{n_k \left(t_{k+1}^2 - t_k^2 \right)}{2nv_k}$$

$$= \sum_{k=1}^m \frac{n_k \left(t_{k+1} + t_k \right)}{2n}$$

$$= \mu_H.$$

This is just the weighted mean of the midpoint of the bins. The sample first moment, of course, is just the sample mean. The bins could be chosen to make the two quantities equal. The higher central moments have more complicated expressions. In general, they are

$$
\begin{aligned}
\operatorname{E}_{\widehat{p_H}}\left((Y - \mu_H)^r\right) &= \int_D (y - \mu_H)^r \widehat{p}_H(y)dy \\
&= \int_D (y - \mu_H)^r \sum_{k=1}^m \frac{n_k}{nv_k} I_{T_k}(y)dy \\
&= \sum_{k=1}^m \int_{T_k} (y - \mu_H)^r \frac{n_k}{nv_k}dy \\
&= \sum_{k=1}^m \frac{n_k\left((t - \mu_H)_{k+1}^{r+1} - (t - \mu_H)_k^{r+1}\right)}{(r+1)nv_k}.
\end{aligned}
$$

For the case of $r = 2$ (that is, for the variance), the expression above can be simplified by using $\operatorname{E}((Y - \operatorname{E}(Y))^2) = \operatorname{E}(Y^2) - (\operatorname{E}(Y))^2$. It is just

$$
\sum_{k=1}^m \frac{n_k\left(t_{k+1}^2 + t_{k+1}t_k + t_k^2\right)}{3n} - m\mu_H^2.
$$

9.16b. Let $K(t) = 1$ if $|t| < 1/2$ and $K(t) = 0$ otherwise.

$$
\begin{aligned}
\operatorname{E}_{\widehat{p_K}}(Y) &= \int_D y\widehat{p}_K(y)dy \\
&= \frac{1}{nh} \sum_{i=1}^n \int_D yK\left(\frac{y - y_i}{h}\right)dy \\
&= \frac{1}{2nh} \sum_{i=1}^n \int_{y_i - h/2}^{y_i + h/2} y^2 dy \\
&= \mu_K \\
&= \bar{y}.
\end{aligned}
$$

The higher central moments have more complicated expressions. In general, they are

$$
\begin{aligned}
\operatorname{E}_{\widehat{p_H}}\left((Y - \mu_K)^r\right) &= \int_D (y - \mu_K)^r \widehat{p}_K(y)dy \\
&= \frac{1}{nh} \sum_{i=1}^n \int_D (y - \mu_K)^r K\left(\frac{y - y_i}{h}\right)dy \\
&= \frac{1}{nh} \sum_{i=1}^n \int_{y_i - h/2}^{y_i + h/2} (y - \mu_K)^r dy. \\
&= \frac{1}{(r+1)nh} \sum_{i=1}^n \left((y_i - \mu_K + h/2)^{r+1} - (y_i - \mu_K - h/2)^{r+1}\right).
\end{aligned}
$$

For the case $r = 2$, as in Exercise 9.16a, this can be simplified considerably:

$$
\operatorname{E}_{\widehat{p_H}}\left((Y - \mu_K)^2\right) = \sum_{i=1}^n y_i^2 - n\bar{y}^2 + \frac{h^3}{12}.
$$

This is the same as the second central sample moment except for the term $\frac{h^3}{12}$.

10.1b. 1

10.1c. .9

10.1d. .8

10.5. This depends on the signal-to-noise. If the ratio is large, then there will be no more than two strong principal components. If x_1 and x_2 are independent, then there will be at least two strong principal components.

10.7b. The optimal projection for the data-generating process is clearly $(0, 1)$. For a given dataset from this process, of course, it may be slightly different.

10.11. 10. This is a simple exercise in the application of the generalized Pythagorean Theorem.

Bibliography

The literature on computational statistics is diverse. Relevant articles are likely to appear in journals devoted to quite different disciplines, especially computer science, numerical analysis, and statistics.

There are at least ten journals and serials whose titles contain some variants of both "computing" and "statistics"; but there are far more journals in numerical analysis and in areas such as "computational physics", "computational biology", and so on that publish articles relevant to the fields of statistical computing and computational statistics. The journals in the mainstream of statistics also have a large proportion of articles in the fields of statistical computing and computational statistics because, as we suggested in the preface, recent developments in statistics and in the computational sciences have paralleled each other to a large extent.

There are two well-known learned societies whose primary focus is in statistical computing: the International Association for Statistical Computing (IASC), which is an affiliated society of the International Statistical Institute, and the Statistical Computing Section of the American Statistical Association (ASA). The Statistical Computing Section of the ASA has a regular newsletter carrying news and notices as well as articles on practicum. Also, the activities of the Society for Industrial and Applied Mathematics (SIAM) are often relevant to computational statistics.

There are two regular conferences in the area of computational statistics: COMPSTAT, held biennially in Europe and sponsored by the IASC, and the Interface Symposium, generally held annually in North America and sponsored by the Interface Foundation of North America with cooperation from the Statistical Computing Section of the ASA.

In addition to literature and learned societies in the traditional forms, an important source of communication and a repository of information are computer databases and forums. In some cases, the databases duplicate what is available in some other form, but often the material and the communications facilities provided by the computer are not available elsewhere.

Literature in Computational Statistics

In the Library of Congress classification scheme, most books on statistics, including statistical computing, are in the QA276 section, although some are classified under H, HA, and HG. Numerical analysis is generally in QA279, and computer science in QA76. Many of the books in the interface of these disciplines are classified in these or other places within QA.

Current Index to Statistics, published annually by the American Statistical Association and the Institute for Mathematical Statistics, contains both author and subject indexes that are useful in finding journal articles or books in statistics. The *Index* is available in hard copy and on CD-ROM. The CD-ROM version with software developed by Ron Thisted and Doug Bates is particularly useful. In passing, I take this opportunity to acknowledge the help this database and software were to me in tracking down references for this book.

The Association for Computing Machinery (ACM) publishes an annual index, by author, title, and keyword, of the literature in the computing sciences.

Mathematical Reviews, published by the American Mathematical Society (AMS), contains brief reviews of articles in all areas of mathematics. The areas of "Statistics", "Numerical Analysis", and "Computer Science" contain reviews of articles relevant to computational statistics. The papers reviewed in *Mathematical Reviews* are categorized according to a standard system that has slowly evolved over the years. In this taxonomy, called the AMS MR classification system, "Statistics" is 62Xyy; "Numerical Analysis", including random number generation, is 65Xyy; and "Computer Science" is 68Xyy. ("X" represents a letter and "yy" represents a two-digit number.) *Mathematical Reviews* is available to subscribers via the World Wide Web at MathSciNet:

`http://www.ams.org/mathscinet/`

There are various handbooks of mathematical functions and formulas that are useful in numerical computations. Three that should be mentioned are Abramowitz and Stegun (1964), Spanier and Oldham (1987), and Thompson (1997). Anyone doing serious scientific computations should have ready access to at least one of these volumes.

Almost all journals in statistics have occasional articles on computational statistics and statistical computing. The following is a list of journals, proceedings, and newsletters that emphasize this field.

ACM Transactions on Mathematical Software, published quarterly by the ACM (Association for Computing Machinery), includes algorithms in Fortran and C. Most of the algorithms are available through `netlib`. The ACM collection of algorithms is sometimes called *CALGO*.

ACM Transactions on Modeling and Computer Simulation, published quarterly by the ACM.

Applied Statistics, published quarterly by the Royal Statistical Society. (Until 1998, it included algorithms in Fortran. Some of these algorithms, with corrections, were collected by Griffiths and Hill, 1985. Most of the algorithms are available through `statlib` at Carnegie Mellon University.)

Communications in Statistics — Simulation and Computation, published quarterly by Marcel Dekker. (Until 1996, included algorithms in Fortran. Until 1982, this journal was designated as *Series B*.)

Computational Statistics, published quarterly by Physica-Verlag (formerly called *Computational Statistics Quarterly*).

Computational Statistics. Proceedings of the xxth Symposium on Computational Statistics (COMPSTAT), published biennially by Physica-Verlag. (It is not refereed.)

Computational Statistics & Data Analysis, published by North Holland. Number of issues per year varies. (This is also the official journal of the International Association for Statistical Computing and as such incorporates the *Statistical Software Newsletter*.)

Computing Science and Statistics. This is an annual publication containing papers presented at the Interface Symposium. Until 1988, these proceedings were named *Computer Science and Statistics: Proceedings of the xxth Symposium on the Interface*. From 1988 until 1992, the proceedings were named *Computing Science and Statistics: Proceedings of the xxth Symposium on the Interface*. (The 24th symposium was held in 1992.) In 1997, Volume 29 was published in two issues: Number 1, which contains the papers of the regular Interface Symposium; and Number 2, which contains papers from another conference. The two numbers are not sequentially paginated. These proceedings are now published by the Interface Foundation of North America. (It is not refereed.)

Journal of Computational and Graphical Statistics, published quarterly by the American Statistical Association.

Journal of Statistical Computation and Simulation, published irregularly in four numbers per volume by Gordon and Breach.

Proceedings of the Statistical Computing Section, published annually by the American Statistical Association. (It is not refereed.)

SIAM Journal on Scientific Computing, published bimonthly by SIAM. This journal was formerly *SIAM Journal on Scientific and Statistical Computing*. (Is this a step backward?)

Statistical Computing & Graphics Newsletter, published quarterly by the Statistical Computing and the Statistical Graphics Sections of the American Statistical Association. (It is not refereed and it is not generally available in libraries.)

Statistics and Computing, published quarterly by Chapman & Hall.

Resources Available over the Internet

The best way of storing information is in a digital format that can be accessed by computers. In some cases, the best way for people to access information is by computers; in other cases, the best way is via hard copy, which means that the information stored on the computer must go through a printing process resulting in books, journals, or loose pages.

A huge amount of information and raw data are available online, much in publicly accessible sites. Some of the repositories give space to ongoing discussions to which anyone can contribute.

For statistics, one of the most useful sites on the Internet is the electronic repository statlib, maintained at Carnegie Mellon University, which contains programs, datasets, and other items of interest. The URL is

```
http://lib.stat.cmu.edu
```

The collection of algorithms published in *Applied Statistics* is available in statlib. These algorithms are sometimes called the *ApStat* algorithms.

The statlib facility can also be accessed by email or anonymous ftp.

Another very useful site for scientific computing is netlib, which was established by research workers at Bell Laboratories and national laboratories, primarily Oak Ridge National Laboratories. The URL is

```
http://www.netlib.org
```

The *Collected Algorithms of the ACM (CALGO)*, which are the Fortran, C, and Algol programs published in *ACM Transactions on Mathematical Software* (or in *Communications of the ACM* prior to 1975), are available in netlib, under the TOMS link.

There is also an X Windows, socket-based system for accessing netlib, called Xnetlib; see Dongarra, Rowan, and Wade (1995).

The *Guide to Available Mathematical Software* (GAMS) can be accessed at

```
http://gams.nist.gov
```

A different interface, using Java, is available at

```
http://math.nist.gov/HotGAMS/
```

A good set of links for software are the Econometric Links of the *Econometrics Journal* (which are not just limited to econometrics):

```
http://www.eur.nl/few/ei/links/software.html
```

There are two major problems in using the WWW to gather information. One is the sheer quantity of information and the number of sites providing information. The other is the "kiosk problem"; anyone can put up material. Sadly, the average quality is affected by a very large denominator. The kiosk problem may be even worse than a random selection of material; the "fools in public places" syndrome is much in evidence.

It is not clear at this time what will be the media for the scientific literature within a few years. Many of the traditional journals will be converted to an electronic version of some kind. Journals will become Web sites. That is for certain; the details, however, are much less certain. Many bulletin boards and discussion groups have already evolved into electronic journals. A useful electronic journal for computational statistics is the *Journal of Statistical Software* at

http://www.jstatsoft.org/

References for Software Packages

There is a wide range of software used in the computational sciences. Some of the software is produced by a single individual who is happy to share the software, sometimes for a fee, but who has no interest in maintaining the software. At the other extreme is software produced by large commercial companies whose continued existence depends on a process of production, distribution, and maintenance of the software. Information on much of the software can be obtained from GAMS. Some of the free software can be obtained from `statlib` or `netlib`.

We refer to several software packages with names that are trademarked or registered. Our reference to these packages without mention of the registration in no way implies that the name carries a generic meaning.

References to the Literature

The following bibliography obviously covers a wide range of topics in statistical computing and computational statistics. Except for a few of the general references, all of these entries have been cited in the text.

The purpose of this bibliography is to help the reader get more information; hence I eschew "personal communications" and references to technical reports that may or may not exist. Those kinds of references are generally for the author rather than for the reader.

In some cases, important original papers have been reprinted in special collections, such as Samuel Kotz and Norman L. Johnson (Editors) (1997), *Breakthroughs in Statistics, Volume III*, Springer-Verlag, New York. In most such cases, because the special collection may be more readily available, I list both sources.

A Note on the Names of Authors

In these references, I have generally used the names of authors as they appear in the original sources. This may mean that the same author will appear with different forms of names, sometimes with given names spelled out, and sometimes abbreviated. In the author index, beginning on page 409, I use a single name for the same author. The name is generally the most unique (i.e., least abbreviated) of any of the names of that author in any of the references. This convention may occasionally result in an entry in the author index that does not occur exactly in any references. For example, a reference to J. Paul Jones together with one to John P. Jones, if I know that the two names refer to the same person, would result in an Author Index entry for John Paul Jones.

Abbott, Edwin A. (1884), *Flatland, A Romance of Many Dimensions*, Seeley & Co. Ltd., London. (Reprinted with an updated introductory note by Dover Publications, New York, 1992).

Abramowitz, Milton, and Irene A. Stegun (Editors) (1964), *Handbook of Mathematical Functions with Formulas, Graphs, and Mathematical Tables*, National Bureau of Standards (NIST), Washington. (Reprinted by Dover Publications, New York, 1974. Work on an updated version is occurring at NIST; see http://dlmf.nist.gov/ for the current status.)

Agresti, Alan (1992), A survey of exact inference for contingency tables (with discussion), *Statistical Science* **7**, 131–177.

Albert, James; Mohan Delampady; and Wolfgang Polasek (1991), A class of distributions for robustness studies, *Journal of Statistical Planning and Inference* **28**, 291–304.

Albert, John (2002), How likelihood and identification went Bayesian, *International Statistical Review* **70**, 79–98.

Allen, David M. (1971), Mean square error of prediction as a criterion for selecting variables (with discussion), *Technometrics* **13**, 469–475.

Allen, David M. (1974), The relationship between variable selection and data augmentation and a method of prediction, *Technometrics* **16**, 125–127.

Amit, Yali, and Donald Geman (1997), Shape quantization and recognition with randomized trees, *Neural Computation* **9** 1545–1588.

Ammann, Larry P. (1989), Robust principal components, *Communications in Statistics — Simulation and Computation* **18**, 857–874.

Ammann, Larry P. (1993), Robust singular value decompositions: A new approach to projection pursuit, *Journal of the American Statistical Association* **88**, 505–514.

Ammann, Larry, and John Van Ness (1988), A routine for converting regression algorithms into corresponding orthogonal regression algorithms, *ACM Transactions on Mathematical Software* **14**, 76–87.

Ammann, Larry, and John Van Ness (1989), Standard and robust orthogonal regression, *Communications in Statistics — Simulation and Computation* **18**, 145–162.

Anderson, E. (1957), A semigraphical method for the analysis of complex problems, *Proceedings of the National Academy of Sciences* **13**, 923–927. (Reprinted in *Technometrics*, 1960, **2**, 387–391.)

Anderson, T. W. (1984), *An Introduction to Multivariate Statistical Analysis*, second edition, John Wiley & Sons, New York.

Andrews, D. F. (1972), Plots of high-dimensional data, *Biometrics* **28**, 125–136.

Andrews, D. F.; P. J. Bickel; F. R. Hampel; P. J. Huber; W. H. Rogers; and J. W. Tukey (1972), *Robust Estimation of Location: Survey and Advances*, Princeton University Press, Princeton.

Antoniadis, A.; G. Gregoire; and I. W. McKeague (1994), Wavelet methods for curve estimation, *Journal of the American Statistical Association* **89**, 1340–1353.

Antoniadis, Anestis, and Georges Oppenheim (Editors) (1995), *Wavelets and Statistics*, Springer-Verlag, New York.

Ash, Peter; Ethan Bolker; Henry Crapo; and Walter Whiteley (1988), Convex polyhedra, Dirichlet tessellations, and spider webs, *Shaping Space. A Polyhedral Approach* (edited by Marjorie Senechal and George Fleck), Birkhäuser, Boston, 231–250.

Asimov, Daniel (1985), The grand tour: A tool for viewing multidimensional data, *SIAM Journal on Scientific and Statistical Computing* **6**, 128–143.

Atkinson, A. C., and H.-M. Mulira (1993), The stalactite plot for the detection of multivariate outliers, *Statistics and Computing* **3**, 27–35.

Aurenhammer, Franz (1991), Voronoi diagrams—a survey of a fundamental geometric data structure, *ACM Computing Surveys* **23**, 345–405.

Banchoff, Thomas F. (1996), *Beyond the Third Dimension: Geometry, Computer Graphics, and Higher Dimensions*, Scientific American Library, A Division of HPHLP, New York.

Banfield, Jeffrey D., and Adrian E. Raftery (1993), Model-based Gaussian and non-Gaussian clustering, *Biometrics* **49**, 803–821.

Banks, David L. (1989), Bayesian sieving, *Proceedings of the Statistical Computing Section, ASA*, 271–276.

Banks, David, and Michael Lavine (1992), The minimal spanning tree for nonparametric regression and structure discovery, *Computing Science and Statistics* **24**, 370–374.

Barbe, Philippe, and Patrice Bertail (1995), *The Weighted Bootstrap*, Springer-Verlag, New York.

Barber, C. Bradford; David P. Dobkin; and Hannu Huhdanpaa (1996), The quickhull algorithm for convex hulls, *ACM Transactions on Mathematical Software* **22**, 469–483.

Barnard, G. A. (1963), Discussion of Bartlett, "The spectral analysis of point processes", *Journal of the Royal Statistical Society, Series B* **25**, 264–296.

Barnett, V. (1976), The ordering of multivariate data (with discussion), *Journal of the Royal Statistical Society, Series A* **139**, 318–352.

Barnett, Vic, and Toby Lewis (1994), *Outliers in Statistical Data*, third edition, John Wiley & Sons, New York.

Bartlett, M. S. (1947), The use of transformations, *Biometrics* **3**, 39–52.

Bassett, Gilbert W. (1991), Equivalent, monotone, 50% breakdown estimators, *The American Statistician* **45**, 135–137.

Becker, Richard A.; John M. Chambers; and Allan R. Wilks (1988), *The New S Language*, Wadsworth & Brooks/Cole, Pacific Grove, California.

Becker, Richard A., and William S. Cleveland (1987), Brushing scatterplots, *Technometrics* **29**, 127–142.

Becker, Richard A.; William S. Cleveland; and Ming-Jen Shyu (1996), The visual design and control of Trellis display, *Journal of Computational and Graphical Statistics* **5**, 123–155.

Beniger, James R., and Dorothy L. Robyn (1978), Quantitative graphics in statistics, *The American Statistician* **32**, 1–11.

Bentley, Jon Louis, and Jerome H. Friedman (1978), Fast algorithms for constructing minimal spanning trees in coordinate systems, *IEEE Transactions on Computers* **27**, 97–105.

Bentley, Jon Louis, and Jerome H. Friedman (1979), Data structures for range searching, *ACM Computing Surveys* **11**, 397–409.

Besag, J. E. (1974), Spatial interaction and the statistical analysis of lattice systems (with discussion), *Journal of the Royal Statistical Society, Series B* **36**, 192–236.

Besag, J., and P. Clifford (1989), Generalized Monte Carlo significance tests, *Biometrika* **76**, 633–642.

Besag, J., and P. Clifford (1991), Sequential Monte Carlo *p*-values, *Biometrika* **78**, 301–304.

Besag, J., and P. J. Diggle (1977), Simple Monte Carlo tests for spatial pattern, *Applied Statistics* **26**, 327–333.

Bézier, Pierre (1986), *The Mathematical Basis of the UNISURF CAD System*, Butterworths, London.

Bhavsar, Suketu P., and E. Nigel Ling (1988), Are the filaments real? *The Astrophysical Journal* **331**, L63–L68.

Birkes, David, and Yadolah Dodge (1993), *Alternative Methods of Regression*, John Wiley & Sons, New York.

Boggs, Paul T.; Janet R. Donaldson; Richard H. Byrd; and Robert B. Schnabel (1989), Algorithm 676: ORDPACK, software for weighted orthogonal distance regression, *ACM Transactions on Mathematical Software* **15**, 348–364.

Bowman, Adrian W., and Adelchi Azzalini (1997), *Applied Smoothing Techniques for Data Analysis*, Clarendon Press, Oxford, United Kingdom.

Bowyer, A. (1981), Computing Dirichlet tessellations, *The Computer Journal* **24**, 162–166.

Box, G. E. P., and D. R. Cox (1964), An analysis of transformations (with discussion), *Journal of the Royal Statistical Society, Series B* **26**, 211–252.

Box, G. E. P., and P. W. Tidwell (1962), Transformation of the independent variables, *Technometrics* **4**, 531–550.

Breiman, Leo (1996a), The heuristics of instability in model selection, *Annals of Statistics* **24**, 2350–2383.

Breiman, Leo (1996b), Bagging predictors, *Machine Learning* **24**, 123–140.

Breiman, Leo (1998), Arcing classifiers (with discussion), *Annals of Statistics* **26**, 801–849.

Breiman, Leo (2000), Randomizing outputs to increase prediction accuracy, *Machine Learning* **40**, 229–242.

Breiman, Leo (2001), Statistical modeling: The two cultures (with discussion), *Statistical Science* **16**, 199–231.

Breiman, Leo, and Jerome H. Friedman (1985a), Estimating optimal transformations for multiple regression and correlation (with discussion), *Journal of the American Statistical Association* **80**, 580–619.

Breiman, Leo, and Jerome H. Friedman (1985b), Estimating optimal transformations for multiple regression, *Computer Science and Statistics: Proceedings of the Sixteenth Symposium on the Interface* (edited by Lynne Billard), North Holland, Amsterdam, 121–134.

Breiman, L.; J. H. Friedman; R. A. Olshen; and C. J. Stone (1984), *Classification and Regression Trees*, Wadsworth Publishing Co., Monterey, California.

Brooks, S. P., and G. O. Roberts (1999) Assessing convergence of iterative simulations, *Statistics and Computing* **8**, 319–335.

Brown, D., and P. Rothery (1978), Randomness and local regularity of points in a plane, *Biometrika* **65**, 115–122.

Buckheit, Jonathan B., and David L. Dohoho (1995), WaveLab and reproducible research, *Wavelets and Statistics* (edited by Anestis Antoniadis and Georges Oppenheim), Springer-Verlag, New York, 55–81.

Buja, Andreas, and Daniel Asimov (1986), Grand tour methods: An outline, *Computer Science and Statistics: Proceedings of the Seventeenth Symposium on the Interface* (edited by D. M. Allen), North-Holland Publishing Company, Amsterdam, 63–67.

Buja, A., and P. A. Tukey (Editors) (1991), *Computing and Graphics in Statistics*, Springer-Verlag, New York.

Burr, I. W. (1942), Cumulative frequency functions, *Annals of Mathematical Statistics* **13**, 215–232.

Burr, Irving W., and Peter J. Cislak (1968), On a general system of distributions. I. Its curve-shape characteristics. II. The sample median, *Journal of the American Statistical Association* **63**, 627–635.

Butucea, Cristina (2001), Numerical results concerning a sharp adaptive density estimator, *Computational Statistics* **16**, 271–298.

Cabrera, Javier, and Dianne Cook (1992), Projection pursuit indices based on fractal dimension, *Computing Science and Statistics* **24**, 474–477.

Campbell, N. A. (1980), Robust procedures in multivariate analysis I: Robust covariance estimation, *Applied Statistics* **29**, 231–237.

Caroni, C. (2000), Outlier detection by robust principal components analysis, *Communications in Statistics — Simulation and Computation* **29**, 139–151.

Carr, Daniel B., and Richard J. Littlefield (1983), Color anaglyph stereo scatterplots—Construction details, *Computer Science and Statistics: The Interface* (edited by James E. Gentle), North-Holland Publishing Company, Amsterdam, 295–299.

Carr, D. B.; R. J. Littlefield; W. L. Nicholson; and J. S. Littlefield (1987), Scatterplot matrix techniques for large N, *Journal of the American Statistical Association* **82**, 424–436.

Carr, D. B., and W. L. Nicholson (1987), EXPLOR4: A program for exploring four-dimensional data using stereo-ray glyphs, dimensional constraints, rotation and masking, *Computer Science and Statistics: Proceedings of the 19th Symposium on the Interface* (edited by Richard M. Heiberger), American Statistical Association, Alexandria, Virginia, 190–196.

Carroll, R. J., and D. Ruppert (1984), Power transformations when fitting theoretical models to data, *Journal of the American Statistical Association* **79**, 321–328.

Carroll, R. J., and D. Ruppert (1988), *Transformation and Weighting in Regression*, Chapman & Hall, New York.

Chambers, John M. (1997), The evolution of the S language, *Computing Science and Statistics* **28**, 331–337.

Chambers, John M.; William S. Cleveland; Beat Kleiner; and Paul A. Tukey (1983), *Graphical Methods for Data Analysis*, Duxbury Press, Boston.

Chan, K. S., and Johannes Ledolter (1995), Monte Carlo EM estimation for time series models involving counts, *Journal of the American Statistical Association* **90**, 242–252.

Cheng, R. C. H., and L. Traylor (1995), Non-regular maximum likelihood problems (with discussion), *Journal of the Royal Statistical Society, Series B* **57**, 3–44.

Chernick, Michael R. (1999), *Bootstrap Methods: A Practitioner's Guide*, John Wiley & Sons, New York.

Chernoff, Herman (1973), The use of faces to represent points in k-dimensional space graphically, *Journal of the American Statistical Association* **68**, 361–368.

Chou, Youn-Min; S. Turner; S. Henson; D. Meyer; and K. S. Chen (1994), On using percentiles to fit data by a Johnson distribution, *Communications in Statistics — Simulation and Computation* **23**, 341–354.

Chui, Charles K. (1988), *Multivariate Splines*, Society for Industrial and Applied Mathematics, Philadelphia.

Clarkson, Douglas B., and James E. Gentle (1986), Methods for multidimensional scaling, *Computer Science and Statistics: The Interface* (edited by D. M. Allen), North-Holland Publishing Company, Amsterdam, 185–192.

Cleveland, William S. (1993), *Visualizing Data*, Hobart Press, Summit, New Jersey.

Cleveland, William S. (1995), *The Elements of Graphing Data*, revised edition, Wadsworth, Monterey, California.

Coleman, Dan; Xioapeng Dong; Johanna Hardin; David M. Rocke; and David L. Woodruff (1999), Some computational issues in cluster analysis with no a priori metric, *Computational Statistics & Data Analysis* **31**, 1–11.

Comon, Pierre (1994), Independent component analysis, a new concept? *Signal Processing* **36**, 287–314.

Conway, J. H., and N. J. A. Sloane (1982), Fast quantizing and decoding algorithms for lattice quantizer and codes, *IEEE Transactions on Information Theory* **28**, 227–231.

Conway, J. H., and N. J. A. Sloane (1999), *Sphere Packings, Lattices and Groups*, third edition, Springer-Verlag, New York.

Cook, Dianne; Andreas Buja; and Javier Cabrera (1993), Projection pursuit indexes based on orthogonal function expansions, *Journal of Computational and Graphical Statistics* **2**, 225–250.

Cook, Dianne; Andreas Buja; Javier Cabrera; and Catherine Hurley (1995), Grand tour and projection pursuit, *Journal of Computational and Graphical Statistics* **4**, 155–172.

Cook, R. D.; D. M. Hawkins; and S. Weisberg (1993), Exact iterative computation of the robust multivariate minimum volume ellipsoid estimator, *Statistics and Probability Letters* **16**, 213–218.

Cowles, Mary Kathryn, and Bradley P. Carlin (1996), Markov chain Monte Carlo convergence diagnostics: A comparative review, *Journal of the American Statistical Association* **91**, 883–904.

Cressie, Noel A. C. (1991), *Statistics for Spatial Data*, John Wiley & Sons, New York.

Cristianini, Nello, and John Shawe-Taylor (2000), *An Introduction to Support Vector Machines*, Cambridge University Press, Cambridge, United Kingdom.

Dale, M. B. (1985), On the comparison of conceptual clustering and numerical taxonomy, *IEEE Transactions on Pattern Analysis and Machine Intelligence* **7**, 241–244.

Davies, P. L. (1993), Aspects of robust linear regression, *Annals of Statistics* **21**, 1843–1899.

Davison, A. C., and D. V. Hinkley (1997), *Bootstrap Methods and Their Application*, Cambridge University Press, Cambridge, United Kingdom.

Davison, A. C., and S. Sardy (2000), The partial scatterplot matrix, *Journal of Computational and Graphical Statistics* **9**, 750–758.

Dawkins, Brian P. (1995), Investigating the geometry of a p-dimensional data set, *Journal of the American Statistical Association* **90**, 350–359.

De Boor, Carl (2002), *A Practical Guide to Splines*, revised edition, Springer-Verlag, New York.

Dempster, A. P.; N. M. Laird; and D. B. Rubin (1977), Maximum likelihood estimation from incomplete data via the EM algorithm (with discussion), *Journal of the Royal Statistical Society, Series B* **45**, 1–37.

Dempster, A. P.; Nan M. Laird; and D. B. Rubin (1980), Iteratively reweighted least squares for linear regression when errors are normal/independent distributed, *Multivariate Analysis V* (edited by P. R. Krishnaiah), Elsevier Science Publishers, Amsterdam, 35–57.

Devroye, Luc (1986), *Non-Uniform Random Variate Generation*, Springer-Verlag, New York.

Diaconis, Persi, and David Freedman (1984), Asymptotics of graphical projection pursuit, *The Annals of Statistics* **12**, 793–815.

DiCiccio, Thomas J., and Bradley Efron (1992), More accurate confidence intervals in exponential families, *Biometrika* **79**, 231–245.

Dielman, Terry E.; Cynthia Lowry; and Roger Pfaffenberger (1994), A comparison of quantile estimators, *Communications in Statistics — Simulation and Computation* **23**, 355–371.

Dielman, Terry E., and Elizabeth L. Rose (1997), A note on hypothesis testing in LAV multiple regression: A small sample comparison, *Computational Statistics & Data Analysis* **23**, 381–388.

Dodge, Yadolah, and Jana Jureckova (2000), *Adaptive Linear Regression*, Springer-Verlag, New York.

Dongarra, Jack; Tom Rowan; and Reed Wade (1995), Software distribution using Xnetlib, *ACM Transactions on Mathematical Software* **21**, 79–88.

Draper, N. R., and H. Smith (1998), *Applied Regression Analysis*, third edition, John Wiley & Sons, New York.

Dryden, Ian L.; Charles C. Taylor; and Mohammad Reza Faghihi (1999), Size analysis of nearly regular Delaunay triangulations, *Methodology and Computing in Applied Probability* **1**, 97–117.

Du, Qiang; Vance Faber; and Max Gunzburger (1999), Centroidal Voronoi tessellations: Applications and algorithms, *SIAM Review* **41**, 637–676.

Dunkl, Charles, and Yuan Xu (2001), *Orthogonal Polynomials of Several Variables*, Cambridge University Press, Cambridge, United Kingdom.

Duran, Benjamin S., and Patrick L. Odell (1974), *Cluster Analysis; A Survey*, Springer-Verlag, New York.

Eckart, Carl, and Gale Young (1936), The approximation of one matrix by another of lower rank, *Psychometrika* **1**, 211–218.

Eddy, William F. (1977), A new convex hull algorithm for planar sets, *ACM Transactions on Mathematical Software* **3**, 398–403.

Eddy, William F. (1981) Comment on Friedman and Rafsky, "Graphics for the multivariate two-sample problem", *Journal of the American Statistical Association* **76**, 287–289.

Eddy, W. F. (1982), Convex hull peeling, *Compstat 1982: Proceedings in Computational Statistics* (edited by H. Caussinus, P. Ettinger, and R. Tomassone), Physica-Verlag, Vienna, 42–47.

Eddy, William F. (1985), Ordering of multivariate data, *Computer Science and Statistics: Proceedings of the Sixteenth Symposium on the Interface* (edited by Lynne Billard), North Holland, Amsterdam, 25–30.

Edgington, Eugene S. (1995), *Randomization tests*, third edition, Marcel Dekker, New York.

Edwards, A. W. F. (1992), *Likelihood*, expanded edition, The Johns Hopkins University Press, Baltimore.

Efron, Bradley (1982), *The Jackknife, the Bootstrap and Other Resampling Methods*, Society for Industrial and Applied Mathematics, Philadelphia.

Efron, Bradley (1987), Better bootstrap confidence intervals (with discussion), *Journal of the American Statistical Association* **82**, 171–200.

Efron, Bradley (1992), Jackknife-after-bootstrap standard errors and influence functions, *Journal of the Royal Statistical Society, Series B* **54**, 83–127.

Efron, Bradley, and Robert J. Tibshirani (1993), *An Introduction to the Bootstrap*, Chapman & Hall, New York.

Efromovich, Sam (1999), *Nonparametric Curve Estimation*, Springer-Verlag, New York.

Epanechnikov, V. A. (1969), Non-parametric estimation of a multivariate probability density, *Theory of Probability and its Applications* **14**, 153–158.

Eubank, Randall L. (1999), *Nonparametric Regression and Spline Smoothing*, second edition, Marcel Dekker, New York.

Everitt, B. S., and D. J. Hand (1981), *Finite Mixture Distributions*, Chapman & Hall, New York.

Faber, Vance (1994), Clustering and the continuous k-means algorithm, *Los Alamos Science* **22**, 138–144.

Farmen, Mark, and J. S. Marron (1999), An assessment of finite sample performance of adaptive methods in density estimation, *Computational Statistics & Data Analysis* **30**, 143–168.

Fayyad, Usama M.; Gregory Piatetsky-Shapiro; and Padhraic Smyth (1996), From data mining to knowledge discovery: An overview, *Advances in Knowledge Discovery and Data Mining*, edited by Usama M. Fayyad, Gregory Piatetsky-Shapiro, Padhraic Smyth, and Ramasamy Uthurusamy, American Association for Artificial Intelligence, Menlo Park, California, 1–34.

Fayyad, Usama M.; Gregory Piatetsky-Shapiro; Padhraic Smyth; and Ramasamy Uthurusamy (Editors) (1996), *Advances in Knowledge Discovery and Data Mining*, American Association for Artificial Intelligence, Menlo Park, California.

Fienberg, Stephen E. (1979), Graphical methods in statistics, *The American Statistician* **33**, 165–178.

Filliben, James J. (1982), DATAPLOT—An interactive, high-level language for graphics, nonlinear fitting, data analysis, and mathematics, *Proceedings of the Statistical Computing Section, ASA*, 268–273.

Fisher, R. A. (1935), *The Design of Experiments*, Oliver and Boyd, Edinburgh.

Fisherkeller, Mary Anne; Jerome H. Friedman; and John W. Tukey (1988), PRIM-9: An interactive multidimensional data display and analysis system *Dynamic Graphics for Statistics* (edited by William S. Cleveland and Marylyn E. McGill), Wadsworth Publishing Company, Belmont, California, 91–109.

Fishman, George S. (1999), An analysis of the Swendsen-Wang and related methods, *Journal of the Royal Statistical Society, Series B* **61**, 623–641.

Fishman, George S., and Louis R. Moore, III (1982), A statistical evaluation of multiplicative random number generators with modulus $2^{31} - 1$, *Journal of the American Statistical Association* **77**, 129–136.

Fishman, George S., and Louis R. Moore, III (1986), An exhaustive analysis of multiplicative congruential random number generators with modulus $2^{31} - 1$, *SIAM Journal on Scientific and Statistical Computing* **7**, 24–45.

Flury, Bernhard, and Alice Zoppè (2000), Exercises in EM, *The American Statistician* **54**, 207–209.

Foley, James D.; Andries van Dam; Steven K. Feiner; and John F. Hughes (1990), *Computer Graphics—Principles and Practice*, second edition, Addison-Wesley Publishing Company, Reading, Massachusetts.

Forster, Jonathan J.; John W. McDonald; and Peter W. F. Smith (1996), Monte Carlo exact conditional tests for log-linear and logistic models, *Journal of the Royal Statistical Society, Series B* **55**, 3–24.

Frank, Ildiko E., and Jerome H. Friedman (1993), A statistical view of some chemometrics regression tools (with discussion), *Technometrics* **35**, 109–148.

Freedman, D., and P. Diaconis (1981a), On the histogram as a density estimator: L_2 theory, *Zeitschrift für Wahrscheinlichkeitstheorie und Verwandte Gebiete* **57**, 453–476.

Freedman, D., and P. Diaconis (1981b), On the maximum deviation between the histogram and the underlying density, *Zeitschrift für Wahrscheinlichkeitstheorie und Verwandte Gebiete* **58**, 139–168.

Freund, Yoav, and Robert E. Schapire (1997), A decision-theoretic generalization of on-line learning and an application in boosting, *Journal of Computer and System Sciences* **55**, 119–139.

Friedman, Jerome H. (1987), Exploratory projection pursuit, *Journal of the American Statistical Association* **82**, 249–266.

Friedman, Jerome H.; Jon Louis Bentley; and Raphael Ari Finkel (1977), An algorithm for finding best matches in logarithmic expected time, *ACM Transactions on Mathematical Software* **3**, 209–226.

Friedman, Jerome H., and Lawrence C. Rafsky (1979a), Multivariate generalizations of the Wald-Wolfowitz and Smirnov two-sample tests, *Annals of Statistics* **7**, 697–717.

Friedman, J. H., and L. C. Rafsky (1979b), Fast algorithms for multivariate lining and planing, *Computer Science and Statistics: Proceedings of the 12th Symposium on the Interface* (edited by Jane F. Gentleman), University of Waterloo, Waterloo, Ontario, 124–129.

Friedman, Jerome H., and Lawrence C. Rafsky (1981), Graphics for the multivariate two-sample problem (with discussion), *Journal of the American Statistical Association* **76**, 277–295.

Friedman, Jerome H., and Werner Stuetzle (1981), Projection pursuit regression, *Journal of the American Statistical Association* **76**, 817–823.

Friendly, Michael (1994), Mosaic displays for multi-way contingency tables, *Journal of the American Statistical Association* **89**, 190–200.

Frigessi, Arnoldo; Fabio Martinelli; and Julian Stander (1997), Computational complexity of Markov chain Monte Carlo methods for finite Markov random fields, *Biometrika* **84**, 1–18.

Fuller, Wayne A. (1987), *Measurement Error Models*, John Wiley & Sons, New York.

Funkhauser, H. G. (1938), Historical development of the graphical representation of statistical data, *Osiris* **3**, 269–404.

Furnas, George W., and Andreas Buja (1994), Prosection views: Dimensional inference through sections and projections (with discussion), *Journal of Computational and Graphical Statistics* **3**, 323–385.

Fushimi, Masanori (1990), Random number generation with the recursion $X_t = X_{t-3p} \oplus X_{t-3q}$, *Journal of Computational and Applied Mathematics* **31**, 105–118.

Gelfand, Alan E., and Adrian F. M. Smith (1990), Sampling-based approaches to calculating marginal densities, *Journal of the American Statistical Association* **85**, 398–409. (Reprinted in Samuel Kotz and Norman L. Johnson (Editors) (1997), *Breakthroughs in Statistics, Volume III*, Springer-Verlag, New York, 526–550.)

Gelfand, Alan E., and Sujit K. Sahu (1994), On Markov chain Monte Carlo acceleration, *Journal of Computational and Graphical Statistics* **3**, 261–276.

Gelman, Andrew, and Donald B. Rubin (1992), A single series from the Gibbs sampler provides a false sense of security, *Bayesian Statistics 4* (edited by J. M. Bernardo, J. O. Berger, A. P. Dawid, and A. F. M. Smith), Oxford University Press, Oxford, United Kingdom, 625–631.

Gelman, Andrew; John B. Carlin; Hal S. Stern; and Donald B. Rubin (1995), *Bayesian Data Analysis*, Chapman & Hall, London.

Geman, Stuart, and Donald Geman (1984), Stochastic relaxation, Gibbs distributions, and the Bayesian restoration of images, *IEEE Transactions on Pattern Analysis and Machine Intelligence* **6**, 721–741.

Gentle, James E. (1998a), *Random Number Generation and Monte Carlo Methods*, Springer-Verlag, New York.

Gentle, James E. (1998b), *Numerical Linear Algebra for Applications in Statistics*, Springer-Verlag, New York.

Gentleman, Robert, and Ross Ihaka (1997), The R language, *Computing Science and Statistics* **28**, 326–330.

Geyer, Charles J. (1991), Markov chain Monte Carlo maximum likelihood, *Computer Science and Statistics: Proceedings of the Twenty-third Symposium on the Interface* (edited by Elaine M. Keramidas), Interface Foundation of North America, Fairfax, Virginia, 156–163.

Geyer, Charles J., and Elizabeth A. Thompson (1995), Annealing Markov chain Monte Carlo with applications to ancestral inference, *Journal of the American Statistical Association* **90**, 909–920.

Gilks, W. R.; A. Thomas; and D. J. Spiegelhalter (1992), Software for the Gibbs sampler, *Computing Science and Statistics* **24**, 439–448.

Girard, Stéphane (2000), A nonlinear PCA based on manifold approximation, *Computational Statistics* **15**, 145–167.

Glaeser, Georg, and Hellmuth Stachel (1999), *Open Geometry: OpenGL + Advanced Geometry*, Springer-Verlag, New York.

Glymour, Clark; David Madigan; Daryl Pregibon; and Padhraic Smyth (1996), Statistical inference and data mining, *Communications of the ACM* **39**, Number 11 (November), 35–41.

Gnanadesikan, R. (1997), *Methods for Statistical Data Analysis of Multivariate Observations*, second edition, John Wiley & Sons, New York.

Golub, Gene, and James M. Ortega (1993), *Scientific Computing. An Introduction with Parallel Computing*, Academic Press, San Diego.

Golub, G. H., and C. F. Van Loan (1980), An analysis of the total least squares problem, *SIAM Journal of Numerical Analysis* **17**, 883–893.

Gordon, A. D. (1999), *Classification*, second edition, Chapman & Hall/CRC, Boca Raton.

Gowda, K. Chidananda, and G. Krishna (1977), Agglomerative clustering using the concept of nearest neighborhood, *Pattern Recognition* **10**, 105–112.

Gower, J. C., and P. Legendre (1986), Metric and Euclidean properties of dissimilarity coefficients, *Journal of Classification* **3**, 5–48.

Gray, A. J. (1994), Simulating posterior Gibbs distributions: A comparison of the Swendsen-Wang and Gibbs sampler methods, *Statistics and Computing* **4**, 189–201.

Gray, H. L., and W. R. Schucany (1972), *The Generalized Jackknife Statistic*, Marcel Dekker, Inc., New York.

Green, P. J., and B. W. Silverman (1994), *Nonparametric Regression and Generalized Linear Models*, Chapman & Hall, London.

Greenwood, J. Arthur (1976), Moments of time to generate random variables by rejection, *Annals of the Institute for Statistical Mathematics* **28**, 399–401.

Grenander, Ulf (1981), *Abstract Inference*, John Wiley & Sons, New York.

Griffiths, P., and I. D. Hill (Editors) (1985), *Applied Statistics Algorithms*, Ellis Horwood Limited, Chichester, United Kingdom.

Hall, Peter (1989), On polynomial-based projection indexes for exploratory projection pursuit, *The Annals of Statistics* **17**, 589–605.

Hall, Peter (1990), Performance of balanced bootstrap resampling in distribution function and quantile problems, *Probability Theory and Related Fields* **85**, 239–260.

Hall, Peter (1992), *The Bootstrap and Edgeworth Expansion*, Springer-Verlag, New York.

Hall, Peter, and D. M. Titterington (1989), The effect of simulation order on level accuracy and power of Monte Carlo tests, *Journal of the Royal Statistical Society, Series B* **51**, 459–467.

Hammersley, J. M., and D. C. Handscomb (1964), *Monte Carlo Methods*, Methuen & Co., London.

Hand, D. J.; F. Daly; A. D. Lunn; K. J. McConway; and E. Ostrowski (1994), *Small Data Sets*, Chapman & Hall, London.

Härdle, W. (1990), *Applied Nonparametric Regression*, Cambridge University Press, Cambridge, United Kingdom.

Härdle, Wolfgang (1991), *Smoothing Techniques with Implementation in S*, Springer-Verlag, New York.

Harrell, Frank E., and C. E. Davis (1982), A new distribution-free quantile estimator, *Biometrika* **69**, 635–640.

Hartigan, John A. (1975), *Clustering Algorithms*, John Wiley & Sons, New York.

Hartigan, J. A., and B. Kleiner (1981), Mosaics for contingency tables, *Computer Science and Statistics: Proceedings of the 13th Symposium on the Interface* (edited by William F. Eddy), Springer-Verlag, New York, 268–273.

Hartigan, J. A., and M. A. Wong (1979), A K-means clustering algorithm, *Applied Statistics* **28**, 100–108. (See England and Beynon, 1981, *Applied Statistics* **30**, 355–356.)

Hastie, Trevor, and Werner Stuetzle (1989), Principal curves, *Journal of the American Statistical Association* **84**, 502–516.

Hastie, Trevor; Robert Tibshirani; and Jerome Friedman (2001), *The Elements of Statistical Learning. Data Mining, Inference, and Prediction*, Springer-Verlag, New York.

Hastings, W. K. (1970), Monte Carlo sampling methods using Markov chains and their applications. *Biometrika* **57**, 97–109. (Reprinted in Samuel Kotz and Norman L. Johnson (Editors) (1997), *Breakthroughs in Statistics, Volume III*, Springer-Verlag, New York, 240–256.)

Hathaway, R. J., and J. C. Bezdek (1988), Recent convergence results for the fuzzy c-means clustering algorithms, *Journal of Classification* **5**, 237–247.

Hausman, Robert E., Jr. (1982), Constrained multivariate analysis, *Optimization in Statistics* (edited by S. H. Zanakis and J. S. Rustagi), North-Holland Publishing Company, Amsterdam, 137–151.

Hawkins, Douglas M. (1993a), A feasible solution algorithm for minimum volume ellipsoid estimator in multivariate data, *Computational Statistics* **8**, 95–107.

Hawkins, Douglas M. (1993b), The feasible set algorithm for least median of squares regression, *Computational Statistics & Data Analysis* **16**, 81–101.

Hawkins, Douglas M. (1993c), The accuracy of elemental set approximations for regression, *Journal of the American Statistical Association* **88**, 580–589.

Hearne, Leonard B., and Edward J. Wegman (1991), Adaptive probability density estimation in lower dimensions using random tessellations, *Computer Science and Statistics: Proceedings of the Twenty-third Symposium on the Interface* (edited by Elaine M. Keramidas), Interface Foundation of North America, Fairfax, Virginia, 241–245.

Heath, D.; S. Kasif; and S. Salzberg (1993), Learning obliques decision trees, *Proceedings of the 13th International Joint Conference on Artificial Intelligence*, Morgan Kaufmann Publishers, San Mateo, California, 1002–1007.

Henery, R. J. (1997), Combining classification procedures, *Machine Learning and Statistics: The Interface* (edited by G. Nakhaeizadeh and C. C. Taylor), John Wiley & Sons, New York.

Hesterberg, Timothy C., and Barry L. Nelson (1998), Control variates for probability and quantile estimation, *Management Science* **44**, 1295–1312.

Hettmansperger, T. P., and S. J. Sheather (1992), A cautionary note on the method of least median squares, *The American Statistician* **46**, 79–83.

Ho, Tin Kam (1998), The random subspace method for constructing decision forests, *IEEE Transactions on Pattern Analysis and Machine Intelligence* **20**, 832–844.

Hoaglin, David C., and David F. Andrews (1975), The reporting of computation-based results in statistics, *The American Statistician* **29**, 122–126.

Hofmann, Thomas (1999), Probabilistic latent semantic indexing, *Proceedings of the 22th International Conference on Research and Development in Information Retrieval* (ACM SIGIR), 50–57.

Hope, A. C. A. (1968), A simplified Monte Carlo significance test procedure, *Journal of the Royal Statistical Society, Series B* **30**, 582–598.

Horowitz, Ellis; Sartaj Sahni; and Sanguthevar Rajasekaran (1998), *Computer Algorithms*, W. H. Freeman and Company, New York.

Huber, Peter J. (1985), Projection pursuit (with discussion), *The Annals of Statistics* **13**, 435–525.

Huber, Peter J. (1994), Huge data sets, *Compstat 1994: Proceedings in Computational Statistics* (edited by R. Dutter and W. Grossmann), Physica-Verlag, Heidelberg, 3–27.

Huber, Peter J. (1996), Massive Data Sets Workshop: The morning after, *Massive Data Sets*, Committee on Applied and Theoretical Statistics, National Research Council, National Academy Press, Washington, 169–184.

Hubert, Lawrence, and Phipps Arabie (1985), Comparing partitions, *Journal of Classification* **2**, 193–218.

Hull, John C. (2000), *Options, Futures, & Other Derivatives*, Prentice-Hall, Englewood Cliffs, New Jersey.

Hunt, Earl B.; Janet Marin; and Philip J. Stone (1966), *Experiments in Induction*, Academic Press, New York.

Hurley, Catherine, and Andreas Buja (1990), Analyzing high-dimensional data with motion graphics, *SIAM Journal on Scientific and Statistical Computing* **11**, 1193–1211.

Huzurbazar, S., and Ronald W. Butler (1998), Importance sampling for p-value computations in multivariate tests, *Journal of Computational and Graphical Statistics* **7**, 342–355.

Hyvärinen, Aapo; Juha Karhunen; and Erkki Oja (2001), *Independent Component Analysis*, John Wiley & Sons, New York.

Inselberg, A. (1985), The plane with parallel coordinates, *The Visual Computer* 1, 69–91.

Inselberg, Alfred (1998), Visual data mining with parallel coordinates, *Computational Statistics* 13, 47–63.

Inselberg, Alfred, and Bernard Dimsdale (1988), Visualizing multi-dimensional geometry with parallel coordinates, *Computer Science and Statistics: 20th Annual Symposium on the Interface* (edited by Edward J. Wegman, Donald T. Gantz, and John J. Miller), American Statistical Association, Alexandria, Virginia, 115–120.

Jacoby, William G. (1998), *Statistical Graphics for Visualizing Multivariate Data*, Sage Publications, Thousand Oaks, California.

Jamshidian, Mortaza, and Robert I. Jennrich (1993), Conjugate gradient acceleration of the EM algorithm, *Journal of the American Statistical Association* 88, 221–228.

Jamshidian, Mortaza, and Robert I. Jennrich (1997), Acceleration of the EM algorithm by using quasi-Newton methods, *Journal of the Royal Statistical Society, Series B* 59, 569–587.

Jolliffe, Ian T., and Mudassir Uddin (2000), The simplified component technique: An alternative to rotated principal components, *Journal of Computational and Graphical Statistics* 9, 689–710.

Jones, M. C., and Robin Sibson (1987), What is projection pursuit (with discussion), *Journal of the Royal Statistical Society, Series A* 150, 1–36.

Jörgensen, B. (1984), The Delta algorithm and GLIM, *International Statistical Review* 52, 283–300.

Julesz, Bela (1986), Texton gradients: The texton theory revisited, *Biological Cybernetics*, 54, 245–251.

Julesz, Bela (1994), *Dialogues on Perception*, The MIT Press, Cambridge, Massachusetts.

Kademan, Edmund; Wei-Yin Loh; and Nunta Vanichsetakul (1989), An improved version of FACT with S front end, *The American Statistician* 43, 273.

Kaigh, W. D., and Peter A. Lachenbruch (1982), A generalized quantile estimator, *Communications in Statistics — Theory and Methods* 11, 2217–2238.

Kao, David T.; R. Daniel Bergeron; and Ted M. Sparr (1998), Efficient proximity search in multivariate data, *Proceedings of the Tenth International Conference on Scientific and Statistical Database Management* (edited by Maurizio Rafanelli and Matthias Jarke), IEEE Computer Society, Los Alamitos, California, 145–154.

Karian, Zaven A., and Edward J. Dudewicz (1999), Fitting the generalized lambda distribution to data: A method based on percentiles, *Communications in Statistics — Simulation and Computation* 28, 793–819.

Karian, Zaven A., and Edward J. Dudewicz (2000), *Fitting Statistical Distributions*, CRC Press, Boca Raton.

Karian, Zaven A.; Edward J. Dudewicz; and Patrick McDonald (1996), The extended generalized lambda distribution system for fitting distributions to data: History, completion of theory, tables, applications, the "final word" on moment fits, *Communications in Statistics — Simulation and Computation* 25, 611–642.

Kass, G. V. (1980), An exploratory technique for investigating large quantities of categorical data, *Applied Statistics* 29, 119–127.

Kaufman, Leonard, and Peter J. Rousseeuw (1990), *Finding Groups in Data: An Introduction to Cluster Analysis*, John Wiley & Sons, New York.

Keim, Daniel A. (1996), Pixel-oriented visualization techniques for exploring very large data bases, *Journal of Computational and Graphical Statistics* 5, 58–77.

Kendall, M. G. (1961), *A Course in the Geometry of n Dimensions*, Charles Griffin & Company Limited, London.

Kennedy, W. J., and T. A. Bancroft (1971), Model building for prediction in regression based upon repeated significance tests, *Annals of Mathematical Statistics* 42, 1273–1284.

Kennedy, William J., and James E. Gentle (1980), *Statistical Computing*, Marcel Dekker, Inc., New York.

Kieffer, J. C. (1983), Uniqueness of locally optimal quantizer for log-concave density and convex error function, *IEEE Transactions in Information Theory* 29, 42–47.

Kim, Dong K., and Jeremy M. G. Taylor (1995), The restricted EM algorithm for maximum likelihood estimation under linear restrictions on the parameters, *Journal of the American Statistical Association* **90**, 708–716.

Kleijnen, Jack P. C. (1977), Robustness of a multiple ranking procedure: A Monte Carlo experiment illustrating design and analysis techniques, *Communications in Statistics — Simulation and Computation* **B6**, 235–262.

Kleiner, B., and J. A. Hartigan (1981), Representing points in many dimensions by trees and castles (with discussion), *Journal of the American Statistical Association* **76**, 260–276.

Klinke, S. (1997), *Data Structures for Computational Statistics*, Springer-Verlag, New York.

Knuth, Donald E. (1973), *The Art of Computer Programming, Volume 3, Sorting and Searching*, Addison-Wesley Publishing Company, Reading, Massachusetts.

Koehler, J. R., and A. B. Owen (1996), Computer experiments, *Handbook of Statistics, Volume 13* (edited by S. Ghosh and C. R. Rao), Elsevier Science Publishers, Amsterdam, 261–308.

Kohn, Robert; Craig F. Ansley; and David Tharm (1991), The performance of cross-validation and maximum likelihood estimators of spline smoothing parameters, *Journal of the American Statistical Association* **86**, 1042–1050.

Kruskal, Joseph B., Jr. (1956), On the shortest spanning subtree of a graph and the traveling salesman problem, *Proceedings of the American Mathematical Society* **7**, 48–50.

Kwon, Sunhee, and Dianne Cook (1998), Grand tour combined with minimal spanning tree in Java for finding structure in high-dimensional data, *Computing Science and Statistics* **30**, 224–228.

Lance, G. N., and W. T. Williams (1966), Computer programs for hierarchical polythetic classification ('similarity analyses'), *Computer Journal* **9**, 60–64.

Lance, G. N., and W. T. Williams (1967a), A general theory of classificatory sorting strategies, *Computer Journal* **9**, 373–380.

Lance, G. N., and W. T. Williams (1967b), Mixed-data classificatory programs. I. Agglomerative systems, *Australian Computer Journal* **1**, 15–20.

Lance, G. N., and W. T. Williams (1968), Mixed-data classificatory programs. II. Divisive systems, *Australian Computer Journal* **1**, 82–85.

Lange, Kenneth (1999), *Numerical Analysis for Statisticians*, Springer-Verlag, New York.

Laviolette, Michael; John W. Seaman, Jr.; J. Douglas Barrett; and William H. Woodall (1995), A probabilistic and statistical view of fuzzy methods (with discussion), *Technometrics* **37**, 249–292.

Lax, David A. (1985), Robust estimators of scale: Finite-sample performance in long-tailed symmetric distributions, *Journal of the American Statistical Association* **80**, 736–741.

Learmonth, G. P., and P. A. W. Lewis (1973), Statistical tests of some widely used and recently proposed uniform random number generators, *Computer Science and Statistics: 7th Annual Symposium on the Interface* (edited by William J. Kennedy), Statistical Laboratory, Iowa State University, Ames, Iowa, 163–171.

Lee, D. T. (1999a), Computational Geometry I, *Algorithms and Theory of Computation Handbook* (edited by Mikhail J. Atallah), CRC Press, Boca Raton, 19-1–19-29.

Lee, D. T. (1999b), Computational Geometry II, *Algorithms and Theory of Computation Handbook* (edited by Mikhail J. Atallah), CRC Press, Boca Raton, 20-1–20-31.

Lee, D. D., and H. S. Seung (1999), Learning the parts of objects by non-negative matrix factorization, *Nature* **401**, 788–793.

Lehmann, E. L., and George Casella (1998), *Theory of Point Estimation*, second edition, Springer-Verlag, New York.

LePage, Raoul, and Lynne Billard (Editors) (1992), *Exploring the Limits of Bootstrap*, John Wiley & Sons, New York.

Lesk, Michael (1997), *Practical Digital Libraries: Books, Bytes, and Bucks*, Morgan Kaufmann Publishers, San Mateo, California.

Levine, Richard A., and George Casella (2001), Implementations of the Monte Carlo EM Algorithm, *Journal of Computational and Graphical Statistics* **10**, 422–439.

Lewis, P. A. W.; A. S. Goodman; and J. M. Miller (1969), A pseudo-random number generator for the System/360, *IBM Systems Journal* **8**, 136–146.

Li, Hongyi, and G. S. Maddala (1996), Bootstrapping time series models (with discussion), *Econometric Reviews* **15**, 115–195.

Liu, Jun S., and Chiara Sabatti (1999), Simulated sintering: Markov chain Monte Carlo with spaces of varying dimensions, *Bayesian Statistics 6* (edited by J. M. Bernardo, J. O. Berger, A. P. Dawid, and A. F. M. Smith), Oxford University Press, Oxford, United Kingdom, 389–413.

Liu, Regina Y. (1990), On a notion of data depth based on random simplices, *Annals of Statistics* **18**, 405–414.

Liu, Regina Y.; Jesse M. Parelius; and Kesar Singh (1999), Multivariate analysis by data depth: Descriptive statistics, graphics and inference (with discussion), *Annals of Statistics* **27**, 783–840.

Lloyd, S. (1982), Least square quantization in PCM, *IEEE Transactions in Information Theory* **28**, 129–137.

Loh, Wei-Yin, and Nunta Vanichsetakul (1988), Tree-structured classification via generalized discriminant analysis (with discussion), *Journal of the American Statistical Association* **83**, 715–728.

Lorensen, William E., and Harvey E. Cline (1988), Marching cubes: A high-resolution 3-D surface construction algorithm, *Computer Graphics, ACM SIGGRAPH Conference Proceedings* **21**, 163–169.

Louis, Thomas A. (1982), Finding the observed information matrix when using the EM algorithm, *Journal of the Royal Statistical Society, Series B* **44**, 226–233.

Lund, Ulric (1999), Cluster analysis for directional data, *Communications in Statistics — Simulation and Computation* **28**, 1001–1009.

Manly, Bryan F. J. (1997), *Randomization, Bootstrap and Monte Carlo Methods in Biology*, second edition, Chapman & Hall, London.

Marazzi, A. (1993), *Algorithms, Routines and S Functions for Robust Statistics* Wadsworth & Brooks/Cole, Pacific Grove, California.

Marchette, David J.; Carey E. Priebe; George W. Rogers; and Jeffry L. Solka (1996), Filtered kernel density estimation, *Computational Statistics* **11**, 95–112.

Maronna, Ricardo A., and Victor J. Yohai (1995), The behavior of the Stahel-Donoho robust multivariate estimator, *Journal of the American Statistical Association* **90**, 330–341.

Marriott, F. H. C. (1979), Barnard's Monte Carlo tests: How many simulations?, *Applied Statistics* **28**, 75–78.

Marron, J. S., and D. Nolan (1988), Canonical kernels for density estimation, *Statistics and Probability Letters* **7** 195–199.

Marron, J. S., and A. B. Tsybakov (1995), Visual criteria for qualitative smoothing, *Journal of the American Statistical Association* **90**, 499–507.

Marron, J. S., and M. P. Wand (1992), Exact mean integrated squared error, *Annals of Statistics* **20**, 343–353.

Marsaglia, George (1985), A current view of random number generators, *Computer Science and Statistics: 16th Symposium on the Interface* (edited by L. Billard), North-Holland, Amsterdam, 3–10.

Marsaglia, George (1995), *The Marsaglia Random Number CDROM, including the DIEHARD Battery of Tests of Randomness*, Department of Statistics, Florida State University, Tallahassee, Florida. Available at http://stat.fsu.edu/~geo/diehard.html .

McCullough, B. D. (1999), Assessing the reliability of statistical software: Part II, *The American Statistician* **53**, 149–159.

McKay, Michael D.; William J. Conover; and Richard J. Beckman (1979), A comparison of three methods for selecting values of input variables in the analysis of output from a computer code, *Technometrics* **21**, 239–245.

McLachlan, Geoffrey J., and Thriyambakam Krishnan (1997), *The EM Algorithm and Extensions*, John Wiley & Sons, New York.

Mead, R. (1974), A test for spatial pattern at several scales using data from a trio of contiguous quadrats, *Biometrics* **30**, 295–307.

Meintanis, S. G., and G. S. Donatos (1997), A comparative study of some robust methods for coefficient-estimation in linear regression, *Computational Statistics & Data Analysis* **23**, 525–540.

Meng, Xiao-Li, and Donald B. Rubin (1991), Using EM to obtain asymptotic variance-covariance matrices: The SEM algorithm, *Journal of the American Statistical Association* **86**, 899–909.

Meng, X.-L., and D. B. Rubin (1993), Maximum likelihood estimation via the ECM algorithm: A general framework, *Biometrika* **80**, 267–278.

Mengersen, Kerrie L.; Christian P. Robert; and Chantal Guihenneuc-Jouyaux (1999), MCMC convergence diagnostics: A reviewwww, *Bayesian Statistics 6* (edited by J. M. Bernardo, J. O. Berger, A. P. Dawid, and A. F. M. Smith), Oxford University Press, Oxford, United Kingdom, 415–440.

Metropolis, N.; A. W. Rosenbluth; M. N. Rosenbluth; A. H. Teller; and E. Teller (1953), Equations of state calculation by fast computing machines, *Journal of Chemical Physics* **21**, 1087–1092. (Reprinted in Samuel Kotz and Norman L. Johnson (Editors) (1997), *Breakthroughs in Statistics, Volume III*, Springer-Verlag, New York, 127–139.)

Michalski, R. S. (1980), Knowledge acquisition through conceptual clustering: A theoretical framework and an algorithm for partitioning data into conjunctive concepts, *Journal of Policy Analysis and Information Systems* **4**, 219–244.

Michalski, R. S., and R. E. Stepp (1983), Automated construction of classifications: Conceptual clustering versus numerical taxonomy, *IEEE Transactions on Pattern Analysis and Machine Intelligence* **5**, 396–409.

Milligan, Glenn W. (1985), An algorithm for generating artificial test clusters, *Psychometrika* **50**, 123–127.

Milligan, Glenn W., and Martha C. Cooper (1985), An examination of procedures for determining the number of clusters in a data set, *Psychometrika* **50**, 159–179.

Monti, Katherine L. (1995), Folded empirical distribution function curves – mountain plots, *The American Statistician* **49**, 342–345.

Morgan, James N., and John A. Sonquist (1963), Problems in the analysis of survey data, and a proposal *Journal of the American Statistical Association* **58**, 415–434.

Mortenson, Michael E. (1995), *Geometric Transformations*, Industrial Press, New York.

Mortenson, Michael E. (1997), *Geometric Modeling*, second edition, John Wiley & Sons, New York.

Morton, Sally C. (1992), Interpretable projection pursuit, *Computer Science and Statistics: Proceedings of the Twenty-second Symposium on the Interface* (edited by Connie Page and Raoul LePage), Springer-Verlag, New York, 470–474.

Murtagh, F. (1984), A review of fast techniques for nearest neighbour searching, *Compstat 1984: Proceedings in Computational Statistics* (edited by T. Havránek, Z. Šidák, and M. Novák), Physica-Verlag, Vienna, 143–147.

Murthy, Sreerama K.; Simon Kasif; and Steven Salzberg (1994), A system for induction of oblique decision trees, *Journal of Artificial Intelligence Research* **2**, 1–32.

Naito, Kanta (1997), A generalized projection pursuit procedure and its significance level, *Hiroshima Mathematical Journal* **27**, 513–554.

Nason, Guy P. (2001), Robust projection indices, *Journal of the Royal Statistical Society, Series B* **63**, 551–567.

Nelder, J. A., and R. W. M. Wedderburn (1972), Generalized linear models, *Journal of the Royal Statistical Society, Series A* **135**, 370–384.

Newton, Carol M. (1978), Graphica: From alpha to omega in data analysis, *Graphical Representation of Multivariate Data* (edited by Peter C. C. Wang), Academic Press, New York, 59–92.

Newman, M. E. J., and G. T. Barkema (1999) *Monte Carlo Methods in Statistical Physics*, Oxford University Press, Oxford, United Kingdom.

Nicole, Sandro (2000), Feedforward neural networks for principal components extraction, *Computational Statistics & Data Analysis* **33**, 425–437.

NIST (2000), *A Statistical Test Suite for Random and Pseudorandom Number Generators for Cryptographic Applications*, NIST Special Publication 800-22, National Institute for Standards and Technology, Gaithersburg, Maryland.

Nummelin, Esa (1984), *General Irreducible Markov Chains and Non-Negative Operators*, Cambridge University Press, Cambridge, United Kingdom.

Obuchowski, Nancy A., and M. L. Lieber (1998), Confidence intervals for the receiver operating characteristic area in studies with small samples, *Academic Radiology* **5**, 561–571.

Okabe, Atsuyuki; Barry Boots; Ksokichi Sugihara; and Sung Nok Chui (2000), *Spatial Tessellations: Concepts & Applications of Voroni Diagrams*, second edition, John Wiley & Sons, New York.

Øksendal, Bernt (1998), *Stochastic Differential Equations. An Introduction with Applications*, fifth edition, Springer-Verlag, Berlin.

OpenGL Architecture Review Board (1992), *OpenGL Reference Manual*, Addison-Wesley Publishing Company, Reading, Massachusetts.

O'Rourke, Joseph (1998) *Computational Geometry in C*, second edition, Cambridge University Press, Cambridge, United Kingdom.

Owen, Art B. (1998), Latin supercube sampling for very high-dimensional simulations, *ACM Transactions on Modeling and Computer Simulation* **8**, 71–102.

Park, Stephen K., and Keith W. Miller (1988), Random number generators: Good ones are hard to find, *Communications of the ACM* **31**, 1192–1201.

Picard, Richard R., and Kenneth N. Berk (1990), Data splitting, *The American Statistician* **44**, 140–147.

Politis, Dimitris N., and Joseph P. Romano (1992), A circular block-resampling procedure for stationary data *Exploring the Limits of the Bootstrap* (edited by Raoul LePage and Lynne Billard), John Wiley & Sons, New York, 263–270.

Politis, Dimitris N., and Joseph P. Romano (1994), The stationary bootstrap, *Journal of the American Statistical Association* **89**, 1303–1313.

Posse, C. (1990), An effective two-dimensional projection pursuit algorithm, *Communications in Statistics — Simulation and Computation* **19** 1143–1164.

Posse, Christian (1995a), Tools for two-dimensional exploratory projection pursuit, *Journal of Computational and Graphical Statistics* **4**, 83–100.

Posse, Christian (1995b), Projection pursuit exploratory data analysis, *Computational Statistics & Data Analysis* **20**, 669–687.

Priebe, Carey E. (1994), Adaptive mixtures, *Journal of the American Statistical Association* **89**, 796–806.

Priebe, Carey E., and David J. Marchette (2000), Alternating kernel and mixture density estimates, *Computational Statistics & Data Analysis* **35**, 43–65.

Quenouille, M. H. (1949), Approximate tests of correlation in time series, *Journal of the Royal Statistical Society, Series B* **11**, 18–84.

Quenouille, M. H. (1956), Notes on bias in estimation, *Biometrika* **43**, 353–360.

Quinlan, J. R. (1986), Induction of decision trees, *Machine Learning* **1**, 81–106.

Quinlan, J. Ross (1993), *C4.5, Programs for Machine Learning*, Morgan Kaufmann, San Mateo, California.

Rai, S. N., and D. E. Matthews (1993), Improving the EM algorithm, *Biometrics* **49**, 587–591.

Ramberg, John S., and Bruce W. Schmeiser (1974), An approximate method for generating asymmetric random variables, *Communications of the ACM* **17**, 78–82.

Ramsay, J. O., and B. W. Silverman (1997), *Functional Data Analysis*, Springer-Verlag, New York.

Rand, William M. (1971), Objective criteria for the evaluation of clustering methods, *Journal of the American Statistical Association* **66**, 846–850.

Rao, J. N. K., and J. T. Webster (1966), On two methods of bias reduction in the estimation of ratios, *Biometrika* **53**, 571–577.

Renka, Robert J. (1997), Algorithm 772: STRIPACK: Delaunay triangulation and Voronoi diagram on the surface of a sphere, *ACM Transactions on Mathematical Software* **23**, 416–434.

Reyment, Richard A., and K. G. Jöreskog (1996), *Applied Factor Analysis in the Natural Sciences*, Cambridge University Press, Cambridge, United Kingdom.

Rice, John R. (1993), *Numerical Methods, Software, and Analysis*, second edition, McGraw-Hill Book Company, New York.

Richeldi, M., and M. Rossotto (1997), Combining statistical techniques and search heuristics to perform effective feature selection, *Machine Learning and Statistics: The Interface* (edited by G. Nakhaeizadeh and C. C. Taylor), John Wiley & Sons, New York.

Riesenfeld, R. F. (1981), Homogeneous coordinates and projective planes in computer graphics, *IEEE Computer Graphics and Applications* **1**, 50–55.

Ripley, B. D. (1979a), Tests of 'randomness' for spatial point patterns, *Journal of the Royal Statistical Society, Series B* **41**, 368–374.

Ripley, B. D. (1979b), Algorithm AS137: Simulating spatial patterns: dependent samples from a multivariate density. *Applied Statistics* **28**, 109–112.

Ripley, Brian D. (1981), *Spatial Statistics*, John Wiley & Sons, New York.

Ripley, Brian D. (1987), *Stochastic Simulation*, John Wiley & Sons, New York.

Ripley, Brian D. (1993), Statistical aspects of neural networks, *Networks and Chaos — Statistical and Probabilistic Aspects* (edited by O. E. Barndorff-Nielsen, J. L. Jensen, and W. S. Kendall), Chapman & Hall, London, 40–123.

Ripley, Brian D. (1994), Neural networks and related methods for classification (with discussion), *Journal of the Royal Statistical Society, Series B* **56**, 409–456.

Ripley, B. D. (1996), *Pattern Recognition and Neural Networks*, Cambridge University Press, Cambridge, United Kingdom.

Robert, Christian P. (1998a), A pathological MCMC algorithm and its use as a benchmark for convergence assessment techniques, *Computational Statistics* **13**, 169–184.

Robert, Christian P. (Editor) (1998b), *Discretization and MCMC Convergence Assessment*, Springer-Verlag, New York.

Robert, Christian P., and George Casella (1999), *Monte Carlo Statistical Methods*, Springer-Verlag, New York.

Roeder, Kathryn, and Larry Wasserman (1997), Practical Bayesian density estimation using mixtures of normals, *Journal of the American Statistical Association* **92**, 894–902.

Rosenblatt, M. (1956), Remarks on some nonparametric estimates of a density function, *Annals of Mathematical Statistics* **27**, 832–835.

Rosenthal, Jeffrey S. (1995), Minorization conditions and convergence rates for Markov chain Monte Carlo, *Journal of the American Statistical Association* **90**, 558–566.

Rousseeuw, P. J. (1984), Least median of squares regression, *Journal of the American Statistical Association* **79**, 871–880. (Reprinted in Samuel Kotz and Norman L. Johnson (Editors) (1997), *Breakthroughs in Statistics, Volume III*, Springer-Verlag, New York, 440–461.)

Rousseeuw, Peter J. (1995), Discussion: Fuzzy clustering at the intersection, *Technometrics* **37**, 283–286.

Rousseeuw, Peter J., and Mia Hubert (1999), Regression depth (with discussion), *Journal of the American Statistical Association* **94**, 388–433.

Rousseeuw, Peter J., and Annick M. Leroy (1987), *Robust Regression and Outlier Detection*, John Wiley & Sons, New York.

Rousseeuw, Peter J., and Ida Ruts (1996), Bivariate location depth, *Applied Statistics* **45**, 516–526.

Rousseeuw, Peter J., and Ida Ruts (1998), Constructing the bivariate Tukey median, *Statistica Sinica* **8**, 827–839.

Rousseeuw, P. J., and B. van Zomeren (1990), Unmasking multivariate outliers and leverage points, *Journal of the American Statistical Association* **85**, 633–651.

Rubin, Donald B. (1987), *Multiple Imputation for Nonresponse in Surveys*, John Wiley & Sons, New York.

Rustagi, Jagdish S. (1994), *Optimization Techniques in Statistics*, Academic Press, Boston.

Ruts, Ida, and Peter J. Rousseeuw (1996), Computing depth contours of bivariate point clouds, *Computational Statistics and Data Analysis* **23**, 153–168.

Sacks, Jerome; William J. Welch; Toby J. Mitchell; and Henry P. Wynn (1989), Design and analysis of computer experiments (with discussion), *Statistical Science* **4**, 409–435.

Sargent, Daniel J.; James S. Hodges; and Bradley P. Carlin (2000), Structured Markov chain Monte Carlo, *Journal of Computational and Graphical Statistics* **9**, 217–234.

Schafer, J. L. (1997), *Analysis of Incomplete Multivariate Data*, Chapman & Hall, London.

Schapire, Robert E. (1990), The strength of weak learnability, *Machine Learning* **5**, 197–227.

Schenker, Nathaniel (1985), Qualms about bootstrap confidence intervals, *Journal of the American Statistical Association* **80**, 360–361.

Schölkopf, Bernhard; Alexander J. Smola; and Klaus-Robert Müller (1999), Kernel principal component analysis, *Advances in Kernel Methods. Support Vector Learning* (edited by Bernhard Schölkopf, Christopher J. C. Burges, and Alexander J. Smola), The MIT Press, Cambridge, Massachusetts, 327–352.

Schroeder, Will; Ken Martin; and Bill Lorensen (1996), *The Visualization Toolkit, An Object-Oriented Approach to 3D Graphics*, second edition, Prentice Hall PTR, Upper Saddle River, New Jersey.

Schucany, W. R.; H. L. Gray; and D. B. Owen (1971), On bias reduction in estimation, *Journal of the American Statistical Association* **66**, 524–533.

Scott, D. W. (1979), On optimal and data-based histograms, *Biometrika* **66**, 605–610.

Scott, David W. (1988), A note on choice of bivariate histogram bin shape, *Journal of Official Statistics* **4**, 47–51.

Scott, David W. (1992), *Multivariate Density Estimation*, John Wiley & Sons, New York.

Scott, D. W.; R. A. Tapia; and J. R. Thompson (1980), Nonparametric probability density estimation by discrete maximum penalized-likelihood criteria, *Annals of Statistics* **8**, 820–832.

Scott, David W., and James R. Thompson (1983), Probability density estimation in higher dimensions, *Computer Science and Statistics: The Interface* (edited by James E. Gentle), North-Holland Publishing Company, Amsterdam, 173–179.

Seaver, Bill; Konstantinos Triantis; and Chip Reeves (1999), The identification of influential subsets in regression using a fuzzy clustering strategy, *Technometrics* **41**, 340–351.

Senchaudhuri, Pralay; Cyrus R. Mehta; and Nitin R. Patel (1995), Estimating exact p values by the method of control variates or Monte Carlo rescue, *Journal of the American Statistical Association* **90**, 640–648.

Sewell, Granville (1988a), Plotting contour surfaces of a function of three variables, *ACM Transactions on Mathematical Software* **14**, 33–41.

Sewell, Granville (1988b), Algorithm 657: Software for plotting contour surfaces of a function of three variables, *ACM Transactions on Mathematical Software* **14**, 42–44.

Shao, Jun, and Dongsheng Tu (1995), *The Jackknife and Bootstrap*, Springer-Verlag, New York.

Sharot, Trevor (1976), The generalized jackknife: Finite samples and subsample sizes, *Journal of the American Statistical Association* **71**, 451–454.

Sherman, Michael, and Edward Carlstein (1996), Replicate histograms, *Journal of the American Statistical Association* **91**, 566–576.

Sibuya, M. (1961), Exponential and other variable generators, *Annals of the Institute for Statistical Mathematics* **13**, 231–237.

Silverman, B. W. (1982), Kernel density estimation using the fast Fourier transform, *Applied Statistics* **31**, 93–97.

Simonoff, Jeffrey S. (1995), The anchor position of histograms and frequency polygons: Quantitative and qualitative smoothing, *Communications in Statistics — Simulation and Computation* **24**, 691–710.

Simonoff, Jeffrey S. (1996), *Smoothing Methods in Statistics*, Springer-Verlag, New York.

Simonoff, Jeffrey S., and Frederic Udina (1997), Measuring the stability of histogram appearance when the anchor position is changed, *Computational Statistics & Data Analysis* **23**, 335–353.

Siu, Cynthia O. (1988), Application of orthogonalization procedures to fitting tree-structured models, *Computer Science and Statistics: Proceedings of the Twentieth Symposium on the Interface* (edited by Edward J. Wegman, Donald T. Gantz, and John J. Miller), American Statistical Association, Alexandria, Virginia, 559–564.

Slifker, James F., and Samuel S. Shapiro (1980), The Johnson system: Selection and parameter estimation, *Technometrics* **22**, 239–246.

Small, Christopher G. (1996), *The Statistical Theory of Shape*, Springer-Verlag, New York.

Solka, Jeffrey L.; Wendy L. Poston; and Edward J. Wegman (1995), A visualization technique for studying the iterative estimation of mixture densities, *Journal of Computational and Graphical Statistics* **4**, 180–198.

Solka, Jeffrey L.; Edward J. Wegman; Carey E. Priebe; Wendy L. Poston; and George W. Rogers (1998), Mixture structure analysis using the Akaike information criterion and the bootstrap, *Statistics and Computing* **8**, 177–188.

Spanier, Jerome, and Keith B. Oldham (1987), *An Atlas of Functions*, Hemisphere Publishing Corporation, Washington (also Springer-Verlag, Berlin).

Sparr, T. M.; R. D. Bergeron; and L. D. Meeker (1993), A visualization-based model for a scientific database system, *Focus on Scientific Visualization* (edited by H. Hagen, H. Müller, and G. M. Nielson), Springer-Verlag, Berlin, 103–121.

Speed, T. P., and Bin Yu (1993), Model selection and prediction: Normal regression, *Annals of the Institute of Statistical Mathematics* **45**, 35–54.

Stevens, S. S. (1946), On the theory of scales of measurement, *Science* **103** 677–680.

Stewart, Ian (2001), *Flatterland: Like Flatland Only More So*, Perseus Books Group, Boulder, Colorado.

Stigler, Stephen M. (1978), Mathematical statistics in the early states, *Annals of Statistics* **6**, 239–265.

Stigler, Stephen M. (1991), Stochastic simulation in the nineteenth century, *Statistical Science* **6**, 89–97.

Stone, Charles J. (1984), An asymptotically optimal window selection rule for kernel density estimates, *Annals of Statistics* **12**, 1285–1297.

Struyf, Anja, and Peter J. Rousseeuw (2000), High-dimensional computation of the deepest location, *Computational Statistics & Data Analysis* **34**, 415–426.

Student (1908a), On the probable error of a mean, *Biometrika* **6**, 1–25.

Student (1908b), Probable error of a correlation coefficient, *Biometrika* **6**, 302–310.

Sullivan, Thomas J. (2002), *Classification Methods for Augmented Arc-Weighted Graphs*, unpublished Ph.D. dissertation, George Mason University, Fairfax, Virginia. Available at http://www.scs.gmu.edu/~tsulliva/csi999/Dissertation.pdf.

Sun, J. (1991), Significance levels in exploratory projection pursuit, *Biometrika* **78**, 759–769.

Sun, Jiayang (1992), Some computational aspects of projection pursuit, *Computer Science and Statistics: Proceedings of the 22nd Symposium on the Interface* (edited by Connie Page and Raoul LePage), Springer-Verlag, New York, 539–543.

Sun, Jiayang (1993), Some practical aspects of exploratory projection pursuit, *SIAM Journal on Scientific and Statistical Computing* **14**, 68–80.

Sutton, Clifton D. (1993), Computer-intensive methods for tests about the mean of an asymmetrical distribution, *Journal of the American Statistical Association* **88**, 802–810.

Swayne, D. F.; D. Cook; and A. Buja (1991), XGobi: Interactive dynamic graphics in the X Window system with a link to S, *Proceedings of the Statistical Computing Section, ASA*, 1–8.

Swendsen, R. H., and J.-S. Wang (1987), Nonuniversal critical dynamics in Monte Carlo simulations, *Physical Review Letters* **58**, 86–88.

Symanzik, J.; D. Cook; B. D. Kohlmeyer; U. Lechner; and C. Cruz-Neira (1997), Dynamic statistical graphics in the C2 virtual reality environment, *Computing Science and Statistics* **29** (2), 41–47.

Tarter, Michael E.; William Freeman; and Alan Hopkins (1986), A Fortran implementation of univariate Fourier series density estimation, *Communications in Statistics — Simulation and Computation* **15**, 855–870.

Tarter, Michael, and Richard Kronmal (1970), On multivariate density estimates based on orthogonal expansions, *Annals of Mathematical Statistics* **41**, 718–722.

Taylor, Malcolm S., and James R. Thompson (1986), Data based random number generation for a multivariate distribution via stochastic simulation, *Computational Statistics & Data Analysis* **4**, 93–101.

Taylor, Walter F. (1992), *The Geometry of Computer Graphics*, Wadsworth & Brooks/Cole, Pacific Grove, California.

Terrell, George R. (1990), The maximal smoothing principle in density estimation, *Journal of the American Statistical Association* **85**, 470–477.

Terrell, George R., and David W. Scott (1992), Variable kernel density estimation, *Annals of Statistics* **20**, 1236–1265.

Theus, Martin (1995), Trellis displays vs. interactive graphics, *Computational Statistics* **10**, 113–127.

Thomas, William (1991), Influence on the cross-validated smoothing parameter in spline smoothing, *Computer Science and Statistics: Proceedings of the Twenty-third Symposium on the Interface* (edited by Elaine M. Keramidas), Interface Foundation of North America, Fairfax, Virginia, 192–195.

Thompson, William J. (1997), *Atlas for Computing Mathematical Functions: An Illustrated Guide for Practitioners with Programs in C and Mathematica*, John Wiley & Sons, New York.

Tibshirani, R. (1988), Estimating transformations for regression via additivity and variance stabilization, *Journal of the American Statistical Association* **83**, 395–405.

Tierney, Luke (1994), Markov chains for exploring posterior distributions (with discussion), *Annals of Statistics* **22**, 1701–1762.

Tierney, Luke (1996), Introduction to general state-space Markov chain theory, *Practical Markov Chain Monte Carlo* (edited by W. R. Gilks, S. Richardson, and D. J. Spiegelhalter), Chapman & Hall, London, 59–74.

Tsianco, Michael C.; K. Ruben Gabriel; Charles L. Odoroff; and Sandra Plumb (1981), BGRAPH: A program for biplot multivariate graphics, *Computer Science and Statistics: The Interface* (edited by William F. Eddy), Springer-Verlag, New York, 344–347.

Tukey, J. W. (1957), On the comparative anatomy of transformations, *Annals of Mathematical Statistics* **28**, 602–632.

Tukey, P. A., and J. W. Tukey (1981), Preparation; prechosen sequences of views, *Interpreting Multivariate Data* (edited by Vic Barnett), John Wiley & Sons, New York, 189–213.

Van Huffel, S., and J. Vandewalle (1991), *The Total Least Squares Problem: Computational Aspects and Analysis*, Society for Industrial and Applied Mathematics, Philadelphia.

Vapnik, Vladimir N. (1999a), *The Nature of Statistical Learning Theory*, second edition, Springer-Verlag, New York.

Vapnik, Vladimir (1999b), Three remarks on the support vector method of function estimation, *Advances in Kernel Methods. Support Vector Learning* (edited by Bernhard Schölkopf, Christopher J. C. Burges, and Alexander J. Smola), The MIT Press, Cambridge, Massachusetts, 25–41.

Velilla, Santiago (1995), Diagnostics and robust estimation in multivariate data transformations, *Journal of the American Statistical Association* **90**, 945–951.

Vidakovic, Brani (1999), *Statistical Modeling by Wavelets*, John Wiley & Sons, New York.

Vines, S. K. (2000), Simple principal components, *Applied Statistics* **49**, 441–451.

Wahba, Grace (1999), Support vector machines, reproducing kernel Hilbert spaces and randomized GACV, *Advances in Kernel Methods. Support Vector Learning* (edited by Bernhard Schölkopf, Christopher J. C. Burges, and Alexander J. Smola), The MIT Press, Cambridge, Massachusetts, 327–352.

Walter, Gilbert G., and Jugal K. Ghorai (1992), Advantages and disadvantages of density estimation with wavelets, *Computing Science and Statistics* **24**, 234–243.

Wan, S. J.; S. K. M. Wong; and P. Prusinkiewicz (1988), An algorithm for multidimensional data clustering, *ACM Transactions on Mathematical Software* **14**, 153–162.

Wand, M. P., and M. C. Jones (1995), *Kernel Smoothing*, Chapman & Hall, London.

Wandell, Brian A. (1995), *Foundations of Vision*, Sinauer, Sunderland, Massachusetts.

Wang, Naisyin, and David Ruppert (1995), Nonparametric estimation of the transformation in the transform-both-sides regression model, *Journal of the American Statistical Association* **90**, 522–534.

Ward, Joe H., Jr. (1963), Hierarchical grouping to optimize an objective function, *Journal of the American Statistical Association* **58**, 236–244.

Ware, Colin (2000), *Information Visualization*, Morgan Kaufmann Publishers, San Mateo, California.

Watson, D. F. (1981), Computing the n-dimensional Delaunay tessellation with application to Voronoi polytopes, *The Computer Journal* **24**, 167–171.

Wedderburn, R. W. M. (1974), Quasi-likelihood functions, generalized linear models, and the Gauss-Newton method, *Biometrika* **61**, 439–447.

Wegman, E. J. (1988), Computational statistics: A new agenda for statistical theory and practice, *Journal of the Washington Academy of Sciences* **78**, 310–322.

Wegman, Edward J. (1990), Hyperdimensional data analysis using parallel coordinates, *Journal of the American Statistical Association* **85**, 664–675.

Wegman, Edward J. (1995), Huge data sets and the frontiers of computational feasibility, *Journal of Computational and Graphical Statistics* **4**, 281–195.

Wegman, Edward J., and Ji Shen (1993), Three-dimensional Andrews plots and the grand tour, *Computing Science and Statistics* **25**, 284–288.

Wei, Greg C. C., and Martin A. Tanner (1990), A Monte Carlo implementation of the EM algorithm and the poor man's data augmentation algorithms, *Journal of the American Statistical Association* **85**, 699–704.

Weisberg, Sanford (1985), *Applied Linear Regression*, second edition, John Wiley & Sons, New York.

Westphal, M., and G. Nakhaeizadeh (1997), Combination of statistical and other learning methods to predict financial time series, *Machine Learning and Statistics: The Interface* (edited by G. Nakhaeizadeh and C. C. Taylor), John Wiley & Sons, New York.

White, A. P., and A. Reed (1989), Probabilistic induction models and logit models, *Machine and Human Learning: Advances in European Research* (edited by Yves Kodratoff and Alan Hutchinson), Kogan Page, London.

Wilkinson, Leland (1997), A graph algebra, *Computing Science and Statistics* **28**, 341–351.

Wilkinson, Leland (1999), *The Grammar of Graphics*, Springer-Verlag, New York.

Wolff, Robert S., and Larry Yaeger (1993), *Visualization of Natural Phenomena*, Springer-Verlag, New York.

Wolpert, D. (1992), Stacked generalization, *Neural Networks* **5**, 241–259.

Woodruff, David L., and David M. Rocke (1993), Heuristic search algorithms for the minimum volume ellipsoid, *Journal of Computational and Graphical Statistics* **2**, 69–95.

Wu, C. F. Jeff (1983), On the convergence properties of the EM algorithm, *Annals of Statistics* **11**, 95–103.

Xiang, Dong, and Grace Wahba (1996), A generalized approximate cross validation for smoothing splines with non-Gaussian data, *Statistica Sinica* **6**, 675–692.

Xu, Chong-Wei, and Wei-Kei Shiue (1993), Parallel algorithms for least median of squares regression, *Computational Statistics & Data Analysis* **16**, 349–362.

Young, Forrest W.; Richard A. Faldowski; and Mary M. McFarlane (1993), Multivariate statistical visualization, *Handbook of Statistics, Volume 9: Computational Statistics* (edited by C. R. Rao), North-Holland, Amsterdam, 959–998.

Young, Forrest W.; Douglas P. Kent; and Warren F. Kuhfeld (1988), Dynamic graphics for exploring multivariate data, *Dynamic Graphics for Statistics* (edited by William S. Cleveland and Marylyn E. McGill), Wadsworth Publishing Company, Belmont, California, 391–424.

Young, Forrest W., and Penny Rheingans (1991), High-dimensional depth-cuing for guided tours of multivariate data, *Computing and Graphics in Statistics* (edited by Andreas Buja and Paul A. Tukey), Springer-Verlag, New York, 239–252.

Young, Martin R. (1992), Estimating optimal transformations for correlation and coherence, *Computer Science and Statistics: Proceedings of the Twenty-second Symposium on the Interface* (edited by Connie Page and Raoul LePage), Springer-Verlag, New York, 571–575.

Zahn, C. T. (1971), Graph-theoretical methods for detecting and describing gestalt clusters, *IEEE Transactions on Computers* **C-20**, 68–86.

Zeger, Kenneth; Jacques Vaisey; and Allen Gersho (1992), Globally optimal vector quantizer design by stochastic relaxation *IEEE Transactions on Signal Processing* **40**, 310–322.

Zuo, Yijun, and Robert Serfling (2000a), General notions of statistical depth function, *Annals of Statistics* **28**, 461–482.

Zuo, Yijun, and Robert Serfling (2000b), Structural properties and convergence results for contours of sample statistical depth functions, *Annals of Statistics* **28**, 483–499.

Author Index

Abbott, Edwin, 290
Abramowitz, Milton, 386
Agresti, Alan, 59
Albert, James, 202
Albert, John, 22
Allen, David M., 75
Amit, Yali, 83, 324
Ammann, Larry P., 122, 319
Anderson, E., 174
Anderson, T. W., 125
Andrews, David F., 176, 340
Ansley, Craig F., 76
Antoniadis, Anestis, 134
Arabie, Phipps, 254
Ash, Peter, 246
Asimov, Daniel, 170, 180
Atkinson, A. C., 178
Aurenhammer, Franz, 246
Azzalini, Adelchi, 162

Banchoff, Thomas F., 154
Bancroft, T. A., 9
Banfield, Jeffrey D., 245
Banks, David L., 207, 257
Barbe, Philippe, 96
Barber, C. Bradford, 258
Barkema, G. T., 215
Barnard, G. A., 58
Barnett, Vic, 255, 258, 276
Barrett, J. Douglas, 251
Bartlett, M. S., 326
Bassett, Gilbert W., 317
Bates, Douglas M., 386
Becker, Richard A., 172, 179, 357
Beckman, Richard J., 349
Beniger, James R., 188
Bentley, Jon Louis, 256, 263
Bergeron, R. Daniel, 174, 246
Berk, Kenneth N., 83
Berry, Michael W., 280
Bertail, Patrice, 96
Besag, Julian E., 59, 68
Bezdek, J. C., 250
Bézier, Pierre, 162
Bhavsar, Suketu P., 256

Bickel, Peter J., 340
Billard, Lynne, 96
Birkes, David, 342
Boggs, Paul T., 319
Bolker, Ethan, 246
Boots, Barry, 215, 246
Bowman, Adrian W., 162
Bowyer, A., 247
Box, G. E. P., 327
Breiman, Leo, 83, 123, 249, 300, 320, 322, 323, 324, 328
Brooks, S. P., 57
Brown, D., 59
Browne, Murray, 280
Buckheit, Jonathan B., xii, 338
Buja, Andreas, 171, 179, 180, 182, 187, 282, 283, 284, 287
Burr, Irving W., 201
Butler, Ronald W., 65
Butucea, Cristina, 226
Byrd, Richard H., 319

Cabrera, Javier, 182, 282, 283, 284, 287
Campbell, N. A., 122, 276
Canty, A. J., 93, 97
Carlin, Bradley P., 57, 66
Carlstein, Edward, 94
Caroni, C., 276
Carr, Daniel B., 167, 174, 182, 228
Carroll, Raymond J., 328
Casella, George, 23, 29, 40
Chambers, John M., 174, 357
Chan, K. S., 29
Chen, K. S., 201
Cheng, R. C. H., 23
Chernick, Michael R., 96
Chernoff, Herman, 173
Chou, Youn-Min, 201
Chui, Charles K., 142
Chui, Sung Nok, 215, 246
Cislak, Peter J., 201
Claerbout, Jon, xii
Clarkson, Douglas B., 122
Cleveland, William S., 172, 174, 178, 179, 183

409

Clifford, P., 59, 68
Cline, Harvey E., 168
Coleman, Dan, 242
Comon, Pierre, 281, 290
Conover, William J., 349
Conway, J. H., 215
Cook, Dianne A., 182, 183, 187, 257, 282, 283, 284, 287
Cook, R. Dennis, 259
Cooper, Martha C., 240
Cowles, Mary Kathryn, 57
Cox, D. R., 327
Crapo, Henry, 246
Cressie, Noel A. C., 68, 71
Cristianini, Nello, 324
Cruz-Neira, C., 183

Dale, M. B., 250
Davies, P. L., 317
Davis, C. E., 14
Davison, A. C., 93, 96, 97, 169
Dawkins, Brian P., 176
De Boor, Carl, 140
Delampady, Mohan, 202
Dempster, Arthur P., 27, 28, 29, 30, 36
Devroye, Luc, 201
Diaconis, Persi, 214, 215, 236, 281
DiCiccio, Thomas, 93
Dielman, Terry E., 14, 318
Diggle, Peter J., 68
Dimsdale, Bernard, 175
Dobkin, David P., 258
Dodge, Yadolah, 318, 342
Donaldson, Janet R., 319
Donatos, G. S., 318
Dong, Xioapeng, 242
Dongarra, Jack J., 388
Donoho, David L., xii, 338
Draper, N. R., 328
Dryden, Ian L., 59
Du, Qiang, 249
Dudewicz, Edward J., 201
Dunkl, Charles, 138
Duran, Benjamin S., 249

Eckart, Carl, 267
Eddy, William F., 255, 258, 259
Edgington, Eugene S., 70
Edwards, A. W. F., 22
Efromovich, Sam, 128
Efron, Bradley, 78, 82, 85, 92, 93, 94, 95, 96
Epanechnikov, V. A., 221
Eubank, Randall L., 162, 332
Everitt, B. S., 202

Faber, Vance, 239, 249

Faghihi, Mohammad Reza, 59
Faldowski, Richard A., 154
Farmen, Mark, 226
Fayyad, Usama M., 124
Feiner, Steven K., 166, 184, 188
Fienberg, Stephen E., 153, 188
Filliben, James J., 154
Finkel, Raphael Ari, 263
Fisher, R. A., 70
Fisherkeller, Mary Anne, 179
Fishman, George S., 66, 354
Flury, Bernhard, 28
Foley, James D., 166, 184, 188
Forster, Jonathan J., 59
Frank, Ildiko E., 317
Freedman, David, 214, 215, 236, 281
Freeman, William, 224
Freund, Yoav, 323
Friedman, Jerome H., 123, 179, 238, 256, 257, 263, 283, 287, 317, 320, 322, 328
Friendly, Michael, 183
Frigessi, Arnoldo, 66
Fuller, Wayne A., 319
Funkhauser, H. G., 188
Furnas, George W., 171
Fushimi, Masanori, 354

Gabriel, K. Ruben, 167
Gelfand, Alan E., 51, 66
Gelman, Andrew, 57
Geman, D., 51
Geman, Donald, 83, 324
Geman, S., 51
Gentle, James E., 17, 53, 76, 114, 122, 315
Gentleman, Robert, 357
Gersho, Allen, 239
Geyer, Charles J., 65
Ghorai, Jugal K, 224
Girard, Stéphane, 289
Glaeser, Georg, 186
Glymour, Clark, 124
Gnanadesikan, R., 125
Golub, Gene H., 319
Goodman, A. S., 354
Gordon, A. D., 238
Gosset, W. S. ("Student"), 337
Gowda, K. Chidananda, 117
Gower, J. C., 119
Gray, A. J., 66
Gray, H. L., 80, 82
Green, Peter J., 331
Greenwood, J. Arthur, 66, 378
Gregoire, G., 134
Grenander, Ulf, 207, 208
Griffiths, P., 387
Guihenneuc-Jouyaux, Chantal, 57

Gunzburger, Max, 249

Hall, Peter, 59, 96, 282, 287
Hammersley, J. M., 338
Hampel, Frank R., 340
Hand, D. J., 202
Handscomb, D. C., 338
Hardin, Johanna, 242
Härdle, Wolfgang, 331
Harrell, Frank E., 14
Hartigan, John A., 174, 183, 239, 240
Hastie, Trevor J., 238, 289
Hastings, W. K., 47
Hathaway, R. J., 250
Hausman, Robert E., Jr., 268
Hawkins, Douglas M., 259, 316, 317, 322, 323
Hearne, Leonard B., 215
Heath, D., 124, 323
Henery, R. J., 323
Henson, S., 201
Hesterberg, Timothy C., 14, 65
Hettmansperger, T. P., 317
Hill, I. D., 387
Hinkley, D. V., 93, 96, 97
Ho, Tin Kam, 323, 324
Hoaglin, David C., 340
Hodges, James S., 66
Hofmann, Thomas, 280
Hope, A. C. A., 58
Hopkins, Alan, 224
Horowitz, Ellis, 256
Huber, Peter J., 124, 283, 340
Hubert, Lawrence, 254
Hubert, Mia, 261
Hughes, John F., 166, 184, 188
Huhdanpaa, Hannu, 258
Hull, John C., 325
Hunt, Earl B., 306
Hurley, Catherine, 182, 287
Huzurbazar, S., 65
Hyvärinen, Aapo, 290

Ihaka, Ross, 357
Inselberg, Alfred, 175

Jacoby, William G., 187
Jamshidian, Mortaza, 30
Jennrich, Robert I., 30
Jolliffe, Ian T., 268, 284
Jones, M. C., 283, 287, 331
Jöreskog, K. G., 276, 280
Jörgensen, B., 26
Julesz, Bela, 183
Jureckova, Jana, 318

Kademan, Edmund, 322

Kaigh, W. D., 14
Kao, David T., 246
Karhunen, Juha, 290
Karian, Zaven A., 201
Kasif, Simon, 124, 321, 323
Kass, Gordon V., 322
Kaufman, Leonard, 245
Keim, Daniel A., 182
Kendall, M. G., 108, 290
Kennedy, William J., 9, 17, 114
Kent, Douglas P., 182
Kieffer, J. C., 248
Kim, Dong K., 30
Kleijnen, Jack P. C., 347
Kleiner, Beat, 174, 183
Klinke, S., 215
Knuth, Donald E., 263
Koehler, J. R., 348
Kohlmeyer, B. D., 183
Kohn, Robert, 76
Krishna, G., 117
Krishnan, Thriyambakam, 27
Kronmal, Richard A., 224
Kruskal, Joseph B., Jr., 255
Kuhfeld, Warren F., 182
Kwon, Sunhee, 257

Lachenbruch, Peter A., 14
Laird, Nan M., 27, 28, 29, 30, 36
Lance, G. N., 115, 116
Lange, Kenneth, vii
Lavine, Michael, 257
Laviolette, Michael, 251
Lax, David A., 214
Learmonth, G. P., 357
Lechner, U., 183
Ledolter, Johannes, 29
Lee, D. D., 280
Lee, D. T., 248
Legendre, P., 119
Lehmann, E. L., 23
LePage, Raoul, 96
Leroy, Annick M., 317
Levine, Richard A., 29
Lewis, P. A. W., 354, 357
Lewis, Toby, 276
Li, Hongyi, 94, 96
Lieber, M. L., 93
Ling, E. Nigel, 256
Littlefield, J. S., 182, 228
Littlefield, Richard J., 167, 182, 228
Liu, Jun S., 65
Liu, Regina Y., 261, 262
Lloyd, S., 248
Loh, Wei-Yin, 322
Lorensen, William E., 168, 187
Louis, Thomas A., 30

Lowry, Cynthia, 14
Lund, Ulric, 119

Maddala, G. S., 94, 96
Madigan, David, 124
Manly, Bryan F. J., 59, 73
Marazzi, A., 122
Marchette, David J., 224, 225
Marin, Janet, 306
Maronna, Ricardo A., 261
Marriott, F. H. C., 58
Marron, J. S., 221
Marron, James S., 183, 226, 229
Marsaglia, George, 40
Martin, Ken, 168, 187
Martinelli, Fabio, 66
Matthews, D. E., 29
McCullough, B. D., 357
McDonald, John W., 59
McDonald, Patrick, 201
McFarlane, Mary M., 154
McKay, Michael D., 349
McKeague, I. W., 134
McLachlan, Geoffrey J., 27
Mead, R., 71
Meeker, L. D., 174
Mehta, Cyrus R., 59, 63, 64
Meintanis, S. G., 318
Meng, Xiao-Li, 29, 30
Mengersen, Kerrie L., 57
Metropolis, N., 47
Meyer, D., 201
Michalski, R. S., 250, 306
Miller, J. M., 354
Miller, Keith W., 351, 354
Milligan, Glenn W., 240, 254
Mitchell, Toby J., 349
Monti, Katherine L., 158
Moore, Louis R., III, 354
Morgan, James N., 322
Mortenson, Michael E., 103, 108, 162
Morton, Sally C., 284
Mulira, H.-M., 178
Müller, Klaus-Robert, 324
Murtagh, F., 264
Murthy, Sreerama K., 124, 321, 323

Naito, Kanta, 284
Nakhaeizadeh, G., 323
Nason, Guy P., 284
Nelder, J. A., 304
Nelson, Barry L., 14, 65
Newman, M. E. J., 215
Newton, Carol M., 179
Nicholson, W. L., 174, 182, 228
Nicole, Sandro, 273
Nolan, D., 221

Nummelin, Esa, 46

O'Rourke, Joseph, 248
Obuchowski, Nancy A., 93
Odell, Patrick L., 249
Odoroff, Charles L., 167
Oja, Erkki, 290
Okabe, Atsuyuki, 215, 246
Oldham, Keith B., 386
Olive, David, 316
Olshen, Richard A., 123, 320, 322
Oppenheim, Georges, 134
Owen, Art B., 348, 349
Owen, D. B., 80

Parelius, Jesse M., 262
Park, Stephen K., 351, 354
Patel, Nitin R., 59, 63, 64
Pfaffenberger, Roger, 14
Piatetsky-Shapiro, Gregory, 124
Picard, Richard R., 83
Plumb, Sandra, 167
Polasek, Wolfgang, 202
Politis, Dimitris N., 94
Posse, Christian, 284, 288
Poston, Wendy L., 202
Pregibon, Daryl, 124
Priebe, Carey E., 202, 224, 225
Prusinkiewicz, P., 245

Quenouille, M. H., 76
Quinlan, J. Ross, 123, 321, 322

Rafsky, Lawrence C., 256, 257
Raftery, Adrian E., 245
Rai, S. N., 29
Rajasekaran, Sanguthevar, 256
Ramberg, J. S., 201
Ramsay, J. O., 113, 128
Rand, William M., 253
Rao, J. N. K., 77, 82
Reed, A., 304
Reeves, Chip, 251
Renka, Robert J., 248
Reyment, Richard A., 276, 280
Rheingans, Penny, 182
Rice, John R., 128
Richeldi, M., 323
Riesenfeld, R. F., 103, 108, 155
Ripley, Brian D., 61, 83, 312
Robert, Christian P., 40, 57, 58
Roberts, G. O., 57
Robyn, Dorothy, 188
Rocke, David M., 242, 259
Roeder, Kathryn, 202
Rogers, George W., 202, 224
Rogers, W. H., 340

Romano, Joseph P., 94
Rose, Elizabeth L., 318
Rosenblatt, M., 205
Rosenbluth, A. W., 47
Rosenbluth, M. N., 47
Rosenthal, Jeffrey S., 57
Rossotto, M., 323
Rothery, P., 59
Rousseeuw, Peter J., 245, 251, 260, 261, 317
Rowan, Tom, 388
Rubin, Donald B., 27, 28, 29, 30, 36, 57, 61
Ruppert, David, 328, 330
Rustagi, Jagdish S., 18
Ruts, Ida, 260, 261

Sabatti, Chiara, 65
Sacks, Jerome, 349
Sahni, Sartaj, 256
Sahu, Sujit K., 66
Salzberg, Steven, 124, 321, 323
Sardy, S., 169
Sargent, Daniel J., 66
Schafer, J. L., 61
Schapire, Robert E., 323
Schenker, Nathaniel, 97
Schmeiser, Bruce W., 201
Schnabel, Robert B., 319
Schölkopf, Bernhard, 324
Schroeder, Will, 168, 187
Schucany, William R., 80, 82
Scott, David W., 168, 208, 215, 216, 224, 228
Seaman, John W., Jr., 251
Seaver, Bill, 251
Senchaudhuri, Pralay, 59, 63, 64
Serfling, Robert, 261
Seung, H. S., 280
Sewell, Granville, 166
Shao, Jun, 82, 96
Shapiro, Samuel S., 201
Sharot, Trevor, 82
Shawe-Taylor, John, 324
Sheather, Simon J., 317
Shen, Ji, 181
Sherman, Michael, 94
Shiue, Wei-Kei, 317
Shyu, Ming-Jen, 172
Sibson, Robin, 283, 287
Sibuya, M., 66
Silverman, Bernard W., 113, 128, 221, 331
Simonoff, Jeffrey S., 157, 158, 162, 216, 331
Singh, Kesar, 262
Siu, Cynthia O., 323
Slifker, James F., 201

Sloane, N. J. A., 215
Small, Christopher G., 128
Smith, Adrian F. M., 51
Smith, H., 328
Smith, Peter W. F., 59
Smola, Alexander J., 324
Smyth, Padhraic, 124
Soffritti, Gabriele, 252
Solka, Jeffrey L., 202, 224
Sonquist, John A., 322
Spanier, Jerome, 386
Sparr, Ted M., 174, 246
Speed, T. P., 9
Stachel, Hellmuth, 186
Stander, Julian, 66
Stegun, Irene A., 386
Stepp, R. E., 250, 306
Stevens, S. S., 99
Stewart, Ian, 290
Stigler, Stephen M., 337
Stone, Charles J., 123, 224, 320, 322
Stone, Philip J., 306
Struyf, Anja, 261
Stuetzle, Werner, 289, 320
Sugihara, Ksokichi, 215, 246
Sullivan, Thomas J., 109
Sun, Jiayang, 284, 287, 288, 289
Sutton, Clifton D., 90
Swayne, D. F., 187
Swendsen, R. H., 66
Symanzik, J., 183

Tanner, Martin A., 29
Tapia, Richard A., 208
Tarter, Michael E., 224
Taylor, Charles C., 59
Taylor, Jeremy M. G., 30
Taylor, Malcolm S., 355
Taylor, Walter F., 188
Teller, A. H., 47
Teller, E., 47
Terrell, George R., 222, 224
Tharm, David, 76
Theus, Martin, 172
Thisted, Ronald A., 386
Thomas, William, 76
Thompson, Elizabeth A., 65
Thompson, James R., 208, 216, 355
Thompson, William J., 386
Tibshirani, Robert J., 82, 95, 96, 238, 329
Tidwell, P. W., 327
Tierney, Luke, 45
Titterington, D. M., 59
Traylor, L., 23
Triantis, Konstantinos, 251
Tsianco, Michael C., 167
Tsybakov, A. B., 183

Tu, Dongsheng, 82, 96
Tukey, John W., 169, 179, 326, 340
Tukey, Paul A., 169, 174, 179
Turner, S., 201

Uddin, Mudassir, 268, 284
Udina, Frederic, 158
Uthurusamy, Ramasamy, 124

Vaisey, Jacques, 239
Van Dam, Andries, 166, 184, 188
Van Huffel, S., 319
Van Loan, Charles F., 319
Van Ness, John, 319
Van Zomeren, B., 317
Vandewalle, J., 319
Vanichsetakul, Nunta, 322
Vapnik, Vladimir N., 324
Velilla, Santiago, 328
Vidakovic, Brani, 224
Vines, S. K., 268, 284

Wade, Reed, 388
Wahba, Grace, 76, 324
Walter, Gilbert G., 224
Wan, S. J., 245
Wand, M. P., 226, 229, 331
Wandell, Brian A., 183
Wang, J.-S., 66
Wang, Naisyin, 330
Ward, Joe H., Jr., 244
Ware, Colin, 188
Wasserman, Larry, 202
Watson, D. F., 247
Webster, J. T., 77, 82
Wedderburn, R. W. M., 304

Wegman, Edward J., 124, 175, 181, 202, 215
Wei, Greg C. C., 29
Weisberg, Sanford, 259, 328
Welch, William J., 349
Westphal, M., 323
White, A. P., 304
Whiteley, Walter, 246
Wilkinson, Leland, 172
Wilks, Allan R., 357
Williams, W. T., 115, 116
Wolff, Robert S., 166, 188
Wolpert, D., 323
Wong, M. A., 239
Wong, S. K. M., 245
Woodall, William H., 251
Woodruff, David L., 242, 259
Wu, C. F. Jeff, 28
Wynn, Henry P., 349

Xiang, Dong, 76
Xu, Chong-Wei, 317
Xu, Yuan, 138

Yaeger, Larry, 166, 188
Yohai, Victor J., 261
Young, Forrest W., 154, 182
Young, Gale, 267
Young, Martin R., 327
Yu, Bin, 9

Zahn, C. T., 256
Zeger, Kenneth, 239
Zoppè, Alice, 28
Zuo, Yijun, 261

Subject Index

ACE (alternating conditional expectation method) 328

ACM Transactions on Mathematical Software 352, 386, 388

ACM Transactions on Modeling and Computer Simulation 386

additivity and variance stabilization (AVAS) 329

affine transformation 103

AID (classification method) 322

alternating conditional expectation (ACE) 328

AMISE (asymptotic mean integrated squared error) 149

AMS MR classification system 386

anaglyph 166

Andrews curve 176

angle between vectors 100, 101

angular separation 116

anisometry 117

ANSI (standards) 186

Applied Statistics 352, 386, 388

arcing 323

ASH (average shifted histogram) 216

aspect ratio 6

asymptotic mean integrated squared error (AMISE) 149

AVAS (additivity and variance stabilization method) 329, 330

average shifted histogram (ASH) 216

AVS (graphics system) 187

B-spline 140

bagging 323

Banach space 132

basis functions 133

batch means for variance estimation 55

Bayes rule 305

Bayesian model 309

BC_a bootstrap 92

Bernstein polynomial 163

beta function 372

beta weight function 163

bias 12

bin smoother 331

binary difference 116

binning 125, 294

blind source separation 289

bona fide density estimator 205

boosting 323

bootstrap bias correction 86

bootstrap confidence interval 89

bootstrap variance estimate 88

bootstrap, parametric 60

bootstrapping regression 93

Box-Cox transformation 327

broken-line ECDF 158

Brownian motion 310

brushing 178

Burr family of distributions 201

Bézier curve 162

C (programming language) 351

C5.0 123, 322

CALGO (Collected Algorithms of the ACM) 386, 388

Canberra distance 115

CART (method and software) 123, 320, 322

casement display 171

categorical variable 111

Cauchy-Schwarz inequality 130

CAVE 183

CDF (cumulative distribution function) 365

centered data 101, 110

centroidal tessellation 248

Chebyshev norm 131

Chernoff face 173

Christoffel-Darboux formula 135

circular data 118

classification tree 123, 238, 320

classification 237, 320

claw density 226

clustered image map 165

clustering 202, 237

Collected Algorithms of the ACM (CALGO) 386, 388

color table 185

color, representation of 184

Communications in Statistics — Simulation and Computation 387
complete linkage clustering 242
complete space 132
COMPSTAT 385, 387
computational feasibility 124
computational inference 10, 58
Computational Statistics 387
Computational Statistics & Data Analysis 387
computer experiment 347
Computing Science and Statistics 387
conceptual clustering 249
conditioning plot 171
coneplots 176
confidence interval 33, 89
conjunctive normal form (CNF) 322
consistent estimator 145
container hull 258
contour plot 164
control variate 63
convergence in mean square 145
convergence in quadratic mean 145
convex hull peeling 258
convex hull 258
coordinate system 108
coplot (conditioning plot) 171
correlation matrix 110
correlation 109
covariance 109
cross validation 74
cumulative distribution function 365
Current Index to Statistics 386
curse of dimensionality 293

data-based random number generation 355
data depth 259
data-generating process 5, 10
data mining 123
data partitioning 69
decomposition of a function 54, 139
Delaunay triangulation 246
Delta algorithm 26
delta method 31
density estimation 197, 205
depth median 261
depth of data 259
device coordinate system 155
device driver 186
DIEHARD tests for random number generators 40, 357
Dijkstra's algorithm 256
dimension reduction 99, 246
Dirac delta function 369
direct volume rendering 166
directional data 118
Dirichlet tessellation 246

discrimination 237
disjunctive normal form (DNF) 322
dissimilarity measure 118
dissimilarity 109, 114
distance 114
dot product 100, 129

ECDF (empirical cumulative distribution function) 11, 158, 194, 365
EDA 123, 300
eigenfunctions 134
eigenvalues 134
elemental regression 323
ellipsoid, minimum volume 259
EM algorithm 27
empirical cumulative distribution function 11, 158, 194, 365
empirical orthogonal functions 265
empirical probability density function (EPDF) 12, 194
empirical quantile 14
EPDF (empirical probability density function) 12, 194
errors-in-variables 318, 319
Euclidean distance 114
Euclidean length 100
EXPLOR4 (software) 174
exploratory data analysis 123, 300
Exponent Graphics (software) 186

factor analysis 265, 276
feature space 289
filter 129, 142
filtered kernel density estimation 224
Fisher scoring 25
flat 101
Fortran 90 351
4-plot 154
Fourier coefficients 134
Fourier series curve 176
fractal dimension 287
frequency polygon 216
functional data 112
fuzzy clustering 250

gamma function 372
GAMS (*Guide to Available Mathematical Software*) 352, 388
GAMS, electronic access 388
Gauss-Newton method 19
generalized jackknife 80, 81
generalized lambda family of distributions 199, 201
generalized linear model 304
geometric Brownian motion 311
geometry 102
Gibbs method 46, 50

Gibbs sampling 51
GIMP (graphics software) 187
GKS 186
glyph 172
GNU Scientific Library (GSL) 352
gnuplot (graphics software) 187
Gram-Charlier series 136
Gram-Schmidt transformation 102, 133
grand tour (in graphics) 180, 257
grand tour in Andrews curves *Exercise 7.9*: 190
grand tour in cone plots *Exercise 7.10*: 190
graphics 153
GSL (GNU Scientific Library) 352

halfspace location depth 259
Hamiltonian circuit 258
Hamming distance 116
Heaviside function 368
Hellinger distance 146
Hermite polynomial 136, 137
hierarchical clustering 240
hierarchical model 309
Hilbert space 132
histogram 155
histospline 216
homogeneous coordinates 106, 155
Hotelling transform 270
Huber estimator 316
hull 258
hypergeometric distribution 199
hypothesis testing 32, 58

IAE (integrated absolute error) 146, 149
ICA (independent components analysis) 281, 289
ideal bootstrap 88
IMAE (integrated mean absolute error) 148
image plot 164
immersive techniques 183
IMPLOM 171, 182
importance sampling 62
imputation 61
IMSE (integrated mean squared error) 147
IMSL Exponent Graphics 186
IMSL Libraries 352, 354
incomplete gamma function 372
independent components analysis 265, 281, 289
indicator function 368
inference, computational 10, 58
inner product 100, 129, 132
integrated absolute bias 147
integrated absolute error (IAE) 146, 149
integrated bias 147

integrated mean absolute error (IMAE) 148
integrated mean squared error (IMSE) 147
integrated squared bias 147
integrated squared error (ISE) 146
integrated variance 147
Interface Symposium 385, 387
International Association of Statistical Computing (IASC) 385, 387
invariance property 102
IRLS (iteratively reweighted least squares) 21, 22
ISE (integrated squared error) 146
ISO (standards) 186
isometric matrix 117
isometric transformation 102, 117, 121
isotropic transformation 102
iteratively reweighted least squares 21, 22
Itô process 311

jackknife 76
jackknife-after-bootstrap 94
Jacobi polynomial 163
Java 3D 186
Jensen's inequality 30
jittering 182
Johnson family of distributions 200
Journal of Computational and Graphical Statistics 188, 387
Journal of Statistical Computation and Simulation 387
Journal of Statistical Software 389

k-d-tree 263
K-means clustering 239, 249
Kagomé lattice 215
Karhunen-Loève transform 265, 270
KDD (knowledge discovery in databases) 123
kernel (function) 142, 218, 324, 331
kernel density estimation 217
kernel estimator 129
kernel regression 331
kernel smoother 331
knowledge discovery in databases (KDD) 123
Kolmogorov distance 146, 148, 161
Kullback-Leibler measure 146

L_1 consistency 149
L_2 consistency 145, 148
L_2 norm 114, 132
L_p norm 115, 132
Laguerre-Fourier index, projection pursuit 287
lambda family of distributions 199, 201
Langevin equation 311

Laplacian operator 370
latent semantic indexing 265, 280
Latin hypercube sampling 293, 348
learning 289
least median of squares regression 317
least squares estimator 17
least squares/normal drift *Exercise 2.6*:
      67
least trimmed absolute values 316
least trimmed squares 316
Legendre polynomial 136
Levenberg-Marquardt algorithm 20
likelihood function 22, 198
linear estimator 31
linear functional 31
lining 257
link function 304
log-likelihood function 24
logit function 304

M-estimator 314
machine learning 237, 289
MAE (mean absolute error) 144
Mahalanobis distance 118, 305
Manhattan distance 115
Markov chain Monte Carlo 47
Mathematical Reviews 386
Matlab (software) 352
Matusita distance 146
maximum absolute error (SAE) 146
maximum difference 115
maximum likelihood method 22, 23, 198,
      206
MCMC (Markov chain Monte Carlo) 47
mean absolute error (MAE) 144
mean integrated absolute error (MIAE)
      148, 149
mean integrated squared error (MISE) 148
mean square consistent 148
mean squared error (MSE) 144, 147
mean squared error 12
mean squared error, of series expansion
      134
mean sup absolute error (MSAE) 148
method of moments 13
metric 109
MIAE (mean integrated absolute error)
      148, 149
minimal spanning tree 255
minimum-volume ellipsoid 259
Minkowski distance 115
MISE (mean integrated squared error) 148
missing data 61
model-based clustering 202
Monte Carlo experimentation 3, 39, 337
Monte Carlo study 337
Monte Carlo test 58

Motif 186
mountain plot 158
MR classification system 386
MSAE (mean sup absolute error) 148
MSE (mean squared error) 144, 147
MST (minimal spanning tree) 255
multidimensional scaling 122
multiple imputation 61
multipolar mapping 246

natural polynomial spline 141
nearest neighbors 235, 263, 264
netlib xii, 352, 386, 388
Newton's method 17
NIST Test Suite, for random number gen-
      erators 40
nonlinear regression 21
nonnegative matrix factorization 280
nonparametric density estimation 205
nonparametric method 299
nonparametric regression 331
norm, function 131, 132
norm, vector 114
normal function 132
numerical data 100

oblique partitioning 124
online algorithm 124
OpenGL (software) 186
order of computations 124
Ornstein-Uhlenbeck process 311
orthogonal distance regression 318, 319
orthogonal polynomials 135
orthogonal transformation 101
orthogonalization transformation 102
out-of-core algorithm 124
outlier 121, 276

p-p plot 257
parallel coordinates 175
parametric bootstrap 60
partial scatter plot matrix 170
PCA (principal components analysis) 264
Pearson family of distributions 199
penalized maximum likelihood method 207
perspective plot 156
PHIGS 186
pivotal value 33
pixel 155, 184, 185
planing 257
plug-in estimator 13, 95
pointwise properties 143
polar coordinates 108, 118, 176, 252
PostScript 186
PRESS 75
PRIM-9 179
principal components 264

principal curves 289
probabilistic latent semantic indexing 280
probability plot 159
probably approximately correct (PAC) model
        305
*Proceedings of the Statistical Computing
        Section* 387
profile likelihood 327
projection pursuit guided tour 182
projection pursuit 281, 319
projection 105, 169
projective transformation 103
prosection 171
proximity search 235, 246
pseudo grand tour 182
pseudovalue 77

q-q plot 159
quad tree 263
quantile plot 199
quantile-quantile plot 159
quasi-Newton method 17, 25

R (software) 187, 352, 357
Rand's statistic 254
random forest 324
rand 353
rank correlation 111
rank transformation 111
raster image 155
recursion formula for orthogonal polyno-
        mials 135
recursive partitioning 123, 238, 245, 321
registration of data 113
regression tree 320, 331
regression 301
regression, bootstrapping 93
regression, nonlinear 21
regularization method 317
reproducible research xii, 338
resampling vector 86
resampling 4, 85
restricted maximum likelihood method 206
robust covariance matrix 121
robust method 121, 315
rotation 103, 180
roughness of a function 150, 212
running smoother 331

S, S-Plus (software) 352, 357
S-Plus (software) 187
SAE (sup absolute error) 146
sample quantile 14
saw-tooth density 226
scaling 117
scatter plot 155, 169
scoring 25

scree plot 271
section 170
See5 123, 322
seed of a random number generator 40,
        351, 354, 356, 359
series estimator 139
series expansion 133
shape of data 291
shearing transformation 103
shrinkage 317
SIAM Journal on Scientific Computing 387
side effect 353
sieve 207
SIGGRAPH 188
signum function 373
similarity 109
similarity measure 110
simplicial location depth 261
simulation 4, 337
single linkage clustering 242
singular value 273
singular value decomposition 273
smooth comb density 226
smoothing matrix 218
smoothing 162, 330
snowflake 173
software engineering 353
sorting of multivariate data 255
SPAVAS (semiparametric AVAS) 330
spectral decomposition 266
sphered data 117, 118, 288
spline smoothing 331
spline 140
SPLOM ("scatter plot matrix") 169
stalactite plot 178
standardized data 117, 235, 265, 266, 267
star diagram 173
Statistical Computing Section of the Amer-
        ican Statistical Association 385,
        387
*Statistical Computing & Graphics Newslet-
        ter* 188, 387
statistical function 12
statistical learning 289
Statistics and Computing 387
statlib xii, 93, 96, 97, 352, 387, 388
stereo-ray glyph 174
stereogram 166
Stevens's scale typology 99
Strauss process 83
structure in data 6, 195
sup absolute error (SAE) 146
support vector machine 324
surface rendering 166
SVD (singular value decomposition) 273
Swendsen-Wang algorithm 66

tensor product 137
tessellation 215, 246, 294
total least squares 318, 319
transform-both-sides 328
transformation of data 326, 328
translation transformation 106
trees and castles 174
trellis display 172
triangle inequality 109
trimmed least squares 316
truncated power function 140
twoing rule 320

ultrametric inequality 109, 244
uniform norm 131

variance estimation 55
variance stabilizing transformation 326
variance 12
variance-covariance matrix 110
vector image 155
virtual reality 183

Visualization Toolkit (software) 187
Voronoi diagram 246
Voronoi tessellation 246
voxel 166
vtk (Visualization Toolkit software) 187

Ward's method of clustering 244
weak convergence in mean square 145
weak convergence in quadratic mean 145
weighted least squares 21
white matrix 118
Wiener process 311
window size 218
wire frame 166
world coordinate system 155

X Windows 186
xfig (graphics software) 187
XGobi (software) 187
Xnetlib 388

z-buffering 166